EXPLAINING THE ECONOMIC PERFORMANCE OF NATIONS

ECONOMISTS OF THE TWENTIETH CENTURY

General Editors: Mark Perlman, *University Professor of Economics, Emeritus, University of Pittsburgh* and Mark Blaug, *Professor Emeritus, University of London; Professor Emeritus, University of Buckingham and Visiting Professor, University of Exeter*

This innovative series comprises specially invited collections of articles and papers by economists whose work has made an important contribution to economics in the late twentieth century.

The proliferation of new journals and the ever-increasing number of new articles make it difficult for even the most assiduous economist to keep track of all the important recent advances. By focusing on those economists whose work is generally recognized to be at the forefront of the discipline, the series will be an essential reference point for the different specialisms included.

A list of published and future titles in this series is printed at the end of this volume.

Explaining the Economic Performance of Nations

Essays in Time and Space

Angus Maddison

ECONOMISTS OF THE TWENTIETH CENTURY

Edward Elgar

Published by
Edward Elgar Publishing Limited
Gower House
Croft Road
Aldershot
Hants GU11 3HR
England

Edward Elgar Publishing Company
Old Post Road
Brookfield
Vermont 05036
USA

British Library Cataloguing in Publication Data
Maddison, Angus
  Explaining the Economic Performance of
  Nations: Essays in Time and Space. –
  (Economists of the Twentieth Century
  Series)
  I. Title II. Series
  338.9

Library of Congress Cataloguing in Publication Data
Maddison, Angus.
    Explaining the economic performance of nations: essays in time
  and space / by Angus Maddison.
      p.   cm. — (Economists of the twentieth century)
    Includes bibliographical references and index.
    1. Economic development — Measurement. 2. Economic policy.
  3. Economic indicators. 4. National income — Accounting. I. Title.
  II. Series.
  HD75.M24   1995
  338.9—dc20   94–37279
                                                         CIP

ISBN 1 85278 600 0

Printed in Great Britain at the University Press, Cambridge

Contents

Acknowledgements   vii
Introduction   ix

PART I   THE ANALYTICAL FRAMEWORK FOR EXPLAINING VARIATIONS
          IN GROWTH PERFORMANCE

1. Reasons for Accelerated Growth and Variations in Performance, pp. 34–62.   7
2. Growth and Slowdown in Advanced Capitalist Economies: Techniques
    of Quantitative Assessment, pp. 649–98.   36 '87
3. Ultimate and Proximate Growth Causality: A Critique of Mancur Olson
    on the Rise and Decline of Nations, pp. 25–9.   86 '88
4. Explaining the Economic Performance of Nations, 1820–1989, pp. 20–61.   91 '94

PART II   INVESTMENT, CAPITAL STOCK AND SAVING

5. Standardised Estimates of Fixed Capital Stock: A Six Country Comparison.   137 new
6. A Long-Run Perspective on Saving, pp. 181–96.   167 '92

PART III MEASURING LEVELS OF ECONOMIC PERFORMANCE

7. A Comparison of Levels of GDP Per Capita in Developed and Developing
    Countries, 1700–1980, pp. 27–41.   189 '83
8. The International Comparison of Value Added, Productivity and Purchasing
    Power Parities in Agriculture (with Harry van Ooststroom).   204
9. International Comparison of Purchasing Power, Real Output and Labour
    Productivity: A Case Study of Brazilian, Mexican and US Manufacturing,
    1975 (with Bart van Ark), pp. 31–55.   227 '89

PART IV   THE ROOTS OF ECONOMIC BACKWARDNESS

10. The Historical Origins of Indian Poverty, pp. 31–81.   257 '70
11. The Historical Roots of Modern Mexico: 1500–1940.   308
12. Dutch Income in and from Indonesia 1700–1938, pp. 645–70.   331 '89

PART V   THE ROLE OF GOVERNMENT POLICY IN THE PERFORMANCE
          OF ADVANCED CAPITALIST COUNTRIES

13. Economic Stagnation Since 1973, Its Nature and Causes: A Six Country Survey,
    pp. 585–608.   361 '83

14. Origins and Impact of the Welfare State, 1883–1983, pp. 55–87.   385   '84

15. What Is Education For?, pp. 19–30.   418   '74

PART VI

16. Confessions of a Chiffrephile, pp. 123–65.   433   '94

Name index   476

Acknowledgements

The publishers wish to thank the following for giving permission for the use of copyright material.

Allen and Unwin Ltd and W.W. Norton and Company for Essay 1, 'Reasons for Accelerated Growth and Variations in Performance', Chapter 2 of A. Maddison, *Economic Progress and Policy in Developing Countries*, London and New York, 1970, pp. 34–62.

The American Economic Association for Essay 2, A. Maddison (1987), 'Growth and Slowdown in Advanced Capitalist Economies: Techniques of Quantitative Assessment', *Journal of Economic Literature*, **XXV**, June, pp. 649–98.

The *Scandinavian Economic History Review* for Essay 3, A. Maddison (1988), 'Ultimate and Proximate Growth Causality: A Critique of Mancur Olson on the Rise and Decline of Nations', *Scandinavian Economic History Review*, **XXXVI**, (2), pp. 25–9.

Oxford University Press for Essay 4, A. Maddison, 'Explaining the Economic Performance of Nations, 1820–1989', Chapter 2 of W.J. Baumol, R.R. Nelson and E.N. Wolff (eds), *Convergence of Productivity: Cross-National Studies and Historical Evidence*, 1994, pp. 20–61.

Innovazione e Materie Prime for an earlier version of Essay 5, A. Maddison (1993), 'Standardised Estimates of Fixed Capital Stock: A Six Country Comparison', *Innovazione e Materie Prime*, April.

The *Scandinavian Journal of Economics* for Essay 6, A. Maddison (1992), 'A Long-Run Perspective on Saving', *Scandinavian Journal of Economics*, **94** (2), pp. 181–96.

The *Journal of Economic History* for Essay 7, A. Maddison (1983), 'A Comparison of Levels of GDP Per Capita in Developed and Developing Countries, 1700–1980', *Journal of Economic History*, **XLIII**, (1), March, pp. 27–41.

The International Association for Research in Income and Wealth for Essay 9, A. Maddison and B. van Ark (1989), 'International Comparison of Purchasing Power, Real Output and Labour Productivity: A Case Study of Brazilian, Mexican and US Manufacturing, 1975', *Review of Income and Wealth*, **35**, (1), March, pp. 31–55.

The *Banca Nazionale del Lavoro Quarterly Review* for Essay 10, A. Maddison (1970), 'The Historical Origins of Indian Poverty', *Banca Nazionale del Lavoro Quarterly Review*, No. 92, March, pp. 31–81; Essay 14, A. Maddison (1984), 'Origins and Impact of the Welfare State, 1883–1983', *Banca Nazionale del Lavoro Quarterly Review*, No 148, March, pp. 55–87; and

Essay 16, A. Maddison (1994), 'Confessions of a Chiffrephile', *Banca Nazionale del Lavoro Quarterly Review*, **XLVII** (189) June, pp. 123–65.

Modern Asian Studies for Essay 12, A. Maddison (1989), 'Dutch Income in and from Indonesia 1700–1938', *Modern Asian Studies*, **23** (4), pp. 645–70.

De Economist for Essay 13, A. Maddison (1983), 'Economic Stagnation Since 1973, Its Nature and Causes: A Six Country Survey', *De Economist*, **131** (4), pp. 585–608.

Lloyds Bank Review for Essay 15, A. Maddison (1974), 'What Is Education For?, *Lloyds Bank Review*, No. 112, April, pp. 19–30.

BK Title:

Introduction

The essays in this book deal with some very broad questions:

a) How fast has economic growth been, and why do growth rates differ between nations?
b) What are the gaps in real income between nations, and why did they arise?
c) Why has the pace of growth varied over time?

The answers to these questions involve an assessment of the comparative performance of nations using an array of quantitative and qualitative evidence across time and space.

It is important to develop quantitative evidence in order to establish what actually happened in the past. Quantification sharpens our appreciation of differences or similarities in the way nations, or distinctive groups of nations, perform. If we have enough comparative evidence it is possible to assess what is 'normal', how potential and performance have changed over time, and whether particular countries have done well or badly. Quantification clarifies issues which qualitative analysis may leave fuzzy. Without it, one cannot readily separate the 'stylised facts' which economic theory seeks to explain from the 'stylised phantasies' which are sometimes perceived to be reality.

Growth analysis benefits greatly from the national income approach which Gregory King pioneered in the 17th century, and which received a major boost in the 20th from the work of Colin Clark, Simon Kuznets and many others. This approach provides a systematic and transparent organisational framework for assembling quantitative evidence in which the boundaries of economic activity are clearly specified. In the comparison of levels, great progress has been made in the past 50 years on lines pioneered by Milton Gilbert and Irving Kravis. The comparative perspective adds an important extra dimension to historical analysis.

Causal analysis of the macroeconomic performance of nations is complex because there are many interactive forces whose individual impact is difficult to identify. Economists often use simple behavioural assumptions to explain the action of individuals or firms. But nation states are much larger units whose performance is strongly affected by governments with coercive power. They have widely differing institutions, traditions, and policies which have a powerful impact on the operation of atomistic market forces.

The first two essays in this volume concentrate on 'proximate' causality where the contribution of the basic factors of production (natural resources, labour supply, human and physical capital) and other complementary influences (structural change, foreign transaction, economies of scale, etc.) can be measured. The two most delicate questions here are the choice of weights in order to arrive at aggregate measures of productivity, and the problem of assessing the impact of technical progress.

In combining the influence of the different measurable elements I used my own adaptation of Denison's growth accounts, which are in their turn an augmented and eclectic version of Solow's neoclassical analysis. This seems to me the most satisfactory and transparent way of merging the available quantitative evidence. There are, of course, other legitimate ways of using the evidence. The econometric approach is less transparent and less sensitive to data quality, but is very useful in checking the plausibility of growth accounting procedures and findings.

No sensible person would claim that growth accounting will tell the whole story. The gaps in levels of real income per head between nations are so wide (a range of 50:1), and the paths of growth in different parts of the world have been so divergent, that 'proximate' analysis still leaves an embarrassing area of ignorance. There is a need to probe beyond the proximate to deeper layers of explanation.

Essay 3 distinguishes between 'ultimate' and 'proximate' layers of explanation. The investigation of 'ultimate' causality involves consideration of institutions, ideologies, socio-economic pressure groups and historical accidents which affect the economic destiny of nations in ways that are difficult to quantify, but nevertheless have a powerful effect on the way resources are mobilised and allocated. Essay 4 combines the 'proximate' and 'ultimate' elements in analysing developments in 43 countries since 1820.

Essays 5 to 9 deal mainly with problems of measurement. Essays 5 and 6 cover savings, investment and capital stock; Essays 7, 8 and 9 deal with levels of aggregate and sectoral performance.

In the three essays in Part IV I return to 'ultimate' levels of causality in greater depth in three case studies of economic backwardness in India, Mexico and Indonesia. Here, I tried to develop a coherent framework for such an analysis, which takes something from Adam Smith, Marx, Max Weber and modern political economists like Buchanan, Olson and Douglass North. I scrutinised a) the sanctions and structure of political power and the extent to which the state is predatory; b) the nature and distribution of property rights and earning capacity; c) the influence of class structure and group conflicts; d) the role of religion and ideology as weapons of social control and legitimation of authority; and e) the interaction between indigenous influences and colonialism.

Essays 13, 14 and 15 deal with the influence of economic and social policy. In Essay 3 I included policy as one of the 'ultimate' elements of causality, but it is not quite the same as the rest as it is more self-consciously directed at influencing particular outcomes. It is therefore an influence that falls somewhere between 'proximate' and 'ultimate'. It is easier to compare the efficacy of economic policy between countries where the institutional and ideological heritage has strong elements of similarity and where per capita incomes are also similar. This is the case for the advanced capitalist countries which are scrutinised in Part V.

Essay 16 is a fragment of professional autobiography which may help to explain why I tackled these issues in the way I did.

PART I

THE ANALYTICAL FRAMEWORK FOR EXPLAINING VARIATIONS IN GROWTH PERFORMANCE

Part I: The analytical framework for explaining variations in growth performance

These four essays provide an analytical framework for causal analysis of growth performance.

Essay 1 was my first effort (Maddison, 1970) to explain economic performance in an articulate growth accounting framework. It covers 22 developing countries, and was strongly influenced by Denison's (1967) attempt to explain why growth rates differ. However, it was adapted to cover countries with a much wider range of incomes; it gave capital a higher weight than is usual in growth accounts; and it tried to bridge the divide between proximate and deeper levels of analysis by incorporating the role of policy.

Essay 2 provides a more complex framework to assess comparative performance of six advanced capitalist economies over the period 1913–1982 (Maddison, 1987). It also surveys the intellectual history of growth accounting and the achievements of its different practitioners. It covers a wide range of causal influences in the Denisonian tradition, but it does not cover 'deeper' levels of causality.

Essay 3 (Maddison, 1988) distinguishes two main levels of causal analysis, i.e. 'proximate', measurable, elements which can be embedded in an articulate accounting framework, and deeper, less tangible, less measurable 'ultimate' influences. Although it developed out of a public debate I had with Mancur Olson, it is not simply a review of his position but presents my own views rather succinctly (see also the essays in Part IV).

Essay 4 is a recent (Maddison, 1994) general survey of variations in growth experience and levels of performance in different parts of the world economy. It covers 43 countries which represent about three-quarters of world population and a larger share of world product. It pushes the quantitative record back to 1820, as far as was possible. It is reasonably representative of the range of country growth experience, though there are important gaps for earlier years, and the information is weakest on African countries. The paper takes cognisance of both proximate and deeper, institutional and policy influences. It was given at a conference which was, in some respects, a reaction to the 'new growth' theory.

As the new growth theory has emerged since Essay 2 was written and is only referred to tangentially in Essay 4, it is useful to note what has emerged from this new wave of interest in economic growth. The two seminal articles are those of Romer (1986) and Lucas (1988). Both authors stressed the interrelationship between the rate of technical advance and the rate of growth of physical and human capital. Unlike Solow, who treated technical progress as exogenous, they assume that it is endogenous to the growth process of each country. Solow argued that diminishing returns would set in if investment were pushed hard, whereas they stress the possibility of technical spillovers which will produce constant or increasing returns. Thus Romer speaks of growth being 'unbounded'. The Solow model distinguished between rich countries near the frontier of technology, and poor countries where the marginal product of capital would be higher, facilitating convergence in growth rates. The new growth theory repudiates the likelihood of convergence, and makes no attempt to differentiate degrees of en-dogeneity and exogeneity. For the lead country it is quite plausible that technological progress is to a large degree endogenous in their sense, particularly as the lead country, the USA, is such a large economy. A large and successful follower country, like Japan, will have elements of endogeneity in its technology, and this is also true of West European countries. But for the rest of the world, technology is probably exogenous.

Romer and Lucas were mainly concerned with theoretical issues, but a new generation with econometric skills was keen to test their ideas empirically. They could do this with relatively little effort, as the Penn World Tables (PWT) of Summers and Heston (1988 and 1991) provided a comprehensive data-set on income levels, growth rates and associated information for 130 countries on diskette, ready for regression.

The most enthusiastic disciples of the increasing returns thesis were De Long and Summers (1991). They concluded that there was a very strong association between equipment investment and growth: 'high rates of investment can, for example, account for nearly all of Japan's extraordinary growth performance'. They have strong policy conclusions: 'the social rate of return to investment is 30 per cent per year, or higher. Much of this return is not captured by private investors. If these results stand up to scrutiny, they have obvious implications. The gains from raising equipment investment through tax or other incentives dwarf losses from any non-neutralities that would result.'

Barro (1991) reached different and more circumspect conclusions from the same evidence. He found human capital to be an important element in growth, but his regression analysis left a good deal of the weak performance of sub-Saharan Africa and Latin America unexplained. He and Sala-i-Martin (1992) found convergence in levels of income between US states for the period since 1840, and suggested that the convergence predictions of the Solow model were likely to be fulfilled when the institutional, political and policy setting was similar. This they characterised as 'conditional' convergence.

Mankiw, Romer and Weil (1992) felt the new growth theorists had been too cavalier in dismissing the conclusions of Solow's (1956) model, so they augmented it to include human capital and tested it with the PWT. They used these selectively, dropping the oil-producing countries from their first sample of 98 countries, then using a 75 nation sample from which they had dropped countries where the data were shaky or idiosyncratic. Finally, they concentrated on 22 OECD countries for which they did find convergence. They concluded that the augmented Solow model was robust if one allowed for the institutional and policy differences between countries, which prevent the expected convergence from occurring.

The new growth theory has been useful in re-emphasising a number of fundamental issues concerning the interrelation of technical progress, economies of scale and formation of physical and human capital. It quite properly directed attention to analysis of convergence and divergence on a world-wide scale. The distinction between the 'conditional' convergence of countries where the institutional policy mix is similar and repudiation of the idea of 'unconditional' convergence (on a global scale) is useful and is one way of bringing attention to the interaction of 'proximate' and 'ultimate' causal influences. It is a fundamental point which has been strongly emphasised by Abramovitz (1989) and it is central to North's (1990) attempt to develop a broader view of growth causality.

The basic contention of the new growth theory about the importance of increasing returns has left most observers as sceptical as an earlier generation was about Kaldor's (1966) arguments in a similar vein. The new growth theorists ignored previous work which was relevant to their discussion of the interaction between investment and technical progress, e.g. Salter's (1960) and Solow's (1962) analysis of vintage effects and the distinction between embodied and disembodied technical progress. They also ignored virtually all the growth accountants whose work is reviewed in Essay 2. The latter have developed a rich and flexible analytical framework more ambitious in scope than acknowledged by the new growth theorists. A greater degree of interaction between the econometricians and the growth accountants is obviously desirable.

References

Abramovitz, M. (1989), *Thinking About Growth*, Cambridge University Press.

Barro, R.J. (1991), 'Economic Growth in A Cross Section of Countries', *Quarterly Journal of Economics*, May, 407–43.

Barro, R.J. and X. Sala-i-Martin (1992), 'Convergence', *Journal of Political Economy*, **100**, 223–51.

De Long, J.B. and L.H. Summers (1991), 'Equipment Investment and Economic Growth', *Quarterly Journal of Economics*, May, 445–502.

Denison, E.F. (1967), *Why Growth Rates Differ: Postwar Experience in Nine Western Countries*, Brookings, Washington DC.

Kaldor, N. (1966), *Causes of the Slow Rate of Growth of the United Kingdom*, Cambridge University Press.

Lucas, R.E. (1988), 'On the Mechanics of Economic Development', *Journal of Monetary Economics*, **22**, 3–42.

Maddison, A. (1970), *Economic Progress and Policy in Developing Countries*, Allen and Unwin, London, and Norton, New York.

Maddison, A. (1987), 'Growth and Slowdown in Advanced Capitalist Economies: Techniques of Quantitative Assessment', *Journal of Economic Literature*, **XXV**, June, 649–98.

Maddison, A. (1988), 'Ultimate and Proximate Growth Causality: A Critique of Mancur Olson on the Rise and Decline of Nations', *Scandinavian Economic History Review*, No. 2.

Maddison, A. (1994), 'Explaining the Economic Performance of Nations, 1820–1989', in W.J. Baumol, R.R. Nelson and E.N. Wolff (eds), *Convergence of Productivity: Cross National Studies and Historical Evidence*, Oxford University Press, New York.

Mankiw, N.G., D. Romer and D. N. Weil (1992), 'A Contribution to the Empirics of Economic Growth', *Quarterly Journal of Economics*, **107**, 407–38.

North, D.C. (1990), *Institutions, Institutional Change and Economic Performance,* Cambridge University Press.

Romer, P.M. (1986), 'Increasing Returns and Long Run Growth', *Journal of Political Economy*, **94**, 1002–37.

Salter, W.E. (1960), *Productivity and Technical Change*, Cambridge University Press.

Solow, R.M. (1956), 'A Contribution to the Theory of Economic Growth', *Quarterly Journal of Economics*, **70**, February, 65–94.

Solow, R.M. (1962), Technical Progress, Capital Formation and Economic Growth', *American Economic Review*, May, 76–86.

Summers, R. and A. Heston (1988), 'A New Set of International Comparisons of Real Product and Prices: Estimates for 130 Countries, 1950–1985', *Review of Income and Wealth*, Series 34, March, 1–43.

Summers, R. and A. Heston (1991), 'The Penn World Table (Mark 5): An Expanded Set of International Comparisons, 1950–1988', *Quarterly Journal of Economics*, May, 327–68.

[1]

NA epc

Chapter II

Reasons for Accelerated Growth and Variations in Performance

Economic growth depends ultimately on the input of productive resources and the efficiency with which they are used. Resource input and efficiency are both affected (*a*) by the spontaneous action of private forces in the economy, (*b*) by government policy. In order to clarify their impact on growth it is useful to set out a simple model in which their relationship and relative importance is made explicit. Our model, like most others, is only a crude approximation to reality because on several important points the quantification is based on judgment rather than evidence, and in the real world there is a more complex interdependence between causal factors than we can hope to numerate. The novel feature of our model is the distinction between autonomous and policy-induced growth. Previous models of economic growth have not set out to do this for developing countries.

Historically, economists have considered land, labour and capital to be the important factors of production. But so much of environment is now man-made, that variations in natural resource endowment are more relevant in explaining the historical differences in level of income than in explaining current rates of growth. In Denison's major work on developed country growth, natural resources play no explanatory role.[1] In developing countries, where

---

[1] See E. F. Denison, *Why Growth Rates Differ*, Brookings Institution, Washington, 1967, and Allen & Unwin, London, 1968. Our own analysis in this chapter is heavily influenced by Denison's work, though the methodology is different on several important points. Denison's approach was first used in his book on the US economy, *The Sources of Economic Growth in the United States and the Alternatives Before Us*, Committee for Economic Development, New York, 1962. This has been subjected to detailed appraisal by M. Abramovitz, 'Economic Growth in the United States', *American Economic Review*, September 1962, pp. 762–82, by R. R. Nelson, 'Aggregate Production Functions and

34

ACCELERATED GROWTH AND VARIATIONS IN PERFORMANCE

man-made capital is scarcer, natural resource endowment looms larger as an explanatory variable, particularly in countries with mineral wealth.

In developed countries where productivity is high and labour scarce, no economist would now think of explaining growth without analysing the labour supply, but developing countries are often assumed to have such a surplus of labour that several quite respectable model-builders have tried to explain performance by models which leave labour out of account.[1] In our view, growth in labour supply has had a substantial influence on output, and it would be absurd to build a model which ignores the advantage to Israel of its 5·4 per cent annual growth in employment as compared with the low 0·7 per cent in Spain. There is also an enormous difference between the productivity of labour in agriculture and non-agriculture which makes it necessary to disaggregate the analysis of labour supply.

The third resource input which economists have considered important is capital. In fact, some growth models consider it the only important source of growth. This is an exaggerated view, but our own conclusion is that the acceleration in investment has been the most important engine of growth in the post-war developing world. We might also have treated research and technical progress explicitly as inputs which affect the quality of capital, but we did not do so as we have already given capital a rather big weight.[2]

Recent analysis of growth has emphasized the importance of non-conventional inputs, particularly education and research. We share the feeling that these have been important, and we treat improved education (and health) as resource inputs which increased the quality of labour.

In analysing the contribution of policy to resource mobilization we have made allowance for constraints imposed by income level. In this respect our model differs from most of those currently used. The result is a better performance rating for some of the low-income countries, e.g. India, than has lately been conventional.

Medium Range Growth Projections', *American Economic Review*, September 1964, and by a group of economists in J. Vaizey, ed. *The Residual Factor in Economic Growth*, OECD, Paris, 1965.

[1] See H. B. Chenery and A. M. Strout, *Foreign Assistance and Economic Development*, AID, Washington, 1965.

[2] See R. M. Solow, 'Technical Progress, Capital Formation, and Economic Growth', *American Economic Review, Proceedings*, May 1962, for a model of 'embodied' technical progress.

ECONOMIC PROGRESS AND POLICY IN DEVELOPING COUNTRIES

We have not treated balance of payments problems as an independent constraint, though they are the most publicized obstacle to faster growth. Developing countries generally do have specific balance of payments constraints because their exports are concentrated on primary products for which demand is sluggish, and some of their potential manufactured exports such as textiles are heavily protected in developed countries. Furthermore, in a period of rapidly rising investment they are heavily dependent on imports. However, balance of payments difficulties are also the reflection of other problems such as inadequate savings, overvalued exchange rates, excessive protection, neglect of agricultural development, etc. As these two sources of payments difficulty are difficult to disentangle in an *ex post* analysis, and as the first kind of problem—the structural one—is characteristic of most developing countries except those with large mineral resources, large-scale aid or tourist earnings, we felt entitled to build a model in which the payments constraint does not figure explicitly. However, the model does give substantial weight to the benefits derived from external finance and mineral resources, so it makes indirect allowance for factors which have affected the payments position of some countries favourably.

As later data are not available for some countries, the model is confined to explaining growth which occurred between 1950 and 1965. However, our other chapters include analysis of policy trends since 1965.

a. *Capital*

In most developing countries, it is only since the last war that investment has risen significantly above the level in Europe in the eighteenth century. The increase has been the biggest factor responsible for accelerated growth.

In the 1950s, economists gave major stress to the importance of high investment in achieving a 'take-off', i.e. in transforming a stagnant economy into a developing one. Arthur Lewis[1] and W. W. Rostow[2] suggested that the critical effort involved in the development process was to increase net investment from 5 to 10 per cent of national income. The argument for a 10 per cent net investment rate implies a target for gross investment, including allowance for replacement, of about 13 or 14 per cent of GDP. In fact, the Lewis–Rostow targets have actually been reached.

[1] See *The Theory of Economic Growth*, Allen & Unwin, London, 1959.
[2] See *The Stages of Economic Growth*, Cambridge, 1960.

36

ACCELERATED GROWTH AND VARIATIONS IN PERFORMANCE

Table II–1

Change in Non-Residential Gross Fixed Investment as Percentage of GDP at Current Market Prices 1950–66

	1950	1966	1950–66 average of annual ratios
Argentina	14·7	13·4	14·3
Brazil	11·3	10·9	12·5
Ceylon	7·1	11·0	10·0
Chile	9·6	10·3	11·7
Colombia	11·4	(12·1)	12·9
Egypt	10·2	(16·3)	11·5
Ghana	7·4	12·0	13·1
Greece	11·7	15·6	11·1
India	7·4	13·8	11·2
Israel	15·6	14·1	17·3
Malaya	5·0	(15·1)	10·3
Mexico	10·8	14·8	13·2
Pakistan	4·8	12·9	9·9
Peru	11·0	13·9	15·3
Philippines	7·4	16·5	10·7
South Korea	5·7	18·1	8·8
Spain	10·3	18·6	13·7
Taiwan	9·8	16·7	12·2
Thailand	11·9	(19·3)	13·9
Turkey	6·9	(10·4)	10·0
Venezuela	20·0	15·6	19·5
Yugoslavia	22·0	18·2	21·1
Average	10·5	14·5	12·9
France	13·6	15·5	14·1
Germany (FR)	14·3	19·9	17·6
Italy	14·8	12·3	15·1
Japan	15·7	(25·2)	23·0
UK	10·3	14·3	12·2
USA	13·7	14·6	13·3
Average	13·7	17·0	15·9

Source: Appendix D, for developing countries, developed countries from sources indicated in A. Maddison, *Economic Growth in Japan and the USSR*, Allen & Unwin, London, 1969, p. 39. Figures in brackets are for 1965. The figures exclude inventories for which data are poor or often not available.

37

ECONOMIC PROGRESS AND POLICY IN DEVELOPING COUNTRIES

For the twenty-two countries combined, gross fixed non-residential investment rose from 10·5 per cent of GDP in 1950 to 14·5 per cent in 1966. The biggest increases occurred in the poorer countries. In Africa and Asia (excluding Israel) the average rose from 7·6 in 1950 to 14·6 per cent in 1966. In Pakistan, Malaya and South Korea the rate has roughly trebled since 1950 and in India, the Philippines and Spain it doubled. In Ceylon, Egypt, Taiwan, Thailand and Turkey it rose by about half. In Latin America, Mexico and Peru made progress, but there were falls in Argentina, Brazil and Venezuela. The investment rate also fell in Israel and Yugoslavia, but in these countries the level was considerably higher than in Asia and Africa.

One difficulty in comparing investment rates is that the price of capital goods varies a good deal. Construction is generally cheaper than in the developed world, and equipment more expensive. The Economic Commission for Latin America found that overall, the relative price of capital goods was higher than in the USA.[1] But as the coverage of developing country estimates is often less complete, these two factors tend to be offsetting.

Figures on investment as a share of GDP show the current financial burden of capital formation. But to measure the effect of investment on output, it is more relevant to see how fast the capital *stock* was growing. Two countries may each devote the same share of GDP to investment, but if GDP is growing faster in one than in the other its capital stock will be rising more quickly. By cumulating the investment which took place between 1950 and 1964 we can arrive at a figure for the gross addition to the capital stock from beginning 1950 to beginning 1965, but to calculate the net increase in capital stock we need to know how much of the new capital formation went to replacement.

As information for 1950 was not generally available, we assumed that the 1950 non-residential capital stock of each of the countries was one and a half times as high as its GDP, i.e. an average initial capital-output ratio of 1·5,[2] and that half of the initial stock was

---

[1] See ECLA, *A Measurement of Price Levels and the Purchasing Power of Currencies in Latin America 1960–62*, E/CN. 12/653, Santiago, March 1963.

[2] It is necessary to make a uniform assumption as estimates are available only for a few countries. In Israel, the ratio was 1·3 in 1957; see A. L. Gaathon, *Capital Stock, Employment and Output in Israel, 1950–59*, Bank of Israel, Jerusalem, 1961, p. 95, for estimates of the Israeli capital stock. In Colombia the ratio was 1·6 in 1953 and in Yugoslavia 2·3 in 1953; see R. W. Goldsmith and C. Saunders, eds., *Income and Wealth Series VIII, The Measurement of*

ACCELERATED GROWTH AND VARIATIONS IN PERFORMANCE

replaced in the fifteen years 1950–64. This implies that assets have
an average useful life of thirty years, and that their age structure
was similar in the different countries in 1950. The assumed life for
assets is a fairly standard one, and although the age and condition
of the capital stock in fact varies a good deal in 1950, our assumption
of similar age structures is the only one that can reasonably be made.
Perhaps more questionable is the assumption that the average
capital-output ratio was similar. The ratio tends to be bigger in
countries which are relatively more advanced and have a more
complex economic structure. Building requirements also vary for
climatic reasons. The kind of building necessary for the rigorous
winters of Yugoslavia is not needed in Egypt. With these caveats,
we nevertheless assume that our estimates provide a crude idea of
differences in the growth of the capital stock, and they are shown
in Table II–2.

The estimates of the growth of the capital stock show big differences between the fast and the slower-growing countries. The
Israeli stock grew 2·4 times as fast as that of India, although her
investment ratio (non-residential) was only 50 per cent higher. On
average, for the twenty-two countries, the capital stock grew by

Table II–2

Rates of Growth of the Non-Residential Fixed Capital Stock
1950–65

Annual average compound growth rates

Argentina	5·6	Pakistan	3·7
Brazil	6·1	Peru	6·8
Ceylon	4·0	Philippines	5·1
Chile	4·9	South Korea	4·4
Colombia	5·8	Spain	7·6
Egypt	5·6	Taiwan	7·0
Ghana	6·0	Thailand	6·8
Greece	5·7	Turkey	5·0
India	4·7	Venezuela	9·3
Israel	11·2	Yugoslavia	9·7
Malaya	3·6		
Mexico	6·4	Average	6·1

Source: Appendix D.

National Wealth, Bowes and Bowes, London, 1959, pp. 9 and 10. In the USA,
the ratio in 1962 was 1·4 excluding government structures and roads; see E.
F. Denison, *Why Growth Rates Differ*, Brookings, Washington DC, p. 415.

ECONOMIC PROGRESS AND POLICY IN DEVELOPING COUNTRIES

6·1 per cent a year. This was considerably faster than the increase in employment and led to rapid growth in capital per head. Unfortunately, data on pre-war investment rates are rare, but it seems likely that pre-war investment was generally below 1950 levels, and the capital stock may well be growing three times as fast as in prewar years.

Our analysis of investment excludes housing because its contribution to productive capacity is rather indirect. Although we would not suggest that the contribution of housing is so negligible that it should be ignored, we have chosen to do so in our model, mainly because data on the housing stock are non-existent for most developing countries, and the statistical coverage of current housing investment is very uneven, with some countries leaving out most of the rural sector.

For what they are worth, the figures on housing investment were as follows:

Table II–3

Average Level of Housing Investment as Percentage of GDP in Current Prices 1950–65

Average of annual ratios

Argentina	4·8	Pakistan	0·9
Brazil	2·2	Peru	4·3
Ceylon	2·9	Philippines	2·5
Chile	3·7	South Korea	1·7
Colombia	3·5	Spain	3·4
Egypt	2·6	Taiwan	1·6
Ghana	1·9	Thailand	1·7
Greece	5·8	Turkey	3·2
India	1·3	Venezuela	2·6
Israel	9·8	Yugoslavia	4·7
Malaya	1·8		
Mexico	1·3	Average	3·1

Source: Appendix D.

b. *Labour*

On average, employment has grown by about 2·1 per cent a year, which is quicker than in pre-war years, and considerably faster than in developed countries. In most cases, the labour force grew more slowly than population. There are two main reasons for this. The

ACCELERATED GROWTH AND VARIATIONS IN PERFORMANCE

fall in death rates was concentrated on children, so there was a decline in the proportion of the population available for work. There were also big increases in school enrolment which reduced the activity rate.

In a few countries the labour force increased faster than population for special reasons. In both countries these special circumstances made the labour force grow considerably faster than population. In Greece the birth rate declined and in Israel there was large-scale immigration.

As we are concerned with growth potential, it might seem reasonable to use the labour force rather than employment as a measure of labour supply. However, unemployment in developing countries is usually due to lack of capital and not to failure of policy to maintain adequate demand. Most of the unemployed could not have been used and it is therefore legitimate to eliminate them in measuring output potential.

Our employment figures are rather rough, because few countries have an adequate statistical reporting system. Only Taiwan and South Korea measure unemployment by a regular sample survey similar to that used in the United States and they are the two countries with the highest recorded unemployment rates, 11·5 per cent for Taiwan and 7·4 per cent for Korea in 1965. It seems likely that several other countries would have had higher unemployment rates, if the figures had been properly recorded.[1]

In calculating the contribution of labour to output, we must take account of the highly dualistic character of these economies. Except in Argentina and Israel, productivity in agriculture is extremely low, on average is only a fifth of that in the rest of the economy (see Table II–4). This low productivity in agriculture is due partly to the fact that farm workers are not fully employed. Some economists argue that a substantial proportion of the agricultural population (30 per cent or more) could be removed without any loss of output. This is the position of Doreen Warriner who first tried to measure 'disguised unemployment' in her pre-war studies of peasant agriculture in eastern Europe. More recently, this view has been contested by writers who have argued that though heavy seasonal unemployment may exist, it is nevertheless impossible to remove

[1] The special ILO sample survey in Ceylon in 1959 found a 10·5 per cent unemployment rate, which is much higher than the unemployment recorded by the census. The figures we have used for Ceylon are based on the sample survey benchmark.

ECONOMIC PROGRESS AND POLICY IN DEVELOPING COUNTRIES

Table II–4

Level of Output per Person Engaged in Agriculture and Non-Agriculture in 1965 and 1950

Dollars at US 1965 relative prices

	1965 Agriculture	1965 Non-agriculture	1950 agriculture	1950 Non-agriculture
Argentina	2,226	3,665	2,001	2,846
Brazil	556	2,372	370	2,018
Ceylon	455	1,524	365	1,347
Chile	644	3,536	504	2,450
Colombia	434	2,004	337	1,503
Egypt	262	1,950	181	1,223
Ghana	211	1,178	n.a.	n.a.
Greece	493	2,629	223	1,470
India	90	1,205	75	1,341
Israel	1,877	3,812	846	1,778
Malaya	515	2,776	363	2,951
Mexico	332	2,401	208	1,828
Pakistan	133	1,381	138	1,148
Peru	550	2,055	373	1,150
Philippines	247	1,591	181	1,450
South Korea	164	1,560	59	1,382
Spain	596	3,574	320	1,582
Taiwan	461	2,551	204	1,103
Thailand	219	1,618	175	1,243
Turkey	240	1,756	161	1,247
Venezuela	599	5,454	301	4,385
Yugoslavia	303	3,179	140	1,751
Average	528	2,444	359	1,783

Source: Appendixes A and B.

any substantial fraction of labour from agriculture without some loss of output.[1]

The burden of modern evidence suggests that there is not a large amount of completely surplus labour in agriculture, but whether or

[1] See C. Clark and M. R. Haswell, *The Economics of Subsistence Agriculture*, Macmillan, London, 1964; A. A. Pepelasis, *Labour Shortages in Greek Agriculture, 1963–73*, Centre of Economic Research, Athens, 1963; and B. Hansen, 'Marginal Productivity Wage Theory and Subsistence Wage Theory in Egyptian Agriculture', *The Journal of Development Studies*, July 1966.

ACCELERATED GROWTH AND VARIATIONS IN PERFORMANCE

not we choose to accept the concept of disguised unemployment, it is quite uncontestable that the productivity of labour in agriculture is low and that additions to farm labour make little contribution to output.

In the past two decades, there has been an absolute increase in farm employment in most developing countries, but the relative share of agriculture has fallen everywhere. In all countries, therefore there has been some improvement in the effectiveness of labour because of this shift to higher productivity employment. However, the higher output per head of non-agriculture is due in part to the fact that it has more capital per head, and we therefore exaggerate somewhat by treating the whole gain from this structural shift as a contribution of labour.

We have divided the employment increase into two parts. The contribution of those entering agriculture is smaller than that of people lucky enough to find jobs in other sectors, and it was assumed that the difference in their 'effectiveness' could be measured in terms of the average productivity of labour in agriculture and non-agriculture.[1] In all countries, the effectiveness of labour increased to some degree and on average, the 'effective' labour supply grew by $3 \cdot 2$ per cent a year compared with an actual employment increase of $2 \cdot 1$ per cent (see Table II–5).

Apart from the improved sectoral distribution of labour there were other improvements in quality which had a significant positive effect on productivity. Rising health standards increased physical working capacity, and probably mental alertness as well. The improvement was particularly important in Asia, where malaria was greatly reduced, thanks to DDT,[2] and the incidence of dysentery declined because of better sanitation. These two illnesses are probably the most debilitating in terms of working efficiency, but there are many others whose impact has faded.[3] Improved nutrition also made

[1] The formula was as follows for the last column of Table II–5:

$$\frac{E_1^a p_0^a + E_1^e p_0^e}{E_0^a p_0^a + E_0^e p_0^e},$$ where E is employment; a is agriculture; e is non-agriculture; and p is labour productivity.

[2] Malaria eradication has proceeded furthest in Ceylon, where 57 per cent of the population had the disease in 1940, 8 per cent in 1950; in 1960 there were only 460 cases in a population of nearly 10 million. See D. R. Snodgrass, *Ceylon: An Export Economy in Transition*, Irwin, Illinois, 1966, p. 87. In Pakistan, malaria still killed 100,000 people a year in 1965.

[3] In East Pakistan there were 79,000 cases of small-pox in 1958 and only fifty in 1964 after the whole population was vaccinated. See *Third Five Year Plan*, Planning Commission, Pakistan, p. 244.

43

ECONOMIC PROGRESS AND POLICY IN DEVELOPING COUNTRIES

Table II–5

Increase in Actual and in 'Effective' Employment 1950–65

Annual average compound growth rates

	Agriculture	Non-agriculture	Actual total	'Effective' total
Argentina	−1·0	2·1	1·4	1·6
Brazil	1·6	4·3	2·9	3·8
Ceylon	0·7	3·0	1·6	2·3
Chile	0·3	1·6	1·3	1·5
Colombia	1·2	3·3	2·3	2·9
Egypt	0·7	2·8	1·5	2·4
Ghana	n.a.	n.a.	n.a.	n.a.
Greece	0·1	2·6	1·2	2·2
India	1·3	4·4	2·2	3·9
Israel	3·8	5·6	5·4	5·5
Malaya	0·0	4·1	1·7	3·5
Mexico	2·2	4·2	3·1	4·0
Pakistan	2·2	3·0	2·4	2·8
Peru	0·1	2·5	1·3	1·9
Philippines	0·7	4·9	2·2	4·1
South Korea	−0·1	5·3	1·8	4·9
Spain	−1·6	2·4	0·7	1·9
Taiwan	0·2	3·0	1·7	2·6
Thailand	2·3	5·6	3·1	4·5
Turkey	1·3	3·3	1·8	2·7
Venezuela	0·9	5·2	3·6	5·1
Yugoslavia	−0·5	3·3	1·0	2·8
Average	0·8	3·6	2·1	3·2
France	−3·2	1·5	0·3	—
Germany (FR)	−3·5	2·8	1·7	—
Italy	−2·5	2·7	0·9	—
Japan	−2·3	4·4	1·9	—
UK	−2·4	0·8	0·7	—
USA	−3·4	1·7	1·3	—
Average	−2·9	2·3	1·1	—

Source: Appendix C for developing countries, developed countries derived from sources described in A. Maddison, *Growth in Japan and the USSR*, Allen & Unwin, London, 1969.

44

ACCELERATED GROWTH AND VARIATIONS IN PERFORMANCE

a contribution in some countries, although there was little significant change in the two poorest countries, India and Pakistan.

It is not easy to quantify the impact of better health and nutrition on working efficiency. In the poorest countries, the improvements must have had some effect, and it was therefore assumed that better physical well-being raised the working efficiency of the labour force in Ceylon, Egypt, Ghana, India, Pakistan, the Philippines, South Korea, Thailand, and Turkey by 3 per cent over the fifteen years under review. In the other countries (where per capita income is above $300 a year) the initial level of health and nutrition was probably high enough to secure reasonable working efficiency. The improvement in standards added to welfare but not to economic potential.

The quality of labour has been improved substantially in terms of education. Table 11–6 gives some rough indicators of the educational attainments of the different countries in 1965. The picture is encouraging, thanks to the vigorous efforts of the past few years. On average, over 70 per cent of the labour force is now literate, and the average employee has 5·4 years of schooling. This is very much better than the record of today's developed countries when they were at similar income levels. The countries with the lowest educational standards were Egypt, Ghana, India, Pakistan, Thailand and Turkey, and those with the highest achievements were Argentina, Chile, Greece and Israel. Educational achievement is positively correlated with the level of income, though there are some low-income countries like South Korea and the Philippines with relatively high standards.

In the 1960s, education received considerable credit as a source of economic growth, and it is now usual to consider it as an 'investment in human resources' as well as an element of communal consumption. In the first flush of enthusiasm for education it was even suggested that it is a more important source of economic growth than investment in physical capital, though most of these claims were not based on a direct identification of its role as a propulsive force, but gave it credit for most of the growth not specifically attributable to other causes.[1] Our own estimates of the role of education are more modest, but they suggest that it added

[1] See R. Solow, 'Technical Change and the Aggregate Production Function', *The Review of Economics and Statistics*, August 1957; O. Aukrust, 'Investment and Economic Growth', *Productivity Measurement Review*, No. 16, OEEC, Paris, 1959.

45

ECONOMIC PROGRESS AND POLICY IN DEVELOPING COUNTRIES

Table II–6
Educational Qualifications of the Labour Force 1965

	Per cent literate	Per cent with high level technical training	Average number of years of primary and secondary education per member of the labour force
Argentina	93·1	0·8	6·9
Brazil	67·3	0·4	3·9
Ceylon	76·0	n.a.	7·5
Chile	86·1	n.a.	6·9
Colombia	65·5	n.a.	3·8
Egypt	36·1	0·3	3·2
Ghana	n.a.	0·05	3·3
Greece	90·1	0·9	7·4
India	35·4	0·35	3·2
Israel	89·3	1·3	8·5
Malaya	64·7	n.a.	5·1
Mexico	70·7	0·3	4·9
Pakistan	27·0	0·08	2·5
Peru	73·0	n.a.	4·9
Philippines	75·6	0·7	7·8
South Korea	82·5	0·9	6·5
Spain	92·1	0·9	5·9
Taiwan	78·9	0·9	5·7
Thailand	74·9	0·1	5·5
Turkey	46·1	0·3	3·7
Venezuela	70·6	n.a.	5·4
Yugoslavia	84·3	0·7	6·0
Average	70·4	n.a.	5·4

Source: Literacy rates for labour force aged 15 to 64 estimated with help of data on literacy by age and sex, data on age structure and activity rates in UNESCO, *Statistical Yearbook* 1965, Paris, 1967, *Yearbook of Labour Statistics*, 1967, ILO, Geneva, 1968, and *Demographic Yearbook* 1966, UN, New York, 1967. Second column refers to scientists and engineers, doctors, dentists and veterinarians. Data derived from A. Maddison, *Foreign Skills and Technical Assistance in Economic Development*, OECD Development Centre, Paris, 1965, F. Harbison and C. A. Myers, *Education, Manpower and Economic Growth*, McGraw Hill, New York, 1964, and data supplied by Mr Jan Auerhan of UNESCO. Years of schooling were calculated from historical data on enrolments as given by UNESCO.

ACCELERATED GROWTH AND VARIATIONS IN PERFORMANCE

0·3 percentage points to the growth rate of the twenty-two countries, which is a sixth of the policy-induced growth.

Almost all countries made big increases in their educational effort. In 1950 just over a third of the children aged 5 to 19 were going to school, and by 1965 the ratio was well over half (see Table II–7). The rise was biggest in Africa. In Ghana enrolments rose from one-seventh to over half of the population of school age.

Table II–7

Ratio of Enrolments in Primary and Secondary Education to Population aged 5 to 19

	1950	1964		1950	1964
Argentina	51	60	Peru	34	50
Brazil	22	46	Philippines	59	57‡
Ceylon*	54	65	South Korea	43	63
Chile	50	63	Spain*	43	59
Colombia	22	45	Taiwan	38	64
Egypt	20	41	Thailand	38	48
Ghana	14	57	Turkey	24	40
Greece	56	60	Venezuela	30	61
India	19	38†	Yugoslavia	44	68
Israel	58	66			
Malaya	35	50	Average	36	54
Mexico	30	52			
Pakistan	16	25	USA	80	84

* Includes pre-school enrolments; † 1963; ‡ seems to exclude private schools.
Source: *Statistical Yearbook*, 1964 and 1966 editions, UNESCO, Paris, 1966 and 1968.

Secondary and higher education expanded much faster than primary, so that the average quality of education may have risen. We have made no allowance for this, as the calculation would be quite complex, and there were offsetting losses in quality due to overcrowded schools and the inadequate supply of teachers. The curricula have remained similar to those in the colonial period and emphasis on scientific and technical training is often inadequate.

Enrolment data of past years enable us to make rough estimates of the change in the educational qualifications between 1950 and 1965. There was a rise of about a quarter in the years of education which an average employee had received (see Table II–8). The problem now is to decide what economic impact this was likely to have had.

ECONOMIC PROGRESS AND POLICY IN DEVELOPING COUNTRIES

Table II–8

Change in Educational Qualifications per Employee 1950–65

	Years of education per employec 1950	Years of education per new employee 1950–65	Proportion of 1950–65 entrants to 1965 employ- ment	Years of education per employee 1965	Difference in years of education per employee 1950–65
Argentina	6·12	8·37	35·5	6·92	0·80
Brazil	2·64	5·22	47·7	3·87	1·23
Ceylon	6·48	8·99	37·4	7·42	0·94
Chile	6·00	8·55	33·6	6·86	0·86
Colombia	2·64	5·15	42·8	3·71	1·07
Egypt	2·40	4·68	36·0	3·22	0·82
Ghana	1·68	5·55	40·6	3·25	1·57
Greece	6·72	8·72	32·7	7·37	0·65
India	2·28	4·47	41·6	3·19	0·91
Israel	6·96	9·35	63·4*	8·48	1·52
Malaya	4·20	6·45	41·3	5·13	0·93
Mexico	3·60	6·27	49·9	4·93	1·33
Pakistan	1·92	3·12	44·1	2·45	0·53
Peru	4·08	6·39	33·3	4·85	0·77
Philippines	7·08	8·70	42·0	7·76	0·68
South Korea	5·16	8·06	38·6	6·28	1·12
Spain	5·16	7·74	28·4	5·89	0·73
Taiwan	4·56	7·79	37·6	5·77	1·21
Thailand	4·56	6·51	49·1	5·52	0·96
Turkey	2·88	4·89	38·9	3·66	0·78
Venezuela	3·60	6·99	53·1	5·40	1·80
Yugoslavia	5·28	7·73	30·9	6·04	0·76
Average	4·36	6·80	40·8	5·36	1·00

* In Israel there was a large influx of immigrants from Asia and Africa with low levels of education, so we may have overstated the increase in the average level of education.

Source: Enrolments are shown in Table II–7 for 1950 and 1965 as a percentage of the population aged 5 to 19. It was assumed that the schooling which had been obtained by the average member of the labour force in 1950 was 80 per cent of the level being provided in 1950, e.g. the 1950 enrolment ratio for Argentina was 51 per cent or 7·65 years of education. 80 per cent of this is 6·12 years. It was assumed that 20 per cent of the labour force of 1950 had retired by 1965, and that the new entrants to the labour force for 1950–65 had a level of schooling equivalent to the average provided in 1950 and 1965.

48

ACCELERATED GROWTH AND VARIATIONS IN PERFORMANCE

The best guide to the economic returns from education is information on the earnings of people with varying qualifications.[1] Earnings are heavily influenced by intelligence and social position and it is difficult to segregate the impact of these from that of education.[2] The earnings structure will also vary over time because of changing demand-supply relations and institutional conventions. In newly independent countries like Ghana where educated people were very scarce and were usually expatriates until very recently, the returns on education have been much higher to those possessing it than in Israel. Ideally therefore we need information on the stock of people with different skills and their relative income for each country. In the absence of such information, we simply assumed that an extra year of schooling added 10 per cent to the quality of the labour force in each country. This is a slightly higher return than Denison obtained for European countries, but the salary differentials for educated people in developing countries are higher than in Europe.[3]

Many of the skills most helpful to efficiency are acquired by on-the-job training and experience. The provisions for practical training are much better in some countries than in others. They are excellent in Brazil and almost non-existent in Pakistan. Work experience—'learning by doing'—is very important in the early stages of industrialization and was significant in all the countries under review. Unfortunately, we have no comparable statistical information on practical training, but the impact of on-the-job training and experience is partially reflected in our earlier adjustment for changes in the sectoral composition of employment.

Table II–9 shows the increase in total human resource inputs from 1950 to 1965 after allowing for improvements in quality due to better industrial composition, better health and education. On average, human resources grew by 3·9 per cent a year or considerably faster than in the developed countries.

[1] See T. W. Schultz, 'Investment in Human Capital', *American Economic Review*, March 1961, and T. W. Schultz, *The Economic Value of Education*, Columbia, New York, 1963. Interestingly enough, Professor Strumilin, the father of Soviet planning, produced estimates similar to those of Schultz in the early 1920s to help justify the Soviet educational effort.

[2] Denison assumed that in Europe and the USA, three-fifths of earnings differentials were due to education and two-fifths to characteristics such as intelligence, social position of parents, etc. See E. F. Denison, *op. cit.*, pp. 83 and 85.

[3] See Denison, *op. cit.*, pp. 103 and 107.

ECONOMIC PROGRESS AND POLICY IN DEVELOPING COUNTRIES

Table II–9

Increase in Total 'Human Resource' Inputs 1950–65

Annual average compound growth rates

Argentina	2·1	Pakistan	3·4
Brazil	4·7	Peru	2·4
Ceylon	3·2	Philippines	4·8
Chile	2·1	South Korea	5·8
Colombia	3·6	Spain	2·4
Egypt	3·1	Taiwan	3·4
Ghana	n.a.	Thailand	5·4
Greece	2·6	Turkey	3·5
India	4·7	Venezuela	6·2
Israel	6·4	Yugoslavia	3·4
Malaya	4·1		
Mexico	4·9	Average	3·9

Source: Derived from Tables II–5 and II–7 with adjustment for health and nutrition.

c. *Natural Resources*

There are big differences in the natural resource endowment of countries. The most important are land, climate and minerals. Table II–10 shows the land-labour ratio for agriculture.

Differences in natural resource endowment are obviously a major historical reason for the high output of farmers in Argentina and for low output in India. Most of the effects of these differences had already made themselves felt before 1950 and there were few significant *changes* in known natural resource endowment in these countries between 1950 and 1965. However, we assumed that countries with less than 1·5 hectares of land per agricultural worker were at a disadvantage, and that this reduced their agricultural growth *potential* by 1 per cent a year. The impact of this drag on growth varies with the importance of agriculture in the economy. Thus a country where agriculture was a third of total output would suffer a reduction in its total growth potential by 0·3 percentage points a year. The countries affected by natural disadvantage were Ceylon, Egypt, India, Pakistan, South Korea, Taiwan and Thailand. In the case of Chile and Venezuela, copper and oil provided government with large revenues from corporate taxation. These two countries were therefore credited with special growth benefits deriving from their mineral endowment. It was assumed that

50

ACCELERATED GROWTH AND VARIATIONS IN PERFORMANCE

Table II–10

The Land-Labour Ratio in Agriculture in 1965

	Hectares per person engaged		Hectares per person engaged
Argentina	91·6	Mexico	14·8
Brazil	11·0	Pakistan	0·9
Ceylon	0·8	Peru	18·8
Chile	21·1	Philippines	1·9
Colombia	8·0	South Korea	0·5
Egypt	0·5	Spain	8·3
Ghana	1·4	Taiwan	0·4
Greece	4·6	Thailand	1·2
India	1·2	Turkey	5·2
Israel	9·8	Venezuela	27·3
Malaya	1·6	Yugoslavia	3·1

Source: *Production Yearbook* 1966, FAO, Rome, 1967, for land area. Appendix B for employment. We have simply added together all agricultural land without adjustment for quality, and this understates the endowment of Egypt and Taiwan where a good deal of land can produce three crops a year, but the differences in land availability are so enormous, that there can be no doubt as to the balance of advantage.

government tax revenue from foreign corporations (2·5 per cent of GDP in Chile and 7 per cent in Venezuela) was a rough measure of this and could be regarded as an external source of finance for capital formation.

GROWTH 'EXPLAINED'

We are now in a position to summarize the contribution of the different influences on the growth of output. We know how the supply of capital and human resources changed, and we need to give each one a weight in order to measure their aggregate impact. In this study of growth in developed countries, Edward Denison[1] has made a composite index of factor inputs, giving each one a weight equivalent to its share in natural income in the country concerned. He assumes that income shares reflect the importance of each factor's contribution to output. Thus, for the USA, he gives labour a weight of 79 per cent, and capital (of all kinds) gets a weight of 21 per cent. For Italy, labour's share is lower at 72 per

[1] See E. F. Denison, *Why Growth Rates Differ*, Brookings, Washington DC, 1967.

51

ECONOMIC PROGRESS AND POLICY IN DEVELOPING COUNTRIES

cent. A recent study on the same lines gives labour a weight from
50 to 60 per cent in Latin American countries.[1] Information on
factor shares in developing countries is scarce but there is a definite
tendency for labour's share to be lower. In these countries this is
to be expected as labour is abundant and capital scarcer than in
the developed world.

In any case, factor rewards are likely to under-state capital's contribution to output. Technical progress is exploited mainly by
being embodied in capital, but the benefits are not monopolized
by capitalists. It is only if the capitalist has secret technical knowledge that he can keep the whole benefit for himself. His profits are
a reward for enterprise and thrift and not for exploiting techniques
which are, for the most part, freely available to any other capitalist.
Therefore, his income is not an adequate reflection of the contribution of capital to the production potential of the economy, unless
we are willing to assume that technical progress is a separate factor
of production which casts its blessings on an economy irrespective
of the investment effort. For these reasons we have given capital a
much greater weight (50 per cent) than in the Denison model.

Table II–11 shows the weighted contribution of factor inputs and
efficiency to economic growth. The first column shows the contribution of human resources (i.e. figures of Table II–9 with 50 per
cent weight) and the second column the contribution of capital (i.e.
figures of Table II–2 with 50 per cent weight). The fourth column
shows the growth of GDP and the fifth column shows the residual
change in efficiency (i.e. the difference between GDP growth and
the growth explained by the increase in factor inputs). In this, and
in subsequent tables, the presence of two decimal points should
not be taken to imply a high degree of accuracy. It is necessary
simply because some influences are very small.

From Table II–11, we can see that Israel, for example, with a
growth in labour supply of 6·4 per cent a year and of capital stock
by 11·2 per cent, increased its total factor input by 8·8 per cent
a year. Labour contributed 3·2 percentage points to the growth
rate (50 per cent of 6·4) and capital 5·6 points (50 per cent of 11·2).
The remaining 1·9 per cent a year of Israeli growth was due to
increased efficiency in resource allocation.[2] Efficiency gains arise

[1] See H. J. Bruton, 'Productivity Growth in Latin America', *American
Economic Review*, December 1967.
[2] If we had used factor income weights labour would have probably been
70 per cent of the total and non-residential capital about 30 per cent. This

52

ACCELERATED GROWTH AND VARIATIONS IN PERFORMANCE

Table II–11

Contribution of Factor Inputs and Increased Efficiency to Economic Growth 1950–65

Percentage point contribution to annual average compound growth rate of GDP

	Human resources	Non-residential capital	Labour and non-residential capital combined	GDP growth rate	Growth due to changes in efficiency
Argentina	1·05	2·80	3·85	3·20	−0·65
Brazil	2·35	3·05	5·40	5·20	−0·20
Ceylon	1·60	2·00	3·60	3·40	−0·20
Chile	1·05	2·45	3·50	4·00	0·50
Colombia	1·80	2·90	4·70	4·60	−0·10
Egypt	1·55	2·80	4·35	5·50	1·15
Ghana	(1·50)	3·00	4·50	4·20	−0·30
Greece	1·30	2·85	4·15	6·40	2·25
India	2·35	2·35	4·70	3·50	−1·20
Israel	3·20	5·60	8·80	10·70	1·90
Malaya	2·05	1·80	3·85	3·50	−0·35
Mexico	2·45	3·20	5·65	6·10	0·45
Pakistan	1·70	1·85	3·55	3·70	0·15
Peru	1·20	3·40	4·60	5·60	1·00
Philippines	2·40	2·55	4·95	5·00	0·05
South Korea	2·90	2·20	5·10	6·20	1·10
Spain	1·20	3·80	5·00	7·50	2·50
Taiwan	1·70	3·50	5·20	8·50	3·30
Thailand	2·70	3·40	6·10	6·30	0·20
Turkey	1·75	2·50	4·25	5·20	0·95
Venezuela	3·10	4·65	7·75	6·70	−1·05
Yugoslavia	1·70	4·85	6·55	7·10	0·55
Average	1·94	3·07	5·00	5·55	0·55

Source: First column derived from Table II–9, second column from Table II–2, both weighted by 50 per cent. Third column is the sum of first and second columns. The fourth column is derived from Table I–1. The fifth column is a residual after deducting third column from fourth column.

would mean, e.g. for Israel, that the labour supply would contribute 4·5 points to the annual growth rate and capital 3·4 points, i.e. a total factor input of 7·9. The residual which we have attributed to efficiency would then be bigger (2·8 points). This is true of most of the countries because capital inputs were generally growing faster than human resource inputs.

53

ECONOMIC PROGRESS AND POLICY IN DEVELOPING COUNTRIES

from several sources. Normally an economy will benefit from economies of scale as production increases. There will be technical improvements which arise independently of expenditure on capital, health and education which we have already accounted for. On the other hand, there may be losses in efficiency if the price system is distorted by inflation, if capacity if left idle by recessions, if inefficient industries are created through excessive tariff protection, or if the balance of payments becomes a bottleneck because of domestic policy mistakes. Thus in some countries, such as Argentina or India, there was an efficiency loss rather than the normal gain.

AUTONOMOUS AND POLICY-INDUCED GROWTH

For our purpose, it is necessary to separate the growth due to policy from that which would have occurred spontaneously. There are, in fact, several growth influences which had little direct connection with government policy in the period under examination. The growth in the labour supply was autonomous, because it was determined by demographic events in an earlier period and could not have been substantially influenced by population policy in the period under review. (Improvements in health and education were due to government policy.) Similarly, a good deal of capital formation was financed from spontaneous private savings or by foreign funds and was not primarily attributable to government domestic policy.

All the countries, except Malaya and Venezuela, were able to draw on external capital. Economic aid and private investment were dominant, but there were also reparations, private gifts (e.g. Jewish community donations to Israel), short-term commercial credit, drawings on exchange reserves, transactions with the IMF, private gold hoarding, and military aid. Some of these were gifts, others were loans which may ultimately have to be repaid, but they were all additions to the resources which the country itself produced within the period.

On average, these resources were equal to 2·8 per cent of GDP.[1]

[1] It should be stressed that our figures (in Table II–12) refer to the net contribution of foreign capital in a national accounting sense, i.e. the balance on trade in goods and services and the balance on factor payments to abroad. Typically a developing country will use external resources both to finance a deficit on goods and services and to pay interest and dividends on foreign capital. Nearly all developing countries are in deficit on 'factor payments' except lucky ones like Greece which have relatively large receipts from emigrants' remittances.

ACCELERATED GROWTH AND VARIATIONS IN PERFORMANCE

But the benefits were very heavily concentrated. In Israel, they were equal to nearly a fifth of GDP, in South Korea 8·3 per cent, in Greece 7·6 per cent and in Taiwan 5·4 per cent. The contribution of these resources was relatively small in Latin America. In India, they were only 1·9 per cent of GDP. In Malaya, there was actually a

Table II–12

External Finance as a Percentage of GDP and Investment 1950–65

Average of annual ratios

	Per cent of GDP	Percentage contribution to non-residential investment		Per cent of GDP	Percentage contribution to non-residential investment
Argentina	0·9	6·3	Pakistan	2·4	24·2
Brazil	1·1	8·8	Peru	3·0	19·6
Ceylon	0·3	3·0	Philippines	2·2	20·6
Chile	1·9	16·2	South Korea	8·3*	94·3
Colombia	1·4	10·9	Spain	1·0	7·3
Egypt	3·4	29·6	Taiwan	5·4	44·3
Ghana	0·4	3·1	Thailand	1·4	10·1
Greece	7·6	68·5	Turkey	2·4	24·0
India	1·9	17·0	Venezuela	−0·2	0·0
Israel	19·1	100·0	Yugoslavia	2·9	13·7
Malaya	−6·5	0·0			
Mexico	1·6	12·1	Average	2·8	24·3

* 1953–65.

Source: First column from Appendix D. The figures are equivalent to the deficit in the balance on trade in goods and services and the deficit on factor payments to abroad. Second column derived from first column of this table and from Appendix D.

large outflow due to repatriation of British capital, and to the traditionally high Chinese remittances.

External resources did not all go to investment. Some were used for military purposes and others went to meet pressing consumption needs. But if they had not been available, domestic investment

For some purposes, however, it is useful to analyse the impact of external resources on a completely net basis and to deduct factor payments. If this is done we get the figures in Table II–13 which some authors describe as the 'net transfer of resources'. On average these transfers were only 1·7 per cent of GDP.

55

ECONOMIC PROGRESS AND POLICY IN DEVELOPING COUNTRIES

would have been the main sufferer. Foreign resources not only financed investment, but also had indirect beneficial effects. They greatly eased balance of payments constraints and the domestic adjustments which would otherwise have been necessary when demand exceeded domestic resources. They provided governments with additional revenue and made it easier to promote development without squeezing consumption and inhibiting production incentives. They enabled countries to be more open to international trade, and thus contributed to the productivity benefits of increased specialization. Considering the importance of these indirect effects it does not seem exaggerated to treat the whole of external resources as a contribution to capital formation.

We must also make some allowance for investment which would have been carried out by the private sector even if there were no government policy for economic growth. We assumed that this autonomous investment would vary directly with the level of per capita income of each country within a range from 4 per cent of GDP in the poorest country to 8 per cent in the richest,[1] and that all domestically financed non-residential investment beyond this level was induced by government policy.

This assumption that poor countries are at a disadvantage in resource mobilization is, curiously enough, not now generally accepted. At one time, it was widely held that the spontaneous propensity to save tends to increase as income rises, and this was the view held by Keynes in his general theory. Since then, however, this idea has been challenged as far as developed countries are concerned,[2] and even for developing countries, many writers assume that the policy problem involved in raising savings or taxation does not depend on the level of income so much as on its distribution. Our own view is therefore an old-fashioned one.

[1] The upper limit of 8 per cent corresponds with the average rate of non-residential fixed investment which prevailed in west European countries before 1913 when there were no significant government policies to stimulate growth, and the lower limit corresponds with the situation in low income Asian countries before their governments started to pursue active growth policies. The actual post-war relation of savings to income does not provide a guide to spontaneous propensities, because the savings ratios are heavily influenced by policy.

[2] See J. S. Duesenberry, *Income, Saving and the Theory of Consumer Behavior*, Harvard, 1949, p. 57, 'According to our hypothesis, the savings rate is independent of the absolute level of income'. Duesenberry's conclusion was based entirely on evidence for the United States. Similarly in Professor Kaldor's writings on taxation it is sometimes suggested that poor countries have just as great a taxation potential as rich ones (see our Chapter III below).

56

ACCELERATED GROWTH AND VARIATIONS IN PERFORMANCE

Table II–13

Net Transfer of Resources as Percentage of GDP 1950–65

Average of annual ratios

Argentina	0·9	Pakistan	2·3
Brazil	0·3	Peru	1·2
Ceylon	−0·5	Philippines	1·2
Chile	0·3	South Korea	9·1*
Colombia	0·2	Spain	0·9
Egypt	2·9	Taiwan	5·3
Ghana	−1·2	Thailand	1·1
Greece	9·3	Turkey	2·1
India	1·6	Venezuela	−9·8
Israel	18·3	Yugoslavia	2·7
Malaya	−11·9		
Mexico	0·4	Average	1·7

* 1953–65.

Source: Appendix D. The figures are equivalent to the deficit on trade in goods and services.

Finally, we must make some allowance for those gains in efficiency which arise from the normal operation of economic forces and which are not due to any special action on the part of government. We assumed that these are 10 per cent of the growth attributable to autonomous factor inputs.

Table II–14 shows the growth which would have been achieved without any policy effort. For the twenty-two countries, growth would have averaged about 3·5 per cent a year if there had been no domestic policy measures to stimulate growth. This is higher than the 2·5 per cent growth average of pre-war years, but in 1950–65 there were recovery factors, a faster growth in labour supply, and two-thirds of external finance consisted of government aid which did not exist in pre-war years.

Autonomous growth varied very widely between countries. In Ceylon, Ghana, India and Malaya it was well under 2.5 per cent a year, whereas in Greece, Israel, South Korea, Taiwan and Venezuela it ranged from 4 to 9 per cent! The wide range of autonomous growth shows that judgements on policy performance will be very misleading if based on crude comparisons of GDP growthrates.

We are now in a position to see how much of growth was due to domestic policy. This is shown in Table II–15. Policy measures

57

Table II-14

Contribution of Autonomous Growth Influences 1950–65

Percentage point contribution to annual average compound growth rate of GDP

	Total GDP growth due to autonomous forces	Contribution of autonomous growth in labour supply	Contribution of external finance	Contribution of autonomous domestic investment	Contribution of natural resources	Autonomous growth in efficiency
Argentina	2·64	0·70	0·18	1·52	0·00	0·24
Brazil	3·26	1·45	0·27	1·24	0·00	0·30
Ceylon	1·58	0·80	0·06	0·88	−0·30	0·14
Chile	3·20	0·65	0·40	1·34	0·52	0·29
Colombia	2·79	1·15	0·32	1·07	0·00	0·25
Egypt	2·71	0·75	0·83	1·09	−0·21	0·25
Ghana	2·29	(1·00)	0·09	0·99	0·00	0·21
Greece	5·05	0·60	1·95	0·90	0·00	1·60*
India	2·26	1·10	0·40	0·86	−0·17	0·07*†
Israel	9·13	2·70	5·60	0·00	0·00	0·83
Malaya	1·91	0·85	0·00	0·89	0·00	0·17
Mexico	3·43	1·55	0·39	1·18	0·00	0·31
Pakistan	2·48	1·20	0·45	0·75	−0·28	0·36*
Peru	2·62	0·65	0·67	1·06	0·00	0·24
Philippines	2·82	1·10	0·53	0·80	0·00	0·39*
South Korea	4·20	0·90	2·07	0·13	−0·10	1·20*
Spain	3·86	0·35	0·28	1·88	0·00	1·35*
Taiwan	5·25	0·85	1·55	1·55	0·00	1·30*
Thailand	3·05	1·55	0·34	1·05	−0·17	0·28
Turkey	2·88	0·90	0·60	1·12	0·00	0·26
Venezuela	5·84	1·80	0·00	1·84	1·67	0·53
Yugoslavia	2·81	0·50	0·66	1·39	0·00	0·26
Average	3·46	1·05	0·80	1·07	0·04	0·49

* Includes impact of recovery bonus as shown in Table I-3, calculated for 1950–65.
† India is the only country in which our measure of output is distorted by the choice of an end-year in which output was below peak. We must make allowance for this, just as we did under (a) above for initial years below peak. We have therefore assumed that the fall in output from 1964 to 1965 reduced Indian growth from 3·8 to 3·5 per cent a year for 1950–65, i.e. imposed an efficiency loss equivalent to 0·3 per cent a year prorated over the whole period.

ACCELERATED GROWTH AND VARIATIONS IN PERFORMANCE

were responsible on average for 2·0 per cent a year of economic growth, with a range from 0.6 per cent in Argentina to 4.3 per cent in Yugoslavia. On average, all the policy-induced growth was due to increased factor inputs, i.e. increases in investment induced by government and improvements in the quality of the labour force because of better structural allocation of labour, and programmes for education and health. In most countries, the government effort at resource mobilization was very impressive by any historical

Table II–15

Economic Growth Attributable to Domestic Policy 1950–65

Percentage point contribution to annual average compound growth rates

	Total GDP growth due to domestic policy	GDP growth due to policy-induced factor inputs	GDP growth due to policy-induced changes in efficiency
Argentina	0·56	1·45	−0·89
Brazil	1·94	2·44	−0·50
Ceylon	1·82	1·86	−0·04
Chile	0·80	0·59	0·21
Colombia	1·81	2·16	−0·35
Egypt	2·79	1·68	1·11
Ghana	1·91	2·42	−0·51
Greece	1·35	0·70	0·65
India	1·24	2·34	−1·10
Israel	1·57	0·50	1·07
Malaya	1·59	2·11	−0·52
Mexico	2·67	2·53	0·14
Pakistan	0·91	1·15	−0·24
Peru	2·98	2·22	0·76
Philippines	2·18	2·52	−0·34
South Korea	2·00	2·00	0·00
Spain	3·64	2·49	1·15
Taiwan	3·25	1·25	2·00
Thailand	3·25	3·16	−0·09
Turkey	2·32	1·63	0·69
Venezuela	0·86	2·44	−1·58
Yugoslavia	4·29	4·00	0·29
Average	2·08	1·98	0·09

Source: Derived from Tables II–11 and II–14.

ECONOMIC PROGRESS AND POLICY IN DEVELOPING COUNTRIES

standards, and particularly high in Yugoslavia. In Greece, Israel, Korea and Taiwan, external finance was so large that governments did not need to make the effort to increase savings. In fact, they reduced private savings below their normal 'autonomous' level and devoted the resources instead to large military programmes.

The government contribution to economic efficiency was very uneven. In Taiwan, policy was particularly conducive to efficiency and accounted for two points a year of the GDP growth. A good deal of this gain was due to active policies of agrarian improvement through extension work and research, and to vigorous efforts to improve industrial efficiency and promote manufactured exports. The efficiency record was also good in Israel and Spain, but on the whole the record was poor and in half the countries there were actually losses due to government policy, the biggest being in Argentina, India, and Venezuela. In Argentina this was due to the deleterious effects of instability and inflation (demand-induced and cost-induced with a strongly entrenched spiral process), to neglect of agriculture, and heavy protection for inefficient industries. In India, the inefficiency was due to excessive use of direct controls, poor agricultural incentives, premature expansion of heavy industry, and badly administered state enterprises. In Venezuela, the efficiency loss seems to have been due primarily to lavish use of capital on massive investment projects which have been slow to produce their yield.

It should be remembered that our efficiency measure is a residual and will be affected by significant errors in the figures for GDP. There is a possibility that GDP growth may be overstated in Ceylon, Egypt and Peru and the efficiency record for these countries may well be worse than Table II–14 indicates.

One objection which may be raised in criticism of our model is that it makes no explicit allowance for balance of payments constraints. Many developing countries are faced with 'structural' payments difficulties because their exports are concentrated on foodstuffs and raw materials for which demand is growing slowly. Prices for their exports have been weak and they have fluctuated a good deal. As they have rather small capital goods industries, the effort to accelerate development usually involves an upsurge in imports of capital goods which is difficult to finance. Most developing countries are faced with these difficulties to a much more serious extent than developed countries, and if our model were trying to compare development and developing countries, it might be worth quantifying these payments constraints. Within the developing world there are

60

ACCELERATED GROWTH AND VARIATIONS IN PERFORMANCE

also important variations in the stringency of payments problems, but we have already made indirect allowance for most of these. We treated the whole of external finance as if it contributed directly to capital formation, whereas we know that some of it was not used for these purposes. In this way we hoped to cover crudely some of the indirect benefits of foreign aid, including its contribution to alleviating payments contraints. Similarly, we have treated Chile and Venezuela as deriving special benefits from their favourable mineral resources, and there would be double counting if we were to attribute payments benefits in addition. However, Mexico and Spain were favoured by particularly high tourist receipts (which were encouraged by policy, but were possible because of geographic and climatic reasons) which eased payments constraints and helped their growth, and we may therefore have given them somewhat higher marks for policy-induced growth than they deserve.

Taking the overall impact of government policy measures (first column of Table II–15) the countries with the best record are Mexico, Peru, Spain, Taiwan, Thailand and Yugoslavia. Those where policy contributed least were Argentina, Chile, India, Pakistan and Venezuela. In the succeeding analysis therefore we must look to the first group of countries for examples worth imitating and to the latter group for most of the illustrations of errors to be avoided. However, the rating of some countries would be changed by using data for a more recent period. This is particularly true of Pakistan which did much better in the 1960s than in the 1950s. The Pakistani case is, in fact, a rather drastic demonstration of the effectiveness and importance of improving development policies.

In any study of performance, the question naturally arises as to how much faster growth might have been if policy had been better. If every country had mobilized domestic resources on the Yugoslav scale and increased efficiency as fast as Taiwan, the policy induced growth would have been 6·0 per cent a year, and total growth would have been 9·5 per cent per annum. This probably represents the upper limit of feasible growth for countries with the political will and competence to reach their maximum potential, but it is not a realistic target as an average for the group. If we were setting targets for this group of countries for the 1970s, a 6·5 per cent rate would seem a reasonable figure to aim at. This would involve an average policy-induced growth of 3 per cent, 1 per cent growth due to external finance, and 2·5 per cent due to spontaneous growth forces of the kind which operated in prewar years. However, we

61

ECONOMIC PROGRESS AND POLICY IN DEVELOPING COUNTRIES

know that our sample has an upward bias of about 0·7 points, so that 6 per cent growth would probably be a reasonable target for developing countries as a whole.

We should note, finally, that the growth capacity of some of the poorer countries such as India will remain below 6 per cent a year because of the smaller size of spontaneous savings, lower taxable capacity and inferior natural resources. This handicap in the spontaneous growth potential of the poorer countries is of fundamental importance in any judgement of past performance, in target setting for the future, and in decisions on aid allocation.

[2]

Journal of Economic Literature
Vol. XXV (June 1987), pp. 649–698

Growth and Slowdown in Advanced Capitalist Economies: Techniques of Quantitative Assessment

By ANGUS MADDISON

University of Groningen

I am indebted to Moses Abramovitz for advice and encouragement; to comments made at a seminar of the Centraal Planbureau, The Hague; to Edward F. Denison, Aerdt Houben, John Kendrick, John Martin, Robin Matthews, Jan Pen, John Pencavel, Peter Sturm, and anonymous referees for discussion and critical comment; and to Derek Blades, Roland Granier, and Micheline Harary for help with statistical source material.

SINCE 1973, economic growth in Western countries has slowed in terms of all relevant measuring rods. The phenomenon has been strikingly general, persistent, and large. Average GDP growth for the major European economies and Japan fell from 5.6 percent in 1950–73 to 2.1 percent thereafter, and for the U.S. from 3.7 to 2.3 percent.

Because the growth process since 1973 was interrupted by important recessions in 1974–75 and 1980–81, by acceleration of inflation, by two oil shocks, and by the collapse of the Bretton Woods payments system, significant conjunctural elements have clearly played a role in the slowdown. Present high levels of European unemployment are an indicator that output is below potential. It is also obvious, however, (see Tables 1 and 2) that the postwar golden age, which ended in 1973, was exceptional. If it were blotted from memory, performance since 1973 would appear less worrisome.

Table 2, on labor productivity, suggests quite strongly that there has not been a simple reversion to historic norms. In Europe and Japan, productivity since 1973 has grown much faster than in the eight decades from 1870 to 1950. By contrast, U.S. productivity growth has fallen well below what was a much more stable long-term norm. The postwar process of convergence by the five follower countries has not been halted since 1973, and the productivity gap with the U.S. (see Table 3) is now smaller than ever. There is no evidence here for the notion of Eurosclerosis, which alleges that Europe's technical dynamism lags behind that of the U.S. One can also see that the Japanese growth advantage over Europe is much smaller than it was in the golden age.

This paper attempts to throw light on the causes of growth acceleration and de-

649

TABLE 1

PHASES OF GDP GROWTH, 1870–1984
(average annual compound growth rates)

	I 1870–1913	II 1913–50	III 1950–73	IV 1973–84	Acceleration from Phase II to Phase III	Slowdown from Phase III to Phase IV
France	1.7	1.1	5.1	2.2	+4.0	−2.9
Germany	2.8	1.3	5.9	1.7	+4.6	−4.2
Japan	2.5	2.2	9.4	3.8	+7.2	−5.6
Netherlands	2.1	2.4	4.7	1.6	+2.3	−3.1
U.K.	1.9	1.3	3.0	1.1	+1.7	−1.9
Five country average	2.2	1.7	5.6	2.1	+4.0	−3.5
U.S.	4.2	2.8	3.7	2.3	+0.9	−1.4

Source: Table A-1.

celeration since 1913 using a simple set of comparative growth accounts for the five biggest and the largest of the smaller capitalist economies. It also reviews the methodology used in 15 other similar studies. For the postwar period these are the pioneer work of Edward Denison (1967) on nine countries, Denison and William Chung (1976) on Japan and the U.S., Laurits Christensen, Dianne Cummings, and Dale Jorgenson (1980) on nine countries, John Kendrick (1981) on seven countries, and John Helliwell, Pe-

ter Sturm, and Gérard Salou (1985) on seven countries. None of these has the long perspective we seek here. Fortunately for four of our six countries, there are historical studies in this vein: Kendrick (1961, 1973) on the U.S., J-J. Carré, P. Dubois, and Edmond Malinvaud (1972) on France, Kazushi Ohkawa and Henry Rosovsky (1973) on Japan, and Robin Matthews, Charles Feinstein, and John Odling-Smee (1982) on the U.K. In addition, there are the four successive studies Denison (1962, 1974, 1979, 1985)

TABLE 2

PHASES OF GROWTH IN LABOR PRODUCTIVITY (GDP PER HOUR WORKED), 1870–1984
(average annual compound growth rates)

	I 1870–1913	II 1913–50	II 1950–73	IV 1973–84	Acceleration from Phase II to Phase III	Slowdown from Phase III to Phase IV
France	1.7	2.0	5.1	3.4	+3.1	−1.7
Germany	1.9	1.0	6.0	3.0	+5.0	−3.0
Japan	1.8	1.7	7.7	3.2	+6.0	−4.5
Netherlands	1.2	1.7	4.4	1.9	+2.7	−2.5
U.K.	1.2	1.6	3.2	2.4	+1.6	−0.8
Five country average	1.6	1.6	5.3	2.8	+3.7	−2.5
U.S.	2.0	2.4	2.5	1.0	+0.1	−1.5

Source: Table A-5.

Maddison: Growth and Slowdown in Advanced Capitalist Economies 651

TABLE 3

COMPARATIVE LEVELS OF PRODUCTIVITY (GDP PER HOUR WORKED), 1870–1984

(U.S. GDP per hour worked = 100)

	1870	1913	1950	1973	1984
France	54.7	49.2	41.5	74.7	97.5
Germany	58.9	55.7	33.6	72.8	90.5
Japan	19.3	18.0	13.9	43.8	55.6
Netherlands	105.2	74.6	56.5	87.5	97.2
U.K.	110.9	80.0	58.6	68.8	80.6
Five country average	70.5	56.2	40.9	69.5	84.3
U.S.	100.0	100.0	100.0	100.0	100.0

Source: Table A-5.

has made for U.S. growth back to 1929, and the Frank Gollop and Dale Jorgenson (1980) study on U.S. performance since 1947.

The works reviewed here raise most of the methodological issues in growth accounting, but we do not aspire to cover the intellectual origins of this approach in full. References to the antecedent literature can be found in Maddison (1972) and in Christensen, Cummings, and Jorgenson (1980).

The present survey is confined to six advanced capitalist countries because for these countries it was possible to check hypotheses quantitatively against historical experience; however, it is desirable to extend the coverage of comparative studies to countries lower down the scale of per capita income and productivity in order to throw more light on the nature of the convergence process and on the "opportunities" or disadvantages of initial backwardness. There are, in fact, some interesting country studies of this kind: Bakul Dholakia (1975) on India, Kwang-Suk Kim and Joon-Kyung Park (1985) on Korea, and Carlos Langoni (1974) on Brazil.

Growth accounting of this type can not provide a full causal story. It deals with "proximate" rather than "ultimate" causality and registers the facts about growth components; it does not explain the ele-

ments of policy or circumstance, national or international, that underlie them, but it does identify which facts need more ultimate explanation. This kind of exercise forces one to merge and match data in a way that provides valuable cross-checks on the consistency and plausibility of the basic growth indicators both for individual countries and across countries. It is particularly useful in avoiding or identifying double counting and in tracking down the complex interactions among causal components.

The comparative approach is of great value in this field. Hypotheses, estimating techniques, and weights that "explain" performance reasonably well in a single country need to be tested in other countries where they may well "overexplain" growth experience.

This technique of diagnosis is most valuable when it is transparent. Transparency is in fact this technique's major charm, for although on significant points there are large judgmental elements, these are not so easily forgotten as they may be in econometric analysis. If all the steps are identified and the statistical appendix provides the basic series, the reader has building bricks for alternate hypotheses. There are no iron laws. The practitioner can augment, truncate, and reshuffle to taste, provided that the "explanations" of growth are logical, consistent, and transparent. This is why the present paper sticks to simple, standardized, and rather conservative hypotheses throughout, so that the impact of a change in assumptions for a particular growth component can be readily traced on a cross-country basis.

Growth accounts can be organized in several ways to serve different purposes. In Denison (1967) the main objective was to explore why growth rates differed among countries. The analysis was concentrated on the period 1950–62, and the accounting covered differences in *level* of performance as well as growth rates.

In the most general form of the accounts, the main item around which the detailed explication is built is total output (which can be measured in different ways, as can be seen below), but if one wants to abstract from differences in demography, activity rates, and working hours, the same basic material can be recast as productivity accounts, where labor productivity is the central point. This approach can be used to give more emphasis to problems of technical progress.

For medium-term conjunctural analysis one can complement the "actual" accounts with an alternative set of counterfactual "potential output" accounts. The confrontation of the two can help identify the losses from macropolicy mistakes or external shocks, as in 1973–84.

Over longer periods, the accounts can be recast as measures of growth acceleration or slowdown, and in this form can help identify the distinctive features of growth momentum in the different phases of development.

This latter approach is used here, as one of our interests is in diagnosing the major changes in momentum, which have been a feature of twentieth-century capitalist development. The timing of these changes has been very similar in all the countries considered here, and the generality of the acceleration/slowdown phenomena is very striking. This can be seen very clearly in Table 21 where only 15 of the 90 growth components were negative in the acceleration phase, and in Table 22 where only 8 of the 90 components were positive in the slowdown phase.

The second main feature of the present analysis is a concern with the nature of the convergence process, in which the follower countries have been catching up with the leader, the U.S. This process has lasted now for four decades, and its nature is important not only for these countries but for countries at much lower levels of productivity and per capita real income.

To study convergence problems fully, the accounts should show levels of performance as well as growth rates. This aspect is not developed extensively here, but levels of real output and productivity are shown corrected for differences in purchasing power of currencies, and Table 13 shows rough estimates of this kind for levels of capital stock and some other relevant magnitudes.

The present estimates cover the period 1913–84, dividing it into three major phases: 1913–50, 1950–73, and 1973–84. Each of the phases in this periodization shows distinctly different features. The use of 1973 as a turning point is hardly controversial. Most observers of the slowdown phenomenon use it, for example, Denison (1985), Federal Reserve Bank of Boston (1980), Shlomo Maital and Noah Meltz (1980), Kendrick (1981, 1984), Assar Lindbeck (1983), Henning Klodt (1984), and William Baumol and Kenneth McLennan (1985). The year 1950 was chosen as the beginning of the postwar period, because it was a year in which reconstruction was reasonably complete; however, in the case of Germany and Japan there was still substantial underuse of labor and capital for which allowance has to be made. Some readers may therefore wish to compare 1973–84 with a shorter part of the golden age, say 1960–73. The period 1913–50 has its unity only as a time of troubles including two world wars and the Great Depression, so one could arguably try to break it down into smaller units. It is regrettable that the 1870–1913 period cannot yet be put into this framework because of gaps in the capital stock estimates and in the disaggregation of GDP by sector. Space did not permit presentation of annual estimates, but for several key magnitudes they can be found in Maddison (1982).

I. *Labor Productivity*

The oldest index of productivity growth is that for labor productivity, $\dot{\Pi}^1$, defined as the difference between the compound rate of increase in output, $\dot{O}$, and the rate of increase in labor input, $\dot{L}$:

$$\dot{\Pi}^1 = \dot{O} - \dot{L}.$$

This indicator has considerable attractions in an economy where labor productivity growth is stable in the long term and where a major social concern is with the level of employment. It is a better measure of long-term technical "progress" or welfare than GDP, which is affected by differences in demographic dynamism, or GDP per head of population, which takes no account of working hours per person, which have declined by almost half over the past century, or of employment rates.

There are two statistical prerequisites for this ratio—measures of output and labor input.

A. *The Output Measure*

Growth accountancy is indebted to pioneers like Colin Clark, Richard Stone, and Simon Kuznets who developed the conceptual framework of national ac-

counts, to scholars who have made historical estimates, to governments who have made official estimates for the postwar period, and to OECD for publishing these official estimates in comparable form. As productivity analysis involves comparisons of levels as well as growth, we are also indebted to those (mainly Milton Gilbert and Irving Kravis) who developed techniques for correcting exchange rate comparisons for purchasing power parities, and the OECD, which now publishes such estimates on an annual basis. The most easily available aggregate for comparative purposes is gross domestic product (GDP), which reflects the whole spectrum of domestic production. This is what I have used here, and this is also true of Matthews, Feinstein, and Odling-Smee (1982) and Carré, Dubois, and Malinvaud (1976). Denison (1967) used net national product (which includes income from abroad), and he and Kendrick (1961) showed both private and total versions of this latter measure as did Denison and Chung (1976). Ohkawa and Rosovsky (1973) analyzed agricultural and private nonagricultural products separately.

In most sectors of the economy, output is produced by both labor and capital, but the housing and government sectors are rather special. The income flow from housing is virtually all a return on capital and very little labor is involved. Conversely, with government activity, as conventionally measured, virtually all the income flow is from labor. Although governments own substantial capital assets, there is generally little operating profit on these, and even depreciation may be significantly understated. For these reasons, and also because of the limited character of market pricing here, the housing and government sectors are often excluded from growth accounts.

The choice of one national accounting aggregate rather than another should not

TABLE 4

RELATIONSHIPS BETWEEN LEVEL OF ALTERNATIVE GROWTH ACCOUNTING AGGREGATES AT NATIONAL PRICES, 1973–82

	Gross National Product at Market Prices	Gross Domestic Product at Market Prices	Gross Domestic Product at Factor Cost	Nonresidential Gross Domestic Product at Factor Cost	Private Gross Domestic Product at Factor Cost	Net Domestic Product at Factor Cost	Net National Product at Factor Cost	Private Nonresidential Net Domestic Product at Factor Cost	Private Nonresidential Net National Product at Factor Cost	Augmented Private GDP at Composite Prices (in 1970)
	(1)	(2)	(3)	(4)	(5)	(6)	(7)	(8)	(9)	(10)
France	114.7	114.2	100.0	93.1	80.1	87.2	87.6	69.3	69.7	109.0
Germany	112.4	112.2	100.0	93.8	80.8	87.4	87.6	70.7	70.9	101.5
Japan	106.0	106.1	100.0	93.3	84.3	85.5	85.4	71.8	71.7	99.3
Netherlands	110.3	110.3	100.0	94.8	79.5	88.7	88.7	69.7	69.7	95.1
U.K.	114.0	113.6	100.0	94.0	80.4	85.4	85.7	67.3	67.6	98.9
U.S.	110.7	109.1	100.0	91.3	77.0	86.6	88.2	64.7	66.3	101.2

Source: This table shows different measures of aggregate product as a percentage of GDP at factor cost averaged over the years 1973–82. Thus French GNP at market prices was 14.7 percent higher than French GDP at factor cost. First nine columns derived from OECD(d). Last column from Christensen, Cummings, and Jorgenson (1980).

be a significant matter of controversy as long as the aggregate used is the same for all the countries in the comparison, but there is a considerable difference in the level of the different aggregates, which must be kept in mind in comparing results of different authors. The first nine columns of Table 4 show different aggregates derivable on a consistent basis from the OECD national accounts, which might all be candidates for growth-accounting purposes. This paper uses estimates based on the column 3 concept. Kendrick (1981) uses a column 5 aggregate and Denison (1967) a column 7 aggregate. In fact the growth movements for all the first nine aggregates are remarkably similar. In practice the main impact of using different aggregates arises when they are used as a denominator for the factor weights.

The last column of Table 4 shows the aggregate used by Christensen, Cummings, and Jorgenson (1980), who exclude government but augment GDP to impute a service flow from consumer durables and who use price conventions that represent neither factor cost nor market prices but depend on their assessment of the incidence of taxes. Indirect taxes "unrelated to factor outlay" are excluded, but some others such as property taxes are included. While the variation between the first nine columns of Table 4 is fairly systematic across countries, this is not true of column 10 where the French aggregate is 9 percent higher than GDP at factor cost and the Netherlands aggregate is 5 percent below.

Table 4 is not an exhaustive listing. Helliwell, Sturm, and Salou (1985) adjust GDP to include the impact of net changes in energy imports because they treat energy as a factor of production. In an exploratory study, Kendrick (1976) took a particularly broad view of capital formation and total output. He augmented 1969 U.S. GNP by 34 percent

by imputing rentals on consumer durables, inventories, government capital, and intangibles such as R and D and earnings foregone by students, none of which are included in the conventional national accounts.

B. *Labor Input*

Construction of labor productivity involves the merger of several sources of data on employment, weekly working hours, and time off for holidays, sickness, strikes, etc., to arrive at total labor input (see Tables A-10 and A-11 and Maddison 1980a on the items required to measure hours).

II. *Capital Productivity*

The next major step in productivity analysis came with the development of capital stock measures using the perpetual inventory method developed by Raymond Goldsmith for cumulating successive increments of capital stock. A prerequisite for such capital stock measures is historical estimates of investment and reasonable price deflators, so estimates of this kind did not begin to appear in a form suitable for cross-country comparison until the 1960s, and even now only three of our six countries (Germany, the U.K., and U.S.) publish official comprehensive estimates of this kind. These measures represent a great step forward for growth analysts compared with the investment to incremental output ratio (ICOR) which was in use in the 1950s.

The capital (K) productivity index

$$\dot{\Pi}^2 = \dot{O} - \dot{K}$$

produces quite different results from that for labor. Labor productivity seldom declines even on an annual basis, and in the long run is always positive whereas capital productivity is only mildly positive and can be substantially negative in depressed business conditions, such as

TABLE 5

CAPITAL PRODUCTIVITY GROWTH, 1913–84

(annual average compound growth rates)

	1913–50	1950–73	1973–84	1913–84
France	0.12	1.50	−1.82	0.23
Germany	0.56	0.57	−1.71	0.20
Japan	0.69	1.39	−3.41	0.28
Netherlands	0.31	0.85	−1.83	0.15
U.K.	0.13	−0.26	−1.45	−0.24
U.S.	0.96	0.34	−0.47	0.55
Average	0.46	0.73	−1.78	0.20

Source: Derived from Tables A-1 and A-15.

those since 1973 (see Table 5). The close correlation between capital and output movements over the long run is the reason simple regressions find capital such a powerful explanation of growth.

Over the long term the gross capital stock (i.e., cumulated gross investment minus scrapping) and net capital stock (i.e., cumulated gross investment minus depreciation) indexes tend to move in a similar way (though the level of the net stock is of course smaller), but when capital formation is accelerating, as in 1950–73, the net stock grows faster than the gross, and, when capital growth slows down, as in 1973–84, the gross stock grows faster than the net (see Raymond Goldsmith 1962 and Michael Ward 1976 for the algebra and Tables A-15 to A-18 below for the figures).

The movement in gross capital stock gives a somewhat exaggerated representation of changes in capital's ability to contribute to production. An automobile is counted at its purchase value in the gross stock until it is scrapped. The car will indeed perform its physical function to the end but its reliability will decline and it will need increasing maintenance. By contrast, the net stock represents the discounted value of the car to its owner, but the declining second-hand value

overstates the decline in functional attributes. The car's contribution to current production is much closer to the gross than the net valuation. I have therefore used the gross stock to measure capital input, but figures on net stock movements are given in the statistical appendix (Tables A-15 to A-18).

Denison (1967) takes a simple average of gross and net stock. Kendrick (1961, 1973) and Matthews, Feinstein, and Odling-Smee (1982) show both concepts separately; Ohkawa and Rosovsky use gross stock, Carré, Dubois, and Malinvaud net stock.

In some growth-accounting exercises, for example, in three of the historical country monographs, the individual items in the capital stock are weighted at their asset values, and it is assumed that the stock thus calculated provides a proxy measure of the potential service flow derivable from the assets; however, the service flow is better approximated by using rental rather than asset weights, particularly when the structure of the gross capital stock is changing between assets with different service lives. There has in fact been a long-term increase in the share of shorter-lived assets (compare the growth of structures and equipment in Table A-17), and this means that the growth in the potential service flow has been bigger than the growth of the gross stock at asset values. The point is clear if one considers two assets such as a house and a car. A $100,000 house has an asset value ten times as big as a $10,000 car, but the annual rental value of the house might well be as low as 5 percent whereas for the car it might be 30 percent (as the annual car rental must cover a much bigger element of depreciation than in the case of the house). Thus the rental weights would be in the ratio of 5:3 compared with 10:1 for the asset ratio.

In Table 5, on capital productivity

growth ($\dot{\Pi}^2$), asset weights were used for capital, but in measuring $\dot{\Pi}^3$, $\dot{\Pi}^4$, and $\dot{\Pi}^5$ below, I used what amounts to rental weights for the two major categories, residential and nonresidential capital, and the average difference between the "capital quantity" thus measured and the growth of the two types of capital amalgamated at asset weights (Table A-15) is 0.2 percent a year for the six countries. However, we could not use rental weights systematically for different kinds of nonresidential assets because no breakdown was available for some of the countries. In this respect, the growth of "capital quantity" is understated here.

Kendrick (1961) was the first analyst to show figures at both net asset and net rental weights. He called the first magnitude the "capital stock" and the second "capital input." For the 68-year period from 1889 to 1957 his figures for the "national economy" show U.S. capital stock increasing at a compound rate of 2.54 per annum whereas his "capital input" grew somewhat faster, at 2.74 per annum (see pp. 320–22 and 328–31). Kendrick did not use rentals by asset type but by industry of use; otherwise the difference between the two concepts might well have been larger. It would certainly be larger if he had used gross weights because these include depreciation provisions that vary much more between assets than the net return.

Christensen, Cummings, and Jorgenson (1980) also draw attention to the difference between asset and rental weights, and the difference between the two is a good deal larger in their study than in Kendrick (1961). Their average capital stock growth rate for the six countries is 5.1 percent per annum (see Table 6) and their capital input grows at 6.2 percent. There are two main reasons why their differential is bigger than Kendrick's. First, they use gross weights; second, they include consumer durables

TABLE 6

MOVEMENT IN PRIVATE DOMESTIC CAPITAL STOCK USING ALTERNATE WEIGHTS, 1950–73
(annual average compound growth rates)

	Asset Weights	Rental Weights	Difference
France	4.68	5.76	1.08
Germany	6.95	7.24	0.29
Japan[a]	7.35	9.48	2.13
Netherlands[b]	4.16	5.70	1.54
U.K.[c]	4.04	4.69	0.65
U.S.	3.15 (3.11)	4.15 (4.39)	1.00 (1.28)

Source: Christensen, Cummings, and Jorgenson (1980, pp. 654–80). These were compiled separately for seven asset classes for the private sector, that is, consumer durables, producer durables, residential structures, nonresidential structures, land, farm inventories, and nonfarm inventories. Each of the seven classes is broken down by four ownership sectors, with adjustment for their different tax burdens, that is, corporate business, noncorporate business, households and nonprofit institutions (see pp. 619–22), so there are 28 categories of capital in their accounts. Figures in parentheses for the U.S. are from Gollop and Jorgenson (1980, p. 87). Here there are six asset classes, as farm and nonfarm inventories are merged, and three ownership sectors, as households and nonprofit institutions are merged. However, the stocks are disaggregated into 51 industries, so there are 918 categories of capital.
[a] 1952–73;   [b] 1951–73;   [c] 1955–73.

that have relatively short lives. Comparisons are further complicated by their use of a price convention different from those of national accounts and by their use of different levels of aggregation. In the parenthetic Gollop and Jorgenson (1980) figures for the U.S. in Table 6, the even wider spread between the two concepts is perhaps due to the use in that study of an extra rapid (double declining balance) replacement pattern.

With the exception of Dutch residential capital and French residential capital from 1966 onward, all the capital stock estimates presented in this paper were derived by the perpetual inventory technique and are more comparable than those Denison had to use for some countries in 1967. There are still differences in assumptions between countries in asset lives, scrapping patterns, depreciation formulas, techniques of price deflation, and years used as benchmarks for weighting purposes (see Maddison 1982, pp. 214–32, for a more detailed analysis of the significance of these variations). Differences in growth of capital stock between countries should therefore be taken only as rough orders of magnitude, and improvement of the historical capital stock estimates is obviously a major priority for better comparative growth analysis.

III. *Joint Factor Productivity*

Once the capital stock is available the next step in growth accounting is an index of joint factor productivity, $\dot{\Pi}^3$, constructed by weighting together the contribution of labor and capital:

$$\dot{\Pi}^3 = \dot{O} - a\dot{L} - (1 - a)\dot{K}.$$

The first comparative approach of this kind was made by Jan Tinbergen in 1942 with crude estimates for 1870–1914 for France, Germany, the U.K., and the U.S. He gave capital a weight of 0.25 and labor 0.75 using Paul Douglas' earlier results from production functions where the two weights were constrained to add to 1 (see Douglas 1948).

The first comprehensive modern study in this field was Kendrick (1961). Kendrick and the authors of all the subsequent historical country monographs have used factor shares in GDP (or in whatever aggregate they used to measure output) as labor and capital weights for their joint factor productivity measures, on the grounds that in neoclassical distribution theory these represent rewards proportional to the contribution of labor and capital to production.

One has only to look at the empirical basis from which the weights are derived

to see that the neoclassical assumptions are very crude. Table 7 gives a breakdown of average income shares of GDP at factor cost for the six countries taken from the OECD(d) for 1973–82.

The first item is rents for dwellings, including depreciation. In all the countries, there are various kinds of rent control and subsidies either to tenants or proprietors that change over time and make the market imperfect. Even without these, this is a sector with fairly long-term private contracts that react with long lags to changes in inflation, mortgage rates, and so on. Finally, one should note that a large part (often more than half) of these incomes has to be imputed, because the houses are occupied by their owners.

The second item of capital income is depreciation that is derived by national income statisticians using guidelines drawn partly from direct estimates of asset lives and partly from the legal provisions for tax relief. These estimates are therefore very crude.

The third item of capital income is the operating surplus on nonresidential capital. This has to be calculated after elimination of the labor component of incomes of self-employed persons, whose incomes are mixed and are included with the operating surplus in the national accounts. The estimates of the labor income of the self-employed in Table 7 were based on the common assumption that their per capita labor compensation was the same as the average for wage and salary earners.

Government-owned assets form a substantial part of the capital stock figures we have used. In 1984, the government share of nonresidential fixed assets (general government and government enterprises combined) was 30 percent in Germany, 38 percent in Japan, 22 percent in the Netherlands, 42 percent in the U.K., and 30 percent in the U.S. How-

Maddison: *Growth and Slowdown in Advanced Capitalist Economies*   659

TABLE 7

DERIVATION OF CAPITAL AND LABOR SHARES IN GDP AT FACTOR COST (AVERAGE FOR 1973–82)
(percentage of GDP)

	Rent and Imputed Rent on Dwellings (Including Depreciation)	Depreciation on Nonresidential Capital	Operating Surplus on Nonresidential Capital	Total Capital Share
France	6.9	10.8	12.8	30.5
Germany	6.2	10.1	13.7	30.0
Japan	6.7	12.5	10.0	29.2
Netherlands	5.2	9.9	14.5	29.6
U.K.	6.0	13.1	6.4	25.5
U.S.	8.7	12.3	5.7	26.7
Average	6.6	11.4	10.5	28.6

	Imputed Labor Income of Self-Employed	Wages and Salaries	Employer Contributions for Social Security, Private Pensions, and Welfare	Total Labor Share
France	7.7	45.7	16.1	69.5
Germany	6.7	52.1	11.2	70.0
Japan	14.1	50.8	5.9	70.8
Netherlands	7.0	48.9	14.5	70.4
U.K.	6.3	59.5	8.7	74.5
U.S.	6.2	56.9	10.2	73.3
Average	8.0	52.3	11.1	71.4

Source: OECD(d) and national sources for GDP components. Proportion of self-employed and family workers in employment are from OECD(c).

ever, no income is imputed in the national accounts (column 3 of Table 7) for general government assets such as roads, schools, or public buildings. Income from government enterprises, which is included, is often depressed by a tendency to underprice their output.

The fourth column of Table 7 is the sum of the first three columns, and represents the total capital share.

The labor share has three components: the imputed labor incomes of the self-employed; wages and salaries; and employer contributions to social security, private pensions, and welfare. The latter are only

very partially determined by market bargaining, and it should be remembered that wages and salaries are also affected by government regulation and by requirements that they include payment for holidays.

Table 7 shows a total capital weight for 1973–82 which averages 28.6 with a dispersion around the average that is not too big. The capital share was somewhat depressed in this period. We were not able to make a comparable estimate for 1950–73 as a whole, but the figure for 1960–73 was about 32 percent.

Table 8 shows the weights used in

TABLE 8

ALTERNATIVE CAPITAL WEIGHTS FOR ESTIMATES OF POSTWAR TOTAL FACTOR PRODUCTIVITY
(percentages of the pertinent aggregate)

	Denison: Share of Net Capital Income in Net National Product at Factor Cost (1950–62)	Share of Gross Capital Income in GDP at Factor Cost (1973–82)	Kendrick: Share of Gross Capital Income in Private GNP at Factor Cost (1960–79)	Helliwell, Sturm, and Salou: Share of Gross Capital Income and Energy Inputs in GDP plus Energy Imports (1962–82)	Christensen, Cummings, and Jorgenson: Share of Augmented Capital Income in Augmented Private Domestic Product at Composite Prices (1950–73)
France	23.0	30.5	38.2	41.0	40.3
Germany	26.3	30.0	34.9	41.0	38.6
Japan	23.7[a]	29.2	33.4	38.0[b]	39.2[c]
Netherlands	26.0	29.6	—	—	44.6[d]
U.K.	22.2	25.5	34.8	38.0	38.5[e]
U.S.	21.4	26.7	37.1	36.0	40.5
Average	23.7	28.6	35.7	38.9	40.3

Source: First column from Denison (1967, p. 38), and, for Japan, from Denison and Chung (1976, p. 30); second column from Table 7 above; third column from Kendrick (1981, p. 127)—he used figures from an unpublished OECD report that refer to 1970 and applied this 1970 weight for both his periods 1960–73 and 1973–79 (pp. 140–41); fourth column from Helliwell, Sturm, and Salou (1985, p. 163); fifth column from Christensen, Cummings, and Jorgenson (1980, p. 620).
[a] 1952–62;   [b] 1967–82;   [c] 1952–73;   [d] 1951–73;   [e] 1955–73.

some other comparative studies. Denison's weights are the lowest because he measures output net of depreciation; Christensen, Cummings, and Jorgenson (1980) have the highest weight because they augment capital to include consumer durables. Helliwell, Sturm, and Salou (1985) also have augmented weights, and Kendrick (1981) has high weights because he excludes government (which has little capital income relative to its share of product).

For earlier years, the four country monographs (see Table 9) show an average weight for capital over the whole period they cover of 34 percent, with a distinct tendency for the weight of capital to fall over time.

The change in weights over time partially reflects underlying real forces such as the change in factor prices, which provides a legitimate reason for using differ-

ent weights for different periods; however, given the crudeness of the statistics, the possible distortion involved because of the large decline in the relative importance of income from self-employment, the increasing legislative squeeze on property shares, and the rising share of government-owned assets, on which rental income is very small, it seemed wise to use the same capital weight for all our periods and countries.

Because GDP is our measure of output, and capital stock is on a gross basis, gross weights are the most appropriate for our purpose. We have therefore given capital a weight of 30 percent in total, with 7 percent for residential capital and 23 percent for other forms. This is a little higher than the figures for 1973–82 in Table 7, but the capital share was depressed somewhat in that period.

We did not include land and invento-

Maddison: Growth and Slowdown in Advanced Capitalist Economies   661

TABLE 9
WEIGHTS USED FOR CAPITAL IN TOTAL FACTOR PRODUCTIVITY MEASURES IN THE HISTORICAL MONOGRAPHS

France	Gross weights, 28 percent throughout (Carré, Dubois, and Malinvaud 1972, p. 248)
Japan	Gross weights, 40 percent for 1913–38, 31 percent for 1954–64 for private nonagricultural output (Ohkawa and Rosovsky 1973, pp. 316–17)
U.K.	Gross weights, 41 percent for 1856–73, 43 percent for 1873–1913, 33 percent for 1913–51, 27 percent for 1951–73 (Matthews, Feinstein, and Odling-Smee 1982, p. 208)
U.S.	Net weights, 35 percent for 1899–1919, 25 percent for 1919–53 for the national economy (Kendrick 1961, p. 85). The revised figure for 1929–53 in (Kendrick 1973, p. 173) averaged 29 percent.

ries in the capital estimates for lack of data.

IV. *Augmentation of Factor Inputs*

Although the total factor productivity approach was a big leap forward in growth analysis, it was clear that a good deal remained unexplained. Kendrick (1961) accounted for less than half of U.S. growth in the period 1869–1957, and subsequent investigators have therefore tried to reduce the size of the productivity component by "augmenting" estimates of factor input. Where K^* is "augmented" capital, and L^* is "augmented" labor, the formula became:

$$\dot{\Pi}^4 = \dot{O} - a\dot{L}^* - (1 - a)\dot{K}^*.$$

A. *Augmenting Labor Input*

Kendrick had already distinguished between the growth of working hours and the growth of "labor input," because he weighted working hours in different industries by their relative average earnings. This "augmented" labor input very little, but under the influence of Theodore Schultz (1961), Denison in his first study for the U.S. (1962) quickly incorporated a sizable adjustment for improvement in educational quality. He also made adjustments for changes in the age-sex composition of employment. Both of these practices have now become general in multifactor growth analysis, though

the old partial measure of labor productivity is almost never expressed with the new augmented denominator.

Virtually all subsequent analysts have taken over the age-sex and education adjustments in one form or other. Here we made no age adjustment because age figures and age-earnings differentials were not reliable for the 1913–50 period. A 0.6 weight was applied to female employment. For education it is generally accepted that some of the wage differential by level of education represents rewards for intelligence, family connections, or the impact of credentialist rules in the public sector and some professions, so some compression of the education weights is warranted. The estimates of education levels are given in Table A-12. In moving from these to the estimates of educational growth in Table 19, we compressed differentials to a degree broadly similar to Denison (1967). See Maddison (1976) for a discussion of the complex role of education, and see George Psacharopoulos (1984) for a discussion of various techniques of measurement.

A more controversial innovation by Denison (1962) was his assumption that there is a compensatory increase in work intensity that partially offsets declines in working hours. Denison assumed that above 2,529 hours a year, reductions in work time are fully compensated for by increased work intensity, and that below

1,762 hours there is no compensating off-set. In between, there was a varying and partial offset. In later studies, Denison refined this assumption for different categories of worker.

This large quality effect seems questionable over the long term. In the short term, a cut in working hours with no corresponding wage reduction may stimulate worker effort and managerial efficiency. But these effects wear off as the memory of the old situation fades. Compared with their grandparents, people now have long holidays, two-day weekends, shorter weekly hours, easy facilities for sickness absence, greater security of employment, more human relations with foremen and supervisors. Their work is less fatiguing, but a lot of the extra reserve of energy goes into leisure pursuits like jogging, skiing, and wind surfing rather than in work effort. I have therefore simply assumed that cuts in working hours lead to an equiproportionate cut in labor input.

Matthews, Feinstein, and Odling-Smee (1982, p. 104) have followed Denison's lead in assuming a work intensity effect; Ohkawa and Rosovsky (1973) ignore it, and Carré, Dubois, and Malinvaud (1972, p. 95) acknowledge that it may play a role, but do not measure it. It is ignored by Kendrick (1981), by Christensen, Cummings, and Jorgensen (1980), and by Helliwell, Sturm, and Salou (1985).

B. *Augmenting Capital Input*

In 1962 Robert Solow suggested incorporation of a hypothetical quality improvement in successive vintages of capital on the grounds that physical investment is the prime vehicle by which technical progress is realized. He overstated the case in assuming, by way of illustration, "that new technology could be introduced into the production process *only* through gross investment in new plant and equipment" (Solow 1962,

p. 76). Later (1963, p. 80), he suggested that plausible rates of quality augmentation for Germany and the U.S. were on the order of 4 or 5 percent a year, which he derived by assuming all progress to be embodied, using a production function where there was no quality improvement for labor, and no "disembodied" technological progress.

Denison rightly rejected the catchall version of the embodiment approach and argued that the high-quality improvement factor was incompatible with what we know about the lives of assets, which would be scrapped earlier than they are if Solow's extreme assumptions were correct.

It is quite clear that some of the impact of technical progress is disembodied and arises from improvement in the content of knowledge acquired by employees and managers in school and on the job, and by retrofitting and recombining old capital assets; however, insertion of a modest element of embodied technical progress in the analysis does illuminate the nature of the growth process and clarifies the impact of changes in the age of capital in a way that is not possible outside the vintage context.

In rejecting Solow's suggestions, Denison (1967, pp. 144–50) argued as if the only legitimate element of the embodiment effect arose in cases where the average age distribution of the capital stock changes (and even this in a very narrow sense, i.e., abstracting from the impact of changes in the distribution of capital between structures and equipment). He assumed that embodied technical progress makes its impact only by changes in age structure and rate of quality improvement, which alter the ratio between average and best practice at different dates, though the embodiment thesis is also (and mainly) concerned with improvements in average practice over time (see Maddison 1972 for a more detailed discussion of the issue).

Perhaps as a result of Denison's opposition and the fact that empirical information about lives of assets and causes of scrapping was poor, growth accounting has proceeded asymmetrically with widespread use of labor augmentation and virtually no capital augmentation (what Christensen, Cummings, and Jorgenson call "capital quality" is something different, as we have seen above).

None of the nine studies we have surveyed carries an embodiment effect as part of its main corpus. Carré, Dubois, and Malinvaud (1972) calculated a substantial embodiment effect, but only as a step in calculating the impact of changes in the average age of capital, which was the only part of the embodiment effect they show in their final statement of sources of growth (p. 275). Denison generally does not include age effects, but he (1967) did so for Denmark, Germany, and Norway 1950–55 using embodiment analysis to estimate their size.

Ohkawa and Rosovsky (1973) and Kendrick (1981) also treat change in the age of assets as a source of growth, but in both cases without working through the embodiment effect. Ohkawa and Rosovsky (p. 64) assume that the reciprocal of average age is a direct indication of capital quality, and they get rather big changes in capital quality over time, for example, 0.7 percent a year for 1917–31 to 4.2 percent a year for 1955–61. Kendrick (1981) calculated an age effect by multiplying changes in average age by changes in the growth rate of the national R and D stock (or the residual), which he took as a proxy for the rate of growth of technical progress. He too gets big jumps in the age effect, which contributed 1.3 percentage points to his Japanese growth for 1960–73 and −0.1 for 1973–79.

The Ohkawa and Rosovsky as well as the Kendrick approaches both involve dubious procedures and their hypothetical magnitudes are implausible because they imply big changes in the rate of embodied progress over time. Because we are dealing with technical progress for the economy as a whole and a large part of progress is small and incremental, it is not likely to be as jerky as they suggest. Indeed our estimates show that we can get a satisfactory explanation of postwar growth acceleration and slowdown without assuming changes in the rate of embodied progress as a causal element. The stability of long-term labor productivity growth in the lead country (the U.S.) is one reason for assuming this. On the basis of their empirical analyses of the processes and impact of innovation, Jacob Schmookler (1966) and the cliometricians (particularly Robert Fogel 1964) have now demolished the Schumpeterian idea of jerky technical improvement.

I have therefore assumed a modest and smooth quality improvement for capital. The particular rate I suggest is meant to be illustrative. While there are strong reasons to suppose that such an influence is operative and fairly smooth in its impact, there is no hard evidence as to what the rate actually is. The 1.5 percent annual improvement that I have assumed, is, however, smaller than that in any of the authors cited above. To assess its impact I have calculated a stylized measure of the growth of capital stock in all the six countries on the uniform assumption that all assets have lives of 30 years. To cover the whole period since 1913 would require figures on investment back to 1883, which are not available for half the countries, so I used investment rates for 1920–84 for the calculations, with allowance for war damage as described in Table 10. Thus for 1950–73 one can see (in Tables 19 and 20) the impact of a steady rate of technical improvement of 1.5 percent a year adjusted for changes in the age of capital. This "capital quality" effect includes the age effect. For 1913–50, for want of data, I assumed that the

TABLE 10

AVERAGE AGE OF THE GROSS NONRESIDENTIAL FIXED CAPITAL STOCK, 1950–84

	1950	1973	1984
France	15.14	9.98	12.01
Germany	16.21	9.72	13.10
Japan	12.48	8.13	10.45
Netherlands	14.71	10.25	13.37
U.K.	13.18	10.93	12.98
U.S.	13.37	11.70	12.50

Source: These estimates assume that all assets have the same 30-year life in all the countries and that the retirement pattern is rectangular; that is, all assets are scrapped on their thirtieth birthday. Annual increments to the stock were calculated by applying the ratio of domestic nonresidential fixed investment to GDP to the index of real GDP (1950 = 100) at constant prices. These increments (all measured as fractions of 1950 GDP) were cumulated over 30 years with adjustment for war damage. Thus the 1950 stock is the sum of the increments from mid-1920 to mid-1950, the 1973 stock the sum of mid-1943 to mid-1973 increments, and the 1984 stock, the sum of the increments from mid-1954 to mid-1984. Because one knows the size and age of all the increments, the average age can be easily calculated. See Maddison (1972, Appendix A) for an illustration of the method used. War damage was derived from Maddison (1976, p. 472) for France (8 percent of the pre-1946 asset formation), Germany (13 percent), and the U.K. (3 percent); from Maddison and Bote Wilpstra (1982, p. 82) for the Netherlands (15 percent); and from Bank of Japan (1966, p. 27) for Japan (25.7 percent). The GDP estimates were from sources cited in Table A-1. Investment coefficients for postwar years are generally from OECD(d), and for earlier years in France from Carré, Dubois, and Malinvaud (1972, p. 652) reduced by 25 percent to eliminate housing and the repairs component of nonresidential construction (1920–21 and 1939–46 investment rates were my estimates); Germany from Wolfgang Kirner (1968, pp. 77, 80–81, 92, 104–07); Japan from Ohkawa and Miyohei Shinohara (1979); Netherlands from Maddison and Wilpstra (1982, pp. 82–84); U.K. from Feinstein (1972); U.S. from Kendrick (1961), Simon Kuznets (1961), Raymond Goldsmith (1955, Vol. I), and for 1929 onward from U.S. Dept. of Commerce publications.

average age of the capital stock did not change.

In all the countries, the average age of the capital stock declined from 1950 to 1973, as the rate of growth of capital stock accelerated a good deal over the previous period. From 1973 to 1984, by contrast, as capital stock growth slowed down, the age of capital rose in all the countries.

Because the weight for capital is 0.3, the contribution of a 1.5 percent capital quality improvement to growth in the standard case (1913–50, where no age adjustment was made) is 0.45 points per annum (see Table 20). The difference between this and the average capital quality contribution (0.55) in 1950–73 for the six countries represents the age effect, that is, an average of about 0.10 for the six countries. These are much smaller than

the age effects in Ohkawa and Rosovsky (1973); Carré, Dubois, and Malinvaud (1972); and Kendrick (1981), but they are similar to the age effect Denison (1967, pp. 304–12) had for Denmark, Germany, and Norway in 1950–55. The main difference between my estimate and the estimates of these authors is that I include the rest of the embodiment effect as well.

It should be noted that the intercountry variation in the capital quality effect cannot be derived directly from Table 10, which shows the average age of the stock, without a vintage effect.

V. *Assessing the Impact of Supplementary Influences Additional to Augmented Joint Factor Productivity*

Some growth analysts stop short after they have measured total factor pro-

TABLE 11a			
JOINT FACTOR PRODUCTIVITY, 1913–84 (annual average compound growth rate)			
	1913–50	1950–73	1973–84
France	1.42	4.02	1.84
Germany	0.86	4.32	1.55
Japan	1.10	5.79	1.21
Netherlands	1.25	3.35	0.81
U.K.	1.15	2.14	1.22
U.S.	1.99	1.85	0.52
Average	1.30	3.58	1.19

Source: Derived from Table 20. Joint factor productivity equals GDP growth minus the contributions of labor quantity, residential capital quantity, and nonresidential capital quantity.

TABLE 11b			
AUGMENTED JOINT FACTOR PRODUCTIVITY, 1913–84 (annual average compound growth rate)			
	1913–50	1950–73	1973–84
France	0.61	3.11	0.93
Germany	0.19	3.61	1.13
Japan	0.04	4.69	0.43
Netherlands	0.53	2.38	0.14
U.K.	0.38	1.53	0.64
U.S.	1.19	1.05	−0.27
Average	0.49	2.73	0.50

Source: Derived from Table 20. Augmented joint factor productivity is equal to joint factor productivity minus the contributions of labor quality and capital quality.

ductivity (see Table 11a or its augmented variant Table 11b). Kendrick (1961) did so because Denison had not then inaugurated the fashion, and Jorgenson, in most of the many studies he has made with various collaborators, has done so out of his strong commitment to neoclassic assumptions. Since Denison's (1962) dazzling tour de force, several other authors, including Kendrick (1981), have followed his example by adding significant supplementary elements. The justification for doing this is clear because the total factor productivity measure, even in its augmented version, still leaves an important amount of growth unexplained, and particularly the growth acceleration of the golden age. This paper therefore incorporates a number of such supplementary influences.

The index for this full-blooded growth accounting approach is:

$$\dot{\Pi}^5 = \dot{O} - a\dot{L}^* - (1 - a)\dot{K}^* - \dot{S}$$

where $\dot{S}$ is the contribution to the rate of growth of a number of supplementary influences. In our case there are nine of these supplementary items. $\dot{\Pi}^5$ is perhaps best referred to as the "residual," which is the residue of unmeasured influ-

ences, including disembodied technical progress, statistical and other error. In comparing different specimens of growth accounting, one must remember that the "residual" may be conceptually different for different authors, as is also the case with augmented total factor productivity, and that its comparative significance depends on what is included in the analysis.

In our approach we have attempted to use the same type of measurement convention across all the countries and periods, but this is not true of all of our nine supplementary influences. Some of them are long term and systematic in character, but some are either cyclical or ad hoc and do not apply to all the periods.

The nine supplementary elements (in order of discussion) derive from:

1. changes in economic structure;
2. the process of convergence (catch-up) of follower countries on the leader (the U.S.);
3. foreign trade effects;
4. economies of scale at the national level;
5. the energy price explosion of 1973–84 and induced energy economy;

6. effects of natural resource discovery;
7. costs of government regulation and crime;
8. labor hoarding/dishoarding;
9. use of capacity effects.

The first four are more or less systematic, the next three are ad hoc, and the last two are of a cyclical/conjunctural nature.

For convenience in comparison, these sources of growth, like the factor inputs, are summarized in Tables 19–22 in additive form as contributions to the overall compound growth rate of GDP, rather than shown as indices that would have to be multiplied together to "explain" growth.

A. *Structural Change*

Economic growth has been accompanied by massive changes in economic structure whose long-run pattern has been similar in all six countries. As can be seen in Table A-13 there has been a steady decline in the share of agriculture in employment, from an average of 34 percent in 1913 to 5.5 percent in 1984, and an equally steady rise in the share of services from 33 to 62 percent. Industrial development has been different. It accounted for 32 percent of employment in 1913, rose to a peak of 39 percent in 1960, and fell back again to 32 percent in 1984. This same bell-shaped pattern of relative industrialization and deindustrialization has affected all of the countries, though its timing has varied, coming earliest in the Netherlands, U.K., and U.S. and latest in Japan. It is clearly a long-run general tendency, though in the 1973–84 period of depressed demand it was exacerbated by the conjunctural situation.

Structural changes reflect two basic forces that have operated on all the countries as they have reached successively higher levels of real income and productivity. The first of these is the elasticity of demand for particular products, which has been rather similar at given levels of income (particularly as relative price structures have moved in a similar direction). These demand forces have reduced the share of agricultural products in consumption and have raised the demand for the products of industry and services. The second basic force has been the differential pace of technological advance between sectors. Productivity growth has been slower in services than commodity production: partly because of the intrinsic character of many personal services; partly because of measurement conventions that exclude the possibility of productivity growth in some services. Structural change has also been affected by other influences such as the size of government activity, foreign trade, etc. (see Maddison 1980b).

If productivity were at the same level and grew at the same pace in each sector, there would be no structural effect, but in fact there are big differences. Historically, agriculture has had low productivity levels, and the exodus from low-productivity employment to higher-productivity employment in industry and services was the important element in structural "progress." After the Second World War, high levels of overall demand speeded up this process, sucking labor out of agriculture at a faster pace. Helped by technical advances, agricultural productivity growth speeded up in the postwar period and has in most cases been faster than that in industry (see Table A-6). Because the relative level of agricultural productivity is a good deal higher now than it was, and employment in agriculture is much smaller, the scope for this kind of sectoral gain has generally eroded. It has not disappeared and still provides scope for significant future gain

TABLE 12

IMPACT OF STRUCTURAL SHIFT IN EMPLOYMENT ON GROWTH OF GDP PER PERSON EMPLOYED, 1950–84
(annual average compound growth rates)

	Actual Rate of Growth of GDP per Person Employed		Rate of Growth of GDP per Person Employed Assuming Employment Structure Unchanged and with Actual In-sector Productivity Growth		Impact of Proportionate Sectoral Shift in Employment on Growth of GDP per Person Employed	
	1950–73	1973–84	1950–73	1973–84	1950–73	1973–84
France	4.65	2.16	4.19	2.28	0.46	−0.12
Germany	4.88	2.29	4.52	2.24	0.36	0.05
Japan	7.67	2.94	6.45	2.73	1.22	0.21
Netherlands	3.62	0.96	3.69	1.26	−0.07	−0.30
U.K.	2.54	1.43	2.44	1.69	0.10	−0.26
U.S.	2.12	0.55	2.00	0.62	0.12	−0.07
Average	4.25	1.72	3.88	1.80	0.37	−0.08

Source: First two columns from Table 19. Otherwise, sectoral GDP from OECD(d) supplemented by national sources; sectoral employment derived from Tables A-7 and A-13. For sectoral productivity growth see Table A-6. Figures on hours worked per person by sector were not available on a reliable basis. For the 1913–50 estimates in Table 19, the sources for GDP by sector were Carré, Dubois, and Malinvaud (1972) for France, Walter Hoffmann (1965) for Germany, Ohkawa and Shinohara (1979) for Japan, Feinstein (1972) for the U.K., and Kendrick (1977) for the U.S.

in Japan, but it is not what it used to be.

In the past there was always some structural "drag" from movement into the slow-growing service sector, but this was compensated for by its being a relatively high productivity sector. Now, however, this "drag" is much bigger than it was. The service sector is bigger than in the past, the level of service productivity is lower than that in industry, and deindustrialization of employment in favor of services is increasingly prevalent.

The contribution of structural change to growth was generally most favorable in 1950–73 and least favorable in 1973–84 (when it was actually negative for four of the countries). Over the whole period since 1913 it was most favorable for Japan, which started with the biggest agricultural sector, and least favorable for the

Netherlands and the U.K., which had the most "mature" economic structures.

Table 12 shows the way in which the structural effect was calculated assuming a three-sector classification of employment in agriculture, industry, or services. It shows what the growth rate of output per man would have been if the structure of employment had not changed and if productivity growth in each sector remained as actually experienced.

Virtually all growth analysts attach importance to structural change, particularly in the form of labor migration from low to high productivity sectors. It is treated as a similar add-on supplement to total factor productivity analysis in the cross-country studies of Denison (1967), Denison and Chung (1976), and Kendrick (1981), as well as in the national

TABLE 13

CHARACTERISTICS OF PERFORMANCE LEVELS IN THE LEAD COUNTRY (U.S.) AND THE FIVE FOLLOWER COUNTRIES IN 1984
(U.S. = 100)

	GDP per Employee	Annual Hours per Employee	GDP per Employee Hour	Sex Mix of Employment	Education per Employee	R and D per Employee	Nonresidential Capital Stock per Employee	Modernity of Nonresidential Capital Stock	Energy Consumption per Employee	Land per Employee	Scale of National Economy	Foreign Trade per Employee
France	93	95	98	101	84	72	101	104	54	29	19	180
Germany	93	103	91	102	73	89	111	95	64	11	22	249
Japan	73	132	56	102	84	68	90	119	39	7	39	102
Netherlands	98	100	97	105	73	72	110	93	72	9	5	497
U.K.	75	93	81	100	81	67	65	96	48	12	17	160
Average for five followers	86	105	84	102	79	74	95	101	55	14	20	238
U.S.	100	100	100	100	100	100	100	100	100	100	100	100

Source: In this table a figure less than 100 represents less favorable performance levels than in the U.S. Most of the figures on levels are derived from the appendix tables with weights similar to those used in Table 20; that is, female employees are weighted 0.6, male employees 1; a year of primary education is given a weight of 1, secondary education 1.4, and higher education 2. The level of the nonresidential capital stock was derived in the same way for all countries as described in Table 10, which produced capital output ratios at constant national prices in 1984 of 3.12 in France, 3.48 in Germany, 3.75 in Japan, 3.60 in the Netherlands, 3.28 in the U.K., and 2.74 in the U.S. These figures were converted into 1984 dollars at U.S. purchasing power parity (PPP) using the GDP figures in Table A-1, and the relative PPPs for investment goods in 1980 in Ward (1985, p. 87). Modernity of capital stock is derived from Table 10, land area from World Bank (1986), scale of economy from Table A-1.

monographs on France, Japan, and the U.K. Kendrick (1961) and Gollop and Jorgenson (1980) in their studies on U.S. growth treat it differently, within their factor productivity analysis, by disaggregating the economy into many more sectors than we have done.

B. *The Catch-Up Bonus*

Between 1913 and 1984, the U.S. had a higher level of real per capita income and labor productivity than all of the other countries, a "leadership" that had emerged around 1890 when U.S. productivity overtook that in the U.K. The initial dynamism of the U.S. came from its comparatively greater advantage in natural resources, its higher investment rates, higher levels of education and research. With time, the larger scale of the U.S. economy became increasingly pronounced, and this also may have contributed something to the U.S. lead. During 1913–50 the leader-follower gap was widened because European and Japanese growth was adversely affected by war.

In the long run, as U.S. natural resource advantages become less significant, as the mechanisms for technical diffusion are improved, as levels of human and physical capital per head in the other countries come closer to U.S. levels, and the scale of markets is widened by international trade, there are strong reasons for expecting a convergence of productivity levels, and indeed, in the period since 1950 this process has been very clear (see Tables 3 and 13).

If the follower countries follow an appropriate policy mix and are not disturbed in the convergence process by war, they should be able to increase productivity at a faster pace than the lead country. They enjoy "opportunities of backwardness," which means that over a considerable range of technology they can emulate the leader and get a given amount of growth with less expenditure

on research and development. They can push the rate of capital formation per worker faster without running into diminishing returns, and structural change is rapid. Most of these effects enter into the accounts elsewhere, but when countries mount a successful process of catch-up, they are in a "virtuous circle" situation, which we have assumed will provide an extra efficiency bonus augmenting the yield of factor inputs and other growth components in a way that is not true of the lead country, which is nearer to a "best-practice" situation over a wide range of productive activity.

I assume this catch-up bonus to be a function of both (*a*) the size of the gap between a particular follower country and the lead country and (*b*) the rate at which the productivity gap is being narrowed. The size of the gap at different periods can be seen in Table 3; the rate of convergence can be seen in Table 19. It was assumed that the rate of bonus when the gap is being narrowed, as it was in 1950–84, was 20 percent of the convergence rate. Although there are strong reasons for thinking that such benefits were a feature of the convergence process, there is no hard evidence for the particular 20 percent coefficient we have chosen, so the magnitude of this element in our growth accounts is rather speculative.

The catch-up effect in the follower countries was biggest in Japan, which had the lowest starting position in 1950 (14 percent of U.S. levels) and the fastest growing economy. It was least in the Netherlands and the U.K., whose position was nearest to the U.S. in 1950. In the U.S., of course, it was zero. When the follower countries have converged on the U.S., this effect will ultimately wither away. High rates of investment will be less profitable and more R and D will be necessary (see Table A-24). Generally speaking, the catch-up effect was weaker in 1973–84 than in the golden age (1950–73) except in the U.K.

It can be seen from Table 13 that the process of convergence has already advanced rather far in this group of countries. The average lag of the followers is now very small for levels of fixed capital, but more marked for education and R and D. The U.S. advantage in natural resource endowment (for which the land and energy ratios are a rough proxy) and in the scale of its internal market is still very large indeed, but these two influences are not very significant now because (a) these particular follower countries have offset the smaller size of their national markets to a large extent by opening their economies to international trade and (b) there have been giant strides in transport technology, which makes the locus of natural resources less important than was once the case.

A catch-up bonus does not figure in many versions of growth accounts, but it plays a major role in Helliwell, Sturm, and Salou (1985) whose hypothesis is different, that is, convergence on growth rates in the lead country rather than on its level. There is an analogous element of this kind in Denison (1967), which he classifies as an economy of scale due to differing "income elasticities." Although Denison's terminology and method of calculation are different, the size of his coefficients and their inverse distribution by initial level of productivity are similar to those presented here.

C. *Foreign Trade Effect*

Since 1913, the foreign trade regimes of these countries have undergone major changes that have had some effect on output growth. In the 1913–50 period, trade was adversely affected by the growth of tariffs, quantitative restrictions, and exchange controls. In 1950–73, tariffs were removed on a great part of the intertrade of the four European countries within the

TABLE 14

RELATION BETWEEN GROWTH OF GDP AND FOREIGN
TRADE VOLUME AVERAGE FOR SIX COUNTRIES
(annual average compound growth rates)

	1913–50	1950–73	1973–84
Average Growth of Trade Volume	0.49	9.42	3.61
Average GDP Growth	1.85	5.31	2.10

Source: Table 19.

European community, and on a worldwide basis for all six countries by successive GATT rounds. Quantitative restrictions on nonagricultural products were greatly reduced, and exchange controls were reduced to negligible proportions.

As a result, foreign trade volume grew more slowly than GDP in all the countries in 1913–50 and faster in all the countries in 1950–73.

After 1973, the tariff reduction process was much less significant, and in some items, quantitative restrictions on trade have grown. Trade volume in 1973–84 was still faster than GDP but to a less marked degree than in 1950–73 (see Table 14).

In 1950–73 the growth of trade strengthened international specialization and competition through the removal of trade barriers and gave the European countries some of the traditional American advantages of large internal markets. The prices of products entering foreign trade, both imports and exports, rose a good deal less than the overall price deflators, in a way that was not true after 1973.

We have assumed that foreign trade produced ten percent economies of scale in the first and last periods, and 20 percent in 1950–73 (see source note for Table 20). For 1950–73, we assumed that the efficiency impact of a given percent-

TABLE 15a

DIFFERENCE BETWEEN GROWTH RATES OF ENERGY CONSUMPTION AND GDP
(annual average compound growth rates)

	1913–50	1950–73	1973–84	Difference 1950–73 Minus 1913–50	Difference 1973–84 Minus 1950–73
France	−0.66	−0.52	−2.06	0.14	−1.54
Germany	−1.30	−1.22	−2.15	0.08	−0.93
Japan	−0.26	−0.16	−3.29	0.10	−3.13
Netherlands	−0.79	1.91	−2.30	2.70	−4.21
U.K.	−1.28	−1.32	−3.17	−0.04	−1.85
U.S.	−0.91	−0.72	−2.24	0.19	−1.52
Average	−0.87	−0.34	−2.54	0.53	−2.20

Source: Table 19.

age expansion of trade was greater because of the intense policy effort to reduce barriers, which produced an unprecedented fall in the relative price of items that entered international trade.

D. *Economies of Scale at the National Level*

In neoclassic versions of growth accounts (e.g., in Jorgenson's work), it is assumed that there are constant returns to scale, but in all of Denison's studies, a significant scale bonus is assumed to occur as national markets increase in size. In Denison (1967), scale economies at the national level represent about 9 percent of growth, and their importance is similar in Kendrick (1981). Ohkawa and Rosovsky (1973) also attribute importance to economies of scale.

In fact, empirical evidence on economies of scale is scarce. Economies of scale are difficult to calculate in cross-section studies because of interfirm variations in vintages of capital, and, in time series, it is difficult to disentangle scale economies from the effects of technical progress. In a careful study, Zvi Griliches and V. Ringstad (1971) found economies of scale in Norwegian manufacturing to be

between 6 and 7 percent, but because Norway is a very small economy, and scale economies are not as likely in the rest of the economy as in manufacturing, I assume that the scale bonus at the national level for these six countries is only 3 percent of GDP growth.

E. *The Energy Effect*

Over the long term, all of these economies have been engaged in a successful process of energy economy. It can be seen from Table 15a that in all our three periods, all six countries had slower growth in energy consumption than GDP (except for the Netherlands in 1950–73).

In 1950–73, there was somewhat less energy economizing than in the previous period, but given the relative cheapness of energy, this change was not big enough to affect aggregate economic growth, except in the Netherlands.

In 1973–84, however, as a result of the OPEC shocks, energy prices rose tenfold in two successive leaps, and this led to a sharp increase in the pace of energy economy. In all countries this process reduced growth rates.

There is considerable controversy about the impact of energy substitution

TABLE 15b

ACTUAL AND HYPOTHETICAL GROWTH OF GDP PLUS ENERGY CONSUMPTION

(annual average compound growth rates)

	Actual		Hypothetical		Actual minus Hypothetical	
	1950–73	1973–84	1950–73	1973–84	1950–73	1973–84
France	5.12	2.07	5.12	2.16	0.00	−0.09
Germany	5.89	1.55	5.89	1.60	0.00	−0.05
Japan	9.37	3.63	9.37	3.77	0.00	−0.14
Netherlands	4.74	1.42	4.69	1.73	0.05	−0.31
U.K.	2.98	0.87	2.98	0.98	0.00	−0.12
U.S.	3.69	2.13	3.69	2.25	0.00	−0.12

Source: Tables 19, A-19, and A-20.

on economic growth. John Tatom (1981) attributed almost all of the 1973 U.S. slowdown to the direct impact of the energy problem, but Denison (1985) gave energy a much more modest role. My procedure for calculating the energy effect is similar to that in Denison (1985).

Viewed over the long run, the energy-economizing processes of 1973–84 look more like a temporarily accentuated version of a long-term trend rather than the catastrophe they seemed to be at the time.

I have made a rather modest estimate of the growth impact of the changed energy situation, as shown in Table 15b. This table compares the actual growth of GDP grossed up by adding energy inputs, with a hypothetical situation that would have occurred if it had been possible to maintain the relation between energy growth and GDP growth in the previous period.

It is clear that the need for energy economy retarded growth generally in 1973–84, and the biggest drag was in the Netherlands, which had built up an industrial structure in the golden age that was energy intensive.

The energy effect thus derived is intended to reflect only the direct impact

on GDP growth. The OPEC shocks clearly had bigger indirect effects on the conjuncture as they exacerbated inflation and created payments problems that induced deflationary policies. They also worsened real GNP (as opposed to GDP) through their terms of trade effect.

F. *Effects of Natural Resource Discovery*

In general I have not taken into account the role of land and natural resources in growth, but it seemed worth considering the role of Dutch exploitation of natural gas discoveries, which boosted output growth strongly from 1968 to 1974, and British exploitation of North Sea oil and gas, which boosted British growth from 1976 to 1983. Neither of these bonanzas had counterparts elsewhere in these countries.

For the 1950–73 period as a whole, natural gas growth accounted for 8 percent of the increment in Dutch real GDP, and in the U.K., in 1973–84, mining output represented 42 percent of U.K GDP growth (measuring in both cases at 1980 prices). If all of the increment in this new energy production in these two countries had been a natural resource windfall, one could say that it raised the Dutch GDP growth rate for 1950–73 from 4.46 to 4.70 percentage points a year, and British GDP growth in 1973–84 from 0.63 to 1.06 percentage points a year.

However, these output gains were not entirely due to natural resource windfalls. North Sea oil exploitation involved heavy capital costs and resource diversion, so we allocate only half of its contribution to natural resource augmentation. In the case of the Netherlands, the resource costs of developing Groningen gas were a good deal smaller, so we have taken 80 percent of the increment as the contribution of natural resources.

G. *Costs of Government Regulation and Crime*

Over the past fifteen years, all these countries stepped up government regulation. To some degree the regulation was intended to improve the quality of the environment, safety, or welfare or to offset the impact of increased criminality or terrorism. The corresponding improvements are not included in measured GDP, but the cost of achieving them has had some retarding impact on output growth. The costs have probably been most marked in the United States, where their impact has been strengthened by the presence of an exceptionally large legal profession, a tradition of litigation, and an adversary relationship between government and business.

Denison (1985, p. 111) estimated for 1973–82 that U.S. government regulation for pollution abatement reduced measured national output growth by 0.09 percentage points a year and that the cost of dishonesty and crime reduced measured growth by 0.05 percentage points a year. Worker safety and health regulation reduced growth by a further 0.02 points, making a total of 0.16 points a year. In 1948–73 the combined drag from these causes was smaller at 0.04 points.

For the U.S. these Denison results are used for our last two periods. For other countries I assume the pollution abatement and crime factors to be only half of that in the U.S. because other countries have fewer lawyers, less crime, and regulatory agencies that are much more sensitive to the wishes of business (see Maddison 1984a for a fuller statement). I assume that new worker safety and health regulation was unimportant in other countries.

H. *Labor Hoarding/Dishoarding*

In normal circumstances one would not expect labor hoarding or dishoarding to be significant in advanced capitalist economies over a period of years because market forces would cause workers to be laid off if they ceased to be productive. Even in cases where labor legislation restricts the freedom to fire and hire, labor turnover will solve the employer profitability problem by attrition over a number of years.

However, Japan differs from the other countries in two respects. First, a very high ratio of employed persons are self-employed or family workers. In 1950 this proportion was approximately 60 percent and in 1984 it was 26 percent; in the U.S., by contrast, the corresponding shares were 20 and 9 percent. Second, a significant portion of wage and salary earners have lifetime job security, which employers can guarantee because wages are very flexible, with mid-, and end-year bonuses that move with business profits and can amount to a third of earnings in normal times. These bonuses can be squeezed to zero in depressed conditions, which makes it fairly easy for employers to retain workers rather than lay them off. In these conditions, one cannot rely on Japanese unemployment figures to provide a guide to labor slack.

In 1950, it is clear that there was a large degree of underemployment in Japan. Official unemployment stood at only 1.9 percent of the labor force, but GDP was only 71.5 percent of its 1939 level. I assumed that labor hoarding amounted to a quarter of employment in 1950 and that this labor had been fully dishoarded by 1973. By 1984, there is likely to have been some element of labor hoarding again in Japan, given the very rapid deceleration in growth rates after 1973, with very little movement in the official unemployment count. I assumed, somewhat arbitrarily, that 3 percent of 1984 employment represented disguised unemployment.

The result of these hypotheses can be seen in Table 20 where labor hoarding had a significant negative impact on growth in 1913–50, and in 1973–84, and dishoarding favored growth in 1950–73.

In Germany too, in 1950, recovery of prewar production levels was not complete, and the production structure was in disequilibrium. There was scope for labor hoarding, for 31 percent of employed persons were self-employed or family workers. For Germany, therefore we assumed 10 percent labor hoarding in 1950, and complete dishoarding over the period 1950–73.

I. *Use of Capacity Effect*

The "use of capacity" adjustment is meant to deal with abnormal situations in terminal or initial years of the periods we have used and was applied only to Germany and Japan in 1950.

In both these economies, I assumed that the slack in the use of physical capital paralleled that in the labor market. In the Japanese case the labor slack consisted of labor hoarding, and in Germany it included both labor hoarding and overt unemployment.

For other countries, no "use of capacity" adjustment was made. The three benchmark years 1913, 1950, and 1973 were all years of high conjuncture in these countries, and although this was definitely not the case for 1984, the low "level of demand" in the latter years was the result of a decade of stagnation in which businessmen had had time to offset the surplus capacity that obviously did prevail within part of the period by reducing the growth of the capital stock below what it would have been at full employment.

It should be noted that accounts such as ours which are concerned with actual growth do not deal fully with the impact of cyclical disturbance. This can only be done by constructing a separate set of "potential output" accounts and comparing the different elements therein with the corresponding "actual accounts" that we have constructed here. The actual accounts include only labor input actually employed, so they are net of cyclical unemployment (which was substantial in 1984).

Table 16 shows what employment inputs would have been in 1973–84 if the 1984 unemployment rate had been at 1973 levels and if everything else had remained as it was. The last column of Table 16 does not figure in our Table 20, because the latter deals with actual and not potential growth.

Denison is the only one of the growth accountants to have developed a full set of "potential output" accounts. In comparing the two sets of accounts in Denison (1985, pp. 111–12), one finds that the two main items are the loss in factor input of 0.71 points in 1973–82, and the loss in output per unit of input 0.35 points. Together they make up 1.06 points, that is, the difference between actual output growth of 1.55 percentage points a year and a potential growth of 2.61 points. The first item is mostly comprised of a loss because of unemployment of 0.68 points and the second is rather similar to the "intensity of demand" ef-

TABLE 16

Direct Impact of Increased Unemployment on Labor Input and Potential Output, 1973–84
(average annual compound growth rates)

	Actual Employment	Potential Employment	Potential Impact on Annual Employment Growth of Reducing Unemployment Rates to 1973 Levels	Potential Output Growth Foregone Because of Rise in Unemployment
France	0.02	0.72	0.70	0.49
Germany	−0.61	0.06	0.67	0.47
Japan	0.84	0.97	0.13	0.09
Netherlands	0.62	1.79	1.17	0.82
U.K.	−0.37	0.59	0.96	0.67
U.S.	1.77	2.02	0.25	0.18
Average	0.38	1.03	0.65	0.45

Source: Tables A-7 and A-8. Column 4 is column 3 multiplied by the factor input weight of 0.7 for labor. As explained in the text, Table 16 shows only part of the output foregone because of cyclical slack. For a fuller analysis, see Maddison (1980a) and Denison (1985).

fect of 0.28 in Denison's "actual" accounts: These two total 0.96 and the rest is due to the imputed effects that full employment would have on working hours, activity rates for women, and structural effects.

Denison's potential output accounts are basically an elaboration of the Keynesian counterfactual first developed by Arthur Okun (1962) and used in simple forms subsequently by the U.S. Council of Economic Advisors. It does not attempt to estimate what output would have been if the capital stock had grown differently.

Several other growth accounts have included an "intensity of demand" effect, for example, Kendrick (1981), Carré, Dubois, and Malinvaud (1972), and Helliwell, Sturm, and Salou (1985). The latter construct their estimate after calculating potential output by regression procedures, and their total cyclical effect is very large for 1973–82. The difficulty with regression analysis, however, is that if some elements are left out of the accounts, those that remain may take over a large part of their "explanatory" power

because of the close correlation of most elements in the growth process. This is well illustrated in our Table 21 where in a situation of acceleration most of the items in the account move in the same direction, and in Table 22, where in a situation of slowdown, most of the explanatory items are negative. I therefore consider that Helliwell, Sturm, and Salou (1985) exaggerate the cyclical element because their accounts leave out the movement in working hours, labor quality, capital quality, and structural effects.

Summary Statement of Growth "Explained"

We have proceeded through the accounts with successive augmentation of their scope. Each of our successive $\dot{\Pi}$s (see Table 17b) is a kind of residual that shows how much growth is left "unexplained." The simplest statement, in terms of labor productivity, $\dot{\Pi}^1$, explains least, and, in particular, does not explain the acceleration/slowdown phenomena. Capital productivity, $\dot{\Pi}^2$, performs much

TABLE 17a

RESIDUAL (UNEXPLAINED) GROWTH (Π^5)
(annual average compound growth rates)

	1913–50	1950–73	1973–84
France	0.48	1.81	0.59
Germany	0.32	1.63	0.69
Japan	0.13	0.64	0.04
Netherlands	0.41	1.06	0.46
U.K.	0.38	1.06	0.49
U.S.	0.81	0.81	−0.01
Average	0.42	1.17	0.38

Source: Table 20.

better in "explaining" output growth and the acceleration phenomenon, but not the post-1973 slowdown. Moreover, we know that this is only a very partial indicator. When capital is linked with labor in the joint factor productivity index Π^3, more of growth is explained than with Π^1 but a large part of the acceleration/slowdown phenomenon is still "unexplained." Augmented joint factor productivity, Π^4, explains more of

growth than $\dot{\Pi}^3$, but is not much good at explaining acceleration and slowdown. In moving from $\dot{\Pi}^4$ to the $\dot{\Pi}^5$ (residual) measure, we added nine components by way of explanation that are quantified in Table 20. For 1950–73, the "golden age," $\dot{\Pi}^5$, "explains" a good deal more of growth than does $\dot{\Pi}^4$, and, as a consequence, it also reduces the mystery concerning acceleration and slowdown. One can therefore see clear gains in carrying the growth accounts beyond factor productivity analysis.

Table 18 summarizes the net explanatory power of the 14 growth components that were deployed in the causal analysis of Tables 20, 21, and 22. On average the degree of explanation is high and consistent, and the same is true for the explanation of the acceleration/slowdown phenomena. However, the degree of explanation varies significantly across countries, and, within each country, between periods. The weakest of the "explanations" is for the U.S. growth slowdown after 1973, and the strongest is for Japanese growth, and its variance between periods.

TABLE 17b

REDUCING THE RESIDUAL: IMPACT OF SUCCESSIVE ROUNDS OF GROWTH ACCOUNTING
(AVERAGE FOR THE SIX COUNTRIES)
(annual average compound growth rates)

	1913–50	1950–73	1973–84	Acceleration 1913–50 to 1950–73	Deceleration 1950–73 to 1973–84
GDP	1.85	5.31	2.10	3.46	−3.21
Labor productivity ($\dot{\Pi}^1$)	1.74	4.84	2.48	3.10	−2.36
Capital productivity (Π^2)	0.46	0.73	−1.78	0.27	−2.51
Joint factor productivity ($\dot{\Pi}^3$)	1.30	3.58	1.19	2.28	−2.39
Augmented joint factor productivity ($\dot{\Pi}^4$)	0.49	2.73	0.50	2.24	−2.23
Residual ($\dot{\Pi}^5$)	0.42	1.17	0.38	0.77	−0.79

Source: Tables 19, 5, 11a, 11b, 20.

TABLE 18

EXPLAINED GROWTH

	1913–50	1950–73	1973–84	Acceleration 1913–50 to 1950–73	Deceleration 1950–73 to 1973–84
	(annual average compound growth rates)			(annual average compound growth rates)	
France	0.58	3.32	1.59	2.74	−1.73
Germany	0.98	4.29	0.99	3.31	−3.30
Japan	2.11	8.73	3.74	6.62	−4.99
Netherlands	2.02	3.64	1.12	1.62	−2.52
U.K.	0.91	1.96	0.57	1.05	−1.39
U.S.	1.97	2.91	2.33	0.94	−0.58
Average	1.43	4.14	1.72	2.71	−2.42
				(percentage explained)	
France	55	65	75	67	59
Germany	75	72	59	72	78
Japan	94	93	99	93	89
Netherlands	83	77	71	71	81
U.K.	71	65	54	61	71
U.S.	71	78	100	100	41
Average	75	75	76	77	70

Source: Tables 20 and 21.

Conclusions

The present survey is intended to show that growth accounts are a useful framework for assembling quantitative "facts" and quantified hypotheses about growth causality in a coherent way. Their usefulness is clear in interpreting developments in six countries over a 71-year period. The explanatory power of the exercise was quite powerful for the countries as a group, though for individual countries the degree to which growth was explained is not always consistent between periods. Some elements in the quantification are much more speculative than others. I therefore tried to keep the assumptions transparent so that the role of different influences can be modified by other analysts who may wish to make partial use of the quantitative framework.

This approach is particularly useful in comparative economic history, which in the past has often been based on loose description, untestable assertions, and literary modes of persuasion. The complexity and interrelatedness of different elements in the growth process, and the variation in momentum over time, make simple or monocausal explanations increasingly suspect. This is recognized by economic historians, who, in the search for better articulation of their facts and hypotheses, have come to use this type of analysis more frequently (see O'Brien 1986).

With the possible exception of those Cambridge economists in the Robinson-Sraffa tradition who still deny the measurability of capital, this approach should not raise serious ideological problems for any economist who concedes that the national accounts are useful. Some growth accountants are rigorously neoclassical, such as Jorgenson, but Denison has both neoclassic and Keynesian elements in his

TABLE 19

BASIC INDICATORS OF GROWTH PERFORMANCE, 1913–84

(annual average compound growth rates)

	1913–50	1950–73	1973–84	1913–50	1950–73	1973–84	1913–50	1950–73	1973–84
	France			Germany			Japan		
Population	0.01	0.96	0.48	0.55	0.94	−0.12	1.31	1.14	0.90
GDP	1.06	5.13	2.18	1.30	5.92	1.68	2.24	9.37	3.78
Employment	−0.24	0.48	0.02	0.55	1.04	−0.61	0.85	1.70	0.84
Hours per employee	−0.71	−0.47	−1.25	−0.30	−1.08	−0.67	−0.33	−0.15	−0.27
Sex mix	−0.01	−0.02	−0.17	−0.04	−0.03	−0.04	0.01	0.00	−0.04
Education	0.52	0.52	0.85	0.35	0.28	0.14	0.86	0.74	0.63
Residential capital	0.39	2.80	2.27	0.40[a]	5.02	3.25	0.12	6.15	6.44
Nonresidential capital	1.21[a]	3.92	4.50	1.02[a]	5.58	3.48	3.36	8.95	7.47
Capital quality	1.50	1.88	1.42	1.50	1.77	1.16	1.50	1.93	1.28
Use of capacity	0.00	0.00	0.00	−0.44	0.82	0.00	−0.80	1.29	0.00
Rate of productivity convergence with lead country	−0.46	2.59	2.45	−1.36	3.42	2.00	−0.70	5.12	2.19
Impact of structural change	0.09	0.46	−0.12	0.20	0.36	0.05	0.62	1.22	0.21
Foreign trade volume	0.69	8.79	3.95	−2.36	11.95	3.36	1.06	15.54	5.25
Energy consumption	0.40	4.61	0.12	0.00	4.70	−0.47	1.98	9.21	0.49
	Netherlands			U.K.			U.S.		
Population	1.35	1.24	0.65	0.45	0.48	0.04	1.21	1.45	1.01
GDP	2.43	4.70	1.58	1.29	3.02	1.06	2.78	3.72	2.32
Employment	1.20	1.08	0.62	0.51	0.48	−0.37	1.26	1.60	1.77
Hours per employee	−0.45	−0.82	−0.97	−0.79	−0.64	−0.96	−0.90	−0.38	−0.42
Sex mix	0.00	−0.05	−0.31	−0.02	−0.16	−0.17	−0.09	−0.17	−0.25
Education	0.38	0.62	0.78	0.47	0.29	0.45	0.59	0.58	0.77
Residential capital	1.94	2.63	2.64	1.65	3.04	2.24	1.82	3.29	2.56
Nonresidential capital	2.21	4.31	3.64	0.95	3.40	2.64	1.78	3.43	2.92
Capital quality	1.50	1.90	1.13	1.50	1.72	1.28	1.50	1.69	1.44
Use of capacity	0.00	0.00	0.00	0.00	0.00	0.00	0.00	0.00	0.00
Rate of productivity convergence with lead country	−0.75	1.92	0.96	−0.84	0.70	1.45	0.00	0.00	0.00
Impact of structural change	n.a.	−0.07	−0.30	−0.04	0.10	−0.26	0.29[b]	0.12	−0.07
Foreign trade volume	1.00	9.26	2.87	0.20	4.50	2.92	2.35	6.47	3.29
Energy consumption	1.64	6.61	−0.72	0.01	1.70	−2.11	1.87	3.00	0.08

Source: Population, GDP, employment, hours, residential and nonresidential capital stock derived from Tables A-2, A-1, A-7, A-9, A-18, and A-16 respectively. Sex mix from Tables A-7 and A-14, giving females a weight of 0.6. Education from Table A-12, giving a weight of 1 to a year of primary education, 1.4 to secondary and 2 to higher, and increments weighted by 0.6. Use of capacity derived from unemployment movements (Table A-8) and labor hoarding estimates as described in the text. Rates of productivity convergence from Table 3. Structural change from Table 12. Foreign trade volume is average of export and import growth in Tables A-21 and A-22. Energy consumption is from Table A-19.
[a] net stock; [b] 1909–48.

TABLE 20

Sources of GDP Growth, Selected Periods, 1913–84

(annual average percentage point contribution to growth rate)

	1913–50	1950–73	1973–84	1913–50	1950–73	1973–84	1913–50	1950–73	1973–84
	France			Germany			Japan		
GDP	1.06	5.13	2.18	1.30	5.92	1.68	2.24	9.37	3.78
Labor quantity	−0.67	0.01	−0.86	0.18	−0.03	−0.90	0.36	1.09	0.40
Labor quality	0.36	0.35	0.48	0.22	0.18	0.07	0.61	0.52	0.41
Labor hoarding	0.00	0.00	0.00	−0.20	0.32	0.00	−0.56	0.90	−0.22
Residential capital quantity	0.03	0.20	0.16	0.03	0.35	0.23	0.01	0.43	0.45
Nonresidential capital quantity	0.28	0.90	1.04	0.23	1.28	0.80	0.77	2.06	1.72
Capital quality	0.45	0.56	0.43	0.45	0.53	0.35	0.45	0.58	0.38
Capacity use effect	0.00	0.00	0.00	−0.13	0.25	0.00	−0.24	0.39	0.00
Catch-up effect	0.00	0.52	0.49	0.00	0.68	0.40	0.00	1.02	0.44
Structural effect	0.09	0.46	−0.12	0.20	0.36	0.05	0.62	1.22	0.21
Foreign trade effect	0.01	0.19	0.06	−0.04	0.21	0.06	0.02	0.26	0.05
Economies of scale	0.03	0.15	0.07	0.04	0.18	0.05	0.07	0.28	0.11
Energy effect	0.00	0.00	−0.09	0.00	0.00	−0.05	0.00	0.00	−0.14
Natural resource effect	0.00	0.00	0.00	0.00	0.00	0.00	0.00	0.00	0.00
Regulation/crime	0.00	−0.02	−0.07	0.00	−0.02	−0.07	0.00	−0.02	−0.07
Total "explained"	0.58	3.32	1.59	0.98	4.29	0.99	2.11	8.73	3.74
Residual	0.48	1.81	0.59	0.32	1.63	0.69	0.13	0.64	0.04
Percentage "explained"	55	65	73	75	72	59	94	93	99
	Netherlands			U.K.			U.S.		
GDP	2.43	4.70	1.58	1.29	3.02	1.06	2.78	3.72	2.32
Labor quantity	0.53	0.18	−0.25	−0.20	−0.11	−0.93	0.25	0.85	0.95
Labor quality	0.27	0.40	0.33	0.32	0.09	0.20	0.35	0.29	0.36
Labor hoarding	0.00	0.00	0.00	0.00	0.00	0.00	0.00	0.00	0.00
Residential capital quantity	0.14	0.18	0.18	0.12	0.21	0.16	0.13	0.23	0.18
Nonresidential capital quantity	0.51	0.99	0.84	0.22	0.78	0.61	0.41	0.79	0.67
Capital quality	0.45	0.57	0.34	0.45	0.52	0.38	0.45	0.51	0.43
Capacity use effect	0.00	0.00	0.00	0.00	0.00	0.00	0.00	0.00	0.00
Catch-up effect	0.00	0.38	0.19	0.00	0.14	0.29	0.00	0.00	0.00
Structural effect	(0.00)	−0.07	−0.30	−0.04	0.10	−0.26	0.29	0.12	−0.07
Foreign trade effect	0.05	0.65	0.12	0.00	0.16	0.06	0.01	0.05	0.02
Economies of scale	0.07	0.14	0.05	0.04	0.09	0.03	0.08	0.11	0.07
Energy effect	0.00	0.05	−0.31	0.00	0.00	−0.12	0.00	0.00	−0.12
Natural resource effect	0.00	0.19	0.00	0.00	0.00	0.22	0.00	0.00	0.00
Regulation/crime	0.00	−0.02	−0.07	0.00	−0.02	−0.07	0.00	−0.04	−0.16
Total "explained"	2.02	3.64	1.12	0.91	1.96	0.57	1.97	2.91	2.33
Residual	0.41	1.06	0.46	0.38	1.06	0.49	0.81	0.81	−0.01
Percentage "explained"	83	77	71	71	65	54	71	78	100

Source: Derived from Table 19, using a weight of 0.70 for the labor components, 0.07 for residential capital, 0.23 for nonresidential capital, and 0.30 for capital quality. The catch-up effect was calculated by assuming a 20 percent bonus from the productivity convergence process; the structural effect is the same as in Table 19; the foreign trade effect is 10 percent of the trade growth shown in Table 19 for the first and last periods and 20 percent for 1950–73 multiplied by the trade to GDP ratios (average for imports and exports) shown in Table A-23. The energy effect is from Table 15b. Natural resource effect is described in the text. The U.S. regulation/crime effect is taken from Denison (1985, p. 111); for other countries the worker safety effect is not counted and the other U.S. effects are assumed to have had half the impact they had in the U.S. Economies of scale are 3 percent of GDP growth rate. Capacity use effect as described in text.

TABLE 21

GROWTH ACCELERATION: 1950–73 PERFORMANCE COMPARED WITH 1913–50

(annual average percentage point contribution to growth acceleration)

	France	Germany	Japan	Netherlands	U.K.	U.S.
GDP	4.07	4.62	7.13	2.27	1.73	0.94
Labor quantity	0.68	−0.21	0.73	−0.35	0.09	0.60
Labor quality	−0.01	−0.04	−0.09	0.13	−0.23	−0.06
Labor hoarding	0.00	0.52	1.46	0.00	0.00	0.00
Residential capital quantity	0.17	0.32	0.42	0.04	0.09	0.10
Nonresidential capital quantity	0.62	1.05	1.29	0.48	0.56	0.38
Capital quality	0.11	0.08	0.13	0.12	0.07	0.06
Capacity use effect	0.00	0.38	0.63	0.00	0.00	0.00
Catch-up effect	0.52	0.68	1.02	0.38	0.14	0.00
Structural effect	0.37	0.16	0.60	−0.07	0.14	−0.17
Foreign trade effect	0.18	0.25	0.24	0.60	0.16	0.04
Economies of scale	0.12	0.14	0.21	0.07	0.05	0.03
Energy effect	0.00	0.00	0.00	0.05	0.00	0.00
Natural resource effect	0.00	0.00	0.00	0.19	0.00	0.00
Regulation/crime	−0.02	−0.02	−0.02	−0.02	−0.02	−0.04
Total "explained"	2.74	3.31	6.62	1.62	1.05	0.94
Residual	1.33	1.31	0.51	0.65	0.68	0.00
Percentage "explained"	67	72	93	71	61	100

Source: Derived from Table 20.

TABLE 22

GROWTH DECELERATION: 1973–84 PERFORMANCE COMPARED WITH 1950–73

(annual average percentage point contribution to growth slowdown)

	France	Germany	Japan	Netherlands	U.K.	U.S.
GDP	−2.95	−4.24	−5.59	−3.12	−1.96	−1.40
Labor quantity	−0.87	−0.87	−0.69	−0.43	−0.82	0.10
Labor quality	0.13	−0.11	−0.11	−0.07	0.11	0.07
Labor hoarding	0.00	−0.32	−1.12	0.00	0.00	0.00
Residential capital quantity	−0.04	−0.12	0.02	0.00	−0.05	−0.05
Nonresidential capital quantity	0.14	−0.48	−0.34	−0.15	−0.17	−0.12
Capital quality	−0.13	−0.18	−0.20	−0.23	−0.14	−0.08
Capacity use effect	0.00	−0.25	−0.39	0.00	0.00	0.00
Catch-up effect	−0.03	−0.28	−0.58	−0.19	0.15	0.00
Structural effect	−0.58	−0.31	−1.01	−0.23	−0.36	−0.19
Foreign trade effect	−0.13	−0.15	−0.21	−0.53	−0.10	−0.03
Economies of scale	−0.08	−0.13	−0.17	−0.09	−0.06	−0.04
Energy effect	−0.09	−0.05	−0.14	−0.36	−0.12	−0.12
Natural resource effect	0.00	0.00	0.00	−0.19	0.22	0.00
Regulation/crime	−0.05	−0.05	−0.05	−0.05	−0.05	−0.12
Total "explained"	−1.73	−3.30	−4.99	−2.52	−1.39	−0.58
Residual	−1.22	−0.94	−0.60	−0.60	−0.57	−0.82
Percentage "explained"	59	78	89	81	71	41

Source: Derived from Table 20.

accounts, plus a large dose of Yankee ingenuity. Indeed, large elements in this kind of approach can be used by Marxists (see Thomas Weisskopf, Samuel Bowles, and David Gordon 1983 for an analogous endeavor).

It must of course be recognized that this approach mixes hard and soft evidence. The harder evidence relates to the measures of GDP, labor input, and capital stock, and even these are subject to revision in the light of more refined use of evidence. Most of the other components are soft evidence based on hypotheses on which there may be quite legitimate differences of opinion. This is true even for measures of the impact of education on labor quality on which there is a huge and very sophisticated literature. It is also clear that there is a great deal of interaction between causes, and particularly between capital growth and technical progress, which makes it difficult to assign separate significance to

each. For this reason, policy inferences from such accounts should be heavily qualified.

It should also be emphasized that this approach deals only with proximate causality, and one has to look behind this to institutions, ideology, sociopolitical conflicts, degree of sophistication of policy, system shocks such as wars, and other historical accidents to get a fuller picture.

This type of analysis would not have been possible 30 years ago, when measures of past growth were much scarcer, so a great deal is owed to the scholars who have prepared the ground. There is little doubt that the analysis can ultimately be pushed back further into the nineteenth century, as estimates of growth, and particularly, of capital stock are improved. This is all the more necessary as circumstances in the decades before 1913 were more normal than in 1913–50.

TABLE A-1

REAL GDP LEVELS AT 1984 PURCHASING POWER PARITY, 1870–1984

($ billion)

	France	Germany	Japan	Netherlands	U.K.	U.S.
1870	59.27	33.98	19.28	8.26	77.95	78.61
1890	78.58	54.43	31.01	n.a.	116.92	188.59
1913	119.99	111.75	54.76	20.33	174.78	454.53
1929	150.93	135.33	97.94	33.86	195.57	740.72
1938	144.93	188.97	134.54	34.89	231.58	698.00
1950	173.49	179.92	124.34	49.40	281.04	1,257.86
1960	271.03	387.21	295.17	76.99	372.80	1,735.92
1973	547.98	675.49	976.50	142.20	556.60	2,911.78
1984	694.70	811.60	1,468.40	168.90	625.20	3,746.50

Source: GDP movement 1870–1952 from Maddison (1982), except Japan 1913–40, from Ohkawa and Miyohei Shinohara (1979, pp. 278–80); 1940–50 derived from pp. 259–69; 1950–52 from Ohkawa and Rosovsky (1973, p. 289). 1952–84 and 1984 purchasing power parities from OECD(d) various issues. The level of U.S. GDP for 1984 was raised by $111.9 billion in line with preliminary U.S. Dept. of Commerce revisions. All figures are adjusted to refer to product within the present-day geographic boundaries of the countries. This article was written before the revised U.S. national income and product accounts were fully available. Revised U.S. GDP in 1984 prices (on an OECD conceptual basis) is now as follows:

1870	80.11	1929	754.80	1960	1,793.38
1890	192.18	1938	708.49	1973	2,931.80
1913	463.18	1950	1,282.81	1984	3,713.02

These revisions (see OECD(d) 1960–85 edition and U.S. Department of Commerce, 1986) came too late to be incorporated in our analysis, but a rough check suggests that they do not lead to any serious change in our findings. In particular, they do not remove the sharp slowdown in the U.S. economy after 1973 which Darby (1984) suggested was an artifact deriving from official mismeasurement of GDP. It should be kept in mind that revisions in growth rates and levels of at least these dimensions can be expected to occur periodically in all the countries.

TABLE A-2

POPULATION ADJUSTED TO PRESENT-DAY BOUNDARIES

(000s at midyear)

	France	Germany	Japan	Netherlands	U.K.	U.S.
1870	38,440	24,870	34,437	3,607	29,185	40,061
1913	41,690	40,825	51,672	6,164	42,622	97,606
1950	41,836	49,983	83,662	10,114	50,363	152,271
1960	45,684	55,433	94,117	11,486	52,559	180,671
1973	52,119	61,976	108,660	13,439	56,210	211,909
1984	54,947	61,175	120,020	14,424	56,488	236,681

Source: Maddison (1982) and OECD(c).

TABLE A-3

POPULATION WITH FRONTIERS OF YEAR CITED[a]

(000s at midyear)

	France	Germany	Japan	Netherlands	U.K.	U.S.
1870	38,440	39,231	34,437	3,607	31,393	39,905
1913	39,770	66,978	51,672	6,164	45,649	97,227
1950	41,836	49,983	82,900	10,114	50,363	151,683
1960	45,684	55,433	93,260	11,486	52,559	180,671
1973	52,119	61,976	108,660	13,439	56,210	211,909
1984	54,947	61,175	120,020	14,424	56,488	236,681

Source: Maddison (1982) and OECD(c).

[a] That is, not adjusted for territorial change.

TABLE A-4

GDP PER HEAD OF POPULATION

	France	Germany	Japan	Netherlands	U.K.	U.S.
1870	1,542	1,366	560	2,290	2,671	1,962
1913	2,878	2,737	1,060	3,298	4,101	4,657
1950	4,147	3,600	1,486	4,884	5,000	8,261
1960	5,933	6,985	3,136	6,703	7,093	9,608
1973	10,514	10,899	8,987	10,581	9,902	13,741
1984	12,643	13,267	12,235	11,710	11,068	15,829

Source: Derived from Tables A-1 and A-2.

TABLE A-5

LABOR PRODUCTIVITY LEVEL (GDP PER HOUR WORKED), 1870–1984

($ at 1984 purchasing power)

	France	Germany	Japan	Netherlands	U.K.	U.S.
1870	1.05	1.13	0.37	2.02	2.13	1.92
1890	1.42	1.63	0.53	n.a.	2.82	2.96
1913	2.21	2.50	0.81	3.35	3.59	4.49
1929	3.21	3.11	1.42	4.96	4.52	6.60
1938	4.14	3.85	1.77	4.91	4.91	7.01
1950	4.54	3.67	1.52	6.17	6.41	10.93
1960	6.95	7.13	2.70	8.62	8.04	13.98
1973	14.31	13.94	8.39	16.77	13.19	19.16
1984	20.78	19.28	11.85	20.72	17.17	21.31

Source: Derived from Tables A-1, A-7, and A-9.

TABLE A-6

SECTORAL LABOR PRODUCTIVITY GROWTH (VALUE ADDED PER PERSON EMPLOYED), 1913–84
(annual average compound growth rate)

	1913–50	1950–73	1973–84
		Agriculture	
France	1.8	5.9	4.8
Germany	−0.4	6.3	4.5
Japan	0.5	7.3	2.1
Netherlands	n.a.	6.0	5.6
U.K.	2.5	4.6	4.2
U.S.	1.6[a]	5.4	2.5
Average	1.2	5.9	4.0
		Industry (Including Construction)	
France	1.4	5.2	3.1
Germany	1.3	5.6	2.7
Japan	0.7	9.5	3.7
Netherlands	n.a.	5.6	2.2
U.K.	1.4	2.9	2.9
U.S.	1.5[a]	2.2	0.8
Average	1.3	5.2	2.6
		Services	
France	0.4	3.0	1.1
Germany	−0.2	2.8	1.7
Japan	0.9	4.0	1.9
Netherlands	n.a.	1.8	0.2
U.K.	0.7	2.0	0.6
U.S.	1.0[a]	1.4	0.4
Average	0.6	2.5	1.0

Source: As for Table A-1.
[a] 1909–48;   [b] 1973–83.

Maddison: Growth and Slowdown in Advanced Capitalist Economies   685

TABLE A-7

EMPLOYMENT (000s)

	France	Germany	Japan	Netherlands	U.K.	U.S.
1870	19,126	10,260	17,685	1,381	12,285	13,826
1890	19,940	12,043	21,174	1,680	14,764	22,817
1913	21,013	17,303	26,046	2,330	18,566	38,821
1929	20,488	19,037	29,171	3,023	18,936	47,915
1938	18,948	21,204	31,855	3,169	20,818	48,271
1950	19,218	21,164	35,683	3,625	22,400	61,651
1960	19,662	26,080	44,670	4,101	24,225	69,195
1973	21,455	26,849	52,590	4,646	24,993	88,868
1984	21,509	25,111	57,660	4,971	23,984	107,734

Source: As described in Maddison (1984a, p. 85), except for France and U.S. France 1870–90 revised from INSEE (1966, p. 43). U.S. 1910–50 from Stanley Lebergott (1964, p. 512) with female farm employment adjusted upward to maintain a uniform female/male farm ratio at Lebergott's 1940 level. See U.S. Dept. of Commerce (1975, Part I, pp. 127–28) for census figures on male and female farm employment. The figures for this period were then adjusted upward by 0.4121 percent to allow for the fact that Alaska and Hawaii were added in 1950. For 1938, New Deal relief workers were added to Lebergott's employment figure (see Michael Darby 1976). For 1870–1910 it was assumed that employment grew parallel with the population aged 15–64. Proportion of working age derived from U.S. Dept. of Commerce (1975, Part I, p. 15). For 1960–84 U.S. employment was augmented to include 14- and 15-year-olds (data supplied by BLS). All figures for all countries are adjusted to refer to the geographic area within 1984 frontiers.

TABLE A-8

UNEMPLOYMENT AS PERCENTAGE OF TOTAL LABOR FORCE

	1913	1950	1973	1984
France	n.a.	2.3	2.6	9.7
Germany	n.a.	8.2	0.7	7.7
Japan	n.a.	1.9	1.3	2.7
Netherlands	n.a.	2.8	3.1	14.7
U.K.	2.1	2.5	3.1	12.8
U.S.	4.3	5.2	4.8	7.4

Source: 1913 and 1950 from Maddison (1982). 1973 and 1984 figures supplied by U.S. Bureau of Labor Statistics. The figures are adjusted to be comparable with U.S. concepts.

TABLE A-9

HOURS WORKED PER PERSON PER YEAR

	France	Germany	Japan	Netherlands	U.K.	U.S.
1870	2,945	2,941	2,945	2,964	2,984	2,964
1890	2,770	2,765	2,770	2,789	2,807	2,789
1913	2,588	2,584	2,588	2,605	2,624	2,605
1929	2,297	2,284	2,364	2,260	2,286	2,342
1938	1,848	2,316	2,391	2,244	2,267	2,062
1950	1,989	2,316	2,289	2,208	1,958	1,867
1960	1,983	2,081	2,450	2,177	1,913	1,795
1973	1,785	1,805	2,213	1,825	1,688	1,710
1984	1,554	1,676	2,149	1,640	1,518	1,632

Source: As described in Maddison (1984a, p. 85). Germany 1960 onward revised from IAB (Institut für Arbeitsmarkt- und Berufsforschung der Bundesanstalt für Arbeit) 1985/1. U.S. 1973 onward revised upward on the basis of Janice Hedges (1977) and Kent Kunze (1984). For 1960 onward the breakdown of the hours estimates was made as shown in Tables A-10 and A-11. For earlier years the procedure was cruder (see Maddison 1980a and Maddison 1982 for further detail of the procedures).

TABLE A-10

ESTIMATED BREAKDOWN OF AVERAGE HOURS PER PERSON EMPLOYED IN 1983

	Net Hours[a] Worked per Day	Days Worked per Year	Hours Worked per Year
France	7.570	206.00	1,560
Germany	7.953	211.45	1,682
Japan	7.956	267.75	2,131
Netherlands	7.758	213.50	1,656
U.K.	7.344	205.83	1,512
U.S.	7.000	231.25	1,619

Source: Estimates derived by merging data from various sources. Methods and sources for France, Germany, and U.K. described in Maddison (1980a); updated figures for France kindly supplied by R. Granier. For other countries from the sources described in Maddison (1984a, p. 85). For the U.S., Kunze (1984) and Hedges (1977) served as guidelines, but I assume somewhat more time off as my employment figures for the U.S. include government workers and 14- and 15-year-olds.

[a] Includes impact of overtime, involuntary short-time, and voluntary part-time working.

TABLE A-11

APPROXIMATE BREAKDOWN OF AVERAGE DAYS OFF PER PERSON EMPLOYED IN 1983

	Weekend Days	Public Holidays	Vacations	Sickness, Strikes, Bad Weather, and Personal
France	105.00	10.00	30.00	14.00
Germany	105.00	9.00	29.10	10.45
Japan	65.25	12.00	12.00	8.00
Netherlands	105.00	6.00	24.50	16.00
U.K.	105.00	8.00	25.02	27.15
U.S.	105.00	9.00	11.35	8.40

Source: See Table A-10.

TABLE A-12

AVERAGE YEARS OF FORMAL EDUCATIONAL EXPERIENCE OF THE POPULATION AGED 15–64
IN 1913, 1950, 1973, AND 1984

		Total	Primary	Secondary	Higher
France	1913	6.18	4.31	1.77	0.10
	1950	8.18	4.96	3.04	0.18
	1973	9.58	5.00	4.11	0.47
	1984	10.79	5.00	4.89	0.90
Germany	1913	6.94	3.50	3.35	0.09
	1950	8.51	4.00	4.37	0.14
	1973	9.31	4.00	5.11	0.20
	1984	9.48	4.00	5.17	0.31
Japan	1913	5.10	4.50	0.56	0.04
	1950	8.12	5.88	2.08	0.16
	1973	10.18	6.00	3.79	0.39
	1984	11.15	6.00	4.56	0.59
Netherlands	1913	6.05	5.30	0.64	0.11
	1950	7.41	6.00	1.17	0.24
	1973	8.88	6.00	2.49	0.39
	1984	9.92	6.00	3.34	0.58
U.K.	1913	7.28	5.30	1.90	0.08
	1950	9.40	6.00	3.27	0.13
	1973	10.24	6.00	3.99	0.25
	1984	10.92	6.00	4.50	0.42
U.S.	1913	6.93	4.90	1.83	0.20
	1950	9.46	5.61	3.40	0.45
	1973	11.31	5.80	4.62	0.89
	1984	12.52	5.80	5.10	1.62

Source: OECD(b) (vol. I, pp. 31–108) and its underlying worksheets, methodology and classification were used for most countries. These give figures for postwar census years. 1913 was derived from postwar census information on education of older cohorts. Thus in the 1950 U.S. census the average levels of education for population aged 15–64 were roughly equivalent to those for people aged 43. It was assumed therefore that the average education level for 1913 would correspond approximately to the education level of people 80 years old in 1950; however, for most European countries, the postwar census simply assumed that everyone had completed the full primary cycle, which was obviously not correct for 80-year-olds. We therefore had to make somewhat rough assumptions for primary education levels in 1913. For France the 1913 levels were derived from Carré, Dubois, and Malinvaud (1972, p. 93), and for Japan the 1913 level is derived from Ohkawa and Rosovsky (1973, pp. 56–57). Matthews, Feinstein, and Odling-Smee (1982, p. 573) give estimates for England and Wales 1871–1961. These provide a cross-check on our crude figures, which are intended to cover the whole of the U.K.

Maddison: *Growth and Slowdown in Advanced Capitalist Economies*   689

TABLE A-13
EMPLOYMENT STRUCTURE, 1870–1984
(percentages of total employment)

		France	Germany	Japan	Netherlands	U.K.	U.S.	Average
Agriculture	1870	49.2	49.5	67.5[a]	37.0	22.7	50.0	46.0
	1913	37.4	34.6	64.3	26.5	11.0	32.3	34.4
	1950	28.5	22.2	48.3	13.9	5.1	13.0	21.8
	1960	21.9	13.8	30.2	9.5	4.6	8.2	14.7
	1973	11.0	7.2	13.4	5.7	2.9	4.1	7.4
	1984	7.6	5.5	8.9	4.9	2.6	3.3	5.5
Industry	1870	27.8	28.7	13.8[a]	29.0	42.3	24.4	27.7
	1913	33.8	37.8	13.9	33.8	44.8	29.3	32.2
	1950	34.8	43.0	22.6	40.2	46.5	33.3	36.7
	1960	36.3	48.2	28.5	39.2	46.7	34.3	38.9
	1973	38.4	46.6	37.2	35.7	41.8	32.5	38.7
	1984	32.0	40.5	34.8	26.4	32.4	28.0	32.4
Services	1870	23.0	21.8	18.7[a]	34.0	35.0	25.6	26.4
	1913	28.8	27.6	21.8	39.7	44.2	38.4	33.4
	1950	36.7	34.8	29.1	45.9	48.4	53.7	41.4
	1960	41.8	38.0	41.3	51.3	48.7	57.5	46.4
	1973	50.6	46.2	49.4	58.6	55.3	63.4	53.9
	1984	60.4	54.0	56.3	68.7	65.0	68.7	62.2

Source: Paul Bairoch (1968) for France 1870 and Netherlands 1870–1913; Carré, Dubois, and Malinvaud (1972) for France 1913–50; Ohkawa and Shinohara (1979) for Japan 1906–50; Feinstein (1972) for U.K. 1870–1950; Kendrick (1961) and Lebergott (1964) for U.S. 1870–1950 (adjusted to correct for census fluctuations in female farm employment). 1960–84 from OECD(c). "Agriculture" comprises agriculture, forestry, and fishing. "Industry" includes mining, manufacturing, electricity, gas, water, and construction. "Services" is a residual covering all other economic activity, private and governmental (including military).

TABLE A-14

FEMALES AS A PROPORTION OF EMPLOYMENT, 1913–84

	1913	1950	1960	1973	1984
France	35.6	36.0	33.4	37.1	41.2
Germany	32.4	35.1	37.4	36.8	37.9
Japan	38.9	38.5	40.4	38.5	39.5
Netherlands	23.6	23.4	22.4	26.4	33.8
U.K.	29.1	30.8	33.7	38.7	42.5
U.S.	21.7	28.8	32.1	37.5	43.0

Source: 1913 from Maddison (1982); 1950–84 from OECD(c).

TABLE A-15

TOTAL REPRODUCIBLE FIXED CAPITAL STOCK (ASSET WEIGHTS) AT MIDYEAR, 1913–84
(1950 = 100.00)

	France	Germany	Japan	Netherlands	U.K.	U.S.
			Gross Stock			
1913	n.a.	n.a.	56.66	45.99	65.17	51.34
1950	100.00	100.00	100.00	100.00	100.00	100.00
1960	126.62	163.09	156.06	138.46	128.51	137.18
1973	226.56	331.78	584.77	238.25	210.13	214.74
1984	348.67	478.99	1,255.23	344.53	276.06	290.66
			Net Stock			
1913	70.61	76.01	n.a.	n.a.	74.29	56.31
1950	100.00	100.00	n.a.	n.a.	100.00	100.00
1960	138.19	190.30	n.a.	n.a.	133.50	147.66
1973	n.a.	404.76	n.a.	n.a.	234.12	242.13
1984	n.a.	563.21	n.a.	n.a.	301.72	316.10

Source: Derived from Tables A-16 and A-18 using asset weights to add the two broad categories of capital (residential and nonresidential) together. Figures refer to midyear. The estimates for Germany and the U.K. are corrected for boundary changes; the French figures are assumed to be so corrected.

Maddison: Growth and Slowdown in Advanced Capitalist Economies   691

TABLE A-16

MIDYEAR NONRESIDENTIAL FIXED CAPITAL STOCK AT CONSTANT PRICES

(1950 = 100.00)

	France	Germany	Japan	Netherlands	U.K.	U.S.
			Gross Stock			
1870	n.a.	n.a.	n.a.	n.a.	35.61	7.04
1913	n.a.	n.a.	29.46	44.54	70.48	52.03
1950	100.00	100.00	100.00	100.00	100.00	100.00
1960	126.20	162.19	175.53	143.07	129.66	135.63
1973	242.20	348.98	717.64	263.86	215.57	217.32
1984	393.02	508.65	1,584.42	390.88	287.04	298.39
			Net Stock			
1870	n.a.	18.58	n.a.	n.a.	49.91	8.01
1913	64.02	68.71	n.a.	n.a.	84.62	57.10
1950	100.00	100.00	n.a.	n.a.	100.00	100.00
1960	133.93	185.67	n.a.	n.a.	137.02	144.97
1973	283.79	414.12	n.a.	n.a.	249.06	245.37
1984	439.10	582.35	n.a.	n.a.	321.30	321.64

Source: France 1913–55 from Carré, Dubois, and Malinvaud (1972, pp. 189, 204, and 659); updated by figures supplied by OECD for 1955–84. Germany 1870–1950 from Maddison (1982) updated from Statistisches Bundesamt (1986). Japan 1913–70 from Ohkawa and Shinohara (1979, pp. 366–69) with rough estimates for the 1940–54 link from capital formation figures in the same source; for 1970 onward the figures were updated by figures supplied by OECD for the private sector, and the increment in the stock of government capital was calculated by cumulating constant price investment figures in OECD(d) with scrapping derived from investment figures for earlier periods from Ohkawa and Shinohara. Netherlands 1913–50 and 1973–84 from methods used in Maddison and Wilpstra (1982) assuming a 1913 capital output ratio of 2.1; 1950–73 from Henk-Jan Brinkman and José Schiphorst (1986). U.K. 1870–1948 from Feinstein (1972); 1948–84 figures supplied by Central Statistical Office, London. U.S. 1870–1926 net stock from Kendrick (1961, pp. 320–25); 1926–84 from John Musgrave (1986). Figures for all countries were adjusted to a midyear basis. The estimates for Germany and the U.K. were corrected for boundary changes, and the estimates for France were presumed to be so adjusted.

TABLE A-17

MIDYEAR STOCK OF NONRESIDENTIAL FIXED CAPITAL BY COMPONENT, 1870–1984

(1950 = 100.00)

	France	Germany	U.K.	U.S.	France	Germany	U.K.	U.S.
	Midyear Stock of Nonresidential Structures at Constant Prices				Midyear Stock of Equipment at Constant Prices			
				Gross Stock				
1870	n.a.	n.a.	40.61	n.a.	n.a.	n.a.	26.62	n.a.
1913	n.a.	n.a.	76.01	n.a.	n.a.	n.a.	60.54	n.a.
1950	100.00	100.00	100.00	100.00	100.00	100.00	100.00	100.00
1960	114.07	157.90	119.75	128.78	158.37	172.30	147.44	155.59
1973	173.55	331.10	190.85	196.91	424.32	391.09	259.95	276.79
1984	246.34	492.77	250.85	250.99	782.20	546.04	352.02	476.45
				Net Stock				
1870	n.a.	21.93	60.98	8.63	n.a.	14.19	31.49	6.35
1913	n.a.	66.63	100.61	62.76	n.a.	71.44	58.00	41.95
1950	100.00	100.00	100.00	100.00	100.00	100.00	100.00	100.00
1960	121.10	176.10	127.99	142.47	163.61	218.70	152.06	151.66
1973	211.17	391.72	239.39	233.88	451.86	491.39	265.15	276.19
1984	292.67	566.18	314.94	286.72	778.00	638.14	331.90	415.24

Source: As for Table A-16.

TABLE A-18

MIDYEAR RESIDENTIAL CAPITAL STOCK AT CONSTANT PRICES, 1870–1984

(1950 = 100.00)

	France	Germany	Japan	Netherlands	U.K.	U.S.
			Gross			
1870	n.a.	n.a.	n.a.	n.a.	29.33	n.a.
1913	86.51	n.a.	95.54	49.20	54.58	51.34
1950	100.00	100.00	100.00	100.00	100.00	100.00
1960	127.64	164.31	128.24	128.24	126.24	139.71
1973	188.85	308.31	394.90	181.51	199.29	210.50
1984	241.72	438.54	784.84	241.85	254.16	277.96
			Net			
1870	n.a.	23.65	n.a.	n.a.	30.41	6.16
1913	89.35	86.20	n.a.	n.a.	56.58	55.09
1950	100.00	100.00	n.a.	n.a.	100.00	100.00
1960	149.55	196.77	n.a.	n.a.	127.45	151.76
1973	n.a.	391.68	n.a.	n.a.	208.51	237.18
1984	n.a.	536.47	n.a.	n.a.	268.14	307.65

Source: France to 1966 from Carré, Dubois, and Malinvaud (1972, pp. 187, 189, and 204); increments to gross stock thereafter calculated from housing construction figures in UN, various issues. Germany, Japan, U.K., and U.S. from same sources as in Table A-16. Netherlands is an average of figures for physical stock of houses and of rooms from CBS (1979) and figures supplied by CBS for later years.

Maddison: Growth and Slowdown in Advanced Capitalist Economies   693

TABLE A-19

ENERGY CONSUMPTION (MILLION TONS OF OIL EQUIVALENT)

	1913	1950	1960	1973	1978	1984
France	55.7	64.6	90.4	182.2	191.8	184.7
Germany	93.8	93.9	145.8	269.8	275.2	256.3
Japan	21.7	44.9	94.7	340.4	362.3	359.3
Netherlands	7.77	14.2	21.9	61.9	65.9	57.2
U.K.	157.5	158.3	169.7	233.2	212.2	184.5
U.S.	436.5	866.0	1,014.2	1,711.0	1,882.3	1,726.3

Source: 1913 European countries from Mitchell (1975, pp. 361–67, 409–18) for coal and oil production and trade, with an addition of 15 percent for other energy sources (wood, water, wind, etc.) for France, 10 percent for Germany, and 4 percent for the U.K. and Netherlands. Japan 1913 from Bank of Japan (1966) data on production and trade in coal and oil, with a 25 percent addition for other energy sources Hiroaki Fukami (1986). U.S. 1913 from J. Frederick Dewhurst (1955, p. 1114). 1950 from W. S. Woytinsky and E. S. Woytinsky (1953, p. 941) converted from coal to oil equivalent (using an adjustment factor of 0.324675). 1960 from OECD(a) (July 1979) and IEA (1979); 1973–84 supplied by IEA. The 1913 figures were adjusted for territorial change, so the estimates refer throughout to consumption within the present area.

TABLE A-20

ENERGY INPUTS AS PERCENTAGE OF REAL GDP AT CURRENT FACTOR COST

	1973	1978	1983
France	1.73	5.21	7.29
Germany	2.06	6.33	8.63
Japan	1.65	4.98	6.20
Netherlands	2.16	6.85	9.23
U.K.	2.14	6.11	8.65
U.S.	2.78	8.95	11.89
Average	2.09	6.41	8.65

Source: Energy consumption from Table A-19 valued at import prices ($19.54 a ton in 1973, $93.98 in 1978, and $212.38 in 1983). GDP at factor cost converted to dollars at OECD purchasing power parities for the given years, from OECD(d) (1985, vol. I).

TABLE A-21

VOLUME OF EXPORTS

(1913 = 100.00)

	France	Germany	Japan	Netherlands	U.K.	U.S.
1913	100.0	100.0	100.0	100.0	100.0	100.0
1929	147.0	91.8	257.9	171.2	81.3	158.2
1938	91.0	57.0	588.3	140.0	57.3	125.7
1950	149.2	34.8	210.1	171.2	100.0	224.6
1960	298.4	154.7	924.4	445.1	120.0	387.9
1973	922.4	514.3	5,672.7	1,632.1	241.9	912.0
1984	1,459.5	774.0	14,425.2	2,383.7	349.1	1,161.5

Source: 1913–73 from Maddison (1982); 1973–84 from IMF.

TABLE A-22

VOLUME OF IMPORTS

(1913 = 100.00)

	France	Germany	Japan	Netherlands	U.K.	U.S.
1913	100.0	100.0	100.0	100.0	100.0	100.0
1929	133.0	99.1	259.8	115.4	125.8	191.7
1938	107.0	87.7	386.9	98.2	127.0	137.7
1950	111.5	48.8	103.4	121.5	115.4	247.7
1960	217.9	191.3	520.2	243.0	182.1	373.5
1973	870.3	594.1	2,943.7	747.7	361.0	1,091.6
1984	1,288.0	815.6	3,525.3	953.3	471.2	1,745.8

Source: 1913–50 Maddison (1962) except for Japan, which is from Ohkawa and Rosovsky (1973, p. 302); 1950–84 from IMF.

Maddison: Growth and Slowdown in Advanced Capitalist Economies   695

TABLE A-23

RATIO OF MERCHANDISE TRADE TO GDP AT CURRENT PRICES

	Exports			Imports		
	1913	1950	1973	1913	1950	1973
France	15.9	10.6	14.3	19.5	10.6	14.7
Germany	17.0	8.5	19.4	18.1	11.6	15.8
Japan	14.9	7.8	9.0	16.5	9.1	9.3
Netherlands	36.8	28.6	39.8	66.8	41.6	40.5
U.K.	19.8	16.7	17.1	24.9	19.3	22.2
U.S.	6.1	3.6	5.3	5.1	3.4	5.5

Source: those cited in Maddison (1983, p. 596) and Maddison (1964, p. 67).

TABLE A-24

RESEARCH AND DEVELOPMENT EXPENDITURE AS PERCENTAGE OF GDP

	1960	1973	1983
France	1.3	1.8	2.1[c]
Germany	1.0	2.1	2.6
Japan	1.4	2.0	2.5[c]
Netherlands	2.0[a]	1.9	2.0[c]
U.K.	2.5	2.1[b]	2.4[d]
U.S.	2.7	2.4	2.7

Source: 1960 from Kendrick (1981, p. 158); other years from OECD Science Directorate.
[a] 1964;   [b] 1972;   [c] 1982;   [d] 1981.

TABLE A-25

RESEARCH AND DEVELOPMENT EXPENDITURE AT 1984 U.S. PRICES
($ billion)

	1960	1973	1984
France	3.52	9.86	14.59
Germany	3.71	14.19	21.10
Japan	4.01	19.53	36.71
Netherlands	1.54	2.70	3.38
U.K.	9.39	11.69	15.00
U.S.	46.35	69.88	101.16
Total	68.52	127.85	191.94
Total as share of six-country GDP	2.2	2.2	2.6
U.S. share of total (percent)	68	55	53

Source: Tables A-1 and A-24.

REFERENCES

ABRAMOVITZ, MOSES. "Rapid Growth Potential and Its Realisation: The Experience of Capitalist Economies in the Postwar Period," in *Economic growth and resources.* Vol. I. Ed.: EDMOND MALINVAUD. London: Macmillan, 1979, pp. 1–30.

BAILY, MARTIN NEIL. "Productivity and the Services of Capital and Labor," *Brookings Pap. Econ. Act.,* 1981, *1,* pp. 1–50.

———. "The Productivity Growth Slowdown by Industry," *Brookings Pap. Econ. Act.,* 1982, *2,* pp. 423–59.

BAIROCH PAUL, *The working population and its structure.* Brussels: Université Libre de Bruxelles, 1968.

BANK OF JAPAN. *Hundred-year statistics of the Japanese economy.* Tokyo, 1966.

BAUMOL, WILLIAM J. AND MCLENNAN, KENNETH. *Productivity growth and U.S. competitiveness.* NY: Oxford U. Press, 1985.

BRINKMAN, HENK–JAN AND SCHIPHORST, JOSÉ. "De omvang van de kapitaalgoederenvoorraad in de perioden 1870–1939, en 1951–1973."Groningen, mimeo., 1986.

CARRÉ, JEAN-JACQUES; DUBOIS, PAUL AND MALINVAUD, EDMOND. *La croissance française.* Paris: Seuil, 1972.

CENTRAAL BUREAU VOOR DE STATISTICK. *Tachtig jaren statistiek in tijdreeksen.* The Hague, 1979.

CHRISTENSEN, LAURITS R.; CUMMINGS, DIANNE AND JORGENSON, DALE W. "Economic Growth, 1947–73: An International Comparison," in JOHN W. KENDRICK AND BEATRICE N. VACCARA, 1980, pp. 595–691.

DARBY, MICHAEL R. "Three-and-a-Half Million U.S. Employees Have Been Mislaid: Or, An Explanation of Unemployment, 1934–1941," *J. Polit. Econ.,* Feb. 1976, *84(1),* pp. 1–16.

———. "The U.S. Productivity Slowdown: A Case of Statistical Myopia," *Amer. Econ. Rev.,* 1984, *74(3),* pp. 301–22.

DENISON, EDWARD F. *The sources of economic growth in the United States and the alternatives before us.* Washington, DC: Committee for Economic Development, 1962.

———. *Why growth rates differ.* Washington, DC: Brookings Inst., 1967.

———. *Accounting for United States economic growth 1929–1969.* Washington, DC: Brookings Inst., 1974.

———. *Accounting for slower economic growth.* Washington, DC: Brookings Inst., 1979.

———. *Trends in American economic growth 1929–1982.* Washington, DC: Brookings Inst., 1985.

DENISON, EDWARD F. AND CHUNG, WILLIAM. *How Japan's economy grew so fast.* Washington, DC: Brookings Inst., 1976.

DEWHURST, J. FREDERIC AND ASSOCIATES. *America's needs and resources.* NY: Twentieth Century Fund, 1955.

DHOLAKIA, BAKUL H. *The sources of economic growth in India.* Baroda: Good Companions, 1974.

DOUGLAS, PAUL H. "Are There Laws of Production?" *Amer. Econ. Rev.,* Mar. 1948, 38(1), pp. 1–41.

FEDERAL RESERVE BANK OF BOSTON. *The decline in productivity growth.* Boston, 1980.

FEINSTEIN, CHARLES H. *National income, expenditure and output of the United Kingdom 1855–1965.* Cambridge: Cambridge U. Press, 1972.

FOGEL, ROBERT W. *Railroads and American economic growth.* Baltimore: Johns Hopkins U. Press, 1964.

FRAUMENI, BARBARA M. AND JORGENSON, DALE W. "The Role of Capital in U.S. Economic Growth, 1948–1979." Discussion Paper no. 1134. Cambridge, MA: Harvard Inst. of Econ. Res., 1985.

FUKAMI, HIROAKI. "The Japanese Economy and Oil Importation," *Proceedings of the Ninth International Economic History Congress.* Berne, 1986.

GOLDSMITH, RAYMOND W. *A study of saving in the United States.* Princeton, NJ: Princeton U. Press, 1955.

———. *The national wealth of the United States in the postwar period.* Princeton: NBER and Princeton U. Press, 1962.

GOLLOP, FRANK M. AND JORGENSON, DALE W. "U.S. Productivity Growth by Industry, 1947–73," in JOHN W. KENDRICK AND BEATRICE N. VACCARA, 1980, pp. 17–124.

GRILICHES, ZVI AND RINGSTAD, V. *Economies of scale and the form of the production function.* Amsterdam: North-Holland, 1971.

HEDGES, JANICE N. "Absence from Work—Measuring the Hours Lost," *Mon. Lab. Rev.,* Oct. 1977, *100(10),* pp. 16–23.

HELLIWELL, JOHN F.; STURM, PETER H. AND SALOU, GÉRARD. "International Comparison of the Sources of Productivity Slowdown 1973–1982," *Europ. Econ. Rev.,* June–July 1985, 28(1–2), pp. 157–91.

HOFFMANN, WALTHER G. *Das Wachstum der deutschen Wirtschaft seit der Mitte des 19 Jahrhunderts.* Berlin: Springer Verlag, 1965.

IAB. *Mitteilungen aus der Arbeitsmarkt und Berufsforschung.* Stuttgart: Kohlhammer, quarterly.

IEA. *1978 Review.* Paris, 1979.

INSEE. *Annuaire statistique de la France, 1966.* Paris, 1966.

KENDRICK, JOHN W. *Productivity trends in the United States.* Princeton: Princeton U. Press, 1961.

———. *Postwar productivity trends in the United States, 1948–1969.* NY: NBER and Columbia U. Press, 1973.

———. *The formation and stocks of total capital.* NY: Columbia U. Press, 1976.

———. *Understanding productivity.* Baltimore: Johns Hopkins U. Press, 1977.

———. "International Comparisons of Recent Productivity Trends," in *Essays in contemporary economic problems.* Ed.: WILLIAM FELLNER. Washington, DC: American Enterprise Inst., 1981, pp. 125–70.

———, ed. *International comparisons of productivity and causes of the slowdown.* Cambridge, MA: Ballinger, 1984.

KENDRICK, JOHN W. AND VACCARA, BEATRICE N.,

eds. *New developments in productivity measurement and analysis.* Chicago: U. of Chicago Press, 1980.

KIM, KWANG-SUK AND PARK, JOON-KYUNG. *Sources of economic growth in Korea: 1963–1982.* Seoul: Korea Development Inst., 1985.

KIRNER, WOLFGANG. *Zeitreihen für das Anlagevermögen der Wirtschaftsbereiche in der Bundesrepublik Deutschland.* Berlin: Duncker and Humblot, 1968.

KLODT, HENNING. *Produktivitätsschwäche in der deutschen Wirtschaft.* Tubingen: J.C.B. Mohr, 1984.

KUNZE, KENT. "A New BLS Survey Measures the Ratio of Hours Worked to Hours Paid," *Mon. Lab. Rev.,* June 1984, *107*(6), pp. 3–7.

KUZNETS, SIMON. *Capital in the American economy.* Princeton: NBER and Princeton U. Press, 1961.

LANGONI, CARLOS GERALDO. *As causas do crescimento economico do Brasil.* Rio de Janeiro: APEC, 1974.

LEBERGOTT, STANLEY. *Manpower in economic growth.* NY: McGraw-Hill, 1964.

LINDBECK, ASSAR. "The Recent Slowdown of Productivity Growth," *Econ. J.,* 1983, *93*(369), pp. 13–34.

MADDISON, ANGUS. "Growth and Fluctuation in the World Economy, 1870–1960," *Banca Naz. Lavoro Quart. Rev.,* June 1962, *61*, pp. 3–17.

―――. *Economic growth in the west.* NY: Twentieth Century Fund, 1964.

―――. "Explaining Economic Growth," *Banca Naz. Lavoro Quart. Rev.,* Sept. 1972, *102*, pp. 211–62.

―――. "What is Education For?" *Lloyds Bank Review,* Apr. 1974, *112*, pp. 19–30.

―――. "Economic Policy and Performance in Europe 1913–1970," in *The Fontana economic history of Europe.* Vol. 5(2). Ed.: CARLO M. CIPOLLA. London: Collins/Fontana Books, 1976, pp. 442–508.

―――. "Long Run Dynamics of Productivity Growth," *Banca Naz. Lavoro Quart. Rev.,* Mar. 1979, *128*, pp. 3–43.

―――. "Monitoring the Labour Market," *Rev. Income Wealth,* June 1980a, *26*(2), pp. 175–217.

―――. "Economic Growth and Structural Change in the Advanced Countries," in *Western economies in transition.* Eds.: IRVING LEVESON AND JIMMY W. WHEELER. London: Croom Helm, 1980b.

―――. *Phases of capitalist development.* Oxford: Oxford U. Press, 1982.

―――. "Economic Stagnation since 1973, Its Nature and Causes: A Six Country Survey," *De Economist,* 1983, *131*(4), pp. 585–608.

―――. "Comparative Analysis of the Productivity Situation in the Advanced Capitalist Countries," in J. W. KENDRICK, 1984a, pp. 59–92.

―――. "Origins and Impact of the Welfare State, 1883–1983," *Banca Naz. Lavoro Quart. Rev.,* 1984b, *148*, pp. 55–87.

MADDISON, ANGUS AND WILPSTRA, BOTE S. *Unemployment: The European perspective.* London: Croom Helm, 1982.

MAITAL, SHLOMO AND MELTZ, NOAH M. *Lagging*

productivity growth. Cambridge, MA: Ballinger, 1980.

MATTHEWS, ROBIN C. O., ed. *Slower growth in the western world.* London: Heinemann, 1982.

MATTHEWS, ROBIN C. O.; FEINSTEIN, CHARLES H. AND ODLING-SMEE, JOHN C. *British economic growth 1856–1973.* Oxford: Clarendon Press, 1982.

MITCHELL, BRIAN R. *European historical statistics 1750–1970.* London: Macmillan, 1975.

MUSGRAVE, JOHN C. "Fixed Reproducible Tangible Wealth in the United States: Revised Estimates," *Surv. Curr. Bus.,* Jan. 1986, *66*(1), pp. 51–76.

NELSON, RICHARD R. "Aggregate Production Functions and Medium-Range Growth Projections," *Amer. Econ. Rev.,* Sept. 1964, *54*, pp. 575–606.

NORDHAUS, WILLIAM D. "Economic Policy in the Face of Declining Productivity Growth," *Europ. Econ. Rev.,* May/June 1982, *18*(1–2), pp. 131–57.

NORSWORTHY, J. R. "Growth Accounting and Productivity Measurement," *Rev. Income Wealth,* Sept. 1984, *30*(3), pp. 309–29.

O'BRIEN, PATRICK, ed. *International productivity comparisons and problems of measurement, 1750–1939.* Berne: Ninth International Economic History Congress, 1986.

OECD. (a) *Economic outlook.* Paris, six-monthly.

―――.(b) *Education, inequality and life chances.* Paris, 1975.

―――.(c) *Labour force statistics.* Paris, annual.

―――.(d) *National accounts.* Paris, annual.

―――.(e) *Quarterly national accounts.* Paris, quarterly.

―――.(f) *Flows and stocks of fixed capital, 1955–80.* Paris, 1983.

OHKAWA, KAZUSHI AND ROSOVSKY, HENRY. *Japanese economic growth.* Stanford, CA: Stanford U. Press, 1973.

OHKAWA, KASUSHI AND SHINOHARA, MIYOHEI, eds. *Patterns of Japanese development: A quantitative appraisal.* New Haven: Yale U. Press, 1979.

OKUN, ARTHUR M. "Potential GNP: Its Measurement and Significance," in *Proceedings of the business and economic statistics section.* American Statistical Association. 1962, pp. 98–104.

PSACHAROPOULOS, GEORGE. "The Contribution of Education to Economic Growth: International Comparisons," in JOHN W. KENDRICK, 1984.

SALTER, WILFRED E. G. *Productivity and technical change.* Cambridge: Cambridge U. Press, 1960.

SCHMOOKLER, JACOB. *Invention and economic growth.* Cambridge, MA: Harvard U. Press, 1966.

SCHULTZ, THEODORE W. "Investment in Human Capital," *Amer. Econ. Rev.,* Mar. 1961, *51*(1), pp. 1–17.

SOLOW, ROBERT M. "Technical Progress, Capital Formation and Economic Growth," *Amer. Econ. Rev.,* May 1962, *52*, pp. 76–86.

―――. *Capital theory and the rate of return.* Amsterdam: North-Holland, 1963.

STATISTISCHES BUNDESAMT. *Volkswirtschaftliches Gesamtrechnungen, Fachserie 18, Reihe S.8, Revidierte Ergebnisse 1960 bis 1984.* Stuttgart: Kohlhammer, 1986.

TATOM, JOHN A. "Energy Prices and Short-Run Economic Performance," *Fed. Res. Bank of St. Louis Rev.*, Jan. 1981, 63(1), pp. 3–17.

TINBERGEN, JAN. "Zur Theorie der langfristigen Wirtschaftsentwicklung," *Weltwirtsch. Arch.*, 1942, 55, B and I, pp. 512–49.

UN. *Monthly bulletin of statistics.* NY, monthly.

U.S. DEPT. OF COMMERCE. "The Measurement of Productivity," *Surv. Curr. Bus.*, May 1972, 52(5), Part II.

_____. *Historical statistics of the United States: Colonial times to 1970.* Washington, DC, 1975.

_____. *The national income and product accounts of the United States, 1929–82. Statistical tables.* Washington, DC, Sept. 1986.

WALTERS, DOROTHY. *Canadian income levels and growth. An international perspective.* Ottawa: Economic Council of Canada, 1968.

WARD, MICHAEL. *The measurement of capital: The methodology of capital stock estimates in OECD countries.* Paris: OECD, 1976.

_____. *Purchasing power parities and real expenditures in the OECD.* Paris: OECD, 1985.

WEISSKOPF, THOMAS E.; BOWLES, SAMUEL AND GORDON, DAVID M. "Hearts and Minds: A Social Model of US Productivity Growth," *Brookings Pap. Econ. Act.*, 1983, 2, pp. 381–450.

WORLD BANK. *World development report 1986.* Washington, DC, 1986.

WOYTINSKY, WLADIMIR S. AND WOYTINSKY, EMMA S. *World population and production.* NY: Twentieth Century Fund, 1953.

86 - 90
(1988)

Ultimate and Proximate Growth Causality:
A Critique of Mancur Olson on the Rise and Decline of Nations[1]

Angus Maddison

In the past three decades analysis of the "proximate" causes of economic growth has been greatly enriched by both theoretical developments and quantitative studies. Technocratic supply-side growth accounts are available in considerable sophistication and detail,[2] but analysis of deeper causality is still rare.

One must therefore welcome a major study which turns back to more "ultimate causes" of growth acceleration and deceleration somewhat in the spirit of Max Weber and which shows some of the links between ultimate and proximate causality. Of course, Olson's evidence is often flimsy but this is, to some extent inevitable, and is not a disadvantage in ventilating a new idea as Weber himself demonstrated.[3]

The hard core of the argument is that various interest groups develop modes of collective action to further their particular interests, and increasingly over time their activities distort the efficiency of resource allocation to a very important degree. The theory derives directly from his earlier book[4], but the new elements are the assertions that these processes cumulate as a very significant growth constraint in countries where the social order has not been interrupted by war or revolution, and that they are always a very powerful, if not the most powerful influence on growth.

As in the earlier book, he argues that it is easier to form small groups than big ones, that the conflict between group and general interest is always larger with small groups, and that some latent groups, e.g. of consumers are not constructable. Some countries are lucky because they tend to develop larger, "encompassing", groups which are less harmful to the general interest, but he rejects the argument of John R.

---

[1] Olson, M., *The Rise and Decline of Nations*, Yale, 1982.

[2] See Maddison, A., "Growth and Slowdown in Advanced Capitalist Economies: Techniques of Quantitative Assessment", *Journal of Economic Literature*, June 1987, for a survey of "proximate" growth accounts.

[3] See the sweeping assertiveness of Weber, M., *The Protestant Ethic and The Spirit of Capitalism*, Unwin, 1971 (first published 1904-5) p.35 where he states (on the basis of some figures "one of my pupils" dug out) "business leaders and owners of capital, as well as the higher grades of skilled labour, and even more the higher technically and commercially trained personnel of modern enterprises, are overwhelmingly Protestant".

[4] Olson, M., *The Logic of Collective Action*, Harvard, 1965.

Commons[5] and J.K. Galbraith[6] that reasonably satisfactory outcomes can be attained by each group exercising countervailing power. He asserts that no country can attain "symmetrical organisation" where interest groups and latent groups can engage in comprehensive bargaining to achieve optimal outcomes.

His strongest evidence concerns the postwar perfomance of advanced capitalist countries, for which he advances a number of quite plausible propositions. Thus the U.K. has had slow growth and relative decline because its ancient social order has not been seriously interrupted by revolution or war. The social order itself and some of the coalitions which it fosters have been of major significance in retarding growth. Sweden, whose traditional order was similarly uninterrupted has done better because its pressure groups are more encompassing. United States postwar growth has been slower than that of the U.K. but it has retained its position as the leader in real income levels, because the country has benefitted from the absence of a medieval past, and from its size. Australia and New Zealand have done badly because pressure group influence has distorted resource allocation through protection. Germany and Japan did very well because defeat in war shattered the old growth impeding coalitions.

As Olson is neither a revolutionary or a warmonger he does not actually recommend periodic destruction of the social order. He would weaken the power of distributional coalitions by free trade, free entry for foreign and multinational investors, and free migration (pp. 141-2). He would dismantle regulation, reduce subsidies and welfare payments (p. 172-5), abandon activist macropolicy aspirations (p. 230) and promote price flexibility (p. 224). He assumes that (a) unconstrained competition is "staggeringly powerful" (p. 59) in producing beneficial outcomes; (b) there are no macroeconomic problems if you get your microeconomics right; and (c) in most cases government intervention to mitigate inequality will make inequality worse.

Olson's basic schema is quite simple. He accepts that GDP (Y) per head of population (D) is a reasonable measure of economic performance. The ultimate influcences on its growth are the institutions (I) that constitute the social order, and the degree of sociopolitical conflict (S) engendered by interest groups within a given order. I and S exert their influence mainly on the efficiency of resource allocation (E). Otherwise the supply potential is more or less given by the available production factors augmented by available technology (F). Olson does not disaggregate the production factors and practically ignores the influcence of I and S on F . Historical events (H) enter into his schema because they (i.e. war and revolution) shake up I and break the constraining power of S. Policy hovers off-stage as an unwelcome phantom. He considers macropolicy to be generally malign in its impact and he wants an economy where discretionary government action virtually disappears.

---

5 Commons, J.R., *The Economics of Collective Action*, Macmillan, New York, 1950.

6 Galbraith, J.K., *American Capitalism*, New York, 1952.

Ultimate and Proximate Growth Causality

One may represent Olson's explanatory schema as follows:

H→$\boxed{\text{I S}}$ Ultimate Causality

$\dfrac{Y}{D} = f\left(\dfrac{F'}{D}\right)E$ Proximate Causality

I have the following comments on Olson's schema:

(a) I would stress the importance and legitimacy of articulate and discretionary macroeconomic policy implemented by governments who exist because they were elected within a framework of universal suffrage. Variations in macropolicy between countries, and changes in policy mix in different phases of capitalist development have had a significant impact on growth. Thus I would add a firm and powerful (P) for policy in the line describing ultimate causality.

(b) I think Olson is right to stress the role of social conflict, but the origins of such conflict go deeper than he suggests. Inequalities which arise from social institutions and market forces are important additional causes. Nevertheless my judgement is that Olson probably exaggerates the causal influence of group conflict as distinct from institutions and policy. This is of course only a hunch, because, like Olson, I do not know how to measure their importance.

(c) Olson's stress on the role of specific historical events is very useful. However, it should be noted that some of these, e.g. the OPEC price rises and the collapse of the Bretton Woods monetary system were oecumenic "system shocks" which have had a simultaneous and similar rather than a differentiating impact on growth performance of different countries.

(d) Olson refers occasionally to the leader-follower dichotomy and the distance from the technical frontier in his treatment of particular countries. In fact, this phenomenon explains a good deal of the postwar differences in growth performance between countries, and should figure explicitly in the growth schema.

(e) The way in which ultimate causality has its impact on growth performance is more complex than Olson suggests. He puts all the weight on efficiency but I, S and P can affect the rate of growth of the physical capital stock, the quality of the labour force, the level and stability of demand, the rate of structural change etc. The growth schema should therefore spell out these proximate influences on growth more fully than Olson does.

(f) Olson more or less rejects the possibility that output may be below potential because of lack of demand. To my mind any schema which deals with comparative growth performance must include at least a crude notion of capacity use.

(g) When dealing with comparative growth performance on a world wide scale, one must allow something for colonial exploitation or conversely for foreign aid. Olson's discussion of pre and postwar Asain development excludes consideration of the malign effect of colonialism or the favourable impact of aid, even though (to quote somewhat extreme cases) the prewar drain from Indonesia took 8 per cent

Scandinavian Economic History Review

from its GDP[7] and postwar aid to Korea added 8 per cent to its GDP[8] in the 1950s and 1960s.

Olson's view of the interaction of ultimate and proximate causality is too simple. I would suggest a more complex explanatory schema, as follows:

An Alternative View of Growth Causality

$$H \rightarrow \boxed{I\,S\,P} \rightarrow \boxed{T}$$ Ultimate Causality

$$\frac{Y}{D} = f\left(\frac{N'\ L'\ K'}{D}\right)EC \pm A$$ Proximate Causality

Y	=	GDP; D = Population
H	=	Significant historical events
I	=	Basic Social order as characterised by Institutions, Beliefs and Ideology
S	=	Degree of Sociopolitical Conflict within a given social order
P	=	Macroeconomic Policies for Growth and Stability
T	=	Distance from Technical Frontier
N'	=	Natural resources developed and augmented
L'	=	Human capital, i.e. labour force augmented by investment in health, education and training
K'	=	Stock of all kinds of physical capital augmented by technical progress
E	=	Efficiency of resource allocation
C	=	Degree of Capacity Use
A	=	Foreign Aid (-) or Plunder (+)

Olson is concerned almost entirely with the relative performance of nations. He says virtually nothing on the reasons why the tempo of growth has varied in different phases of capitalist development. In a way he gives some sort of explanation of why there was a golden age between the end of the war and 1973, though his explanation could have been richer if his model had been more articulate about the general significance of the catch-up phenomenon which separated the USA from the rest. However he does not make any serious attempt to explain or measure the general slowdown since 1973 apart from suggesting that apparently all countries suffer from an increasing price stickiness.

It is useful for economists to specify their theory of the state, and it seems to me that four are available. One is the Marxist view that the state is an organ which the ruling class uses as an instrument of exploitation. This rules out the Olson thesis and he naturally rejects Marxism hook line and sinker. The second view is the social engineering one which assumes that rational state action can achieve optimal out-

---

[7]   See Maddison, A., Dutch Income in and from Indonesia, 1700-1938, in Maddison, A. and Prince, G., eds., *Economic Growth in Indonesia 1820-1940*, KITLV, Leiden, 1988.

[8]   Maddison, A., *Economic Progress and Policy in Developing Countries*, Allen and Unwin, London, 1970, pp. 310-11.

Ultimate and Proximate Growth Causality

comes. This Olson would reject as naive. Olson's own theory is an ethereal version of the liberal one. His objectives are similar to Hayek's, but for Olson the state is a piece of scenery - all real action is concentrated on his distributional coalitions. He does not mention bureaucratic power and threats to freedom, which are central to Hayek.

My own theory of society and the state is more eclectic than Olson's. I share the liberal concern with the dangers and distortions of bureaucracy, and am all in favour of a hands-off policy in most microeconomic matters. In macroeconomic matters I think there is a strong case for articulate and activist policy. On distributive issues, some degree of conflict is always present in the socioeconomic process, but the nature and locus of conflict varies over time, and is not necessarily cumulative. I also believe that state redistributive action has played an important and useful role in mitigating social conflict over the past century.

The original context of Olson's theory of collective action was the United States economy. It seems legitimate to extend it to the advanced capitalist countries as a group, even though there are differences in constitutions, party systems, proportional representation etc., which affect the way in which distributive coalitions operate. However, he is on thin ground when claiming that his theory can be readily applied to third world countries which are not pluralist democracies, or when he tells the citizens of the biggest third world democracy that they would have been better off to remain a colony of the slowest growing capitalist country (p.179).

My final problem with Olson's approach is that he is vague about measurement. He does not tell us how to measure the strength of distributive coalitions, how to measure the degree to which they are encompassing, or how to measure allocative efficiency. He does not tell us how to rebut alternative explanations of the growth phenomena he discusses. He is obviously aware of the need for some quantitative evidence because he includes 20 pages of Kwang Choi's analysis of growth experience within the USA. Unfortunately this regional evidence is irrelevant in a study of the rise and decline of nations.

[4]

2

Explaining the Economic Performance of Nations, 1820–1989

ANGUS MADDISON

The aim of this chapter is to establish how Western countries became rich and to understand why the rest of the world is poorer. I first measure the extent of real-income disparities to see how they have changed since 1820. I examine the causal role of quantifiable factors—natural resources, raw labor, human capital, and physical capital—and speculate on their interaction with demographic change, the growth and diffusion of technology, the growth of international trade and capital flows, and changes in economic structure. There are also deeper and less tangible layers of causality related to the character of basic institutions, the degree of social conflict, the international order, ideology, and the nature of economic policy. These underlie, interact with, and complement the "proximate" causality.

The Unit of Analysis

As in most growth analyses, the unit considered here is the nation-state. Since 1820, the constellation of states has varied as countries have split up, merged, or changed their boundaries. It is therefore not possible to identify all of them or to monitor their experience over the past 17 decades.

The maximum number of states has probably been below 200 over the whole period. Writing in 1951, Kuznets counted 85 independent states (including "such curiosities as Monaco, the Vatican and Andorra") and 111 non-self-governing units. In 1992, we have 175 member countries of the United Nations and a much smaller number of non-self-governing units.

The type of economic reasoning that is appropriate to such a restricted universe is different for that which is normally used to analyze the behavior of individual economic "agents" (about 5.5 billion people), "firms" (several million), or "regions" (several thousand).

When we consider economic agents or firms, it is legitimate to disregard the institutional or policy context and assume that resource allocation, resource accumulation, transmission of information, and technology occur through disembodied competitive market forces. But the performance of nation-states is strongly influenced by governments with coercive power. These governments have widely differing institutions, policies, interests, traditions, and beliefs, and the degree of freedom they permit for economic transmission mechanisms to operate across their borders is usually much more limited than the freedom for homogenizing forces to operate internally.

This, of course, is a rather self-evident point and fully reflected in what I consider to be the mainstream literature on economic growth, for example, by analysts like Kuznets or Denison. However, some of the new growth theory that has emerged since 1986 does not adequately acknowledge the specificity of the nation-state as the basic unit of analysis, and it tries to assimilate the problem of explaining the growth performance of nations to that of explaining the equilibrium behavior of individuals or firms. Paul Romer's (1986 and 1990) influential essays are a good example of this. His analytical model concentrates on the behavior of "profit-maximizing agents" or modes of transmission of knowledge and technology between "firms."

Establishing the Basic Facts About Income Growth and Its Dispersion

Table 2-1 gives a representative portrayal of comparative growth performance and income dispersion between nations since 1820, that is, for the whole period of modern economic growth.[1] It measures the gross domestic product (GDP) per capita. The logic of national accounts was developed by some of the finest minds in the economic profession, and there is wide agreement as to the scope, coverage, and boundaries of this indicator. Nevertheless, to measure output over such a long period means comparing the present situation with that of dead ancestors who had no experience of air and motor transport, radio, television, cinema, or household electrical appliances. Similarly, it means comparing incomes across countries whose life-styles are vastly different, so one cannot hope to get more than rough estimates covering such large interspatial and intertemporal distances.

The estimates of Table 2-1 merge four kinds of information: (1) historical national accounts built up mainly by academic research; (2) postwar official national accounts that are based on the UN/OECD/Eurostat standardized system but whose quality is often weak in poor countries; (3) purchasing power parity (PPP) converters provided by the joint International Comparisons Project (ICP) of Eurostat/OECD and the United Nations; and (4) estimates of population that are still subject to significant error in the poor countries (most egregiously so in Nigeria).

For the former communist countries and the African countries, we must use GDP estimates that are a good deal weaker than those for the OECD countries. We must also include some countries for which the historical record does not reach earlier than 1950. In order to express GDP in a common currency (1985 dollars at U.S. relative prices), we have to splice the results for the 1980 and 1985 ICP rounds and make some use of the proxy PPP converters developed by Robert Summers and Alan Heston (1988 and 1991).

Our sample covers 43 countries in 1989 and 21 in 1820. It represents about three-

Table 2-1. GDP per Capita in Our Sample of 43 Countries, 1820–1989
($ at 1985 U.S. relative prices)

	1820	1870	1890	1913	1950	1973	1989
The West European capitalist core and its offshoots (14 countries)							
Austria	1,048	1,442	1,892	2,683	2,869	8,697	12,519
Belgium	1,025	2,089	2,654	3,267	4,229	9,417	12,875
Denmark	980	1,543	1,944	3,014	5,227	10,527	13,822
Finland	639	933	1,130	1,727	3,481	9,073	14,015
France	1,059	1,582	1,955	2,746	4,176	10,351	13,952
Germany	902	1,251	1,660	2,506	3,295	10,124	13,752
Italy	965	1,216	1,352	2,079	2,840	8.631	12,989
Netherlands	1,308	2,065	2,568	3,179	4,708	10,271	12,669
Norway	856	1,190	1,477	2,079	4,541	9,347	15,202
Sweden	1,008	1,401	1,757	2,607	5,673	11,362	14,824
United Kingdom	1,450	2,693	3,383	4,152	5,651	10,079	13,519
Australia	1,250	3,143	3,949	4,553	5,970	10,369	13,538
Canada		1,330	1,846	3,515	6,112	11,835	17,236
United States	1,219	2,244	3,101	4,846	8,605	14,093	18,282
Average	1,055	1,723	2,191	3,068	4,813	10,298	14,228
European periphery (7 countries)							
Czechoslovakia	836	1,153	1,515	2,075	3,465	6,980	8,538
Greece				1,211	1,456	5,781	7,564
Hungary		1,139	1,439	1,883	2,481	5,517	6,722
Ireland				2,003	2,600	5,248	8,285
Portugal		833	950	967	1,608	5,598	7,383
Spain	900	1,221	1,355	2,212	2,405	7,581	10,081
Soviet Union		792	828	1,138	2,647	5,920	6,970
Average	868	1,028	1,217	1,641	2,381	6,089	7,931
Latin America (6 countries)							
Argentina		1,039	1,515	2,370	3,112	4,972	4,080
Brazil	556	615	641	697	1,434	3,356	4,402
Chile			1,073	1,735	3,255	4,281	5,406
Colombia				1,078	1,876	2,996	3,979
Mexico	584	700	762	1,121	1,594	3,202	3,728
Peru				1,099	1,809	3,160	2,601
Average	570	785	998	1,350	2,180	3,661	4,033
Asia (9 countries)							
Bangladesh				519	463	391	551
China	497	497	526	557	454	1,039	2,538
India	490	490	521	559	502	719	1,093
Indonesia	533	585	640	710	650	1,056	1,790
Japan	609	640	842	1,153	1,620	9,524	15,336
Korea			680	819	757	2,404	6,503
Pakistan				611	545	823	1,283
Taiwan			564	608	706	2,803	7,252
Thailand		741	801	876	874	1,794	4,008
Average	532	591	653	712	730	2,284	4,484

EXPLAINING THE ECONOMIC PERFORMANCE OF NATIONS   23

	1820	1870	1890	1913	1950	1973	1989
Africa (7 countries)							
Côte d'Ivoire					888	1,699	1,401
Ghana				484	733	724	575
Kenya					438	794	886
Morocco					1,105	1,293	1,844
Nigeria					608	1,040	823
South Africa				2,037	3,204	5,466	5,627
Tanzania					334	578	463
Average	400ª	400ª	400ª	580ª	1,044	1,656	1,660

Source: OECD countries from A. Maddison 1991 at 1985 U.S. relative prices, using Paasche PPPs supplied by Eurostat from the ICP V exercise. For non-OECD countries, from sources indicated in Maddison (1989 and 1990b) whose figures were in 1980 international dollars with PPPs derived mainly from UN/Eurostat (1986, pp. 7 and 8). I have converted them into dollars at 1985 U.S. relative prices, using a multiplier of 1.343. This crude adjustment reflects both the rise in price level between 1980 and 1985 in the United States (the numeraire country) and the average difference between the Paasche PPP and the Geary–Khamis PPP for the OECD countries. For China, Taiwan, and Mexico, the 1980 levels were derived as described in Maddison 1989, p. 111. For Czechoslovakia and the Soviet Union, the 1980 levels were derived from Summers and Heston 1988 relative to per-capita product in Hungary and, for Ghana, from their figure relative to Nigeria. The figures are adjusted to eliminate the effects of boundary changes.

ªRough guesses, assuming no progress in the nineteenth century.

quarters of the world population and an even larger share of the world product. In terms of income spreads, the sample is fairly complete. Summers and Heston (1991) record only 4 countries with an income level somewhat below that of Tanzania (Ethiopia, Mali, Uganda, and Zaire) and only 1 (United Arab Republics) with an income level marginally higher than that of the United States.

The following facts emerge from the evidence of Tables 2-1 through 2-5.

1. Between 1820 and 1989 there was a substantial increase in real income in all countries outside Africa (see Figure 2-1).

2. The rates of growth in these countries varied considerably, and there was a clear divergence in performance over the long run. In 1820 the intercountry income spread was probably about 4:1; in 1913 it was 10:1; in 1950 it was 26:1; in 1973 it was 36:1; and in 1989 it was 39:1. Between 1913 and 1950, not only was there increasing divergence on the global level; there was also an increase in the proportional gap between the lead country and 30 of the 37 follower countries for which we have evidence. However, the widening in the spread between 1950 and 1989 was due entirely to disappointing performance in very poor countries. The percentage gap between the lead country, the United States, and 30 of the 42 follower countries was reduced and often very significantly reduced between 1950 and 1989 (i.e., in all 18 European countries, in Australia and Canada, in 8 Asian countries, and in 2 Latin American countries). Clearly, there was a good deal of "catch-up" within a global framework of "divergence" (see Table 2-3).

3. Our 43 sample countries are divided into five separate groups. Except for Asia, their in-group performance has had some degree of homogeneity.

The capitalist core countries have had the highest incomes and the fastest long-term growth. Already in 1820 these countries had a clear lead, because of their slow but significant growth in the protocapitalist period.[2] Between 1820 and 1989 their average real income rose thirteenfold, and there was intergroup convergence from an income spread of 2.3:1 in 1820 to 1.5:1 in 1989.

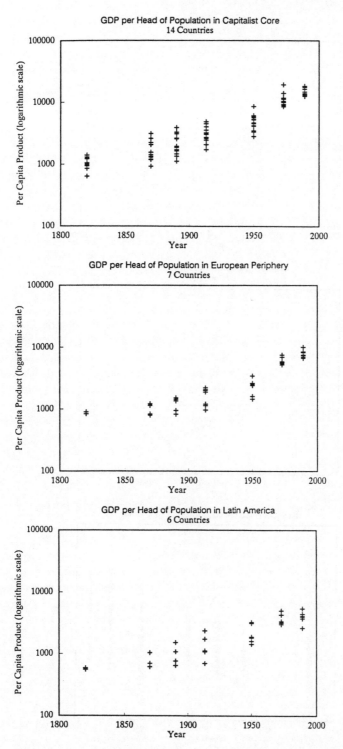

Figure 2-1. a–f: Divergence and convergence in GDP per capita, 1820–1989.

Continued overleaf

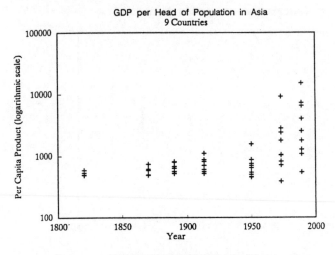

GDP per Head of Population in Asia
9 Countries

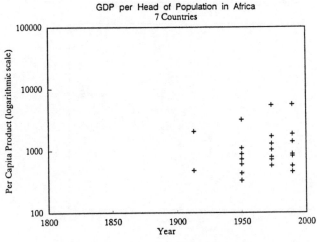

GDP per Head of Population in Africa
7 Countries

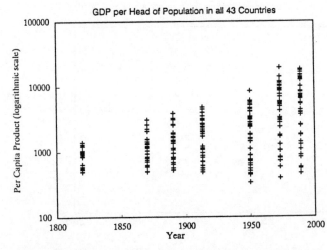

GDP per Head of Population in all 43 Countries

Table 2-2. Rates of Growth of GDP per Capita in Our 43-Country Sample, 1820–1989
(annual average compound rate of growth)

	1820–70	1870–1913	1913–50	1950–73	1973–89
The European capitalist core and its offshoots					
Austria	0.6	1.5	0.2	4.9	2.3
Belgium	1.4	1.0	0.7	3.5	2.0
Denmark	0.9	1.6	1.5	3.1	1.7
Finland	0.8	1.4	1.9	4.3	2.8
France	0.8	1.3	1.1	4.0	1.9
Germany	0.7	1.6	0.7	5.0	1.9
Italy	0.4	1.3	0.8	5.0	2.6
Netherlands	0.9	1.0	1.1	3.4	1.3
Norway	0.7	1.3	2.1	3.2	3.1
Sweden	0.7	1.5	2.1	3.1	1.7
United Kingdom	1.2	1.0	0.8	2.5	1.9
Australia	1.9	0.9	0.7	2.4	1.7
Canada		2.3	1.5	2.9	2.4
United States	1.2	1.8	1.6	2.2	1.6
Average	0.9	1.4	1.2	3.5	2.1
European periphery					
Czechoslovakia	0.6	1.4	1.4	3.1	1.3
Greece			0.5	6.2	1.7
Hungary		1.2	1.2	3.5	1.2
Ireland			0.7	3.1	2.9
Portugal		0.3	1.4	5.6	1.7
Spain	0.6	1.4	0.2	5.1	1.8
Soviet Union		0.8	2.3	3.6	1.0
Average	0.6	1.0	1.1	4.3	1.7
Latin America					
Argentina		1.9	0.7	2.1	−1.2
Brazil	0.2	0.3	2.0	3.8	1.7
Chile			1.7	1.2	1.5
Colombia			1.5	2.1	1.8
Mexico	0.4	1.1	1.0	3.1	1.0
Peru			1.4	2.5	−1.2
Average	0.3	1.1	1.4	2.5	0.6
Asia					
Bangladesh			−0.3	−0.7	2.2
China	0.0	0.3	−0.5	3.7	5.7
India	0.0	0.3	−0.3	1.6	2.7
Indonesia	0.2	0.5	−0.2	2.1	3.4
Japan	0.1	1.4	0.9	8.0	3.0
Korea			−0.2	5.2	6.4
Pakistan			−0.3	1.8	2.8
Taiwan			0.4	6.2	6.1
Thailand		0.4	0.0	3.2	5.2
Average	0.1	0.6	−0.1	3.5	4.2

Continued overleaf

	1820–70	1870–1913	1913–50	1950–73	1973–89
Africa					
Côte d'Ivoire				2.9	−1.2
Ghana			1.1	−0.1	−1.4
Kenya				2.6	0.7
Morocco				0.7	2.2
Nigeria				2.4	−1.5
South Africa			1.2	2.3	0.2
Tanzania				2.4	−1.4
Average			1.2	1.9	−0.3

Source: Data derived from Table 2-1.

The European periphery has the second-highest level of income. Since 1820 its average real income has risen ninefold, and the intercountry income spread within this group was probably similar in 1820 to what it is now, that is, about 1.5:1.[3]

Latin America was the third most prosperous group for most of the period, and its average per-capita income rose sevenfold. The 1989 income spread within our Latin American sample was about 1.6:1, which is probably similar to that in 1820.[4]

Table 2-3. Rates of Catch-up on the per-Capita GDP Level of the Lead Country (the United States), 1913–89
(annual average compound rate of growth)

	1913–50	1950–89		1913–50	1950–89
Austria	−1.4	1.9	Argentina	−0.8	−1.2
Belgium	−0.9	0.9	Brazil	0.4	0.9
Denmark	−0.1	0.6	Chile	0.2	−0.6
Finland	0.3	1.7	Colombia	0.0	0.0
France	−0.4	1.2	Mexico	−0.7	0.3
Germany	−0.8	1.7	Peru	−0.2	−1.0
Italy	−0.7	2.0	Bangladesh	−1.8	−1.5
Netherlands	−0.5	0.6	China	−2.1	2.5
Norway	0.6	1.2	India	−1.8	0.1
Sweden	0.6	0.5	Indonesia	−1.8	0.7
United Kingdom	−0.7	0.3	Japan	−0.6	3.9
Australia	−0.8	0.2	Korea	−1.7	3.6
Canada	−0.1	0.7	Pakistan	−1.9	0.3
Czechoslovakia	−0.2	0.4	Taiwan	−1.1	4.1
Greece	−1.0	2.3	Thailand	−1.5	2.0
Hungary	−0.8	0.6	Côte d'Ivoire	n.a.	−0.8
Ireland	−0.8	1.0	Ghana	−0.4	−2.6
Portugal	−0.2	2.0	Kenya	n.a.	−0.2
Spain	−1.3	1.8	Morocco	n.a.	−0.6
Soviet Union	0.7	0.6	Nigeria	n.a.	−1.2
			South Africa	−0.3	−0.5
			Tanzania	n.a.	−1.1

Source: Data derived from Table 2-1, taking rates of growth between the standing of the country relative to the United States in the years in question.

Table 2-4. Population of Our Sample of 43 Countries, 1820–1989
(000s at midyear, adjusted to 1989 boundaries to exclude impact of frontier changes)

	1820	1870	1913	1950	1973	1989
The European capitalist core and its offshoots						
Austria	3,189	4,520	6,967	6,935	7,586	7.624
Belgium	3,424	5,096	7,666	8,640	9,739	9,938
Denmark	1,155	1,888	2,983	4,269	5,022	5,132
Finland	1,169	1,754	3,027	4,009	4,666	4,964
France	31,250	38,440	41,690	41,836	52,118	56,160
Germany	15,788	24,870	40,825	49,983	61,976	62,063
Italy	19,000	27,888	37,248	47,105	54,779	57,525
Netherlands	2,355	3,615	6,164	10,114	13,439	14,846
Norway	970	1,735	2,447	3,265	3,961	4,227
Sweden	2,585	4,164	5,621	7,015	8,137	8,493
United Kingdom	19,832	29,312	42,622	50,363	56,210	57,236
Australia	33[a]	1,620	4,821	8.177	13,505	16,807
Canada	657[a]	3,736	7,582	13,737	22,072	26,248
United States	9,656[a]	40,061	97,606	152,271	211,909	248,777
European periphery						
Czechoslovakia	7,190	9,876	13,245	12,389	14,560	15,643
Greece			5,425	7,566	8.929	10,033
Hungary	4,571	5,717	7,840	9,338	10,426	10,587
Ireland			3,110	2,969	3,073	3,515
Portugal	3,420	4,370	6,001	8,441	8,316	9,793
Spain	12,958	16,213	20,330	27,977	34,810	38,888
Soviet Union	50,392	79,354	158,371	180,050	249,800	288,887
Latin America						
Argentina	534	1,796	7,653	17,150	25,195	31,883
Brazil	4,507	9,797	23,660	51,941	99,836	147,473
Chile	885	1,943	3,491	6,082	10,012	12,961
Colombia	1,206	2,392	5,195	11,597	22,916	32,335
Mexico	6,587	9,219	14,971	27,376	56,481	84,330
Peru	1,317	2,606	4,507	7,630	14,347	21,142
Asia						
Bangladesh			31,786	43,135	74,368	106,510
China	350,000	350,000	430,000	546,815	881,940	1,105,000
India	172,383	208,674	251,826	359,943	579,000	811,820
Indonesia	16,443	26,528	48,150	72,747	124,189	179,140
Japan	31,000	34,437	51,672	83,662	108,660	123,120
Korea			10,277	20,557	34,103	42,894
Pakistan			20,007	37,646	66,669	109,950
Taiwan			3,469	7,882	15,427	20,050
Thailand	4,665	5,775	8,690	19,553	39,527	55,450
Africa						
Côte d'Ivoire				3,091	6,235	11,713
Ghana	885	1,403	2,085	4,368	9,388	14,425
Kenya				6,556	12,770	23,277

Continued overleaf

	1820	1870	1913	1950	1973	1989
Morocco				9,142	16,511	24,567
Nigeria				40,588[b]	71,361[b]	113,665[b]
South Africa			6,214	13,863	24,158	34,925
Tanzania				8,341	14,927	24,728

Source: Maddison 1989, OECD Development Centre data bank, World Bank, *World Tables,* and national sources. As far as possible, the figures are adjusted to refer to populations within the 1989 boundaries, although this was not possible for Indonesia. The 14-country sample for Group 1 had a 1989 population of 580 million, or 98 percent of the population of the 18 countries in this category; the 7 countries in the European periphery had 377 million, or 79 percent of the 13 countries in this category; the 6 countries in Latin America had 330 million, or 75 percent of the population of the 33 countries in this category; the 9 Asian countries in our sample had a population 2,554 million, or 83 percent of the population of the 44 countries in Asia; the 7 countries in our African sample had 217 million, or 38 percent of the population of the 53 countries of Africa in 1989 (see *Population et sociétés,* July–August 1989).

[a]Excludes indigenous populations.

[b]*Population et sociétés,* October 1992, suggests revising the figures for Nigeria in the light of the 1991 census: 1950 would become 36,147; 1973 would become 56,450; and 1989 would become 82,244.

Table 2-5. Rates of Growth of Population in Our 43-Country Sample, 1820–1989
(annual average compound growth rate adjusted to 1989 boundaries to exclude impact of frontier changes)

	1820–70	1870–1913	1913–50	1950–73	1973–89
Capitalist core					
Austria	0.7	1.0	0.0	0.4	0.0
Belgium	0.8	1.0	0.3	0.5	0.1
Denmark	1.0	1.1	1.0	0.7	0.1
Finland	0.8	1.3	0.8	0.7	0.4
France	0.4	0.2	0.0	1.0	0.5
Germany	0.9	1.2	0.5	0.9	0.0
Italy	0.8	0.7	0.6	0.7	0.3
Netherlands	0.9	1.2	1.3	1.2	0.6
Norway	1.2	0.8	0.8	0.8	0.4
Sweden	1.0	0.7	0.6	0.6	0.2
United Kingdom	0.8	0.9	0.5	0.5	0.1
Australia	8.1[a]	2.6	1.4	2.2	1.4
Canada	3.5[a]	1.7	1.6	2.1	1.1
United States	2.9[a]	2.1	1.2	1.4	1.0
European periphery					
Czechoslovakia	0.6	0.7	−0.2	0.7	0.4
Greece			0.9	0.7	0.7
Hungary	0.4	0.7	0.5	0.5	0.1
Ireland			−0.1	0.1	0.8
Portugal	0.5	0.7	0.9	−0.1	1.0
Spain	0.4	0.5	0.9	1.0	0.7
Soviet Union	0.9	1.6	0.3	1.4	0.9
Latin America					
Argentina	2.5	3.4	2.2	1.7	1.5
Brazil	1.6	2.1	2.1	2.9	2.5
Chile	1.6	1.4	1.5	2.2	1.6

Table 2-5. Rates of Growth of Population in Our 43-Country Sample,
1820–1989 (*continued*)

	1820–70	*1870–1913*	*1913–50*	*1950–73*	*1973–89*
Colombia	1.4	1.8	2.2	3.0	2.2
Mexico	0.7	1.1	1.6	3.2	2.5
Peru	1.4	1.3	1.4	2.8	2.5
Asia					
Bangladesh			0.8	2.4	2.3
China	0.0	0.5	0.7	2.1	1.4
India	0.4	0.4	1.0	2.1	2.1
Indonesia	1.0	1.4	1.1	2.4	2.3
Japan	0.2	0.9	1.3	1.1	0.8
Korea			1.9	2.2	1.4
Pakistan			1.7	2.5	3.2
Taiwan			2.2	3.0	1.7
Thailand	0.4	1.0	2.2	3.1	2.1
Africa					
Côte d'Ivoire				3.1	4.0
Ghana	0.9	0.9	2.0	3.4	2.7
Kenya				2.9	3.8
Morocco				2.6	2.5
Nigeria				2.5[a]	3.0[a]
South Africa			2.2	2.4	2.3
Tanzania				2.6	3.2

Source: Data derived from Table 2-4.

[a]With INED revisions (see note b to Table 2-4), these rates become 2.0 and 2.5, respectively.

The Asian sample is much more heterogeneous than any of the others. Its income spread in 1820 was rather narrow but since 1950 has widened very sharply and in 1989 was 27:1. The average income of the group has risen eightfold since 1820. Originally this group was poorer than the first three, but the average income is now above that in Latin America, and it contains one country, Japan, whose income has risen above the average for the advanced capitalist group.

The African group has the lowest income level. The average now is not very different from that of the capitalist core 120 years ago. The quality and quantity of evidence for this group are weaker than for all the others. The divergence in performance within the group is higher than in the first three groups but narrower than in Asia. The current spread of income within the group is about 12:1.

4. The pace of growth over the 17 decades has not been steady. In all areas and in all countries (except Bangladesh, Chile, and Ghana) the years between 1950 and 1973 were a golden age when the growth in real income per capita was much faster than ever recorded before. The acceleration was most marked in Asia and least so in Latin America and Africa. Since 1973 this growth has slackened appreciably in all areas except Asia, and in Africa, income actually declined (see Table 2-2 and Figure 2-2).

5. The in-group homogeneity of the long-run performance record suggests that the countries in each group had common institutional or policy characteristics that distinguished them from the members of the other groups. The universality of the

EXPLAINING THE ECONOMIC PERFORMANCE OF NATIONS   31

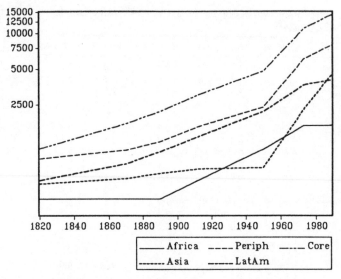

Figure 2-2. Comparative growth of GDP per capita by area, 1820–1989.

acceleration in the golden age does suggest, on the other hand, that there are some ecumenical influences powerful enough to have had a global effect. These forces generally originated in the first group and diffused their negative influences between 1913 and 1950 and their positive impact between 1950 and 1973.

6. The first group has provided "leadership" in productivity and technology for the past six centuries. Northern Italy and Flanders played this role from 1400 to 1600, the Netherlands from 1600 to 1820. Since 1820, there have been two successive "leaders." The United Kingdom had the highest level of labor productivity from 1820 to 1890, and the United States in the century since then.[5] To a significant degree, at least in the twentieth century, the lead country has determined the potential performance of the other countries. In most sectors of activity, the technical frontier has been in the United States. The other countries have been followers, and their performance over the past century has been substantially influenced by the diffusion of technology from the lead country.

7. Population growth in Western Europe has been modest over the long run. The long experience of declining mortality was matched by gradual reductions in fertility, although family tradition had already imposed constraints on fertility before the mortality rate began to fall. For several hundred years, Europe has had a later marriage age and a greater incidence of celibacy than Africa, Asia, or Latin America have had, and more widespread, checks on fertility within marriage. Australia, Canada, and the United States have had higher population growth because of their large-scale immigration and higher fertility, but their fertility is now low by Asian, African, or Latin American standards. In the European periphery, demographic growth has been near the West European range. With the exception of Japan, whose demographic experience lies within the European range, the Asian countries have had a much faster nat-

ural rate of increase since 1950 than Europe or Japan have ever had. The sharp decline in mortality, due to rising living standards, better sanitation, and the rapid impact of improved medical technology, was not matched by a falling fertility rate, though there was some decline after 1973. The significant demographic differences between the rich and poor countries have undoubtedly had some impact on their per-capita growth potential, though the relationship has not always been clear-cut.

Causal Analysis, Ultimate and Proximate

When assessing the reasons for nations' differing growth performance, one can operate at two levels: "ultimate" and "proximate" causality.[6] An investigation of ultimate causality involves consideration of institutions, ideologies, socioeconomic pressure groups, historical accidents, and national economic policy. It also involves consideration of the international economic "order," foreign ideologies or shocks from friendly or unfriendly neighbors. All these "ultimate" features are part of the historians' traditional domain (e.g., Gibbon on the Roman Empire) or sociologists (e.g., Max Weber on the Protestant ethic). They are virtually impossible to quantify, and thus there will always be legitimate scope for disagreement on what is important. However, it is a mistake to ignore causality at this level, particularly if one is tackling such a wide range of experience in time and space.[7] The serious problems that the Soviet Union and Eastern Europe have had in switching to capitalism have made it abundantly clear that the capitalist model is not simply a reliance on market forces but has a complex institutional underpinning.

"Proximate" areas of causality are those where measures and models have been developed by economists, econometricians, and statisticians.[8] Here the relative importance of different influences can be more readily assessed. At this level, one can derive significant insight from comparative macroeconomic performance accounts (i.e., growth accounts, level accounts, and acceleration and slowdown accounts; see Maddison 1987). The most difficult problem at the "proximate" level of explanation is analyzing the role of technical progress, which interacts in myriad ways with other items in the growth accounts.[9] Hence technical progress must be treated separately from other elements of proximate causality, because it is almost as difficult to quantify satisfactorily as are the elements of ultimate causality.

I have tried to illustrate the operation of ultimate causality in two major respects: (1) "institutional" features of advanced Western capitalist economies which enabled them to embark on modern economic growth and do better than the rest of the world and (2) the changes in policy and circumstance underlying the postwar acceleration of growth.

Socioinstitutional Basis for the Early Western Lead and Greater Dynamism Until 1950

The fact that the West established an early lead which reached such gigantic proportions by 1950 is due in part to distinctive socioinstitutional characteristics that the Western countries acquired gradually during the Renaissance and the Enlightenment.

The most fundamental of these was the recognition of human capacity to transform the forces of nature through rational investigation and experiment. By the seventeenth century, Western elites had abandoned superstition, magic, and submission to religious authority. The Western scientific tradition that underlies the modern approach to technical change and innovation had clearly emerged and impregnated the educational system. Circumscribed horizons were abandoned, and the quest for change and improvement was unleashed. This characteristic of the West is brought out clearly by David Landes (1969), who rightly contrasts this European spirit with that in Asian countries.

The ending of feudal constraints on the free purchase and sale of property was followed by a whole series of developments which gave scope for successful entrepreneurship. A nondiscretionary legal system protected property rights. The development of accountancy helped further in making contracts enforceable. State fiscal levies became more predictable and less arbitrary. The growth of trustworthy financial institutions and instruments provided access to credit and insurance, which made it easier to assess risk and to organize business rationally on a large scale over a wide area. Techniques of organization, management, and labor discipline were also improved.

A third distinctive feature of Western Europe was the emergence of a system of nation-states in close propinquity, which had significant trading relations and relatively easy intellectual interchange in spite of their linguistic and cultural differences. This stimulated competition and innovation. Migration to or refuge in a different culture and environment were options open to adventurous minds; printing presses and universities added to the ease of interchange.

The Western family system was different from that in other parts of the world. It involved controls over fertility and limited obligations to more distant kin, which reinforced the possibilities for accumulation.

Since 1820, the institutional arrangements of advanced capitalist countries have not stood still. The degree of democratic participation and the socioeconomic role of government have changed a good deal in ways that have generally been positive for growth. In the postwar period, interrelations between these countries have involved articulate cooperation and some rudiments of a managed international order. This, too, has been favorable to economic growth.

The European "periphery" has an institutional heritage which is not the same as those of the advanced European countries. There are quite separate kinds of periphery. In the east, Russian traditional institutions were as much Asian as European and were further differentiated from the Western model from 1917 onward by the advent of communism. The East European countries had dirigiste central planning imposed on them for more than 40 years. In the Czech and Hungarian cases, they were plucked from the advanced capitalist group to be put into the communist camp. Some other East European countries with lower incomes (Albania, Bulgaria, Greece, Romania, and Yugoslavia) were part of the Ottoman Empire until the nineteenth century and so were isolated from the West European mainstream. This was also true of Poland, most of which was part of Russia until 1918.

The Western European periphery consists mainly of the two Iberian countries. Spain and Portugal were institutionally different from the advanced capitalist group in their degree of religious bigotry, censorship, neglect of popular education, and fiscal irresponsibility. Their colonization policy in Latin America reordered indigenous institutions very much in their own image.

Although Latin America became independent in the 1820s, it retained many of the Iberian institutional characteristics. The Latin American heritage of peonage and slavery led to very wide disparities in income, wealth, and economic opportunity, with neglect of popular education, heavy-handed regulatory tendencies in government, and fiscal irresponsibility. The last characteristic has led to chronic inflation, which in the past decade has brought Latin America close to societal collapse.

Historically, the performance of the Asian and African countries has been hampered by two types of constraint. Indigenous institutions were less favorable to growth than those in the West and most of them were colonies of the West in ways which also hampered their development (see Maddison 1990a). By Western standards, all of these countries except Japan remained relatively stagnant until 1950.

In China, bureaucratic control and excessive respect for tradition impeded the emergence of a modern scientific approach and held back a civilization that had earlier shown greater promise than Europe's had. The Chinese experience in this respect is laid out in Needham's huge multivolume study (1954). The essentially defensive and static character of India's social institutions also exerted a depressive influence on growth potential (see Lal 1980 and Maddison 1971).

Within Asia, Japan was unique in its early mimicry of Western institutions in the Meiji reforms of 1867, and its growth performance is the most striking in our whole array of 43 countries. Its per-capita income level has risen twenty-six-fold since 1820 and is now well within the range of the advanced capitalist countries.

Policy and Circumstances Underlying Postwar Growth

The Capitalist Core

The postwar boom in Western Europe was not due to an acceleration of technical change but was to a large extent a catch-up phenomenon. Over several decades, European productivity had fallen behind that in the United States, which was the country closest to the frontiers of technology. However, there was no automaticity or inevitability about the catch-up. It did not happen after the first world war, and its importance after the second depended strongly on policy improvements. With the stimulus of Marshall aid and new forms of international cooperation, liberal policies were reapplied to international trade, and international capital markets were reopened. High levels of domestic demand promoted full employment, better internal resource allocation and led to an unparalleled investment boom. This European boom—together with enlightened international economic policy in the United States, the abandonment of colonialism, and its replacement by aid programs—was basically responsible for the worldwide diffusion of the postwar golden age.

The long postwar boom in Europe was due, in large part, to the exploitation of once-for-all opportunities that had been missed earlier because of two world wars and the protectionist, dirigiste, and otherwise defensive policies of the interwar years.[10] The boom was biggest in those countries that had suffered most from these policies. By the end of the boom, the productivity gap between the advanced European countries and the United States had been considerably reduced. There was a convergence in levels of per-capita income and productivity that was normal for countries with close cooperation, similar institutions, similar human capital, and convergent economic policies. If there had indeed been a postwar acceleration of technical progress, one would have expected the postwar supergrowth in the advanced European countries to continue. But the fact that there was no postwar acceleration in productivity growth in the United States—the frontier country—meant that the advanced European countries would eventually reach a point at which the payoff for such high levels of investment was bound to falter.

The slowdown after 1973 was quite general and quite sharp. It did not simply reflect a gradual erosion of supergrowth possibilities. Its sharpness was due to three closely clustered and interactive developments that forced major changes in policy: the acceleration of the inflationary momentum that accompanied the prolonged boom, the collapse of the postwar monetary order—the dollar-based, fixed exchange-rate system established at Bretton Woods—and the OPEC shocks. By any reasonable accounting, the most sophisticated governments could be expected to lose output when dealing with these shocks in such open economies, because they involved new risks and transition problems in devising and learning to use new policy weapons, such as floating exchange rates. This was equally true of entrepreneurial and trade union decision makers whose reactions significantly affect macroeconomic outcomes.

Another influence that reinforced the sharpness of the slowdown was the basic change in the "establishment view" of economic policy objectives. The new consensus emerged as a response to events, but it also helped mold them. The shock of inflation, the new wave of payments problems, and speculative possibilities brought a profound switch away from Keynesian type attitudes toward demand management and full employment. Most countries gave overriding priority to combating inflation and safeguarding the balance of payments. Unemployment was allowed to rise to prewar levels. Even when oil prices collapsed and the momentum of world inflation was broken in the early 1980s, the new orthodoxy continued to stress the dangers of expansionary policy in spite of widespread unemployment and strong payments positions. It looked to a self-starting recovery rather than one induced by policy. A further reason for the cautiousness of policy compared with that of the golden age is the greater vulnerability to speculative capital movements in a world without exchange controls, and a dichotomous monetary order—the precariously frozen parities of European countries within the European monetary system, on the one hand, and the floaters (the United States and Japan), on the other.

The European Periphery

The postwar growth acceleration in the "capitalist" part of the European periphery had much the same causes as in the European core, but the results were better, partly because the starting point was lower and partly because the degree of institutional modernization was bigger. These economies benefited greatly from their proximity to the European core, which provided them with booming export markets and very large earnings from tourism and emigrants' remittances. More recently they have received large grant aid from the European community.

The sharp slowdown after 1973 was due to some of the same reasons as that in the core, and the close integration of the European economies meant that the periphery felt the full retarding influence of the slowdown in the core. The peripheral countries had even bigger problems in controlling inflation and dealing with payments disequilibria than did the core.

The performance of the communist economies is less well documented than that of OECD countries. Their own yardsticks for measuring growth and levels of performance have hitherto differed from those in the West. We have had to rely on the skill of Kremlinologists for measures of performance comparable in kind to those we use for OECD countries, and the CIA growth estimates (which I use here) have now come under challenge for exaggerating growth and levels of performance.[11] The communist countries did not benefit from the Marshall Plan and were relatively isolated from the new liberalism in the world economy. The acceleration in their growth involved a government effort to mobilize very high rates of investment. The poorer results were due to less efficient resource allocation, greater diversion of resources to military spending, and the deleterious effect of censorship and thought control on processes of innovation.

After 1973, the performance of these economies deteriorated sharply. Their slowdown was influenced to some extent by that of the capitalist countries, but it also reflected the increasing problems of running a command economy efficiently at increasingly sophisticated levels of demand. More recently (since 1989, when our tables end) they have fallen into a condition of deep crisis with some similarities to the Latin American situation (hyperinflation, fiscal crisis, indebtedness), plus the unprecedented problems of switching from a command to a market economy, dismantling the old apparatus of power (party, secret police, armed forces, and administration), and privatizing economies in which virtually all assets belonged to the state.

Latin America

Between 1913 and 1950, the Latin American countries performed very well compared with most of the rest of the world. They did not suffer significantly from the two world wars, and they offset the effects of the 1930s depression by successful import substitution and industrialization. In the early postwar years they had advantageous terms of trade.

Because they had no wartime backlogs to make good, were fairly content with the dirigiste and corporative policies of the 1930s and 1940s, and were not influenced by the liberalism that went with the Marshall Plan, Latin American countries chose to remain fairly isolated from the world economy for a fairly long time after the war. They did not have a postwar golden age. Although their experience between 1950 and 1973 was better in per-capita terms than that before 1950, it was not on the scale seen in Europe and Asia.

Latin American growth did not deteriorate sharply in 1973 as did that of the capitalist core, and Latin America generally did not react with the same caution as did most of the world to the OPEC shocks. The governments felt they could accommodate high rates of inflation, and they were able to borrow on a large scale to cover payments deficits incurred as a result of their expansionary policies. The crunch came in the

1980s, after the Mexican suspension of debt service, when their supply of new foreign funds dried up and service costs of existing debt soared because of rising interest rates. Since 1982 most of Latin America has had negative real income growth.

The dramatic Latin American slowdown was not caused by a sudden drying up of supply potential or by any unfairness in the operation of the international economy. Rather, it was the result of misguided domestic policies. The Latin American economies suffer from four basic problems:

1. *Heavy foreign debt.* Amortization payments generally stopped, but interest payments are a very heavy burden for the balance of payments and governmental budgets. The bleak outlook here led to major capital flight and undermined the governments' domestic and international creditworthiness.
2. *Fiscal crisis.* Governments find it very difficult to maintain revenues or borrow.
3. *Hyperinflation* and the exhaustion of a whole menu of heterodox methods of dealing with it.
4. *Distortions in resource allocation* due initially to excessive government intervention and protectionism, which were further complicated by hyperinflation.

Asia

The great postwar acceleration in Asian growth can be traced to several influences:

1. The rise to power of new national elites, and the development of an indigenous capitalist class willing to keep their savings at home and free to pursue their own interests.
2. Virtually all the Asian countries followed the advice of development economists like Arthur Lewis, Walt Rostow, and Paul Rosenstein Rodan in mounting a big push in investment rates and an even bigger acceleration in the growth of capital stock.
3. They also followed the advice of Theodore Schultz to improve human capital. In 1950 their educational stock was a quarter of that in Europe, but it has grown prodigiously and, in some of the supergrowth countries, is now close to European levels.
4. The colonial drain was replaced by a new inflow of foreign capital and aid. In prewar years Asia had big trade surpluses, which have now become deficits. Between 1913 and 1938, the average Asian ratio of exports to imports was 1.22, whereas between 1950 and 1986 it was .85.
5. The postwar period was one of buoyant world trade, thanks to the faster growth in the capitalist core and the reduction of trade barriers. Many Asian countries, particularly those with supergrowth, took advantage of those new trade outlets by remaining competitive and aggressively seeking new markets. The opening up of their economies improved their efficiency and facilitated their growth.
6. Many of the Asian countries have had high per-capita labor inputs, with working years much higher than those in other parts of the world.

7. Finally, Asian countries were able to get a large catch-up bonus because their starting levels of productivity were so low and they were so far from the productivity frontier.

The continuation of the Asian countries' fast growth since 1973 (except in Japan, which is the nearest to the productivity frontier) makes one realize that there were other elements in their menu of progrowth policies whose importance was not so obvious in the golden age. These Asian characteristics now stand out more clearly because they were so lacking in Latin America.

8. Inflation was actually better controlled in the Asian countries after 1973 than between 1950 and 1973. Their average annual rate of price increase dropped from 17 percent a year between 1950 and 1973 to 11 percent between 1973 and 1982, and 6 percent between 1982 and 1987. In Latin America, by contrast, inflation accelerated from an average of 21 percent a year to 110 percent between 1973 and 1982 and 122 percent a year between 1982 and 1987.

9. The fiscal and monetary policies of the Asian countries were generally more prudent than those of the Latin American countries.

10. The Asian countries' foreign borrowing was more judicious. On a per-capita basis their borrowing averaged only a third of that of Latin America, and so with the exception of the Philippines, they remained creditworthy and did not face the crunch that hit Latin America in the 1980s. Furthermore, less of their debt to commercial bank lenders was incurred on a floating-rate basis.

11. They generally maintained their export competitiveness.

12. Most of the conuntries' economies had more flexible wage and price structures than did those of the capitalist core or Latin America.

It is the combination of these macropolicy virtues with continuing catch-up possibilities that has been the basis of Asian success since 1973. It should also be remembered that the Asian countries generally do not have as extreme inequalities in income and wealth as do the Latin American countries. This fact probably gave them greater sociopolitical coherence and meant that they were less subject to short-term vagaries in populist policies.

In terms of more proximate growth accounting there is nothing mysterious or miraculous in the postwar Asian experience (see Maddison 1989 for the relevant growth accounts). Asian growth has required fast-growing labor and capital inputs. Except for Japan, total factor productivity even in the supergrowth countries was not out of line with that of some of the European countries in the golden age, and this has been true since 1973 (see Maddison 1989).

Africa

In the postwar golden age, economic growth in Africa was much slower than in any other major world area. In the slowdown since 1973, their average incomes have actually fallen (see Table 2-2). African countries were the last to emerge from colonialism, and their education, health, and infrastructure are very poor. Their populations are growing twelve times as fast as those in the advanced capitalist countries of Europe are, and they are still accelerating. Another major problem is the newness of the nation-states whose rulers have often tried to forge a national unity by creating one-party regimes. This has reinforced a tendency for dirigisme that has led to big market distortions, artificial exchange rates, and policies harmful to agriculture. It was also a major barrier to corrective changes in policy. Sub-Saharan Africa has already received much foreign aid, and it is likely that it will continue, but a real turnaround in growth prospects will depend heavily on changes in domestic policy.

Proximate Influences on Economic Performance

We can now turn to proximate growth causality, an area that has attracted more precise technocratic analysis, because the important elements can be more readily measured. The degree to which they can be accurately measured leaves a good deal to be desired, however, and it should be stressed that these proximate influences are not independent of what I have called ultimate causes. Rather, to a significant degree they are dimensions through which ultimate causes can be seen to operate.

Table 2-6 compares the major characteristics that generally figure in growth accounts. We concentrate on a 1989 cross-section view and try to see what we can deduce about causality from this in an illustrative way. It would, of course, be useful to be more rigorous and to have all these indicators on a historical basis as well, but this is too big an exercise for this chapter.

Table 2-6. Comparative Characteristics of Economic Performance Near 1989 (U.S.A. = 100)

	Level of GDP per Capita	Labor Input per Capita	GDP per Hour Worked	Education per Capita	Land Area per Capita	Gross Capital Stock per Capita	Exports per Capita	Scale of Economy
Austria	68.5	91.2	75.1		29.6	106.2	286.5	2.1
Belgium	70.4	79.5	88.6	84.9	8.7	80.8	663.2	2.8
Denmark	75.6	114.2	66.2	78.1	22.6	89.9	374.6	1.6
Finland	76.7	109.8	69.9		166.6	110.9	321.1	1.5
France	76.3	80.1	95.3	84.7	26.6	90.8	218.5	17.2
Germany	75.2	95.4	78.8	70.9	10.6	101.7	376.5	18.8
Italy	71.0	88.2	80.5	59.1	13.9	79.3	167.1	16.4
Netherlands	69.3	75.0	92.4	73.2	6.3	81.1	503.0	4.1
Norway	83.2	100.1	83.1	77.6	197.3	154.5	437.8	1.4
Sweden	81.1	100.5	80.7	77.8	132.6	88.6	417.8	2.8
United Kingdom	73.9	91.0	81.2	79.8	11.4	69.9	182.1	17.0
Australia	74.1	95.5	77.6		1,231.8	91.1	153.3	5.0
Canada	94.3	103.5	91.1	84.7	954.6	102.0	313.3	10.0
United States	100.0	100.0	100.0	100.0	100.0	100.0	100.0	100.0
Czechoslovakia	46.7	124.3	37.6		21.7		63.2	2.9
Greece	41.4	87.3	47.4	61.2	35.3		51.4	1.7

Table 2-6. Comparative Characteristics of Economic Performance Near 1989
(U.S.A. = 100) (*continued*)

	Level of GDP per Capita	Labor Input per Capita	GDP per Hour Worked	Education per Capita	Land Area per Capita	Gross Capital Stock per Capita	Exports per Capita	Scale of Economy
Hungary	36.8	111.4	33.0		23.6		65.0	1.6
Ireland	45.3	69.6	65.1		53.3		402.2	0.6
Portugal	40.4	98.0	41.2	48.3	25.5	34.3	89.3	1.6
Spain	55.1	78.5	70.2	57.4	34.8	51.7	78.1	8.7
Soviet Union	38.1	123.9	30.8	68.1	209.5		25.7	44.5
Argentina	22.3	86.1	25.9	59.3	233.2	19.5	20.5	2.9
Brazil	24.1	100.1	24.1	36.8	155.7	25.5	15.9	14.4
Chile	29.6	73.4	40.3	61.6	157.1	17.4	43.2	1.5
Colombia	21.8	77.0	28.3	39.4	87.2		12.1	2.8
Mexico	20.4	73.4	27.8	46.3	62.0	21.8	18.7	7.0
Peru	14.2	82.5	17.2		164.4		11.3	1.2
Bangladesh	3.0	82.6	3.6		3.5		0.8	1.3
China	13.9	140.2	9.9	37.2	22.8		3.3	61.9
India	6.0	115.9	5.1	25.9	10.1		1.4	19.6
Indonesia	9.8	109.3	8.9		27.4	5.0	8.5	7.0
Japan	83.9	129.9	64.6	83.1	8.4	92.2	152.2	41.5
Korea	35.6	131.1	27.2	78.3	6.3	23.7	99.5	6.1
Pakistan	7.0	87.0	8.1		19.0		2.9	3.1
Taiwan	39.7	157.8	25.2	87.4	4.9	28.1	173.2	3.2
Thailand	21.9	145.2	15.1		25.0		24.8	4.9
Côte d'Ivoire	7.7	70.3	11.0		73.6		16.1	0.4
Ghana	3.1	71.6	4.3		43.2		3.6	0.2
Kenya	4.8	75.7	6.4		66.6		2.9	0.5
Morocco	10.1	57.2	17.6		49.5		9.2	1.0
Nigeria	4.5	67.7	6.6		21.7		4.7	2.1
South Africa	30.8	64.5	47.8		94.8		43.5	4.3
Tanzania	2.5	89.6	2.8		97.3		0.8	0.3

Source: Column 1 from Table 2-1, Column 2 from Table 2-8, Column 3 from Columns 1 and 2, Column 4 from Table 2-9, Column 5 from Table 2-7. The estimates of capital stock in Column 6 were made by cumulating investment at constant national prices for 30 years and converting it to 1985 dollars at U.S. relative prices, using same sources for investment as for the GDP estimates in Table 2-1. This measure of capital stock is very rough indeed compared with the estimates cited in Table 2-10. Exports were taken from IMF, *International Financial Statistics,* February 1992. Scale of economy was derived from Tables 2-1 and 2-4.

I deal first with the role of the traditional factors of production, land, labor, and capital and then turn to influences on the efficiency with which they are used, that is, the degree of openness to international trade and economies of scale.

Natural Resource Endowment per Capita

In the early literature on economic growth, and particularly in the work of Thomas Malthus, the fixed character of natural resources was regarded as a major constraint that would ultimately result in a stationary state because of population pressure. Natural resource constraints have also been strongly emphasized by military thinkers, who regard them as an important problem in wartime when foreign trade is difficult.

No measures of aggregate natural resources are available, and as a crude proxy, Table 2-7 shows the comparative endowment of land per capita. Within our 43 countries, there is a very wide dispersion of land availability. Australia is the most favored with nearly 350 times as much per capita as Bangladesh, which has the poorest endowment. However, there is no discernible relationship between contemporary incomes per capita and natural resources per capita. Australia is 150 times better endowed than Japan is, but it has a lower per-capita GDP. The Netherlands has 0.23 hectares per capita, but it also has an extremely high labor productivity in agriculture, closer to that of the United States than any of the other advanced countries. Argentina has 46 times as much land per person as Taiwan does, but its per-capita product is half that of Taiwan. It is clear (see Figure 2-3), therefore, that in contemporary circumstances, natural resource endowment has a negligible effect on the growth potential of different nations, and the inexorable decline in the ratio between resources and population has little effect on contemporary per-capita growth performance. This does not mean, however, that we can ignore the historical role of natural resources, which were in fact influential in fostering the early dynamism of the United States and Australia.

Table 2-7. Land Area per Capita in 1989
(hectares per capita)

Capitalist core		Latin America	
Austria	1.09	Argentina	8.58
Belgium	.32	Brazil	5.73
Denmark	.83	Chile	5.78
Finland	6.13	Colombia	3.21
France	.98	Mexico	2.28
Germany	.39	Peru	6.05
Italy	.51	*Asia*	
Netherlands	.23		
Norway	7.26	Bangladesh	.13
Sweden	4.88	China	.84
United Kingdom	.42	India	.37
		Indonesia	1.01
Australia	45.33	Japan	.31
Canada	35.13	Korea	.23
United States	3.68	Pakistan	.70
European periphery		Taiwan	.18
		Thailand	.92
Czechoslovakia	.80	*Africa*	
Greece	1.30		
Hungary	.87	Côte d'Ivoire	2.71
Ireland	1.96	Ghana	1.59
Portugal	.94	Kenya	2.45
Spain	1.28	Morocco	1.82
Soviet Union	7.71	Nigeria	.80
		South Africa	3.49
		Tanzania	3.58

Source: Land area from FAO, *Production Yearbook*, Rome 1988. Population from Table 2-4.

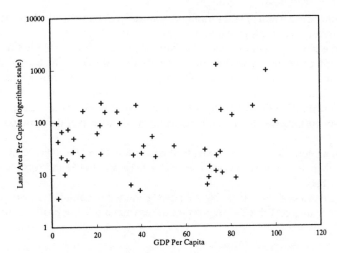

Figure 2-3. Relationship between endowment of natural resources and GDP per capita in 1989 (43 countries).

Labor Input per Capita (Raw Labor Input)

There is a significant variation in labor input per capita (though the intercountry variance in this characteristic is modest compared with that for the other characteristics shown in Table 2-6). This measure is rough even for the advanced countries, which have regular labor force surveys, but whose statistics on working hours are of varying quality. The lower down we go in the income scale, the worse the quality of the information is. However, the figures are robust enough to demonstrate that the advanced capitalist countries, the communist countries, Japan, Korea, and Taiwan have a much higher proportion of employed people than is the norm elsewhere. To some extent these variations in activity rates are a reflection of social institutions (with regard to female employment) or of deliberate policy to promote participation (e.g., in the communist countries), but a predominant influence is simply the age structure of the population as a result of demographic trends.

The demographic pattern in Europe and Japan increases the relative size of the active population by reducing the proportion of children and freeing women to enter the labor force. Thus in Japan 20 percent of the population are children under the age of 15, which is about half the share in the Third World, and about 40 percent of the labor force are women, compared with under 30 percent in the Third World. As a result, about half the Japanese population are employed, compared with 29 percent in Mexico, which is the extreme case of low activity rates. These differences in demographic structure and labor force activity help explain why Japan can save such a high proportion of its income, why a greater proportion of investment can go to capital deepening rather than providing for social infrastructure and capital widening, and why it can afford to educate its population so well.

The other dimension of labor input is the number of hours worked by those who are economically active. Not many countries have effective surveys of working hours for the whole economy, but one can get a reasonable representation of the situation in the advanced countries as well as the three Asian countries with the most rapid growth—Japan, Korea, and Taiwan. These figures demonstrate unequivocally that these three Asian countries have much longer working hours than does the capitalist core. It also seems that this is true of most Asian countries. For Africa, there is no real evidence on working hours, and so I have simply assumed that they are lower than elsewhere.

When we combine the two elements of labor input to get the average labor input per capita, there is a large variation, from 1,188 in Taiwan to 431 in Morocco, that is, a range of 2.8:1.

The estimates of hours in Table 2-8 have been used in conjunction with the per-capita GDP figures of Table 2-1 to produce the estimates of labor productivity.

Table 2-8. Labor Input per Capita, 1987

	Proportion of Population Employed	Average Annual Number of Hours per Person Employed	Annual Number of Hours Worked per Capita
Capitalist core			
Austria	43.0	1,595	687
Belgium	37.0	1,620	599
Denmark	51.6	1,669	860
Finland	49.7	1,663	827
France	39.1	1,543	603
Germany	44.3	1,620	718
Italy	43.5	1,528	664
Netherlands	40.8	1,387	565
Norway	50.8	1,486	754
Sweden	51.6	1,466	757
United Kingdom	44.0	1,557	685
Australia	44.1	1,631	719
Canada	46.6	1,673	779
United States	46.8	1,608	753
European periphery			
Czechoslovakia	49.9	1,875	936
Greece	36.5	1,800	657
Hungary	48.5	1,730	839
Ireland	30.8	1,700	524
Portugal	43.4	1,700	738
Spain	31.1	1,900	591
Soviet Union	52.1	1,791	933
Latin America			
Argentina	34.1	1,900	648
Brazil	39.7	1,900	754
Chile	29.1	1,900	553
Colombia	30.5	1,900	580

Table 2-8. Labor Input per Capita, 1987 (*continued*)

	Proportion of Population Employed	Average Annual Number of Hours per Person Employed	Annual Number of Hours Worked per Capita
Mexico	29.1	1,900	553
Peru	32.7	1,900	621
Asia			
Bangladesh	28.3	(2,200)	622
China	48.0	(2,200)	1,056
India	39.7	(2,200)	873
Indonesia	37.4	(2,200)	823
Japan	48.4	2,020	978
Korea	38.4	2,570	987
Pakistan	29.8	(2,200)	655
Taiwan	47.5	2,500	1,188
Thailand	49.7	(2,200)	1,093
Africa			
Côte d'Ivoire	37.8	1,400	529
Ghana	38.5	1,400	539
Kenya	40.7	1,400	570
Morocco	30.8	1,400	431
Nigeria	36.4	1,400	510
South Africa	34.7	1,400	486
Tanzania	48.2	1,400	675

Source: A. Maddison 1989 and 1991, ILO, and national sources. For the African countries, the employment ratios are in fact ratios of labor force to population as recorded in World Bank, *Social Indicators of Development 1989* (Baltimore: Johns Hopkins University Press, 1989), and the figures on working hours are a guess. For the first 14 countries and Japan, the figures refer to 1987 and for the other countries, to 1986.

Education and Skills per Capita

A significant characteristic of the advanced capitalist countries is the effort they have made over the long run to raise the level of education of their populations. In 1820, their average education level[12] for both sexes combined was probably about 2 years, and by 1989 this figure had risen about sevenfold (see Table 2-9). Furthermore, education is now more evenly spread, thanks to universal attendance in the primary and some of the secondary school years.

The higher the average level of education is, the easier it is for a working population to understand and apply the fruits of technical progress (see Figure 2-4). It is difficult to be at all precise about the impact of rising educational standards on productivity, but most growth analysts consider it to have been substantial, and levels of education have a significant positive relationship to the economic distance between nations. Within the advanced countries, differences in income and levels of education are now not too large by international standards, but the lead country, the United States, has a clear lead over the rest. The educational gap between the rich and the

Table 2-9. Levels of Formal Education per Person Aged
15 and Over, 1913–87
(average for both sexes, in equivalent years of primary
education)

	1913	1950	1987
Belgium	n.a.	9.85	14.34
Denmark	n.a.	10.44	13.19
France	6.99	9.58	14.31
Germany	8.37	10.40	11.97
Italy	n.a.	5.49	9.99
Netherlands	6.42	8.12	12.37
Norway	n.a.	8.44	13.10
Sweden			13.14
United Kingdom	8.12	10.84	13.47
Canada	n.a.	9.84	14.31
United States	7.86	11.27	16.89
Soviet Union	n.a.	4.10	11.50
Greece		4.16	10.34
Portugal	n.a.	2.49	8.15
Spain	n.a.	4.76	9.69
Argentina	n.a.	4.80	10.01
Brazil	n.a.	2.05	6.22
Chile	n.a.	6.09	10.41
Colombia		3.93	6.65
Mexico	n.a.	2.60	7.82
China	n.a.	2.20	6.28
India	n.a.	1.35	4.38
Japan	5.36	9.11	14.04
Korea	n.a.	3.36	13.22
Taiwan	n.a.	3.62	14.76

Source: See sources cited in Maddison 1989, p. 136. Primary education is
given a weight of 1, secondary 1.4, and higher 2.

poorer countries of the world is significant (even though the divergence is smaller than
for some other characteristics). In Asia, the link among education, real income levels,
and rates of growth is also striking, with India being the worst off and Taiwan, Japan,
and Korea in the lead. In 1950, the average educational levels in India were well below
those in Europe in 1820, as were its income and productivity levels. In the poorer
countries some people never go to school, and many drop out very early, so that these
countries' dispersion around the averages in Table 2-9 is greater than that of the
advanced countries. In addition, the quality of education is generally worse in the
poorer countries.

Physical Capital Stocks and Level of Investment

A necessary condition for exploiting the possibilities offered by technical progress is
an increase in the stock of machinery and equipment in which this technology is
embodied, and in the buildings and infrastructure in which they operate. There is a

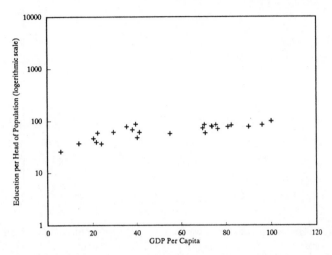

Figure 2-4. Relationship between education per capita and GDP per capita in 1989 (25 countries).

clear positive relationship between the level of GDP per capita and the level of capital stock: It is stronger than for the other inputs we have considered (compare Figure 2-5 with Figures 2-3 and 2-4).

All the advanced countries of Group 1 have accumulated huge stocks of physical capital. In the lead country, the United States, the capital stock has, until recently, been much higher per capita than in the other advanced countries, which have had lower productivity levels. This characteristic of the U.S. economy has been clearly discernible since it took over as the lead country in around 1890 (see Tables 2-10 and 2-11).

Over time there has been a rise in the capital output ratio in the advanced capitalist countries other than the United States, with the most marked rise in Japan, the country whose growth was fastest. This can be seen clearly in Table 2-12, which shows the sharp long-term rise in the capital output ratio in Japan compared with its relative

Table 2-10. Gross Fixed Nonresidential Capital Stock per Capita for
Selected Countries, 1820–1989
(at 1985 U.S. relative prices)

	1820	1890	1913	1950	1973	1989
France	n.a.	n.a.	n.a.	6,861	17,925	33,210
Germany	n.a.	n.a.	n.a.	7,410	24,672	41,500
Japan	n.a.	568	1,068	2,994	17,373	44,064
Netherlands	n.a.	n.a.	n.a.	11,502	24,262	34,213
United Kingdom	1,203	3,399[a]	4,243	6,038	17,010	27,174
United States	1,016	8,221	14,421	19,438	28,999	40,913

Source: Maddison 1992c.
[a]1891.

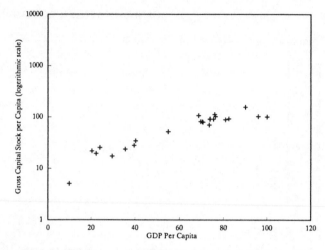

Figure 2-5. Relationship between gross capital stock per capita and GDP per capita in 1989 (24 countries).

Table 2-11. Rate of Growth of Gross Fixed Nonresidential Capital Stock per Capita, 1820–1989
(annual average compound growth rate)

	1820–90	1890–1913	1913–50	1950–73	1973–89
France				4.3	3.9
Germany				5.4	3.3
Japan		2.8	2.8	7.9	6.0
Netherlands				3.3	2.2
United Kingdom	1.5	1.0	1.0	4.6	3.0
United States	3.1	2.3	0.8	1.8	2.2

Source: Maddison 1992c.

Table 2-12. Ratio of Gross Nonresidential Fixed Capital Stock to GDP, 1820–1989
(at 1985 U.S. relative prices)

	1820	1890	1913	1950	1973	1989
France	n.a.	n.a.	n.a.	1.64	1.73	2.38
Germany	n.a.	n.a.	n.a.	2.24	2.44	3.01
Japan	n.a.	0.74	0.93	1.85	1.82	2.87
Netherlands	n.a.	n.a.	n.a.	2.44	2.36	2.70
United Kingdom	0.86	1.05	1.06	1.06	1.69	2.01
United States	0.83	2.77	2.96	2.26	2.06	2.24

Source: Maddison 1992c.

stability in the United States. This intensified capitalization of the economy is a characteristic of countries engaged in the process of catch-up. It also applied to the United States when it was overtaking the United Kingdom as leader. But in the lead country, which is the closest to the frontier of technology, capitalization cannot be sharply increased without running into diminishing returns.

The information on the developing countries' capital stocks is more rudimentary than that on the advanced countries, because their construction requires very long series of investment data, and it is more difficult to estimate differences in the relative price of investment goods. There is nothing in this past history of capital formation, however, to suggest that fast growth can be attained without a major effort to sustain high rates of capital formation.

Structural Change

Economic growth has been accompanied by massive changes in economic structure whose long-term pattern has been similar in most countries. There has been a steady decline in the share of agriculture in employment and value, and a rise in the share of services, which was sharpest in countries with the highest income levels. Industry has shown a bell-shaped pattern of development, with an increasing share as incomes rose in the nineteenth and twentieth centuries and a fall in the advanced capitalist countries in the past two decades (see Table 2-13).

Levels of labor productivity are generally much lower in agriculture than in the rest of the economy, so some analysts treat the structural changes as an independent source of growth due to improved resource allocation. But, it is necessary to treat the role of structural change with caution, as many of the apparent gains from resource reallocation are in fact due to increased inputs of physical and human capital in the nonagricultural sectors.

Table 2-13. Long-Term Changes in the Structure of Employment and Output (percentages of total employment and GDP)

	Employment			Value Added		
	Agriculture	*Industry*	*Services*	*Agriculture*	*Industry*	*Services*
			OECD countries			
1870	49	27	24	39	26	35
1950	25	36	39	15	41	44
1987	6	30	64	4	36	60
			Latin America			
1950	50	22	28	23	30	47
1986	24	28	48	11	38	51
			Asia			
1950	73	8	19	49	15	36
1986	57[a]	17[a]	26[a]	25	34	41

Source: A. Maddison, *The World Economy in the Twentieth Century* (Paris: OECD, 1989), p. 20.
[a]1980.

Structural changes reflect two basic forces that operate in all the countries when they reach successively higher levels of real income and productivity. The first of these is the elasticity of demand for particular products, which has been similar at given levels of income (particularly as relative price structures have moved in a similar direction). These demand forces have reduced the share of agricultural products in consumption and have raised the demand for the products of industry and services. The second force is the various sectors' differing pace of technological advance. Productivity growth has been slower in many services than commodity production has been, partly because of the intrinsic character of many personal services and partly because of measurement conventions that exclude the possibility of productivity growth in some services. Structural change has also been affected by other influences such as the size of government activity, the share and pattern of foreign trade, the rate of investment, and natural resource endowments and their rate of depletion (see Maddison 1980).

Foreign Trade

There are many ways in which nations interact with one another, and their degree of openness has an important impact on their growth potential. The main ways in which they interact are through the exchange of goods and services, migration of people, exchange of ideas and skills or tourism, and movements of capital, private or public. Foreign contacts and foreign trade are a major source of new technology, and they help determine the degree of economic specialization and economic structure, particularly for the follower countries. The state of the world economy also affects the level of demand, the rate of inflation, and fashions in economic policy. Although we cannot consider here the impact of all these external influences on growth, we can note some basic facts about the relationship of trade and growth of real income.

Over the long run, trade has grown faster than output, but the impact has varied over time. For instance, 1913 to 1950 was a period of neomercantilism, with the blockades imposed during the two world wars and the discriminatory policies, higher tariffs, quantitative restrictions, exchange controls, and other autarkic measures sparked off by the world depression of 1929–32.

After the second World War, the golden age was characterized by a revival of liberalism in commercial policy that was concentrated in the advanced countries but had

Table 2-14. Comparative Size of Manufacturing Plants in Six Advanced Capitalist Countries Around 1987
(number of persons engaged)

	France 1988	Germany 1987	Japan 1987	Netherlands 1985	United Kingdom 1988	United States 1987
Average size	19	30	16	34	30	49
Median size	146	318	166	254	240	263

Source: B. van Ark, "International Comparisons of Output and Productivity" (Ph.D. diss., University of Groningen, 1993), Table 6.6. Plant is a somewhat narrower definition than establishment. Plant is a local unit at a single postal address. Median is defined here in relation to total manufacturing employment. Half the employees are in smaller plants than the median, half in plants above that size.

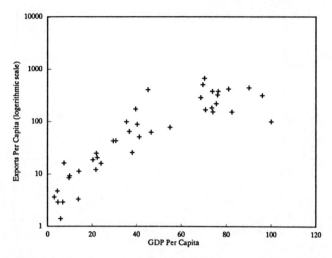

Figure 2-6. Relationship of exports per capita and GDP per capita in 1989 (43 countries).

worldwide effects in those countries that chose to benefit from the opportunity. Some of this growth-stimulating impact faded after 1973, as the effect of trade liberalization was absorbed, but international trade has continued to rise faster than output and has contributed to growth. Figure 2-6 shows the relationship between exports per capita and GDP per capita in 1989. Compared with some of the other characteristics, the positive relationship is rather strong.

Economies of Scale

There is a very wide range (500:1) in the size of our 43 economies, but there is no significant relationship between their size and their per-capita income performance (see Figure 2-7). Some small economies, like those of Norway and Sweden, have much higher per-capita incomes than large economies, like those of the Soviet Union or China. Most of the benefits of specialization and scale can be obtained by small countries through international trade.

In fact, the average size of productive establishments in advanced capitalist countries is much smaller than is often imagined (see Tables 2-14 and 2-15). In the private sector of the U.S. economy, there were 5.8 million establishments in 1986, and on average they employed 14 people; manufacturing had the largest establishments, with an average employment of 54 persons. The median size is much bigger than the average. In 1987 the median U.S. manufacturing plant employed 263 people (half those employed worked in bigger plants, and half worked in smaller plants). The median size of a U.S. plant was only marginally different from that in the Netherlands and the United Kingdom, and it was smaller than that in Germany. There is thus little evidence that big countries have much of a scale advantage, and again, small countries

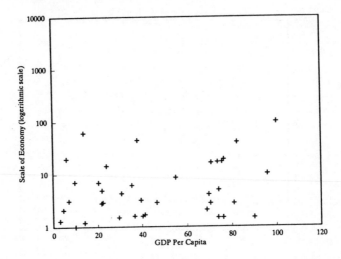

Figure 2-7. Relationship between size of economy and GDP per capita in 1989 (43 countries).

can get most of the benefits of specialization between firms through international trade.

Between 1899 and 1986 the average U.S. manufacturing establishment rose in size from 24 to 54 employees (see Table 2-16). The rise in median size may well have been bigger, although there is little evidence in these numbers that scale economies played more than a modest role in U.S. productivity. The United States' GDP per person employed rose almost fourfold between 1900 and 1989; the proportion of people with higher education rose ninefold; and the stock of machinery and equipment per person employed rose about fifteenfold. It is not easy to give a summary statistic on research activity, but according to the evidence presented in Mowery and Rosenberg (1989), it seems likely that it rose as fast proportionately as did inputs of machinery and equipment. Despite this evidence, many authors, for example, Kaldor and

Table 2-15. Average Number of Establishments, Employees, and Employees per Establishment in the United States in 1986

	Agriculture	Contract Construction	Private Services	Transportation	Mining	Manufacturing	Total
Establishments (thousands)	68	492	41,960	210	35	355	5,807
Employees (thousands)	412	4,659	55,524	4,884	847	19,142	83,380
Employees per establishment	6.1	9.5	13.2	23.3	24.2	53.9	14.4

Source: U.S. Department of Commerce, *Statistical Abstract of the United States 1989* (Washington DC: U.S. Government Printing Office, 1989), p. 523.

Table 2-16. Average Number of Establishments, Employees, and Number of Employees per Establishment in U.S. Manufacturing, 1899–1986

	Employees	Establishments	Employees
1986	53.9	355	19,142
1980	66.3	319	21,185
1950	55.6	260	14,467
1929	46.7	207	9,660
1899	23.7	205	4,850

Source: Data for 1980 and 1986 are the same as for Table 2-15; data for 1899 to 1950 from *Historical Statistics of the United States: Colonial Times to 1970, Part 2* (Washington, DC: U.S. Government Printing Office, 1975), p. 666. The rise in the size of establishments between 1899 and 1929 is exaggerated because the cutoff point for inclusion in the census was raised in 1921 from annual shipments of $500 to $5,000. This source also gives figures for 1840–99 that suggest that the average establishment size rose by about 28 percent between those dates. Note that there was a substantial rise in the share of administrative and supervisory personnel. In 1899 "nonproduction" workers made up 7 percent of the total, and in 1970 this had risen to 25 percent.

Chandler, have held scale economies to be of major importance, though they usually mix up scale economies with other influences.

Alfred Chandler (1990) argues that the growth of large multiunit firms has been the major force underlying economic growth in the United States and that the greater degree of corporativeness in the USA has been the major source of the U.S. productivity advantage over that of the United Kingdom. He puts considerable emphasis on scope, that is, the vertical and horizontal integration of multifold activities within big

Table 2-17. Comparative Levels of Labor Productivity in the Economy as a Whole, 1913–89 (U.S. GDP per labor hour = 100)

	1913	1950	1973	1989
Austria	48	27	59	75
Belgium	61	42	64	89
Denmark	58	43	63	66
Finland	33	31	57	70
France	48	40	70	95
Germany	50	30	64	79
Italy	37	31	64	81
Netherlands	69	46	77	92
Norway	43	43	64	83
Sweden	44	49	76	81
United Kingdom	78	57	67	81
Australia	93	67	70	78
Canada	75	75	83	91
United States	100	100	100	100
Japan	18	15	46	65

Source: Data for 1913–73 from Maddison 1991, p. 53; data for 1989 from Table 2-6. GDP is measured in 1985 U.S. relative prices (Paasche PPP converter).

corporations. This is, of course, contrary to the usual view that specialization is important. Chandler's analysis of scale and scope is not based on quantitative evidence, nor does he separate the impact of organizational advance from the role of improvements in technology and increases in physical and human capital inputs. His comparison with the United Kingdom ignores the fact that until recently Britain had much less capital per worker than did the United States. Furthermore, the evidence that Prais and associates (1981) and Caves and Krause (1980) found suggests that British firms have been too big rather than too small. In the 1980s, the size of British firms fell, and their productivity accelerated.

My own view is that scale economies are rather modest and that government efforts to promote bigness have generally been a failure, particularly so in Eastern Europe and the Soviet Union where industrial and agricultural establishments have been much bigger than in the West (see Ehrlich 1985).

Technical Progress

Technical progress is the most essential characteristic of economic growth. If there had been no technical progress, the whole process of capital accumulation would have been much more modest. Massive investment in transport was rational when railways, automobiles, and aircraft brought progressively bigger possibilities for reliability, speed, and comfort at low cost. Massive investment in horse-drawn carriages obviously would not have produced the same result.

A substantial part of technical progress must be embodied in new capital goods to be exploited effectively;[13] some of it becomes operational mainly through improvements in the skill and knowledge of the labor force; and some progress is due to improvements in management and organization. Because technical progress is continuous and substantial, economies never function at a technical optimum. There is a continuous process of learning by doing in which those using a new machine become familiar with its potential. By the time the new technique has been fully mastered in a given establishment, new and better techniques will become available and will be used in competitive establishments that will begin the process of learning by doing all over again. Firms vary in the vintages of capital they can deploy and in their level of organizational skill. Thus, the average level at which all advancing economies operate is below feasible best practice, and they have a variety of techniques in operation.

If labor productivity is used as a crude proxy measure of average technological levels, it is clear that the United States has been the lead country for all of the twentieth century. We can make such measures with any semblance of accuracy only for the countries in Group 1 and for Japan, but if the United States was unequivocally the productivity leader among these countries, it must also have been the world leader. Table 2-17 shows clearly that the United States was still the lead country in 1989, though its leadership edge had greatly eroded since 1950.

From the information we have by industry of origin, it seems probable that the U.S. lead prevailed in all major sectors of the economy and in virtually all branches of manufacturing. This is still the case, except for Japan. Japan's overall productivity standing is not impressive compared with that of the European countries, but its economic performance by sector and branch is more uneven than that of the European

Table 2-18. Comparative Levels of Labor
Productivity in Manufacturing, 1950–89
(U.S. manufacturing output per labor hour
= 100)

	1950	1973	1989
Germany	39	75	80
United Kingdom	40	52	61
Brazil	18	36	26
Mexico	18	32	30
India	5	5	6
Korea	5	11	20
Japan	18	56	80
United States	100	100	100

Source: B. van Ark 1993. Output was measured using a
Fisher PPP (geometric average of Paasche and Laspeyres
measures).

countries. Its manufacturing productivity was 80 percent of that of the United States
in 1989, and its productivity in the machinery and equipment sector was above that
of the United States (see Tables 2-18 and 2-19).

The reasons why the United States has been the lead country in the twentieth
century are that it had the highest levels of capital per capita until very recently (Table
2-10), it has had and still has the most highly educated labor force (Table 2-9), and it
had an even larger lead in expenditures on research and development (Table 2-20),
which it still maintains.[14] All of these characteristics interacted to make the United
States the technical leader and to produce a steady stream of technical improvement
at a faster pace than the United Kingdom (the old leader) produced in the nineteenth
century.

It seems legitimate to describe U.S. technical progress as steady, because U.S.
labor productivity growth was rather steady over the long haul from 1890 to 1973 (the
slowdown of 1929–38 being compensated in 1938–50). Since 1973 the rate of U.S.
productivity growth has decelerated markedly. As this slowdown has now lasted for
two decades, there are some grounds for thinking that the rate of technical progress
has decelerated particularly because the other advanced capitalist countries are now

Table 2-19. Comparative Levels of Labor Productivity in Branches of
Manufacturing, 1988

	Germany	United Kingdom	Japan	United States
Food products	69	49	24	100
Textiles	86	69	64	100
Chemicals	68	75	69	100
Basic metals	84	78	90	100
Machinery	80	62	114	100
Other	80	57	56	100

Source: Update of D. Pilat and B. van Ark 1991. Output was measured using Fisher PPP converters.

Table 2-20. Research and Development
Expenditure per Person Employed, Six
Countries, 1960–87
($ in 1985 U.S. relative prices)

	1960	1973	1987
France	207	448	761
Germany	179	475	848
Japan	89	342	757
Netherlands	291	514	687
United Kingdom	343	480	650
United States	809	814	1074

Source: Maddison 1991, p. 152.

much nearer to U.S. levels of performance and have stepped up their own research
and development efforts, which one would normally have expected to reinforce the
rate of technical progress.

One of the most ambitious analysts of technical progress (Schmookler 1966)
argued that the development of new processes and products is induced by demand.
"We are, and evidently for some time have been able to extend the technological frontier perceptibly at virtually all points" (p. 210). He buttresses his argument with evidence drawn from U.S. patent statistics (and chronologies of major inventions) covering a period of a century and a half "A million dollars spent on one kind of good is
likely to induce about as much invention as the same sum spent on any other good"
(p. 172). In effect, Schmookler says that there are constant returns to inventive effort,
a viewpoint that may have seemed plausible in the 1960s but is much less so today.

Rosenberg (1976) challenged Schmookler's view on this issue and argued that science and technology are not omnicompetent, that certain obvious human needs "have
long gone either unsatisfied or very badly catered for in spite of a well-established
demand" (p. 267) and that attempts to quicken, or even maintain, the pace of technical progress may run into decreasing returns because the necessary process of trial
and error imposes constraints on the pace of development of knowledge.

As productivity growth has slowed down in all the countries of Group 1 and in
Japan as well, there is some reason to believe that the pace of technical progress has
slowed down. One can subscribe to this proposition without being an adherent of
the Kondratieff–Schumpeter hypothesis about the presence of long waves in technology.

The main burden of innovation in new processes and products has been borne
by the advanced countries, and with some lag, follower countries can usually mimic
the technology and copy the leaders. The advantage to a backward country is that it
can grow faster than the leader when it is catching up and can mount a bigger investment effort without running so easily into a zone of diminishing returns. However, the
Japanese experience shows that a substantial degree of catch-up requires great effort
sustained over a long period to build up human capital, to accumulate physical capital,
and to adapt technology to its own needs (see Hayami and Ruttan 1985, who show
why the difference in factor endowment between Japanese and U.S. agriculture made
it necessary for Japan to develop an idiosyncratic technology path in this sector).

Mimicry of the lead country's technology by follower countries is too facile a description of the process. Most technology needs to be carefully adapted to local needs and local skills, so it cannot be transplanted successfully without a reasonable level of education and skills in the follower country and some experience in adaptive R&D and in the installation of new capital. It requires a fair degree of what Abramovitz calls "technical congruence."

The Outlook for Growth and Convergence

In all the countries we have surveyed here, the major engine of growth has been advancing knowledge and technical progress, which needs to be embodied in human and physical capital in order to have an impact. There is no reason to suspect that this will change.

At the frontiers of knowledge and technology, economic progress is necessarily rather gradual, and there have been no big leaps forward in productivity. The United States—the lead country for a century in terms of living standards and level of performance—had a rather steady pace of advance in both labor and total factor productivity until the 1970s, at which time there was a distinct slowdown, which has persisted now for nearly two decades. If it continues in the long term, it will have a major influence on the pace of growth in the twenty-first century because the slowdown has also affected productivity growth in all of the other advanced countries and there is no clear prospect of a new leader emerging.

Within the world economy, there are large spreads in per-capita income and productivity. Some countries that were well below the frontier of technology at the beginning of the century were able to grow much faster than the lead country when they mounted the necessary effort in terms of human and physical capital. Japan, Korea, and Taiwan did a fair amount of catching up, but they are still significantly below U.S. productivity levels. Japan's experience suggests that supergrowth cannot be sustained indefinitely, for its productivity growth has not surpassed that of the top European performers in the past decade. Countries like Korea and Taiwan also seem likely to converge to slower growth paths within the next two decades.

Progress in many of the poor countries, particularly in Asia, was faster in the second half of the twentieth century than it was in the first, partly because the abolition of colonialism gave these countries greater freedom to control their destiny, a freedom that they generally used in a very positive manner. Progress was also helped by buoyancy in the world economy, better opportunities for trade and the transfer of technology, and, to a modest extent, because the advanced countries provided some aid for development. Nevertheless, despite significant gains in income and productivity, many of these poorer countries are not catching up to or keeping up the pace of growth in the advanced countries. Convergence in per-capita income levels is by no means inevitable, particularly in countries with a rapidly growing population.

It is clear that the eighth and ninth decades were not the twentieth century's best. Only the Asian countries grew rapidly. Latin America, Africa, Eastern Europe, and the former Soviet Union are in the middle of complex "adjustment" crises, and the performance of Western and Southern Europe is well below that of the postwar golden age.

The slowdown in the advanced countries was due in part to the erosion of once-for-all elements in the postwar golden age. It is nearer to being satisfactory than that in some other parts of the world economy. But growth and employment are below their potential because of caution about inflation and balance-of-payment risks, induced in part by problems of living in a world with unrestricted freedom for international capital movements and fluctuating exchange rates. Growth did not accelerate significantly in the 1980s despite the waning of inflation and the reduced power of OPEC. Mutual consultation has been successful in avoiding beggar-your-neighbor policies but very slow in getting remedial action to reduce payments disequilibria or to induce changes in the U.S. fiscal–monetary policy mix.

The general economic situation in Latin America is one of major crisis—worse than anything previously experienced in the twentieth century. Since 1982 these countries have had 10 years in the wilderness trying to tackle a multiplicity of problems with desperate remedies. There are four characteristic and interrelated problems: a fiscal crisis, galloping inflation, very heavy external indebtedness, and distortions in resource allocation that derived originally from excessive protectionism, subsidies, and dirigisme and have been complicated by inflation and depression. To solve all of them by means of orthodox policy measures has proved very painful, but heterodox alternatives have proved disastrous.

In the former Soviet Union and in Eastern Europe there is also a crisis of a different origin. The Stalinist model of authoritarian centralized controls has lost its legitimacy, because it produced low growth, shoddy products, queues, and shortages. The transition to a more market-oriented economy, with private ownership of means of production, more consumer choice, and scope for entrepreneurial initiative is being held back by both vested interests remaining from the old system and the inherent difficulty of the task. The remarkable results of liberalization in China are not much of a guide to what can be expected from changes in Eastern Europe and the former Soviet Union, because they were applied to a much more primitive economy. As Russia liberalizes, its problems will probably resemble more closely those of Latin America.

Notes

I am grateful to Gjalt de Jong for help in preparing the graphs and to Moe Abramovitz, Bart van Ark, William Baumol, and André Hofman for comments on the text. I also benefited from comments received during the two seminars organized by W. Baumol, R. Nelson, and E. N. Wolff, Historical Perspectives on the International Convergence of Productivity, in November 1991 and April 1992.

1. The importance of getting a representative sample of countries is clear from the exchange between Baumol (1986) and De Long (1988), which opened up the recent discussion on convergence. Baumol concentrated on evidence for 16 rich countries from Maddison (1982), and De Long pointed out that convergence was much weaker when the sample of countries was expanded. One of the striking features of the new growth economics that has emerged since 1986 is the fact that it takes a global view of economic growth and jettisons the old dichotomy between "growth" (of advanced countries) and "development" (of poor countries).

2. Simon Kuznets (1966) put the turning point for "modern economic growth" at 1750, but in the light of recent evidence suggesting that growth in the eighteenth century was slower than previously thought (Crafts 1985), I prefer to put the turning point at 1820. Furthermore, I think recent evidence has falsified the earlier view (espoused most strongly by Rostow 1960 and Gerschenkron 1965) that there was a long, drawn-out sequence of staggered "takeoffs" in West European countries throughout the nineteenth century. It now seems clear that growth was generally much faster after 1820 than it was in the "protocapitalist" period from 1500 to 1820, when Western Europe was slowly pulling ahead of the rest of the world. For evidence on the pace of growth in Flanders for 1500 to 1812, see van der Wee and Blomme (1992) who estimate a growth rate in GDP of 0.2 percent per year over these three centuries.

3. Within the European periphery, the countries excluded from our sample (Albania, Bulgaria, Poland, Romania, and Yugoslavia) probably have income levels below those of the Soviet Union, and so the degree of convergence is somewhat exaggerated by our sample.

4. Our Latin American sample excludes the Caribbean area where there are several countries below the income range in our 6 sample countries. In Latin America proper, some countries, like Bolivia and Ecuador, are below the level of Peru (the poorest of our sample countries), and two countries may have a higher income than our sample (Uruguay and Venezuela). See Summers and Heston 1991, pp. 351–52 for rough 1988 estimates for 29 countries in the region.

5. In defining productivity leadership, I have ignored the special case of Australia, whose impressive achievements before the first World War were due largely to its natural resource advantages rather than to its technical achievements and the stock of man-made capital.

6. For a more elaborate statement of my causal schema, see Maddison 1988 and 1991, p. 12. Maddison 1970, chap. 2, was an attempt to measure the interaction of different layers of causality.

7. This "ultimate" level of causality is generally missing in the new growth theory, which seeks to find comprehensive explanations by sticking to the proximate domain (see the contributions to the May 1991 issue of the *Quarterly Journal of Economics*). Lucas (1988, p. 5) is the most straightforward in recognizing these limitations:

> The term "theory" is used in so many different ways, even within economics, that if I do not clarify what I mean by it early on, the gap between what I think I am saying and what you think you are hearing will grow too wide for us to have a serious discussion. I prefer to use the term "theory" in a very narrow sense, to refer to an explicit dynamic system, something that can be put on a computer and *run*.

Adam Smith and Simon Kuznets, the fathers of modern growth analysis, clearly operated across a broader spectrum of causality. Kuznets did not claim to have a general theory but stuck to rather simple presentations of quantitative evidence, avoided econometrics, and made very sparing use of regressions. He used his imagination to fill empty economic boxes and to make strategic interconnections (see Lundberg 1971). Abramovitz (1989) approaches growth in the same way and refers frequently to the "ultimate" domain in terms of nations' differential "social capability," different degrees of "technical congruence," or differences in institutions and policy. See also Cipolla 1991 for a contrast between the approach of economists and that of economic historians.

8. There are two main schools of "proximate" analysis. The first consists of the growth accountants, whose guru is Ed Denison. Denison's (1967) analytic framework contains some neoclassic elements, particularly in his use of factor weights, but he is eclectic in his procedures. The new growth economists either ignore his work (as Paul Romer does) or label it without adequate qualification as neoclassic (as Lucas does). The advantage of the growth-accounting approach as Denison developed it is that the accounts are completely transparent and great care is given to what exactly the measures mean. The other school of proximate analysis is econometric, as represented by Chenery or Barro who tend to be "maximalist" in their willingness to use data of widely varying reliability. They also use less transparent procedures. Jorgenson falls somewhat between the two approaches. He is more strictly neoclassical than Denison, makes greater use of econometric techniques, and is less transparent, but he is generally more fastidious about the data he uses than are the maximalists.

9. See Abramovitz (1989, p. 23) for a cautionary note on interactive causality:

> Growth accounting—holds that the sources it measures act independently of one another so that each makes its own contribution. There are good reasons, however, to question that claim. The growth sources feed from one another. The most important interactions are those between technological progress and the accumulation of tangible capital and between technological progress and the build-up of human capital through education and training.

10. See Maddison 1991 for the relevant growth accounts and a more detailed analysis of policy. Kindleberger 1992 provides an excellent survey of the variety of interpretations of the golden age.

11. It is too early to try to improve on the old CIA estimates until we have better evidence. However, it is now clear that the East German Statistical Office deliberately misrepresented economic growth. The same is probably true of Romania. In other East European countries the problem appears not to have been cheating but the inappropriateness of the data collection system for generating the statistics needed to estimate real GDP. For revisionist estimates for the Soviet Union, see Bergson 1991 and Khanin 1988. I have dropped the estimates for Bulgaria, Poland, Romania, and Yugoslavia that I included in Maddison 1990.

12. I have measured human capital characteristics in terms of the stock of formal education embodied in the population. I think this is preferable to flow data on educational enrollments which some analysts use as a proxy measure, for example, Easterlin 1981 or Barro 1991:

13. The interaction of investment, capital stock, and technical progress is shown most clearly in Salter 1960.

14. The R&D effort of the United States compared with that of the United Kingdom is analyzed and documented with great clarity in Mowery and Rosenberg 1989. They also show that the U.S. educational system and the direction of research in U.S. universities was well designed to foster the acquisition of technical skills and to nurture technical progress.

References

Abramovitz, M. (1989). *Thinking About Growth.* Cambridge: Cambridge University Press.

van Ark, B. (1993). "The ICOP Approach—Its Implications and Applicability." In A. Szirmai, B. van Ark, and D. Pilat, eds., *Explaining Economic Growth.* Amsterdam: North Holland.

Barro, R. J. (1991). "Economic Growth in a Cross Section of Countries." *Quarterly Journal of Economics,* May, pp. 407–43.

Baumol, W. J. (1986). "Productivity Growth, Convergence and Welfare: What the Long-Run Data Show." *American Economic Review,* December, pp. 1072–86.

Baumol, W. J., and Wolff, E. W. (1988). "Productivity, Convergence and Welfare: Reply." *American Economic Review,* December, pp. 1155–59.

Bergson, A. (1991). "The USSR Before the Fall: How Poor and Why." *Journal of Economic Perspectives,* Fall, pp. 29–44.

Caves, R. E., and L. B. Krause. (1980). *Britain's Economic Performance.* Washington, DC: Brookings Institution.

Chandler, A. D., Jr. (1990). *Scale and Scope: The Dynamics of Industrial Capitalism.* Cambridge, MA: Harvard University Press.

Chernery, H. and M. Syrquin. (1975). *Patterns of Development, 1950–1970.* Oxford: Oxford University Press.

Cipolla, C. M. (1991). *Between History and Economics: An Introduction to Economic History.* Oxford: Basil Blackwell.

Crafts, N.F.R. (1985). *British Economic Growth During the Industrial Revolution.* Oxford: Oxford University Press.

De Long, J. Bradford. (1988). "Productivity, Convergence and Welfare: Comment." *American Economic Review,* December, pp. 1138–54.

De Long, J. Bradford, and L. H. Summers. (1991). "Equipment Investment and Economic Growth." *Quarterly Journal of Economics,* May, pp. 445–502.

Denison, E. F. (1967). *Why Growth Rates Differ.* Washington, DC: Brookings Institution.

Dosi, G., C. Freeman, R. Nelson, G. Silverberg, and L. Soete. (1988). *Technical Change and Economic Theory.* London: Francis Pinter.

Easterlin, R. (1981). "Why Isn't the Whole World Developed?" *Journal of Economic History,* March, pp. 1–19.

Ehrlich, E. (1985). "The Size Structure of Manufacturing Establishments and Enterprises: An International Comparison." *Journal of Comparative Economics* 9:267–95.

Gerschenkron, A. (1965). *Economic Backwardness in Historical Perspective*. New York: Praeger.

Hayami, Y., and V. W. Ruttan. (1985). *Agricultural Development: An International Perspective*. Baltimore: Johns Hopkins University Press.

Hofman, A. A. (1991). "The Role of Capital in Latin America: A Comparative Perspective of Six Countries for 1950–1989." Working Paper no. 4, ECLAC, Santiago, December.

Khanin, G. (1988). "Ekonomicheski rost, alternativnaia otsenka." *Kommunist* 17:83–90.

Kindleberger, C. (1992). "Why did the Golden Age Last So Long?" In F. Cairncross and A. Cairncross, eds., *The Legacy of the Golden Age*. London: Routledge & Paul Kegan.

Kuznets, S. (1951). "The State as a Unit in Study of Economic Growth." *Journal of Economic History*, pp. 25–41.

Lal, D. (1988). *The Hindu Equilibrium*. Vol. 1. Oxford: Oxford University Press.

Landes, D. S. (1969). *The Unbound Prometheus*. Cambridge: Cambridge University Press.

Lucas, R. E. (1988). "On the Mechanics of Economic Development." *Journal of Monetary Economics* 22:3–42.

Lundberg, E. (1971). "Simon Kuznets' Contribution to Economics." *Scandinavian Journal of Economics*, pp. 444–61.

Maddison, A. (1970). *Economic Progress and Policy in Developing Countries*. New York: Norton.

———. (1971). *Class Structure and Economic Growth: India and Pakistan Since the Moghuls*. London: Allen & Unwin.

———. (1980). "Economic Growth and Structural Change in the Advanced Countries." In I. Leveson and J. W. Wheeler, eds., *Western Economies in Transition*. London: Croom Helm, pp. 41–66.

———. (1982). *Phases of Capitalist Development*. Oxford: Oxford University Press.

———. (1987). "Growth and Slowdown in Advanced Capitalist Economies: Techniques of Quantitative Assessment." *Journal of Economic Literature*, June, pp. 649–98.

———. (1988). "Ultimate and Proximate Growth Causality: A Critique of Mancur Olson on the Rise and Decline of Nations." *Scandinavian Economic History Review* 36:25–29.

———. (1989). *The World Economy in the Twentieth Century*. Paris: OECD Development Centre.

———. (1990a). "The Colonial Burden: A Comparative Perspective." In M.Scott and D. Lal, eds., *Public Policy and Economic Development*. Oxford: Oxford University Press, pp. 361–75.

———. (1990b). "Measuring European Growth: The Core and the Periphery." In E. Aerts and N. Valerio, eds., *Growth and Stagnation in the Mediterranean World in the 19th and 20th Centuries*. Leuven University Press.

———. (1991). *Dynamic Forces in Capitalist Development*. Oxford: Oxford University Press.

———. (1992a). "A Long-Run Perspective on Saving." *Scandinavian Journal of Economics*, June, pp. 181–213.

———. (1992b). *The Political Economy of Poverty Equity and Growth: Brazil and Mexico*. New York: Oxford University Press.

———. (1992c). "Standardised Estimates of Fixed Investment and Capital Stock at Constant Prices: A Long Run Survey for Six Countries." Paper presented at IARIW meetings, Flims, September.

Mowery, D. C., and N. Rosenberg. (1989). *Technology and the Pursuit of Economic Growth*. Cambridge: Cambridge University Press.

Needham, J. (1954–). *Science and Society in China*. Cambridge: Cambridge University Press.

Pilat, D., and B. van Ark. (1991). "Productivity Leadership in Manufacturing, Germany, Japan and the United States, 1973–1989." *Research Memorandum* no. 456, Institute of Economic Research, University of Groningen.

Prais, S. J., A. Daly, D. T. Jones, and K. Wagner (1981). *Productivity and Industrial Structure*. Cambridge: Cambridge University Press.

Pratten, C. (1988). "A Survey of Economies of Scale." Department of Applied Economics, Cambridge University, October.

Romer, P. M. (1986). "Increasing Returns and Long-Run Growth." *Journal of Political Economy* 94:1002–37.

———. (1990). "Endogenous Technical Change." *Journal of Political Economy* 98:S71–S102.

Rosenberg, N. (1976). *Perspectives on Technology*. Cambridge: Cambridge University Press.

Rostow, W. W. (1960). *The Stages of Economic Growth*. Cambridge: Cambridge University Press.

Salter, W.E.G. (1960). *Productivity and Technical Change*. Cambridge: Cambridge University Press.

Schmookler, J. (1966). *Invention and Economic Growth*. Cambridge, MA: Harvard University Press.

Summers, R., and A. Heston. (1988). "A New Set of International Comparisons of Real Product and Prices: Estimates for 130 Countries, 1950–1985." *Review of Income and Wealth*, March, pp. 1–25.

————. (1991). "The Penn World Table (Mark 5): An Expanded Set of International Comparisons, 1950–1988." *Quarterly Journal of Economics,* May, pp. 327–68.

United Nations/Eurostat. (1986). *World Comparisons of Purchasing Power and Real Product for 1980.* New York: United Nations/Eurostat.

van der Wee, H., and J. Blomme. (1992). "The Belgian Economy in the Very Long Run: A Case Study of Economic Development in the Flanders/Brabant Region 1500–1812." Paper presented at IARIW meetings, Flims, September.

PART II

INVESTMENT, CAPITAL STOCK
AND SAVING

Part II: Investment, capital stock and saving

In the 1950s and 1960s, the literature devoted to 'explaining' economic growth relied a good deal on rates of investment to illustrate changes in the productive contribution of capital. Thus Maddison (1964) and ECE (1964) used investment-output ratios (average investment rates related to output growth rates over the same period). At that time very few countries had satisfactory or comparable estimates of capital stock, so the investment-output ratio (sometimes called an incremental capital-output ratio) was one of the few ways of trying to assess the impact of capital formation on growth.

In the past 30 years, statistical offices in OECD countries have made a serious effort to measure the capital stock, using the perpetual inventory technique pioneered by Raymond Goldsmith (1951). The task has become easier as the run of years for which reliable investment series are available has lengthened.

The advantages in using capital stocks rather than investment ratios are several. They provide a better measure of the production capacity available to different economies; it is easy to identify the age structure and composition of these assets, to assess the likely spread between 'best practice' and 'average practice' techniques and to experiment with different 'vintage' hypotheses about the interrelationship between capital formation and technical change. These advantages were clearly demonstrated in Salter's (1960) analysis of productivity and technical change.

For this reason I have, since 1970, always used capital stocks rather than investment ratios in trying to 'explain' growth. Sometimes this involved crude estimates. Where the run of years for investment was inadequate one had to make a hypothesis about the initial level of the stock (see Essays 1 and 4 and Maddison, 1972). Summers and Heston (1991) also did this when constructing their capital stocks. This procedure is preferable to using investment ratios as a proxy for the capital stock, because there is not a close relationship between investment ratios and growth of capital stock, e.g. in the UK the capital stock rose about five times as fast in 1950–73 as it did in 1913–50 whereas the investment rate only doubled. In 1950–73 the UK capital stock was growing twice as fast as that of the USA, but their investment rates were similar (see Denison, 1967, pp. 121 and 138 on the weak relationship between investment rates and growth of capital stock).

For most OECD countries it is no longer necessary to make such crude measures. In Maddison (1982) I used the official capital stocks for postwar years and linked them with more or less comparable scholarly estimates for prewar years. In Essay 2 I did the same thing in a more elaborate growth accounting approach for six countries. In Maddison (1991), I moved a step further towards comparable estimates. There I re-estimated the capital stocks for six countries with common assumptions about asset lives and a conversion at purchasing power parities rather than exchange rates. Thus one can better compare both growth rates and levels and get a more accurate and consistent view of age structure and vintage effects.

Essay 5 is a detailed presentation (Maddison, 1993) of the standardised estimates of capital stock, which makes the procedure transparent, and provides the underlying investment series in national prices as well as in the international *numeraire*. The new estimates falsify the notion that capital-output ratios have been stable over time. They also show the US economic leadership involved capital-output ratios higher than other countries.

There are some analysts who still use investment ratios instead of capital stock in their growth accounting or econometrics. Most of them are using investment ratios as a proxy. This is not the case with Maurice Scott (1989). His analysis has some similarities to the new growth theorists, but his framework is in the heterodox tradition (with strong echoes of Kaldor) and is not at all neoclassical. He is more extreme than the new growth theorists about the strength of the endogenous link between investment and technical progress. He is at pains to reject the usefulness of capital stock measures. I disagree with him on this, but he does throw light on the interaction of technical progress and capital formation and he provides an illuminating analysis of the whole literature in this field (see Denison's 1991 review of Scott).

Essay 6 is a survey (Maddison, 1992) of the historical evidence on savings behaviour for 11 countries which together account for half of world savings. Unlike most recent analysts who have focused on a narrow time period, I look at evidence for more than 100 years. The paper makes two important points: (a) savings rates in the 1950s and 1960s were exceptionally high, and their recent decline can just as well be interpreted as a reversion towards the longer run average rather than a deviation from what shorter term analysis took to be normality; (b) influential theories of saving, both the life cycle hypothesis and the permanent income hypothesis (which rejects Keynes' notion that savings rise with income) are based almost entirely on US savings experience. However, the US savings record is atypical and the general record is more favourable to Keynes' view.

This essay was written as a background paper for a conference on savings behaviour funded by the Finnish Savings Bank Research Foundation, so it is not directed explicitly to explaining economic growth. However, the underlying statistical information on investment in current prices is complementary to and more or less congruent with the analysis of investment in constant prices in Essay 5. The statistical appendix was too long to include in the paper but is available from the author, as is the data diskette.

References

Denison, E.F. (1967), *Why Growth Rates Differ*, Brookings.
Denison, E.F. (1991), 'Scott's "A New View of Economic Growth": A Review Article', *Oxford Economic Papers* (43).
Economic Commission for Europe (1964), *Some Factors in Economic Growth in Europe During the 1950s*, UN, Geneva.
Goldsmith, R.W. (1951), 'A Perpetual Inventory of National Wealth', in M.R. Gainsburgh, *Studies in Income and Wealth*, Vol. 14, Princeton.
Maddison, A. (1964), *Economic Growth in the West*, Allen and Unwin, London, and Twentieth Century Fund, New York.
Maddison, A. (1972), 'Explaining Economic Growth', *Banca Nazionale del Lavoro Quarterly Review*, September.
Maddison, A. (1982), *Phases of Capitalist Development*, Oxford University Press.
Maddison, A. (1991), *Dynamic Forces in Capitalist Development*, Oxford University Press.
Maddison, A. (1992), 'A Long Run Perspective on Saving', *Scandinavian Journal of Economics*, **94**, 2.
Maddison, A. (1993), 'Standardised Estimates of Fixed Capital Stock: A Six Country Comparison', *Innovazione et Materie Prime*, April.
Salter, W. (1960), *Productivity and Technical Change*, Cambridge University Press.
Scott, M.Fg. (1989), *A New View of Economic Growth*, Clarendon Press, Oxford.
Summers, R. and A. Heston (1991), 'The Penn World Table (Mark 5): An Expanded Set of International Comparisons 1950–1988', *Quarterly Journal of Economics*, May.

[5]

Standardised Estimates of Fixed Capital Stock: A Six Country Comparison*

Angus Maddison

Historical and methodological background

In the past 50 years, the quantitative study of economic growth has been sharpened and enriched by improved measures of capital stock. When Tinbergen (1942) made his pioneering international comparison of joint factor productivity, he had to cobble together miscellaneous physical indicators of the stock of animals, ships, locomotives, industrial horsepower, dwellings, etc., with very crude weights. His *Kapitalmenge* could better be translated as a heap than a stock. For the USA, there was better wealth survey material from censuses going back to 1850, but this too was difficult to aggregate with consistent valuations (Kuznets, 1946).

In 1951, Goldsmith pioneered the perpetual inventory method in which the stock estimates for the USA were derived from investment series in constant prices from the national accounts. Here the coverage and valuation methods were more consistent and transparent and much greater information was available on the age structure of assets. Kendrick (1961) used this method to produce the capital stock estimates he needed in his study of joint factor productivity for 1889–1957 in the USA. In order to go back so far he had to merge some rough benchmark estimates with a perpetual inventory approach for subsequent years. In the 1970s the US Department of Commerce started to produce comprehensive annual capital stock estimates on a regular basis. These begin with the year 1925 and are based entirely on the perpetual inventory technique. The asset lives the Department uses are generally shorter than those of Kendrick.

In the UK, the pioneer official exercise was Dean (1964) which led to regular official publication of estimates for 1947 onwards. Feinstein (1965, 1972 and 1988) provided an exemplary series of British investment and capital stock estimates which go back much further in time than those for any other country. Kirner (1968) and Lützel (1977) laid the basis for the official German estimates which go back to 1950. The publication of Ward (1976) encouraged the adoption of such measures in other OECD countries (OECD, 1993c).

*I am grateful to Nanno Mulder and Gjalt de Jong for help in preparing the stock estimates, and to Bart van Ark, Derek Blades, Peter Groote, André Hofman, Dirk Pilat, Eddy Szirmai and Michael Ward for comments on earlier drafts. John C. Musgrave of the US Department of Commerce answered many questions on the US official figures, the British and Dutch statistical authorities (CSO and CBS) supplied information on investment and I also received information from official sources in Germany. Hugo Krijnse-Locker of Eurostat advised on PPPs. An earlier version of this paper (with the same title) appeared in *Innovazione e Materie Prime* in April 1993. In the earlier version I used the bilateral Paasche PPP at US prices, whereas here I use the more conventional multilateral PPP measure, i.e. Geary Khamis international dollars.

We now have official capital stock estimates for several countries (Australia, Canada, Germany, the UK, the USA and Scandinavian countries) which are comprehensive in scope and based entirely on the perpetual inventory technique. For a number of other countries there are estimates which resemble those of Kendrick (1961) or Maddison (1972) in that they involve a mix of a base year wealth survey and subsequent use of the perpetual inventory technique (as was the case in Japan), or a rough benchmark based on some assumption about the base year capital–output ratio and subsequent use of the perpetual inventory technique. The OECD secretariat has estimates of 'business' capital stocks of this type for 18 countries in its econometric data base which are increasingly used by joint factor productivity analysts (see Kendrick, 1993).

The major element of incomparability in the official estimates is that assumptions about the length of life of assets vary more between countries than seems legitimate (see Blades, 1983). It is not easy to measure exactly what these differences are in the aggregate, as the detail is not always publicly available, or is available in different degrees of disaggregation. In Germany, however, we know that the average life assumed for non-residential structures is 57 years (Schmidt, 1986) whereas it is about 39 years in the USA, and O'Mahony (1993) estimates it to be 66 years in the UK. For machinery and equipment, the German and US official estimates of asset life are similar at 14 years, but O'Mahony (1993) suggests that the average UK life is 25 years. These differing assumptions have a significant effect on the comparative levels and rates of growth exhibited by the official stocks.

It is sometimes argued that the official estimates reflect real intercountry differences in average age of capital. One must concede that this is correct so far as compositional differences are concerned. Within a very broad category such as non-residential structures, one country may have a bigger proportion of long-life assets such as roads and canals and the same is true of the broad category machinery and equipment. However, when countries, which, by world standards, are so similar have very different assumptions about virtually identical assets, it seems likely that there is a significant element of incomparability. If the major purpose of stock comparisons is catch-up analysis, i.e. measurement of the distance between the lead country, the USA, and follower countries such as Germany and the UK, it is appropriate to give a zero value to British and German assets which US statisticians would consider to be junk. Conversely it would be legitimate to impute the longer British lives to German and US assets when looking at the world from the UK standpoint.

The major novelty in my standardisation procedure is to assume asset lives which approximate as closely as possible to those in the USA for all six countries under review, i.e. 39 years for non-residential structures and 14 years for machinery and equipment. I also assume that all assets are scrapped when their expected life expires. This (rectangular) assumption makes no allowance for accidents, fire damage, etc., but from evidence for countries where alternative retirement patterns have been tested (i.e. France, Germany, the UK and USA) capital stock estimates are not very sensitive to plausible variations in retirement patterns.

I corrected the capital stock estimates for war damage, assuming 3 per cent loss in the UK from the second world war, 8 per cent in France, 10 per cent in the Netherlands, 16 per cent in Germany and 25.7 per cent in Japan. For France I also assumed 8 per cent war damage in the 1914–18 war. The source of these estimates is indicated in the country notes. For simplicity of calculation, I assumed the impact of the damage to be concentrated on the year 1945. I assumed that war damage affected all of the relevant vintages of capital equally. Thus for non-residential structures, the impact of the second world war on retirements lasted until 1984, and for machinery and equipment until 1959. Most descriptions of official estimates of capital stock make no mention of how or whether war damage is incorporated in the calculations.

My estimates are for mid-year. Thus, the stock estimates shown in Tables 7a to 7f are derived by cumulating investment (from Tables 8a to 8f) over the expected life of the relevant asset. For machinery and equipment, gross investment in the 14 years 1978–91 is cumulated to get the end 1991 stock, and the end 1990 stock represents cumulation over the years 1977–90. The mid-year 1991 stock shown in Tables 7a to 7f is the average of the end year figures for 1990 and 1991. This holds true in all cases except when war damage was involved.

The estimates include all non-residential structures, machinery, equipment and vehicles. They exclude land and natural resources, intangibles such as human capital or the stock of knowledge, precious metals, international monetary reserves, foreign assets, increases in inventories, livestock, consumer durables, ancient monuments, works of art and military items.

My estimates are carried back a good deal further than official estimates, i.e. to 1820 for the UK, 1890 for the USA, 1900 and 1925 for Japan, 1935 for Germany, and 1950 for France and the Netherlands. In the case of Japan and the USA, I have linked my perpetual inventory estimates to those of other investigators for earlier years, so that we have a three-country comparison for 1890 and a crude binary comparison for the UK and USA for 1820.

In order to enhance intercountry comparability I have shown all the capital stock estimates in 1990 'international' dollars, using the Geary-Khamis purchasing power parity (PPP) converters of OECD (1993a), rather than exchange rates. I have also presented the estimates in national currency, so it is relatively easy for the reader to use one of the other PPPs which are available (Paasche, Laspeyres or Fisher).

The major data problem in deriving such estimates is the assembly of the relevant investment series for the two major asset classes in constant prices. Except in the USA, where a more or less complete investment series at 1987 prices was available from the US Department of Commerce, the constant price investment series involved linkage of separate segments with different weighting bases which were converted into a single national *numeraire*, e.g. the UK investment figures were expressed in 1985 prices, but in fact they involve linkage of figures from 1780 to 1851 at 1851–60 prices, 1851–1920 at 1900 prices, 1920–48 at 1938 prices, and 1948–91 at 1985 prices. There is no clear case for preferring the US procedure of a single weighting system for such a long period instead of a linked segment approach. However, the fact that there are differences in the temporal segments between countries does reduce the comparability of the results. Standardisation of the national weighting bases, and testing the sensitivity of the results to such variations is obviously a desirable target for future research. However, it should be stressed that this element of non-comparability in the present standardisation exercise is also a shortcoming of the existing official estimates which are based on similar linkages.

There are some breaks in the historical investment series or inadequate continuity in the price deflators, and for this reason there was some degree of interpolation of investment in war years in France, Japan and the Netherlands as indicated in the country notes. There was also a discrepancy between the Feinstein (1972) and Feinstein (1988) estimates for the link year 1920. Feinstein (1988) estimates 1920 investment in non-residential structures to be about 30 per cent higher and machinery and equipment about 22 per cent higher than Feinstein (1972) (in both cases I have adjusted for the change in geographic coverage for that year). By linking the two estimates I ignored these differences in level. The investment series used by the CSO in constructing the official capital stock take no cognisance of Feinstein (1972) and (1988), but only of Feinstein (1965).

The advantage of a do-it-yourself approach to estimating capital stock is not only that it corrects for incomparabilities in official stock estimates and permits one to push back the estimates further than the official measures, but it also provides comparable information on the age structure of assets which is not always available from official sources, and it enables one to experiment with and test the sensitivity of the results of alternative assumptions about asset lives and retirement patterns. It is possible to incorporate vintage assumptions about the impact of embodied technical change, to estimate net as well as gross stocks. In the process of making such comparisons, one becomes more intimate with some of the flaws in the existing investment series which would not otherwise be obvious. It is also possible to use the present material with alternative PPP converters to those which I have used.

In view of these advantages, it is not surprising that the practice of standardising capital stock measures has spread rapidly. Approaches similar to mine (which I first developed in Maddison, 1991) can be found in Hofman (1992), O'Mahony (1992 and 1993) and van Ark (1993). Summers and Heston (1991) incorporated standardised estimates of net stock per worker for 40 countries into their Penn World Tables for the years 1980–88. However, as they have only a short time series for investment, have rather short asset lives and assume very rapid depreciation, their results are not too compatible with mine.

Confrontation of official and standardised estimates in national currencies
Table 1 compares my results with the official estimates for Germany, the UK, and the USA. Such a comparison with the Netherlands is not possible as there are no official estimates for the whole economy. For France and Japan it would be misleading because the official figures exclude all publicly owned assets.

In 1950 the British official non-residential capital stock levels were 91 per cent higher than my standardised estimate and for Germany they were 39 per cent higher. The differences in level narrow over time, because both Germany and the UK assume declining lives of assets. As a consequence the official British and German estimates show slower growth rates for 1950–73 than the standardised figures.

The official estimates are more finely disaggregated than mine. Germany has 207 different types of non-residential asset (Lützel, 1977, p. 65). The UK has four types of non-residential asset whose lives vary across 36 industry divisions (CSO, 1985, p. 200). However these compositional differences are not likely to be a major reason for differences between the standardised and the official estimates, because my crude two-way asset breakdown replicates rather closely the US official figures though the latter are disaggregated into 64 kinds of equipment and 32 types of non-residential structures.

Conversion to a common numeraire by use of PPPs rather than exchange rates
I converted all the constant price capital stock estimates at national prices into 1990 prices and then converted them into 1990 international dollars using the multilateral (Geary-Khamis) purchasing power parities (PPPs) as a converter rather than the exchange rate (see Table 2a).

Table 1
Confrontation of Official Estimates of Non-Residential
Gross Fixed Capital Stocks
and My Standardised Estimates (in National Prices)
(all figures are adjusted to a mid-year basis)

	Standardised Estimate	Official Estimates	Ratio Official/ Standardised
Germany (billion 1985 DM)			
1950	766.3	1,062.3	139
1973	3,245.1	3,678.6	113
1987	5,159.6	5,729.8	111
UK (billion 1985 pounds)			
1950	178.7	341.6	191
1973	570.1	745.7	131
1987	870.3	1,055.2	121
USA (billion 1982 dollars)			
1926	1,952.6	2,055.1	105
1950	2,902.2	2,843.9	98
1973	6,053.2	6,180.4	102
1987	9,535.5	9,332.9	98

Sources: See Maddison (1993). This table is based on an earlier version of the present estimates where the national *numeraires* were for the years stated.

It can be seen from Table 2b that that price level for all these expenditure categories was higher in 1990 in the five follower countries than in the USA, and that the price of investment goods was higher than that for GDP as a whole in most cases. In all countries except the UK, the relative price of machinery and equipment was higher than for structures.

Some significant results
The main purpose of this paper is to provide standardised annual estimates of capital stock as a working tool for analysts of comparative economic performance, catch-up and convergence. However, it is worth highlighting some of the major results which emerge.

1. We can see in Table 4a that the ratio of the non-residential capital stock to GDP (the capital–output ratio) has not been stable over the long term, and has varied a good deal between countries. In the USA, the capital output ratio peaked in 1913 at a level more than three and a half times that in the UK and Japan. In the postwar period, in which the follower

Table 2a
1990 Geary Khamis Purchasing Power Parities and Exchange Rates
(units of national currency per US dollar)

	Machinery & Equipment	Non-Residential Structures	GDP	Exchange Rate
France	9.1100	6.1513	6.4502	5.43
Germany	2.7200	2.09512	2.0518	1.61
Japan	229.230	197.560	185.271	145.00
Netherlands	2.7900	2.4921	2.0840	1.82
UK	0.84622	0.8600	0.58695	0.561
USA	1.00000	1.00000	1.00000	1.00000

Table 2b
1990 Price Level Relative to USA
(purchasing power parity divided by exchange rate)

	Investment in Machinery & Equipment	Investment in Non-Residential Structures	Expenditure on GDP
France	1.678	1.133	1.188
Germany	1.689	1.301	1.274
Japan	1.581	1.362	1.278
Netherlands	1.533	1.369	1.145
UK	1.508	1.533	1.046
USA	1.000	1.000	1.000

Source: PPPs and exchange rates derived from OECD (1993a). Non-residential construction is the weighted average for each country of 'non-residential construction', and 'civil engineering works'.

countries made significant headway in catching up on the USA, their capital stock (see Table 3b) grew at unprecedented rates. Their capital–output ratios have risen sharply, and are now much closer to that in the USA. Thus the evidence flatly contradicts Kaldor's (1961) assumption, which was widely shared, that the capital–output ratio has been steady over long periods in capitalist countries. He asserted (p. 178) as a 'stylised fact', 'the near-identity of the percentage rates of growth of production and of the capital stock'.

2.   In the process of attaining economic leadership in the nineteenth century, the USA achieved a huge advantage over the old leader, the UK, in terms of capital stock per head and capital stock in relation to GDP. Thus our evidence flatly contradicts Field (1983) p. 407 when he asserts that the capital–labour and the capital–output ratios 'in Britain exceeded their American values by a factor of at least three in midcentury'. Thus my estimates throw new light on an old controversy about the roots of US economic growth. It must be added that the margin of error in my calculations for this period is significant, but within the

Table 3a
Level of Total Gross Fixed Non-Residential Capital Stock
Per Capita 1820–1991
(in 1990 Geary Khamis $)

	1820	1890	1913	1950	1973	1991
France	n.a.	n.a.	n.a.	8,516	20,075	39,341
Germany	n.a.	n.a.	n.a.	7,754	25,510	44,918
Japan	n.a.	691	1,180	3,337	19,209	55,097
Netherlands	n.a.	n.a.	n.a.	12,403	25,210	37,786
UK	1,201	3,438	4,230	5,535	15,792	27,640
USA	1,222	10,355	17,514	23,321	35,127	51,932

Source: Tables 7a-7f divided by population. US capital stock for 1820 derived from Gallmann (1986 and 1987) as described in the country notes for the USA.

Table 3b
Rate of Growth of Total Fixed Non-Residential Capital Stock per Capita
(annual average compound growth rate, in 1990 Geary Khamis $)

	1820–90	1890–1913	1913–50	1950–73	1973–91
France	n.a.	n.a.	n.a.	3.8	3.8
Germany	n.a.	n.a.	n.a.	5.3	3.2
Japan	n.a.	1.6	2.8	7.9	6.0
Netherlands	n.a.	n.a.	n.a.	3.3	2.3
UK	1.5	0.9	0.7	4.7	3.2
USA	3.1	2.3	0.8	1.8	2.2

Source: Derived from Table 3(a).

Table 4a
Ratio of Total Gross Non-Residential Capital Stock to GDP 1820–1991
(in 1990 Geary Khamis $)

	1820	1890	1913	1950	1973	1991
France	n.a.	n.a.	n.a.	1.63	1.55	2.22
Germany	n.a.	n.a.	n.a.	1.81	1.94	2.32
Japan	n.a.	0.71	0.88	1.77	1.74	2.86
Netherlands	n.a.	n.a.	n.a.	2.06	1.98	2.25
UK	0.68	0.84	0.87	0.81	1.32	1.74
USA	0.95	3.05	3.30	2.44	2.12	2.43

Source: Capital stock derived from Tables 7a to 7f, GDP from Maddison (1994).

Table 4b

Ratio of Gross Stock of Machinery and Equipment to Total Non-Residential
Gross Stock (mid-year estimates)
(at 1990 relative prices)

	1820	1890	1913	1950	1973	1991
France	n.a.	n.a.	n.a.	0.13	0.32	0.33
Germany	n.a.	n.a.	n.a.	0.22	0.32	0.31
Japan	n.a.	0.14	0.28	0.42	0.33	0.35
Netherlands	n.a.	n.a.	n.a.	0.13	0.31	0.34
UK	0.08	0.14	0.22	0.38	0.39	0.36
USA	0.07	0.15	0.16	0.26	0.31	0.35

Source: Derived from Tables 7a to 7f.

Table 5a

Average Age (in years) of Non-Residential Structures at end-year

	1890	1913	1950	1973	1991
France	n.a.	n.a.	19.88	12.60	15.40
Germany	n.a.	n.a.	18.85	12.37	16.99
Japan	n.a.	n.a.	14.70	8.78	13.06
Netherlands	n.a.	n.a.	19.78	13.48	17.74[a]
UK	18.29	18.81	18.14	12.57	16.44
USA	14.69	15.05	19.28	14.78	17.59

a) 1990.

Table 5b

Average Age (in years) of Machinery and Equipment at end-year

	1890	1913	1950	1973	1991
France	n.a.	n.a.	6.32	6.15	6.90
Germany	n.a.	n.a.	8.02	6.61	6.95
Japan	n.a.	5.87	8.40	5.59	6.05
Netherlands	n.a.	n.a.	5.88	6.75	6.76[a]
UK	7.48	7.60	7.25	6.93	6.81
USA	7.20	6.85	6.35	6.48	7.08

a) 1990.

Source: Derived from computer worksheets

margins which seem likely, there is no possibility that Field's assertion can be correct. Nevertheless, his belief is shared by others, e.g. James and Skinner (1985, p. 514), Engerman (in Gallman and Wallis, 1992, p. 119) and Broadberry (1993, p. 783).

Table 6
Total Gross Non-Residential Capital Stock of the USA
and the Five Follower Countries 1950 and 1991
(billion 1990 Geary Khamis dollars)

	——— 1950 ———		——— 1991 ———	
	USA	Five Followers	USA	Five Followers
Machinery and Equipment	930	368	4,622	4,741
Non-Residential Structures	2,621	1,053	8,501	9,364
Total Non-Residential	3,551	1,421	13,123	14,105

Source: Derived from Tables 7a to 7f.

3. We can get some clues about the changing composition and age structure of the capital stock which throw some light on possible changes in the rate at which technical change has been embodied in the capital stock. Thus we see over the very long run that the share of machinery and equipment in the total stock has risen (Table 4b). As there is reason to think that technical progress may be faster in machinery and equipment than in structures, this may help explain why productivity growth has been faster in the twentieth century than in the nineteenth. However, it should be noted that the equipment share has not risen monotonically. We can also see that the average age of the capital stock fell in the follower countries in the postwar golden age. The accelerated growth of capital stock led to a larger share for the newer vintages of capital. When economic growth slowed down after 1973, the average age of capital rose in virtually all cases (Tables 5a and 5b).

4. We can also get some idea of the changing geographic locus of the technological frontier. Table 6 compares the level of the aggregate non-residential capital stock in the USA and the five follower countries. In 1950 the total stock in the five follower countries was only two fifths of that in the USA, whereas in 1991 it was bigger. Technological progress depends to an important extent on the scope which engineers, entrepreneurs and managers have to test out new ideas by embodying them in the capital stock. In the past the scope in this respect for Americans was clearly bigger than in the follower countries. Now the followers have a relatively greater scope for experimentation and learning-from-doing. This means that the sources of technological progress have become more widely diffused, all the more so as the ease of transnational communication between the follower countries has improved dramatically in the past half-century.

Country Source Notes

France

1910–38 investment in structures and 1935–38 in equipment from Carré, Dubois and Malinvaud (1972), p. 652, with interpolation where necessary for 1913–22. 1938–50 investment from Maddison (1972) assuming both types of investment to move parallel; 1950–68 from OECD (1970) at 1963 prices, linked to 1968–75 at 1970 prices; 1975–91 at 1980 prices from subsequent issues of the same OECD publication. Eight per cent war damage was assumed for each of the two world wars: see Présidence du Conseil (1948–51).

Germany

1950–91 investment at 1985 prices from Federal Statistical Office (1991) and OECD national accounts, linked to earlier years at 1954 prices from Kirner (1968) pp. 103–5 for non-residential structures (back to 1850) and pp. 106–7 for equipment (partial from 1900, complete from 1930). Kirner estimated war damage to be about 16 per cent. The official capital stock estimates quoted in Table 1 above for 1960–87 are from the Federal Statistical Office (1991) linked to earlier official estimates for 1950–60. The official estimates of capital stock are based on the same investment series I used for 1950 onwards. For earlier years the statistical office also used Kirner's estimates but made some adjustments based on postwar wealth surveys. The detail of these adjustments is not in the public domain.

Japan

1885–1940 investment by type of asset at 1934–6 prices from Ohkawa and Shinohara (1979), p. 357–61. 1940–52 total non-residential investment at 1934–6 prices (adjusted to a calendar year basis) from Ohkawa and Rosovsky (1973) pp. 292–3. 1945 gross investment was missing and was assumed to be half that of 1944. This source does not show a breakdown of non-residential investment by type of asset at constant prices, so 1941–5 machinery and equipment investment was assumed to be the same proportion of total non-residential fixed investment as in 1940 and for 1946–51 it was assumed to be the same proportion of the total as in 1952. 1952–70 investment by type of asset at current prices from EPA (Economic Planning Agency) (1969) and EPA (1975) adjusted to a calendar year basis. EPA does not provide deflators for 1952–70, so I deflated each type of asset by the overall deflator (in 1965 prices) for non-residential investment which is implicit in Ohkawa and Shinohara (1979) pp. 363 and 365. 1970–91 investment in 1985 prices from EPA (1990 and 1991) and OECD National accounts. The volume movements for earlier years were linked at 1970. War damage was taken to be 25.7 per cent of pre-1946 investment, see Bank of Japan (1966), p. 27. As a proxy for the 1890–1924 stock of non-residential structures, and for the 1890–99 stock of machinery and equipment I used the stock estimates in Ohkawa and Shinohara, pp. 366–7, to link with my perpetual inventory estimates.

Netherlands

Gross investment 1921–39 and 1948–90 at 1980 prices by type of asset was supplied by CBS. 1910–21 and 1939–48 figures were not available from CBS and as a proxy I assumed both types of asset to move parallel to machinery and equipment investment by enterprises at 1970 prices from Appendix 7.2 of den Hartog and Tjan (1979). This source puts war damage at 35 per cent, probably based on the official (*Memorandum*, 1945) estimates made to back claims for reparations. However, this is well out of line with Kirner's estimate of 16 per cent war damage for Germany. Van Zanden and Griffiths (1989), pp. 185–7, acknowledge the overestimate of war damage in the official sources, which apart from being exaggerated for bargaining purposes, also included disinvestment and a very large estimate for inventory losses. I assumed Dutch war damage to have been 10 per cent of pre-1946 investment, i.e. significantly less than in Germany. The Netherlands does not yet have a comprehensive official estimate of capital stock. So far estimates have been prepared for agriculture, mining, manufacturing and dwellings, see CBS (1991).

United Kingdom
Annual estimates of fixed investment at 1985 prices for 1948 to 1991 were provided by the Central Statistical Office. These were linked to 1920–48 estimates in 1938 prices from Feinstein (1972). These were, in their turn, linked backward to the movement shown for 1780–1920 in Feinstein (1988), pp. 446–7. For 1851–1920 they are at 1900 prices and include the whole of Ireland. For 1780–1851 they exclude Ireland and are at 1851–60 prices; for this period I had to unscramble Feinstein's decade averages, prorating growth between the decade midpoints to get rough annual figures. I assumed war damage to be 3 per cent of pre-1946 investment. Hancock and Gowing (1949), p. 551 give a figure of 10 per cent for physical destruction and domestic disinvestment. But I have excluded the latter, as its effects are already contained in our accumulation accounts.

United States
United States official (US Department of Commerce, 1993) capital stock figures start with the year 1925, and the official investment figures were assembled with this date in mind. Hence there are zero entries for several kinds of investment for early years as these were not necessary for the official purpose. As my annual estimates of capital stock start in 1890, I had to make a rough estimate for investment missing in the official figures, i.e. 1850–93 for private non-residential structures and 1875–97 for private investment in equipment. Detailed figures for 22 types of equipment, 6 types of non-residential building and eight other types of structure are given by the Department of Commerce. For the missing categories, I simply assumed that investment in the earlier years with a zero entry was the same as in the year for which the first entry was available (excluding items such as autos and aircraft where such an assumption would have been anachronistic). The missing items were particularly large for equipment in the early years and not negligible for structures. In Table 3 I have included a rough estimate for US capital stock per capita in 1820. The link 1820–90 was derived from volume movements shown in Gallman (1986 and 1987). Gallman (1987) gives alternative perpetual inventory estimates of gross stock for 1840–90. I selected the option where his asset life assumptions were nearest to mine. The 1820–40 movement I derived from the wealth survey estimates in Gallman (1986). The 1820 figure for the gross stock of non-residential structures was 10,876 million 1990 dollars, for machinery and equipment 873 million.

Table 7a
France: Gross Stock of Fixed Non-Residential Capital at 1990 Prices at Midyear

Year	Gross Stock of Non-Residential Structures	Gross Stock of Machinery and Equipment	Gross Stock of Non-Residential Structures	Gross Stock of Machinery and Equipment
	(million 1990 Francs)		(million 1990 Geary-Khamis $)	
1950	1,910,411	416,415	310,572	45,710
1951	1,935,269	439,909	314,613	48,289
1952	1,952,692	464,102	317,446	50,944
1953	1,967,593	491,091	319,868	53,907
1954	1,990,245	530,499	323,551	58,233
1955	2,025,644	588,475	329,306	64,597
1956	2,070,932	658,281	336,668	72,259
1957	2,130,003	739,078	346,271	81,128
1958	2,199,557	827,872	357,578	90,875
1959	2,272,603	924,087	369,453	101,437
1960	2,351,199	1,020,020	382,231	111,967
1961	2,438,171	1,113,536	396,369	122,232
1962	2,533,464	1,209,365	411,861	132,751
1963	2,629,428	1,309,839	427,462	143,780
1964	2,735,108	1,422,465	444,642	156,143
1965	2,853,876	1,543,201	463,950	169,396
1966	2,993,654	1,676,233	486,673	183,999
1967	3,158,146	1,824,931	513,414	200,322
1968	3,325,522	1,985,492	540,624	217,946
1969	3,495,637	2,168,223	568,280	238,005
1970	3,684,030	2,369,339	598,907	260,081
1971	3,891,398	2,584,124	632,618	283,658
1972	4,116,523	2,820,780	669,216	309,636
1973	4,355,753	3,080,870	708,107	338,185
1974	4,598,931	3,345,441	747,640	367,227
1975	4,844,016	3,582,509	787,484	393,250
1976	5,091,747	3,811,701	827,757	418,408
1977	5,340,043	4,046,230	868,122	444,153
1978	5,585,706	4,270,864	908,059	468,811
1979	5,850,734	4,498,259	951,144	493,772
1980	6,139,962	4,735,372	998,163	519,799
1981	6,433,191	4,965,870	1,045,833	545,101
1982	6,726,937	5,177,098	1,093,587	568,287
1983	7,014,966	5,352,244	1,140,411	587,513
1984	7,294,706	5,487,177	1,185,888	602,325
1985	7,559,599	5,611,736	1,228,951	615,997
1986	7,814,500	5,737,877	1,270,390	629,844
1987	8,067,622	5,862,776	1,311,540	643,554
1988	8,331,907	6,018,649	1,354,504	660,664
1989	8,620,018	6,243,326	1,401,342	685,327
1990	8,929,259	6,496,667	1,451,615	713,136
1991	9,261,557	6,730,298	1,505,636	738,781

Table 7b
Germany: Gross Stock of Fixed Non-Residential Capital in 1990 Prices at Midyear

Year	Gross Stock of Non-Residential Structures	Gross Stock of Machinery and Equipment	Gross Stock of Non-Residential Structures	Gross Stock of Machinery and Equipment
	(million 1990 DM)		(million 1990 Geary-Khamis $)	
1935	734,348	188,705	350,504	69,377
1936	743,947	189,326	355,085	69,605
1937	755,693	193,210	360,692	71,033
1938	770,691	201,344	367,851	74,024
1939	787,647	210,905	375,944	77,539
1940	800,214	220,057	381,942	80,903
1941	805,740	227,881	384,579	83,780
1942	803,308	233,982	383,419	86,023
1943	792,604	238,953	378,310	87,850
1944	776,438	241,198	370,593	88,676
1945	705,791	223,019	336,874	81,992
1946	638,366	205,068	304,692	75,393
1947	629,819	205,896	300,613	75,697
1948	628,513	208,794	299,989	76,762
1949	631,806	216,354	301,561	79,542
1950	636,897	227,275	303,990	83,557
1951	643,833	238,623	307,301	87,729
1952	654,816	249,546	312,544	91,745
1953	673,244	260,913	321,339	95,924
1954	699,498	276,204	333,870	101,546
1955	735,658	299,132	351,129	109,975
1956	782,158	328,204	373,324	120,663
1957	835,260	359,417	398,669	132,139
1958	892,378	395,754	425,932	145,498
1959	953,070	443,002	454,900	162,868
1960	1,017,471	501,082	485,639	184,221
1961	1,084,974	566,667	517,858	208,333
1962	1,158,329	634,482	552,870	233,265
1963	1,237,804	697,675	590,803	256,498
1964	1,325,145	758,870	632,491	278,996
1965	1,419,506	823,994	677,530	302,939
1966	1,513,845	889,428	722,558	326,995
1967	1,600,905	947,603	764,112	348,384
1968	1,684,485	1,000,472	804,004	367,821
1969	1,778,674	1,058,341	848,961	389,096
1970	1,889,817	1,128,665	902,009	414,951
1971	2,014,251	1,210,153	961,401	444,909
1972	2,140,189	1,292,128	1,021,511	475,047
1973	2,258,880	1,367,667	1,078,163	502,819
1974	2,369,407	1,427,749	1,130,917	524,908
1975	2,471,623	1,471,674	1,179,705	541,057
1976	2,568,015	1,512,344	1,225,713	556,009
1977	2,660,538	1,558,586	1,269,874	573,010
1978	2,752,242	1,611,539	1,313,644	592,477
1979	2,852,551	1,669,482	1,361,522	613,780
1980	2,962,310	1,733,348	1,413,910	637,260
1981	3,073,801	1,800,345	1,467,124	661,892
1982	3,184,163	1,859,103	1,519,800	683,494
1983	3,295,424	1,903,981	1,572,905	699,993
1984	3,408,006	1,934,074	1,626,640	711,057
1985	3,519,064	1,958,633	1,679,648	720,086
1986	3,630,739	1,992,161	1,732,950	732,412
1987	3,742,241	2,035,239	1,786,170	748,250
1988	3,848,860	2,095,664	1,837,059	770,465
1989	3,953,250	2,177,543	1,886,885	800,567
1990	4,059,255	2,277,851	1,937,481	837,445
1991	4,168,681	2,393,748	1,989,710	880,054

Table 7c
Japan: Gross Stock of Fixed Non-Residential Capital in 1990 Prices at Midyear

Year	Gross Stock of Non-Residential Structures	Gross Stock of Machinery and Equipment	Gross Stock of Non-Residential Structures	Gross Stock of Machinery and Equipment
	(Billion 1990 Yen)		(Million 1990 Geary-Khamis $)	
1890	5,448 *	779 *	23,767 *	3,946
1891	5,480 *	814 *	23,907 *	4,122
1892	5,606 *	842 *	24,455 *	4,261
1893	5,656 *	882 *	24,676 *	4,465
1894	5,787 *	970 *	25,246 *	4,910
1895	5,925 *	1,046 *	25,849 *	5,295
1896	6,168 *	1,132 *	26,908 *	5,731
1897	6,417 *	1,271 *	27,995 *	6,435
1898	6,521 *	1,426 *	28,447 *	7,219
1899	6,648 *	1,520 *	29,001 *	7,692
1900	6,802 *	1,639	29,674 *	8,294
1901	6,918 *	1,713	30,179 *	8,671
1902	7,061 *	1,759	30,803 *	8,901
1903	7,174 *	1,795	31,298 *	9,087
1904	7,267 *	1,857	31,702 *	9,400
1905	7,426 *	1,978	32,396 *	10,014
1906	7,654 *	2,144	33,391 *	10,851
1907	7,971 *	2,302	34,773 *	11,654
1908	8,251 *	2,461	35,994 *	12,456
1909	8,584 *	2,605	37,447 *	13,187
1910	8,921 *	2,724	38,916 *	13,789
1911	9,319 *	2,871	40,653 *	14,530
1912	9,741 *	3,076	42,493 *	15,568
1913	10,088 *	3,354	44,010 *	16,979
1914	10,399 *	3,659	45,366 *	18,522
1915	10,709 *	3,920	46,716 *	19,840
1916	10,984 *	4,226	47,916 *	21,392
1917	11,329 *	4,739	49,422 *	23,987
1918	11,638 *	5,549	50,772 *	28,089
1919	12,038 *	6,505	52,515 *	32,928
1920	12,615 *	7,458	55,033 *	37,748
1921	13,123 *	8,272	57,249 *	41,872
1922	13,751 *	8,821	59,987 *	44,648
1923	14,301 *	9,188	62,386 *	46,506
1924	14,855 *	9,503	64,802 *	48,103
1925	15,580	9,784	67,968	49,524
1926	16,706	10,022	72,878	50,731
1927	17,932	10,271	78,227	51,989
1928	19,119	10,557	83,404	53,438
1929	20,268	10,934	88,416	55,344
1930	21,406	11,317	93,380	57,282
1931	22,484	11,396	98,083	57,684
1932	23,489	11,058	102,467	55,972
1933	24,475	10,593	106,772	53,617
1934	25,536	10,313	111,399	52,201
1935	26,730	10,417	116,606	52,730
1936	27,984	10,932	122,080	55,337
1937	29,228	11,712	127,507	59,282
1938	30,507	12,835	133,085	64,967
1939	31,912	14,597	139,214	73,887
1940	33,113	16,923	144,452	85,659
1941	34,027	19,488	148,441	98,646
1942	34,891	21,916	152,212	110,932
1943	35,823	24,398	156,275	123,496
1944	36,891	27,181	160,933	137,584
1945	32,732	25,371	142,791	128,423
1946	28,863	22,279	125,914	112,773
1947	30,777	22,591	134,264	114,349
1948	33,031	22,868	144,094	115,752
1949	35,205	22,956	153,581	116,198

Table 7c (cont.)
Japan: Gross Stock of Fixed Non-Residential Capital in 1990 Prices at Midyear

Year	Gross Stock of Non-Residential Structures	Gross Stock of Machinery and Equipment	Gross Stock of Non-Residential Structures	Gross Stock of Machinery and Equipment
	(Billion 1990 Yen)		(Million 1990 Geary-Khamis $)	
1950	36,957	22,800	161,223	115,409
1951	38,644	22,548	168,583	114,131
1952	40,774	22,219	177,874	112,466
1953	43,459	21,648	189,586	109,578
1954	46,606	20,806	203,314	105,315
1955	50,024	19,753	218,224	99,985
1956	53,879	18,952	235,043	95,928
1957	58,275	18,468	254,220	93,482
1958	63,027	18,088	274,949	91,559
1959	68,254	18,702	297,753	94,665
1960	74,578	21,030	325,340	106,446
1961	82,736	24,596	360,928	124,498
1962	92,646	28,843	404,161	145,999
1963	103,717	33,667	452,457	170,414
1964	115,877	39,282	505,505	198,837
1965	128,596	45,396	560,990	229,782
1966	141,985	51,804	619,398	262,217
1967	159,598	59,103	696,235	299,163
1968	180,120	68,336	785,762	345,899
1969	201,798	80,182	880,330	405,861
1970	227,175	93,859	991,034	475,090
1971	255,323	107,932	1,113,831	546,324
1972	285,533	122,250	1,245,617	618,798
1973	318,282	138,051	1,388,481	698,778
1974	351,335	153,382	1,532,674	776,379
1975	383,573	166,007	1,673,312	840,286
1976	415,859	177,587	1,814,156	898,899
1977	448,472	189,364	1,956,429	958,513
1978	482,783	201,713	2,106,106	1,021,024
1979	519,867	215,624	2,267,885	1,091,437
1980	559,105	230,567	2,439,055	1,167,072
1981	599,302	245,440	2,614,412	1,242,354
1982	639,348	259,387	2,789,110	1,312,951
1983	678,353	271,594	2,959,266	1,374,742
1984	717,221	284,058	3,128,826	1,437,830
1985	756,014	299,219	3,298,060	1,514,571
1986	794,599	316,413	3,466,384	1,601,603
1987	834,174	334,477	3,639,027	1,693,039
1988	876,103	357,288	3,821,937	1,808,504
1989	921,812	388,148	4,021,341	1,964,712
1990	971,241	425,531	4,236,974	2,153,935
1991	1,023,677	466,623	4,465,722	2,361,932

* these figures are not derived by the perpetual inventory method, but are estimates derived from Ohkawa and Shinohara (1979), pp. 366-8.

Table 7d
Netherlands: Gross Stock of Fixed Non-Residential Capital in 1990 Prices

Year	Gross Stock of Non-Residential Structures	Gross Stock of Machinery and Equipment	Gross Stock of Non-Residential Structures	Gross Stock of Machinery and Equipment
	(million 1990 guilders)		(million 1990 Geary-Khamis $)	
1950	263,733	44,580	105,827	15,978
1951	269,258	48,550	108,045	17,401
1952	274,016	51,229	109,954	18,362
1953	279,995	53,727	112,353	19,257
1954	287,183	58,594	115,237	21,002
1955	294,663	66,761	118,239	23,929
1956	303,208	77,588	121,668	27,809
1957	312,144	90,240	125,253	32,344
1958	320,342	102,420	128,543	36,710
1959	328,415	114,289	131,783	40,964
1960	337,878	126,920	135,580	45,491
1961	348,995	138,892	140,040	49,782
1962	361,778	150,007	145,170	53,766
1963	375,540	160,784	150,692	57,629
1964	392,077	171,506	157,328	61,472
1965	410,523	183,161	164,730	65,649
1966	429,182	196,807	172,217	70,540
1967	449,631	211,564	180,422	75,829
1968	472,183	226,675	189,472	81,246
1969	494,526	240,369	198,437	86,154
1970	516,102	252,994	207,095	90,679
1971	539,127	265,589	216,334	95,193
1972	561,840	278,266	225,449	99,737
1973	582,585	293,024	233,773	105,027
1974	602,393	308,348	241,721	110,519
1975	622,298	321,539	249,708	115,247
1976	642,499	331,693	257,814	118,886
1977	661,755	342,379	265,541	122,716
1978	680,117	355,125	272,909	127,285
1979	700,355	367,810	281,030	131,831
1980	723,456	378,571	290,300	135,688
1981	746,730	385,621	299,639	138,216
1982	768,529	389,314	308,386	139,539
1983	789,819	393,822	316,929	141,155
1984	811,698	400,261	325,709	143,463
1985	832,984	411,815	334,250	147,604
1986	851,760	430,954	341,784	154,464
1987	868,302	450,692	348,422	161,538
1988	884,933	467,732	355,095	167,646
1989	902,782	486,441	362,257	174,352
1990	921,382	510,187	369,721	182,863
1991	941,235	534,981	377,687	191,749
1992	960,562	557,846	385,443	199,945

Table 7e
UK: Gross Stock of Fixed Non-Residential Capital in 1990 Prices at Midyear

Year	Gross Stock of Non-Residential Structures	Gross Stock of Machinery and Equipment	Gross Stock of Non-Residential Structures	Gross Stock of Machinery and Equipment
	(Million 1990 Pounds)		(million 1990 Geary-Khamis $)	
1820	18,546	1,633	21,916	1,899
1821	18,847	1,665	22,272	1,936
1822	19,147	1,701	22,627	1,978
1823	19,455	1,741	22,990	2,025
1824	19,768	1,785	23,360	2,076
1825	20,087	1,834	23,738	2,132
1826	20,415	1,888	24,124	2,195
1827	20,756	1,946	24,528	2,263
1828	21,117	2,009	24,955	2,336
1829	21,499	2,078	25,406	2,416
1830	21,895	2,152	25,873	2,502
1831	22,308	2,230	26,362	2,593
1832	22,749	2,312	26,883	2,689
1833	23,214	2,398	27,433	2,788
1834	23,705	2,488	28,012	2,893
1835	24,224	2,581	28,626	3,001
1836	24,781	2,677	29,284	3,113
1837	25,384	2,777	29,997	3,229
1838	26,039	2,880	30,771	3,349
1839	26,749	2,988	31,610	3,474
1840	27,523	3,100	32,525	3,604
1841	28,440	3,214	33,609	3,737
1842	29,500	3,329	34,860	3,871
1843	30,634	3,448	36,202	4,010
1844	31,849	3,571	37,637	4,152
1845	33,147	3,697	39,171	4,299
1846	34,499	3,828	40,769	4,451
1847	35,843	3,964	42,356	4,609
1848	37,146	4,107	43,896	4,776
1849	38,408	4,258	45,388	4,951
1850	39,630	4,416	46,832	5,135
1851	40,744	4,586	48,148	5,333
1852	41,791	4,769	49,385	5,546
1853	42,807	4,973	50,586	5,782
1854	43,797	5,239	51,756	6,092
1855	44,802	5,552	52,943	6,456
1856	45,747	5,807	54,061	6,752
1857	46,671	5,971	55,152	6,943
1858	47,619	6,085	56,272	7,076
1859	48,650	6,188	57,491	7,196
1860	49,784	6,335	58,831	7,366
1861	51,042	6,532	60,317	7,596
1862	52,415	6,764	61,940	7,866
1863	53,898	7,070	63,692	8,221
1864	55,496	7,484	65,581	8,702
1865	57,234	7,941	67,635	9,234
1866	59,009	8,346	69,733	9,704
1867	60,543	8,642	71,545	10,048
1868	61,821	8,797	73,055	10,230
1869	62,957	8,880	74,398	10,325
1870	64,082	9,064	75,727	10,539
1871	65,336	9,443	77,210	10,981
1872	66,754	9,950	78,885	11,570
1873	68,267	10,447	80,673	12,148
1874	69,956	10,913	82,669	12,689
1875	71,793	11,372	84,840	13,223
1876	73,635	11,788	87,016	13,707
1877	75,451	12,152	89,163	14,130
1878	77,184	12,364	91,210	14,377
1879	78,752	12,453	93,064	14,480

Continued overleaf

Table 7e (cont.)
UK: Gross Stock of Fixed Non-Residential Capital in 1990 Prices at Midyear

Year	Gross Stock of Non-Residential Structures	Gross Stock of Machinery and Equipment	Gross Stock of Non-Residential Structures	Gross Stock of Machinery and Equipment
	(Million 1990 Pounds)		(million 1990 Geary-Khamis $)	
1880	80,020	12,558	94,562	14,602
1881	81,100	12,788	95,838	14,869
1882	82,078	13,147	96,993	15,287
1883	82,909	13,606	97,976	15,821
1884	83,785	13,979	99,011	16,255
1885	84,600	14,126	99,974	16,426
1886	85,202	14,102	100,686	16,398
1887	85,748	14,048	101,331	16,334
1888	86,302	14,067	101,985	16,356
1889	86,897	14,179	102,688	16,487
1890	87,666	14,385	103,597	16,727
1891	88,599	14,606	104,700	16,984
1892	89,616	14,900	105,901	17,325
1893	90,710	15,247	107,194	17,729
1894	91,862	15,619	108,556	18,161
1895	93,163	16,019	110,094	18,627
1896	94,602	16,458	111,794	19,137
1897	96,220	16,962	113,705	19,724
1898	98,062	17,748	115,883	20,638
1899	100,031	18,911	118,209	21,990
1900	101,988	20,295	120,522	23,599
1901	103,982	21,831	122,878	25,385
1902	106,124	23,375	125,409	27,180
1903	108,184	24,822	127,844	28,862
1904	109,951	26,230	129,931	30,500
1905	111,513	27,641	131,777	32,140
1906	113,136	28,927	133,695	33,636
1907	114,697	30,007	135,540	34,892
1908	115,873	30,746	136,930	35,752
1909	116,806	31,330	138,033	36,430
1910	117,652	31,981	139,032	37,188
1911	118,337	32,640	139,841	37,953
1912	118,883	33,199	140,487	38,604
1913	119,427	33,673	141,130	39,155
1914	119,915	34,211	141,707	39,780
1915	119,829	34,476	141,605	40,088
1916	118,998	34,177	140,623	39,741
1917	117,865	33,761	139,285	39,257
1918	116,886	33,761	138,127	39,257
1919	116,556	34,430	137,737	40,035
1920	117,294	35,577	138,610	41,369
1921	118,387	37,204	139,901	43,260
1922	119,114	39,267	140,760	45,659
1923	119,856	41,265	141,637	47,983
1924	120,951	43,376	142,931	50,437
1925	122,633	45,793	144,919	53,248
1926	124,386	47,914	146,990	55,714
1927	125,885	49,935	148,762	58,064
1928	127,377	52,577	150,525	61,136
1929	129,128	55,623	152,594	64,678
1930	131,573	58,788	155,484	68,358
1931	133,957	61,964	158,301	72,051
1932	135,447	64,269	160,061	74,731
1933	136,334	65,056	161,109	75,646
1934	137,289	65,859	162,238	76,580
1935	138,619	67,342	163,809	78,305
1936	140,217	69,406	165,698	80,704
1937	142,330	72,076	168,195	83,810
1938	144,657	74,693	170,945	86,853
1939	147,126	76,756	173,863	89,252

Table 7e (cont.)
UK: Gross Stock of Fixed Non-Residential Capital in 1990 Prices at Midyear

Year	Gross Stock of Non-Residential Structures	Gross Stock of Machinery and Equipment	Gross Stock of Non-Residential Structures	Gross Stock of Machinery and Equipment
	(Million 1990 Pounds)		(million 1990 Geary-Khamis $)	
1940	148,318	79,467	175,271	92,403
1941	147,287	82,231	174,053	95,618
1942	145,654	83,229	172,123	96,778
1943	143,787	82,770	169,916	96,244
1944	141,505	81,300	167,221	94,535
1945	137,388	78,171	162,355	90,897
1946	135,188	76,715	159,755	89,203
1947	136,904	79,577	161,783	92,532
1948	139,111	83,517	164,392	97,113
1949	141,807	87,642	167,577	101,910
1950	145,434	91,920	171,863	106,884
1951	149,552	96,253	176,730	111,923
1952	153,517	100,258	181,416	116,579
1953	157,901	104,143	186,596	121,097
1954	163,580	108,294	193,307	125,923
1955	170,911	113,506	201,970	131,984
1956	179,745	120,397	212,409	139,997
1957	189,557	129,143	224,005	150,166
1958	199,701	139,837	235,992	162,601
1959	209,142	151,571	247,149	176,245
1960	219,402	163,047	259,273	189,590
1961	232,216	173,551	274,415	201,804
1962	246,117	182,921	290,843	212,699
1963	259,790	191,217	307,000	222,346
1964	274,293	200,182	324,140	232,770
1965	290,804	210,373	343,650	244,620
1966	308,281	221,830	364,303	257,942
1967	326,947	234,402	386,362	272,561
1968	347,018	247,066	410,081	287,287
1969	367,070	258,746	433,776	300,867
1970	387,928	269,949	458,425	313,894
1971	410,527	280,721	485,130	326,419
1972	433,439	290,163	512,206	337,399
1973	456,016	299,956	538,886	348,786
1974	477,514	310,405	564,291	360,936
1975	498,131	318,955	588,654	370,878
1976	518,395	326,949	612,601	380,174
1977	537,508	336,131	635,187	390,851
1978	555,424	345,486	656,359	401,728
1979	573,917	355,563	678,212	413,445
1980	593,288	364,895	701,104	424,297
1981	612,250	370,735	723,512	431,087
1982	632,354	374,111	747,269	435,013
1983	654,332	378,128	773,241	439,683
1984	677,561	384,039	800,691	446,557
1985	700,308	393,050	827,572	457,034
1986	722,235	404,594	853,483	470,458
1987	746,482	416,461	882,137	484,257
1988	774,241	430,657	914,941	500,764
1989	804,086	450,619	950,209	523,976
1990	835,498	472,228	987,330	549,102
1991	867,486	488,710	1,025,131	568,268

Table 7f
USA: Gross Stock of Fixed Non-Residential Capital in 1990 Prices at Midyear

Year	Gross Stock of Non-Residential Structures	Gross Stock of Machinery and Equipment	Year	Gross Stock of Non-Residential Structures	Gross Stock of Machinery and Equipment
	(million 1990 US$)			(million 1990 US$)	
1890	554,811	98,120	1940	2,484,977	438,281
1891	581,630	100,171	1941	2,508,931	448,161
1892	606,240	102,640	1942	2,531,869	472,954
1893	630,305	105,416	1943	2,538,743	511,343
1894	652,516	107,486	1944	2,530,761	557,455
1895	674,295	108,813	1945	2,522,821	610,347
1896	698,889	111,450	1946	2,526,588	668,864
1897	727,006	114,016	1947	2,543,146	736,514
1898	756,602	115,708	1948	2,566,002	812,050
1899	787,785	119,173	1949	2,591,536	875,941
1900	821,937	125,216	1950	2,620,695	930,386
1901	858,859	131,974	1951	2,658,250	985,605
1902	903,732	139,372	1952	2,701,940	1,048,233
1903	955,856	148,819	1953	2,758,111	1,117,880
1904	1,006,309	157,742	1954	2,830,890	1,180,296
1905	1,052,355	166,468	1955	2,910,861	1,233,434
1906	1,097,129	179,300	1956	2,998,397	1,279,688
1907	1,144,931	196,131	1957	3,098,349	1,309,743
1908	1,192,147	209,596	1958	3,200,357	1,322,863
1909	1,236,948	218,865	1959	3,293,465	1,335,407
1910	1,285,273	228,940	1960	3,388,731	1,360,669
1911	1,334,914	239,522	1961	3,491,483	1,382,686
1912	1,383,992	252,504	1962	3,592,296	1,397,754
1913	1,434,437	268,359	1963	3,694,714	1,427,915
1914	1,481,147	279,966	1964	3,807,875	1,472,607
1915	1,521,509	286,427	1965	3,934,062	1,529,449
1916	1,560,749	295,676	1966	4,069,575	1,603,031
1917	1,597,759	310,459	1967	4,208,297	1,681,563
1918	1,628,151	329,925	1968	4,347,000	1,765,499
1919	1,656,709	348,081	1969	4,488,452	1,859,394
1920	1,690,594	359,068	1970	4,638,086	1,950,578
1921	1,724,916	362,168	1971	4,802,265	2,037,060
1922	1,761,938	368,157	1972	4,979,241	2,142,504
1923	1,810,124	386,088	1973	5,163,463	2,280,228
1924	1,866,459	404,133	1974	5,347,089	2,431,580
1925	1,926,503	420,813	1975	5,508,789	2,568,874
1926	1,987,233	438,940	1976	5,650,200	2,690,015
1927	2,049,487	451,559	1977	5,791,755	2,822,551
1928	2,112,771	464,531	1978	5,942,856	2,976,429
1929	2,174,926	485,301	1979	6,114,925	3,134,464
1930	2,235,522	501,160	1980	6,298,494	3,269,826
1931	2,285,266	499,005	1981	6,486,419	3,387,035
1932	2,314,108	482,122	1982	6,693,444	3,484,898
1933	2,327,677	461,374	1983	6,904,958	3,562,727
1934	2,339,968	446,025	1984	7,119,846	3,664,626
1935	2,354,055	440,714	1985	7,348,410	3,804,318
1936	2,375,093	444,045	1986	7,565,627	3,949,120
1937	2,404,966	446,989	1987	7,762,728	4,067,936
1938	2,432,557	444,826	1988	7,950,724	4,177,069
1939	2,459,316	440,140	1989	8,138,481	4,321,616
			1990	8,327,004	4,487,613
			1991	8,500,883	4,621,782
			1992	8,654,232	4,723,222

Table 8a
France: Gross Investment in Non-Residential Structures and Machinery
and Equipment (million 1990 Francs)

Year	Gross Investment in Non-Residential Structures	Gross Investment in Machinery and Equipment	Year	Gross Investment in Non-Residential Structures	Gross Investment in Machinery and Equipment
1910	61,670		1950	82,908	60,693
1911	65,095		1951	79,622	64,241
1912	69,207		1952	70,916	61,245
1913	68,521		1953	68,725	61,955
1914	62,238		1954	70,224	66,210
1915	49,244		1955	76,969	76,182
1916	41,702		1956	83,138	85,601
1917	41,075		1957	90,807	96,399
1918	25,357		1958	96,457	99,788
1919	29,192		1959	107,412	110,705
1920	33,606		1960	116,291	121,622
1921	38,689		1961	134,221	138,688
1922	44,538		1962	147,770	153,428
1923	54,816		1963	157,629	165,960
1924	68,521		1964	177,289	180,188
1925	65,780		1965	193,260	186,218
1926	78,800		1966	217,417	205,332
1927	63,724		1967	236,386	215,264
1928	71,948		1968	242,727	234,024
1929	84,966		1969	260,774	273,829
1930	92,503		1970	279,915	290,185
1931	85,651		1971	282,333	321,384
1932	74,688		1972	299,668	348,116
1933	68,521		1973	298,568	382,558
1934	61,670		1974	298,109	378,913
1935	58,243	34,868	1975	299,860	355,533
1936	58,928	38,538	1976	302,138	394,967
1937	56,872	46,184	1977	294,059	393,477
1938	51,391	37,621	1978	291,826	401,940
1939	51,391	37,621	1979	305,646	419,256
1940	21,886	16,021	1980	308,928	446,522
1941	17,373	12,718	1981	307,817	435,069
1942	15,546	11,380	1982	307,549	436,675
1943	14,752	10,800	1983	293,915	421,472
1944	12,863	9,416	1984	290,242	412,409
1945	13,960	10,220	1985	294,816	448,277
1946	42,429	31,060	1986	315,086	473,505
1947	57,670	42,218	1987	328,384	506,965
1948	79,555	58,239	1988	361,980	566,252
1949	82,238	60,202	1989	379,388	617,549
			1990	401,624	639,632
			1991	413,510	616,075

Table 8b
Germany: Gross Investment in Non-Residential Structures and Machinery and Equipment (million 1990 DM)

Year	Gross Investment in Non-Residential Structures	Gross Investment in Machinery and Equipment	Year	Gross Investment in Non-Residential Structures	Gross Investment in Machinery and Equipment
1880	11,241		1935	24,818	14,800
1881	11,493		1936	28,670	17,032
1882	10,167		1937	31,702	19,941
1883	10,041		1938	37,701	23,133
1884	10,230		1939	35,364	24,404
1885	10,167		1940	26,397	24,008
1886	10,799		1941	22,671	24,517
1887	11,557		1942	17,745	23,528
1888	12,062		1943	13,009	20,562
1889	12,125		1944	7,831	13,303
1890	12,441		1945	6,883	5,593
1891	12,883		1946	8,384	6,063
1892	13,262		1947	10,942	7,938
1893	13,830		1948	17,965	15,364
1894	14,335		1949	25,260	23,253
1895	15,661		1950	30,704	26,029
1896	16,419		1951	29,988	28,540
1897	17,872		1952	32,100	30,437
1898	19,008		1953	38,726	33,278
1899	20,398		1954	42,743	39,038
1900	18,756		1955	53,205	48,650
1901	17,872		1956	61,299	50,911
1902	20,145		1957	62,161	49,525
1903	25,134		1958	63,290	52,342
1904	27,028		1959	73,338	58,444
1905	26,144		1960	82,792	68,601
1906	26,776		1961	88,091	76,569
1907	23,492		1962	91,719	82,364
1908	18,756		1963	95,267	82,641
1909	17,808		1964	109,031	89,032
1910	24,692		1965	112,302	95,785
1911	28,418		1966	113,776	94,060
1912	25,892		1967	99,379	86,007
1913	20,650		1968	104,527	92,047
1914	18,756		1969	116,299	111,380
1915	14,840		1970	131,192	128,829
1916	12,567		1971	136,133	134,581
1917	12,378		1972	134,797	131,236
1918	7,641		1973	132,528	130,629
1919	5,368		1974	128,485	116,579
1920	12,314	12,428	1975	122,058	116,440
1921	19,387	14,800	1976	122,772	123,833
1922	22,229	15,789	1977	122,104	133,654
1923	16,167	13,416	1978	124,292	143,923
1924	16,356	13,388	1979	129,568	156,781
1925	17,998	15,026	1980	132,251	160,796
1926	19,829	15,083	1981	125,571	153,265
1927	23,555	17,794	1982	121,666	142,304
1928	21,724	18,049	1983	118,821	150,879
1929	20,903	16,100	1984	119,028	149,516
1930	16,735	13,275	1985	117,404	163,012
1931	12,504	9,208	1986	125,271	169,862
1932	8,904	6,468	1987	126,642	178,160
1933	13,198	7,852	1988	129,821	189,899
1934	21,534	12,456	1989	134,923	206,878
			1990	137,780	234,010
			1991	143,159	255,272

Table 8c
Japan: Gross Investment in Non-Residential Structures and Machinery
and Equipment (Billion 1990 Yen)

Year	Gross Investment in Non-Residential Structures	Gross Investment in Machinery and Equipment	Year	Gross Investment in Non-Residential Structures	Gross Investment in Machinery and Equipment
1885	97	48	1940	1,158	3,157
1886	93	53	1941	1,221	3,331
1887	96	59	1942	1,083	2,956
1888	108	81	1943	1,300	3,543
1889	121	72	1944	1,332	3,634
1890	135	82	1945	666	1,817
1891	159	98	1946	1,911	722
1892	134	87	1947	2,498	943
1893	136	107	1948	2,631	994
1894	151	149	1949	2,459	929
1895	157	144	1950	2,024	765
1896	195	177	1951	2,293	866
1897	264	188	1952	2,724	1,029
1898	266	187	1953	3,408	1,354
1899	255	115	1954	3,608	1,354
1900	264	135	1955	3,877	1,361
1901	275	126	1956	4,516	1,707
1902	276	105	1957	5,048	2,154
1903	300	121	1958	5,268	2,418
1904	221	156	1959	6,198	2,859
1905	276	266	1960	7,655	3,868
1906	340	250	1961	9,920	4,930
1907	369	261	1962	11,128	5,502
1908	412	311	1963	12,345	6,067
1909	425	270	1964	13,591	6,858
1910	571	288	1965	13,659	7,001
1911	747	369	1966	15,092	7,710
1912	522	415	1967	22,068	9,271
1913	497	444	1968	20,874	11,904
1914	529	415	1969	24,392	14,503
1915	443	366	1970	28,181	15,919
1916	431	479	1971	29,811	16,089
1917	488	772	1972	32,287	17,120
1918	553	1,126	1973	35,015	19,759
1919	542	1,208	1974	33,126	17,630
1920	819	1,212	1975	33,556	16,419
1921	804	929	1976	33,258	17,173
1922	891	741	1977	34,255	17,951
1923	762	575	1978	36,839	19,673
1924	1,029	614	1979	39,514	22,007
1925	1,145	604	1980	40,728	22,589
1926	1,295	657	1981	41,378	24,138
1927	1,361	700	1982	40,484	24,931
1928	1,241	732	1983	39,481	25,891
1929	1,313	802	1984	39,740	29,458
1930	1,257	809	1985	40,252	32,871
1931	1,192	601	1986	41,327	34,726
1932	1,089	620	1987	42,952	38,282
1933	1,172	784	1988	45,994	44,730
1934	1,257	1,077	1989	49,907	51,039
1935	1,481	1,272	1990	53,269	57,318
1936	1,487	1,427	1991	56,620	59,989
1937	1,531	1,448			
1938	1,547	1,988			
1939	1,782	2,755			

Table 8d
Netherlands: Gross Investment in Non-Residential Structures and Machinery
and Equipment (million 1990 Guilders)

Year	Gross Investment in Non-Residential Structures	Gross Investment in Machinery and Equipment	Year	Gross Investment in Non-Residential Structures	Gross Investment in Machinery and Equipment
1910	5,633		1950	10,758	7,567
1911	5,624		1951	10,842	7,114
1912	6,097		1952	9,903	6,511
1913	6,379		1953	13,283	7,397
1914	6,097		1954	12,322	9,341
1915	6,379		1955	14,337	11,312
1916	6,620		1956	14,189	13,173
1917	6,088		1957	14,231	13,973
1918	5,633		1958	13,655	11,203
1919	7,132		1959	15,590	12,536
1920	7,422		1960	17,121	15,087
1921	7,895		1961	18,409	16,261
1922	6,878		1962	19,316	17,300
1923	6,632		1963	20,178	17,281
1924	6,668		1964	25,011	18,466
1925	6,792		1965	25,101	19,525
1926	7,899		1966	27,092	21,394
1927	8,627		1967	30,157	22,028
1928	9,542		1968	33,098	24,933
1929	10,624		1969	31,656	23,107
1930	11,676		1970	33,292	26,627
1931	12,541		1971	34,043	25,707
1932	11,108		1972	30,215	24,824
1933	9,816		1973	28,967	28,430
1934	9,843		1974	28,010	29,841
1935	9,446	2,961	1975	28,264	27,891
1936	8,848	3,220	1976	28,155	25,977
1937	8,949	4,271	1977	27,792	29,976
1938	10,423	4,915	1978	28,276	31,263
1939	11,071	4,988	1979	27,743	32,097
1940	6,202	2,794	1980	28,046	30,344
1941	4,451	2,005	1981	24,787	27,179
1942	2,531	1,141	1982	22,897	27,167
1943	2,011	906	1983	21,492	29,890
1944	0	0	1984	22,267	32,723
1945	0	0	1985	24,060	42,720
1946	3,757	2,362	1986	25,270	46,090
1947	8,020	5,041	1987	25,840	46,640
1948	10,006	6,289	1988	27,980	45,710
1949	10,553	6,737	1989	29,030	49,440
			1990	29,770	51,920
			1991	30,680	53,620
			1992	31,160	53,350

Table 8e
UK: Gross Investment in Non-Residential Structures and Machinery
and Equipment (million 1990 pounds)

Year	Gross Investment in Non-Residential Structures	Gross Investment in Machinery and Equipment	Year	Gross Investment in Non-Residential Structures	Gross Investment in Machinery and Equipment
1780	324		1840	1,293	282
1781	324		1841	1,509	288
1782	328		1842	1,586	299
1783	334		1843	1,668	309
1784	339		1844	1,755	320
1785	345		1845	1,845	332
1786	352		1846	1,876	345
1787	362		1847	1,842	359
1788	373		1848	1,809	375
1789	383		1849	1,776	391
1790	393		1850	1,743	408
1791	419		1851	1,575	431
1792	430		1852	1,625	452
1793	442		1853	1,529	491
1794	455		1854	1,589	597
1795	466		1855	1,575	597
1796	475		1856	1,493	499
1797	479		1857	1,553	437
1798	483		1858	1,565	421
1799	488		1859	1,743	437
1800	492	96	1860	1,779	532
1801	482	98	1861	1,999	567
1802	486	100	1862	2,034	632
1803	490	102	1863	2,244	746
1804	495	103	1864	2,290	881
1805	499	104	1865	2,556	872
1806	505	107	1866	2,412	820
1807	512	108	1867	2,132	714
1808	519	109	1868	1,963	686
1809	526	110	1869	1,912	673
1810	534	113	1870	2,014	791
1811	542	110	1871	2,250	906
1812	549	113	1872	2,412	966
1813	557	114	1873	2,516	885
1814	565	115	1874	2,842	1,016
1815	572	117	1875	2,898	1,000
1816	583	120	1876	2,954	1,031
1817	594	123	1877	2,960	1,073
1818	606	128	1878	2,904	979
1819	617	132	1879	2,756	951
1820	629	136	1880	2,582	953
1821	626	142	1881	2,674	1,040
1822	637	147	1882	2,536	1,079
1823	650	153	1883	2,550	1,200
1824	662	158	1884	2,802	1,011
1825	675	162	1885	2,550	979
1826	695	168	1886	2,372	844
1827	723	174	1887	2,372	899
1828	754	181	1888	2,321	1,041
1829	785	188	1889	2,388	1,200
1830	817	196	1890	2,470	1,245
1831	859	204	1891	2,596	1,302
1832	895	212	1892	2,592	1,338
1833	932	219	1893	2,714	1,286
1834	969	228	1894	2,756	1,361
1835	1,010	237	1895	2,914	1,432
1836	1,057	245	1896	3,010	1,564
1837	1,112	254	1897	3,343	1,725
1838	1,169	263	1898	3,650	2,058
1839	1,230	273	1899	3,809	2,258

Continued overleaf

Table 8e (cont.)
UK: Gross Investment in Non-Residential Structures and Machinery
and Equipment (million 1990 pounds)

Year	Gross Investment in Non-Residential Structures	Gross Investment in Machinery and Equipment	Year	Gross Investment in Non-Residential Structures	Gross Investment in Machinery and Equipment
1900	3,885	2,333	1950	7,138	10,541
1901	4,135	2,481	1951	6,937	11,024
1902	4,427	2,546	1952	7,246	10,328
1903	4,227	2,588	1953	8,036	10,600
1904	4,151	2,673	1954	8,831	11,829
1905	3,941	2,694	1955	9,956	12,984
1906	3,849	2,519	1956	11,202	13,356
1907	3,369	2,265	1957	12,013	14,339
1908	2,858	1,860	1958	12,815	14,636
1909	2,934	2,099	1959	12,597	15,372
1910	3,020	2,200	1960	15,094	16,655
1911	3,010	2,405	1961	16,880	18,109
1912	3,010	2,496	1962	17,553	17,351
1913	3,435	2,767	1963	17,109	18,165
1914	3,282	2,899	1964	19,935	20,327
1915	2,398	2,444	1965	21,087	21,619
1916	1,855	1,987	1966	21,327	22,648
1917	1,743	2,315	1967	23,469	23,424
1918	1,958	2,946	1968	24,783	24,334
1919	2,720	3,759	1969	24,976	23,837
1920	4,013	3,749	1970	26,397	24,909
1921	3,381	4,288	1971	26,836	24,329
1922	3,159	3,964	1972	26,494	26,065
1923	3,678	3,991	1973	26,494	26,065
1924	3,865	4,531	1974	24,828	26,861
1925	4,421	4,909	1975	25,668	25,002
1926	3,827	4,234	1976	25,746	26,446
1927	3,865	5,071	1977	24,227	27,434
1928	3,827	5,880	1978	23,890	29,768
1929	4,532	5,556	1979	23,157	32,333
1930	5,424	5,205	1980	21,891	30,599
1931	4,532	5,448	1981	21,260	27,153
1932	3,753	4,423	1982	23,450	27,357
1933	3,492	3,856	1983	23,931	28,848
1934	4,088	5,258	1984	26,133	31,720
1935	4,496	5,744	1985	26,166	35,539
1936	5,053	6,635	1986	27,164	35,409
1937	6,167	6,662	1987	31,361	37,920
1938	5,945	7,093	1988	35,328	43,397
1939	6,688	6,472	1989	37,466	48,390
1940	3,715	8,092	1990	39,434	46,276
1941	2,786	6,743	1991	38,725	40,569
1942	2,600	6,203			
1943	2,044	4,315			
1944	1,486	3,506			
1945	2,162	3,140			
1946	4,644	5,934			
1947	4,830	7,821			
1948	5,202	8,900			
1949	5,966	10,023			

Table 8f
USA: Gross Investment in Non-Residential Structures and
Machinery and Equipment (million 1990 US$)

Year	Gross Investment in Non-Residential Structures	Gross Investment in Machinery and Equipment	Year	Gross Investment in Non-Residential Structures	Gross Investment in Machinery and Equipment
1850	6,304		1900	42,601	13,922
1851	6,463		1901	44,520	14,000
1852	8,009		1902	54,828	16,150
1853	7,930		1903	58,267	18,431
1854	9,843		1904	53,461	15,364
1855	8,941		1905	50,462	18,531
1856	7,200		1906	53,913	24,294
1857	8,556		1907	58,820	27,167
1858	8,708		1908	56,289	16,534
1859	7,863		1909	61,700	18,726
1860	7,158		1910	68,031	21,975
1861	7,035		1911	67,082	19,132
1862	6,242		1912	67,791	24,413
1863	3,359		1913	65,698	27,910
1864	5,488		1914	56,042	20,758
1865	5,334		1915	51,304	20,086
1866	6,498		1916	54,561	28,563
1867	8,328		1917	49,354	35,584
1868	8,799		1918	42,201	37,141
1869	11,878		1919	46,707	33,066
1870	16,510		1920	65,888	31,734
1871	16,571		1921	58,556	25,927
1872	19,260		1922	67,337	29,753
1873	17,457		1923	75,148	41,368
1874	15,144		1924	78,227	35,421
1875	13,176	6,169	1925	77,856	39,047
1876	13,444	6,169	1926	88,980	40,751
1877	13,941	6,169	1927	91,870	36,810
1878	15,954	6,056	1928	92,266	37,801
1879	14,818	6,190	1929	96,768	44,583
1880	16,974	6,441	1930	92,534	35,784
1881	27,849	7,627	1931	72,115	24,054
1882	27,951	7,647	1932	51,471	14,904
1883	23,897	7,164	1933	38,875	13,808
1884	22,216	7,032	1934	45,405	20,293
1885	18,490	6,651	1935	47,713	26,745
1886	17,505	6,717	1936	67,861	35,596
1887	27,871	7,689	1937	67,648	41,416
1888	28,469	7,664	1938	64,919	31,047
1889	29,099	8,023	1939	71,095	34,049
1890	35,626	7,925	1940	67,349	42,030
1891	32,484	8,517	1941	79,906	55,291
1892	32,676	8,646	1942	79,067	68,908
1893	33,226	9,154	1943	46,407	90,254
1894	29,982	7,617	1944	41,552	82,337
1895	29,717	9,106	1945	46,943	83,284
1896	35,227	11,443	1946	73,322	72,707
1897	38,270	8,500	1947	74,902	91,305
1898	37,493	9,080	1948	88,799	93,870
1899	39,895	11,533	1949	92,000	80,950

Continued overleaf

Table 8f (cont.)
USA: Gross Investment in Non-Residential Structures and
Machinery and Equipment (million 1990 US$)

Year	Gross Investment in Non-Residential Structures	Gross Investment in Machinery and Equipment	Year	Gross Investment in Non-Residential Structures	Gross Investment in Machinery and Equipment
1950	101,431	90,281	1970	228,097	197,058
1951	108,553	97,167	1971	223,848	195,178
1952	112,317	100,552	1972	220,449	214,539
1953	121,765	103,837	1973	232,274	251,619
1954	131,137	97,075	1974	228,097	257,601
1955	134,670	106,521	1975	210,878	225,032
1956	144,319	110,186	1976	207,453	232,562
1957	147,141	109,086	1977	208,225	267,651
1958	145,783	89,744	1978	229,992	300,721
1959	153,028	100,966	1979	252,588	316,479
1960	161,948	105,549	1980	261,804	299,130
1961	169,449	102,498	1981	273,020	296,739
1962	174,663	112,814	1982	266,505	267,772
1963	183,549	122,327	1983	244,482	279,273
1964	198,857	138,289	1984	273,789	323,599
1965	220,352	162,843	1985	303,604	348,023
1966	231,525	182,041	1986	279,055	351,298
1967	230,054	179,412	1987	278,848	352,492
1968	236,386	189,372	1988	277,943	374,995
1969	235,820	202,016	1989	291,003	396,733
			1990	296,027	392,854
			1991	272,601	375,697
			1992	268,178	395,555

References

Bank of Japan, *Hundred Year Statistics of the Japanese Economy*, Tokyo, 1966.
Blades, D., 'Service Lives of Fixed Assets', *ESD Working Papers*, No. 4, OECD, Paris, 1983.
Broadberry, S.N., 'Manufacturing and the Convergence Hypothesis: What the Long Run Data Show', *Journal of Economic History*, December 1993.
Carré, J.-J., P. Dubois and E. Malinvaud, *La croissance française*, Seuil, Paris, 1972.
CBS, *Kapitaalgoederenvoorraad 1990*, The Hague, 1991.
CSO, *UK National Accounts: Sources and Methods*, HMSO, London, 1985.
Dean, G., 'The Stock of Fixed Capital in the United Kingdom in 1961', *Journal of the Royal Statistical Society*, Series A, **127** (3), 1964.
Den Hartog, H. and T.S. Tjan, 'A Clay-Clay Vintage Model Approach for Sectors of Industry in the Netherlands', Central Planning Bureau, The Hague, September 1979.
Economic Planning Agency, *Revised Report on National Income Statistics 1951–1967*, Tokyo, 1969.
Economic Planning Agency, *Annual Report on National Income Statistics*, Tokyo, 1975.
Economic Planning Agency, *Revised Accounts on the Basis of 1985*, Tokyo, October 1990.
Economic Planning Agency, *Annual Report on National Accounts*, Tokyo, 1991.
Federal Statistical Office, *Volkswirtschaftliche Gesamtrechnungen*, Fachserie 18, Reihe S. 15, *Revidierte Ergebnisse 1950 bis 1990*, Wiesbaden, 1991.
Feinstein, C.H., *Domestic Capital Formation in the United Kingdom 1920–1938*, Cambridge University Press, 1965.
Feinstein, C.H *National Income, Expenditure and Output of the United Kingdom 1855–1965*, Cambridge University Press, 1972.
Feinstein, C.H., 'National Statistics, 1760–1920' in C.H. Feinstein and S. Pollard (eds), *Studies in Capital Formation in the United Kingdom 1750–1920*, Oxford University Press, 1988.
Field, A.J., 'Land Abundance, Interest/Profit Rates, and Nineteenth-Century American and British Technology', *Journal of Economic History*, June 1983.
Gallman, R.E., 'The United States Capital Stock in the Nineteenth Century', in S.L. Engerman and R.E. Gallman (eds), *Long Term Factors in American Economic Growth*, University of Chicago, 1986.
Gallman, R.E., 'Investment Flows and Capital Stocks: US Experience in the Nineteenth Century', in P. Kilby (ed.), *Quantity and Quiddity: Essays in US Economic History*, Wesleyan University Press, Middletown, 1987.
Gallman, R.E. and J.J. Wallis, *American Economic Growth and Standards of Living Before the Civil War*, NBER, University of Chicago, 1992.
Goldsmith, R.W., 'A Perpetual Inventory of National Wealth', in M.R. Gainsburgh, *Studies in Income and Wealth*, Vol. 14, Princeton, 1951.
Hancock, W.K. and M.M. Gowing, *British War Economy*, HMSO, London, 1949.
Hofman, André A., 'Capital Accumulation in Latin America: A Six Country Comparison for 1950–89', *Review of Income and Wealth*, December 1992.
IMF, *International Financial Statistics*, various issues.
James, J.A., and J.S. Skinner, 'The Resolution of the Labor-Scarcity Paradox', *Journal of Economic History*, September 1985.
Kaldor, N. 'Capital Accumulation and Economic Growth', in F.A. Lutz and D. Hague, (eds), *The Theory of Capital*, Macmillan, London, 1961.
Kendrick, J., *Productivity Trends in the United States*, Princeton University Press, 1961.
Kendrick, J., 'How Much Does Capital Explain?', in A. Szirmai, B. van Ark and D. Pilat (eds), *Explaining Economic Growth: Essays in Honour of Angus Maddison*, Elsevier, North Holland, Amsterdam, 1993.
Kirner, W., *Zeitreihen für das Anlagevermögen der Wirtschaftsbereiche in der Bundesrepublik Deutschland*, Duncker and Humblot, Berlin, 1968.
Kuznets, S., *National Product since 1869*, NBER, New York, 1946.
Lützel, H., 'Estimates of Capital Stock by Industries in the Federal Republic of Germany', *Review of Income and Wealth*, March 1977.
Maddison, A., 'Explaining Economic Growth', *Banca Nazionale del Lavoro Quarterly Review*, September 1972.
Maddison, A., *Dynamic Forces in Capitalist Development*, Oxford University Press, 1991.
Maddison, A., 'A Long Run Perspective on Saving', *Scandinavian Journal of Economics*, June 1992.
Maddison, A., 'Standardised Estimates of Fixed Capital Stock: A Six Country Comparison', *Innovazione e Materie prime*, Milan, April 1993.
Maddison, A., *Monitoring the World Economy 1820–1992*, OECD Development Centre, Paris, 1994.
Memorandum van de Nederlandsche Regeering inzake de door Nederland van Duitschland te eischen schadevergoeding, The Hague, 1945.
OECD, *National Accounts 1950–1968*, Paris, 1970.

OECD, *Purchasing Power Parities and Real Expenditures: GK Results*, Vol. 2, 1990, Paris, 1993a.
OECD, *National Accounts 1979–1991*, vol. 2, Paris, 1993b.
OECD, *Methods used by OECD Countries to Measure Stocks of Fixed Capital*, Paris, 1993c.
Ohkawa, K. and H. Rosovsky, *Japanese Economic Growth*, Stanford University Press, 1973.
Ohkawa K. and M. Shinohara, *Patterns of Japanese Economic Development* Yale University Press, 1979.
O'Mahony, Mary, 'Productivity Levels in British and German Manufacturing', *National Institute Economic Review*, February 1992.
O'Mahony, Mary, 'Capital Stocks and Productivity in Industrial Nations', NIESR, London, mimeographed, 1993.
Présidence du Conseil, *Dommages subis par la France et l'Union française du fait de la guerre et de l'occupation ennemie*, Paris, 1948–51.
Schmidt, L., 'Reproduzierbares Anlagevermögen', *Wirtschaft und Statistik*, July 1986.
Summers, R. and A. Heston, 'The Penn World Table (Mark 5): An Expanded Set of International Comparisons 1950–1988', *Quarterly Journal of Economics*, May 1991.
Tinbergen, J. 'Zur Theorie der langfristigen Wirtschaftsentwicklung', *Weltwirtschaftliches Archiv*, **55**, 1942.
US Department of Commerce, Bureau of Economic Analysis, *Fixed Reproducible Tangible Wealth in the United States 1925–89*, Washington DC, January 1993.
van Ark, Bart, *International Comparisons of Output and Productivity*, PhD thesis, University of Groningen, 1993.
Ward, Michael, *The Measurement of Capital: The Methodology of Capital Stock Estimates in OECD Countries*, OECD, Paris, 1976.
Zanden, J.L. van and R.T. Griffiths, *Economische Geschiedenis van Nederland in de 20e eeuw*, Aula, Utrecht, 1989.

[6]

Scand. J. of Economics 94(2), 181–196, 1992

A Long-Run Perspective on Saving

Angus Maddison*

University of Groningen, The Netherlands

Abstract

Historical estimates of long-run gross savings rates are provided for 11 countries, which represent about 48 per cent of world product in real terms and close to half of world savings. Even though savings rates declined over the past decade in nine of the 11 countries, present rates are usually well above their prewar levels. Factors which influence savings rates are also examined.

I. Introduction

Recent comparative surveys of savings behaviour have focused on a rather narrow time period; see Dean *et al.* (1990) and Agherli *et al.* (1990). This affects the validity of their general finding that savings rates in the 1980s have been at historic lows.

This paper provides longer term evidence on gross savings rates in 11 countries (Australia 1870–1988, Canada 1870–1988, France 1820–1913 and 1950–88, Germany 1870–1913, 1925–39 and 1950–88, Korea 1911–38 and 1953–88, India 1870–1988, Japan 1885–1988, Netherlands 1921–39 and 1950–88, Taiwan 1903–38 and 1951–88, U.K. 1870–1988 and U.S.A. 1870–1988). My coverage of the historical evidence is not exhaustive (more countries could be included, and for some of those included it may be possible to go further back).[1] Neverthe-less the 11 countries in this paper represent about 48 per cent of world

---

*I am grateful to Nanno Mulder for help in preparing the graphs and statistical appendix. The original version of this paper contained a statistical appendix of 50 pages with detailed figures and sources underlying the diagrams and tables. This is available from the author.
[1] Kuznets (1961b) provides a comparative survey of long term investment and savings experience. He covers 12 countries (Argentina, Australia, Canada, Denmark, Germany, Italy, Japan, Norway, South Africa, Sweden, U.K. and U.S.A.). In Maddison (1964, pp. 234–42), I presented long term investment ratios for some countries not included in this paper (Denmark, Italy, Norway and Sweden) and discussed some of the problems of comparability and measurement in more detail.

182   *A. Maddison*

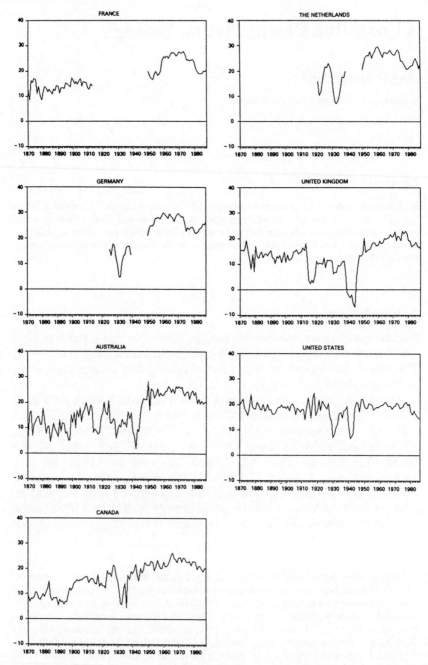

Fig. 1. Gross national saving as percentage of GDP at current prices.

A long-run perspective on saving   183

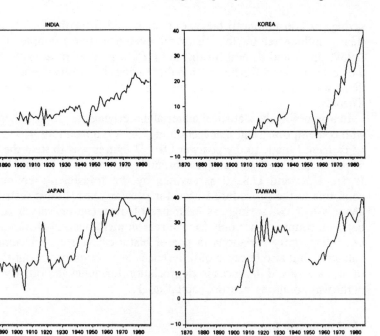

Fig. 1 — Continued

product in real terms and probably about half of world savings. They are also countries which are or have been important in the international flow of capital.

The historical evidence on savings is best summarised in Figure 1, which presents the record for the 11 countries in comparable form. The decline in savings rates over the past decade is clearly confirmed in nine of the 11 countries. The only exceptions are Korea and Taiwan. However, in most countries, the savings rates of the 1950s and 1960s were very high in terms of historical experience. Even at their present reduced level, savings rates in most of the countries are usually well above their prewar levels. It would therefore be just as feasible to conceive of recent savings patterns as a reversion towards longer term "norms" after an unusually prolonged postwar boom, as it is to consider them as an aberration from postwar normality.

It is also clear from inspection of Figure 1 that U.S. long run experience has not conformed to the norm for the other countries. In most of the other cases, it is possible to discern an upward trend in the long term savings rate, whereas this is not the case in the U.S.A. The atypicality of U.S. experience is important because a good deal of the theorising about saving (or consumption) behaviour emanated from the U.S.A. and was clearly influenced by the historical evidence. For example, Friedman (1957, pp. 3 and 4) and Modigliani (1986, p. 298) have explained how they came to reject Keynes' notion that savings rise with income — because there was no upward trend in the U.S. savings estimates developed by Kuznets.

In assembling the statistical material underlying the graphs, I kept in line with contemporary national accounting (SNA) conventions. However, one adjustment I made to the postwar OECD figures was to treat the balance of payments item "net transfers abroad" (substantial in France, Germany, Japan, U.K. and U.S.A.) as savings by the transferring country. This conforms to the procedure I used for prewar years. I have restricted the analysis to gross savings, as estimates of depreciation vary a good deal between countries, not only for the reason mentioned in Horioka (1990), i.e., intercountry variations in use of historical versus replacement cost valuation, but also because of differences in assumptions about the length of life of assets, differences in depreciation formulae and other variations in the way countries measure capital stock.

II. Domestic Investment

Figure 2 shows the behaviour of domestic investment. It is interesting to compare the contours of these diagrams with those in Figure 1 on total savings. In general the two sets of contours are not too different, except for the U.K., where pre-1913 investment was significantly lower than savings, so that its long run domestic investment trend is more clearly upwards than is the case for savings. For Canada, the contour for long term investment is significantly different from that for long term saving. There are also important differences for Taiwan where domestic investment rates have dropped considerably in recent years, but savings have continued to be very high.

III. Investment Abroad

Figure 3 presents the record for investment abroad. Suprisingly, Taiwan has proportionately had the biggest investment abroad, both in recent years and in the colonial period (when its experience was very different from that of the other Japanese colony, Korea). Over the long haul, Australia has been the most consistent foreign borrower, though not on as large a scale as pre-1913 Canada. Of the European countries, the U.K. appears as the biggest pre-1913 foreign investor (though its lending proportion may have been below that of the Netherlands in that period). In the postwar period the Netherlands and Germany have been lenders on a

Table 1a. *Total gross savings as a ratio of GDP at current market prices*

	1870–89	1890–1913	1914–38	1939–49	1950–73	1974–87	1950–9	1960–73	1974–80	1981–87
Australia	11.2a	13.0a	12.4	13.8	24.4	22.0	23.5	25.1	23.5	20.7
Canada	9.1b	12.2b	14.4b	19.3	22.5	21.5	21.4	23.4	22.7	20.4
France	12.8	14.7	n.a.	n.a.	23.5	22.3	18.8	26.8	24.9	20.0
Germany	n.a.	n.a.	12.9c	6.7	27.5	24.0	25.9	28.6	24.1	24.0
India	n.a.	5.8d	7.4	23.3e	12.8	20.2	10.8	14.3	20.7	17.3
Japan	12.4e	12.3e	16.7e	n.a.	32.8	32.9	28.1	36.1	33.0	32.8
Korea	n.a.	n.a.	4.3f	n.a.	8.1g	27.9	4.0h	10.1	24.3	31.0
Netherlands	n.a.	n.a.	15.2i	n.a.	26.8	22.9	25.8	27.4	23.2	22.7
Taiwan	n.a.	9.6j	25.5k	n.a.	19.9	33.2	14.7	23.2	31.9	34.5
U.K.	13.9	13.6	8.3	1.6	17.9	19.2	15.7	19.5	20.9	17.5
U.S.A.	19.1	18.3	17.0	15.2	19.7	18.0	19.7	19.7	19.7	16.7

(a) Excludes inventories; (b) 1870–1926 excludes inventories; (c) 1925–38 excludes inventories; (d) 1900–13; (e) 1885–1940 excludes inventories and first entry is for 1885–9; (f) excludes part of inventories; (g) 1953–73; (h) 1953–9; (i) 1921–38; (j) 1903–13 and excludes part of inventories; (k) excludes part of inventories.
Source: Appendix, Table 2.

Table 1b. *Gross fixed domestic investment as a ratio of GDP at current market prices*

	1870–89	1890–1913	1914–38	1939–49	1950–73	1974–87	1950–9	1960–73	1974–80	1981–87
Australia	16.5	13.4	15.0	11.9	25.0	24.3	24.3	25.4	24.0	24.6
Canada	16.0	19.4	15.2	12.9	22.4	22.3	22.3	22.2	23.6	21.2
France	12.8	13.9	16.1a	n.a.	21.2	21.7	17.5	23.8	23.5	20.2
Germany	n.a.	n.a.	12.9b	n.a.	23.2	20.6	20.8	24.9	21.1	20.2
India	4.5c	5.6c	7.0	7.8	12.5	17.7	10.2	14.2	17.2	19.2
Japan	12.6d	14.4	16.2	18.6	28.3	30.4	22.3	32.6	31.7	29.2
Korea	n.a.	4.9e	7.0	n.a.	15.9f	28.9	9.8g	18.9	29.4	28.6
Netherlands	n.a.	n.a.	17.5h	n.a.	23.8	20.2	22.3	25.0	21.0	19.4
Taiwan	n.a.	n.a.	15.6	n.a.	17.0j	24.6	13.0k	19.5	28.3	21.8
U.K.	8.4	8.7i	7.8	6.5	16.3	17.7	14.1	17.9	18.8	16.5
U.S.A.	16.3	15.9	14.2	13.1	18.0	18.0	18.4	17.8	18.4	17.7

(a) 1922–38; (b) 1925–38; (c) in separating fixed investment from inventories it was assumed for 1870–99 that inventories averaged 0.6 per cent of GDP; (d) 1885–9; (e) 1911–13; (f) 1953–73; (g) 1953–9; (h) 1921–38; (i) 1903–13; (j) 1951–73; (k) 1951–9.
Source: Appendix, Table 2.

Table 1c. *Net investment in inventories as a ratio of GDP at current market prices*

	1870–89	1890–1913	1914–38	1939–49	1950–73	1974–87	1950–9	1960–73	1974–80	1981–87
Australia	n.a.	1.7	0.8	1.2	1.2	0.5	1.2	1.1	0.7	0.2
Canada	n.a.	n.a.	0.3	1.0	1.3	0.5	1.5	1.1	1.1	0.0
France	0.0	0.2	n.a.	n.a.	1.9	0.5	1.9	1.9	1.1	0.1
Germany	n.a.	n.a.	0.1h	n.a.	1.9	0.4	2.5	1.6	0.8	0.0
India	0.6	0.6	0.4	0.2	1.9	3.4a	1.8	1.9	3.5	3.3b
Japan	n.a.	n.a.	n.a.	7.7	3.8	0.6	5.2	2.7	0.9	0.4
Korea	n.a.	n.a.	n.a.	n.a.	1.9c	1.1	2.8d	1.4	1.6	0.7
Netherlands	n.a.	n.a.	-2.7e	n.a.	1.8	0.2	2.1	1.5	0.7	-0.4
Taiwan	n.a.	n.a.	n.a.	n.a.	3.1f	2.1	2.7g	3.4	3.7	0.8
U.K.	0.9	0.6	-0.2	0.4	0.9	0.3	0.9	1.0	0.4	0.2
U.S.A.	3.5	1.9	0.9	0.9	0.9	0.6	1.0	0.9	0.6	0.5

(a) 1974–87; (b) 1981–7; (c) 1953–73; (d) 1953–73; (e) 1921–38; (f) 1951–73; (g) 1951–9; (h) 1925–38.
Source: Appendix, Table 2.

Table 1d. Net investment abroad as a ratio of GDP at current market prices

	1870-89	1890-1913	1914-38	1939-49	1950-73	1974-87	1950-9	1960-73	1974-80	1981-87
Australia	-5.4	-1.5	-3.5	0.7	-1.7	-2.8	-2.0	-1.5	-1.3	-4.2
Canada	-6.9	-7.1	-0.9	5.4	-1.1	-1.3	-2.5	-0.2	-1.9	-0.7
France	-0.1	0.6	n.a.	n.a.	0.4	-0.2	-0.6	1.1	0.3	-0.3
Germany	1.7	1.5	-0.1a	n.a.	2.4	3.1	2.7	2.1	2.3	3.8
India	n.a.	0.2	0.0	-1.3	-1.5	-0.9	-1.3	-1.8	0.0	-1.9
Japan	-0.3	-2.1	0.5	-1.9	0.7	1.8	0.7	0.7	0.4	3.1
Korea	n.a.	n.a.	-2.7	n.a.	-9.7b	-2.2	-8.7c	-10.2	-6.6	1.7
Netherlands	n.a.	n.a.	0.4d	n.a.	1.2	2.7	1.5	0.9	1.4	3.7
Taiwan	n.a.	0.9e	9.9	n.a.	-0.2f	6.4	-1.0g	0.3	-0.1	11.8
U.K.	4.5	4.6	0.7	-5.3	0.6	0.9	0.7	0.6	1.7	0.3
U.S.A.	-0.7	0.5	2.0	1.3	0.8	-0.6	0.4	1.0	0.7	-1.6

(a) 1925-38; (b) 1953-73; (c) 1953-9; (d) 1921-38; (e) 1903-13; (f) 1951-73; (g) 1951-9.
Source: Appendix, Table 2. Negative sign means negative investment (borrowing).

188   *A. Maddison*

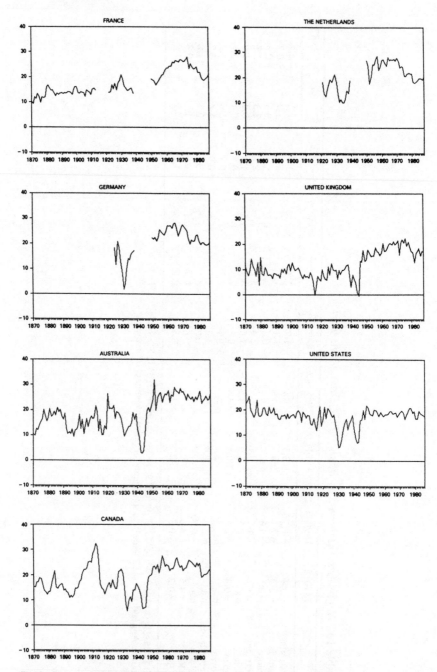

Fig. 2. Gross domestic investment as percentage of GDP at current prices.

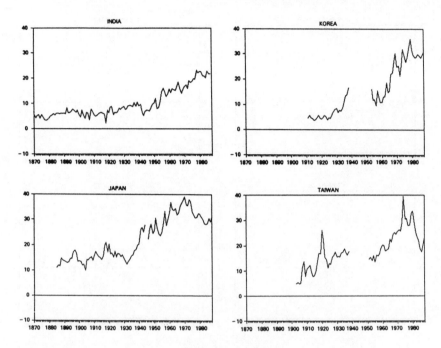

Fig. 2 — Continued

larger scale than the U.K., whose investment abroad has been modest by historical standards. France has also been relatively modest in its postwar lending abroad. The U.S.A. has been the most consistent in lending abroad in the twentieth century and its recent borrowing abroad is clearly an unusual break with precedent.

IV. Absolute Importance of Savers

All the graphs are in proportionate terms, showing total savings and uses of savings in relation to GDP in the country concerned. However, the importance of individual countries in the international market for savings depends not only on their savings rate but also on the absolute size of the country, its propensity to invest abroad, and the extent to which its exchange rate deviates from purchasing power parity. This is illustrated in Table 2, which shows the situation in 1988.

Thus it can be seen that Japan had the biggest savings in 1988 — $974 billion compared with $700 billion in the U.S.A., in spite of the fact that the real GDP of Japan was only 40 per cent of that of the U.S.A. Japan's

190   *A. Maddison*

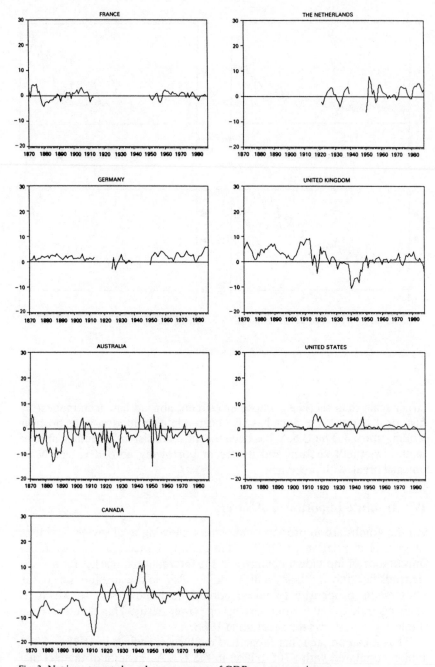

Fig. 3. Net investment abroad as percentage of GDP at current prices.

A long-run perspective on saving 191

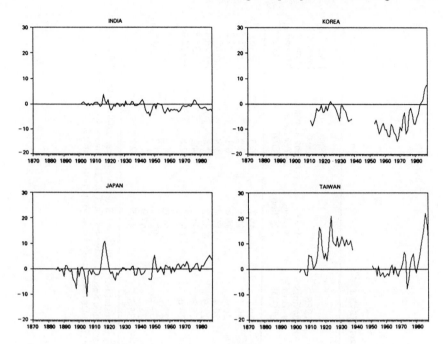

Fig. 3 — Continued

savings were high relative to the U.S.A. because it had one of the highest savings rates (34.2 per cent of GDP), whereas the U.S.A. had the lowest in our group (at 14.6 per cent of GDP). Japan also had the biggest deviation between its exchange rate and the purchasing power of its currency. In real terms, converting GDP at national prices with purchasing power parities supplied by Eurostat, its GDP was only 40 per cent of that in the U.S.A., but in money terms, with conversion at the exchange rate, it was 59 per cent of that in the U.S.A. The comparison between India and Japan is even more strongly affected by use of PPP rather than an exchange rate converter. In money terms Japanese GDP was 10 times that of India, but in real terms it was only twice as high.

As Japanese investment abroad was 3.2 per cent of GDP in 1988 whereas U.S. investment was negative — at − 28 per cent — the contrast in the position of the two countries was most striking in this respect: the U.S.A. being the biggest borrower ($132 billion) and Japan being the biggest investor ($92 billion).

Thus there are serious problems of aggregation if one wants to estimate savings trends for our eleven countries combined.

Table 2. Comparative levels of real GDP, money GDP and savings in 1988

	1988 GDP at U.S. Relative Prices $ Billion	1988 GDP Converted at Exchange Rate $ Billion	1988 Price Level Relative to U.S.A.	1988 Savings as Per Cent of GDP	1988 Savings $ Billion	1988 Investment Abroad as Per Cent of GDP	1988 Investment Abroad $ Billion
Australia	236.6	247.0	1.13	20.1	49.7	-6.7	-16.6
Canada	482.1	486.0	1.10	19.7	95.5	-2.7	-13.3
France	816.7	955.7	1.27	20.9	199.4	-0.1	-1.2
Germany	906.5	1,201.8	1.44	26.4	316.7	5.8	69.9
Netherlands	197.3	227.4	1.25	22.9	52.0	2.8	6.4
U.K.	815.5	833.8	1.11	15.8	131.6	-4.2	-35.3
U.S.A.	4,809.1	4,809.1	1.00	14.6	699.9	-2.8	-132.4
India	899.4	281.1	0.34	21.0	59.0	-3.0	-8.4
Japan	1,926.3	2,848.9	1.61	34.2	973.5	3.2	91.6
Korea	286.3	174.9	0.66	38.3	67.0	7.7	13.5
Taiwan	146.5	123.3	0.91	35.3	43.5	12.0	14.8

Source: First column represents GDP in national currencies converted by Eurostat ICP V PPPs at US relative prices, adjusted to 1988 basis; Indian, Korean and Taiwanese GDP converted by ICP IV PPPs updated to 1988. Second column from OECD sources. Column 3 is equal to column 2 divided by column 1. Colums 5 and 7 converted at exchange rate. Savings rates derived from Appendix, Table 2.

V. Factors Influencing Savings Rates

The main purpose of this paper is to provide estimates of savings rates over the long run for a significant sample of countries, and I cannot hope to make much of a contribution to diagnosing reasons for variation in such a complex phenomenon. However, it is worth looking at long term changes in some characteristics which savings theorists have considered to be important.

Most analysts of saving behaviour are concerned with identifying the motivations of various categories of savers — individuals, corporations or governments and their interaction (e.g. the impact of obligatory social security systems or fiscal deficits on private thrift). By contrast, the statistical evidence I present here concentrates on the uses of savings — for residential and non-residential fixed investment, for inventories, and for foreign investment — magnitudes which help illuminate business cycle or secular growth experience rather than intertemporal optimisation of individuals. As current saving and investment flows are equal at the aggregate level, there are obvious benefits from confrontation of the source of savings and use of savings approaches.

Tables 3 and 4 show absolute levels and growth of per capita real income in comparable units for the eleven sample countries. There has been very substantial long run growth in real income per head in all of these countries except India. This growth was generally fastest in the 1950–73 period and has slowed down appreciably since then, except in India, Korea and Taiwan. There is a general positive relationship between the faster postwar growth in output per head and the acceleration in savings rates, and a similar positive relation in the post 1973 slowdown. The U.S.A., which has the smallest postwar acceleration in per capita

Table 3. *GDP per capita in 1985 dollars at U.S. prices*

	1870	1913	1950	1973	1989
Australia	3,123	4,523	5,931	10,331	13,584
Canada	1,347	3,560	6,113	11,866	17,576
France	1,571	2,734	4,149	10,323	13,837
Germany	1,300	2,606	3,339	10,110	13,989
Netherlands	2,064	3,178	4,706	10,267	12,737
U.K.	2,610	4,024	5,651	10,063	13,468
U.S.A.	2,247	4,854	8,611	14,103	18,317
India	470	536	482	689	1,065
Japan	618	1,114	1,563	9,237	15,101
Korea	n.a.	819	757	2,404	6,503
Taiwan	n.a.	608	706	2,803	7,252

Source: Maddison (1991).

194   *A. Maddison*

Table 4. *Rate of growth of GDP per capita (annual average compound growth rate)*

	1870–1913	1913–50	1950–73	1973–89
Australia	0.9	0.7	2.5	1.7
Canada	2.3	1.5	2.9	2.5
France	1.3	1.1	4.1	1.8
Germany	1.6	0.7	4.9	2.0
Netherlands	1.0	1.1	3.5	1.4
U.K.	1.0	0.8	2.5	1.8
U.S.A.	2.0	1.6	2.2	1.6
Average	1.4	1.1	4.0	1.8
India	0.3	−0.3	1.6	2.8
Japan	1.4	0.9	8.0	3.1
Korea	n.a.	−0.2	5.2	6.4
Taiwan	n.a.	0.4	6.2	6.1
Average	n.a.	0.2	5.3	4.6

Source: Derived from Table 3.

growth, was also the country with least change in its long run savings habits.

Contemporary rates of saving are, if anything, negatively related to per capita income levels, as the richest country, the U.S.A., has the lowest saving level and the highest levels are in two relatively low income countries — Korea and Taiwan. Even a very low income country like India has a higher savings ratio than the U.S.A. When we match the real income evidence of Table 3 with the savings ratios of Table 1, it appears that the savings ratio is more responsive to investment opportunity than to income.

When there are realistic opportunities for economic catch-up — produced by accelerated international diffusion of technology, increased absorptive capacity due to improvements in human capital, effective pro-growth policies, better international cooperation, or liberation from a colonial yoke — then the improvement in prospective returns seem to induce a rise in savings and investment in follower countries (whatever their level of income). The lead country — the U.S.A. — did not have this experience; hence, its savings behaved differently.

As follower countries aproach the leader more closely (the European and Japanese case), their opportunities for catch-up fade and this may help explain the fall in savings ratios since 1973. The lower-income Asian countries (India, Korea and Taiwan) are not yet in this situation (though the causes of the recent sharp fall in Taiwanese domestic investment rates are worth closer scrutiny).

The fall in savings rates in OECD countries since 1973 has been greater than would be warranted by the erosion of special opportunities for catch-

Table 5. *Changes in demographic structure, 1870–1987*

	Percentage of population aged 65 and over					Percentage of population 0–14				
	1870	1910	1950	1973	1987	1870	1910	1950	1973	1987
Australia	1.8	4.0	8.1	8.5	10.7	42.3	35.2	26.6	28.2	22.6
Canada	3.7	4.7	7.4	8.3	10.9	41.6	33.1	29.7	28.0	21.2
France	7.4	8.4	11.4	13.2	13.5	27.1	25.8	22.7	24.4	20.6
Germany	4.6	4.9	(9.2)	13.9	15.1	34.0	33.9	(23.5)	22.4	14.9
Netherlands	5.5	6.1	7.7	10.5	12.4	33.6	34.5	29.3	26.4	18.6
U.K.	5.0	5.3	10.7	13.6	15.5	36.1	30.8	22.3	23.9	18.9
U.S.A.	3.0	4.3	8.1	10.2	12.2	39.2	32.1	26.8	26.5	21.5
India	3.2a	2.4	3.6	3.4	4.4	34.9a	38.5	37.5	42.0	37.2
Japan	5.3	5.3b	5.2	7.3	10.8	33.7	36.5b	35.3	24.2	20.4
Korea	n.a.	n.a.	3.9c	3.5d	4.8	n.a.	n.a.	43.2c	28.1d	27.3
Taiwan	n.a.	2.4e	n.a.	3.2	5.3	n.a.	35.9e	39.0	37.1	28.6

(a) 1881; (b) 1920; (c) 1944; (d) 1975; (e) 1905. German figures in brackets exclude Berlin.
Source: OECD countries from OECD, *Labour Force Statistics*, various issues, OECD *Demographic Trends 1950–1990*, Paris, 1979, and B. Mueller, *A Statistical Handbook of the North Atlantic Area*, Twentieth Century Fund, New York, 1965. Asian countries from B. R. Mitchell, *International Historical Statistics: Africa and Asia*, Macmillan, London, 1982, World Bank, *World Development Report 1990*, and UN, *The Aging of Populations and Its Economic and Social Implications*, New York, 1956.

up. There has been a constellation of other influences which have generally had an adverse effect on savings — the oil shocks, the switch in policy emphasis towards anti-inflationary rather than full-employment objectives, the aberrant fiscal-monetary policy mix in the U.S.A., the greater caution in macropolicy which results from the great openness which has developed in international capital markets; see Maddison (1984 and 1991). These causal influences require very careful scrutiny before one can jump to conclusions about a "shortage" of world savings, or the efficacy of policy action specifically directed to enhance savings incentives.

Some of the savings literature stresses the possibility that the ageing of the population and the swelling cohorts of elderly citizens will reduce the incentive or capacity to save, or that the decline in the proportion of children will reduce the incentive to provide for posterity. It is clear from Table 5 that ageing has been important in the advanced capitalist countries and is starting in Asia, but the timing and pattern of change in savings ratios has not been very obviously affected by this.

Even more striking than the demographic changes of Table 5 are the changes in institutional arrangements that have led to the massive increase in the governmental role in the economy (see Table 6). On average, government spending on goods, services, and transfers accounted for 46 per cent of GDP in 1987 compared with 12 per cent in 1913. A significant

196   *A. Maddison*

Table 6. *Total government expenditures as a percentage of GDP at current prices, 1913–87*

	1913	1929	1938	1950	1973	1987
France	8.9	12.4	23.2	27.3	38.8	56.6[b]
Germany	17.7	30.6	42.4	30.4	42.0	47.3
Japan	14.2	18.8	30.3	19.8	22.9	33.9
Netherlands	8.2[a]	11.2	21.7	26.8	45.5	59.7
U.K.	13.3	23.8	28.8	34.2	41.5	45.2[b]
U.S.A.	8.0	10.0	19.8	21.4	31.1	37.0
Average	11.7	17.8	27.7	26.7	37.0	46.0

(a) 1910; (b) 1986.
Source: Maddison (1991).

proportion of these expenditures involve governmental takeover of provision for old age, or coverage of risks which were previously borne by individuals. This has obviously had an impact on the way savings are formed, but it is not so clear what the impact has been on overall rates of saving.

References

Agherli, B. B., Boughton, J. M., Montiel, P. J., Villanueva, D. & Woglom, G.: The role of national saving in the world economy. *Occasional Paper,* No. 67, IMF, Washington DC, 1990.

Blades, D.: Alternative measures of saving. *OECD Economic Outlook, Occasional Studies,* June 1983.

Dean, A., Durand, M., Fallon, J. & Hoeller, P.: Savings trends and behaviour in OECD countries. *OECD Economic Studies,* No. 14, Spring 1990.

Friedman, M.: *A Theory of the Consumption Function.* NBER, Princeton, 1957.

Horioka, C. Y.: Why is Japan's household saving rate so high? A literature survey. *Journal of Japanese and International Economies 4,* 1990.

Kuznets, S.: *Capital in the American Economy: Its Formation and Financing.* NBER, Princeton, 1961a.

Kuznets, S.: Long term trends in capital formation proportions. *Economic Development and Cultural Change,* July 1961b.

Kuznets, S.: Capital formation in modern economic growth. In his *Population, Capital and Growth: Selected Essays,* Heinemann, London, 1974.

Maddison, A.: *Economic Growth in the West,* Allen and Unwin, London, 1964.

Maddison, A.: Comparative analysis of the productivity situation in the advanced capitalist countries. In J. W. Kendrick (ed.), *International Comparisons of Productivity and Causes of the Slowdown.* Ballinger, Cambridge, MA, 1984.

Maddison, A.: *Dynamic Forces in Capitalist Development.* Oxford University Press, 1991.

Modigliani, F.: Life cycle, individual thrift, and the wealth of nations. *American Economic Review,* June 1986.

Sturm, P. H.: Determinants of saving: Theory and evidence. *OECD Economic Studies,* No. 1, Autumn 1983.

PART III

MEASURING LEVELS OF ECONOMIC PERFORMANCE

Part III: Measuring levels of economic performance

My interest in measuring spreads in performance of nations goes back to the 1940s when I read the pioneer works of Colin Clark (1940) and Rostas (1948). I did research on comparative manufacturing productivity levels in Canada, the UK and USA when I was a graduate student in McGill and Johns Hopkins Universities.

In the 1950s I had close colleagues (Beckerman, Bombach, Edelman, Gilbert, Kravis, Marris, Stuvel and Teichert) in OEEC who were engaged on major studies of real expenditure and product purchasing power parities. I myself did not work on these, but I was an enthusiastic user in monitoring performance of the OEEC economies. Studies of this kind add a sharper comparative perspective for assessing performance and potential.

In 1960 I became involved in development and foreign aid issues as the secretary of the Development Assistance Group (DAG) which later became a major OECD committee. We devised a framework for measuring the foreign aid efforts of donor countries, and for assessing its impact on recipient countries. In this field of burden sharing and foreign aid, it was of fundamental importance to have a measure of comparative levels of real product.

At that time, we had only rough World Bank guesstimates from various bits of evidence including the implications of the Gilbert-Kravis comparisons for OEEC countries. The Bank estimates were very different from exchange rate comparisons. For Japan (which at that time had an undervalued currency) they meant raising GDP per capita from 18 per cent to 31 per cent of the US level. As one of the early DAG meetings was in Tokyo in 1961, I had long discussions of this problem with Kazushi Ohkawa and Saburo Okita who were at first taken aback by this upward revision of Japan's living standard by three-quarters, but agreed on the importance of further research in this area. Ohkawa invited me to Hitotsubashi University for a seminar where I met Miyohei Shinohara, who subsequently made international comparisons for manufacturing, and Okita persuaded the Economic Planning Agency to take up research of this kind.

When I moved to the OECD Development Centre in 1964, Raymond Goldsmith and I tried to strengthen our assessment of Third World performance by setting up a systematic reporting procedure for national accounts, and pressed for action to improve level comparisons. The Centre commissioned Wilfred Beckerman (1966) to make a preliminary survey of the literature and produce surrogate non-monetary indicators. Irving Kravis was willing to undertake the bigger project, and in 1968 the Ford Foundation agreed to finance it. Kravis worked out a deal to locate the ICP (International Comparisons Project) in the University of Pennsylvania in cooperation with the UN Statistical Office.

The ICP expenditure approach is now a joint exercise of EUROSTAT/OECD/UN and has produced real output and PPP estimates for about 80 countries, with supplementary short-cut estimates by Summers and Heston which have now raised coverage to 150 countries.

The ICP studies did not start appearing until 1975 so I decided to make my own comparisons (Maddison, 1970) from the production side which I needed as a statistical frame for a survey of postwar economic performance. I made estimates of value added and productivity in agriculture, industry and services in US relative prices for 29 countries for 1965. The agriculture estimates were made from FAO sources, and for manufacturing I used a modified version of the estimates Shinohara had derived for manufacturing. For services I had no direct estimates, but I used employment figures and assumed that productivity in services varied *pro rata* with that in the commodity sector.

Kravis, Heston and Summers (1982) published expenditure-side estimates for 34 countries for 1975, and 18 of these overlapped with my 29 countries for 1965.

Essay 7 (Maddison, 1983) is a confrontation of my production-side estimates with theirs. I also used the two sets of estimates as benchmarks for merger with historical national accounts to see what the implications were for comparative levels of performance at the beginning of the capitalist epoch. I concluded provisionally that the Kravis-Heston-Summers approach probably exaggerated service output in the poorer countries, but an authoritative view on this topic required a new and more careful study from the production side than that which I had done in 1970. I therefore set up the ICOP programme (International Comparisons of Output and Productivity) at the University of Groningen in 1983. About 60 research memoranda or publications appeared in the 10 years 1983–93 including two outstanding PhD theses by van Ark (1993) and Pilat (1993). A survey of the ICOP work can be found in Maddison and van Ark (1994).

Essays 8 and 9 emerged from this research programme and they explain the problems and the methods used in such comparisons. Agriculture (see Essay 8 with Harry van Ooststroom) was the first sector we tackled and the approach was basically a more sophisticated replication of what I had done in 1970. An earlier version of this paper had considerable influence on Prasada Rao in his work on the official FAO estimates.

Essay 9 (Maddison and van Ark, 1989) was the first of the ICOP comparisons for manufacturing (of which there are now more than 20). It tackled the main analytic problems, surveyed the previous literature, and devised matching procedures which exploited the potential of modern computer technology which was not available to earlier investigators like Rostas (1948) and Paige and Bombach (1959). A fuller description of the procedures can be found in Maddison and van Ark (1988).

References

van Ark, B. (1993), 'International Comparisons of Output and Productivity', PhD, University of Groningen, April.

Beckerman, W. (1966), *International Comparisons of Real Incomes*, OECD Development Centre.

Clark, C. (1940), *Conditions of Economic Progress*, Macmillan, London.

Gilbert, M. and I. B. Kravis (1954), *An International Comparison of National Products and the Purchasing Power Parity of Currencies*, OEEC, Paris.

Kravis, I.B., A. Heston and R. Summers (1982), *World Product and Income*, Johns Hopkins, Baltimore.

Maddison, A. (1970), *Economic Progress and Policy in Developing Countries*, Allen and Unwin, London, and Norton, New York.

Maddison, A. (1983), 'A Comparison of Levels of GDP Per Capita in Developed and Developing Countries, 1700–1980', *Journal of Economic History*, March.

Maddison, A. and B. van Ark (1988), *Comparisons of Real Output in Manufacturing*, Working Paper WPS 5, World Bank, Washington DC, April.

Maddison, A. and B. van Ark (1989), 'International Comparison of Purchasing Power, Real Output and Labour Productivity: A Case Study of Brazilian, Mexican and US Manufacturing, 1975', *Review of Income and Wealth*, March.

Maddison, A. and B. van Ark (1994), 'International Comparisons of Real Output and Productivity', Research Memorandum, Groningen Growth and Development Centre.

Maddison, A. and H. van Ooststroom (1993), 'The International Comparison of Value Added, Productivity and Purchasing Power Parities in Agriculture', Research Memorandum, Groningen Growth and Development Centre.

Paige, D. and G. Bombach (1959), *A Comparison of National Output and Productivity of the United Kingdom and United States*, OEEC, Paris.

Pilat, D. (1993), 'The Economics of Catch Up: The Experience of Japan and Korea', PhD Thesis, University of Groningen, November.

Rostas, L. (1948), *Comparative Productivity in British and American Industry*, Cambridge University Press.

LDC
MDC

189- 203
(1983) N10

[7]

047 0412
K1230
C82 2210
2260
047

A Comparison of Levels of GDP Per Capita in Developed and Developing Countries, 1700–1980

ANGUS MADDISON

This paper examines the evolution of the per capita income gap between developed and developing countries. Landes and Kuznets suggest that Western countries already had a big lead before their economic growth accelerated, but Bairoch has recently claimed that European living standards in the mid-eighteenth century were lower than in the rest of the world. I think the existing evidence supports the Landes-Kuznets position, and that Bairoch probably overstates the contemporary income gap and understates per capita income growth in the developing world. But there are contradictory elements in the evidence, on which further research is needed.

O NE of the most interesting questions in comparative economic history is the gap in levels of real income between developed and developing countries. We know that this gap is large today and infer that it was smaller in the past because the available growth record shows much slower per capita growth in the developing world over the past 160 years (Table 1). But there is disagreement about the size of the gap in the eighteenth century, before the great acceleration in Western growth.

David Landes wrote in 1969: "Western Europe . . . was already rich before the Industrial Revolution—rich by comparison with other parts of the world of that day and with the pre-industrial world of today. This wealth was the product of centuries of slow accumulation, based in turn on investment, the appropriation of extra-European resources and labour, and substantial technological progress, not only in the production of material goods, but in the organization and financing of their exchange and distribution."[1]

Landes's benchmarks for Europe were Phyllis Deane's estimate for Britain and Marczewski's for France. His figures for real income levels in developing countries in 1961 were derived from Rosenstein-Rodan, who had made a rough upward adjustment from official exchange rate figures averaging 59 percent for the developing world.[2] Landes offset

Journal of Economic History, Vol. XLIII, No. 1 (March 1983). © The Economic History Association. All rights reserved. ISSN 0022-0507.

The author is Professor of Economic History at the University of Groningen, Netherlands. He is grateful for comments on an earlier draft from Paul Bairoch, Raymond Goldsmith, Irving Kravis, and Simon Kuznets, and for bibliographic help from Carlos Diaz Alejandro and Billie Salter, but does not suggest that they agree with the findings here.

[1] See David S. Landes, *The Unbound Prometheus* (Cambridge, 1969), pp. 13–14.

[2] See Phyllis Deane, *The First Industrial Revolution* (Cambridge, 1965), p. 7; and P. N. Rosenstein-Rodan, "International Aid for Underdeveloped Countries," *Review of Economics and Statistics* (May 1961), 118–22.

27

TABLE 1
GROWTH OF GDP PER HEAD OF POPULATION
(annual average compound growth rates)

Country	1820–1870	1870–1913	1913–1950	1950–1973	1973–1980
Argentina		1.5	0.6	2.2	0.1
Bangladesh				−0.7	2.5
Brazil	0.1	1.2	1.6	4.3	5.0
China	(0.0)	0.5	−0.4	4.0	3.7
Colombia			1.3	2.3	3.1
Egypt			0.2	1.7	6.6
Ghana		0.9	1.1	1.2	−3.0
India	(0.0)	0.6	−0.1	1.4	1.7
Mexico	0.0[a]	0.8[b]	1.7[c]	3.1	2.4
Pakistan				1.7	2.2
Peru			2.2	2.7	−0.7
Philippines			−0.3	2.9	3.6
South Korea			−0.9	4.7	4.9
Spain			−0.3	5.9	1.0
Thailand				4.0	4.4
Turkey				3.2	2.3
Arithmetic Average	(0.0)	(0.9)	0.6	2.8	2.5
Advanced Country Average	1.1	1.4	1.2	3.8	1.8

[a] 1803–1877.
[b] 1877/78–1910.
[c] 1910–1950.
Source: Developing countries from Tables 5 and 7. Average for 16 advanced countries from Angus
Maddison, *Phases of Capitalist Development* (London and New York, 1982).

most of this by an unwarranted augmentation of Phyllis Deane's (and
implicitly Marczewski's) estimates by one-third. The Landes conclusion was endorsed by Kuznets in his Nobel Prize lecture in 1971: "The
less developed areas that account for the largest part of the world
population today are at much lower per capita product levels than were
the developed countries just before their industrialization."[3]

More recently, Paul Bairoch has taken quite the opposite view: "It is
very likely that, in the middle of the eighteenth century, the average
standard of living in Europe was a little bit lower than that of the rest of
the world."[4] Bairoch's results derive from a bigger upward adjustment

[3] See Simon Kuznets, *Population, Capital and Growth* (London, 1974), p. 179. The underlying
evidence for his conclusion is presented in Kuznets, *Economic Growth of Nations*, (Cambridge,
Massachusetts, 1971), chap. 1. The benchmark for comparison there is 1965 levels of per capita
income converted at exchange rates. He also makes the dubious Rostow-type assumption (p. 25)
that modern economic growth in most of the developed world began at dates staggered throughout
the nineteenth century, and is therefore comparing developed world performance at a later date
than Landes. In an earlier consideration of the same problem (*Modern Economic Growth* [New
Haven, 1966], chap. 7), Kuznets had augmented the relative per capita GDP of developing
countries using purchasing power rather than exchange rate conversions, and reached conclusions
about the Western lead that were distinctly more cautious.
[4] See P. Bairoch and M. Lévy-Leboyer, eds., *Disparities in Economic Development since the
Industrial Revolution* (London, 1981), p. 7.

Levels of GDP Per Capita 29

of present-day third world income than that of Landes and Kuznets by a multiplier of 1.95, and from very low estimates of third world per capita growth (8 percent from 1800 to 1950).[5]

These remarkably different quantitative conclusions have very different analytical implications. If Bairoch is right, then much more of the backwardness of the third world presumably has to be explained by colonial exploitation and much less of Europe's advantage can be due to scientific precocity, centuries of slow accumulation, and organizational and financial superiority.

Here I am mainly concerned with the evidence currently available on the benchmark problem. On growth rates I have merely presented what seemed to me the best currently available estimates of GDP and population growth, indicating the sources used. These can be compared in detail with the Bairoch estimates when the latter become available, but it seems clear that my sources show somewhat faster growth than he suggests.

THE BENCHMARK COMPARISON OF LEVELS

In Table 2 I have linked my own benchmark estimates of comparative real product per head in 1965 in American prices (second column of Table 3) with my preferred estimates of 1820–1980 per capita growth rates (derived from Tables 4 and 5). The results of this comparison come much closer to the Landes-Kuznets conclusion than to that of Bairoch. For 1820 the unweighted average is $113 per capita for four big developing countries (Brazil, China, India, and Mexico) compared with an average of $280 for France, Britain, and the United States. The three advanced countries shown in Table 2 were about 15 percent above the Western average in 1820, but even so the Western lead over the developing world is 2:1. Going back to the mid-eighteenth century (1760) and assuming that the third world per capita product stagnated before 1820, one still finds a clear lead in France and Britain.

My benchmark estimates for 1965 represent levels of net output for five sectors of the economy, using 80 quantitative indicators of output in agriculture, forestry, and fishing, 70 for industry, and estimates for services based on employment data and relative productivity assumptions.[6] They were made quite independently of the national accounts estimates for all countries except the United States. They differ from the

---

[5] This seems to be a "synthesis" from shortcut estimates of Beckerman and Bacon, Bennett, Braithwaite, Colin Clark, Delahaut and Kirschen, Kravis, Heston, and Summers, and Niewaroski; see P. Bairoch, "Ecarts Internationaux des Niveaux de Vie avant La Révolution Industrielle," *Les Annales* (Jan.-Feb. 1979), 155.

[6] See Angus Maddison, *Economic Progress and Policy in Developing Countries* (New York, 1970), pp. 278–96. This study covered 22 developing countries and compared their per capita production with that of seven developed countries (France, Germany, Italy, Japan, Britain, the United States, and the Soviet Union).

TABLE 2
LEVELS OF REAL DOMESTIC PRODUCT AT FACTOR COST PER HEAD OF
POPULATION
(at 1965 United States factor cost)

Country	1980	1965	1950	1913	1870	1820	1760	1700
Argentina	1,632	1,301	1,013	804	420			
Bangladesh	133	136	132					
Brazil	1,113	479	309	169	101	97		
China	404	224	127	149	118	118		
Colombia	608	371	302	184				
Egypt	528	301	231	213				
Ghana	190	232	236	156	104			
India	235	186	152	159	123	123		
Mexico	643	427	282	143[a]	110[b]	112[c]		
Pakistan	257	187	152					
Peru	463	401	269	121				
Philippines	430	279	175	195				
South Korea	645	262	163	232				
Spain	1,608	976	401	444				
Thailand	505	258	160					
Turkey	451	295	191					
France	3,374	2,025	1,142	794	423	254	198	185
United Kingdom	2,544	2,046	1,439	1,025	668	312	233	205
United States	4,295	3,229	2,384	1,344	567	276		

[a] 1910.
[b] 1877/1878.
[c] 1803.
Source: 1965 level derived from column 2 of Table 3 and time series from sources cited for Table 1.

sources used by Landes and Bairoch, which were mostly shortcut procedures extrapolating from the evidence of expenditure studies for purchasing power parity of developed countries.

Recently Kravis, Heston, and Summers have produced an ambitious 34-country study of real GDP levels in international dollars for 1975, which provides an alternative estimate of contemporary performance levels in 18 developing and 16 developed countries.[7] They use an "expenditure" approach which compares prices for 151 components of final consumption, investment, government spending, and foreign balance. They compare national prices with "world" prices and then convert the exchange rate GDP figure into "world" prices. Table 3 compares the Kravis-Heston-Summers estimates of per capita product for 1965 with those from my production approach. For the five developed countries in the table the "expenditure" and "product" approaches give similar results—an average of 56.2 percent of American per capita product for my approach, and 58.2 percent for theirs—a difference of less than 4 percent. For Britain the results were identical,

[7] See I. B. Kravis, A. Heston, and R. Summers, *World Product and Income* (Baltimore, 1982).

Levels of GDP Per Capita 31

TABLE 3

ALTERNATIVE MEASURES OF REAL GDP PER HEAD OF POPULATION IN 1965

(United States GDP per capita = 100.00)

Country	At Official Exchange Rate	At 1965 United States Factor Cost (Maddison)	At 1975 Multilateral Weights (Kravis)	At 1970 Multilateral Weights (Kravis Shortcut)
Argentina	27.89	40.30		40.00
Bangladesh	1.98	4.22[b]		6.52
Brazil	7.26[a]	14.82	16.66	19.99
China		6.94[c]	9.76	
Colombia	9.66	11.48	18.96	16.58
Egypt	5.05	9.32		11.46
Ghana	7.14	7.19		13.15
India	2.94	5.76	6.81	6.68
Mexico	14.56	13.24	30.66	24.01
Pakistan	3.22	5.79[b]	8.57	9.06
Peru	9.34[a]	12.41		22.98
Philippines	5.52	8.63	12.62	12.37
South Korea	3.11	8.11	11.86	9.63
Spain	22.57	30.22	41.76	34.10
Thailand	3.63	7.99	9.59	8.07
Turkey	7.61	9.14		16.44
France	53.05	62.71	65.39	63.05
Germany	53.22	66.73[d]	74.85	71.14
Italy	31.27	42.14	46.28	42.26
Japan	26.27	46.01	41.09	40.54
United Kingdom	49.89	63.35	63.31	62.98
United States	100.00	100.00	100.00	100.00

[a] Excludes depreciation.

[b] Derived from estimate for original Pakistan. Interwing split (Bangladesh 45.1, present Pakistan 54.9 percent of GDP of former Pakistan) from *Reports of the Advisory Panels for the Fourth Five Year Plan 1970–1975*, vol. 1 (Islamabad, 1970).

[c] Derived from Kravis 1975 estimate, linked via Philippines, the country nearest Chinese 1975 GDP levels per capita in Kravis estimate.

[d] Excludes Berlin.

Sources: Column One: 1965 GDP at factor cost and official exchange rates from World Bank, *World Tables* (Baltimore, 1980); population from *World Tables* except for European countries and Japan, which are from O.E.C.D., *Labour Force Statistics*.

Column Two: GDP estimates at factor cost converted at United States relative prices from Angus Maddison, *Economic Progress and Policy in Countries* (New York, 1970), p. 295, divided by population as above and adjusted for revision in benchmark United States GDP at factor cost $618,609 million to $627,600 million (from *World Tables*).

Column Three: Real GDP per capita at multilateral weights and market prices extrapolated from 1975 phase III results from I. B. Kravis, A. Heston, and R. Summers, *World Product and Income* (Baltimore, 1982), p. 333, except China, which is from the 1975 estimate of I. B. Kravis, "An Approximation of the Relative Real Per Capita GDP of the People's Republic of China," *Journal of Comparative Economics*, 5 (1981) backcast to 1965 from movement of Chinese per capita GDP 1965–1975 relative to that in the United States.

Column Four: Per capita GDP at market prices from R. Summers, I. B. Kravis, and A. Heston, "International Comparison of Real Product and its Composition: 1950–77," *Review of Income and Wealth* (March 1980), 44–46.

which was also the case of the earlier British/American comparisons by the two methods for 1950.[8]

For the developing countries the two methods diverge much more. For the ten countries in the third column of Table 3, the expenditure approach yields per capita GDPs averaging 16.73 percent of the United States, whereas the product method yields an average of 11.30. My estimate for all the countries except China involves multiplying the 1965 exchange rate valuation by a factor of 1.43, whereas the Kravis-Heston-Summers procedure involves a multiplier of 2.04.[9]

Before noting the possible causes for this, it is well to look at the implications of the Kravis-Heston-Summers estimates for historical comparisons. Extrapolating from their benchmark (with the figures from Tables 4 and 5), the average per capita product of the four developing countries in 1820 was 60 percent of the three Western countries. Going back to 1760, and again assuming stagnant per capita performance in the developing countries, one finds the four developing average 77 percent of per capita levels in Britain and France. This is not quite the Bairoch position but is nearer to it than to that of Landes-Kuznets. If we use the Kravis-Heston-Summers estimates at American prices instead of their preferred multilateral weights, the 1760 position would be virtually as Bairoch claims.

Thus a good deal hangs on the benchmark comparisons. The Kravis-Heston-Summers study is more recent, more sophisticated, and more painstaking than mine, but I do not think one can reject the results of the "production" approach as implausible simply because they differ from the results of the expenditure approach.[10] There are many differences in the two benchmark approaches and for a proper reconciliation one would need estimates of both kinds for the same year and a set of input-output tables for each country, because in the expenditure approach the breakdown of the economy by sectors is not the same as in the production approach.

The most important issue determining the outcome of real income comparisons that cover countries at widely differing levels is the treatment of services. For many of these the output or quality of output is difficult to measure, and one is often forced to rely on employment (or employment-adjusted) comparisons as a rough proxy for a substantial portion of service output. In my study I assumed that productivity in services was related to that in commodity production, with a floor level

[8] See Kravis, Heston, and Summers, *World Product*, p. 27, which compares the Bombach-Paige study with the Gilbert-Kravis study.

[9] The Kravis-Heston-Summers multiplier is even bigger at American prices. For 1975 it was 2.77 compared with 2.29 for the comparison (including China) at their international prices (see Table 10).

[10] See Kuznets (*Population, Capital and Growth*, p. 333), who rejects my results because they did not conform to his expectations of relative price differentials (expectations derived from his interpretation of the results of previous expenditure-type comparisons).

Levels of GDP Per Capita   33

TABLE 4
INDEX OF GDP AT CONSTANT PRICES
(1950 = 100.00)

Country	1820	1870	1913	1950	1965	1973	1980
Argentina		4.34	35.40	100.0	166.1	234.7	260.3
Bangladesh				100.0	150.3	154.1	224.3
Brazil	2.68	6.08	24.41	100.0	241.9	504.8	809.2
China	59.51	59.51	92.18	100.0	231.9	395.6	567.9
Colombia			25.70	100.0	195.9	319.1	463.7
Egypt			54.80	100.0	187.1	248.5	443.9
Ghana		12.89	30.84	100.0	174.8	212.6	215.8
India	36.93	47.06	72.76	100.0	164.5	220.9	286.7
Mexico	8.71[a]	14.15[b]	28.80[c]	100.0	244.1	405.3	578.2
Pakistan				100.0	176.6	266.1	381.1
Peru			25.30	100.0	222.8	339.8	386.4
Philippines			51.28	100.0	241.0	369.0	562.2
South Korea			71.97	100.0	222.3	468.0	749.7
Spain			81.10	100.0	278.4	466.5	537.6
Thailand				100.0	247.2	459.7	734.2
Turkey				100.0	231.0	370.8	514.7

[a] 1803.
[b] 1877/78.
[c] 1910.

Sources: 1950 onwards generally from World Bank, *World Tables, 1980* (Washington, D.C., 1980) and idem, *World Development Report, 1981* (Washington, D.C., 1981). Otherwise as follows:

Argentina: 1870–1950 from C. F. Diaz Alejandro, *Essays on the Economic History of the Argentine Republic* (New Haven, 1970), pp. 3, 417–20.

Bangladesh: 1950–1960 from Angus Maddison, *Class Structure and Economic Growth* (London, 1971), p. 171.

Brazil: 1870–1950 real GDP from C. R. Contador and C. L. Haddad, "Produto Real, Moeda e Preços: A Experiência Brasileira No Periodo 1861–1870," *Revista Brasileira de Estadistica* (July–Sept. 1975). Table C-2 1820–1870 derived from N. H. Leff, *Undevelopment and Development in Brazil* (London, 1982), vol. 1, pp. 33–34.

China: 1914/18 from D. W. Perkins, *China's Modern Economy in Historical Perspective* (Stanford, 1975), p. 117. For 1950–1977, calculated from A. G. Ashbrook's estimates for agriculture and industry in U.S. Congress, Joint Economic Committee, *Chinese Economy Post-Mao* (Washington, D.C., 1978), vol. 1, p. 231; assuming construction and modern-type transport and communication to increase parallel to average for agricultural and industrial product; assuming services to move parallel to population. Sector weights for 1952 from T-C. Liu and K-C. Yeh, *The Economy of the Chinese Mainland: National Income and Economic Development, 1933–1959* (Princeton, 1965), p. 66. For 1973–1980, derived from World Bank, *World Development Report* (Washington, D.C., 1982), p. 8. For 1870–1913 it was assumed that GDP per head grew at the same rate as for 1914/18–1933 as measured by Perkins, and that prior to 1870 it did not increase.

Colombia: 1929–1950 supplied by Statistics Division, ECLA, Santiago; 1913–1929 derived from L. J. Zimmerman, *Arme en RijkeLanden* (The Hague, 1964).

Egypt: 1911–1950 GDP at 1954 prices derived from B. Hansen and G. A. Marzouk, *Development and Economic Policy in the UAR (Egypt)* (Amsterdam, 1965), p. 3.

Ghana: 1870–1950 derived from R. Szereszewski, *Structural Changes in the Economy of Ghana* (London, 1965), who gives detailed estimates for the 1891–1911 period when per capita income first began to rise (p. 149) and who suggests (p. 92) that per capita growth from 1911 to 1955 was at 1.2 percent a year. I assumed that there was no increase in per capita product before 1891.

India: 1870–1950 from A. Heston, "National Income," in *Cambridge Economic History* (forthcoming). I assume that there was no rise in per capita GDP from 1820 to 1870 for

34   *Maddison*

of service productivity (a quarter of that of the United States) in the
country where commodity (agriculture plus industry) productivity was
lowest. In earlier studies Kravis, Heston, and Summers had assumed
for "comparison resistant" services that the productivity of inputs was
the same in developed and developing countries. In their latest study
they sift various kinds of evidence which leads them to assume that the
productivity of medical personnel is a good deal lower in developing
than in developed countries, but for teachers and civil servants they
assume only a small productivity gap. Indeed for several poor countries
they assume higher teacher productivity than in developed countries
because classes are bigger. Table 6 compares their productivity assumptions with mine. For "comparison resistant" services as a group they
assume very much higher productivity than I do, and this difference
helps to explain why Kravis-Heston-Summers have a higher real GDP
per head for the poorer countries. But this is only part of the service
story.

The Kravis-Heston-Summers approach identifies only about a quarter of GDP as services, because its view of the economy is an end-use
perspective. Many activities which are "services" from a production
perspective are "disguised" in the Kravis-Heston-Summers approach
because they are embedded in the end-use product. Thus consumption
of rice, meat, fish, milk, and so on are "commodity" activities valued at
retail market prices, whereas the production approach measures the
agricultural and the trading components separately at factor cost. The
importance of this can readily be seen in Table 7, which compares the
share of services in GDP at national prices as defined by the expenditure
and the production approaches. For the developing countries shown

---

reasons explained in Angus Maddison, *Class Structure and Economic Growth: India
and Pakistan since the Moghuls* (London, 1971), pp. 67–70.

Mexico: Derived from C. W. Reynolds, *The Mexican Economy: Twentieth-Century
Structure and Growth* (New Haven, 1970), 1900–1950 from pp. 340–41. For 1877/78–
1900 movements in agricultural and industrial output, *Fuerza de Trabajo y Actividad
Economica* (Mexico City, 1964), movement in services assumed parallel to population
growth, and sector weights from Reynolds, *Mexican Economy*, for 1900. Reynolds
cites the Humboldt-Aubrey estimates for 1803 on p. 313, and I used the lowest of these.

Peru: 1913–1941 from C. A. Boloña Behr, "Tariff Policies in Peru, 1880–1980," (Ph.D.
thesis, Oxford, 1981). For 1942–1950, ECLA, "Cuadros del Producto Interno Bruto a
Precios del Mecado en dolares de 1950" (Santiago, 1962), mimeo.

Philippines: Derived by interpolation from figures for 1902, 1918, 1948, and 1961 in
R. W. Hooley, "Long-Term Growth of the Philippine Economy, 1902–1961," *The
Philippine Economic Journal* (First semester, 1968).

South Korea: Commodity output for 1910–1940 from Sang-Chul Suh, *Growth and
Structural Changes in the Korean Economy, 1910–40* (Cambridge, Massachusetts,
1978), p. 171, and 1950–1953 from Kwang Suk Kim and M. Roemer, *Growth and
Structural Transformation* (Cambridge, Massachusetts, 1979), p. 35. It was assumed
that service output moved parallel to population, and sector weights for 1953 were
taken from Kim and Roemer, p. 35. For 1950–1953, GDP at factor cost from United
Nations, *The Growth of World Industry, 1938–61* (New York, 1963), p. 484.

Spain: 1913–1950 derived from Consejo de Economia Nacional, *La Renta Nacional de
Espagna 1940–1964* (Madrid, 1965), pp. 112, 164.

Levels of GDP Per Capita   35

TABLE 5
POPULATION
(thousands)

Country	1820	1870	1913	1950	1973	1980
Argentina	534	1,796	7,653	17,150	24,709	27,700
Bangladesh	a	a	a	40,574	73,146	90,200
Brazil	4,540	9,797	23,660	52,901	103,659	118,700
China	350,000	350,000	430,000	547,100	877,400	976,700
Colombia	1,240	2,560	4,885	11,597	22,623	26,700
Egypt	3,190	5,873	12,170	20,461	34,629	39,800
Ghana	(800)	(1,275)	2,042	4,368	9,415	11,700
India	199,700[a]	253,200[a]	303,700[a]	361,575	583,107	673,200
Mexico	6,530	9,002	15,160[b]	26,606	55,493	67,500
Pakistan	a	a	a	36,450	66,162	82,200
Peru	1,600	2,592	4,400	7,832	14,660	17,600
Philippines	2,176	5,063	9,384	20,895	39,991	47,900
South Korea	5,900	7,000	10,277	20,356	33,304	38,500
Spain	12,206	16,213	20,435	27,868	34,858	37,400
Thailand	4,000	5,700	8,492	20,010	39,015	46,500
Turkey	6,900	10,700	14,860	20,809	38,094	45,400
Total	599,316	680,771	867,118	1,232,184	2,050,265	2,347,700
Total Advanced Countries	151,170	240,350	387,290	494,979	639,685	671,166

[a] Figures for India, 1820–1913, include present areas of Bangladesh and Pakistan.
[b] 1910.

Sources: Argentina: 1820–1913 from C. F. Diaz Alejandro, *Essays*, p. 421.

Brazil: 1820 derived from T. W. Merrick and D. H. Graham, *Population and Economic Development in Brazil* (Baltimore, 1979), p. 31; 1870–1913 from *O Brasil em Numeros*, IBGE (Rio de Janeiro, 1960), p. 5.

China: 1820–1913 from D. H. Perkins, *Agricultural Development in China 1368–1968* (Chicago, 1969), p. 16; 1950 onwards from World Bank.

Colombia: 1820–1913 derived from W. P. McGreevey, *An Economic History of Colombia, 1845–1930* (Cambridge, 1971), p. 287.

Egypt: 1820–1913 from Hansen and Marzouk, *Development and Economic Policy*, pp. 22–23.

Ghana: 1820–1913, no estimates are available, so population assumed to grow at same rate as in other 15 countries.

India: 1820–1913 from Maddison, *Class Structure and Economic Growth: India and Pakistan*, pp. 164–65.

Mexico: 1820–1913 derived from Reynolds, *Mexican Economy*, p. 384.

Peru: 1820–1870 from *Encyclopaedia Britannica*, 1885 edition.

Philippines: 1820–1913 from Kirsten, Buchholz, and Köllmann, *Raum und Bevölkerung in der Weltgeschichte* (Wurzburg, 1956).

South Korea: 1820–1913 assumed to grow at same pace as Japan. For 1913–1940, growth for Korea as a whole from Sang-Chul Suh, *Growth and Structural Change*, p. 41. For 1940–1953, from Kim and Roemer, *Growth and Structural Transformation*, p. 35.

Thailand: 1820–1870 based on Bowring's estimates as cited by J. C. Ingram, *Economic Change in Thailand, 1850–1970* (Stanford, 1971), p. 7.

Turkey: 1820–1913 derived from M. G. Mulhall, *The Dictionary of Statistics* (London, 1899), p. 450, and Kirsten, Buchholz, and Köllmann, *Raum und Bevölkerung*, vol. 2, p. 247.

Otherwise 1870–1913 figures are from Angus Maddison, *Economic Progress and Policy in Developing Countries* (New York, 1970); 1950–1973 from World Bank, *World Tables*; 1980 from O.E.C.D., *Geographical Distribution of Financial Flows to Developing Countries, 1977/1980* (Paris, 1981).

36   *Maddison*

TABLE 6
A COMPARISON OF KRAVIS-HESTON-SUMMERS AND MADDISON ASSUMPTIONS
ABOUT LEVEL OF PRODUCTIVITY IN SERVICES

	Kravis-Heston-Summers Hypotheses				*Maddison Hypothesis for Services*
Country	*Medical Personnel*	*First- and Second-Level Teachers*	*Third-Level Teachers*	*Civil Servants*	
Brazil	50.0	82.5	91.9	95.5	34.5
Colombia	50.0	98.2	71.7	95.5	48.2
India	32.0	93.9	107.4	95.5	25.0
Mexico	70.0	123.9	96.2	97.7	33.2
Pakistan	32.0	127.7	112.0	95.5	25.5
Philippines	32.0	89.6	123.0	95.5	32.3
South Korea	50.0	128.3	109.7	95.5	26.5
Spain	83.0	109.3	93.2	100.0	46.6
Thailand	32.0	95.3	65.9	95.5	26.1
Average Developing	47.9	105.4	96.8	96.2	33.1
United States	100.0	100.0	100.0	100.0	100.0

Sources: Kravis, Heston, and Summers, *World Product*, pp. 149 and 155 for medical personnel; p.
157 for first- and second-level teachers (ratio of column 5 to column 2); p. 160 for third-
level teachers (ratio of column 3 to column 1); pp. 141 and 159 for civil servants.
Maddison, *Economic Progress and Policy in Developing Countries*, p. 291.

there, 44.2 percent of GDP is services when one looks at production,
but only 24.6 percent when one looks at final expenditure. The main
difference between the two is the trading activities, which in the
expenditure approach are embedded in "commodity" activity. Such
disguised services are bigger than the comparison-resistant services
discussed above. The latter are about 42 percent of the Kravis-Heston-
Summers definition of services, or around 10 percent of GDP, whereas
the disguised service output is almost 20 percent of GDP (44.2–24.6, see
Table 7).

Kravis, Heston, and Summers define their approach to the problem
as follows: "The ICP method of international comparisons. . . . simply
compares the extent to which each economy delivered meat and
potatoes, shoes and stockings, and other commodities to its residents
without regard to the extent or nature of the accompanying services.
The extent and nature of the bias that result from the omission of these
general quality factors are difficult to judge."[11] Their basic procedure is
the potato-is-a-potato rule. "A potato with given physical characteristics was treated not only as the same product but also as the same
quantity, whether it was purchased in the country, or in the city, in
January, or in June, by the piece or by the bushel, and whether it was

[11] See Kravis, Heston, Summers, *World Product*, pp. 30–33 for a discussion of the problem.

Levels of GDP Per Capita   37

TABLE 7

A COMPARISON OF THE RELATIVE SHARE OF "SERVICES" IN GDP AT
NATIONAL PRICES IN 1975 USING EXPENDITURE AND PRODUCTION APPROACHES

Country	Expenditure Approach	Production Approach
Brazil	27.3	50.9
Colombia	32.6	42.4
India	16.3	34.3
Mexico	26.2	52.2
Pakistan	20.9	44.7
Philippines	19.1	37.5
South Korea	28.4	42.1
Spain	29.4	50.3
Thailand	21.4	43.2
Average	24.6	44.2
France	35.4	57.4
Germany	37.5	48.7
Italy	33.7	50.1
Japan	34.3	54.2
United Kingdom	42.7	60.5
Average	36.7	54.2

Sources: First column at national prices from Kravis, Heston, and Summers, *World Product*,
Table 6–10, p. 194 (Kravis classification of services is on p. 69). Second column from
World Bank, *World Tables* (1980), GDP by industrial origin at current national prices;
"services" includes "transport and communications, trade and finance, public administration and defense, other branches."

purchased at a retail market or consumed out of own production." They
adjust for differences in quality and for some variations in packaging,
but not for variations in the amount of distributive service per unit of
consumption. For most consumption items the distributive and transport markups are large in developed countries.[12] It seems possible that
the lack of adjustment for variations in this proportion may lead to
overstatement of developing country real product.

My conclusion on the benchmark comparison is that the Kravis-
Heston-Summers expenditure-type comparison may well tend system-

[12] The distributive margin (for transport, wholesale, and retail trade) added 47 percent to
American producer prices for food in the United States in 1967, 70 percent for apparel, 74 percent
for footwear, and 111 percent for petroleum products. See "The Input-Output Structure of the U.S.
Economy: 1967," *Survey of Current Business* (Feb. 1974), 28. The evidence on distributive output
in developing countries is generally weak. P. T. Bauer and B. S. Yamey, *The Economics of
Underdeveloped Countries* (Cambridge, 1957), pp. 37–42, stress that distributive activity in these
countries is understated by occupational statistics, and it is clear that the distributive content of
items sold in very small quantities may be quite high. Nevertheless Kravis, Heston, and Summers
themselves mention several factors that suggest higher proportionate trade content in developed
countries, due to greater urbanization and the fact that people generally do not grow their own
food. They also acknowledge that in intertemporal comparisons the shift from farm to urban
consumption would usually lead to an increase in distributive output, which they do not measure in
their intercountry approach. (See Kravis, Heston, and Summers, *World Product*, p. 32.)

38   *Maddison*

TABLE 8
RATIO OF NATIONAL PRICE LEVEL TO UNITED STATES PRICE LEVEL BY SECTOR

Country	As Calculated by Kravis for 1975		As Calculated by Maddison for 1965			
	Services	Commodities	Services	Commodities	Agriculture	Industry
Brazil	41.0	80.7	46.5	53.7	44.4	59.7
Colombia	23.0	45.4	59.2	128.2	168.6	99.5
India	10.7	48.0	23.4	116.2	166.8	72.5
Mexico	38.8	74.2	120.5	102.5	125.7	94.4
Philippines	15.1	61.6	50.6	101.3	104.1	112.2
South Korea	23.7	50.5	18.5	99.7	138.3	68.1
Spain	52.3	89.9	74.5	76.8	149.0	64.6
Thailand	23.7	47.2	34.3	83.6	66.5	138.4
Average	28.5	62.2	53.4	95.3	120.4	88.7
France	95.8	121.4	111.1	90.3	135.0	84.7
Germany	105.4	122.9	87.6	102.8	201.5	98.9
Italy	68.4	105.3	90.9	79.4	163.6	68.7
Japan	79.2	101.9	54.9	70.6	151.5	63.4
United Kingdom	68.2	106.5	90.4	93.7	101.0	93.2
Average	83.4	111.6	87.0	87.4	150.5	81.8

Sources: First and second columns from Kravis, Heston, and Summers, *World Product*, Table 6–12, p. 196 (services are as defined by Kravis on p. 69). Last four columns derived from *World Tables*, valuation of 1965 sector output in 1965 prices converted by official exchange rate and divided by sector output at 1965 U.S. prices in A. Maddison, *Economic Progress and Policy in Developing Countries*, p. 294 with construction allocated to industry and transport and communications to services on basis of *World Tables* proportion. Commodities include output of agriculture, forestry, and fishing plus industry (mining, manufacturing, gas, water, electricity, and construction).

atically to overvalue developing country real product levels because of its treatment of comparison-resistant and disguised services. This bias does not appear to operate for comparisons of developed countries. My own preference is for the production-type benchmark which supports the Landes-Kuznets view; but my earlier benchmark study needs to be updated in more detail and crosschecked more carefully with the Kravis-Heston-Summers results. There is also need for more explicit confrontation of my evidence on growth trends with that which Bairoch is preparing.

RELIABILITY OF OFFICIAL DEVELOPING COUNTRY GROWTH RATES

Kuznets criticized the results of my production approach mainly because he considered implausible the relative price structure that emerged. He expected (from results of earlier expenditure comparisons) that developing countries would have a relative price advantage for agricultural products, but not for industry and services. He argued that

TABLE 9

GROWTH OF OUTPUT (GDP AT FACTOR COST) BY SECTOR 1950–1973

(annual average compound rate of growth)

Country	Agriculture, Forestry, and Fishing	Industry (Mining Manufacturing, Utilities, and Construction)	Services	Total	Reweighted Totals at U.S. Prices
Argentina	2.0	5.2	3.2	3.8	3.3
Bangladesh	1.4	5.2	2.1	1.9	n.a.
Brazil	4.1	8.7	7.2	7.3	7.1
China	3.5	12.3	2.7	6.2	n.a.
Colombia	3.5	6.6	5.7	5.2	5.5
Egypt	2.7	5.2	4.8	4.0	4.5
Ghana	3.7[a]	4.9[a]	0.0[a]	3.3	—
India	2.3	5.3	4.6	3.5	4.3
Mexico	3.6	7.7	6.1	6.3	6.5
Pakistan	2.8	8.6	4.5	4.3	n.a.
Peru	3.1	6.5	5.7	5.5	5.4
Philippines	4.0	7.4	6.4	5.8	6.1
South Korea	4.0	13.0	7.3	6.9	7.8
Spain	3.2[b]	9.5[b]	7.3[b]	6.9	—
Thailand	5.3	8.8	7.3	6.9	6.9
Turkey	2.8	7.6	7.8	5.9	6.3
Arithmetic Average	3.3	7.7	5.2	5.2[c]	5.8[d]

[a] 1965–1973.

[b] 1960–1973.

[c] The average of the 12 countries represented in the last column is 5.6.

[d] Average of 12 countries.

Source: See text.

because developing countries' national prices probably overvalue non-agricultural output their growth statistics exaggerate the importance of the most rapidly growing sectors. "The ratios of prices of industrial products to those of agricultural products are generally much higher in the less-developed than in the developed countries, according to a few tested price comparisons available. Consequently the I (and perhaps the S) sector has a greater weight in the current price estimates for the LDCs than it would have in those for the DCs; and some adjustment to assure better comparability is called for."[13] He assumes that the I/A ratio in developing countries is 1.5 of that in the developed and the S/A ratio 1.25 and then recalculates developing country growth rates with the weight of the I sector reduced by one-third and that of the S sector reduced by one-fifth. This reduces growth rates because the more rapidly growing sectors are given lower weights.

Table 8 shows that my estimates resulted in quite different sector weights. For the eight developing countries shown there my I/A ratio

[13] See Kuznets, *Population, Capital and Growth*, pp. 333, 336.

40   *Maddison*

TABLE 10

KRAVIS-HESTON-SUMMERS ALTERNATIVE MEASURES OF REAL GDP PER HEAD
OF POPULATION IN 1975

(United States per capita GDP = 100.00)

Country	Valued at Exchange Rates	Valued at Own Country Weights	Valued at United States Weights	Valued at Multilateral Weights
Brazil	16.00	19.30	30.70	25.20
China	2.60	5.00	21.00	12.30
Colombia	7.92	14.00	26.70	22.40
India	2.03	4.10	9.00	6.56
Korea	8.12	12.90	24.80	20.70
Mexico	20.40	30.00	42.20	34.70
Pakistan	2.64	4.60	9.30	8.23
Philippines	5.24	9.10	15.90	13.20
Thailand	5.00	7.70	15.10	13.00
Spain	41.00	47.20	62.00	55.90
Average	9.26	15.39	25.67	21.22
France	89.60	73.70	89.50	81.90
United Kingdom	57.60	60.80	73.50	63.90
United States	100.00	100.00	100.00	100.00

Sources: Kravis, Heston, and Summers, *World Product*, Tables 1–2, 7–3 to 7–30, and 3–6. China
from I. B. Kravis, "An Approximation of the Relative Real Per Capita GDP of the
People's Republic of China," *Journal of Comparative Economics*, 5 (1981).

was 88.7/120.4 (that is, 0.74) and my S/A ratio was 53.4/120.4 (that is,
0.44).[14] When I use American relative prices as weights, I therefore
increase the weight of industry and services relative to that for
agriculture, and hence give the faster growing sectors a bigger weight.
Thus for the 12 countries in Table 9 where it is possible to apply
American relative price weights, one gets a growth rate of GDP at factor
cost of 5.8 percent per year instead of the 5.6 percent recorded at
national prices by the World Bank's *World Tables* for 1950–1973.

It is clear from Table 8 that services are relatively cheaper than
commodities in developing countries whether one uses the Kravis-
Heston-Summers or Maddison approach, and it was already clear that
the Bombach-Paige study for Britain and the United States did not
confirm the Kuznets inference about sector price ratios from expenditure-type estimates.[15]

[14] See D. Paige and G. Bombach, *A Comparison of National Output and Productivity*, O.E.E.C.
(Paris, 1959), p. 19, from which sector price relatives can be derived comparable with those in the
last four columns of Table 8. For Britain in 1950 they were 44.8 for services, 70.9 for commodities,
86.6 for agriculture, and 69.3 for industry (that is, the I/A ratio was 0.80 and S/A ratio was 0.52).
Kuznets had an I/A ratio of 1.26 for Britain and an S/A ratio of 0.75. See S. Kuznets, *Economic
Growth of Nations* (Cambridge, Massachusetts, 1971), p. 137.
[15] Ibid.

Levels of GDP Per Capita 41

In short, the Kuznets-type manipulation of the earlier (Gilbert-Kravis) expenditure comparisons to derive proxies for the sector-weights emerging from a production approach is unlikely to produce reliable estimates because the two approaches are so different. The expenditure approach does not break down services and commodities in the same way as the product approach; it uses market price valuations that include the impact of tariffs, indirect taxes, and subsidies, and it relies on the validity of the national accounts of the developing countries in a way that is not true of the production approach.

8

The International Comparison of Value Added, Productivity and Purchasing Power Parities in Agriculture*

Angus Maddison and Harry van Ooststroom
University of Groningen

This study is part of the ICOP (International Comparison of Output and Productivity) project of the University of Groningen. It presents international comparisons of levels of value added, productivity and purchasing power parities (PPPs) in agriculture for 13 countries for 1975. An early version of this paper was issued in 1984 (Research Memorandum 162 of the Institute of Economic Research, Groningen). In 1985 a slightly revised version was given limited circulation. The present paper contains further revisions, makes an assessment of other studies in this field, confronts our results with those of Prasada Rao (1986 and 1992) and contains suggestions for further research.

I Our methodology and its relation to other studies

There were three stages in our procedure for estimating gross value added in agriculture.

a. We estimated the gross value of farm output from quantitative information on commodity production from FAO *Production Yearbooks*. We adopted a maximalist approach, including item headings for all products listed by FAO, and for some others for which we received supplementary FAO information. In this revised version of our estimates, wine is excluded as it is, in fact, a manufactured product and involved double counting. Thus we listed 149 potential product items (excluding wine) under 13 basic headings (cereals, vegetables, etc.). There were quite a few of these items for which FAO recorded no production in any of our 13 country sample, so a listing of 110 products (excluding wine) would have been adequate for our purpose. For China, 90 commodities were specified, the USA 84, Mexico 83, India 78, Brazil and Argentina 76, Japan 68, France 66, Korea 60, Germany 47, Indonesia 45, Netherlands and the UK 43 items.

  The quantities were valued at US producer prices as given in FAO's *Statistics on Prices Received by Farmers*. For commodities which did not exist in the USA we used 'shadow' US prices (derived from wheat or rice price relatives for 5 other countries) as

*We are grateful to the following persons who were kind enough to comment on earlier drafts: Bart van Ark, Derek Blades, Tom Elfring, Cees van der Meer, D.S. Prasada Rao, Vernon W. Ruttan, Robbin Shoemaker, Albert Simantov, Adolf Weber and Saburo Yamada. We are indebted to Maria Alice de Gusmao Veloso and Jagdish Kumar who gave us access to the detailed national accounts for agriculture in Brazil and India, to G. Parniczky and Nurul Islam of FAO, who provided a substantial amount of unpublished FAO material for 1975, to Robert Ballance of UNIDO for documentation on input–output structures and to Paul Wieringa, who assisted with preliminary data assessment.

well as some proxy prices. The proportionate importance of shadow and proxy pricing is indicated in the notes to Table 1.

The quality and amount of market information was better in the USA than in most countries. There were very few price holes for the USA, i.e. commodities where we had production but no price information from FAO. We had prices for 81 US items compared with no prices for China, 30 for Indonesia, 40 for the UK, 44 Netherlands, 46 Germany, 49 Japan, 50 India, 53 Korea, 69 Argentina and Brazil, 75 France, 81 Mexico. Reliance on shadow pricing was minimised by having the USA as the benchmark. As the USA was the lead country in terms of productivity, its price structure seemed the most appropriate for analysing problems of convergence and catch-up which were our central concern. However, it would be useful to expand the analysis of the present data set to cover the full range of bilateral measures (i.e. Paasche, Laspeyres and Fisher variants used in other ICOP studies for manufacturing as well as the Geary–Khamis multilateral measures used by ICP and FAO. This expansion of the present paper is contained in Prasada Rao and Maddison (1994).

b. The second stage in our calculation was to deduct inputs of feed and seed, which we derived from FAO *Food Balance Sheets* and valued at the same price as the outputs.

c. The third step was to estimate non-farm inputs. Fertiliser and pesticide inputs were derived from FAO publications, energy inputs from OECD sources. These were revalued at prices paid by US farmers. Quantitative indicators for other inputs for administrative, veterinary, irrigation, insurance, repair and maintenance costs etc., were not available. Values of these inputs were assumed to have the same proportionate relation to the combined value of fertiliser, pesticide and energy input in US dollars as they did in national currencies (this is equivalent to assuming their PPPs to be the same). The relevant values in national currency were mostly taken from FAO and OECD 'economic accounts' for agriculture.

Section II (below) provides a summary of the methods used in 9 other studies as well as the two earlier versions of the present study. These studies have a strong 'family' resemblance. Our own 1984/5 work was most strongly influenced by Paige and Bombach (1959) and Maddison (1970). In this revision we have paid particular attention to the lessons that can be derived from Prasada Rao (1986 and 1992) and van der Meer and Yamada (1988 and 1990).

All the studies summarised in Section II attempted to estimate value added. In some cases the allowance for non-agricultural inputs was crude as in Maddison (1970), Hayami and Ruttan (1971) and Prasada Rao (1986 and 1992). Terluin did not attempt to deduct for non-agricultural services. The most detailed attempt to measure inputs was in the van der Meer and Yamada studies (1988 and 1990); they also deducted depreciation (as did Mensink) in order to estimate net value added.

All the studies measured output of two or more countries in a common set of prices (purchasing power parities – PPPs). In binary studies, the PPPs were shown at own country and other country quantity weights (Paasche and Laspeyres variants). In multilateral studies, practice has varied. We showed our results in terms of US prices (Paasche PPP) and offered 6 other national price variants. Prasada Rao (1986 and 1992) used the multilateral Geary–Khamis PPP procedure favoured by the United Nations International Comparison Project.

This is a weighted average price system for all countries in the comparison which is meant to approximate to average world prices. This price system is transitive and is invariant to choice of base country. Terluin used the Gerardi PPP procedure, which has similar properties, but gives equal weight to all the EC countries involved in her comparison, whereas the Geary–Khamis variant gives weights according to the relative size of farm output in the countries considered. Hayami and Ruttan used a hybrid procedure – a geometric average of Japanese, Indian and US prices for measuring gross output, and a geometric average of Japanese and US prices for inputs. Our own preference is for simple, transparent, weighting systems, but, in future studies we would favour presenting as wide a range of alternative price systems as is feasible, because the array of different possible answers provides useful analytical information.

Most of the studies derive their measure of the value of gross output from detailed price and quantity information for individual commodities. Van der Meer and Yamada use a different approach in their binary comparison of Japan and the Netherlands. One might term it the 'accounts' approach as distinct from our 'commodity' approach. They start with value aggregates from the 'economic accounts' for agriculture, and deflate them by a composite price index to get an indirect measure of comparative output volume on a highly aggregate basis (with a threefold breakdown for crops, livestock, and horticultural products). Terluin used a similar procedure.

Most binary comparisons have made some kind of coverage adjustment for items not included in their detailed commodity specification. The van der Meer–Yamada approach involves an implicit coverage adjustment in that their value aggregates are comprehensive in coverage, whereas the commodities included in their composite price index are limited to 88/89 items. Implicitly they assume that the intercountry price variance for non-covered items is the same as the average for covered items. None of the multilateral studies (except that of Terluin, whose procedure is similar to that of van der Meer and Yamada) made an adjustment for non-covered items, i.e. they define the boundaries of agriculture in terms of the array of commodities they are able to specify and measure. Implicitly, they assume that the intercountry quantity variance for non-covered items is the same as the average for covered items.

The data available in internationally comparable form from FAO on quantity and price of agricultural products are much richer than those for manufacturing in UNIDO statistics. The structure of commodity output and inputs in agriculture is very much simpler than that in manufacturing, and FAO (together with its predecessor, the International Institute for Agriculture) has been working towards data standardisation and enhanced international comparability for nearly 70 years. It is quite striking that none of the cross-country comparisons listed in Section II was based on agricultural censuses, because of the wealth of information from secondary sources. This is in contrast with the situation for manufacturing, where the ICOP programme has relied almost exclusively on census material. In manufacturing, there are major problems in making matches for products which vary in quality and specification, whereas these problems can and have been largely ignored in agricultural comparisons. None of the agricultural studies makes any adjustment for intercountry variation in the quality of products.

II Summary description of previous studies of agricultural value added, productivity, and/or PPPs

PAIGE and BOMBACH (1959). 2 Countries. 62 Farm Products.
(Part of gross value added, labour productivity and PPP comparison for total GNP in UK/ USA 1959)

> Individual products in each country were weighted by own prices and other country prices to produce Paasche and Laspeyres output estimates. Where British prices were missing, e.g. for tobacco, corn and citrus fruit, import prices were used. UK output data were available net of feed and seed. Some minor use of coverage adjustments with both equiprice and equiquantity assumptions. No quality adjustments. End result adjusted to a national accounts basis, i.e. agricultural contribution to gross national product. Fishery output measured crudely by total weight of fish catch. No mention of forestry. Productivity measured in terms of output per 'worker'. Official UK and US sources.

MENSINK (1966). 2 Countries. 35 Farm and Horticulture Products.
(Part of comparison of net value added and labour productivity in manufacturing and agriculture UK/Netherlands 1958/9)

> Similar to Paige and Bombach, showing Paasche and Laspeyres variants. Greater use of coverage adjustment for non-specified products. All such adjustments were on an equiprice basis. No quality adjustments. Paasche and Laspeyres comparisons were shown. End result more or less on a national accounts basis, with a rough adjustment for depreciation. Butter and cheese processing treated as part of agriculture. Productivity measured in terms of output per man year. Sources are UK official publications and Dutch CBS files.

MADDISON (1970). 29 Countries. 89 Farm Products, 3 Fishery and 4 Forestry Products.
(Part of industry of origin comparison of gross value added, and labour productivity for GDP at factor cost in 1965)

> Similar to Paige and Bombach. All estimates at US prices (FAO North American wheat relatives converted into dollars). Commodity quantities from FAO sources. Detailed information on non-farm inputs was available only for a few countries, so fertiliser inputs were used as a proxy in most cases to arrive at estimate of agricultural contribution to GDP at factor cost. Productivity measured in terms of output per person engaged. Also included estimates of food consumption.

HAYAMI and RUTTAN (1971). 43 Countries. 53 Farm Products.
(Estimate of farm output, net of feed and seed, and approximate gross value added 1957–62)

> Individual product output, feed and seed inputs for each country weighted by FAO wheat price relatives for India, Japan and USA. Composite indicator derived as geometric average of 3 weighting systems. No coverage or quality adjustments. Crude measures of gross value added using benchmark data on non-farm inputs in Japan and USA; inputs in other countries proxied by fertiliser use and stock of farm machinery; composite indicator of these inputs using geometric average of 2 weighting systems. Hayami and Ruttan were rather dubious about the quality of their value added estimates and used their gross output benchmark for intertemporal extrapolation. In the 1985 update of their book the attempt to measure gross value added was dropped.

SMITH, HITCHENS and DAVIES (1982). 3 Countries. 38 Farm Products.
(Part of comparison of gross value added and labour productivity in commodity-producing sectors, UK/USA, UK/Germany in 1974)
> Paasche and Laspeyres quantity comparison. Seems to have involved weighting of commodities by prices of each country, with some use of shadow prices and coverage adjustments. No adjustment for quality. Forestry and fishing measured roughly. Fertiliser input adjusted by FAO price data, other inputs adjusted by output prices. Official national sources were used.

VAN OOSTSTROOM and MADDISON (1984 and 1985). 14 Countries. 150 Farm Products.
(Estimate of gross value added, land and labour productivity and producer PPPs for agriculture, forestry and fishing in 1975)
> Quantities of individual commodities, feed and seed inputs, were weighted by US prices. No adjustment for coverage or quality. Four categories of non-farm inputs were measured, fertilisers, pesticides, energy and service inputs. Energy input measured by proxy. Service inputs by value ratios in national currencies. Paasche PPPs shown only for gross value of farm output, productivity in terms of land and persons engaged. Material nearly all from FAO. The 1985 paper was a revised and expanded version of the 1984 study with 11 appendices instead of 5, with revised estimates of feed and seed inputs, minor modification in the measure for service inputs, and improved estimates for forestry. Paasche PPPs shown for gross output, total inputs and gross value added. Supplementary estimates were presented for output of grass and hay, dung, the increment in livestock herds and food consumption levels.

PRASADA RAO (1986). 95 Countries. 173 Farm Products.
(Estimate of gross value added, labour productivity and Geary–Khamis PPPs for 1970, 1975 and 1980)
> Quantities of individual commodities, feed and seed inputs, were weighted by Geary–Khamis average world prices (using price data for all 95 countries). No coverage or quality adjustment. Non-farm input values from FAO farm accounts were divided by Geary–Khamis fertiliser prices as a proxy for all input prices. The 29 country input proxy was regressed against 6 variables representing levels of development, and reproxied for a further 53 countries for which the 6 indicators were available. Rough estimate of gross value added presented for 82 countries (for 13 communist countries, the reproxying procedure not feasible).

VAN DER MEER and YAMADA (1988 and 1990). 2 Countries. 3 Product Groups,
deflated by composite interspatial Paasche and Laspeyres price indices.
(Full binary comparison for Japan/Netherlands of net value added, land and labour productivity in 1975. Rough quadrilateral comparison including Taiwan and USA. Supplementary 26 country comparison of gross value added (1975) adjusting FAO (1986) estimates by input value ratio from farm accounts at national prices)
> They derive price indices for three categories of farm output (arable crops, horticulture and livestock), for 9 Japanese and 12 Dutch input categories, and for depreciation. These

are then applied to the corresponding value estimates from the farm accounts to derive intercountry comparisons of the volume of output and input. The results are generally shown on both a Paasche and Laspeyres basis. For Japan 88 product prices were used, for the Netherlands 89. The Netherlands does not produce rice, so the Italian rice/wheat price ratio was used as a Dutch shadow price. As rice had a weight of 34 per cent in the Japanese price index, this procedure had a large effect on their results. Their method involves an implicit, equiprice, coverage adjustment. Labour productivity is measured in man hours, and they also show land productivity. The basis for the Taiwan and US comparisons is not very clearly described. All their comparisons are reviewed in the context of developments since 1880, with some merger of time series and benchmark estimates.

TERLUIN (1990). 9/10 Countries. 20 Product Groups deflated by composite Gerardi interspatial price indices.
(Estimate of farm output, inputs except services, and surrogate gross value added – without deduction for service inputs, 9 EC countries for 1975, 10 for 1980 and 1985)
Gerardi price indices are applied to values from Eurostat economic accounts for 14 groups of crop products, 6 livestock groups, and 3 types of input (fertiliser, feeding stuffs and energy) to get a surrogate valuation of gross value added. PPPs for output and input are shown in units of national currency per ECU. Outputs and inputs are also repriced using Eurostat's 1985 Gerardi PPPs for GDP, with backward extrapolation of these parities to 1975 and 1980 (the method by which the extrapolation was made is not explained, but the GDP PPPs for 1975 and 1980 are different from Eurostat's earlier set of such PPPs for 1975 and 1980).

PRASADA RAO (1992). 103 Countries. 185 Farm Products.
(Estimate of gross value added, labour productivity and Geary–Khamis PPPs for 1985. New estimates of gross output, feed and seed inputs for 1970, 1975, 1985, and 1990, together with corresponding Geary–Khamis PPPs)
Procedure similar to that in (1986) study, except that feed and seed input prices are different from output prices. Prices are again expressed with the US dollar as the *numeraire*, but also in a new composite agricultural commodity unit (ACU).

III   Gross value of farm output
Gross value for each product was calculated by multiplying production quantities by 'prices received by farmers' (at the 'farm gate', or first point of sale), excluding indirect taxes and subsidies. The sum of these is the gross value of farm output.

It can be seen from Table 1, that in 1975 agricultural products were very cheap in Argentina, relatively cheap in Brazil, India, and Indonesia. The opposite was the case for Korea, Mexico, France, Germany, Japan, Netherlands and the UK. In the latter cases the exchange rate conversions would exaggerate the real output of the countries concerned in 1975, whereas in the former countries real output would be understated by such a procedure.

Table 1   Gross Value of Farm Output, Purchasing Power Parities and Price Levels in 1975

	(1) Gross Value at US plus shadow and proxy US Prices (mln. $)	(2) Gross Value at Country's own Prices (mln. national currency units)	(3) Paasche Purchasing Power Parities: Units of National Currency per US $	(4) Exchange Rate Units of National Currency per US $	(5) Producer Price Level Relative to USA (PPP:Exchange rate)
Argentina	11,316	148,653	13.18	36.57	36.0
Brazil	23,600	173,311	7.34	8.127	90.3
China	112,960	n.a.	n.a.	1.86	n.a.
India	49,104	404,993	8.25	8.653	95.3
Indonesia	10,480	3,734,909	356.38	415.0	85.9
Korea	3,348	2,294,940	685.47	484.00	141.6
Mexico	9,042	121,712	13.46	12.50	107.7
France	21,649	118,471	5.47	4.29	127.5
Germany(FR)	15,843	51,174	3.23	2.46	131.3
Japan	12,505	8,721,990	697.48	296.79	235.0
Netherlands	5,912	17,881	3.02	2.53	119.4
UK	9,999	4,926	0.49	0.45	108.9
USA	92,863	92,863	1.00	1.00	100.0

Note: n.a. = not available

Sources: Van Ooststroom and Maddison (1985). First and second columns derived from FAO, *Production Yearbooks* for quantities, and FAO, *Statistics on Prices Received by Farmers*, FAO, Rome, 1982 for prices. In the first column, the valuations are at US prices or where there was no US price available, we used proxy or shadow US prices. The proxy/shadow component of the US valuations in the first column was 17.9 per cent for Argentina, 6.4 per cent for Brazil, 1.8 per cent for China, 14.3 per cent for India, 16.3 per cent for Indonesia, 1.1 per cent for Korea, 4.5 per cent for Mexico, 1.1 per cent for France, 0.3 per cent for Germany, 1.7 per cent for Japan, 0.2 per cent for the Netherlands and the UK and 0.1 per cent for the USA. In the second column, there is also a significant element of shadow pricing because there were items where production was reported by FAO, but FAO supplied no prices for the product in that country. These 'holes' in our national price information were biggest for Indonesia. There were also cases of redundant prices, i.e. FAO prices were available in some cases for products not produced in the country. The third column was derived by dividing column 2 by column 1. Fourth column from IMF, *International Financial Statistics*. Fifth column derived by dividing column 3 by column 4.

IV   The cost of inputs and the derivation of gross value added

In order to arrive at value added we must deduct inputs. It is convenient to distinguish:

a.   Inputs of agricultural products, i.e. feed and seed,
b.   Inputs of goods purchased from outside agriculture, i.e. fertilisers, pesticides, fuel, lubricants and electricity,
c.   Inputs of services supplied from outside agriculture, i.e. maintenance and minor repairs of fixed capital assets, rentals of machinery and equipment, overhead and other costs.

(a) Agricultural inputs

Agricultural items which we deducted included feeding stuffs for livestock used during the reference period, eggs for hatching and crop items used for seed.

The FAO *Food Balance Sheets, 1975–77 Average* (1980), provide data on feed and seed, whether domestically produced or imported for 1975–77. FAO kindly provided the figures for 1975 from their basic data files. These 1975 feed and seed input quantities were valued by the same prices as we used for gross output.

Table 2 shows the value of feed and seed inputs. Hay, green feed, silage, and grass for grazing are excluded from the FAO production statistics and for that reason are not included in either our agricultural input or our gross output measure. However, the relative availability of these items helps to explain some of the intercountry variation in inputs of feeding stuffs. Argentina's large area of lush grass obviously helps to explain its relatively low feed ratio.

Table 3 shows the value of farm output net of feed and seed in 1975. It is derived by deducting the inputs shown in Table 2 from the gross value of physical output shown in Table 1: the results are shown in terms of US relative prices and at national prices, together with the implicit PPPs, which are very close to those in Table 1.

(b) Identifiable inputs of goods purchased outside agriculture

Fertiliser inputs were taken from the *1978 F.A.O. Fertilizer Yearbook* (1979). They are given in metric tons of plant nutrients of nitrogen (N), phosphate (P_2O_5) and potash (K_2O). The fertiliser registration year covers the period starting and ending the first of July. We therefore averaged 1974/75 and 1975/76 consumption to derive the estimate for 1975. FAO does not quote a US price for each type of fertiliser, so we estimated average prices for three groups of fertilisers (nitrogenous, phosphate and potash) using quantities consumed in the USA as weights. In this manner we determined the average unit value of nitrogenous fertilisers (440 US dollars per metric ton), phosphate fertilisers (454 US dollars per metric ton) and potash fertilisers (182 US dollars per metric ton).

Figures on consumption of pesticides are from the *1977 F.A.O. Production Yearbook* (1978). A quantity ratio relative to the value of US consumption of chemical products was applied, to obtain the value of chemical product consumption in the other countries. Our source did not give pesticide inputs for Brazil, China, Japan, Netherlands and the UK. For Brazil we used the figure for 1977 as given in *Brasil Series Estatisticas Retrospectivas* (1977). Pesticide use in China was assumed to be the same per hectare of agricultural land as in India and it was assumed that the average pesticide input coefficient of France and Germany was valid for Japan, the Netherlands and the UK.

Energy inputs in equivalent tons of oil are available from the International Energy Agency (see *Energy Balances of OECD Countries 1970–1985*, Paris, 1987 for OECD countries, and *World Energy Statistics and Balances 1971–1987*, Paris, 1988 for non-OECD countries). These were converted into dollars at US prices from data on the value of US agricultural energy consumption in the OECD economic accounts for US agriculture.

(c) Other inputs

It was not possible with the information we had, to identify specific inputs of administrative, veterinary, irrigation, insurance and other services and costs of repair and maintenance of

Table 2   Value of Feed and Seed Inputs in 1975

	Seed Input at US prices (mln $)	Feed Input at US prices (mln $)	Feed as % of livestock output (%)
Argentina	184	1,238	23.6
Brazil	369	2,630	38.4
China	2,389	11,193	43.5
India	2,052	3,170	55.2
Indonesia	96	270	42.9
Korea	43	259	57.3
Mexico	74	1,102	36.8
France	232	4,856	40.0
Germany	229	5,429	51.7
Japan	119	2,197	44.5
Netherlands	58	1,269	44.3
UK	165	2,050	29.3
USA	1,265	15,701	38.5

Sources: van Ooststroom and Maddison (1985).

Table 3   Value of Farm Output Net of Feed and Seed in 1975

	Value at US (plus shadow and proxy US) Prices $ million	Value in National Prices million national currency units	Paasche PPP
Argentina	9,894	132,887	13.43
Brazil	20,601	151,148	7.34
China	99,378	n.a.	n.a.
India	43,882	358,975	8.18
Indonesia	10,114	3,612,423	357.17
Korea	3,046	2,092,442	686.95
Mexico	7,866	102,248	13.00
France	16,561	92,986	5.61
Germany	10,185	33,873	3.33
Japan	10,189	6,816,961	669.05
Netherlands	4,585	13,877	3.03
UK	7,784	3,858	0.496
USA	75,897	75,897	1.00

Source: Derived from Tables 1 and 2. See notes to Table 1.

Table 4   Value of Non-Agricultural Inputs into Agriculture in 1975 at US Relative Prices (millions of 1975 US dollars)

	Fertilisers ($ mln)	Pesticides ($ mln)	Energy ($ mln)	Other Non- agricultural Inputs ($ mln)	Total Non- Agricultural Inputs ($ mln)
Argentina	29	47	337	548	961
Brazil	715	73	361	1,149	2,298
China	2,512	270	562	538	3,882
India	1,130	122	401	266	1,919
Indonesia	212	1	a	270	483
Korea	340	15	2	165	522
Mexico	460	45	474	863	1,842
France	1,730	140	778	1,831	4,479
Germany(FR)	1,117	66	591	1,435	3,209
Japan	712	26	668	1,214	2,620
Netherlands	254	10	283	691	1,238
UK	679	86	501	1,321	2,587
USA	6,599	1,780	3,918	16,619	28,916

Note: a)   Included in fourth column.

Source: As described in text.

Table 5   Value of Inputs at National Prices (million units of national currency)

	Feed	Seed	Fertiliser	Pesticides	Energy	Services & Other Inputs
Argentina	13,196	2,570	5,718	a	815	8,673
Brazil	18,486	3,677	5,398	a	1,989	7,387
India	29,474	16,544	17,249	3,625	9,919	4,957
Indonesia	86,127	36,359	38,600	a	b	428,000
Korea	176,730	25,768	89,990	41,990	120,150	116,450
Mexico	18,365	1,099	5,777	2,809	2,467	9,740
France	24,385	1,100	8,103	3,342	3,010	9,993
Germany	16,478	823	3,417	585	3,125	5,766
Japan	1,839,413	65,620	612,000	282,000	198,000	943,000
Netherlands	3,787	217	660	160	510	1,680
UK	982	86	342	87	187	643
USA	15,701	1,265	6,599	1,780	3,918	16,619

Notes:
a)   Included with fertilisers
b)   Included in last column.

Source: First two columns derived by multiplying FAO quantity figures by FAO prices (or our shadow prices, where relevant). For Argentina and Brazil, input/output tables were used for fertilisers, energy and other inputs. Other entries were generally derived from economic accounts for agriculture.

fixed capital assets in quantifiable terms. As a proxy we took the ratio of the aggregate value of these inputs to inputs of fertiliser, pesticides and energy as recorded in the 'economic accounts' in national prices. Our sources were the replies to the FAO *Questionnaire on Economic Accounts for Agriculture*, 1980/81, for India, Korea and Mexico; input/output tables for Argentina, and national accounts for Brazil. For China we assumed the ratio to be the same as in India. For OECD countries, non-agricultural inputs in national prices were taken from OECD, *Economic Accounts for Agriculture 1975–1987*, Paris, 1990.

(d)   Total inputs
Total inputs in US prices are shown in Tables 2 (for feed and seed) and 4 (for non-farm inputs). Table 5 shows the value of farm inputs in national currencies.

(e)   Gross value added
Table 6 shows gross value added in farming in US prices which was derived from Tables 1, 2 and 4. Gross value added is also shown in national prices together with the Paasche PPP for value added which is derived by dividing column 2 of Table 6 by column 1. The last column of Table 6 shows the Paasche PPP for non-agricultural inputs.

Table 6   Gross Value Added in 1975 in US Prices, in National Prices and the Paasche PPPs for Gross Value Added and Non-Agricultural Inputs

	Gross Value Added at US Prices (Million $)	Gross Value Added in million National Currency Units	PPP for Gross Value Added Units of National Currency per $	Non-Agricultural Inputs at US Prices (Million $)	Non-Agricultural Inputs in Million National Currency Units	PPP for Non-Agricultural Inputs
Argentina	8,933	117,681	13.17	961	15,206	15.82
Brazil	18,303	136,374	7.47	2,298	14,774	6.42
China	95,496	n.a.	n.a.	3,882	n.a.	n.a.
India	41,963	323,225	7.70	1,919	35,750	18.63
Indonesia	9,631	3,145,823	326.64	483	466,600	966.05
Korea	2,524	1,723,862	682.99	522	368,580	706.09
Mexico	6,024	81,455	13.52	1,842	20,793	11.29
France	12,082	68,538	5.67	4,479	24,448	5.46
Germany	6,976	20,980	3.01	3,209	12,893	4.02
Japan	7,569	4,781,961	631.78	2,620	2,035,000	776.72
Netherlands	3,347	10,867	3.25	1,238	3,010	2.43
UK	5,197	2,599	.50	2,587	1,259	.487
USA	46,981	46,981	1.00	28,916	28,916	1.00

Source: Derived from Tables 1, 2, 4 and 5. US prices means US plus US shadow and proxy prices.

V   Comparative levels of economic performance in agriculture

Table 7 provides some of the major indicators of comparative levels of performance in agriculture, which can be derived from our estimates of gross output and value added, when they are considered in relation to employment, land availability and population.

Column 1 shows clearly that the USA is the world productivity leader in agriculture. The Netherlands was the only close competitor at 90 per cent of the US level. The UK was in third place with only 55 per cent of US productivity. Argentina came next but had less than half the US level. Some countries with high levels of performance in manufacturing had poor performance in agriculture. French farm productivity was 40 per cent of that in the USA. German farm productivity was less than a third of that in the USA. Japanese productivity was abysmal at only 8.8 per cent of the USA. India had the worst performance at 1.9 per cent of the US level, and performance in China and Indonesia was not much better.

A major reason for US productivity leadership in agriculture is its abundant supply of land. In terms of land productivity, US performance is only one-fourteenth of that in the Netherlands. In fact the only countries with lower levels of land productivity than the USA were Argentina, Brazil and Mexico.

It would, of course, be desirable to supplement our productivity measures by estimates of the stock of physical capital and human capital (education and skills embodied in the labour

Table 7   Comparative Performance in Agriculture in 1975

	Gross Value Added Per Person Engaged	Gross Value Added Per Hectare of Agricultural Land	Gross Value Added Per Head of Population	Utilisation of Agricultural Products Per Head of Population	Agricultural Employment 000s	Area of Agricultural Land 000 ha.
Argentina	43.9	48.0	157.7	74.9	1,389	170,550
Brazil	10.0	81.7	80.2	44.5	12,468	205,001
China	2.3	218.2	47.9	33.0	281,378	400,710
India	1.9	212.4	31.4	21.5	147,936	180,858
Indonesia	2.4	275.6	33.3	20.6	27,400	31,996
Korea	3.6	1,015.5	32.9	30.4	4,831	2,272
Mexico	6.7	56.1	46.0	40.1	6,134	98,339
France	39.8	341.9	105.4	106.1	2,074	32,357
Germany	30.1	511.1	51.9	102.2	1,585	12,496
Japan	8.8	1,243.5	31.2	39.9	5,870	5,573
Netherlands	90.0	1,441.4	112.6	72.7	254	2,126
UK	54.7	256.1	42.5	81.7	649	18,583
USA	100.0	100.0	100.0	100.0	3,208	430,158

Source: The first two columns are derived from the last two columns and from Table 6. Column 3 from Table 6 divided by population. Fourth column derived from Table 8. Employment in India, Indonesia, Korea and Japan from van der Meer and Yamada (1990), p. 175; China from *Statistical Yearbook of China 1984*, Hong Kong, 1984, pp. 104 and 109. For other countries, the available employment figures included forestry and fishing; we excluded forestry and fishing for France, Germany and the Netherlands by using indications of their share in employment for neighbouring years. For the other five countries we assumed productivity in agriculture to be the same as in agriculture, forestry and fishing. Employment for OECD countries from *Labour Force Statistics* and *National Accounts*, OECD, Paris. Employment in Latin American countries was supplied by ECLAC. Land area from Prasada Rao (1992), Table 5.101.

Table 8   Domestic Utilisation of Farm Products in 1975

	Gross Value of Farm Output	Imports	Exports	Domestic Utilisation	Per Capita Domestic Utilisation
	——————————— million dollars ———————————				$
Argentina	11,316	485	4,520	7,281	2,795
Brazil	23,600	1,367	7,545	17,422	1,661
China	112,960	2,323	2,498	112,785	1,231
India	49,104	2,119	2,031	49,193	802
Indonesia	10,480	872	1,106	10,246	770
Korea	3,348	873	216	4,005	1,135
Mexico	9,042	673	717	8,998	1,496
France	21,649	6,797	7,588	20,857	3,958
Germany (FR)	15,843	11,537	3,807	23,574	3,813
Japan	12,505	4,247	140	16,613	1,490
Netherlands	5,912	4,622	6,830	3,703	2,710
UK	9,999	10,480	3,347	17,132	3,048
USA	92,863	10,149	22,459	80,553	3,730

Source: Column 1 from Table 1. Imports and exports from FAO, *Trade Yearbook, 1977* (1978), converted to dollars with our PPP converters in Table 1, except for China where we had no PPPs and used the exchange rate. Domestic utilisation equals output, plus imports, minus exports.

force). With such information we would be able to make estimates of total factor productivity which would give better insight into the efficiency of agriculture in the different countries.

As agriculture supplies basic necessities for human subsistence, it is clear that low productivity countries have to offset their low agricultural productivity by keeping large fractions of their population in agricultural employment. In the USA, only 1.5 persons per 100 members of the population are engaged in agriculture, whereas in China the figure is 31 and India 24. The only country with a lower ratio is the UK where only 1.2 persons are in agriculture per 100 members of the population. The UK has had the lowest ratio of farm employment over the past 150 years since it embraced free trade in 1848, and for this reason it is a big net importer of agricultural products.

The third column of Table 7 shows gross value added per head of population. This was biggest in Argentina which is proportionately the biggest net exporter of agricultural products. France and the Netherlands also had bigger ratios of value added per head of population than the USA, and were also net exporters of agricultural products. Gross value added per head of population was lowest in Japan.

The fifth column of Table 7 shows total utilisation of agricultural products per head of population. Utilisation is equal to gross output as shown in our Table 1 adjusted for the net balance on foreign trade in agricultural products (as derived from the FAO, *Trade Yearbook*). Here we can see that France and Germany were the only countries with higher per capita utilisation than the United States. The lowest utilisation levels were in the poorest countries, India and Indonesia, but they were also remarkably low in Japan. It should be remembered that utilisation levels are not a good index of food consumption as agriculture includes items like tobacco, textile fibres, hides and skins. Furthermore, fish are an important source of food, particularly in Japan (see Appendix A on forestry and fishing output).

VI   Comparison of our results with those of other recent studies

a)   Prasada Rao (1986 and 1992)

It is interesting to compare our results with those of Prasada Rao (1986 and 1992), as his sources and a good deal of his methodology were similar to ours.

In fact, his results for gross agricultural output are not very different from ours, as can be seen in Table 9. The major exception to this was China, where our estimate was over 40 per cent higher than his, for reasons which will not be clear until we can compare his detailed worksheets with ours.

There are two main differences between his studies and ours. The least significant is probably the difference in commodity coverage. He specified a potential 173 commodities in the 1986 study and 185 in 1992, which may account for the fact that his 1992 results are generally somewhat higher than those of 1986 (though not for China, Korea and Japan). We specified 149 commodities which should have produced slightly lower figures than his. The difference would not be too large as we included some generic residual items (e.g. cereals not elsewhere specified). The de facto differences in our coverage of production were small. We both excluded production of grass, hay and dung, and we both measured animal production for meat in terms of meat slaughterings (valued at prices received by farmers). It is clear on inspection of updated FAO worksheets that there were some revisions in FAO production statistics Prasada Rao used but none of those were very dramatic.

Prasada Rao valued farm output at 'Geary–Khamis international' prices, which could be expected to produce lower values than with our US and US proxy/shadow prices (Paasche PPPs). There is a persistent and very general tendency of this kind (the Gerschenkron effect) which can be observed in those ICP studies where the impact of different price systems can be observed. For OECD countries the Paasche GDP PPPs tend to produce a measure of output volume about 7 per cent higher on average than the Geary–Khamis PPPs. His 1986 results (excluding China) averaged about 5 per cent lower than ours and in his 1992 study the corresponding average was 3 per cent lower. This type of discrepancy between the Paasche and the Geary–Khamis approaches is more or less what we might expect. However, it would clearly be useful for FAO to augment its future estimates by publishing results on a Paasche and Laspeyres basis as well as the Geary–Khamis results.

For gross value added in 1975, Prasada Rao's 1986 estimates differed from ours in both positive and negative fashion, with a range of the ratios from 0.82 to 1.28 (excluding China, for which he did not calculate value added). In Table 10 one can see what were the main identifiable differences between his studies and ours, as far as inputs are concerned. Our feed and seed estimates were significantly higher than his, by a ratio which varied from 1.2 for the USA to 3.4 for the Netherlands, with an average for the 13 countries of 1.9 for his 1986 study. His 1992 study showed higher feed and seed inputs in all cases; they were much

Table 9　Comparison of Our Estimate of Gross Output and Gross Value Added in Agriculture and those of Rao for 1975

| | Gross Farm Output | | | | | Gross Value Added | | |
	Rao (1986) (million Geary–Khamis $)	Rao (1992) (million Geary–Khamis $)	Our Estimate (million Paasche $)	Ratio of Our Estimate to that of Rao(1986)	Ratio of Our Estimate to that of Rao (1992)	Rao (1986) (million Geary–Khamis $)	Our Estimate (Million Paasche $)	Ratio of Our Estimate to that of Rao
Argentina	11,377	11,500	11,316	0.99	0.98	9,551	8,933	0.94[a]
Brazil	21,721	22,234	23,600	1.09	1.06	18,122	18,303	1.01[a]
China	80,264	79,277	112,960	1.41	1.43	n.a.	95,496	n.a.
India	47,294	48,287	49,104	1.04	1.02	38,837	41,963	1.08
Indonesia	8,981	9,827	10,480	1.17	1.07	8,601	9,631	1.12[a]
Korea	3,244	3,141	3,348	1.03	1.07	2,956	2,424	0.82[a]
Mexico	8,331	9,387	9,042	1.09	0.96	4,757	6,024	1.27
France	21,450	21,632	21,649	1.01	1.00	10,833	12,082	1.12
Germany	14,920	15,073	15,843	1.06	1.05	6,432	6,976	1.08
Japan	12,484	12,245	12,505	1.00	1.02	5,906	7,569	1.28
Netherlands	5,297	5,313	5,912	1.12	1.11	3,646	3,347	0.92
UK	9,409	9,521	9,999	1.06	1.05	5,976	5,197	0.87
USA	91,350	91,758	92,863	1.02	1.01	56,626	46,981	0.83

Note:　a)　For these countries, Prasada Rao's estimate of non-agricultural inputs was extremely rough.

Source:　Prasada Rao (1986), pp. 31 and 46 (1992), Table 5.4. Our estimates from Tables 1 and 6 above. Prasada Rao (1992) did not contain estimates of 1975 value added.

Table 10 Comparison of Our Estimate of Inputs in Agriculture and those of Rao for 1975

	Feed and Seed					Non-Agricultural Inputs		
	Rao (1986) (million Geary–Khamis $)	Rao (1992) (million Geary–Khamis $)	Our Estimate (million Paasche $)	Ratio of Our Estimate to that of Rao (1986)	Ratio of Our Estimate to that of Rao (1992)	Rao (1986) (million Geary–Khamis $)	Our Estimate (Million Paasche $)	Ratio of Our Estimate to that of Rao
Argentina	867	999	1,422	1.64	1.42	960	961	1.00
Brazil	2,418	2,689	2,999	1.24	1.12	1,181	2,298	1.95
China	5,046	10,312	13,582	2.69	1.32	n.a.	3,882	n.a.
India	2,443	4,145	5,222	2.14	1.26	6,015	1,919	0.32
Indonesia	199	365	366	1.84	1.00	180	483	2.68
Korea	125	279	302	2.42	1.08	162	522	3.22
Mexico	845	1,117	1,176	1.39	1.05	2,729	1,842	0.68
France	3,095	3,701	5,088	1.64	1.38	7,522	4,479	0.60
Germany	2,579	3,583	5,658	2.19	1.58	5,909	3,209	0.54
Japan	1,057	2,341	2,316	2.19	0.99	5,522	2,620	0.47
Netherlands	387	1,102	1,327	3.43	1.20	1,265	1,238	0.98
UK	1,438	1,969	2,215	1.54	1.13	1,995	2,587	1.30
USA	13,940	17,134	16,966	1.22	0.99	20,785	28,916	1.39

Source: Prasada Rao (1986), p. 31 for col. 1 and p. 96 for col. 4, (1992) Table 5.4. Our estimates from Tables 2 and 6 above.

closer to our estimates with a range from 1 in Indonesia, Japan and the USA to 1.6 for Germany, and an average difference in the ratio for these inputs of 1.2.

Table 10 also shows the difference between his 1986 estimate for non-agricultural inputs and our figures. There is a wide range of discrepancies with the ratio of the two estimates ranging from 0.3 for India to 3.2 for Korea. Unfortunately his 1992 study did not show a revised estimate of these inputs for 1975.

It seems clear that the biggest reconciliation problem concerns the measurement of non-agricultural inputs and this is the area where further research would probably be most fruitful. We regard our method as preferable to that of Prasada Rao because it involves more detailed specification of the components of these inputs. However, this does not mean that our ratios are necessarily better than his, as he had better information than we had, and there is plenty of scope for error in our procedures.

Table 11 provides a rough guide to the plausibility of the different ratios. It shows our ratio of gross value added to gross output in US prices and Prasada Rao's ratio in Geary–Khamis prices. Column 3 shows our estimate of the ratio in national prices. This is a hybrid measure, because our measure of gross output, feed and seed inputs is derived from our 'commodity' approach, whereas the valuation of non-agricultural inputs was predominantly from the economic accounts for agriculture. The fourth column is the ratio shown by van der Meer and Yamada (1990) relying entirely on the 'accounting' approach in national prices. All the van der Meer–Yamada ratios, except that for Brazil, are closer to our results than to those of Prasada Rao. All of our national price ratios are nearer to our US dollar estimate than to Prasada Rao except for India and Germany.

Table 11   Ratio of Gross Value Added to Gross Output in Agriculture in 1975

	Our Estimate (in Paasche $)	Prasada Rao (1986) (in Geary–Khamis units)	Our Estimate in National Prices	V.der Meer & Yamada National Prices
Argentina	78.9	84.0	79.2	71.5
Brazil	77.6	83.4	78.7	87.7
China	84.5	n.a.	n.a.	n.a.
India	85.5	82.1	79.8	91.7
Indonesia	91.9	95.8	83.0	91.4
Korea	75.4	91.1	75.1	81.6
Mexico	66.6	57.1	66.9	65.9
France	55.8	50.5	57.9	62.1
Germany	44.5	43.1	41.0	54.3
Japan	60.5	47.3	54.8	61.1
Netherlands	56.6	68.8	60.8	50.8
UK	52.0	63.5	52.8	45.8
USA	50.6	62.0	50.6	49.9

Source: First two columns derived from Table 9 above, third column from Tables 1 and 6 above, fourth column from van der Meer and Yamada (1990), pp. 171–2.

Prasada Rao presents estimates of land and labour productivity. As we used his estimates for land, the differences in land productivity between his estimates and ours are attributable entirely to the reasons already discussed. In the case of employment, his estimates are invariably higher than ours, and may perhaps refer to persons engaged in forestry and fishing as well as agriculture. Our figures for employment are more or less the same as those of van der Meer and Yamada.

b)   Van der Meer and Yamada (1990)
Van der Meer and Yamada made two kinds of estimate. The closest of these to our work was their estimate of gross value added, land and labour productivity for 26 countries (Chapter 3 and Appendix B of their book). For 1975, they simply used the gross value estimates of Prasada Rao (1986) in Geary-Khamis international dollars and multiplied them by the ratios of gross value added to gross value which they derived from 'economic accounts' for agriculture (see last column of our Table 11). Their value added estimate is therefore of a hybrid character as the output and inputs are calculated in different price systems. Furthermore, they assume that the basic ingredients (i.e. price and quantity measures) in the economic accounts are compatible with those in the 'commodity' approach.

The second part of the Van der Meer and Yamada study is a very detailed binary comparison of value added in the Netherlands and Japan, which they supplement with a rougher estimate on the same lines for the USA and Taiwan. This part of their work contains some important innovations.

An important difference between our study and that of van der Meer and Yamada is that we measure gross value added, whereas they deducted depreciation to arrive at net value added. Their procedure here is in line with their general methodology. They deflate the value of depreciation as recorded in the national sector accounts by an interspatial price index for costs of building and prices of farm machinery. In the case of depreciation there is likely to be more variation of a misleading kind between valuations in the 'economic accounts' than there is in most of the other items, because the depreciation rules vary between countries for fiscal reasons. Although the theoretical reasons for using a net valuation are unimpeachable, in practice we feel that this procedure is likely to lead to error. In our manufacturing studies we estimated capital stocks using standardised asset lives for each country, and from these one can derive more comparable estimates of capital consumption. An alternative way of bringing capital into the accounts, is to use such estimates to measure joint factor productivity as a supplement to the labour and land productivity measures. Where information is available on human capital it is also possible to augment the accounts to include human capital.

Van der Meer and Yamada measured labour input in terms of working hours rather than employment. This is clearly an advance on the procedure used in our study or by Prasada Rao. The main problem is that it is much more difficult to find source material on hours for most countries than it was for Japan, Netherlands, Taiwan and the USA. In their 26 country comparison they did not attempt to make such a measure. Nevertheless, the differences in agricultural working hours which they found are quite significant (1778 a year in Japan, 787 in the Netherlands and 2113 in the USA – see pp. 175 and 188) and this is an area where further research is needed.

Van der Meer and Yamada make much greater use of the 'economic accounts' for agriculture than most other studies we have cited (except that of Terluin). However, we have strong doubts about the usefulness of a general switch from our 'commodity' approach to measurement of gross output, feed and seed, towards their 'accounts', given the present state of ignorance about the way in which such accounts are compiled and their compatibility with FAO commodity information.

The problem with using their approach as a general multicountry procedure is that the FAO farm accounts are not available for all countries; they vary in commodity coverage, and in the pricing conventions which they use, in ways that are not always explicit. It would clearly be risky to use FAO's price information to divide into the economic accounts valuations in order to derive intercountry estimates, as the FAO prices may well be different from those embedded in the farm accounts.

The Van der Meer–Yamada technique is not the only way of dealing with the coverage problem. There are more direct ways of dealing with deficiencies in the coverage of FAO's commodity estimates. They can be supplemented by estimates for missing items. However, van der Meer and Yamada have put their finger on a weakness in our estimates which is not easy to remedy.

Van der Meer and Yamada suggest that our commodity approach tends fairly systematically to understate gross output compared with that in the agricultural accounts (see their pp. 181–2). This is true in Japan and the Netherlands in which they were most interested, and the difference was probably due to the reasons they identify. However, in some cases our method produced significantly higher estimates than the farm accounts. In Brazil our estimate was 24 per cent higher and in India 18 per cent (see Table 12).

In the case of Brazil, the national accounts included some items we had omitted, notably the increase in the size and value of livestock herds, the increase in the stock and value of coffee trees, and a small item (about 0.2 per cent of output) for flowers. Together these three items amounted to 14.6 billion cruzeiros. However, this was more than offset by discrepancies arising from differences in the quantities and prices for individual items. The biggest discrepancy was for coffee, where the Brazilian price was about a fifth of that recorded by FAO and production was twice as high. If the Brazilian authorities had valued coffee at the FAO price, their total output would have been 49.6 billion cruzeiros greater. For Brazil, unlike the other countries in our sample, the FAO prices for 1975 were nearly all estimates. Errors in Brazilian prices are not a problem for our volume estimates as we valued all output at US prices, but the differences in the quantity estimates are disconcerting. As there was an agricultural census for Brazil in 1975, on which the national accounts estimates are based, the latter are obviously more reliable than the estimates of FAO. Our estimate for Brazil must therefore be regarded as weak.

In India, the national accounts for agriculture are published in more detail than for most countries, and were identical with the FAO farm accounts. They include some small items we omitted, e.g. straw, ghee and increases in the value of livestock, but these differences in item coverage are not a major source of discrepancy. The Indian authorities supplied their quantity and price estimate for 33 crops which we could check with the FAO commodity data. There were discrepancies in both directions for both prices and quantities, but a major difference was for rice where the FAO production estimate was nearly 25 million tons (tonnes) higher than that of FAO. If the Indian authorities had used the FAO quantity

Table 12   Gross Value of Farm Output in 1975: Our Measure and that of Economic Accounts (million units of national currency)

	Our Method	Economic Accounts	Our Estimate as Percent of Accounts
Brazil	173,311	140,537[a]	123
India	404,993	342,175	118
Indonesia	3,470,260	3,730,400	93
Korea	2,294,940	2,645,420	87
Mexico	121,712	160,408[a]	76
France	118,471	128,999	92
Germany	51,174	50,295	102
Japan	8,721,990	9,719,700	90
Netherlands	17,881	18,539	96
UK	4,926	4,768	103
USA	92,863	92,878	100

Note: a)   National accounts. For Mexico the FAO farm account figure was 153,776.

Source: Column 1 from our Table 1. Column 2 derived from FAO economic accounts worksheets supplied by FAO in 1983. The Brazilian national accounts worksheets of the Vargas Foundation were supplied by Maria Alice de Gusmao Veloso. Mexican national accounts from SPP/Bank of Mexico, *Sistema de Cuentas Nacionales de Mexico*, Vol. II, January 1981.

estimate their output would have been raised by about 40 million rupees. Here again we must assume that the national accounts estimate for rice was better than that of FAO.

In Mexico, the national accounts give considerable detail by value of commodity but not by quantity. The national accounts figure for gross output was 160 billion pesos (excluding agricultural services). Of this total 10.8 billion consisted of items not included in our estimates (alfalfa, hay, other forage, flowers and own account capital formation in livestock and crops). For wheat, rice and maize, the national account values were virtually identical with those we derived from FAO and for several other groups, the differences were not large. However, the national accounts estimates for vegetables and meat were both around twice as big as those we derived from FAO, and together they were big enough to explain the difference in the two sources. In our ICOP studies for manufacturing we found a systematic tendency in the Mexican national accounts to make large-scale imputations for items not fully covered in censuses, and this also appears to be true for agriculture.

There is clearly a need to reconcile the commodity data of FAO with the valuations and the underlying quantitative and price information in the economic accounts for agriculture and in the national accounts.

Appendix A   Output in forestry and fishery

For forestry and fishing FAO does not supply information on inputs, so we could only measure the gross output volume relatives and benchmark them on US gross value added in each of the two sectors. This procedure is equivalent to assuming that all countries had the same input–output coefficients as the USA.

The FAO *Yearbook of Forest Products 1969–80* (1982), provides qualitative information on output of 12 categories of forest products. It gives export unit values but no domestic price information. We derived volume relatives using US export unit values as weights.

Estimates of the total volume of fish catch (in tons) were taken from the *F.A.O. Food Balance Sheets* (1980). No price information was available so we simply assumed that value added was proportionate to the ratio of the total weight of the fish catch in the country concerned to that in the USA.

Table 13 shows our crude estimates of value added in forestry and fishing, together with agricultural value added and total value added for the three sectors combined.

Table 14 shows land productivity in forestry and Table 15 shows labour productivity in agriculture, forestry and fishing as a whole.

Table 13   Gross Value Added in Agriculture, Forestry and Fishery in 1975 ($ millions at 1975 US prices)

	Gross Agricultural Value Added	Gross Value Added in Forestry	Gross Value Added in Fishery	Total Gross Value Added in the three sectors combined
Argentina	9,279	55	59	9,393
Brazil	18,342	963	197	19,502
China	95,496	1,377	1,759	98,632
India	41,963	805	595	43,361
Indonesia	9,631	804	355	10,790
Korea	2,524	268	546	3,338
Mexico	6,027	97	128	6,252
France	13,278	425	206	13,909
Germany(FR)	7,119	375	113	7,607
Japan	7,573	862	2,691	11,126
Netherlands	3,347	9	90	3,446
UK	5,197	53	255	5,505
USA	47,184	3,664 ·	741	51,589

Source: Tables 7, D1 and D2. Total combined value added of US forestry and fisheries output in 1975 from FAO, *Economic Accounts Questionnaire 1980/81*. 1975 Value added in fisheries in USA from *Institute of Developing Economics*, Tokyo, 1982.

Table 14   Output of Forestry per Hectare of Forest and Woodland in 1975

	Value Added in Forestry at US rel. prices (mln. US $)	Forest and Woodland in 1975 (1000 ha.)	Forest and Woodland as % of Total Land Area (%)	Forest Output Per Hectare of Forest Land (US $ct)	Forest Output Per Hectare of Forest Land (US=100.0)
Argentina	55	60,700	22.1	91	7.5
Brazil	963	510,000	60.3	189	15.7
China	1,377	151,800	16.3	907	75.4
India	805	67,400	22.7	1,194	99.2
Indonesia	804	121,400	67.0	662	55.0
Korea	268	6,628	67.5	4,043	335.9
Mexico	97	71,600	36.3	135	11.3
France	425	14,610	26.8	2,909	241.7
Germany	375	7,162	29.3	5,236	435.0
Japan	862	25,043	67.5	3,442	286.0
Netherlands	9	308	9.1	2,922	242.8
UK	53	2,020	8.4	2,624	218.0
USA	3,664	304,400	33.4	1,204	100.0

Source: Figures on forest and woodland and total land area from *1976 F.A.O. Production Yearbook* (1977). Forest land and woodland refers to land under natural or planted stands of trees, whether or not they are productive.

Table 15   Labour Productivity: Output in Agriculture, Forestry and Fishing per Person employed in these sectors in 1975

	Value Added in Agriculture, Forestry and Fisheries at US prices (mln. US $)	Econ. Active Population in Agriculture Forestry and Fisheries (000s)	id. as % of Total Employment (%)	Value Added Per Person Employed (US $)	Value Added Per Person Employed (USA=100.0)
Argentina	9,393	1,406	15.0	6,681	45.4
Brazil	19,502	13,256	37.4	1,471	10.0
China	98,632	293,410	77.7	336	2.3
India	43,361	161,439	66.6	269	1.8
Indonesia	10,790	29,378	62.6	367	2.5
Korea	3,338	5,773	44.7	578	3.9
Mexico	6,252	6,363	39.4	983	6.7
France	13,909	2,156	10.0	6,451	43.9
Germany(FR)	7,607	1,749	6.9	4,349	29.6
Japan	11,126	6,610	12.7	1,683	11.4
Netherlands	3,446	263	5.5	13,103	89.1
UK	5,505	687	2.7	8,013	54.5
USA	51,589	3,507	4.0	14,710	100.0

Sources: Data on the economically active population in agriculture for Argentina, Brazil, and Mexico supplied by ECLA. France, Germany, Japan, Netherlands, UK and USA employment figures from OECD, *Labour Force Statistics (1970–1990). 1982 F.A.O. Production Yearbook* (1983) for the remaining countries, except China which was taken from the *Statistical Yearbook of China*, 1984, State Statistical Bureau, PRC, Economic Information and Agency, Hong Kong, 1984 (p.109 for labour force, adjusted to a mid-year basis).

References to citations in Section I

Y. Hayami and Y.W. Ruttan, *Agricultural Development: An International Perspective*, Johns Hopkins, Baltimore, 1971 and revised edition 1985.

A. Maddison, *Economic Progress and Policy in Developing Countries*, Norton, New York, 1970.

G.J.A. Mensink, *Comparisons of Labour Productivity in the United States and the Netherlands*, CBS, The Hague, 1966.

D. Paige and G. Bombach, *A Comparison of National Output and Productivity*, OEEC, Paris, 1959.

D.S. Prasada Rao, *Inter-Country Comparisons of Agricultural Production Aggregates*, FAO, Rome, 1986.

D.S. Prasada Rao, *Inter-Country Comparisons of Agricultural Output and Productivity*, FAO, Rome, 1992.

D.S. Prasada Rao and A. Maddison, *A Generalized Approach to International Comparison of Agricultural Output and Productivity*, mimeographed, University of New England, Armidale, Australia, 1994.

A.D. Smith, D.M.W.N. Hitchens and S.W. Davies, *International Industrial Productivity: A Comparison of Britain, America and Germany*, Cambridge University Press, Cambridge, 1982.

I.J. Terluin, *Comparison of Real Output, Productivity and Price Levels in Agriculture in the EC: A Reconnaissance*, Agricultural Research Institute, The Hague, 1990.

C.L.J. van der Meer and S. Yamada, 'Comparison of Real Output, Productivity and Effective Protection in Dutch and Japanese Agriculture for 1975, 1980 and 1984', *Research Memorandum 267*, Institute of Economic Research, Groningen, 1988.

C.L.J. van der Meer and S. Yamada, *Japanese Agriculture: A Comparative Economic Analysis*, Routledge, London 1990.

H. van Ooststroom and A. Maddison, 'An International Comparison of Levels of Real Output and Productivity in Agriculture in 1975', *Research Memorandum 162*, Institute of Economic Research, University of Groningen, 1984, 67 pp. A slightly revised text with five additional annexes was privately circulated in April 1985, 112 pp.

9

Review of Income and Wealth
Series 35, Number 1, March 1989

INTERNATIONAL COMPARISON OF PURCHASING POWER, REAL OUTPUT AND LABOUR PRODUCTIVITY: A CASE STUDY OF BRAZILIAN, MEXICAN AND U.S. MANUFACTURING, 1975

By Angus Maddison and Bart van Ark

This study has a twofold objective: (a) a substantive analysis of purchasing power parities (PPP's), real output and labour productivity in Brazil, Mexico and the U.S.A.; and (b) a methodological survey of the analytic problems in measuring PPP's from the production side, rather than the expenditure approach used by the United Nations (ICP). Our main substantive findings were that PPP's for manufacturing did not vary greatly from the 1975 exchange rates, that labour productivity was surprisingly high in the two Latin American countries, and that there are substantial differences in the coverage of national accounts between Mexico and Brazil. We found census concepts of value added to be rather anachronistic, particularly in the U.S.A.; we developed a new short-cut matching procedure for industries with a complex product structure; and we found the unit value approach not inferior to the specification pricing practiced by ICP.

1. Introduction

The most direct way of comparing levels of output in different countries is to use the official exchange rate to convert GDP in one country's prices into the prices of another country, and, in multicountry comparisons, to use some key currency, such as the U.S. dollar, as a numéraire. However, exchange rates do not indicate the average purchasing power of currencies over all goods and services, but mainly reflect their purchasing power over tradeables. Furthermore exchange rates are subject to fluctuation, and capital movements play a major role in determining their level, so even for tradeables, they could be substantially misleading as indicators of purchasing power. Hence measurement of real output across countries is closely intertwined with the assessment of purchasing power.

Research on purchasing power parities (PPP's) has been under way for over three decades in international agencies concerned with burden sharing or with the relative need for aid. Hence the early work of OEEC (1954, 1958, 1959) for Western countries, of Gosplan (1965) for the CMEA countries, and ECLA (1963)

Note: University of Groningen (The Netherlands). The authors are grateful to Harry van Ooststroom and Paul Wieringa who helped launch the investigation, and to Aerdt Houben, Dirk Pilat, and Eddy Szirmai who helped in the end phase. We had extensive and very helpful discussions with Derek Blades. For help in interpreting and gathering data for particular countries, the authors are grateful to Jerome Mark, Arthur Neef, Robert Parker, Angelo de Souza, Thomas Tibbetts, Victor Urquidi, Maria Alice Gusmao Veloso, Gaylord Worden and Ralph Zerkowsky. Useful comments were also received from Sultan Ahmad, Robert Ballance, Jean Baneth, Stephen Davies, Laszlo Drechsler, Arun Ghosh, Alan Heston, Irving Kravis, Hugo Krijnse Locker, Valentin Kudrov, Jagdish Kumar, Arabinda Kundu, Jaroslav Kux, Kees van der Meer, Jan Pen, Sigbert Prais, Anthony Smith, Robert Summers and Michael Ward. We are also grateful to the World Bank both for intellectual cooperation, and for meeting some of our research expenses, particularly those for travel and translation.

31

for Latin America. This kind of measure is also useful in analysing military or geopolitical potential: see the CIA studies of Block (1981) and Schroeder and Edwards (1981); and U.S. Congress Joint Economic Committee studies (1981) and (1982) on Eastern Europe and the U.S.S.R.

Most of the above studies develop PPP's for final demand components (consumption, investment, etc.) The largest and most sustained scholarly effort using this "expenditure approach" was the International Comparisons Project (ICP) of the United Nations. The results of the first four phases are published in Kravis, Kenessey, Heston and Summers (1975), Kravis, Heston and Summers (1978) and (1982), and UN (1986). ICP methods are now used on a regional basis by Eurostat (1983) and OECD (Ward, 1985).

The expenditure approach is useful for analysis of macreconomic perform-ance, but cannot be directly used for sectoral analysis since it does not show real product by industry. This handicaps comparative structural analysis, work on labour or total factor productivity, growth accounting, and studies of technologi-cal performance. This latter group of problems is better illuminated by the alternative "industry of origin" approach which we use here.

This study has a twofold objective:

(a) substantive analysis of manufacturing output levels, purchasing power parities, and labour productivity in Brazil, Mexico and the U.S.A.;

(b) a methodological survey of the analytical problems inherent in such an exercise for any group of countries, in order to facilitate the task of researchers who may wish to replicate our approach.

The present study is part of a series of comparative industry of origin investigations in which we and our colleagues have been engaged. Houben (1988) covers the mining sector in Brazil, Mexico and the U.S.A. Comparisons for the manufacturing sectors for India/U.S.A. (Van Ark, 1987) and Brazil/U.K. (Van Ark, 1988) are available, and others are underway for Japan, Korea, France and The Netherlands. A fourteen country comparison is available for agriculture by Van Ooststroom and Maddison (1985). The 1975 benchmark was chosen to facilitate comparison with the third phase of the ICP. The basic source is censuses of manufacturing which provide quantitative indicators of output levels in con-siderable detail as well as information on employment, gross output, value added, and inputs at national prices.

2. Previous Real Product Comparisons for Manufacturing

Some economists have manipulated real expenditure PPP's to produce proxy estimates of real output levels by sector (see Table 1). Thus Simon Kuznets (1972) used OEEC and ECLA real expenditure studies to derive estimates of real output for agriculture and industry. Jones (1976) used Kravis, Kenessey, Heston and Summers (1975) expenditure PPP's to estimate manufacturing output levels, A. D. Roy (1982) used the same procedure with Kravis, Heston and Summers (1978), and Prais (1981) followed a moré detailed procedure, using about half of the expenditure items listed in Kravis, Kenessey, Heston and Summers (1975) to derive a weighted average PPP for manufacturing. Klodt (1984), Jorgenson,

TABLE 1
PROXY COMPARISONS OF REAL OUTPUT LEVELS IN MANUFACTURING USING ANALOGOUS
ICP EXPENDITURE COMPONENTS

Kuznets (1972)	Used reweighted OEEC and ECLA expenditure PPP's to estimate sector PPP's for large groups of countries.
Jones (1976)	Used reweighted Kravis, Kenessey, Heston and Summers (1975) expenditure PPP's to derive sector PPP's.
Prais (1981)	Used reweighted Kravis, Kenessey, Heston and Summers (1975) expenditure PPP's to derive PPP's for 10 manufacturing industries in Germany, U.K. and U.S.A.
Roy, A. D. (1982)	Used reweighted Kravis, Heston and Summers (1978) expenditure PPP's to derive sector PPP's.
Klodt (1984)	Applied Kravis, Heston and Summers (1978) PPP's to 16 branches of manufacturing for Germany, Japan and U.S.A., 1960, 1970 and 1978.
Guinchard (1984)	Uses Kravis, Heston and Summers (1982) expenditure PPP's (with adjustment for taxes and trade margins) to derive PPP's for some branches of manufacturing. For intermediate products he used the exchange rate.
Jorgenson, Kuroda and Nishimizu (1986)	Applied "remapped" Kravis *et al.* (1975, 1978) PPP's to estimate productivity differentials in Japan and U.S.A. (1960–79).
Roy, D. J. (1987)	Used reweighted expenditure PPP's from ICP IV, derived from a tape provided by UNSO, for 60 countries for 1980.

Sources: See bibliographic references.

Kuroda and Nishimizu (1986), and D. J. Roy (1987) are the latest in this tradition.

Procedures of this type need to be crosschecked with independent estimates by industry of origin such as we present here. Until this is done for a reasonable sample of countries, one must be sceptical about the value of such proxies.

The initial impetus to "industry of origin" comparisons was given by Rostas (1948). The studies of Maddison (1952), Galenson (1955), Frankel (1957) and Yukizawa (1978) replicated his method for measuring real output, which concentrated on comparisons of "physical" gross output of different countries. The most ambitious studies in terms of sample size were those of Paige and Bombach (1959), Kudrov (1969), West (1971), Smith, Hitchens and Davies (1982), and Smith (1985). Table 2 shows their coverage so far as we could determine. Another indicator of the adequacy of their sample is the number of items matched. On the latter criterion, our study is amongst the most comprehensive. Some of the studies cited used a mixed methodology, in the sense that they combined independently determined PPP's by industry of origin with some proxy PPP's derived from expenditure studies. This was true of Paige and Bombach, and to smaller extent also of Smith, Hitchens and Davies (1982) and Smith (1985). In our study we kept strictly to the industry of origin approach, without using proxy PPP's. It should be noted that Table 2 is not exhaustive. See also Heath (1957), Maizels (1958), Frank (1977), Davies and Caves (1987), van Ark (1988), Szirmai and Pilat (1989), as well as the short-cut approach of Shinohara (1966) and Maddison (1970).

33

3. Comparisons of Purchasing Power, Real Output and Labour Productivity for Brazil/USA and Mexico/USA

Our analysis covered 17 industries, which were assumed to be representative for total manufacturing. The sample accounted for about 40 percent of gross value of output in Brazil and Mexico, and almost 28 percent in the U.S.A.

TABLE 2

13 Studies of Real Output Levels in Manufacturing

Author	Number of Products Sampled	Size of Sample	Country Coverage	Reference Years
Rostas (1948)	108	22 percent of 1937 U.S. employment	U.K./U.S.A.	1935 to 1939
Maddison (1952)	34	15 percent of Canadian, 14 per-cent of U.K., and 8 percent of U.S. employment in 1935	Canada/U.K./ U.S.A.	1935
Galenson (1955)	23	17 per cent of U.S. industrial gross output in 1939[a]	U.S.S.R./U.S.A.	1936 to 1939
Frankel (1957)	50[b]	18 percent of 1947 U.S. employment, 16 percent of U.K. 1948 employment	U.K./U.S.A.	1948/7
Paige and Bombach (1959)	380	51 percent of U.K., and 48 percent of U.S. manufacturing value added	U.K./U.S.A.	1950
Mensink (1966)	78	14 percent of U.K. 1958 employment	Netherlands/U.K.	1958
Kudrov (1969)	224[c]	substantial, but not stated	U.S.S.R./U.S.A.	1963
Czech Statistical Office/INSEE (1969)	113	substantial, but not stated	Czechslovakia/ France	1962 and 1967
West (1971)	150[b]	31 percent[d] of U.S. shipments	Canada/U.S.A.	1963
Yukizawa (1978)	60	26 percent of Japanese and 24 percent of U.S. value added in 1972	Japan/U.S.A.	1958/9, 1963 1967, 1972
Smith, Hitchens and Davies (1982)	487[ce] 350	substantial, but not stated	U.K./U.S.A. Germany/U.K.	1968/7 1967/8
Smith (1985)	386[ce]	55 percent of U.K. value added and 53 percent of U.S. value added	U.K./U.S.A.	1977
Maddison and Van Ark (present study)	171–372 192–342 200–157	33 percent of value added in Brazil, 39 percent in Mexico, 20 percent in U.S.A	Brazil/U.S.A. Mexico/U.S.A. Mexico/Brazil	1975 1975 1975

[a]Galenson includes three mining industries (coal, iron ore, oil and natural gas).
[b]In the absence of information from the authors, these are rough estimates.
[c]Information supplied by the authors.
[d]West does not say how his sample is, but we derived this figure by comparing the large industry codes he uses (pp. 59-61) with 1963 information in the *General Summary* volume of the *1977 Census of Manufactures.*
[e]Refers to number of "matches" instead of number of matched products.

The basic procedure involved weighting physical output of individual commodities by a common set of price weights. These "prices" were unit values derived from production censuses[1] by dividing gross value of output by corresponding quantities. Two sets of binary comparisons were made, i.e. Brazil/U.S.A. and Mexico/U.S.A.[2] Each involved (a) unit value weights of country X (Brazil or Mexico) to compare gross volume of output of that country with that in the United States:

$$\frac{\sum (Q_y^{X} * P_y^{X})}{\sum (Q_y^{U} * P_y^{X})} \tag{1a}$$

and each (b) used the unit value weights of the U.S.A. to derive a quantity ratio between country X and the United States as follows:

$$\frac{\sum (Q_y^{X} * P_y^{U})}{\sum (Q_y^{U} * P_y^{U})} \tag{1b}$$

with Q_y = quantity of product y, P_y = unit value of product y, X = country X. U = United States.

It is usually not possible to make these quantitative comparisons for all products of an industry, because:

(a) one cannot match each product with a corresponding one in the U.S. Census;

(b) some products are only specified by value and not by quantity.

In the Brazil/U.S.A. comparison 171 Brazilian product items and 372 U.S. product items were matched; and in the Mexico/U.S.A. comparison 192 Mexican product items and 342 U.S. product items were matched. Table 3 shows the ratios of covered output to total gross value of output for each of the 17 industries. In only two cases, i.e. the Brazilian motor vehicle industry and petroleum refining industry, was the coverage below 40 percent—because of the unusually large amount of "non-specified" output. On average the sample coverage ratios were between 58 and 73 percent.

There are two alternative procedures to move from the "covered output" comparison to one for the industry as a whole. It can be assumed that the quantity relationship between matched output in country X and country U applies to the industry as a whole, or that the price (unit value) relationship for covered output is representative for the entire industry. These two alternatives have been extensively discussed in the literature on measurement of production trends since Mills first raised the issue (Mills, 1932). Burns (1934, pp. 260–261) stressed that prices of different commodities are likely to be under the general influence of "common monetary factors", whereas there is no such "single dominant force acting pervasively" on quantitative movements for different commodities. Fabricant (1940) also preferred price indicators because "prices probably move together within closer limits than do quantities." Stone (1956) stated that completeness of coverage is of less importance with price indicators compared to quantity

---

[1]For an extensive discussion of the scope of the production censuses in Brazil, Mexico and the U.S.A. see Maddison and Van Ark (1987).

[2]In fact we also made a binary comparison of Brazil/Mexico, which is not shown here.

TABLE 3

COVERAGE RATIOS: GROSS VALUE OF MATCHED ITEMS AS A PERCENTAGE OF TOTAL GROSS VALUE OF OUTPUT (NATIONAL CURRENCIES)

	Brazil/U.S.A.		Mexico/U.S.A.	
	Brazil (1975)	U.S.A. (1977)	Mexico (1975)	U.S.A. (1977)
Grain Mill Products	83.17	58.06	65.51	59.89
Sugar and Sugar Products	94.83	72.41	85.68	72.41
Malt and Malt Beverages	88.05	93.67	89.08	93.67
Tobacco and Tobacco Products	90.15	94.19	98.05	89.76
Textiles	86.37	83.13	42.11	82.18
Footwear and Leather Products	56.28	52.29	53.72	61.01
Pulp and Paper	77.78	75.62	66.23	81.79
Soap and Detergents	94.79	48.84	81.57	61.51
Paints	45.32	44.83	69.30	44.83
Agricultural Fertilizers	82.68	83.90	66.88	83.90
Petroleum Refining and Products	38.19	86.60	75.42	82.01
Tires and Inner Tubes	79.48	58.11	48.72	53.58
Cement	86.64	65.00	59.22	66.04
Bricks	51.73	47.17	70.07	45.08
Iron and Steel	53.86	58.02	72.50	57.31
Radio and TV Receivers	62.17	64.80	68.75	63.23
Motor Vehicles	34.21	68.86	59.86	66.68
Weighted Average 17 industries	57.61	72.78	67.23	71.32

Note: For details on matching for individual industries see "Statistical Appendix" to our original, much larger, research report (Maddison and Van Ark, 1987).

indicators, because "prices charged for close substitutes by different firms or in different parts of a country are likely, in many cases, to show similar movements even if their absolute level is a little different." We agree with the statements above. Therefore our coverage adjustments are entirely based on the price indicator method.

As a result the price ratios (or PPP's) for an industry as a whole were assumed to be similar to the derived PPP's for the covered part of output. PPP's were either weighted by quantities of the United States, i.e.

$$\frac{\sum (Q_y^{U} * P_y^{X})_c}{\sum (Q_y^{U} * P_y^{U})_c} = \frac{\sum (Q_y^{U} * P_y^{X})}{\sum (Q_y^{U} * P_y^{U})} = PPP^{U} \tag{2a}$$

or by quantity weights of country X:

$$\frac{\sum (Q_y^{X} * P_y^{X})_c}{\sum (Q_y^{X} * P_y^{U})_c} = \frac{\sum (Q_y^{X} * P_y^{X})}{\sum (Q_y^{X} * P_y^{U})} = PPP^{X}. \tag{2b}$$

with "c" indicating covered output

PPP^{X} = purchasing power parity using quantity weights of country X

PPP^{U} = purchasing power parity using quantity weights of the U.S.A.

Table 4 presents the 1975 PPP estimates in terms of the number of currency units of country X to the U.S. dollar for the 17 individual industries and compares

TABLE 4

PURCHASING POWER PARITIES, BRAZIL/U.S.A. (CRUZEIROS TO THE U.S.$) AND MEXICO/U.S.A.
(PESOS TO THE U.S.$), 1975

	PPP: Cruzeiros/U.S. $			PPP: Pesos/U.S. $		
	U.S. Quantity Weights (1)	Brazil Quantity Weights (2)	Geometric Average (3)	U.S. Quantity Weights (4)	Mexico Quantity Weights (5)	Geometric Average (6)
Grain Mill Products	7.58	6.94	7.25	13.13	12.34	12.73
Sugar and Sugar Products	2.48	2.14	2.30	3.74	3.62	3.68
Malt and Malt Beverages	8.10	7.73	7.91	17.66	17.66	17.66
Tobacco and Tobacco Products	4.94	4.38	4.65	9.35	7.64	8.45
Textiles	13.33	9.81	11.44	18.69	17.45	18.06
Footwear and Leather Products	5.62	4.77	5.18	12.85	11.32	12.06
Pulp and Paper	10.53	8.24	9.31	22.77	19.83	21.25
Soap and Detergents	8.45	4.39	6.09	11.55	9.07	10.24
Paints	4.07	4.39	4.23	15.41	14.76	15.08
Agricultural Fertilizers	12.01	11.77	11.89	8.40	7.61	8.00
Petroleum Refining and Products	14.56	14.39	14.47	11.02	10.76	10.89
Tires and Inner Tubes	13.17	11.64	12.38	32.68	29.29	30.94
Cement	9.90	9.90	9.90	12.18	12.11	12.14
Bricks	4.03	3.62	3.82	9.79	13.60	11.54
Iron and Steel	8.95	7.27	8.07	14.09	11.25	12.59
Radio and TV Receivers	7.72	7.64	7.68	8.92	11.39	10.08
Motor Vehicles	6.49	6.32	6.40	13.74	13.55	13.64
Exchange Rates	8.13	8.13	8.13	12.50	12.50	12.50

Source and note: Includes adjustments for indirect taxes and subsidies for malt and malt beverages
tobacco and tobacco products and petroleum refining and products in the Mexico-U comparison,
and for quality differences in the motor vehicles industry in both country comparisons.

them with the official 1975 exchange rates, i.e. 8.13 cruzeiros to the U.S. dollar
and 12.5 Mexican pesos to the U.S. dollar.

Thus the PPP's in the first and fourth columns of Table 4 are weighted by
U.S. quantities, and those in the second and fifth columns by the quantities of
each of the Latin American countries. Geometric averages (Fisher indices) of
the two PPP's are also presented in the third and sixth columns. In the
Brazil/U.S.A. comparison 31 of the 51 PPP's were below the exchange rate, and
in the Mexico/U.S.A. comparison 27 of the 51 PPP's.[3]

Corresponding quantity relatives can be derived by applying the PPP's of
Table 4 to the gross value of output at national prices, because price and quantity
relatives are complementary to each other. The value ratio between country X
and base country U is divided by a Laspeyres price ratio, i.e. using quantity

[3]At this stage the 1977 U.S. census figures were adjusted to a 1975 basis. Volume adjustment
were derived from the *1982 Industrial Outlook,* in which gross value of output is shown at constant
1972 U.S.$ for separate product groups. These ratios were applied to the 1977 U.S. census gross value
of output. The resulting 1975 figures at 1977 prices were compared with the product group figures
for 1975 at 1975 prices derived from the *Annual Survey of Manufactures 1975-1976* (ASM). From
this latter comparison we derived our unit value indices for 1975 relative to 1977.

37

weights of the base country (see formula (2a)). Thus the derived quantity ratio is of the Paasche type, i.e. using unit value weights of country X (see formula 1a):

$$\frac{\sum (Q_y^X * P_y^X)}{\sum (Q_y^U * P_y^U)} \bigg/ \frac{\sum (Q_y^U * P_y^X)}{\sum (Q_y^U * P_y^U)} = \frac{\sum (Q_y^X * P_y^X)}{\sum (Q_y^U * P_y^X)}. \tag{3a}$$

The same is true for a combination of a Paasche price index and a Laspeyres quantity index, i.e.:

$$\frac{\sum (Q_y^X * P_y^X)}{\sum (Q_y^U * P_y^U)} \bigg/ \frac{\sum (Q_y^X * P_y^X)}{\sum (Q_y^X * P_y^U)} = \frac{\sum (Q_y^X * P_y^U)}{\sum (Q_y^U * P_y^U)}. \tag{3b}$$

Thus far the procedure described relates to gross value of output, but in order to avoid double-counting in aggregating the individual industry results, we must move on to derive quantity relatives for value added. The best way to do this would be to make separate comparison of outputs and inputs (so-called "double deflation"). Unfortunately, the production censuses do not give figures for individual inputs at the product level, so we had to tackle the problem by making a proportionate adjustment at national prices of the ratio of gross output to value added.

It would be desirable to adjust the value added concept used in the censuses to a national accounts basis. The "national accounts" concept of value added avoids all duplication, because it deducts all inputs. The Brazilian and Mexican censuses provide enough detailed information to reconcile census value added to a national accounts basis, but this was not possible for the U.S.A.

In the detailed value added comparisons for the 17 industries, we were therefore obliged to adjust the value added specifications in the three production censuses to a common basis using the "U.S. census concept" of value added. According to this concept only inputs directly related to the production process (i.e. raw materials, energy consumption, and packing expenses) are deducted from gross output.[4]

Table 5 shows Brazilian and Mexican value added ("U.S. census concept") converted to U.S. dollars at the official exchange rate, compared with the 1975 U.S. figures for value added derived from *Annual Survey of Manufactures*. Tables 6 and 7 show the results of applying the PPP's from Table 4 to the figures of value added in order to convert them to a common currency unit for the Brazil/U.S.A. and Mexico/U.S.A. comparison respectively. The first two columns show the results of the calculations in Brazilian and Mexican unit values respectively, and the fourth and fifth columns show value added at U.S. unit values. The third and last columns show the ratios of value added in Brazil and Mexico to the U.S.A.

---

[4]For the estimates at branch level and manufacturing as a whole we were able to use the "former national accounts" concept of value added, which is completely free of duplication. The "former" concept is preferred, because it deducts inputs of financial services at the branch level, whereas this particular input is usually deducted on a global basis for the economy as a whole in present national accounting practice.

TABLE 5

VALUE ADDED (U.S. CENSUS CONCEPT) IN BRAZIL, MEXICO AND THE U.S.A. IN 1975, AT
OFFICIAL EXCHANGE RATES (1975 U.S. DOLLARS)

	Brazil (million dollars)	Mexico (million dollars)	U.S.A. (million dollars)
Total Manufacturing Value Added	37,748.2	17,585.6[ab]	442,485.2
Grain Mill Products	236.0	207.3	1,587.8
Sugar and Sugar Products	571.4	257.3	933.9
Malt and Malt Beverages	248.7	550.0[a]	2,129.8
Tobacco and Tobacco Products	395.0	145.3[a]	3,721.5
Textiles	1,260.4	669.2	6,217.3
Footwear and Leather Products	583.8	266.4	2,941.6
Pulp and Paper	571.6	502.3	7,626.1
Soap and Detergents	169.7	216.3	2,419.7
Paints	350.8	127.8	2,126.3
Agricultural Fertilizers	445.5	180.9	3,306.1
Petroleum Refining and Products	1,883.0	684.9[ab]	9,332.3
Tires and Inner Tubes	388.6	236.4	3,462.8
Cement	382.3	276.0	1,332.9
Bricks	542.2	69.4	715.7
Iron and Steel	2,223.8	1,082.8	15,783.2
Radio and TV Receivers	447.3	205.3	1,542.5
Motor Vehicles	1,772.6	1,163.3	21,465.9
Total in our sample	12,472.8	6,840.9	86,645.4
as % of Total Manufacturing	33.04	38.90	19.58

Source: Figures for Brazil from *Censo Industrial*, figures for Mexico from *Resumen General* (except for figures mentioned under footnotes (a) and (b)), and figures for U.S.A. from the *Annual Survey of Manufactures 1975-1976*.

Note: Figures are converted at the exchange rate of 8.13 cruzeiros to the U.S. dollar and 12.5 pesos to the U.S. dollar.

[a] Indirect taxes and subsidies are deducted (see Table 2.3).

[b] Includes 571.8 million U.S. dollars (excl. indirect taxes and subsidies) for petroleum refining, not shown in the census, but taken from *Sistema de Cuentas Nacionales de Mexico*.

BLOWING UP OUR SAMPLE TO MAKE ESTIMATES FOR MANUFACTURING
AS A WHOLE

Previous investigators have followed different options in order to blow up their sample for manufacturing as a whole. Rostas (1948), Maddison (1952), Galenson (1955), Frankel (1957), Mensink (1966), and Yukizawa (1978) simply assumed that their sample results were representative for manufacturing as a whole (either explicitly or implicitly). They gave the overall result in terms of labour productivity, not output or PPP's. Sometimes, as with Rostas and Yukizawa, the sample aggregate result was derived by using labour weights.

Three studies explicitly discuss the aggregation problem in all three dimensions (output, PPP's and labour productivity), i.e. Paige and Bombach (1959), the Czech Statistical Office/INSEE (1969) and West (1971), but they each followed different methods.

39

TABLE 6

QUANTITIES (VALUE ADDED, U.S. CENSUS CONCEPT), BRAZIL/U.S.A., 1975

	At Brazilian "Prices"			At U.S. "Prices"		
	Brazil 1975	U.S.A. 1975	Brazil U.S.A. (%)	Brazil 1975	U.S.A. 1975	Brazil U.S.A. (%)
	(1975 Cr. million)			(1975 U.S.$ million)		
Grain Mill Products	1,918.7	12,038.2	15.94	276.5	1,587.8	17.41
Sugar and Sugar Products	4,645.4	2,320.0	200.24	2,167.8	933.9	232.13
Malt and Malt Beverages	2,021.9	17,259.0	11.72	261.4	2,129.8	12.27
Tobacco and Tobacco Products	3,211.7	18,392.9	17.46	733.2	3.721.5	19.70
Textiles	10,246.9	82,852.7	12.37	1,044.6	6,217.3	16.80
Footwear and Leather Products	4,746.0	16,531.3	28.71	994.4	2,941.6	33.80
Pulp and Paper	4,647.5	80,326.6	5.79	564.1	7,626.1	7.40
Soap and Detergents	1,379.8	20,504.5	6.73	314.5	2,419.7	13.00
Paints	2,852.3	8,654.5	32.96	649.4	2,126.3	30.54
Agricultural Fertilizers	3,621.5	36,696.6	9.12	307.6	3,306.1	9.30
Petroleum Refining and Products	15,309.0	135,912.4	11.26	1,064.0	9,332.3	11.40
Tires and Inner Tubes	3,159.1	45,600.3	6.93	271.4	3,462.8	7.84
Cement	3,107.7	13,194.5	23.55	313.9	1,332.9	23.55
Bricks	4,408.5	2,884.2	152.85	1,217.2	715.7	170.07
Iron and Steel	18,079.7	141,222.5	12.80	2,487.0	15,783.2	15.76
Radio and TV Receivers	3,636.9	11,902.2	30.56	475.8	1,542.5	30.84
Motor Vehicles	14,411.4	139,258.3	10.35	2,279.4	21,465.9	10.62
Total in our sample	101,404.1	788,550.7	12.86	15,422.2	86,645.4	17.80

Note: Includes adjustment for quality differences in the motor vehicles industry.

Paige and Bombach covered about half of output in their two countries, i.e. the U.K. and the U.S.A., and their average result is very similar to that for their sample, as they predominantly assumed their quantitative relationships to be representative (see p. 102). They got their total for manufacturing by blowing up the industries they covered to represent the situation by major branch (using quantity relationships of their sample in 59 percent of cases, PPP relatives for 19 percent, other price information for 10 percent, and employment for 12 percent).

West did not make estimates by major branch, but assumed the average PPP for his sample (with value added weights) was representative for the non-sampled industries, using the sample average PPP to derive real output in the non-covered sector (see p. 26). His overall labour productivity result was significantly lower than that for his sample.

The authors of the Czech–French study used an unweighted average of their sample PPP's (by branch) to get a PPP for each branch, with output derived for the branch by applying this PPP to calculate branch value added in real terms. Their manufacturing total was derived by summing branch totals. A similar procedure was used by Smith, Hitchens and Davies (1982), and Smith (1985).

TABLE 7

QUANTITIES (VALUE ADDED, U.S. CENSUS CONCEPT), MEXICO/U.S., 1975

	At Mexican "Prices"			At US "Prices"		
	Mexico 1975	U.S.A. 1975	Mexico U.S.A.	Mexico 1975	U.S.A. 1975	Mexico U.S.A.
	(1975 Ps. million)		(%)	(1975 U.S.$ million)		(%)
Grain Mill Products	2,591.8	20,842.0	12.44	210.0	1,587.8	13.22
Sugar and Sugar Products	3,216.1	3,490.8	92.13	888.3	933.9	95.12
Malt and Malt Beverages	6,874.8	37,615.8	18.28	389.2	2,129.8	18.28
Tobacco and Tobacco Products	1,816.8	34,777.7	5.22	237.9	3,721.5	6.39
Textiles	8,364.7	116,206.3	7.20	479.4	6,217.3	7.71
Footwear and Leather Products	3,329.5	37.784.9	8.81	294.1	2,941.6	10.00
Pulp and Paper	6,278.8	173, 674.5	3.62	316.6	7,626.1	4.15
Soap and Detergents	2,704.2	28,005.9	9.66	298.1	2,419.7	12.32
Paints	1,597.0	32,770.7	4.87	108.2	2,126.3	5.09
Agricultural Fertilizers	2,261.7	27.775.3	8.14	297.1	3,306.1	8.99
Petroleum Refining and Products	8,561.7	102,884.8	8.32	795.9	9,332.3	8.53
Tires and Inner Tubes	2,954.4	113.178.8	2.61	100.9	3,462.8	2.91
Cement	3,449.5	16,239.0	21.24	284.9	1,332.9	21.38
Bricks	867.2	7,009.2	12.37	63.8	715.7	8.91
Iron and Steel	13,535.1	222,453.8	6.08	1,203.2	15,783.2	7.62
Radio and TV Receivers	2,565.7	13,751.5	18.66	225.2	1,542.5	14.60
Motor Vehicles	14,541.6	295,020.1	4.93	1,073.5	21,465.9	5.00
Total in our sample	85,510.9	1,283,481.2	6.66	7,266.2	86,645.4	8.39

Note: Includes adjustments to exclude indirect taxes and subsidies for malt and malt beverages, tobacco and tobacco products and petroleum refining and products, and for quality differences in the motor vehicles industry.

Our approach comes closest to that of the Czech–French study. We assumed that the PPP's for our sample were representative for the non-sampled industries in the same manufacturing branch. For reasons already explained above, we feel that the PPP relationships are more representative than the quantitative relationships which Paige and Bombach predominantly used to establish their aggregate result. Unlike the Czech–French study, we used a weighted average of our individual industry PPP's to arrive at the PPP for each branch. For example our PPP for the food products branch is the average of the price ratios for grain mill and sugar and confectionery products weighted by value added (U.S. census concept). Table 8 shows our PPP's by manufacturing branch. They were used to convert branch value added at national prices to a common currency unit (see the quantity relatives in Tables 9 and 10).

LABOUR PRODUCTIVITY

One of the major purposes of our approach is to estimate comparative levels of labour (and ultimately of total factor) productivity. Labour productivity is here expressed as output per person engaged. Figures on working hours are

41

TABLE 8

PURCHASING POWER PARITIES BY MAJOR BRANCH OF MANUFACTURING BRAZIL/U.S.A. (CRUZEIROS TO THE U.S. DOLLAR) AND MEXICO/U.S. (PESOS TO THE U.S. DOLLAR), 1975

	PPP: Cruzeiros/U.S. dollar			PPP: Pesos/U.S. dollar		
	U.S. Quantity Weights	Brazil Quantity Weights	Geometric Average	U.S. Quantity Weights	Mexico Quantity Weights	Geometric Average
Food Products	5.69	2.69	3.91	9.65	5.29	7.14
Beverage Products	8.10	7.73	7.92	17.66	17.66	17.66
Tobacco Products	4.94	4.38	4.65	9.35	7.64	8.45
Textiles and Wearing Apparel	13.33	9.81	11.43	18.69	17.45	18.06
Footwear and Leather Products	5.62	4.77	5.18	12.85	11.32	12.06
Wood and Paper Products	10.53	8.24	9.32	22.77	19.83	21.25
Chemical Products	11.92	9.92	10.87	11.14	10.09	10.60
Rubber and Plastic Products	13.17	11.64	12.38	32.68	29.28	30.94
Stone, Clay and Glass Products	7.85	4.91	6.21	11.35	12.38	11.85
Metal Products	8.95	7.27	8.07	14.09	11.25	12.59
Electrical Machinery	7.72	7.64	7.68	8.92	11.39	10.07
Machinery and Transport Equipment	6.49	6.32	6.40	13.74	13.55	13.64
Other	8.79	6.26	7.42	14.92	10.94	12.77
Total	8.79	6.26	7.42	14.92	10.94	12.77

Source and note: PPP's from Table 4. The PPP for food products is the weighted average for grain mill products and sugar and confectionery products. The PPP for chemical products is a weighted average for soap and detergents, paints, agricultural fertilizers and petroleum refining and products. The PPP for stone, clay and glass products is a weighted average for cement and bricks. In all cases value added (U.S. census concept) was used as weights. The Cruzeiro/U.S. dollar PPP's and Peso/U.S. dollar PPP's for "Other Manufacturing" and "Total Manufacturing" are derived from the sum of the branch values in Tables 9 and 10, respectively.

generally not available for Brazil, and there are only rough figures for Mexico. In 1975, average working hours in Mexico were 44.05 per week compared with 39.50 for production and non-supervisory workers in U.S. manufacturing.[5] Reliable comparative information on time off for holidays and sickness is not available, so output per man hour cannot be calculated with any accuracy, but it seems probable that aggregate hours per person engaged were longer in Brazil and Mexico than in the U.S.A., perhaps around 10 percent higher.

The labour productivity ratios presented here do not account for activities of head offices and auxiliaries in any of the three counties. We do not believe that the ratios would change significantly by including such activity. The head office share of total manufacturing employment was 14 percent in both Brazil and Mexico and 16 percent in the U.S.A.

Table 12 presents ratios of value added per person engaged in manufacturing branches for the Brazil/U.S.A. and the Mexico/U.S.A. comparison. The produc-

[5]For Mexico, see INEGI (1985), Vol. 1, p. 60; for the U.S.A., see *Employment and Earnings*, December 1978, p. 85.

TABLE 9

QUANTITIES (VALUE ADDED, FORMER NATIONAL ACCOUNTS CONCEPT) BY MAJOR BRANCH
OF MANUFACTURING, BRAZIL/U.S.A. 1975

	At Brazilian "Prices"			At U.S. "Prices"		
	Brazil 1975 (1975 Cr.million)	U.S.A. 1975	Brazile U.S.A. (%)	Brazil 1975 (1975 U.S.$ million)	U.S.A. 1975	Brazil U.S.A. (%)
Food Products	27,759	144,744	19.18	10,337	25,421	40.66
Beverages	4,565	41,774	10.93	590	5,155	11.45
Tobacco Products	2,987	12,203	24.48	682	2,469	27.62
Textiles and Wearing Apparel	22,940[a]	270,854	8.47	2,339	20,325	11.51
Footwear and Leather Products	3,977[a]	13,145	30.26	833	2,339	35.63
Wood and Paper Products	27,696	482,290	5.74	3,362	45,788	7.34
Chemical Products	42,511	388,781	10.93	4,286	32,627	13.14
Rubber and Plastic Products	10,260	121,560	8.44	881	9,231	9.55
Stone, Clay and Glass Products	15,365	84,899	18.10	3,130	10,817	28.93
Metal Products	31,176	470,798	6.62	4,289	52,617	8.15
Electrical Machinery	15,437	211,184	7.31	2,020	27,369	7.38
Machinery and Transport Equipment	44,231	513,071	8.62	6,996	79,087	8.85
Other	8,109	132,811	6.11	1,295	15,099	8.58
Total	257,012	2,888,112	8.90	41,039	328,343	12.50

Source: Brazil value added in national currencies from *Censo Industrial*, U.S. value added in national currencies from *National Income and Products Accounts of the United States: 1929–76 Statistical Tables* (1981c) after adjustment for inventories indirect taxes and subsidies and net interest. PPP's from Table 8.

Note: The breakdown between food products and beverages for the U.S. on a national accounts basis was assumed to be proportionately the same as on a U.S. Census basis (1975 figures derived from *Annual Survey of Manufactures*).

[a]The footwear industry (2,675.9 million cruzeiros) was reallocated from wearing apparel to footwear and leather.

tivity ratios show a very clear U.S. productivity advantage over both the other countries.

In the Brazil/U.S.A. comparison labour productivity (the geometric "Fisher" index) varied between 33 percent of the U.S. for wood and wood products to 76 percent for food products, with a weighted average of 49 percent for manufacturing as a whole. The average Mexico/U.S.A. ratio is below that for Brazil/U.S.A., namely 39 percent, with a minimum of 22 percent of the U.S. level for wood and paper products and a high of 48 percent for food products.

4. REVIEW OF THE RESULTS

The most interesting feature of our results is that our PPP's (Table 13) do not vary greatly from the exchange rate.[6]

[6]It should be stressed that the PPP's in Table 13 are our preferred summary measures, and are not unique in character. As in all such studies the final outcome can be stated in alternative ways, i.e. the price relations can be measured with the "quantity" weights of either one of the two countries involved in each binary comparison. In complementary fashion, our quantity relations (see Table 15) can be measured using the "price" weights of either one of the countries involved in each binary comparison. The measure we show in Table 13 is a geometric (Fisher) average of these alternatives.

TABLE 10

QUANTITIES (VALUE ADDED, FORMER NATIONAL ACCOUNTS CONCEPT) BY MAJOR BRANCH
OF MANUFACTURING, MEXICO/U.S.A., 1975

	At Mexican "Prices"			At U.S. "Prices"		
	Mexico 1975	U.S.A. 1975	Mexico U.S.A.	Mexico 1975	U.S.A. 1975	Mexico U.S.A.
	(1975 Ps. million)		(%)	(1975 U.S.$ million)		(%)
Food Products	20,446	245,296	8.34	3,866	25,421	15.21
Beverages	8,170[a]	91,046	8.97	462	5,155	8.97
Tobacco Products	1,177[a]	23,073	5.10	154	2,469	6.24
Textiles and Wearing Apparel	15,334	379,890	4.04	879	20,325	4.32
Footwear and Leather Products	2,472	30,044	8.23	218	2,339	9.34
Wood and Paper Products	13,121	1,042,762	1.26	662	45,788	1.44
Chemical Products	26,226[ab]	363,469	7.22	2,600	32,627	7.97
Rubber and Plastic Products	6,264	301,708	2.08	214	9,231	2.32
Stone, Clay and Glass Products	8,857	122,755	7.21	715	10,817	6.61
Metal Products	23,949	741,602	3.23	2,129	52,617	4.05
Electrical Machinery	9,557	243,997	3.92	839	27,369	3.06
Machinery and Transport Equipment	19,423	1,086,945	1.79	1,434	79,087	1.81
Other	2,494	225,228	1.11	228	15,099	1.51
Total	157,488	4,897,816	3.22	14,401	328,343	4.39

Source: Mexican value added in national currencies from *Resumen General*, U.S. value added in national currencies from *National Income and Products Accounts of the United States: 1929–76 Statistical Tables* (1981c) after adjustment for inventories indirect taxes and subsidies and net interest. PPP's from Table 8.

Note: The breakdown between food products and beverages for the U.S. on a national accounts basis was assumed to be proportionately the same as on a U.S. Census basis (1975 figures derived from *Annual Survey of Manufactures*).

[a]Indirect taxes and subsidies are deducted.

[b]Includes 3,831.7 million pesos (excl. indirect taxes and subsidies) for petroleum refining, not shown in the census *Resumen General*, but taken from *Sistema de Cuentas Nacionales de Mexico*.

In fact the purchasing power of the Brazilian currency was somewhat greater for manufactured products than suggested by the exchange rate, while in Mexico the reverse situation prevailed. These conclusions seem quite plausible. After the first OPEC shock Brazil took steps to make its effective exchange rate more competitive in 1974 and 1975, whereas the Mexican currency is generally held to have been overvalued in 1975, since the exchange rate had been unchanged since 1954. The currency was substantially devalued in 1976.

Our PPP's and exchange rate deviation indices (Table 13) are quite different from those of the ICP for GDP. This in itself does not mean that they are incompatible as the ICP figures are strongly affected by services where their exchange rate deviation index is particularly extreme.

Although the ICP authors have never used their results to derive proxy estimates for sectors of output, several other investigators have done so (see Table 1). Using the same technique as such analysts, we can use ICP material to derive the PPP's for manufacturing in Table 14. The proxy PPP for manufactur-

TABLE 11

	Brazil	Mexico	U.S.A.
Food Products	482,434	309,651	1,321,400
Beverages	52,080	69,392	203,800
Tobacco Products	23,965	8,645	66,200
Textiles and Wearing Apparel	507,593[a]	229,027	2,049,300
Footwear and Leather Products	129,231[a]	48,101	239,700
Wood and Paper Products	524,402	164,595	2,642,700
Chemical Products	177,920	157,170[b]	983,100
Rubber and Plastic Products	120,866	53,363	585,000
Stone, Clay and Glass Products	311,361	100,714	588,800
Metal Products	429,539	206,509	2,505,800
Electrical Machinery	170,425	114,382	1,523,600
Machinery and Transport Equipment	595,580	178,678	3,571,200
Other	146,260	34,113	893,200
Total Manufacturing	3,671,656	1,674,340	17,173,800[c]

Source: Brazil from IBGE, *Censo Industrial* (1981a), Mexico from SPP, *Resumen General* (1979a), USA from U.S. Dept. of Commerce, *Annual Survey of Manufactures 1975-76* (1979).

[a]Employment in the footwear industry (95,358 employees) was reallocated from wearing apparel to footwear and leather.

[b]Includes 25,989 employees in petroleum refining which are not covered by the industrial census *Resumen General*, but taken from SPI, 1981.

[c]Excludes employees in administrative offices and auxiliaries, i.e. 152,682 in Brazil, 69,448 in Mexico, and 1,128,200 in the U.S.A.

ing is identical with our average PPP result in the Brazil/U.S.A. comparison, but substantially different for the Mexico/U.S.A. comparison.

Apart from the possible shortcomings of proxy PPP's, there is also a substantial problem when they are applied (see D. J. Roy, 1987) to the respective national accounts at national prices, without adjustment for differences in the coverage of such accounts. The Mexican national accounts make a very large imputation for manufacturing activity in the informal sector, whereas the Brazilian accounts make virtually no adjustment. As there is no reason to expect the relative size of the informal sector to be much different in the two countries, use of inconsistent national accounts can have serious results. The typical shortcut proxy procedure would overstate Mexico's output position relative to Brazil's for two reasons:

(a) by overstating the relative PPP of the peso, and

(b) overstating Mexico's output in national currency terms vis-à-vis Brazil.

Table 15 shows the quantitative results (geometric averages) of our study for the Brazil/U.S.A. and Mexico/U.S.A. comparison. The figures show clearly that Brazil had a better performance than Mexico both in terms of labour productivity and output per head of population, but it appears that the Latin American performance per head of population is much lower than the productivity standing, because manufacturing employment is relatively smaller than it is in the U.S.A.

Table 16 compares our labour productivity results for Brazil, Mexico and the U.S.A. with those of analogous studies for other countries. The studies of Paige and Bombach for 1950, Smith, Hitchens and Davies for 1967–68, and Smith

TABLE 12

Productivity Ratios (Value Added, Former National Accounts Concept) per Person Engaged by Major Branch of Manufacturing, Brazil/U.S.A. and Mexico/U.S.A., 1975

	Brazil/U.S.A.			Mexico/U.S.A.		
	Brazil Unit Value Weights	U.S.A. Unit Value Weights	Geometric Average	Mexico Unit Value Weights	U.S.A. Unit Value Weights	Geometric Average
Food Products	52.53	111.37	76.49	35.57	64.90	48.05
Beverages	42.76	44.80	43.77	26.35	26.35	26.35
Tobacco Products	67.61	76.28	71.82	39.06	47.80	43.21
Textiles and Wearing Apparel	34.19	46.45	39.85	36.12	38.69	37.38
Footwear and Leather Products	56.12	66.08	60.90	41.00	46.52	43.68
Wood and Paper Products	28.94	37.00	32.72	20.20	23.20	21.65
Chemical Products	60.42	72.59	66.23	45.13	49.84	47.43
Rubber and Plastic Products	40.85	46.22	43.45	22.76	25.40	24.05
Stone, Clay and Glass Products	34.22	54.72	43.27	42.18	38.67	40.39
Metal Products	38.63	47.55	42.86	39.19	49.10	43.86
Electrical Machinery	65.35	65.97	65.66	52.17	40.82	46.15
Machinery and Transport Equipment	51.69	53.04	52.36	35.71	36.24	35.97
Other	37.29	52.37	44.19	28.99	39.55	33.86
Total Manufacturing	41.62	58.64	49.33	32.98	44.99	38.52

Source: Value added from Tables 9 and 10 for the Brazil/U.S.A. and Mexico/U.S.A. comparison respectively. Persons engaged from Table 11.

TABLE 13

Confrontation of Our PPP's for Manufacturing with the Exchange Rate and with the PPP's of ICP for 1975

	Brazil/U.S.A. (Cr./U.S.$)	Mexico/U.S.A. (Ps. /U.S.$)
Our PPP's for Manufacturing (weighted by major branch)	7.42	12.77
ICP (Augmented Binary) PPP's for GDP	5.40	7.17
Exchange Rate	8.13	12.50
Our Exchange Rate Deviation Index for Manufacturing	1.10	0.98
ICP Exchange Rate Deviation Index for GDP (augmented Binaries)	1.51	1.74

Source: Our PPP's for Brazil/U.S.A. derived from Table 9 and for Mexico/U.S.A. from Table 10, respectively; ICP augmented binaries from Kravis, Heston and Summers (1982), pp. 255, 272. In fact the preferred ICP PPP's are multilaterally weighted, but we have shown their augmented binaries here because they are conceptually closer to ours. The multilaterally weighted PPP's of ICP did not vary greatly, i.e. 5.20 and 7.40, respectively for 1975 (see Kravis, Heston and Summers, 1982, p. 177). Exchange rates from IMF.

Note: The exchange rate deviation index is the ratio of the exchange rate to the PPP.

TABLE 14

CONFRONTATION OF OUR PPP's FOR MANUFACTURING WITH THE PROXY PPP's DERIVED
FROM THE ICP 1975 AUGMENTED BINARY RESULTS

	Brazil/U.S.A. (Cr./U.S.$)	Mexico/U.S.A. (Ps. /U.S.$)
Our PPP's for Manufacturing (weighted by major branch)	7.42	12.77
Proxy PPP's for Manufacturing Derived from ICP Augmented Binaries	7.42	10.66
Ratio of Our PPP/Proxy ICP PPP	1.00	1.20

Source: Top line from Table 13; Second line derived from Kravis, Heston and Summers (1982), pp. 255, 272 and 313 as follows: the ICP III augmented binary PPP's for expenditure on the consumer items food, beverages, tobacco, clothing, footwear, furniture, appliances and transport equipment, and for producer durables were used to make the weighted average. These are the ICP PPP's which are conceptually closest to our type of comparison. The preferred PPP's of the ICP itself are in "international dollars."

TABLE 15

SUMMARY RESULTS FOR MANUFACTURING OUTPUT AND PRODUCTIVITY BRAZIL/U.S.A. AND
MEXICO/U.S.A. (1975)

	Brazil/U.S.A.	Mexico/U.S.A.
Value Added (Former National Accounts Concept) as a Percentage of the U.S.A.	10.55	3.76
Value Added (Former National Accounts Concept) per Person engaged as a Percentage of the U.S.A.	49.33	38.52
Value Added (Former National Accounts Concept) per Head of Population as a Percentage of the U.S.A.	21.72	13.48
Persons Engaged in Manufacturing as a Percentage of the U.S.A.	21.38	9.75
Population as a Percentage of the U.S.A.	48.55	27.85

Source: Value added from Tables 9 and 10; value added per person employed from Table 12; population figures for Brazil from IBGE, *Censo Demografico* (1983), Mexico from Bank of Mexico, *Indicadores Economicos* (1986), U.S.A. from OECD, *Labour Force Statistics* (1987).
Note: Figures in the three upper lines are geometric averages.

for 1977 all found the U.K. productivity ratio to the U.S.A. (value added per person employed) to be similar to what we found for Mexico/U.S.A. for 1975, and below the Brazil/U.S.A. ratio we obtained for 1975.

Confirmation of the rather high level of productivity in Brazilian manufacturing can be found in a recent direct comparison by Van Ark (1988) of labour productivity in Brazil and the United Kingdom for 1975. Using the same methods as this study for a larger sample of 23 industries, it showed average Brazilian output per person engaged to be not far from that of the U.K. in 1975.

It is at first sight surprising that real productivity levels in Brazilian and Mexican manufacturing are as high by international standards as they appear. However, evidence from estimates at national prices appears to confirm that Brazil and Mexico have much higher productivity levels in manufacturing compared with the rest of the economy than is the case in the more advanced countries.

47

TABLE 16

RESULTS OF PREVIOUS STUDIES AND OUR STUDY OF OUTPUT PER PERSON ENGAGED IN
MANUFACTURING AS A WHOLE, AS A PERCENTAGE OF THE U.S.A.

	At Local Prices	At U.S. Prices	Geometric Average
		Brazil/U.S.A. (1975)	
Present study	41.6	58.5	49.3
		Mexico/U.S.A. (1975)	
Present study	33.0	45.0	38.6
		U.K./U.S.A. (1950)	
Paige and Bombach (1959)	34.2	39.1	36.6
		U.K. (1968)/U.S. (1967)	
Smith, Hitchens and Davies (1982)	36.2	39.7	37.9
		U.K./U.S.A. (1977)	
Smith (1985)	38.3	41.5	39.9
		U.S.S.R./U.S.A. (1963)	
Kudrov (1969)	33.6	36.8	35.3
		Japan/U.S.A. (1972)	
Yukizawa (1978)	78.2	62.1	69.9
		Canada/U.S.A. (1963)	
West (1971)	64.4	68.5	66.4

Sources: See bibliographic references.

There are several reasons for this relatively high level of labour productivity in the manufacturing sectors of Brazil and Mexico. One is that in many sectors of manufacturing, the nature of technology is such that it is often rational to use processes which are labour saving and capital intensive, even in countries with low wages. Low income countries do have some leeway in adapting technology to a situation of low labour costs, but a large part of industrial technology was developed in countries where labour is more expensive, and there are problems in adapting it to different factor cost situations.

A second reason for relatively high labour productivity in Brazilian and Mexican manufacturing is the importance of policies which subsidize capital inputs. As a result, scarce capital is funnelled by priority towards industry. These policies are probably operative to a greater degree than in the OECD countries.

A few additional remarks should be added on the relatively high productivity standing of Brazil and Mexico compared to the other countries. Firstly, the Latin American standing in terms of output per man hour, which could not be measured accurately, is probably lower than the productivity ratio in terms of output per person engaged, because working hours appear to be higher than in the U.S.A. Secondly, in comparison with the U.S.A. there is probably a greater amount of informal manufacturing activity outside the scope of the census in Latin America where productivity is lower. Thirdly, as already noted, Latin American performance per head of population is much lower than their productivity standing, because manufacturing employment is relatively much smaller than it is in the U.S.A.

The present article deals with two binary comparisons, one between Brazil and the U.S.A. and the other between Mexico and the U.S.A., and made some inferences about the relative productivity standing of Brazil/Mexico from the two other binaries. In fact we also made a direct binary comparison between Brazil and Mexico, without using the U.S.A. as an intermediary, but have not presented the details here as the quantitative results were not substantially different from the inferential comparison. The geometric average of the Mexico/Brazil ratio of value added per person engaged was 82.70 percent in the direct binary comparison against 78.09 percent according to the inferential comparison (which can be derived from Table 12).

5. Results of Methodological Endeavours

One of the objectives of the present study was to provide a systematic methodological survey of the analytical problems inherent in the industry of origin approach, with whatever pragmatic contribution or recommendations we could make to mitigate or solve those which characteristically emerge.

(a) *An Integrated Three-Dimensional Approach*

We tried to give full attention to each of the three main dimensions of international comparison—real output, PPP's and productivity, and to set out their interrelation and complementary character clearly. Here our exposure to ICP methodology was very useful, as its rigour in this respect is exemplary. We feel that a good deal of previous work on industry-of-origin lines has suffered from concentrating only on the productivity aspects (this is true of all studies listed in Table 2 except Paige and Bombach, the Czech/INSEE study and that of West).

(b) *Reconciliation with the National Accounts Framework*

There are obvious advantages in making sectoral output and productivity studies of this kind in a conceptual framework compatible with the national accounts. We made a careful confrontation between the census and the national accounts, from which it appeared that the Mexican national accounts make extensive (and perhaps excessive) allowance for informal activity not recorded in the manufacturing censuses.

It is also clear that census definitions of value added vary between countries, and need adjustment to bring the comparisons for the three countries to a common conceptual basis as is used in national accounting. The "national accounts" concept of value added is obviously preferable to the census concepts, which are becoming increasingly anachronistic by neglecting to deduct service inputs in measuring value added.

(c) *Adjustment to a Common Benchmark Year*

Our study meets the problem of comparing countries whose census dates fall in different years. Our adjustment procedures have general applicability, and they were applied here to the U.S.A., whose performance is often a yardstick for comparison in such studies. In fact, using our approach, U.S. data can be adjusted to any intercensal year needed for purposes of international comparison.

49

(d) *A Systematic Shortcut Procedure for Matching*

None of the previous studies mentioned in Table 2 used a systematic procedure to select the particular "representative" products on which price and quantity comparisons are ultimately based. We therefore developed criteria for a systematic matching procedure which is economical in terms of time and effort.

Exact-matching is difficult to realize because strictly identical products are only rarely available in two or more countries at the same date. In consequence, lower degrees of product comparability have to be accepted for international comparisons than for inter-temporal comparisons within a single country. This is true not only for the present product-based study, but also for expenditure-based studies such as the ICP.

The maximalist approach tries to match as many items as possible, but often results in very wide ranges of PPP's within an industry. These widely divergent PPP's for different products are a signal to the possibility that some of the matches are false. In spite of having similar (or even identical) descriptions, we inferred that some of these outliers were, in reality, different products.

For complex multiproduct industries, we therefore developed a procedure which confines matching to the most important products. Only products that accounted for more than 1 percent of the gross value of output of an industry were considered for matching. Smaller items were only included when they matched a similar product of importance in the other country, or when they were required to complete a "match" with an important product.

The advantages of a systematic matching procedure is important, when one has to deal with:

—a large industry with many product items, for example, textiles or footwear and leatherware, and/or

—a technically complicated industry producing items difficult for a technically inexperienced researcher to characterize, for example motor vehicles or iron and steel.

In these cases, an important risk of mismatching occurs when a less systematic approach is used. For smaller, simpler industries the maximalist approach was used.

(e) *The Unit Value Approach is not Inferior to Specification Pricing*

It is sometimes suggested that unit values such as we derived from census information are inherently inferior to specification pricing as practiced by ICP, but we do not believe this to be the case.

Specification pricing involves meticulous characterisation of the items chosen as representative, whereas our "prices" are unit values derived by confrontation of census information on values and quantities of product. In practice the "products" may be a mix of items and qualities and be very far from the ideal of specification pricing, but there are compensatory advantages in the industry of origin approach:

(1) the unit values are average transaction values for the whole year for all producing locations of the countries compared, whereas ICP prices are quotes, shelf, list or monitored prices for one point in the year in a limited number of locations,

50

(2) with the census one can judge the representativity of the "unit values" which are selected from a much wider range of information than ICP had at its disposal. For instance, our 17 industry sample yielded 1,434 Mexican unit values from which 192 were chosen to match with the U.S.A., and 543 Brazilian unit values of which 171 were matched with the U.S.A. ICP, by contrast, had to use what it got from national statistical offices (at least for consumption goods). For Mexico it received only 284 of the much larger number of consumer prices it requested, as compared with 359 for Brazil and 571 for the U.S.A. (Kravis, Heston and Summers, 1982, p. 45).

Our unit value specification was particularly poor in the case of motor vehicles, largely because of census confidentiality rules. The census information was therefore supplemented in this case by using information on output and consumer price structures from trade sources. *Automotive News* provides figures furnished by trade associations from trade sources which are reasonably reliable (see the "Statistical Appendix" in Maddison and Van Ark, 1988). Producer prices would have been preferable to consumer prices, but the U.S. producer price index is based on information for only a limited number of models, and is as confidential as the census itself. Our method of handling the problem produced a reasonable, though not an optimal, adjustment for quality. In any case, we would stress that our approach is not inferior to that of ICP for this particular industry. As the ICP approach is a multilateral one, its products have to be "representative" in a global sense. ICP III used passenger car models which were characteristic across its 34 countries, and its comparison for Brazil/U.S.A. and Mexico/U.S.A. was based largely on Japanese and European models which were quite unrepresentative of the situation in these three markets.

(f) *The Adequacy of the Sample*

Our sample size (39 percent of Mexican, 33 percent of Brazilian and 20 per cent of U.S. value added) was certainly large enough to illustrate most of the methodological problems one is likely to encounter in this kind of study and to help elaborate pragmatic solutions to them. Except as noted under (g) below, the only failure in this respect was the problem of unique products, such as atomic weaponry, guided missiles and space vehicles, which are unique to the U.S.A. and for which it would be difficult to derive dummy Brazilian and Mexican prices. There are also industries which are not unique, but near enough to impede comparison (such as aircraft, computers, oil drilling and other specialized machinery). These unique and quasi-unique industries were about 7 percent of total U.S. manufacturing output in 1975. Otherwise, there are very few industries which are truly comparison resistant, particularly if one makes supplementary inquiries with trade associations (which we did for motor vehicles, paints, petroleum products and bricks) where there were national idiosyncracies in measurement units or gaps in the census due to confidentiality rules. From the point of view of our other objective of comparing output, productivity and PPP outcomes for the three countries, the results can always be improved by increasing the sample size, but we felt that there was already reasonable coverage of major

51

industry branches in Brazil and Mexico, and weaknesses only for food products and electrical machinery for the U.S.A.

(g) *Approaches to the Problem of Double Deflation*

The important unsolved problem in this study is that of double deflation. Virtually all analysts who have used the industry of origin approach have been unable to find separate PPP's for inputs. The double deflation approach is feasible for agriculture (van Ooststroom and Maddison 1985), but it was not feasible for manufacturing for these three countries, because the Brazilian and Mexican censuses give global value figures on inputs with no detailed quantitative information, and the U.S. census gives detailed figures only for energy consumption, contract work and inputs directly related to the production process.

In agriculture the difference between the gross output PPP's and the double deflated PPP's was rather small. For Brazil the 1975 PPP (Brazil quantity weights) was 7.35 cruzeiros to the U.S. dollar, 6.63 for inputs and 7.57 for value added. For Mexico the 1975 PPP (Mexican weights) was 13.46 pesos to the U.S. dollar, 13.68 for inputs and 13.36 for value added.

In manufacturing, inputs are much bigger in relation to gross output than in agriculture, but in the U.S.A. 60 percent of these are from manufacturing itself and in Mexico 48 percent. For manufacturing as a whole therefore, it does not seem *a priori* likely that the PPP's resulting from "double deflation" would be very different from those in our study, but for particular branches they might vary a good deal more.

Previous investigators who have discussed this problem, have been able to make only very partial adjustments for inputs. Paige and Bombach did this for fuel inputs on an aggregate basis, and Smith, Hitchens and Davies made some illustrative calculations (whose basis is not clear) for fuels and raw materials. However, a close look at the input–output tables which are available for Mexico (SPP, 1981) and the U.S.A. (U.S. Dept. of Commerce, 1984a and 1984b) shows that fuel and raw material inputs are only a small part of the problem in most industries.

Our analysis of the relation of census to GDP concepts of value added helps to clarify the nature of double deflation because it demonstrates the need to deal with all inputs. Further progress can best be made, when industry of origin studies such as the present one are available for all the major sectors of the economy, i.e. for agriculture, mining, manufacturing, utilities, construction and services. With this information and input–output tables for each of the countries under comparison, one can return to the problem of double deflation much better equipped to do a thorough job. In the case of Mexico and the U.S.A., input–output tables are available for the census years we covered, and the 1975 table for Brazil is due to be published soon, so for these three countries, this work should be feasible.

REFERENCES

Ahmad, S., *Approaches to Purchasing Power Parity and Real Product Comparisons Using Shortcuts and Reduced Information*, World Bank Staff Working Paper, No. 418, Washington D.C., processed, 1980.

Van Ark, B., "Time and Country Comparisons of Real Output and Productivity: A Case Study for the Manufacturing Sectors of India and the USA," revised version of paper presented at IARIW meeting, Rocca di Papa, processed, 1987.

———, "Labour Productivity in Manufacturing: A Comparison of Brazil and the United Kingdom for 1975," Research Memorandum 259, Groningen, 1988.

Beckerman, W., *International Comparisons of Real Incomes*, OECD Development Centre, Paris, 1966.

———, "Updating Short-Cut Methods for Predicting 'Real' Per Capita GDP," World Bank, September, processed, 1984.

Bergson, A., "Comparative Productivity: The USSR, Eastern Europe, and the West," *American Economic Review*, June, 1987.

Blades, D. W., "Short-cut comparisons of U.S.A. and U.S.S.R. GDP," International Association for Research in Income and Wealth, Luxembourg (mimeographed), 1982.

Block, H., *The Planetary Product in 1980: A Creative Pause?* C.I.A., Washington DC, 1981.

Board of Governors of the Federal Reserve System, *Industrial Production 1986 Edition*, Washington D.C, 1986.

Burns, A. F., *Production Trends in the United States Since 1870*, NBER, New York, 1934.

Czechoslovak Statistical Office/INSEE, "Comparison of Levels of Labour Productivity in Industry in Czechoslovakia and France," ECE, Geneva, November, processed, 1969.

Christensen L. R., and Cummings, D., "Relative Productivity Levels, 1947-1973: An International Comparison," *European Review*, May, 1981.

Conference of European Statisticians, "Comparisons of Labour Productivity in Industry in Austria, Czechoslovakia, France and Hungary," Conf. Eur. Stats./WG 21, Geneva, also in *Statistical Standards and Studies*, No. 24, UN, New York, 1972.

Davies, S., and Caves, R. E., *Britain's Productivity Gap*, NIESR, Cambridge, 1987.

Drechsler, L., and Kux, J., *Mezinarodni Srovnani Produktivity Prace*, Central Statistical Office, Prague, 1972.

Economic Commission for Europe, "Comparative GDP Levels, "*Economic Bulletin for Europe*, 1980.

ECLA, *A Measurement of Price Levels and the Purchasing Power of Currencies*, Santiago, processed, 1963.

Eurostat, *Comparison in Real Values of the Aggregates of ESA*: 1980, Luxembourg, 1983.

Fabricant, S., *The Output of Manufacturing Industries*, 1899-1937, NBER, New York, 1940.

Flux, A. W., "Industrial Productivity in Britain and the United States," *Quarterly Journal of Economics*, November, 1933.

Frank, J. G., *Assessing Trends in Canada's Competitive Position: The Case of Canada and the United States*, Conference Board in Canada, Ottawa, 1977.

Frankel, M., *British and American Manufacturing Productivity*, University of Illinois, Urbana, 1957.

Fundacao Getulio Vargas, *Contas Nacionais do Brasil: Metodologia e Tabelas Estatisticas*, Rio de Janeiro, 1984.

Galenson, W., *Labour Productivity in Soviet and American Industry*, Columbia University Press, New York, 1955.

Ghosh, A., "Some Problems Relating to the Selection of Representative Commodity Baskets, the Problem of Quality Differences and the Treatment of Comparison Resistant Services in the ICP," Bellagio, processed, September, 1984.

———, "Comparison of Structurally Divergent Economies, Problems and Limitations," *Economic and Political Weekly*, January 19th, 1984.

Gilbert, C. L., "Short-Cut Methods of Estimating Per Capita GDP and Tentative Results on the Distribution and Growth of Real GDP," *Oxford Economic Papers*, November, 1982.

Gilbert, M., and Beckerman, W., "International Comparison of Real Product and Productivity by Final Expenditures and by Industry," in NBER, *Output, Input and Productivity Measurement*, New York, 1961.

Gilbert, M., and Kravis, I. B., *An International Comparison of National Products and the Purchasing Power of Currencies*, OEEC, Paris, 1954.

Gilbert, M., and Associates, *Comparative National Products and Price Levels*, OEEC, Paris, 1958.

Gollop, F. M., and Jorgenson, D. W., "US Productivity Growth by Industry 1947-1973" in J. W. Kendrick and B. N. Vaccara, eds. *New Developments in Productivity Measurement and Analysis*, University of Chicago Press, Chicago, 1980.

Gosplan, *Sopostavlennie Urovnei Ekonomicheskovo Razvitia Sotsialisticheskikh Stran*, Moscow, 1965.

Guinchard P., "Productivité et Competitivité des Grands Pays Industriels," Economie et Statistique, January 1984.

de Gusmao Veloso, M. A., "Brazilian National Accounts 1947-1985, "IBGE, Rio de Janeiro, August, 1987.

Haig, B. D., *Real Product, Income and Relative Prices in Australia and the United Kingdom*, ANU, Canberra, 1968.

53

Heath, J. B., "British–Canadian Industrial Productivity." *Economic Journal* 1957.

Houben, A., "An International Comparison of Real Output, Labour Productivity and Purchasing Power in the Mineral Industries in the United States, Brazil and Mexico for 1975," University of Groningen, MA thesis, processed, 1988.

IBGE, *Censo Industrial: Brasil, Serie Nacional*, Vol. 2, Part 1, Rio de Janeiro, 1981a.

——, *Censo Industrial: Brasil, Producão Fisica, Serie Nacional*, Vol. 2, Part 2, Rio de Janeiro, 1981b.

——, *Censo Demografico: Mão de Obra*, Vol. I, Tomo 5, No. 1, Rio de Janeiro, 1983.

——, *Censo Industrial: Dados Gerais: Brasil*, Vol. 3, Tomo 2, Rio de Janeiro, 1984.

ILO, *International Recommendations on Labour Statistics*, Geneva, 1976.

INEGI, *Estadisticas Historicas de México*, Mexico, 1985.

Joint Economic Committee, *East European Economic Assessment*, U.S. Congress, Washington DC, 1981.

Joint Economic Committee, *USSR: Measures of Economic Growth and Development*, 1950–1980, U.S. Congress, Washington D.C., 1982.

Jones, D. T., "Output, Employment and Labour Productivity in Europe since 1955, "*National Institute Economic Review*, London, August, 1976.

Jorgenson, D. W., Kuroda, M., and Nishimizu, M., "Japan–US Industry Level Productivity Comparisons, 1960–1979," Harvard Institute of Economic Research, *Discussion Paper* No. 1254, July, 1986.

Klodt, H., *Produktivitätsschwäche in der deutschen Wirtschaft*, Mohr, Tübingen, 1985.

Kravis, I. B., "A Survey of International Comparisons of Productivity," *Economic Journal*, March, 1976.

——, "Comparative Studies of National Incomes and Prices," *Journal of Economic Literature*, March, 1984.

——, "The Three Faces of the International Comparison Project", *World Bank Research Observer*, January, 1986.

Kravis, I. B., Kennessey, Z., Heston, A., and Summers, R., *A System of International Comparisons of Gross Product and Purchasing Power*, Johns Hopkins, Baltimore, 1975.

Kravis, I. B., Heston, A., and Summers, R., A System of International *Comparisons of Real Product and Purchasing Power*, Johns Hopkins, Baltimore, 1978a.

——, "Real GDP per Capita for More than One Hundred Countries," *Economic Journal*, June, 1978b.

——, *World Product and Income*, Johns Hopkins, Baltimore, 1982.

Kravis, I. B., and Lipsey, R. E., *Price Competitiveness in World Trade*, NBER, New York, 1971.

Krijnse-Locker, H., "On Estimation of Purchasing Power Parities on the Basic Heading Level," *Review of Income and Wealth*, June, 1984.

Kudov, V. M., "Problemi Sopostavlenii Proizvoditelnosti Truda v Promischlennosti S.S.S.R. i S.Sch.A.", *Vestnik Moscovskovo Universiteta*, No. 1, 1969.

Kuznets, S., "Problems in Comparing Recent Growth Rates for Developed and Less-Developed Countries," *Economic Development and Cultural Change*, January, 1972.

Maddison, A., "Productivity in Canada, the United Kingdom, and the United States," *Oxford Economic Papers*, October, 1952.

——, "Comparative Productivity Levels in the Developed Countries," *Banca Nazionale del Lavoro Quarterly Review*, December, 1967.

——, *Economic Progress and Policy in Developing Countries*, Allen and Unwin, London, 1970.

——, "Monitoring the Labour Market," *Review of Income and Wealth*, June, 1980.

——, *Phases of Capitalist Development*, Oxford, 1982.

——, "A Comparison of Levels of GDP per Capita in Developed and Developing Countries, 1700–1980," *Journal of Economic History*, March, 1983.

——, "Growth and Slowdown in Advanced Capitalist Economies," *Journal of Economic Literature*, June, 1987.

Maddison, A., and Van Ark, B., "The International Comparison of Real Output, Purchasing Power and Labour Productivity in Manufacturing Industries: A Pilot Study for Brazil, Mexico and the USA for 1975," *Memorandum*, Institute of Economic Research, No. 231, Groningen, 1987.

——, *Comparisons of Real Output in Manufacturing*, Working Papers WPS5 World Bank, Washington D.C., 1988.

Maizels, A., 'Comparative Productivity in Manufacturing Industry: A Case Study of Australia and Canada," *Economic Record*, April 1958.

Mensink, G. J. A., *Comparisons of Labour Productivity in the United Kingdom and the Netherlands, 1958*, CBS, The Hague, January (*Statistical Studies*, no. 18), 1966.

Mills, F. C., *Economic Tendencies in the United States: Aspects of Pre-War and Post-War Changes*, NBER, New York, 1932.

Van Ooststroom, H. and Maddison, A., "An International Comparison of Levels of Real Output and Productivity in Agriculture in 1975," revised version, Groningen, processed, 1985.

Paige, D. and Bombach, G., *A Comparison of National Output and Productivity*, OECC, Paris, 1959.

Prais, S. J., *Productivity and Industrial Structure*, Cambridge, 1981.

Roman, Z., *Productivity and Economic Growth*, Akademiai Kiado, Budapest, 1982.

Rostas, L., *Comparative Productivity in British and American Industry*, Cambridge, 1948.

Roy, A. D., "Labour Productivity in 1980: An International Comparison," *National Institute Economic Review*, 1982.

Roy, D. J. "International Comparisons of Real Value Added, Productivity and Energy Intensity in 1980," *Economic Trends*, June, 1987.

Schroeder, G. E. and Edwards, I., *Consumption in the USSR: An International Comparison*, CIA study published by Joint Economic Committee, U.S. Congress, Washington D.C., 1981.

Shinohara, M., *Japan's Industrial Level in International Perspective*, Ministry of Foreign Affairs, Tokyo, March, 1966.

Smith, A. D., "Changes in Comparative Anglo-American Productivity in Manufacturing Industries," *NIESR Discussion Papers*, London, 1985.

Smith, A. D., Hitchens, D. M. W. N., and Davies, S. W., *International Industrial Productivity*, NIESR, Cambridge, 1982.

SPP, *X Censo Industrial 1976, Datos de 1975, Resumen General*, Tomo 1, Mexico, 1979a.

———, *X Censo Industrial 1976, Datos de 1975, Desglose de Productos Obtenidos por Clase de Actividad*, Mexico, 1979b.

———, *Sistema de Cuentas Nacionales de Mexico*, Tomos I-VII, Mexico, 1981.

Stone, R., *Quantity and Price Indices in National Accounts*, OEEC, Paris, 1956.

Summers, R. and Heston, A., "Improved International Comparisons of Real Product and Its Composition, 1950-80," *Review of Income and Wealth*, June, 1984.

Szitmai, A., and Pilat D., "A comparison of Real Output and Labour Productivity in Manufacturing in Japan, Korea and the USA 1975," University of Groningen, processed, 1989.

Taussig, F. W., "Labor Costs in the United States Compared with Costs Elsewhere," *Quarterly Journal of Economics*, November, 1924.

United Nations, *World Comparisons of Purchasing Power and Real Product for 1980, Phase IV of the International Comparison Project, Part One*, 1986, *Part Two*, 1987, New York, 1986-87.

U.S. Dept. of Commerce, *Annual Survey of Manufactures 1975-1976*, Bureau of the Census, Washington D.C., May, 1979.

———, *1977 Census of Manufactures, General Summary*, Bureau of the Census, Washington D.C., April, 1981a.

———, *1977 Census of Manufactures, Final Report Volumes*, Volume 2, *Industry Statistics*, Part I, *Major Groups 20-26*, Part II, *Major Groups 27-34*, Part III, *Major Groups 35-59*, Bureau of the Census, Washington D.C., August, 1981b.

———, *1982 US Industrial Outlook*, Bureau of Industrial Statistics, Washington D.C., 1982.

———, *The National Income and Product Accounts of the United States 1929-82, Statistical Tables*, BEA, Washington D.C., September, 1986.

Ward, M., *Purchasing Power Parities and Real Expenditures in the OECD*, Paris, 1985.

West, E. C., *Canada-United States Price and Productivity Differences in Manufacturing Industries, 1963*, Economic Council of Canada, Ottawa, 1971.

Yukizawa, K., "The Relative Productivity of Labour in American and Japanese Industry and Its Change, 1958-1972," Kyoto Institute of Economic Research, *Reprint Series*, No. 147, 1978.

PART IV

THE ROOTS OF ECONOMIC BACKWARDNESS

Part IV: The roots of economic backwardness

If we are to explain why the economic growth experience of nations has been so diverse and why income spreads are now so wide, it is necessary to go beyond proximate and measurable elements of causality and examine institutional and social influences which may retard or encourage economic development. Economic 'backwardness' is a topic which has concerned economic historians for decades. Gerschenkron (1962) drew attention to the problem and correctly stressed the need for historical perspective, but his spatial perspective was concentrated on European countries. North and Thomas (1973) and North (1981) are other important and influential books on this theme, but also deal with a limited range of backwardness, i.e. varieties of European experience.

In a world perspective, the gaps in performance between Western countries have been rather narrow, and their institutions and mentalités have a lot in common. Rosenberg and Birdzell (1986) show how Western countries were able to generate technical progress and adapt their institutions to exploit its production potential, both in a protocapitalist period of 300 years or so, and in the period of more rapid growth in the past 200 years.

Over the past five centuries, the influence of indigenous social and institutional forces in retarding growth were much stronger in Africa, Asia and Latin America than in the West, but have received much less attention from Western economists and economic historians. The role of colonialism in retarding development has also been largely ignored. These three essays are a contribution to filling this gap.

The analytic framework of Essays 10 (on India) and 11 (on Mexico) is rather similar. They (a) scrutinise the sanctions and structure of political power, the extent to which the state is predatory; (b) scrutinise the nature and distribution of property rights and earning capacity; (c) analyse the class structure and the nature of group conflicts; (d) investigate the role of religion and ideology as weapons of social control and legitimation of authority; and (e) examine the interaction between indigenous influences and colonialism.

Essay 12 (on Indonesia) is mainly concerned with the last topic.

For other pieces on these themes, see Maddison (1969, 1971 and 1992) and Maddison and Prince (1989). In the autobiographical note (Part VI) I have given a more cursory account of the variety of institutional and policy forces operative in other countries in Asia, Latin America and Africa.

References

Gerschenkron, A. (1962), *Economic Backwardness in Historical Perspective*, Harvard University Press.
Maddison, A. (1969), *Economic Growth in Japan and the USSR*, Allen and Unwin, London and Norton, New York.
Maddison, A. (1970), 'The Historical Origins of Indian Poverty', *Banca Nazionale del Lavoro Quarterly Review*, March.
Maddison, A. (1971), *Class Structure and Economic Growth: India and Pakistan since the Moghuls*, Allen and Unwin, London and Norton, New York.
Maddison, A. (1989), 'Dutch Income in and from Indonesia 1700–1938', *Modern Asian Studies*, **23**, 4.
Maddison, A. (1992), *The Political Economy of Poverty, Equity and Growth: Brazil and Mexico*, Oxford University Press, New York.
Maddison, A. and G. Prince (eds) (1989), *Economic Growth in Indonesia, 1820–1940*, Foris, Dordrecht.
North, D.C. (1981), *Structure and Change in Economic History*, Norton, New York.
North D.C. and R.P. Thomas (1973), *The Rise of the Western World*, Cambridge University Press.
Rosenberg, N. and E. Birdzell Jnr (1986), *How the West Grew Rich*, Basic Books, New York.

[10]

The Historical Origins of Indian Poverty

The Indian subcontinent is today the poorest area in the world. Its living standard is wretched, both through Western eyes, and from the perspective of most other developing countries. But in the sixteenth century, India was considered wealthy by Europeans. This paper attempts to analyse the reasons for the decline in India's relative economic status from the time of the Moghuls up to independence. Such an exercise is essential if we are to make a valid assessment of the tasks and performance of economic policy in India and Pakistan since independence. It may also contribute something of general interest to the economic analysis of colonialism (which is still in a primitive state).

Unfortunately, Indian economic history has been written largely by people with a political axe to grind. Nationalists like Romesh Dutt put most of the blame for Indian poverty on the British raj, and claim that the period preceding British rule was a golden age. More extreme writers see malice in everything done by the British and some seem to imply that India would have attained Western living standards if it had not been for British policy. The nationalist school found support from autocritical British bureaucrats like William Digby and from anglophobe Americans like Brooks Adams. By contrast, academic defenders of the British raj, like Vera Anstey, attribute India's backwardness mainly to its own social institutions, and stress the blessings brought by British law and order, and railways. Now that the British Empire has gone, it is possible to take a more detached view, and to remove some of the mythology.

In this paper, which is intended as no more than an interpretative essay, we examine briefly the nature of the Moghul economy and then analyse the main ways in which British rule promoted or retarded economic growth. Some of the conclusions are novel. Most of them are tentative.

Moghul India

Before the British conquest, India had been dominated by the Moghul Empire. The first Moghul Emperor, Babur (a descendant of both Ghengis Khan and Timur), came to India from central Asia in 1526 (1). Before he came, India was politically divided with the Muslim sultanate of Delhi (founded in 1192) in loose control of the North and the powerful Hindu Kingdom of Vijayanagar in the South. The Moghuls established control over the North of India as well as retaining Afghanistan, and eventually, under Aurangzeb, controlled most of the South as well.

The Muslim population was always a minority but in the Moghul period it had probably become about a fifth or a quarter of the total. A minority of Indian Muslims (about 10 per cent) were descended from the Islamic conquerors (Turks, Afghans and Mongols) who had come to India via the Khyber Pass. The rest included some forcibly converted Hindus, and many more voluntary converts — low-caste Hindus attracted by the more egalitarian Muslim society. The Muslim ratio grew over time because polygamy and widow remarriage gave them greater fertility than Hindus. Muslims were highly concentrated in the North, in the Indo-Gangetic plain. In the South they were mainly in court towns and much more thinly spread. The first Muslim invaders carried out forcible conversions, but later rulers restrained their evangelising activities partly because of Hindu resistance, partly because they realised that this would reduce their elite status. The only area where the indigenous population was converted to Islam *en masse* was East Bengal which had had a strong Buddhist tradition and looked on the Islamic invaders as liberators from Hindu rule.

At the height of its power under Akbar, the Moghul Empire exercised religious tolerance. This is one of the reasons why it was more successful in maintaining an extensive domain than the earlier Muslim sultanates of Delhi. There were some attempts to fuse Islamic doctrine with Hinduism of which the main one was the Sikh religion, but this had a very limited success and Sikhs are still only

---

(1) The Moghul emperors were Babur 1526-1530, Humayun 1530-1556 (whose reign was interrupted from 1540 to 1555 by the Afghans, Sher Shah and Islam Shah), Akbar 1556-1605, Jehangir 1605-27, Shah Jehan 1627-58, Aurangzeb 1658-1707. After Aurangzeb the Moghul Empire collapsed, though its nominal existence continued until 1857.

1 per cent of the population of the subcontinent. There was some interpenetration of religious practices, with the Muslims retaining some elements of caste prejudice, adopting saints and holy men, and the Hindus accepting purdah and the segregation of women. In effect, however, the Muslim rulers did not succeed in creating an integrated society, but simply imposed themselves on top of the Hindus as a new caste segregated by different dietary and social habits, with a ban on intermarriage with infidels.

At the base of economic life was the Hindu village which had changed little for 2,000 years. The villages were defensive self-contained units, designed for survival in periods of war and alien domination. The chief characteristic which differentiates the Indian village from other types of society is the institution of caste. This system divided the population into rigid hereditary groups whose economic and social functions were clearly defined. There are thousands of castes and sub-castes, but the four main groups are *brahmins*, a caste of Hindu priests at the top of the social scale whose ceremonial purity was not to be polluted by manual labour; next in priority came the *kshatriyas* or warriors, thirdly the *vaishyas* or traders, and finally the *sudras*, i.e. the farmers. Below this there were outcastes to perform menial and unclean tasks. Members of different castes could not intermarry or eat together, and kept apart in their social life. Outcastes were not even allowed in the temples, and any kind of physical contact with them was regarded as pollution. This system encouraged sanctimonious arrogance at the top and obsequious submission at the bottom. It prevented social mobility and the development of a strong national sense. Hence the relative passivity of India towards foreign invaders and rulers. The rigidity of the system prevented foreigners from assimilating. They were faced with either the enormous task of destroying the system or the relatively easy task of establishing themselves as a separate caste. The latter was the choice exercised by both the Muslim and the British conquerors. Newcomers to India did not enter a melting pot out of which they fused a homogeneous society, they simply added a fresh slice to a stale and desiccated layer cake. To add to the segregation, India was also split into more than a dozen major language groups, several of them with different scripts.

Landholding within the villages was based on custom rather than precise legal rights. In relations with the State, the village usually acted as a community. In particular, land taxes were usually paid collectively and the internal allocation of the burden was a village responsibility. Unlike feudal Europe, the upper classes were not landlords cultivating holdings with the help of serf labour. Instead they collected a land tax from the peasants, part of which they kept for themselves and part of which went to the central power. In India the cultivation unit has always been small scale. This arrangement in which the upper class had no deep roots in the production process made the political structure unstable and provided no incentive to increase productivity. Furthermore, the religions of India, both Islam and Hinduism, did not have the elaborate hierarchic structure and political influence which the Catholic church enjoyed in Europe. These organisational weaknesses were perhaps the reason why village society developed such rigid institutions to hold itself together, and why, having elaborated them, it was so indifferent to what happened on the national level.

Because of poor transport facilities, villages were largely self sufficient. In the South of India there was no wheeled transport, and goods were carried on pack animals. In the North transport was confined to bullock carts. Horses were a luxury item and not used for transport of goods. Within each village there was a class of artisans who catered to local needs for non-agricultural commodities and services, e.g. the blacksmith, carpenter, potter, cobbler, weaver, washerman, barber, water carrier, astrologer, watchman and occasionally a dancing girl. Spinning was not a specialised craft but was carried out by village women. There was also a group of village servants to perform menial tasks, i.e. sweeping, removal of human and animal manure, etc. Probably 10 to 20 per cent of the village labour force was engaged in non-agricultural activity. Village servants and artisans had a guaranteed income paid collectively by the village and did not sell their services piece-meal to individuals. This rigid caste division of labour prevented people switching jobs or learning new skills and is still a deeply ingrained characteristic of the Indian and Pakistani labour force. Each household operated on a joint family basis. All generations of the family lived together and pooled their income, with little distinction between brothers and cousins in terms of family obligations. This system inhibited individual incentives to work or save, and provided no motive for limiting family size.

From the time of Akbar to Shah Jehan the Moghul court was one of the most brilliant in the world. It was cosmopolitan and religiously tolerant. Literature and painting flourished and there were magnificent palaces and mosques at Agra, Delhi, Fatehpur Sikri and Lahore. The Moghul nobility had a very luxurious style of life, living in walled castles with harems, gardens, fountains and large retinues of slaves and servants. They were particularly addicted to splendid garments of fine cotton and silk and had huge wardrobes.

In order to cater to their needs, a number of handicraft industries produced high quality cotton textiles, silks, jewellery, decorative swords and weapons. These luxury industries grew up in urban centres. The urban population was bigger in the Muslim period than it had been under Hindu rulers, for caste restrictions had previously kept artisans out of towns (2). Most urban workers were Muslims (3). The main market for these urban products was domestic but a significant portion of luxury textiles was exported either to Europe or South East Asia. Other export items were saltpetre (for gunpowder), indigo, sugar, opium, and ginger. Imports were mainly precious metals, woollens and metals. It is sometimes suggested that India's export trade was of vast proportions (4), but, in fact, Indian exports in the mid-eighteenth century were much smaller than those of the U.K. which had less than a tenth of its population. At the middle of the eighteenth century, India's exports were probably no more than 2 per cent of its G.N.P. The main factor limiting exports was that India had little taste for the goods which Europe could offer in exchange so Europe had to pay for its imports largely with silver and gold (5).

---

(2) See B. N. GANGULI, ed., *Readings in Indian Economic History*, Asia Publishing House, Bombay, 1964, p. 55.

(3) See I. H. QURESHI, *The Muslim Community of the Indo-Pakistan Sub-Continent (610-1947)*, Mouton, The Hague, 1962, p. 219 " The courts had been great consumers of the various articles produced by Muslim craftsmen. All the finer qualities of textiles like Dacca muslin and Kashmir shawls were woven by Muslim master weavers. The manufacture of rich carpets was a Muslim monopoly. The rich brocades which had been in fashion both among men and women of means were made by Muslims. The manufacture of the more delicately finished jewellery, inlay work in silver and gold, and the creation of many articles of beauty so highly prized by the wealthy classes were almost entirely in Muslim hands ".

(4) See R. C. DUTT, *The Economic History of India 1757-1837*, Government of India, reprint, Delhi 1963, p. XXV, " India in the eighteenth century was a great manufacturing as well as a great agricultural country, and the products of the Indian loom supplied the markets of Asia and Europe ".

(5) The same was true in China whose Emperor wrote to George III, " The Celestial Empire possesses all things in prolific abundance and lacks no product within its borders. There is therefore no need to import the manufactures of outside barbarians in exchange for our own products ". See E. BACKHOUSE and J. O. P. BLAND, *Annals and Memoirs of the Court of Peking*, 1914, p. 326.

According to the testimony of European travellers, some of the urban centres of Moghul India were bigger than the biggest cities in Europe at the same period (6). The reason was primarily that the climate made it possible to get double and treble cropping in some areas, and hence, for a given transport system, it was possible to support bigger concentrations of urban population than in Europe ((7). But the ratio of urban to total population may have been no greater than in Europe (8).

Because of the luxury of court life, the large size and splendour of some Indian cities, and the disdain for European products, Moghul India was generally regarded as a wealthy country by contemporary Europe. Some Indian nationalist historians claim that the Moghul period was a golden age. However, it seems likely that the *average* living standard was somewhat lower than that in sixteenth or seventeenth century Europe, because the mass of the population were poorer than Europeans. In the eighteenth century, when modern economic growth began in Europe and the Moghul Empire was in decline, it seems certain that average Indian standards were lower than those in Europe.

In spite of India's reputation as a cloth producer, the average level of textile consumption was lower than in Europe. Abul Fazl, the sixteenth century chronicler of Akbar makes reference to the lack of clothing. In Bengal " men and women for the most part go naked wearing only a cloth about the loins ". In Orissa " the women cover only the lower part of the body and may make themselves coverings of the leaves of trees " (9). Such people also lacked do-

---

(6) For example, Clive considered that Murshidabad was more prosperous than London, see J. NEHRU, *Glimpses of World History*, Lindsay Drummond, London, 1945, p. 417 " Clive has described the city of Murshidabad in Bengal in 1757, as a city 'as extensive, populous, and rich as the city of London, with this difference, that there are individuals in the first possessing infinitely greater property than in the last' ".

(7) See B. H. SLICHER VAN BATH, *The Agrarian History of Western Europe, A.D. 500-1850*, Arnold, London, 1963, pp. 14-15, " As long as transport methods remained primitive, the population of a town could not rise above a certain maximum level dependent on the agricultural production from the rural area surrounding it. It has been calculated that to feed a city of 3,000 inhabitants in the Middle Ages required an arable of 3,000 hectares as well as the necessary pasture for the cattle ".

(8) There are no statistics on the size of the urban population before the 1872 census when it was 10 per cent of total population. Prof. Gadgil suggests that the proportion was probably about the same at the beginning of British rule. See D. R. GADGIL, *The Industrial Evolution of India in Modern Times*, Oxford, 1950, p. 6.

(9) See H. S. JARRETT and J. SARKAR, eds., *Ain-I-Akbari of Abul Fazl-I-Allami*, Vol. II, Calcutta, 1949, pp. 134 and 138.

mestic linen, sheets, and blankets, which would probably have been owned by their European counterparts. Their loincloths were often of jute rather than cotton. In terms of housing and furniture the Indian peasantry were worse off than Europeans and their diet was also poorer (10).

The technical level of agriculture was lower than in many other Asian countries, with fairly large areas devoted to production of low-quality grains like bajra or jowar. The unreliable weather was one of the reasons for growing low quality grains for they were more resistant to weather fluctuation than wheat or rice. Farm implements were poor and ploughs were made of wood. The huge cow population was not used for meat. A large number of cows were completely unproductive and competed for food with humans rather than meeting their needs. Religious prejudice also impeded the development of pig production. The brahmins and a large part of the rest of the population were vegetarians, though they did use livestock products such as milk. Cow dung was used as a fuel or building material rather than for manure, and there was little use of human excrement, bone meal and oil seeds for manure as in China or Japan. Crops were damaged by rodent and insect pests which were not checked for religious reasons. Indian agriculture did not benefit as much as Europe and Africa from the new American crops available from the sixteenth century onwards. Potatoes, maize and cassava remained unimportant, and tobacco was the only significant novelty.

Life expectation was lower in India than in Europe, but fertility was higher because there were virtually no bachelors, no celibate priests and virtually all girls were married before puberty. Death rates were higher for several reasons. As a result of poor transport and storage facilities, a near to subsistence standard at the best of times, highly fluctuating monsoon weather conditions, droughts and floods, famines were experienced more frequently than had ever been the case in Europe. War and civil disorders were practically continuous and must have led to more mortality than in Europe. Health conditions were worse than in Europe, partly because of poor diet, partly for other reasons. The climate was more debilitating. There were tropical diseases as well as all the European ones. Hindu tabus against killing rodents and insects led to longer persistence of bubonic

---

(10) See W. H. MORELAND, *India at the Death of Akbar*, A. Ram, Delhi, 1962, for a description of living conditions at the end of the sixteenth century.

plague. Hindu distaste for touching refuse or excreta led to greater squalor and lack of sanitation. Finally, infanticide of daughters added substantially to mortality in some areas.

The population of Moghul India was probably the same as it had been 2,000 years earlier (about 100-125 million) (11), but the static population is not evidence that India had reached a Malthusian equilibrium. As we have seen, there were factors other than capacity to produce food which limited population growth. But the tax levy on the mass of the peasantry was so high, that most of them were living very close to bare subsistence.

Educational facilities and the content of education were no better than in medieval Europe, and much worse than in Europe after the Renaissance. Muslim education was entirely religious and carried out in madrassas where boys learned the Koran in Arabic. Although the Moghul period was distinguished for its architecture, painting, poetry, and music, these were largely derived from foreign models, particularly those of Safavid Persia. India was never the intellectual centre of the Muslim world. Hindu education was confined to religious instruction for higher caste boys in Sanskrit. Neither religious group provided education for women. It has been suggested that at the time of the British takeover about a quarter of the male population had received a few years of schooling, that most Brahmins could read and write, and that the literacy rate was about 5 per cent (12). There was no Hindu higher education of a secular character. Earlier Indian Buddhist universities (e.g. Nalanda) had been destroyed by the Muslim invaders. Neither the social system nor the theology of

---

(11) See K. DAVIS, *The Population of India and Pakistan*, Princeton, 1951, p. 24, " During the two thousand years that intervened between the ancient and the modern period India's population could not have grown rapidly. It must have remained virtually stationary. The usual course was surely a gradual growth for a short period followed by an abrupt decline. The population would tend to grow slightly in 'normal'times, because the customs governing fertility would provide a birth rate slightly higher than the usual death rate. This would build up a population surplus as a sort of demographic insurance against catastrophe. Inevitably, however, the catastrophe would come in the form of warfare, famine or epidemic, and the increase of population would suddenly be wiped out. Thus while there would be short-run periods of population growth and decline, the long-run trend would be one of virtual fixity of numbers. No real change could have occurred in this condition until the coming of European control, and then only slowly ".

(12) See S. NURULLAH and J. P. NAIK, *A Hisory of Education in India*, Macmillan, Bombay, 1951. Teaching was done largely on a monitorial system, which was copied in England on the first few decades of the nineteenth century where it was known as the Madras system.

Hinduism encouraged the growth of rational analysis or scientific thought.

The Moghul regime concentrated power on the royal court and a bureaucratic aristocracy. The Moghul aristocracy itself was not, in principle, hereditary, and a considerable part of it consisted of foreigners. They were nominated by the Emperor, and did not pass an examination like the Chinese bureaucracy. Moghul practice derived from the traditions of the nomadic societies which had created Islam in Arabia as well as similar Turkic traditions. Under this system, Moghul nobles were paid either in cash, or, more usually, were allocated the revenues from a *jagir*. The *jagir* was a collection of villages, and there were independent Moghul officials who acted as a check on the holder of the *jagir*. The main officials were the *qanungo* (accountant) and *qazi* (judge who settled criminal and revenue cases) (13). *Jagirdars* were regularly posted from one *jagir* to another and their property was liable to forfeit on death. Because of their non-hereditary status there was little incentive to build up property on a long term basis, and in fact the optimum situation was to die in debt to the state. However, as the central Moghul power declined, *jagirs* tended to become hereditary. Waste land which the *jagirdars* developed became their personal property and they often collected much more revenue from the peasantry than they remitted to the central power. There were also some Hindu landlords (*zamindars*) (14) who retained traditional hereditary control over village revenues, and Hindu princes who continued to rule and collect revenue in autonomous states within the Moghul Empire, e.g. in Rajputana.

The income of Moghul officials was high, and they had many dependents to support, both because of the practice of polygamy and the vast retinues of slaves and servants they maintained. The military were also a considerable burden on society because their number was so large, and they were very frequently engaged in wars. Religion was possibly a bigger economic burden than in Europe, but not in such a direct way. Religious property was smaller, with rather

---

(13) For a description of the system, see M. A. ALI, *The Moghul Nobility under Aurangzeb*, Asia Publishing House, London, 1966.
(14) In Bengal, in the 1720s, under the Muslim subahdar, Murshid Quli, " more than three-fourths of the zamindars, big and small, and most of talukdars were Hindus ". N. K. SINHA, *The Economic History of Bengal*, Mukhopadhyay, Calcutta, 1961, p. 4. This was the case in a province where the majority of peasants were Muslims.

modest tax free land grants and no hierarchically organised priesthood. But there was a vast band of religious mendicants to be
supported and considerable expense in carrying out weddings and
funerals in a way which satisfied religious scruples. The burden of
supporting the ruling class, religion, the military and governmental
apparatus was almost certainly larger than in Europe, given the
greater poverty of the mass of the population.

The main revenues of the Moghul State were derived from the
land tax which was about a third of the gross crop production (perhaps a fifth of total agricultural output including livestock products).
Other levies, tolls and taxes were of much smaller importance. Land
revenue collected by *jagirdars* was handed over to the Empire or
used to support troops. Tribute or troops were also demanded from
zamindars and native princes. In some areas, revenue was paid in
cash, in others in kind, or a mixture of both. The levy was usually
fixed over a period of years and did not vary with each year's crop,
but the law was administered flexibly with some allowance for
vagaries in weather and crops. Peasants were not dispossessed for
non-payment, and payments were often delinquent. It is not clear
how the revenue assessments of the Moghuls and the preceding
Muslim rulers compared with those of previous Hindu rulers. Probably they were rather similar as they varied a good deal from region
to region to conform with local custom. The Hindu religious text,
the laws of Manu, prescribed a land revenue share of one sixth for
the sovereign, which is only half of the Moghul claim, but there is
no evidence from Hindu provinces that the laws of Manu were
actually practiced (15).

European traders dominated the export business from the sixteenth century onwards. Before that Indian and Arab merchants
had traded in textile products with East Africa, the Persian Gulf,
Malaya and Indonesia. The Portuguese opened up new markets in
Europe, West Africa and the Philippines, and being organised on a
large scale brought more capital into the business. In the seventeenth
century the Portuguese monopoly ended and more competition and
capital were brought in by the Dutch, British and French and on a

---

(15) Moreland suggests that the revenue demand in the Hindu Kingdom of Vijayanagar
was bigger than in Moghul territories. See W. H. MORELAND, *Op. cit.*, Mrs. Boserup also
quotes evidence that revenue demands in pre-Muslim times could be much bigger than
prescribed by the laws of Manu. See E. BOSERUP, *The Conditions of Agricultural Growth*,
Allen and Unwin, London, 1965, p. 98.

lesser scale by the Danes and Swedes. This further expanded both Asian and European markets and the trading companies built up production centres for textiles, indigo and saltpetre in Gujarat, Coromandel and Bengal. Europeans also introduced factory production and wage labour, as well as a putting out system. Their impact was to increase the productivity of the economy and was not exploitative (16), except in the Portuguese phase, and in the thirty years after the East India Company conquered Bengal, when there was severe monopolistic exploitation which was damaging to the economy, and even more harmful to the interests of Indian merchants, bankers, and weavers, and to the other European trading companies.

Moghul control of India disintegrated after the death of Aurangzeb in 1707. Given the size of the country which was as big as the whole of Europe, its racial and linguistic complexity and the great conflicts of interest which existed within the system, it is not surprising that it fell apart. Aurangzeb is often blamed for the collapse because he was too ambitious. He turned away from Akbar's policy of religious tolerance, destroyed Hindu temples, reimposed the *jizya* (a capitation tax on non-Muslims) and confiscated some non-Muslim princely states when titles lapsed. As a result Aurangzeb was engaged in a constant series of wars to hold his Empire together (17). After his death, it split into several parts. In Western

---

(16) See T. RAYCHAUDHURI, " European Commercial Activity and the Organisation of India's Commerce and Industrial Production 1500-1750 ", in B. N. GANGULI, *Op. cit.*, pp. 75-6, " To sum up, the impact of European commerce with India on a competitive basis was in many ways beneficient. New markets were opened for Indian exports and the existing ones further deepened. For the limited areas supplying the staples of export, this meant an increase in production and probably also in productivity, partly through the extension of the putting out system as well as the localization of industries. Thus, in certain parts of the country at least, the possibility of further signficant changes in the volume, technique and organization of production had been opened. But the initiative in innovation remained throughout in the hands of certain foreign companies of monopolistic merchant capital whose interest in reorganizing production was necessarily limited "... " Certain new techniques in dyeing and silk-winding were introduced by European experts working for the companies. In short, within the limits already defined, new elements of efficiency were introduced in production, probably resulting in an increased productivity ".

(17) It has also been argued that the Moghul Empire declined because it had become too liberal under Akbar and that the Moghul collapse would have occurred earlier if it had not benefited from Aurangzeb's efforts to consolidate in religiously and to extend its area by military conquest. See I. H. QURESHI, *Op. cit.*, p. 168 " Akbar had strengthened his dynasty but made it subservient to interests other than those of Islam to a remarkable degree, so that it took three generations to restore the laws of Islam to their previous position "... " Empires which are established by a numerically inferior community over a larger population always find themselves on the horns of a dilemma. They endure only so long as they can

India, the Mahrattas established an independent Hindu state with their capital at Poona. The *Nizam-ul-Mulk*, a high Moghul official who foresaw the collapse of the Empire, installed himself as the autonomous ruler of Hyderabad in 1724. In 1739, the Persian emperor Nadir Shah invaded India, massacred the population of Delhi and took away so much booty (including Shah Jehan's peacock throne and the Kohinoor diamond) that he was able to remit Persian taxes for three years. He probably damaged the economy as much as Timur had done in 1398. The Sikhs took over Punjab and set up an independent Kingdom in Lahore. In other areas which nominally remained in the Empire, e.g. Bengal, Mysore, and Oudh, the power of the Moghul emperor declined, as did his revenue. Continuous warfare weakened the economy and trade of the country, and put some irrigation canals out of action, e.g. the Jumna canal. Internal trade was further hampered by the imposition of local transit tolls which the Moghuls had kept in check.

British India

Because of the Moghul collapse, the European powers were able to expand their control in India. They did so partly to step into a political vacuum, partly to protect their commercial interests, and partly as an extension of their conflicts in other parts of the world (particularly the rivalry between the British and French). In the event, it was the British who won control by conquering Bengal in 1757 and taking over the government there in 1765. In 1803, they extended their control to Madras and Bombay and became masters of India. In 1849, they completed their territorial acquisitions by taking over the Punjab and Sindh.

Bengal was the biggest province of the old Moghul Empire, and provided lavish spoils for the handful of East India Company servants who had conquered it and, in particular, Robert Clive who took a quarter million pounds for himself as well as a *jagir* worth £27,000 a year. The first two decades of British rule under Clive and Warren Hastings were ones of ruthless exploitation but the

---

maintain the delicate balance between dominance and surrender. The difficulty with surrender is that it does not succeed unless it is complete. Akbar gave away so much, yet he was not able to reconcile the Hindu sentiment completely "... " conciliation, however deep, never takes the sting away from the sense of radical or national humiliation of the subject people. The best that such policies can achieve is the neutrality of large masses of people by looking after their interests ".

British did not pillage on the scale of Nadir Shah who probably took as much from India in one year as the East India Company did in the 20 years following the Battle of Plassey (18). The British were also shrewd enough to realise that it was not in their long run interest to devastate the country.

The main reason the British were successful in retaining control of India was through the creation of an efficient bureaucracy and army. The traditional system of the East India Company had been to pay its servants fairly modest salaries, and to let them augment their income from private transactions. This arrangement worked reasonably well before the conquest of Bengal, but was inefficient as a way of remunerating the officials of a substantial territorial Empire (a) because too much of the profit went into private hands rather than the Company's coffers; (b) an over-rapacious short-term policy was damaging to the productive capacity of the economy and likely to drive the local population to revolt, both of which were against the Company's longer-term interests. Clive had operated a " dual " system, i.e. Company power and a puppet Nawab. Warren Hastings displaced the Nawab and took over direct administration, but he retained Indian officials. Finally, in 1785, Cornwallis created a professional cadre of Company servants who were paid on a princely scale, had no private interests, enjoyed the prospect of regular promotions and were entitled to pensions (19). All high level posts were reserved for the British, and Indians were excluded. Cornwallis

---

(18) There is a tendency amongst Marxist and anti-British historians to exaggerate the size of the Indian plunder. R. P. Dutt argues that " the spoliation of India was the hidden source of accumulation which played an all important role in helping to make possible the Industrial Revolution in England ", see R. P. DUTT, *India To-day*, Gollancz, London, 1940. A even more extreme view is taken by P. A. BARAN, *The Political Economy of Growth*, Prometheus, New York, 1957, p. 145. See also B. ADAMS, *The Law of Civilisation and Decay*, New York, 1910 and W. DIGBY, *Prosperous British India*, 1901. In fact a good deal of the Indian revenue was used to finance local wars and did not get to the U.K. The latest scholarly estimates suggest that the transfer to the U.K. was about one tenth of the amounts estimated by Digby.

(19) See *Report of the Pay and Services Commission, 1959-62*, Government of Pakistan, Karachi, 1969, p. 23 " The term 'Civil Service' was used for the first time by the East India Company which maintained military forces side by side with a body of 'merchants, factors and writers' exclusively recruited in England whose functions, with the onward march of the Company's administrative responsibilities, underwent a process of transformation into those of local administrators while the Company's trading activities gradually declined. Thus the civil administration of the country passed by degrees into the hands of those employees of the Company, whose careers were secured by the terms of covenants executed in England, before they left for India, and who were therefore known as Covenanted Servants of the Company ".

introduced British law of property and administration, appointed British judges, and established British officials as revenue collectors and magistrates in each district of Bengal.

In 1806 the Company began to train its young recruits in Hailey-bury College near London. Appointments to the Company were still organised on a system of patronage, but after 1833 the Company selected amongst its nominated candidates by competitive examination. After 1853, the examination was thrown open to any British candidate. The examination system was influenced by the Chinese model, which had worked well for 2,000 years and had a similar emphasis on classical learning and literary competence. The Indian civil service was able to secure high quality people because (a) it was very highly paid; (b) it enjoyed political power which no bureaucrat could have had in England. In 1829 the system was strengthened by establishing districts throughout British India small enough to be effectively controlled by an individual British official who acted as revenue collector, judge and chief of police. This arrangement later became the cornerstone of Imperial administration throughout the British Empire. As the civil service was ultimately subject to the control of the British parliament, and the British community in India was subject to close mutual surveillance, the administation was virtually incorruptible.

The army of the Company was a local mercenary force with 20,000-30,000 British officers and troops. It was by far the most modern and efficient army in Asia. After the Mutiny in 1857, the size of the British contingent was raised to a third of the total strength and all officers were British until the 1920s when a very small contingent of Indians was recruited. Normally the total strength of the army was about 200,000. This army was very much smaller than those of Moghul India, but it had better training and equipment, and the railway network (which was constructed partly for military reasons) gave it greater mobility, better logistics and intelligence.

The army officer corps and the higher ranks of the administration remained almost entirely British until 1928 when the Indian civil service examinations began to be held in India as well as the U.K. (20). In addition, there was a whole hierarchy of separate

---

(20) The army was more exclusive than the civil service and in 1911 had practically no Indians and only 135 Anglo-Indians as compared with 4,378 British officers, see *Census of India, 1911*, P. Woodruff, *The Men who Ruled India, The Guardians*, Cape, London,

bureaucracies in which the higher ranks were British, i.e. the revenue, justice, police, education, medical, public works, engineering, postal and railway services. India thus offered highly-paid careers to large numbers of the British middle and upper classes (particularly for its peripheral members from Scotland and Ireland).

British salaries were high, the Viceroy received £25,000 a year, and governors £10,000. The starting salary in the engineering service was £420 a year or about 60 times the average income of the Indian labour force. From 1757 to 1919, India also had to meet administrative expenses in London, first of the East India Company, and then of the India Office, as well as other minor but irritatingly extraneous charges. The cost of British staff was raised by long home leave in the U.K., early retirement, and lavish amenities in the form of subsidised housing, utilities, rest houses, etc.

Like all conquerors of India, the British had to decide what accommodation to make with the local ruling class and prevailing social institutions. In the first phase of British rule there was a fairly strong urge for change. The British stamped out infanticide and ritual suicide of widows (*sati*). They abolished slavery, and eliminated *dacoits* (religious thugs) from the highways. They legalised the remarriage of widows and allowed Hindu converts to Christianity to lay claim to their share of joint family property. They introduced English education and a codified version of British law. In the 1850s, the Governor General, Dalhousie, extended the area of British rule by taking over native states whose kings had left no direct heirs. It seemed to be British policy to take over the whole of India, and, at least partially, to westernise it. There was a strong streak of Benthamite radicalism in the East India Company administration. James Mill became a senior company official in 1819 after writing a monumental and contemptuous history of India without having visited the country. From 1831 to 1836 he was the chief executive officer of the E.I.C. and his even more distinguished son worked for the Company from 1823 to 1858. Haileybury teaching was also strongly influenced by utilitarianism. The utilitarians deliberately used India to try out experiments and ideas (e.g. competitive entry for the civil service) which they would have liked to apply in England. The utilitarians were strong supporters of laisser faire and

---

1963, p. 363 shows the composition of the I.C.S. (the top rank of the civil service) from 1859 to 1939. In 1869 there were 882 Europeans and 1 Indian, in 1909, 1,082 Europeans and 60 Indians, and in 1939 759 Europeans and 540 Indians.

abhorred any kind of state interference to promote economic development. Thus they tended to rely on market forces to deal with famine problems, they did nothing to stimulate agriculture or protect industry. This *laisser faire* tradition was more deeply embedded in the Indian civil service than the U.K., and persisted very strongly until the late 1920s. The administration was efficient and incorruptible, but the state apparatus was of a watchdog character with few development ambitions. Even in 1936, more than half of government spending was for the military, justice, police and jails, and less than 3 per cent for agriculture (21).

Until 1857, it was possible to entertain the view that the British might eventually transform the nature of Indian society. But activist Westernising policies provoked both the Hindu and Moslem communities into rebellion in the Mutiny of 1857, which almost suceeded in defeating the British.

After the Mutiny, British policy towards Indian institutions and society became much more conservative. The Crown took over direct responsibility and the East India Company was disbanded. The Indian civil service attracted fewer people with innovating ideas than had the East India Company and was more closely controlled from London. The British forged an alliance with the remaining native princes and stopped taking over new territory. Until the end of British rule about a quarter of the Indian population remained in quasi-autonomous native states. These had official British residents but were fairly free in internal policy.

Thus nothing was done to break the many traditional obstacles to development which were more severe and persistent in India than anywhere else in the developing world. There were many of these such as the caste system, the fatalistic ascetism, resignation and renunciation of Hindu religion in which people accepted their lot passively, the preference for magic rather than science, the maintenance of enormous numbers of cows with low productivity, debilitating vegetarianism, insanitary habits with regard of washing and sewerage, refusal to kill rats and pests, wasteful ceremony and marriage feasts, the joint family system which reduced incentives to work and save, and the low status of women.

The British gave up the attempt to change Indian society, and established themselves as a separate ruling caste. Like other Indian

(21) See V. ANSTEY, *The Economic Development of India*, Longmans Green, London, 1952, p. 540.

castes they did not normally intermarry or eat with the lower (native) castes. Thanks to the British public school system, their children were shipped off and did not mingle with the natives. At the end of their professional careers they returned home. The small creole class of Anglo-Indians were outcastes unable to integrate into Indian or local British society (22). The British kept to their clubs and bungalows in special suburbs known as cantonments and civil lines. They maintained the Moghul tradition of official pomp, sumptuary residences, and retinues of servants (23). They did not adopt the Moghul custom of polygamy, but remained monogamous and brought in their own women (24). The British ruled India in much the same way as the Roman consuls in Africa 2,000 years earlier, and were very conscious of the Roman paradigm. The elite with its classical education and contempt for business were quite happy establishing law and order, and keeping barbarians at bay on the frontier of the raj with the Imperial army (25). Apart from building railways and canals, they did almost nothing to promote economic development.

The most striking thing about the British raj is that it was operated by such a small number of people. There were only 31,000

---

(22) The situation was totally different in the Portuguese colony of Goa. The Portuguese intermarried with the natives, broke down caste barriers, brought in Jesuit priests, imposed Catholicism, imported a saint, buried him locally and thus established a centre for pilgrimage. Spanish practice in the Philippines was similar. The British deliberately kept out missionaries until 1813, which is when they brought in their first bishop.

(23) See Lord Beveridge's life of his parents, *India Called Them*, Allen and Unwin, 1947. Beveridge's father did not have a very successful career, but had 21 servants to start married life, 39 when he had three children and cut down to 18 when living on his own. The 18 servants cost him less than 6 per cent of his salary.

(24) The change in British attitudes in the early nineteenth century is noted in M. EDWARDES, *British India 1772-1947*, Sudwick and Jackson, London, 1967, p. 33. " There were other factors which contributed to the growing estrangement between Indians and the British. One of these was the growing number of women in the British settlements. They tended to bring with them the prejudices of their time. Their attitude, generally speaking was Christian, and narrowly so. They brought, too, a new sense of family life, and their arrival resulted in the expulsion of native mistresses who had at least injected something of India into the world of the British. The women had little to occupy their minds. Their life was a tedious social round. But they did have gossip ".

(25) The connections with India had a substantial impact on British domestic institutions and attitudes. The British civil service, with its tradition of generalists and brahminical status of the administrative class is derived from the Indian model. The British " public " school system was greatly strengthened by the needs of expatriate families. The domestic status of royalty was enhanced by the Imperial connection. The close contact with Hindu casteism strengthened British snobbery and helped to make the British somewhat more racist towards subject peoples than the French and Dutch who intermarried much more with colonials.

British in India in 1805 (of which 22,000 in the army and 2,000 in civil government) (26). The number increased substantially after the Mutiny, but thereafter remained fairly steady. In 1911, there were 164,000 British (106,000 employed, of which 66,000 in the army and police and 4,000 in civil government) (27). In 1931, there were 168,000 (90,000 employed, 60,000 in the army and police and 4,000 in civil government). They were a thinner layer than the muslim rulers had been (never more than 0.05 per cent of the population) and were a smaller portion of the population than were the Dutch and French in their Asian colonies.

Because of the small size of the British administration and its philosophy of minimum government responsibility outside the field of law and order, India ended the colonial period with a very low level of taxation. In 1936, central and provincial taxes amounted to only 6.6 per cent of G.N.P. (28) and they were not very much different in 1947. In most Western countries, the tax ratio was about three times higher than in India by the 1930s.

The evolution of the tax burden in India under the British was therefore different from that in most other countries. Whilst other countries were increasing the tax ratio and the role of government, they were being reduced in India. The administrative burden declined because the British establishment remained static in an economy which was growing in size. The British inherited the Moghul tax system which provided the state with revenue on a more lavish scale than in Europe and they gradually reduced the tax burden over time. This was particularly true of land tax which had been a third of the crop in Moghul times and was only 5 per cent of the crop in 1936.

It should also be remembered that the British dispossessed an important part of the native ruling class. They made some conces-

---

(26) See D. A. B. BHATTACHARYA, ed., *Report on the Population Estimates of India (1820-30)*, *Census of India 1961*, Government of India, Registrar General Delhi, 1963, pp. 4-5.

(27) See *Census of India 1911*, Vol. I, *India*, Part II, *Tables*, Calcutta, 1913, pp. 374-6. The total population of all India (including native states) was 313 million and the total labour force 149 million. It is interesting to note that the European population of India was of relatively much lower importance than in Indonesia, where there were 81,000 Europeans in a population of 38 million in 1905, see J. S. FURNIVALL, *Colonial Policy and Practice*, Cambridge, 1948, p. 255 or in French Indo-China with 42,000 Europeans and a total population of 23 million in 1937, see C. ROBEQUAIN, *The Economic Development of French Indo-China*, Oxford University Press, London, 1944.

(28) For tax receipts see V. ANSTEY, *Op. cit.*, p. 540; G.N.P. derived from S. SIVASUBRAMONIAN, *National Income of India 1900-01 to 1946-47*, Delhi, 1965.

sions to vested interest by maintaining Indian princes in power in a quarter of the country, but they made few other concessions to local economic interests. Therefore the joint burden of supporting a ruling class, a civilian bureaucracy and an army (29) was smaller under the British raj than under the Moghuls.

We may now ask what were the economic results of lowering the tax burden. In Bengal and other areas of zamindar settlement, the chief effect was to increase the income of landlords, in other areas the benefit accrued to peasants. The gains of the peasantry probably went to increase population rather than per capita income. Because they were able to retain a higher proportion of their product, peasants were able to subsist on land of lower productivity. Hence when India became independent, her tax base was very low and there was probably a larger proportion of poor peasants and landless labourers in the population than there had been under the Moghuls. The economy had a much smaller " surplus " mobilisable for development purposes than there had been in Meiji Japan on the eve of her modernisation efforts.

In the nineteenth century, the British were accused by Indian nationalists of overtaxing the country. Both Naraoji and Dutt constantly urged lower taxes and retrenchment. They particularly attacked the land tax. They were both Gladstonian liberals in matters of public finance. In fact, the British government did what Naraoji and Dutt suggested. It would have been better for the economy if they had maintained higher taxes and spent more on development, as happened in Japan.

The Economic Burden of Foreign Rule

The major burden of foreign rule arose from the fact that the British raj was a regime of expatriates. Under an Indian administration income from government service would have accrued to the local inhabitants and not to foreigners. The diversion of this upper class income into the hands of foreigners inhibited the development of local industry because it put purchasing power into the hands of

---

(29) Moreland suggests that in the time of Akbar the military strength of India was well over a million men, i.e. more than twice the size of the armies maintained in British India and the princely states, and much bigger in relation to population. See W. H. MORELAND, *India at the Death of Akbar*, A. Ram, Delhi, 1962, p. 72.

people with a taste for foreign goods. This increased imports and was particularly damaging to the luxury handicraft industries.

An even more important effect of foreign rule on the long run growth potential of the economy was the fact that a large part of its potential savings were siphoned abroad. The " drain " of funds from India to the U.K. which occurred under British rule has been a point of major controversy between Indian nationalist historians and defenders of the British raj. However, the only real grounds for controversy are statistical. There can be no denial that there was a substantial outflow which lasted for 190 years. If these funds had been invested in India they could have made a major contribution to raising income levels.

Before the British conquered Bengal, they had paid for imports mainly by exporting silver and gold bullion. Only about a quarter of their purchases were covered by commodity exports. The same was true for other European traders with India. The total annual bullion inflow to Bengal was about £780,000 (30). Indian exports were about £1 million a year of which about a third were bought by the East India Company, a third by the Dutch and a third by the French (31).

After the conquest of Bengal, the East India Company acquired a substantial income from its official revenues and its servants had a bigger income because of their increased monopolistic power and participation in local trade. As a result, the Company no longer had to pay in bullion for most of its imports from India (32). In fact, it had a revenue surplus bigger than the Indian surplus on commodity trade with the U.K. In order to effect the transfer of these additional resources, some Indian bullion and diamonds were shipped to the U.K. and Bengal silver was exported to China to finance British purchases of Chinese tea. In addition, Company servants sold their rupee profits to foreign trading companies against European bills of exchange, which supplanted other countries' exports of bullion to India. Bengal had a surplus on trade with other parts of India and these revenues were used by the East India Com-

---

(30) See K. DATTA, *Survey of India's Social Life and Economic Condition in the Eighteenth Century,* Mukhopadhyay, Calcutta, 1961, p. 138.

(31) See N. K. SINHA, *The Economic History of Bengal,* Vol. I, Mukhopadhyay, Calcutta, 1961.

(32) Bullion exports did not end. In fact, they eventually rose to higher levels than before Plassey (along with the rise in British imports). See C. H. PHILIPS, *The East India Company 1784-1834,* Manchester, 1961, p. 106.

pany to finance military campaigns in Madras and Bombay. Bengal revenues and profits were also used to finance the local costs of a larger contingent of Company servants and private traders. The annual net real transfer of resources to the U.K. amounted to about £1.8 million a year in the 1780s. This was also the size of India's exports (33).

Under the rule of the East India Company, official transfers to the U.K. rose gradually until they reached about £3.5 million in 1856, the year before the mutiny. In addition, there were private remittances. In the 20 years 1835-54, India's average annual balance on trade and bullion was favourable by about £4.3 million a year.

During the period of direct British rule from 1858 to 1947, official transfers of funds to the U.K. by the colonial government were called the "Home Charges". They mainly represented debt service, pensions, India Office expenses in the U.K., purchases of military items and railway equipment. Government procurement of civilian goods, armaments, and shipping was carried out almost exclusively in the U.K. By the 1930s these home charges were in the range of £40 to 50 million a year. Some of these flows would have occurred in a non-colonial economy, e.g. debt service on loans used to finance railway development, but a large part of the debt was incurred as a result of colonial wars. Some government expenditure was on imports which an independent government would have bought from local manufacturers. Of these official payments, we can legitimately consider service charges on non-productive debt, pensions and furlough payments as a balance of payments drain due to colonialism.

There were also substantial private remittances by British officials in India either as savings or to meet educational and other family charges in the U.K. In the interwar period, these amounted to about £10 million a year, and Naoroji estimated that they were running at the same level in 1887 (34). These items were clearly

(33) See N. K. Sinha, *Op. cit.*, p. 236 who cites the estimates of Grant and of Furber. According to Grant £1 million represented E.I.C. exports, £600,000 exports of other European companies and private traders, and £200,000 exports to China.

(34) See A. K. Banerji, *India's Balance of Payments*, Asia Publishing House, Bombay, 1963, p. 137; D. Naoroji, *Poverty and Un-British Rule in India*, London, 1901 (Government of India reprint), Delhi, 1962, p. 223. C. Lewis, *America's Stake in International Investments*, Brookings, Washington, D.C., 1938, p. 462 suggests that the annual remittances, including business profits, from India and China were already £6 million in 1838. The bulk of this would be from India as at that time there were probably less than 250 British residing in China, see C. Lewis, *Op. cit.*, p. 176.

the result of colonialism. In addition, there were dividend and interest remittances by shipping and banking interests, plantations, and other British investors; to some extent, these were normal commercial transactions, but there was a large element of monopoly profit due to the privileged position of British business in India; and in many cases, the original assets were not acquired by remittance of funds to India but by savings derived from official employment in India, or by purchase of Indian property on favourable terms, e.g. the land acquisitions of plantation companies. About a third of the private profit remittances should therefore be treated as the profits of colonialism (35).

The total " drain " due to government pensions and leave payments, interest on non-railway official debt, private remittances for education and savings, and a third of commercial profits amounted to about 1.7 per cent of the G.N.P. of undivided India from 1921 to 1938 (36) and was probably a little larger before that. Gross investment was about 6 per cent of G.N.P. at the end of British rule, and net investment was probably about half this level. Roughly a third of Indian net savings was therefore transferred out of the economy, and foreign exchange was lost which could have paid for imports of capital goods. As a consequence of this foreign drain the Indian balance on trade and bullion (37) was always positive as can be seen in Table 1. If we take Table 1 as a rough indicator of the *movement* in the colonial burden (though not of the absolute level) it would seem that it was biggest around the 1880s. Since independence the picture has been completely reversed and there is now a substantial inflow of resources because of foreign aid.

In judging the Indian situation in the colonial era, we must not forget that its experience was not unique. There was a drain of this kind from most countries under colonial rule, and it is not clear that India's experience was worse than that of other colonies. Even nominally independent countries, such as Mexico, granted land and

---

(35) Some writers have treated the whole of these service payments as a drain due to colonialism, e.g. K. T. SHAH and K. J. KHAMBATA in *Wealth and Taxable Capacity of India*, London, 1924, p. 232. This is an exaggeration.

(36) "Drain" estimate derived from A. K. BANERJI, *India's Balance of Payments*, Asia Publishing House, London, 1963, and G.N.P. derived from national income figures (grossed up 12.5 per cent) of S. SIVASUBRAMONIAN, *National Income of India 1900-01 to 1946-47*, Delhi School of Economics, 1965.

(37) India continued to be a massive net importer of bullion under British rule.

TABLE I
INDIA'S BALANCE ON MERCHANDISE AND BULLION

	Balance in current prices	Balance in 1948-49 prices	Per capita balance at 1948-49 prices
	annual average £ million		£
1835-54	4.5	n.a.	n.a.
1855-74	7.3	50.0	0.21
1875-94	13.4	80.0	0.30
1895-1913	16.8	77.6	0.26
1914-34	22.5	59.2	0.19
1935-46	27.9	66.1	0.17
1948-57 (India & Pakistan)	− 99.9	− 97.6	−0.21
1958-67 (India & Pakistan)	− 472.7	−384.7	−0.67

Note: This table understates the Indian surplus (and overstates the deficit) because imports are recorded c.i.f. and exports f.o.b. Constant price figures derived by using national income deflator.

oil concessions to foreigners which were just as favourable as those which private British capital received in India.

In spite of its constant favourable balance of trade, India acquired substantial debts. By 1939 foreign assets in India amounted to $2.8 billion of which about $1.5 billion was Government bonded debt and the rest represented direct investment (mainly tea, other plantations and the jute industry). Although the debt was large in absolute terms, foreign investment was modest in relation to the size of the economy. Almost every other developing country except China received proportionately more than India and although in China foreign investment per head was less than that in India a larger part of it represented a genuine inflow of resources. In China there was no large scale foreign administration, and there was, in addition, a considerable remittance of savings from Chinese migrants overseas. As a result China was able to run a substantial trade deficit from the 1870s onwards (38).

During the first world war, India did not reduce its foreign debt as many other developing countries did. Instead, there were

(38) See C. F. REMER, *The Foreign Trade of China*, Commercial Press, Shanghai, 1926.

two " voluntary " war gifts to the U.K. amounting to £150 million
($730 million). India also contributed one and a quarter million
troops, which were financed from the Indian budget. The " drain "
of funds to England continued in the interwar years because of home
charges and profit remittances. There was also a small outflow of
British capital.

During the depression of 1929-33, many developing countries
defaulted on foreign debt or froze dividend transfers, but this was
not possible for India (39). The currency was kept at par with
sterling and devalued in 1931, but the decisions were based on British
rather than Indian needs. Furthermore, the salaries of civil servants
remained at high levels (40), and the burden of official transfers increased in a period of falling prices.

During the second world war, India's international financial
position was transformed. The U.K. had enormous military expenditures for its own troops in India and also financed local costs of
allied troops under Lease-Lend arrangements. Indian war finance
was much more inflationary than in the U.K. and prices rose three-
fold, so these local costs of troop support were extremely high in
terms of sterling, as the exchange rate remained unchanged. As a
result, India was able to liquidate $1.2 billion of prewar debt and
acquired reserve assets of $5.1 billion, ending the war a large net
creditor (41). These new assets and the disappearance of the colonial
drain gave a formidable boost to postwar development policy.

---

(39) The developing countries which were politically free to do so went into default
over the bulk of their bonded indebtedness in this period. Of the $5.3 billion South American
securities outstanding in 1938, $3 billion were in default compared with $340 million in 1913
and about $1.4 billion in 1929. The proportion of defaulted East European, Greek and
Yugoslav bonds seems to have been even higher. China and Turkey were also defaulters.
See C. Lewis, *The United States and Foreign Investment Problems*, Brookings, Washington,
D.C., 1948, p. 42, and *The Problem of International Investment*, Royal Institute of International Affairs, O.U.P., London, 1937, p. 303. A good deal of this default was ultimately
accepted by the creditors (mainly the U.K. and U.S.A.) in war-time and post-war debt
settlements. There was also debt default by developed countries. All European governments
except Finland defaulted on repayment of war debt to the U.S.A. This position was later
legally endorsed by an official U.S. moratorium and eventual cancellation of war debts.
Germany stopped paying reparations and set a moratorium on interest payments on other debt.
(40) There was a cut in civil service salaries in 1931, but it applied only to new
recruits.
(41) In 1939, India had a foreign debt of 4,485 million rupees and assets of 739 million.
In 1945 its official debt was only 175 million and its assets 17,243 million rupees. See
K. C. Chacko, *The Monetary and Fiscal Policy of India*, Vora, Bombay, 1957.

TABLE 2

FOREIGN CAPITAL INVESTED IN DEVELOPING COUNTRIES
PER HEAD OF POPULATION IN 1938

	U.S. Dollars		U.S. Dollars
Chile	268	Indonesia	35
Argentina	228	Turkey	35
Malaya	170	Egypt	32
Uruguay	118	Yugoslavia	21
Venezuela	105	Philippines	20
Mexico	95	Thailand	14
Greece	69	Iran	12
Brazil	51	India	7
Peru	49	China (inc. Manchuria) .	6
Colombia	38		

Source: CHI-MING HOU, *Foreign Investment and Economic Development in China 1840-1937*, Harvard, 1965, p. 98. India from C. LEWIS, *The United States and Foreign Investment Problems*, Brookings, Washington D.C., 1948.

Agriculture

When the British left India three quarters of the population were engaged in agriculture and it produced more than half the national income. It is therefore obvious that aggregate economic welfare depended a great deal on the performance of farmers. We have no reliable agricultural statistics before 1900 but we know that from 1900 to 1947 food consumption per head of the population declined and so did output per man and it seems perfectly feasible that food consumption and productivity levels were lower in 1947 than they had been two centuries earlier.

In setting up their administration in India, the British were strongly influenced by Moghul practice, and the basic source of revenue remained the land tax. But Indian notions of property were not at all like those in England, and the system itself was in flux because of the collapse of the Moghul Empire. Furthermore, the British, like any conquerors, had to displace the property rights of at least part of the existing ruling class in order to provide something for themselves. In the course of defining their revenue system, the British therefore redefined property rights.

In Bengal, they displaced the Nawab and took over the revenues he received from zamindars but their Permanent Settlement of 1793 gave zamindars the right to extract rent from tenants on their own account as landlords. Originally zamindars had kept only a tenth of land revenue for themselves and passed the rest to the State. By the end of British rule, Bengal landlord income from rents was a multiple of the land tax. In Madras and Bombay, the British pushed out the whole of the upper class (nobility and zamindars) and levied land taxes directly on individual peasants who thus became proprietors. The revenue assessment in Bengal was fixed in perpetuity whereas elsewhere it was temporary and could be raised every 30 years (20 years in the Punjab and Central Provinces) (42). In Northern India (United Provinces of Agra and Oudh, and in the Punjab), tax was levied collectively on villages (mahalwari settlement). This system tended to preserve the Indian village community in these areas.

The initial British revenue demands were probably similar to those of the Moghuls, though it is sometimes suggested that they were higher. However, prices were rising in the troubled period of British takeover, and immediately preceding this, the Moghul revenue system was in a state of collapse, so comparison is difficult. A further complication is that British land assessment was made as a percentage of net rental value (50 per cent) rather than gross product. At first, British land assessments seem to have been about a third of the crop, but the proportion fell over time as other sources of revenue emerged. In Bengal, revenues were unchanged in absolute terms from 1793 until independence in 1947 and although they were changed periodically elsewhere they also fell substantially as a share of the crop. By 1936, land tax represented only 5 per cent of the gross value of crop output in British India and about 3.5 per cent of total primary production. During the second world war, the three-fold rise in the agricultural price level and the static level of land taxes reduced the incidence of land taxation to that of a very minor levy.

---

(42) Just before the second world war, 122 million acres of land were subject to permanent settlement in British India (in Bengal, Bihar, parts of Madras, Orissa, U.P., Anam and Ajmer). The other 389 million assessed acres were under various kinds of temporary settlement, see R. C. Desai, *Standard of Living in India and Pakistan*, Popular Book Depot, Bombay, 1953, p. 6. At that time the actual cultivated area seems to have been somewhat over 300 million acres in British India, see Desai, *Op. cit.*, p. 27.

The introduction of a clearer, more legalistic, view of tax obligations and delinquencies, the collection of taxes in cash not kind, the conversion of zamindar rights into landlord rights, the insistence in ryotwari areas of individual responsibility for taxes, weakened the power of the village community and strengthened individual property rights. It increased the possibility for sale or distraint of peasant property and led to land transfers on a much larger scale. There was also a substantial growth in moneylending and peasant indebtedness. Previously the State had been more willing to make allowances for bad harvests, to take payment in kind, to tolerate delay or even default in payments. Muslim antipathy to usury, the strength of the village community in allocating land and the fuzziness of the law about debt had also acted as impediments to moneylending which were now removed (43). As a result many peasants lost their land and became landless labourers or very insecure tenants, in spite of later government efforts to restrict the rights of moneylenders and increase security of tenure. The weakening of community ties and growing competition from manufactured goods also weakened the position of village artisans who no longer had a guaranteed source of income, and some of them became landless labourers. During the period of British rule the proportion of landless labourers and tenants therefore grew considerably, and by the end of it many provinces had a very complex structure of sub-tenants. There was also a decline in the average size of plots (44), and an increase in land values due to population pressure. The basic cultivation unit remained small except in the limited areas where the British operated plantations. Most Indian landlords leased their land to peasants and were not capitalist farmers. There was very little private investment in agriculture.

The main contribution of British policy towards increased agricultural output was through irrigation. During the period of British

---

(43) For a description of the changed status of the moneylender in the Punjab under British rule, see M. L. DARLING, *The Punjab Peasant in Prosperity and Debt*, p. 178 " For centuries he was nothing but a servile adjunct to the Muhammadan cultivator, who despised him as much for his trade as for his religion. Forbidden to wear a turban and allowed to ride only on a donkey, and often the object of 'unmentionable indignities' sufferance was the badge of all his tribe; but when British rule freed him from restraint and armed him with the power of the law, he became as oppressive as he had hitherto been submissive ".

(44) See H. H. MANN, *Land and Labour in A Deccan Village*, who traces the history of a village near Poona where the average landholding fell from 40 acres in 1771 to 7 acres in 1914-15.

rule the irrigated area was increased more than threefold, and when they left a quarter of the land was irrigated. Before the British came, irrigation was provided by storage tanks in the South, canals and dams in the North and wells to exploit subsurface water in various parts of the country. Most of the well irrigation was private, but the canals and tanks were operated by government, and the water was sold to private users. The tanks were of ancient origin in Southern India, but the Northern canals were mostly built by Muslim rulers. During the eighteenth century disturbances, the Northern canals fell into disrepair.

The East India Company repaired the Ganges and the Jumna canals and the Grand Anicut on the Cauvery early in the nineteenth century. Later the British extended irrigation considerably, particularly in the North, both as a source of revenue and as a measure against famine. British irrigation activity was greatest in the 1890s and the beginning of this century, when the Punjab canal colonies were created. The motive here was to provide land for retired Indian army personnel, a large part of which came from the Punjab, and to build up population in an area which bordered on the disputed frontier with Afghanistan. There were also large-scale irrigation works in Sind. These areas, which formerly had been desert, became the biggest irrigated area in the world, and a major producer of wheat and cotton, both for export and for sale in other parts of India. Most of it is now in West Pakistan.

Improvements in transport facilities (particularly railways) enabled agriculture to specialise to some degree on cash crops in which each area had a comparative advantage. This probably helped increase yields somewhat, but the bulk of the country stuck to subsistence farming. The British added to agricultural output by developing specialist plantation agriculture for export crops. These included indigo, sugar, and jute. In the 1850s came tea, the biggest of the plantation crops. These items made a significant contribution to Indian exports, but in the context of Indian agriculture as a whole, they were very much less important than in Ceylon or Malaya (45).

---

(45) In 1946, the two primary staples, tea and jute, were only 3.9 per cent of the gross value of crop output, see S. Sivasubramonian, *National Income of India 1900-01 to 1946-47*, Delhi School of Economics, Delhi, 1965, whereas in Ceylon tea, rubber, coconuts and other estate crops were threequarters of agricultural output in 1950, see D. R. Snodgrass, *Ceylon: An Export Economy in Transition*, Irwin, Illinois, 1966, p. 128.

They were, however, more significant than in China which had no plantation agriculture and whose tea exports suffered as a result of Indian competition.

Many developing countries, particularly in Latin America or Africa, and some Asian countries, such as Burma, Ceylon, Malaya, and Thailand had large areas of uncultivated fertile land which could be mobilised to produce export crops when the transport re-volution gave a major boost to international trade in the second half of the nineteenth century. In some Asian countries there was also a good deal of idle labour which could be mobilized. By exploiting this " vent for surplus ", international trade made possible a once-for-all rise in their standard of living (46). There was a rapid rise in cultivated area and agricultural output bigger than the increase in population (47).

In India, agricultural settlement was too ancient and population too dense to have left as big an excess of land or surplus labour. There was substantial waste land available for development, but the expansion of cultivated area did not keep pace with population.

The new land in India was less fertile on average than the old. There was only minor improvement in seeds during British rule, little increase in manuring or fertiliser use, or improvement in live-stock, and increased fragmentation of holdings, so yields of individual crops are unlikely to have risen in spite of increased specialisation and irrigation (48). Per acre yields were amongst the lowest in the

---

(46) See the theoretical analysis of the process by Professor H. Myint, " The Classical Theory of International Trade and the Underdeveloped Countries », *Economic Journal*, June 1958, and R. E. Caves, " Vent for Surplus' Models of Trade and Growth ", in R. E. Caves, H. G. Johnson and P. B. Kenen, *Trade Growh and the Balance of Payments*, North Holland, Amsterdam, 1965.

(47) In Thailand there was surplus land in the main paddy area of the country where the crop area doubled from 1850 to 1913. This was done with no investment in irrigation or change in technology. The paddy area doubled again from 1913 to 1938 but this required some investment in railways and brought areas under cultivation with lower yields. 95 per cent of the agricultural area was devoted to rice and exports rose from 5 per cent of produc-tion in 1850 to 50 per cent in 1907. See J. C. Ingram, *Economic Change in Thailand since 1850*, Stanford, 1955.

(48) M. D. Morris suggests that there was an increase in both yield and area cultivated in the nineteenth century because of improvements in public order and transport, but gives no real evidence, see " Towards a Reinterpretation of Nineteenth Century Indian Economic History ", *Journal of Economic History*, December 1963, p. 612. W. C. Neale, *Economic Change in Rural India*, Yale, 1962, pp. 143-4 gives evidence of rise in area and yields in Uttar Pradesh.

world at the end of British rule (49). Agricultural output per head of total population was lower than almost anywhere else in the world.

The British did very little to promote technical improvements. The first agricultural research institute was started only in 1905 and this was initially financed by a private American donation. At about the same time a veterinary service was created and experimental stations set up. There was consequently very little improvement in seeds, no extension service (50), no improvement in livestock and no official encouragement to use fertiliser. Lord Mayo, the Governor General, said in 1870 " I do not know what is precisely meant by ammoniac manure. If it means guano, superphosphate or any other artificial product of that kind, we might as well ask the people of India to manure their ground with champagne " (51).

The contrast between experience in India and that in Japan and the Japanese colony of Taiwan was very striking indeed. Japanese farm practice, seeds and yields were already much superior to those in India in the Tokugawa period, but from the 1870s onward, Meiji policy produced major improvements in yields and from 1895 improved those in Taiwan. Government sponsored research and extension, improved seeds and fertiliser made the major contribution. The Japanese, like the Indians, had been vegetarians before 1867 because of Buddhist religious beliefs. However, the Japanese government imported foreign strains of cattle, horses, sheep, pigs and poultry in order to diversify the diet, to provide traction power and manure. The government sponsored literature on livestock farming and trained veterinarians. In India there was no progress at all with livestock breeding.

British rule reduced some of the old checks on Indian population growth. The main contribution was the ending of internal warfare and local banditry. Better transport and more reliable water supply through irrigation reduced the incidence of famine. Famines did not disappear, but it is noteworthy that the decades in which they

---

(49) See V. D. WICKIZER and M. K. BENNETT, *The Rice Economy of Monsoon Asia*, Stanford, 1940, p. 318-9 who show average 1935-9 rice yields in India as 8.8 quintals of cleaned rice per hectare compared with 27.1 in Japan, 19.0 in Taiwan, 17.6 in Korea, 10.0 in Java and Madura, and 9.6 in Burma. Yields were lower in three countries, Indo-China 6.9, Philippines 7.3, and Thailand 7.9.

(50) " In the sphere of agricultural education India has, no doubt, been held back by the fact that until the last decade of the nineteenth century England herself was very deficient in that respect ". See V. ANSTEY, *The Economic Development of India*, London, 1929, p. 178.

(51) See M. EDWARDES, *Op. cit.*, p. 219.

occurred were ones in which population was static rather than falling (52). The death rate was also reduced to some degree by making infanticide illegal, and the British made a marginal contribution to public health by some smallpox vaccination, killing rats, and better quarantine procedures. As a result, the death rate fell (53) and the population of India grew. By 1913 it was a little over 300 million, and, by 1946, 425 million, whereas at the time of the conquest of Bengal it was in the range of 100-125 million.

There was a very substantial increase in agricultural production in the period of British rule but it is not possible to determine whether farm output grew as fast as population in the nineteenth century (54). But it is quite possible that farm productivity may have declined somewhat even if peasant living standards remained unchanged. Firstly, the peasant was probably getting a larger share of what he produced at the end of British rule than two centuries earlier, because the combined burden of taxes, rent, and usury charges was proportionately lower. Secondly, better transport reduced wastage, by enabling surplus areas to sell their grains (55). This means that more of the crop was actually consumed. Thirdly, it is conceivable that peasants worked harder. Fourthly, the huge cow population may have been getting less to eat (56).

In the last half century of British rule for which agricultural statistics are available, there is evidence of a substantial drop in farm output per head of population. Per capita output of crops, livestock, and fisheries fell 15 per cent from 1900-3 to 1944-6 (57). There was also a drop in wheat exports and a rise in rice imports, so that at

(52) See K. Davis, *Op. cit.*, p. 28. In the 1870s Indian population was static, in the 1880s it rose 9 per cent, in the 1890s 1 per cent, the first decade of the twentieth century 6 per cent, and the second less than 1 per cent.

(53) The fall in death rates was not spectacular. In 1931 life expectation was 27 years, i.e. about the same level as in Europe up to the eighteenth century. Surveys of ancient Greek cemeteries and those of Restoration England show average life expectation at birth of less than 30 years. See L. I. Dublin, A. J. Lotka and M. Spiegelman, *Length of Life*, Ronald, New York, 1949, p. 42.

(54) Moreland argues quite convincingly that there was a rise in living standards of the masses between the time of Akbar and 1920, but the rise mainly affected non-food items and there was certainly a fall in per capita food consumption from 1920 to independence. See W. H. Moreland, *Op. cit.*

(55) See M. L. Darling, *Op. cit.*, p. 172.

(56) On the two latter points see E. Boserup, *The Conditions of Agricultural Growth*, Allen and Unwin, London, 1965, p. 37 and 53.

(57) See S. Sivasubramonian, *Op. cit.* Similar results can be seen in G. Blyn, *Agricultural Trends in India, 1891-1947*, Philadelphia, 1966, p. 251.

the time of independence, India was a net importer of grain. This stagnation in farm output was unique to India, and did not occur elsewhere in Asia.

TABLE 3

RICE PRODUCTION IN MONSOON ASIA
million metric tons of cleaned rice

	Burma	India	Indo-China	Japan	Java and Madura	Korea	Philip-pines	Thai-wan	Thai-land
Average 1910-14	3.74	25.10	3.66	6.78	2.77	1.56	0.54	0.60	1.92
Average 1935-39	4.94	25.77	3.94	8.64	4.00	2.73	1.44	1.24	2.71

Source: V. D. WICKIZER and M. K. BENNETT, *Op. cit.*, pp. 316-7.

The Indian population continued to have a living standard very close to subsistence and remained subject to famines and epidemic diseases whose impact was greatly accentuated by malnutrition. In 1876-8 and 1899-1900 famine killed millions of people. In the 1890s there was a widespread outbreak of bubonic plague and in 1919 a great influenza epidemic. In the 1920s and 1930s there were no famines, and the 1944 famine in Bengal was due to war conditions and transport difficulties rather than crop failure. However, the expe-rience after 1920 was probably due as much to a break in the weather cycle rather than to a new stability of agriculture (58).

It is sometimes asserted by Indian nationalist historians that British policy increased the incidence of famine in India (59), part-icularly in the nineteenth century. Unfortunately we do not have any figures on agricultural production for the nineteenth century. It is difficult to base a judgement merely on catalogues of famine years whose intensity we cannot measure. Furthermore, there seem

---

(58) See S. R. SEN, *Growth and Stability in Indian Agriculture*, Waltair, January 1967.

(59) This is the argument of Romesh Dutt and also of the British author William Digby, (*Prosperous British India*, London, 1901). More recently their assertion that the incidence of famine increased under British rule has been repeated in B. M. BHATIA, *Famines in India*, Asia Publishing House, Bombay, 1963, pp. 7-8. " The frequency of famine showed a disconcerting increase in the nineteenth century ». However, there is no evidence to support this statement. In the period of British rule, the population started to increase which must have been due to some degree to a reduction in the impact of crop failure on mortality.

to be long cycles in Indian weather conditions which make output unstable over a period of decades. As agriculture was extended to more marginal land one would have expected output to become more volatile. However, this was offset to a considerable extent by the major improvement in transport brought by railways, and the greater security of water supply brought by irrigation.

Industry

British rule dispossessed a large part of the Muslim aristocracy, destroyed court life in many places and substituted a bureaucracy with European tastes. As a result, there was a decline in domestic demand for fine muslins, traditional shoes, decorative swords and weapons, and other luxury handicrafts. In some cases, the previous rulers had run State manufactories which had guaranteed employment to artisans, and except in the remaining princely states, these disappeared. This change in tastes applied not only to the ruling class but also to the male members of the new Indian middle class which arose to act as their clerks and intermediaries. Domestic demand and production capacity were further affected by the drop in population following the famine of 1770, which is reputed to have reduced the population of Bengal by a third (and of India by 10 per cent).

The area worst hit by the decline in the market for high class textiles was Dacca, which had been the production centre for fine muslins. The population of Dacca declined from about 300,000 in the eighteenth century to 50,000 in the mid-nineteenth. This change in Dacca is not a representative indicator of the effects of British de-industrialisation, because the decline of Dacca's population also had another cause. Its production had already been hit before the British came by the removal of the Nawab's court from Dacca to Murshidabad. Later it was affected by the rise of Calcutta as the major urban centre of Bengal (60).

The second major blow to Indian cotton textiles came from British cloth which began to enter India round 1815, and which

---

(60) The decline in the Indian textile industry before the industrial revolution is noted by C. J. HAMILTON, *The Trade Relations between England and India 1600-1896*, Calcutta, 1919, p. 198, who suggests that the value of textile output in Dacca fell from £300,000 in 1766 to £200,000 in 1776.

had hit Indian exports a little earlier. Indian exports to Europe fell during the Napoleonic wars, partly because of the drastic reduction in British domestic production costs in the textile industry, partly because of higher wartime tariffs in the U.K. and the British blockade of continental Europe. The new British competitiveness was the result of a vastly improved technology which provided better quality goods at much lower prices than before (61). In fact the Napoleonic wars helped the Indian textile industry by delaying the arrival of cheap British textiles on the Indian market. Indian economic historians often emphasise the impact of these imports in displacing handloom spinners and weavers who usually had no alternative employment but to become agricultural labourers, but we must not forget that these cheap and superior cotton textiles enabled a large section of the Indian population to increase its textile consumption and to switch from jute to cotton clothing. The cost situation was such that manufactured goods would have ousted handloom products in any case. There is no doubt that large numbers of Indians lost employment in cotton spinning and weaving, particularly in high class textiles, but the British certainly did not wipe out textile handicrafts. Handloom weaving still persists in India and the availability of cheap yarn may even have given a boost to handloom weaving for crude textiles.

The change in the pattern of Indian textile trade and production was not determined wholly by changes in demand and technology but was also affected by commercial policy.

It is sometimes suggested that commercial policy in the U.K. dealt a major blow to Indian textiles. It is true that British protectionist interests were very powerful throughout the eighteenth century in restricting imports of Indian goods. Imports of silk manufactures were actually prohibited between 1700 and 1825, and there were protective duties on cotton textiles which were raised for revenue purposes in 1797 during the Napoleonic wars. These high duties lasted till 1824. But between 1825 and 1842 British import duties on textiles were gradually reduced to 10 per cent as the U.K.

---

(61) See H. HEATON, *Economic History of Europe*, Harper and Row, New York, 1965, p. 491, " Between 1779 and 1812 the cost of making cotton yarn dropped nine tenths. The mule's fine cheap yarn 'brought to the masses of the people better goods than even the rich had been able to afford in the earlier period' ". There was almost equal cost reduction in the weaving process. British textile exports rose 30 fold in volume between the 1780s and the end of the Napoleonic wars, see P. DEANE, *The First Industrial Revolution*, Cambridge, 1965, p. 89.

moved steadily towards free trade. The prohibition on manufactured silk imports was removed in 1825. Thus British policy on textile imports became less protectionist after India became a colony than it had been before.

We may however ask why India did not react quickly to the new technical possibilities and start factory production of textiles herself. She had, after all, been exposed to these new industrial products much earlier than China or Japan. Why could India not have copied Lancashire technology as quickly as France which had 3.5 million spindles by 1847? (62). Indian historians attribute the delay primarily to the lack of protective tariffs, and British imposition of a policy of free trade. British imports entered India duty free and when a small tariff was required for revenue purposes, Lancashire pressure led to the imposition of a corresponding excise duty on Indian products to prevent them gaining a competitive advantage. This undoubtedly handicapped industrial development. If India had been politically independent, her tax structure could have been completely different. In the 1880s, Indian customs revenues were only 2.2 per cent of the trade turnover, i.e. the lowest ratio in any country. In Brazil import duties at that period were 21 per cent of trade turnover. In the 1870s only 4 per cent of Indian government revenues were derived from customs duties whereas in Brazil the proportion was 72 per cent (63). As a result of this tax structure, Brazilian industrialisation got a much bigger push than that of India.

Another major reason why textile mills were not started earlier in India is that there was no Indian capitalist class, and no opportunity to attain the necessary technical knowledge quickly. By the 1850s, a new Indian middle class had begun to emerge which had made its money trading with the British and had acquired some education in English, and it was they who launched the Bombay textile industry with financial and managerial help from British trading companies which became managing agencies. These first Indian entrepreneurs tended to come from minority groups like the Parsees who did not have the same disdain for productive activity as upper class Hindus and Muslims.

---

(62) See J. H. CLAPHAM, *Economic Development of France and Germany 1815-1914*, Cambridge, 1963, p. 65.
(63) See M. G. MULHALL, *The Dictionary of Statistics*, Routledge, London, 1899, p. 172 and 258.

In fact, India was the first country in Asia to have a modern cotton textile industry, preceding Japan by 20 years and China by 40 years. It started in Bombay in 1851, and concentrated on coarse yarns which were sold domestically and to China and Japan. Yarn exports were about half of output. At that time, all Asian countries practised free trade which had been forced upon them by colonial treaties, and India enjoyed open access to the Chinese and Japanese markets. Japan did not have protective tariffs until 1911 and China until 1931.

Modern jute manufacturing started about the same time as textiles. The first jute mill was built in 1854 and the industry expanded rapidly in the vicinity of Calcutta. The industry was largely in the hands of foreigners (mainly Scottish), and most of the product was exported. India also continued to export raw jute which was used by the industry in Dundee. Between 1879 and 1913 the number of jute spindles rose tenfold — much faster than the cotton textile industry.

Coal mining was another industry which achieved significance. Its output largely met the demand of the Indian railways. By 1914 output reached 15.7 million tons. Most of it was in Bengal.

In 1911, the first Indian steel mill was built by the Tata Company at Jamshedpur in Bihar. However, production did not take place on a significant scale before the first world war. The Indian steel industry started 15 years later than in China, where the first steel mill was built at Hangyang in 1896. The first Japanese mill was built in 1898. In both China and Japan the first steel mills (and the first textile mills) were government enterprises.

Indian industrialisation was given a boost in 1905 by the *swadeshi* movement, which was the result of nationalist pressure, and involved a boycott of British goods in favour of Indian enterprise. Its results were not spectacular as British enterprise was too well entrenched to be pushed aside but it did help some industries and gave a fillip to Indian insurance and banking.

During the first world war the Indian textile industry managed to build up its home market for piece goods at the expense of British imports, and in the interwar period this process of import substitution for British cloth continued. Total imports of cloth fell from 3.2 billion yards in 1913-14 to 1.9 billion in 1929-30. However, Japanese products entered the market for cheaper textiles on a large scale during the first world war. In the 1930's, Japan supplied half of Indian cloth imports whereas the U.K. had provided virtually all imports in 1913.

Under nationalist pressure, there were some changes in British policy in India in the 1920s. During the first world war, tariffs had been raised for revenue purposes. In 1921, the government agreed to create a tariff commission and although it worked slowly, it did start raising tariffs for protective reasons. By 1925, the average tariff level was 14 per cent (64) compared with 5 per cent pre-war. The procedure for fixing tariffs was lengthy and tariff protection was granted more readily to foreign-owned than to Indian firms (65). As a result of these measures, there was a considerable substitution of Indian textile production for imports. At the end of the nineteenth century Indian mills supplied 10 per cent of total cloth consumption, hand-looms 27 per cent and imports 63 per cent. In 1931-2 the percentages were 56 for local mills, 30 for hand-looms and 14 for imports (66).

The government was more willing to protect the textile industry when the threat came from Japan and not the U.K. At the beginning of 1930, the tariff on cotton cloth was raised from 11 to 15 per cent for British imports and 20 per cent for others, with a minimum specific rate to discriminate against cheaper grades. In March 1931 the tariff on Japanese goods was raised to 25 per cent, in September 1931 to 31¼ per cent. As the Japanese devalued the yen from 2.1 rupees to an eventual rate of 0.8, they were able to break through these tariffs which were raised to 50 per cent in August 1932 and to 75 per cent in 1933. The Japanese responded by boycotting imports of Indian raw cotton, and this forced the Indian government into a quota agreement in January 1934 by which Japan's export markets for cloth were geared to her purchases of raw cotton, and the duty was reduced to 50 per cent. In all of these tariff arrangements, British imports were accorded a margin of preference.

Japanese competitiveness was due in part to an overvalued Indian currency, to government support and protection, greater access to finance and technical training, aggressive export marketing, bulk purchase of raw materials and skilful mixing procedures for

(64) See W. A. Lewis. *Economic Survey, 1919-39*, Allen & Unwin, London, 1949. p. 48.

(65) See M. Kidron, *Foreign Investments in India*, London, 1965, p. 13.

(66) See D. H. Buchanan, *The Development of Capitalistic Enterprise in India*, Cass, London, 1966, p. 222.

different types of raw cotton. It was also helped by the fact that
80 per cent of the Japanese labour force were girls, whereas in India
80 per cent were men, whose wages had to support families and
who were much more active in trade unions which went in for
strikes and restrictive practices, particularly during the deflationary
years 1928-34 when the millowners were trying to reduce wages.
Most Japanese mills had their workers living in dormitories and
found it easier to use equipment intensively by shift working. Japanese workers had better health and education, whereas Indian
workers were debilitated by disease and malnutrition. Japanese
wages were higher than those in India, but by the later 1930s, each
Japanese operative worked three times as many spindles as an Indian.
Indian efficiency was greatly hindered by the managing agency
system under which the management was foreign, expensive and
inefficient (67); the exclusive use of jobbers for hiring workers and
maintaining discipline, and a completely unskilled group of workers
who had to bribe the jobbers to get and retain their jobs. There
were also problems of race, language and caste distinctions between
management, supervisors and workers. The small size and very
diversified output of the enterprises hindered efficiency.

Indian yarn exports to Japan dropped sharply from 8,400 tons
in 1890 to practically nothing in 1898, and India also suffered from
Japanese competition in China. The Japanese set up factories in
China after the Sino-Japanese War of 1894-5. Before this, India
had supplied 96 per cent of Chinese yarn imports, the U.K. 4 per
cent, and Japan none. Within three years the Japanese had a quarter
of Chinese imports and by 1914 India was exporting less yarn to
China than was Japan. During the first world war Japan made
further progress in the Chinese market and by 1924 supplied three-
quarters of Chinese imports. By 1928 India was exporting only
3 per cent of her yarn output.

---

(67) This raised the cost of management. In 1925, 28 per cent of the managerial and
supervisory staff in the Bombay textile mills were English, even though the plants were
owned by Indians. In 1895 the proportion was 42 per cent. Very few Indians got technical
training in the U.K. This was totally different from the situation in Japan. See D. H.
BUCHANAN, *Op. cit.*, p. 211. Elsewhere (p. 321) Buchanan gives figures of the cost of
European managerial personnel. In the Tata steel works in 1921-2 the average salary of
foreign supervisory staff was 13,527 rupees a year, whereas Indian workers got 240 rupees.
These foreigners cost twice as much as in the U.S.A. and were usually less efficient. Use of
foreign staff often led to inappropriate design, e.g. multi-story mills in a hot climate or use
of mule instead of ring spindles.

By the end of the 1930s, Indian exports of yarn to China and Japan had disappeared, piece goods exports had fallen off, and India imported both yarn and piece goods from China and Japan. She had made progress in substituting for British imports, but the net result was that the Indian textile industry was less dynamic than it had been in the second half of the nineteenth century.

Other Indian industries did better than textiles in the interwar period. There was some stimulus to import substitution during the first world war and in the 1920s certain steel products got tariff protection and bounties as well as government orders. It would appear that the Indian iron and steel industry grew faster than that of China. In the 1930s the industry produced over a million tons of pig iron and half a million tons of steel (68). Indian enterprises also started to grow rapidly in electricity, cement and sugar. British enterprises remained dominant in transport, coal, plantation crops and jute. In 1928, under nationalist pressure, the government started to favour Indian enterprises in its purchase of stores, and departments of industry were set up at the centre and in each province. The second world war gave a fillip to Indian industrial output, but there was not much increase in capacity because of the difficulty of importing capital goods and the lack of a domestic capital goods industry.

The British policy of segregating Indians from positions of responsibility and power greatly weakened the entrepreneurial dynamism which Western influence and foreign trade might have introduced. The early monopolistic position of the East India Company meant that a good deal of the most lucrative commercial, financial, business, and plantation opportunities were absorbed by foreigners. British monopoly of high level jobs and neglect of technical education effectively prevented the diffusion of skills to an Indian elite and perpetuated the privileged British position. British influence was further increased through the system of " managing agencies ". These agencies were used to manage industrial enterprises, and handled most of India's international trade.

---

(68) In China, pig iron output rose more slowly from 354,000 tons in 1915-18 to 735,000 in 1935-7, see CHI-MING HOU, *Op. cit.*, pp. 230-1. But in coal, the pace of growth was faster in China where production rose from 18 million tons in 1918 to 39 million in 1936. Indian production rose from 19 million in 1916-18 to 23 million in 1936.

They were closely linked with British banks (69), insurance and shipping companies. Usually they were shareholders in the companies they managed, but they were paid commissions based on gross profits or total sales and were often agents for the raw materials used by the companies they managed. The origins of the system go back to the agency houses founded by ex-Company servants in the eighteenth century in Bengal, who controlled internal trade, the indigo and sugar industry, ran banks and insurance companies and tendered for government contracts. They also dominated the trade of China, Burma and Malaya, and until 1900, that of Japan. In 1913 the managing agencies of Calcutta " managed 116 coal mines, 43 jute mills, 19 railways and steam navigation companies, 6 cotton mills and 42 miscellaneous joint stock companies " (70).

These agencies were in many ways able to take decisions favourable to their own interests rather than those of shareholders. The government of British India did nothing to check their powers. Indian shipping was entirely in the hands of British companies, and of course, the British administration would never have dreamt of subsidising a local shipping line in the way which was done so successfully in Japan. Even less would they have thought of building up big Indian companies to rival the managing agencies in export promotion, or of creating a bank for export credit as the Japanese government did. The foreign firms and the government were not active in promoting training for Indians or in upgrading them to managerial positions. Even in the Bombay textile industry, where most of the capital was Indian, there was usually a heavy British component of management. The managing agencies were so powerful because they had a quasi-monopoly in access to capital (71), and

---

(69) As Keynes said " Indian exchange banking is no business for speculative or enterprising outsiders, and the large profits which it earns are protected by established and not easily assailable advantages ". See J. M. KEYNES, *Indian Currency and Finance*, London, 1913, p. 208.

(70) See S. K. SEN, *Studies in Industrial Policy and Development of India*, (1858-1914), Progressive Publishers, Calcutta, 1964, p. 145. See also D. H. BUCHANAN, *The Development of Capitalistic Enterprise in India*, New York, 1934.

(71) In 1913, foreign banks held over threequarters of total deposits, Indian Joint Stock Banks less than one fourth. In the eighteenth century there had been very powerful Indian banking houses (dominated by the Jagath Seths) which handled revenue remittances and advances for the Moghul Empire, the Nawab of Bengal, the East India Company, other foreign companies, and Indian traders, and which also carried out arbitrage between Indian currency of different areas and vintages. These indigenous banking houses were largely pushed out by the British.

they had interlocking directorships which gave them control over supplies and markets. They dominated the foreign markets in Asia. They had better access to government officials than did Indians.

The major act of British policy to promote Indian development was the construction of railways which were started in the 1850s. They made an enormous difference to Indian transport, for goods had previously moved by bullock cart or pack animal (i.e. usually less than walking pace). However, the degree of railway development was not very large. In relation to the size of the country and its population India remained worse off than most developing countries except China, Thailand and Indonesia. At first, railways were developed by private companies with British capital and a government guarantee of interest on the bonds. They were later taken over by government. Railway development was criticised in India because of these large government subsidies, because there were not enough feeder lines, and because their location was not optimum in terms of industrial development. It was also argued that too much was spent on railway development and not enough on irrigation. However, the economics of Indian railway development were no worse than in most countries, except that foreign investors did much better than in the U.S.A. or South America where there were major losses from default on bonds.

One major effect of railway development in India was to reduce the impact of famines by enabling grain to be shipped from surplus to deficit areas.

The basic limitations on the growth of industrial output in India were the extreme poverty of the local population, the fact that a large proportion of the elite had a taste for imported goods or exported their purchasing power, the fact that there was no tariff protection, or government preference for local products. The government itself did not create industrial plants or sponsor development banks which could have helped. The banking system gave little help to industry and technical education was poor. This contrasted sharply with the situation in Japan. In Japan the government promoted industrialisation by setting up State industry on an experimental basis and then selling off the plants to private enterprise (72).

---

(72) Lord Curzon had had the idea of doing the same in India, but these policies were vetoed by Lord Morley, as Secretary of State for India.

TABLE 4

DENSITY OF RAILWAY DEVELOPMENT IN 1913
Kilometres of Railways per Million Inhabitant-Kilometres

Belgium	355.8	Mexico	22.8
U.S.A.	186.1	Chile	15.4
Switzerland	160.3	Greece	15.3
France	123.5	Russia (European) . . .	5.8
Germany	112.1	Egypt	3.2
U.K.	99.6	Brazil	3.0
Argentina	81.5	Japan	2.9
Netherlands	54.9	India	2.0
Italy	31.1	Indonesia	0.5
Malaya	30.7	Thailand	0.2
Canada	30.4	China	0.03
Spain	25.4		

Source: Statistisches Jahrbuch für das deutsche Reich, 1915.

It favoured domestic firms in State contracts, e.g. for railway equipment. It manufactured its own military equipment, built its own naval vessels and subsidised private shipbuilding. It created a Japanese banking system which favoured local industry and it also set up State development banks and a bank to promote exports. It developed technical education on a large scale. The government also supported the growth of Japanese business trusts (zaibatsu) which were able to drive out the foreign trading companies and build up close subcontracting relations with local small-scale industry. An independent India could have done many of these things.

By the time of independence, large scale factory industry in India employed less than 3 million people as compared with twelve and quarter million in small scale industry and handicrafts, and a labour force of 160 million (73).

If we compare Indian industrialisation with that of Japan the record of British rule looks very poor. If we compare India with other countries in Asia which were colonies, the record is much more favourable, because India's per capita industrial output at independence was higher than elsewhere in Asia outside Japan, and more than half of India's exports were manufactures. British policy was less repressive to local industry than that of other colonial powers.

(73) See S. SIVASUBRAMONIAN, *Op. cit.*

The comparison with China is also interesting, because China was never colonised to the same degree as India. Chinese development is perhaps similar to what would have occurred in India, if the eighteenth century political pattern had prevailed for another two centuries, i.e. limited foreign enclaves, with most of the country under weak and xenophobic indigenous rulers. China had a smaller degree of industrial development than India at independence, poorer transport facilities and a smaller elite with knowledge of English and access to foreign technology, but from the 1890s onwards, the rate of industrial expansion was probably faster because government policy in the late Manchu period (74) and under the Nationalists was more active than in India. China also benefited substantially from massive Japanese investment in Manchuria, and if it had not been for civil war and the war with Japan, the degree of industrialisation might have been higher than in India in the early 1940s.

Foreign Trade

Until the end of the Napoleonic wars, cotton manufactures had been India's main export. They reached their peak in 1798, and in 1813 they still amounted to £2 million (75), but thereafter they fell rapidly. Thirty years later, half of Indian imports were cotton textiles from Manchester. This collapse in India's main export caused a problem for the Company which had to find ways to convert its rupee revenue into resources transferable to the U.K. The Company therefore promoted exports of raw materials on a larger scale including sugar, silk, saltpetre, and indigo, and greatly increased exports of opium which were traded against Chinese tea. These dope-peddling efforts provoked the Anglo-Chinese war of 1842 after which access to the Chinese market was greatly widened. By the middle of the nineteenth century opium was by far the biggest export of India, and remained in this position until the 1880s when

---

(74) The Manchu government built its own armament factories and created a number of industrial enterprises. Although they were run in a very bureaucratic way and were financial failures in some cases, they helped familiarise the Chinese with modern industry, and probably helped provoke foreign interest in direct investment in China from the 1890s onwards. For a description of Chinese policy, see A. FEUERWERKER, *China's Early Industrialisation: Sheng - Hsuan - huai and Mandarin Enterprise*, Harvard, 1958.

(75) See R. DUTT, *Economic History of India*, Vol. I, Government of India reprint, Delhi, 1963, p. 202.

its relative and absolute importance began to decline. Another new export was raw cotton, which could not compete very well in European markets against higher quality American and Egyptian cottons (except during the U.S. Civil War), but found a market in Japan and China. Sugar exports were built up after 1833 when the abolition of slavery raised West Indian production costs, but India had no long-run comparative advantage in sugar exports. Indigo (used to dye textiles) was an important export until the 1890s when it was hit by competition from German synthetic dyes. The jute industry boomed from the time of the Crimean War onwards, when the U.K. stopped importing flax from Russia. In addition to raw jute (shipped for manufacture in Dundee) India exported jute manufactures. Grain exports were also built up on a sizeable scale, mainly from the newly irrigated area of the Punjab. The tea industry was introduced to India from China and built up on a plantation basis. Tea exports became important from the 1860s onwards. Hides and skins and oil cake (used as animal feed and fertiliser) were also important raw material exports.

Manufactured textile exports from India began to increase in the 1850s when the first modern mills were established. The bulk of exports were yarn and crude piece goods which were sold in China and Japan. Indian jute manufactures were exported mainly to Europe and the U.S.A.

TABLE 5

LEVEL OF ASIAN EXPORTS F.O.B. 1850-1950

Dollars million

	1850	1913	1937	1950
Ceylon	5	76	124	328
China	24	294	516	(700)
India	89	786	717	1,178
Indonesia	24	270	550	800
Japan	1	354	1,207	820
Malaya	24	193	522	1,312
Philippines	n.a.	48	153	331
Thailand	3	43	76	304

N. B. - Trade figures refer to customs area of the year concerned. In 1850 and 1913 the Indian area included Burma. The comparability of 1937 and 1950 figures is affected by the separation of Pakistan.

Indian exports grew fairly rapidly in the period up to 1913, but their growth was slower than that of most other Asian countries which had a natural resource endowment offering greater opportunities for trade. As a consequence, in 1913, India had a smaller trade per head than most countries except China. Nevertheless exports were 11.7 per cent of G.N.P., probably a higher ratio than has been reached before or since.

Until 1898, India, like most Asian countries, was on the silver standard. In the 1870s, the price of silver began to fall and the rupee depreciated against sterling. This led to some rise in the internal price level, but it helped to make Indian exports more competitive with those of the U.K., e.g. in the Chinese textile market. In 1898, India adopted a gold exchange standard which tied the rupee to sterling at a fixed value of 15 to 1. This weakened her competitiveness vis-à-vis China which remained on a depreciating silver standard, but its potential adverse effects were mitigated because Japan went on to the gold exchange standard at the same time.

During the first world war, when the sterling exchange rate was allowed to float, the rupee appreciated. Unfortunately, when sterling resumed a fixed (and overvalued) parity in 1925, the rupee exchange rate was fixed above the pre-war level. This overvaluation eased the fiscal problems of government in making transfers to the U.K. and enabled British residents in India or those on Indian pensions in the U.K. to get more sterling for their rupees, but it made it necessary for domestic economic policy to be deflationary (in cutting wages) and greatly hindered Indian exports particularly those to or competing with China and Japan.

As a result, Indian exports fell from 1913 to 1937, a poorer performance than that of almost any other country. By 1937 exports were only 7.6 per cent of G.N.P. and at independence they were only 4.4 per cent. If we look at Indian export performance from 1850 to 1950 it was worse than that of any other country in Asia (see Table 5).

Education

When the Company's commercial activities ended in 1833 and the first Viceroy was installed, he brought Macaulay as his legal advisor to codify the law, and to decide on the educational system. Macaulay's Minute on Education had a decisive impact on British educational policy in India and is a classic example of a Western rationalist approach to Indian civilisation. Before the British took over, the Court Language of the Moghuls was Persian and the Muslim population used Urdu, a mixture of Persian, Arabic and Sanskrit. Higher education was largely religious and stressed knowledge of Arabic and Sanskrit. The Company had given some financial support to a Calcutta Madrasa (1781), and a Sanskrit college at Benares (1792). Warren Hastings, as governor general from 1782 to 1795 had himself learned Sanskrit and Persian, and several other Company officials were oriental scholars. One of them, Sir William Jones, had translated a great mass of Sanskrit literature and had founded the Asiatic Society of Bengal in 1785. But Macaulay was strongly opposed to this orientalism:

> " I believe that the present system tends, not to accelerate the progress of truth, but to delay the natural death of expiring errors. We are a Board for wasting public money, for printing books which are less value than the paper on which they are printed was while it was blank; for giving artificial encouragement to absurd history, absurd metaphysics, absurd physics, absurd theology.".... " I have no knowledge of either Sanskrit or Arabic... But I have done what I could to form a correct estimate of their value "... " who could deny that a single shelf of a good European library was worth the whole native literature of India and Arabia. " ... " all the historical information which has been collected from all the books written in the Sanskrit language is less valuable than what may be found in the most paltry abridgements used at preparatory schools in England. "

For these reasons Macaulay had no hesitation in deciding in favour of English education, but it was not to be for the masses:

> " it is impossible for us, with our limited means to attempt to educate the body of the people. We must at present do our best to form a class who may be interpreters between us and the millions whom we govern; a class of persons, Indian in blood and colour, but English in taste, in opinions, in morals, and in intellect. To that class we may leave it to refine the vernacular dialects of the country, to enrich those dialects with terms of science borrowed from the Western nomenclature, and to render them by degrees fit vehicles for conveying knowledge to the great mass of the population." (76).

---

(76) Quoted from the text as given in M. EDWARDES, *British India 1772-1947*, Sidgwick and Jackson, London, 1967.

In fact, the education system which developed in British India was a very pale reflection of that in the U.K. Three universities were set up in 1857 in Calcutta, Madras and Bombay, but they were merely examining bodies and did no teaching. Higher education was carried out in affiliated colleges which gave a two year B.A. course and gave heavy emphasis to rote learning and examinations. Drop-out ratios were always very high. They did little to promote analytic capacity or independent thinking and produced a group of graduates with a halfbaked knowledge of English, but sufficiently westernised to be alienated from their own culture (77). The Indian Educational Service was created in 1896 to strengthen college teaching, but it never attracted very high quality people and was not very large. It was not until the 1920s that Indian universities provided teaching facilities and then only for M.A. students. The only way in which an Indian could acquire a high quality Western education was to attend a British public school and university. This possibility was, of course, open only to an infinitely small fraction of the population. Furthermore, Indian education was of a predominantly literary character and the provision for technical training was much less than in any European country. Very little was done to provide education for girls who were almost totally ignored throughout the nineteenth century. Because higher education was in English there was no official effort to translate Western literature into the vernacular. Nor was there any attempt to standardise and simplify Indian scripts whose variety is a major barrier to multilingualism amongst educated Indians.

Primary education was not taken very seriously as a government obligation and was financed largely by the weak local authorities. As a result, the great mass of the population had no access to education and at independence in 1947, 88 per cent was illiterate. In other Asian countries education was more highly developed than in India. This is particularly true of Japan, Formosa and the Philippines. Progress was accelerated from the 1930s onwards, but at independence only a fifth of children were receiving any primary schooling.

Education could have played a major role in promoting democracy, encouraging social mobility, developing aesthetic sensitivity, eliminating religious superstition, unifying different linguistic and

---

(77) See the Kothari Report, *Report of the Education Commission 1964-66*, Government of India, Delhi, 1966.

racial groups, increasing productivity and uplifting the status of women. Instead it was used mainly to train clerical labour to work in a stilted and obsequious version of the English language.

Conclusions

There has been a good deal of controversy amongst statisticians about the rate of growth of income in India in the colonial period. The argument is politically coloured and the statistics are poor (78). The latest estimates suggest that per capita income rose by about a quarter between the 1870s and 1947 (79). There are no estimates for the movement in Indian income from Clive's conquest to the 1870s, but there could not have been much net progress in real income per head before the development of railways, modern industry, irrigation and the big expansion in international trade. From the beginning of British conquest in 1757 to independence, it therefore seems unlikely that per capita income increased by more than a third. In other developing countries for which records exist there seems to have been a substantially bigger increase than in India (80). In the U.K. itself there was a tenfold increase (81).

The main increase in the standard of living in the British period was in textile consumption, transport and some service industries. The mass of the labour force remained in agriculture and the urban population was relatively small — about 12 per cent of the total at independence. The total product of the economy was probably more than four times as big in 1947 as it had been in 1757, but most of the increase had been absorbed by the rise in population from 125 to about 425 million. The degree of development varied a good deal from one part of India to another. In Rajastan, Mysore, Orissa and Bihar per capita income was only a half to two thirds of that

(78) For a survey of the literature, see D. & A. THORNER, *Land and Labour in India*. Chapter vii, and S. J. PATEL, " Long-term Changes in Output and Income in India: 1896-1960 ", *Indian Economic Journal*, January 1958.

(79) Estimates provided by M. Mukherjee of the Indian Statistical Institute. S. SIVA-SUBRAMONIAN, *Op. cit.*, shows a rise of a little less than a quarter from 1900 to 1946.

(80) See A. MADDISON, *Economic Progress and Policy in Developing Countries*, Allen and Unwin, London, 1970.

(81) See P. DEANE and W. A. COLE, *British Economic Growth 1688-1959*, Cambridge, 1964, pp. 78, 282, 329-30, and A. MADDISON, *Economic Growth in Japan and the U.S.S.R.*, Allen and Unwin, London, 1969, p. 159.

in West Bengal and the Punjab, but even the advanced areas of India were not particularly prosperous by Asian standards.

The reasons for India's poverty and slow growth can be summarised as follows:

(a) India was not a rich country when conquered by the British. It had a wealthy ruling class whose sumptuary standards may have surpassed those in eighteenth century Europe, and it had a relatively small industrial sector providing them with luxury handicrafts. But the mass of the population was subjected to a greater degree of exploitation than in Europe. This " oriental despotism " was possible because of the passivity induced by the caste structure of village society. Agricultural productivity was lowered by religious tabus which inhibited animal husbandry, and by a social system which provided little incentive to agricultural investment;

(b) the ratio of population to natural resources was less favourable than in Latin America or Africa, so that there were fewer benefits to be reaped from large scale international trade which the transport revolution made possible in the second half of the nineteenth century;

(c) the British dispossessed a substantial part of the old ruling class and revamped the state apparatus. They substituted an efficient Benthamite bureaucracy and a modern army which absorbed a smaller fraction of national income than the *ancien regime*. The benefits of a reduced degree of exploitation, improved law and order and better communications were largely absorbed by increases in population rather than per capita income. A significant fraction of the income of the new ruling class was siphoned out of the country, not formally as Imperial tribute (such as the Spaniards had levied in Mexico) but in more respectable guise as pensions, school fees, savings, and profits on enterprises which enjoyed monopolistic privileges. After independence, therefore, India had only a very small economic " surplus " which could be mobilised for development either through taxation of upper income groups, or by incentives to a wealthy class to use their wealth for productive investment;

(d) agricultural productivity showed no progress under British rule and may even have declined. Removal of some of the non-nutritional checks on population growth pushed the economy closer to a Malthusian equilibrium;

(e) industry got very little help from government. Managerial and technical competence were severely inhibited by British monopoly power in managing agencies, banking, shipping and insurance. Industrial efficiency was damaged by the poverty of human resources in terms of education and health, and by caste and religious prejudices which restricted entrepreneurial activity to a limited group. The poverty of the agricultural population (extreme even for Asia), and the thinness of the upper class stratum were a major handicap to growth in demand for industrial products. Nevertheless, industry developed further than in other Asian countries except Japan, and British policy was less repressive to industrial development than that of other colonial powers;

(f) English education created a small elite which was more westernised than in any other Asian country, but also more alienated from the mass of the population. Their standards and aspirations were largely British, and after independence they took over the special caste attributes which the British had created for themselves in India (except expatriate status). Independence brought a takeover, not a revolution, and preserved many of the static elements in the society and economy. This had some shortrun advantages as it led to greater political stability than elsewhere in Asia, but the preservation of caste, social immobility, and excessive respect for bureaucracy were probably harmful to long run economic growth.

It is interesting to speculate on India's potential economic fate if it had not been subjected to British rule. There are three major alternatives which can be seriously considered. One would have been the maintenance of indigenous rule with a few foreign enclaves, as in China. Given the fissiparous forces in Indian society, it is likely that there would have been major civil wars as in China in the second half of the nineteenth century and the first half of the twentieth century. Without direct foreign interference with its educational system, it is less likely that India would have developed a modernising intelligentsia than China, because Indian society was less rational and more conservative, and the Chinese had a much more homogeneous civilisation around which to build their reactive nationalism. If this situation had prevailed, population would certainly have grown less but the average standard of living might possibly have been a little higher because of the bigger upper class, and the smaller drain of resources abroad. Another alternative to

British rule would have been conquest and maintenance of power by some other West European country such as France or Holland. This probably would not have produced results very different in economic terms from British rule. The third hypothesis is perhaps the most intriguing, i.e. early conquest by the evangelising Portuguese. If they had succeeded in India as they did in Brazil they would have transformed social attitudes, language and religion, and created a new creole ruling class which would probably have rebelled and thrown off metropolitan domination. Thus the country would have been westernised more thoroughly and have been independent longer. This may have been the optimum solution, but would probably not have been feasible even if the Moghul Empire had been in a state of collapse when the Portuguese came. Indian society and religion were too strong for Aurangzeb to change, and it is unlikely that the Portuguese could have succeeded where he failed.

Harvard Advisory Group   ANGUS MADDISON

Islamabad

[11]

The Historical Roots of Modern Mexico, 1500–1940*

Angus Maddison
University of Groningen

Present-day Mexico covers 2 million square kilometres. This is bigger than the area of Aztec civilisation in Central Mexico, but considerably smaller than the Spanish colony of New Spain which also included sparsely settled land corresponding to present-day Arizona, California, Colorado, Florida, Louisiana, Nevada, New Mexico, Texas and Utah. Spain lost Louisiana to France which sold it to the USA in 1803, and it ceded Florida in 1819. Mexico lost more than half (2.4 million square kilometres) of its original territory to the USA in 1848–53, and was at war with France after the French invasion in the 1860s. This experience of foreign intervention and territorial loss had a substantial effect on the character of Mexican nationalism.

Independent Mexico also experienced major domestic turmoil. In 1810–21 there was significant economic loss and human sacrifice in the struggle for independence, there was a prolonged period of internal unrest from then to 1877, and in 1910–20 there were again major losses in the process of revolution.

Ethnically, Mexico consists essentially of three layers: the indigenous Indian stock, the descendants of Spanish settlers, and a large mestizo group in between. There is a very small fraction from other areas and races, but it is much less diverse than Brazil or the USA.

In order to understand the complex nature of Mexico's political system, its brand of economic nationalism and contemporary social forces, it is necessary to look at history. It is helpful to do this in a comparative vein, keeping in mind the differences in its history, institutions and colonial heritage from the United States whose development started later but which has become a much richer country.

For our purposes Mexican economic history can conveniently be divided into eight stages. The first five are covered in the paper, the last three in Maddison and Associates (1992):

1. The indigenous Indian economy and society;
2. the colonial period: New Spain 1519–1821;
3. the first chaotic phase of independence 1821–77;
4. the developmentalist dictatorship of Porfirio Diaz 1877–1910;

*My biggest debt is to Victor Urquidi with whom I have had a more or less continuous discussion on Mexican history and politics over the past thirty years. I am also very grateful to André Hofman for help in analysing Mexican population developments in the early sixteenth century, to Noel Butlin, John Coatsworth, Paul Lamartine Yates, Nanno Mulder and Bartolomé Yun for comments on earlier drafts.

5. the revolution, its aftermath and consolidation 1910–40;
6. political stability, rapid growth and sensible macropolicy 1940–70;
7. developmentalist populism, oil bonanza and debt delinquency 1970–82;
8. crisis, inflation and stabilisation since 1982.

1) The pre-Columbian situation

Before Mexico was conquered by Cortés for the Spanish crown in 1519–21 it consisted of three main Indian groups. Central Mexico, from about 100 miles north of Mexico City to about 300 miles South, was occupied by settled agriculturalists, dominated politically by the Aztec confederacy. Although this area is in the tropics, most of it is a high plateau with a non-tropical climate. Agricultural productivity was sufficiently high to provide an economic surplus, which was appropriated by the Aztec nobility and priesthood with an Emperor and a sizeable imperial city (Tenochtitlan–Tlaltelolco) on the site of present-day Mexico City. The Aztecs operated as predatory war lords over the Tlaxcalans in the East and other Indians in Central Mexico who paid tribute, which, on the evidence of the *Codex Mendoza*, seems to have been fixed *ad hoc* after battles rather than being a coherent tax system. These subject Indians proved to be willing allies for the Spaniards. The Conquest was a quick success due to their defection and the superiority of Spanish military technology and organisation.

As the indigenous population had been cut off from other continents for thousands of years, its basic technology was more limited than that which Spain could command. The basic diet was close to vegetarianism as there were no cattle, sheep, pigs or hens. Meat consisted mainly of turkeys, birds and dogs, with venison and pheasant in Yucatan. Crop, fruit and vegetable production (mostly maize, beans, cassava, yams, chilis, tomatoes and pineapples) was labour intensive, with use of canals for irrigation, as well as the *chinampa* technique (a kind of horticulture on floats in the lake which was later drained to form present-day Mexico City) which permitted multicropping and dense settlement in the Aztec capital. However, there were no ploughs and agricultural tools seem to have consisted of hoes and sticks. The absence of horses, oxen, donkeys and wheeled vehicles meant that land transport possibilities were confined to human porterage. There were canals, but no seagoing ships or knowledge of navigation. Precious metals were worked, but there were no metal weapons or tools. The Aztecs had only wooden swords against the steel armour and weapons of the Spaniards. There were major public buildings, a knowledge of astronomy, mathematics and architecture, and a pictographic form of writing, but there was no satisfactory system of public accounts or currency. Market transactions were based on barter or use of cocoa beans as a medium of exchange.

The sanctions for the Aztec social order were a priesthood and religion whose gods required frequent human sacrifice, a military elite of nobles, and rigid codes of social discipline. Private property in land seems to have been confined to the upper social groups.

The bulk of the population was organised in *calpulli* (kinship groups) on inalienable communal land. A lower social order of commoners provided tribute in kind to the nobility and priesthood and worked the *calpulli* land. Below them were *mayeques* who provided labour services on the private lands of the nobility more or less as serfs, and there was an underclass of slaves generally occupied as household servants.

The size of the Aztec population is a matter of considerable controversy, as the evidence is weak. It clearly declined substantially after the Conquest, mainly because of the ravages of disease. As the native population had been isolated over millenia from foreign microbes, they suffered major epidemics from European diseases, such as smallpox and measles, which were new to them.

Table 1   Alternative Estimates of the Population of Central Mexico

	Rosenblat (1945)	Cook and Simpson (1948)	Borah and Cook (1963)	Sanders (1976)	Zambardino (1980)
1492	4.50				
1518					5.0–10.0
1519		11.02	25.20	11.26	
1532			16.80		
1540		6.43			
1548			6.30		2.7–4.5
1565		4.41			
1568			2.65	2.54	2.2–3.0
1570	3.56				
1580		1.90			
1595			1.38		
1597		2.50			
1605			1.08		
1607		2.01			
1650	3.80	1.50			
1700		2.00			
1825	6.80				

Sources: Column 1 from Rosenblat (1945), pp. 36, 57, 81 and 92. Rosenblat in fact refers to Mexico as a whole and not just to Central Mexico. Column 2 from Cook and Simpson (1948) pp. 16, 38, 43, 45 and 46. Column 3 from Borah and Cook (1963) pp. 4, 88 and 157. Column 4 derived from Sanders in Denevan (1976) pp. 115, 120 and 131 (his sample blown up to cover Central Mexico). Column 5 from Zambardino (1980).

In an assessment based mainly on a careful survey of literary evidence and documents in Spanish archives, Angel Rosenblat (1945) estimated the pre-Conquest population of present day Mexico to have been 4.5 million (See Table 1). The Berkeley school (Cook and Simpson, 1948) first estimated the figure for Central Mexico alone to have been 11 million. This was based on various flimsy suppositions, e.g. multiplying the number of Franciscans by baptismal coefficients or inferring population from the size of the Aztec armies as estimated by those who fought them. Later (Borah and Cook, 1963) estimated the 1519 population of Central Mexico (i.e. about a quarter of the territory of present-day Mexico) to be 25 million on the basis of ambiguous pictographs describing the 'incidence' of Aztec tribute. The Berkeley school is now generally given credence by historians even though their evidence is weaker than Rosenblat's. Borah and Cook suggest a mortality for Indians of 95 per cent, i.e. a decline from 25 million in 1519 to 1 million in 1605. There is no doubt that European contact with microbially isolated peoples sparked off demographic collapse through disease in Mexico as it did in Peru and Australia, but this phenomenon is usually followed by recovery as immunities develop in later generations. This kind of recovery happened in Europe after the Black Death, and more recently in Australia where total population is now a very large multiple of what it was when European settlement began in 1788. It seems most implausible that the population of Central Mexico did not recover its alleged 1519 level until 1970 in spite of the additions the Spaniards made to productive potential by the import of European livestock, transport and other technology. One cannot completely reject the Berkeley estimates, but their scholarly character is inferior to those of Butlin (1983) for Australia, or of Cook (1981) for Peru who both try to be more specific in modelling plausible sources of mortality. The Berkeley school never bothered to respond to Rosenblat's (1967) criticism of their work. Sanders in Denevan (1976) made a detailed critique of the Berkeley estimates and suggested a figure less than half of theirs. Zambardino (1980) suggests a plausible 1519 range of 5–10 million which is much nearer to Rosenblat's estimate.

The range of opinions about the size of the Aztec capital is even bigger than those for Mexico as a whole. Cortés, in his history of the conquest, himself compared Tenochtitlan with Cordoba and Seville (Cortés 1982, p. 127) which had a combined population of around 75 thousand in his time (Collantes de Téran, 1977). Adam Smith suggested a population of 20,000 at the time of Montezuma (Smith, 1776, Bk. IV, Chapter VII, Part II). Morgan, the American anthropologist, suggested 30,000 (see Morgan, 1877, p. 195). The Berkeley group (Borah and Cook, 1963, p. 79) suggest a figure of 360,000; this originates from a purported count of 60,000 households made by the Spanish conquerors (multiplied by 6), but it is not certain if the oft-quoted 60,000 refers to houses or people. The eighteenth-century Scottish historian Robertson (1778) took it to refer to people. The most egregious estimate is that of Soustelle who suggested somewhere between 500,000 to 1 million (Soustelle, 1977, p. 27).

To the North of the settled Aztec Indians there was a desert area which reaches to the borders of present-day Mexico and well beyond, which was sparsely inhabited by hunter-gatherer Indian tribes (whom the Aztecs called Chichimecs), who did not produce the 'surplus' beyond subsistence which was required by the more advanced civilisation of the Aztecs.

The Yucatan peninsula was the third characteristic area. Its tropical jungle was sparsely inhabited by Mayans outside the sphere of Aztec control and contact. They were the descendants of what had been a higher civilisation which, perhaps through ecological mishap, had reverted to a lower productivity level than the Aztecs.

2) New Spain 1521–1821

The nature of Spanish colonialism was different from that of other European powers like the British, French, or Dutch who conquered sizeable indigenous populations. These countries also had a phase in which they contemplated cultural conquest, but they eventually compromised with indigenous institutions. Spain, by contrast, steadfastly followed a policy of conquest imperialism. Having divided and conquered the Aztec confederacy, the colonial power destroyed indigenous religion, even in the territory of its allies. They dispossessed the indigenous ruling class of their land and appropriated the economic surplus the Aztec nobility had levied in kind, gradually transforming the nature of landed property rights and taxation. Most indigenous buildings were destroyed. Churches and convents were built on the remains of Aztec temples.

A major reason for this approach was the fact that Spain itself had gone through several centuries in reconquest of its territory from the Islamic Moors. The process ended just before the New World was discovered. Thus the Spanish had the military know-how and organisation for conquest, and a church organisation for evangelising, converting and indoctrinating a conquered population. Islam and judaism were proscribed in Spain, just as the Aztec religion was to be extirpated in Mexico. Furthermore, the Catholic church in Spain was firmly under national control; the king was free to appoint bishops under a sixteenth-century treaty with the Papacy. Centuries of militant struggle had concentrated power and legitimacy on the Spanish monarchy as the ultimate arbiter, against which rebellion even in very distant colonies was seldom imagined.

What was remarkable in New Spain, was the power of this regalist state apparatus to impose an effective *pax hispanica* without a large and costly military arm. Between 1535 and 1816 there was a steady succession of 60 viceroys whose authority was not seriously challenged.

As a result of the destruction of the Aztec state system and religion, Indians became a homogenous social group of paupers within the new system, most of them living in nucleated self-sufficient villages with communal land, under the supervision of local bosses (*caciques*) who were used by the Spanish to collect labour services and a poll tax tribute which was increasingly levied in money rather than kind. The need to pay tribute was a major factor encouraging Indians to sell their labour in the Spanish hacienda sector of the economy. Traditional agricultural crops and techniques in villages were augmented by the new livestock and transport facilities and by use of the plough.

Indians were treated as inferiors throughout Spanish rule with the legal status of minors. Social control was established by three main mendicant orders, the Franciscans, Dominicans and Augustinians. In the first generation, they were often utopians committed to frugal lives, study of native languages, and a new kind of social order. Once the basic task of evangelism was fulfilled, the regular priesthood stepped in to consolidate Spanish authority. The church stressed veneration of saints, provided elaborate processions, and developed the popularity of the dark-skinned Virgin of Guadalupe as an Indian saint. There were elements of syncretism with Aztec and other indigenous religions, but heresy was fiercely punished. Throughout Spanish rule, the church virtually excluded Indians from holy orders. Most priests and members of mendicant orders were immigrant Spaniards under firm control by their bishops. From 1536 to 1820, the Inquisition reinforced orthodoxy by banishing and occasionally killing jews and protestants, repressing witchcraft and sexual deviancy.

The administrative head of New Spain, under the Crown, was the Viceroy. He controlled the church via the bishops who were nominated by the Crown. Under him, the civil administration was capped by the *Audiencia* of judges in Mexico City; local authority was in the hands of *corregidores*, with town councils of notables. Fiscal levies were collected by tax farmers. At the lower levels of government, officials were not well remunerated. Their income was largely derived from selling monopoly rights, administrative favours, etc. in a highly regulated and controlled economy. There were several official monopolies (*estancos*) for tobacco, salt, dye, etc. Bureaucratic leverage over the private sector was strengthened by the absence of a legal basis for corporate enterprise, so that traders and merchants had to operate as individuals. However, the *consulado*, a kind of Chamber of Commerce for regulating trade, emerged in the sixteenth and flourished in the eighteenth century.

There were many restrictions on production, prices, and foreign trade. Trade with other Spanish colonies such as Peru was prohibited. In 1678 the Viceroy of Peru was dismissed for permitting trade with Mexico. All trade with Spain was funnelled through Veracruz in biennial convoys to Cadiz and Seville, and all trade with Manila in the Spanish colony of the Philippines had to pass through the port of Acapulco. Trade with foreigners was considered as piracy; and many of the limited trading opportunities were in the hands of peninsular Spaniards in receipt of official favours.

A major purpose of colonisation was to extract a surplus for the metropole. To provide for this and the cost of local administration, a royal 'fifth' was levied on the produce of silver mines and on agriculture. Between 1503 and 1660 (according to Hamilton, 1934, pp. 32–45), Spain imported about 16.9 thousand metric tons of silver and 181 tons of gold from the New World. About 40 per cent of this came from New Spain, 26 per cent was on government account and represented a fiscal transfer. This official 'drain' varied between a quarter and a half of government revenue in New Spain. The rest was on private account. Some of this was for imports of merchandise but a good deal represented remitted profits and savings of Spaniards.

This tribute system differed from most other European colonialisms which generally got their benefits in the form of a trading profit flowing to the private sector. Portuguese income from Brazil was mainly trading profit; the tribute element was much smaller than in Spanish colonies.

The mining industry was a Spanish creation. Although the Aztecs had precious metals they were an accumulation of nuggets and native metal amassed from alluvial gatherings over the centuries. Mining was started in 1545 in Guanajuato and Zacatecas, northwest of Mexico City, after the Spaniards had disposed of most of the original hoard. Silver output was greatly facilitated by use of mercury in the patio amalgamation process from 1555 onwards. This permitted a high rate of extraction from low-grade ores.

Plantations were also developed for production and refining of sugar cane. In both the plantations and the mines negro slaves were imported as labour, because the work was heavier than Indians were willing or able to perform. However, plantation agriculture was never so important in production and export in New Spain as it was in Brazil or the Caribbean. Furthermore, the cost of slave labour was rather high given the presence of a large and docile Indian population. In the course of the seventeenth century slave imports petered out, and the recognisable black population was relatively small by the time of independence.

Apart from mining and sugar, the other export-oriented activities were hides derived from the massive growth of livestock, a blue vegetable dye – indigo, and a red dye – cochineal, developed by crushing insects.

In terms of landed property outside the Indian villages, the dominant form by the end of Spanish rule was large *haciendas* worked by peons, who were legally wage labourers, but many were in debt to the hacienda (for purchases from the hacienda shop – *tienda de raya* – and cash advances needed to pay their poll tax), and therefore unable to leave. Runaway peasants who were caught were compelled to return and vagrancy laws further discouraged such action. Discipline was often enforced by flogging on a whipping post and social control was strengthened by the hacienda priest. Casual labour was hired from neighbouring Indian villages. Many haciendas sublet land to tenants who usually paid by providing labour services. According to Brading (1971, p. 215) there were 4,945 haciendas in 1809, 6,680 much smaller *ranchos*, and 4,680 Indian villages.

A substantial portion of haciendas was owned by the church. The most efficient of the church entrepreneurs was the Jesuit order which was in Mexico from 1572 to 1767, and used the profits from its investments to fund educational work and hospitals. There were also large ecclesiastical assets in mortgages (*censos*) taken out by hacienda owners in need of funds. The church was the major financial institution in Mexico. Its income was bigger than its expenses and it made loans at low interest rates. It enjoyed a substantial income from tithes, mortgages and financial commitments by hacienda owners who wanted masses said or who endowed other kinds of religious activity in perpetuity (chantries and *capellanias*). These latter payments were guaranteed by giving the church a lien on landed property or urban real estate. As the church had a close interrelation with landed proprietors, the latter frequently ran arrears on their debts without foreclosure, and also enjoyed lower interest rates than those prevailing in the limited financial sector outside church control.

Although haciendas met most of their own food needs and sometimes had a fortress character in Northern territories from which Indian marauders never disappeared, they were not self-sufficient 'feudal' units. This was the interpretation of the Berkeley school (see Borah, 1951 and Simpson's introduction to Chevalier, 1963). Since then Bakewell (1971), Brading (1971) and van Young (1981) have stressed the importance of trading networks in which haciendas played a role as providers of supplies to mining camps and to urban settlements. However, it is clear that they were not nearly as outward oriented as plantation agriculture in Brazil. Ownership of haciendas was important in conferring social status, which some owners managed to augment by purchasing titles of nobility.

Hacienda properties were originally acquired by government gifts, by takeovers of 'empty' land, by purchase, and by dubious practices associated with a patrimonial state dominated by *peninsulares* (officials born in Spain) conscious of the need to keep property in the hands of their cronies. The titles were usually legitimated by subsequent composition fees to the government. Although, in general, New Spain followed Castilian inheritance law which split property at death, many haciendas were covered by special dispensations or entails (*mayorazgos*), which permitted them to remain as large properties between generations by concentrating the inheritance on the first born. However, there is also clear evidence that many haciendas were bought or sold.

The hacienda form of enterprise was Spanish, not an evolution from the Aztec system. Before it developed there were two other forms of Spanish income from land which were derivative from the pre-Columbian situation.

In the first division of spoils, the Spanish conquerors created *encomiendas*, i.e. the right to collect Aztec-style tribute and labour services in a specific geographic area. This was not an ownership title, though titles were often granted separately to *encomenderos*. *Encomiendas* were not popular with the Crown and were gradually suppressed. By 1642, there were only 140 left (Israel, 1975, p.79).

The Crown tried to gain control of Indian labour by allocating it to Spaniards through *repartimiento*, a contract for a temporary pool of labour at a fixed wage for a given period, with individual labourers returning to their own villages after their stint of compulsory service. This bureaucratic system had obvious inefficiencies and was officially abolished in 1633, although it lasted in some places until the eighteenth century.

The seventeenth century has traditionally been regarded as one of economic decline (see Borah, 1951), when Spanish revenues from Mexico fell and the economic system was generally inefficient. However, this view has been challenged by TePaske and Klein (1981) who show that public revenue held up better than had been thought and by Morineau (1985) who cites evidence of substantial bullion shipments to destinations other than Spain, which suggests that the total flow was far higher in the second half of the seventeenth century than Hamilton (1934) thought.

What is uncontestable is that in the second half of the eighteenth century Spain made a number of changes intended to increase efficiency and improve the yield of the colony, which had at least some of the intended effect.

In 1778, the obligation to channel all trade to Spain via Veracruz and Cadiz was ended, and all Mexican ports were gradually opened for trade with Spain and its colonies. Taxation of mining was changed to increase production incentives and a mining college was created. The bulk of exports came from the mines. As a result, government revenue rose from around 3 million pesos at the beginning of the eighteenth century to over twenty million at the end (Humboldt, 1978, p. 540). About a quarter of this was remitted directly to Spain, and another quarter was used for Spanish administrative purposes outside Mexico.

Greater stress was given to military sanctions for Spanish power, and the leverage of the church was reduced. By 1810 the government had built up an armed force of 40,000 troops of whom half were Spaniards. The bureaucracy was modernised and became less patrimonial. Bureaucratic control was strengthened with abolition of tax farming and the establishment of 12 intendancies in 1776. The hold of the *peninsulares* on the economy was increased, and the power of local magnates and municipal *cabildos* was weakened.

The most wealthy, powerful, and independent church order, the Jesuits, were expelled in 1767, with government confiscation of its assets. The assets were sold to provide government revenue, but many of the sales were well below assessed values, and the beneficiaries of this were the large landowners who purchased new holdings at low cost (Bauer, 1971).

The privileges, jurisdiction and immunities of the other clergy were reduced. In 1804 the government agreed to pay the church the annual income it had derived from landowners for chantries and capellanias, and landowners were obliged to pay the government the corresponding capital value (11 million pesos) between 1804 and 1813. However, the government then defaulted on the interest payments to the church. This action antagonised both the lay and the ecclesiastical elites of New Spain (see Lavrin, 1963).

In 1825, just after Spanish rule ended, the population of Mexico was about 6.8 million (Rosenblat, 1945, p. 36).

At the top of the scale was a thin layer of peninsular Spaniards (about 70,000 including family members, see Humboldt, 1978, p. 540) who ran the army, the administration, the church, trading monopolies and part of the professions. Their income claims were high as they aspired to a baroque lifestyle with sumptuous residences and retinues of servants. In 1810 there were 4,176 regular clergy and more than 5,000 monks and nuns in religious orders (Canga Argüelles, 1834). Thus there was one ecclesiastic for every 660 persons in the population as compared with a 1980 figure of 9,800 priests and 1,177 in religious orders, i.e. one for every 6,300 persons.

The second group consisted of 1.2 million *criollos*, i.e. whites of Spanish origin (Rosenblat, 1945 p. 36) who had been born in Mexico. They were hacienda owners, merchants, and part of the clergy. This group was particularly discontented with the Bourbon reforms which had squeezed their income and weakened the political and social standing they had had in the less formal system of administration that had prevailed earlier.

The third social group was more heterogeneous. There were 1.9 million mestizos or *castas*. Most of them originated from unions between whites and Indians. Some were simply Indians who had abandoned their rural lifestyle, wore Spanish-type clothes and lived in urban areas. There were also mulattoes and about 10,000 negro slaves still on plantations at the time of independence. In the hierarchical society of New Spain the *castas* were virtually excluded from government employment and were weakly represented in the church. In an economy which had depended so heavily on official favours and cronyism, mestizos were only very weakly represented as owners of haciendas, or as merchants. In the North the more prosperous of them were rancheros, but the bulk were urban workers, servants and farm hands. A sizeable number were engaged in smuggling and banditry.

At the bottom of the social scale were the rural Indians (3.7 million) living mostly in nucleated pueblos, engaged in subsistence agriculture, wearing traditional dress, and maintaining their own languages and customs except religion. In the North there was a much smaller number of untamed Indians (Navajos and Apaches).

Thus colonial society was segregated, and skin colour was important. Spain had had a system of blood purity certificates from 1547 onwards for those who wanted to prove themselves free of moorish or jewish ancestry, and this spirit still lingered in New Spain. Speech, lifestyle and occupational status were additional criteria for segregation, and were reinforced by explicit legal differentiation of rights.

It is interesting to try to get some comparative perspective on the economy at the end of the colonial epoch. It was generally agreed by contemporaries that New Spain was the most prosperous of the Spanish colonies. It was the only one to boast a domestic nobility, which included both peninsular settlers and creoles, who were richer than the upper crust elsewhere in Spanish America. Humboldt met families in New Spain with an annual income of 200,000 pesos, whereas in Lima, 6,500 pesos was the top level. However average real income per head in New Spain was substantially below that in the United States.

The main reasons for Mexican backwardness compared with the ex-British colonies in North America were probably as follows:

a. The Spanish colony was subject to a bigger drain of resources to the metropole. In the first place a considerable part of domestic income went into the pockets of peninsular Spaniards who did not stay in the colony but took their savings back to Spain. Secondly, there was official tribute which Rosenzweig (1963) estimated to have been 9.5 million pesos a year: 1.64 pesos per capita or about 2.7 per cent of GDP (see rough estimate in Table 2).

b. The British colonial regime imposed mercantilist restrictions on foreign trade, but they were lighter than in New Spain. Thomas (1965) has suggested that the net cost of British trade restrictions was about 42 cents per head in the American colonies in 1770. Coatsworth (1978) believes that the burden was considerably larger in New Spain. The North American colonies had a prosperous shipping industry and trade with the Caribbean. New Spain also had some trade with the Caribbean, but it had a surreptitious contraband character.

Table 2 Rough Estimate of the GDP of New Spain (Average Level for the Years 1791–1809)

million pesos

Agriculture	128
Manufacturing	55
Mining	28
Other	140
GDP	351

Source: First three items from Rosenzweig (1963, p. 492) with agriculture augmented by 21.6 for undercount of beef production (see Ladd (1976), p. 26). I have added a rough estimate for other sectors (services and construction) equal to two-thirds of the combined output of the first three sectors. Rosenzweig's estimates are derived from Quiros (1817). Aubrey had an alternative (much lower) estimate based on Humboldt (see Reynolds (1970), pp. 311–14).

c. The British colonies had a better educated population, greater intellectual freedom and social mobility. Education was secular with an emphasis on pragmatic skills and yankee ingenuity of which Ben Franklin was the prototype. Spanish education was reserved for *letrados* with the long fingernail mentality. Whilst the 13 British colonies had 9 university institutions in 1776 for 2.5 million people (Judges, 1965, p. 149), New Spain, with 5 million had only 2 universities, in Mexico City and Guadalajara, which concentrated on theology and law. Throughout the colonial period the Inquisition kept a tight censorship and suppressed heterodox thinking.

d. In New Spain, the best land was engrossed by hacienda owners. In North America the white population had much easier access to land, and in New England small-scale farming enterprise was typical. Restricted access to land was recognised as a hindrance to economic growth both by Adam Smith and the Viceroy of New Spain. Rosenzweig (1963) quotes the latter (Revillagigedo) as follows (my translation): 'Maldistribution of land is a major obstacle to the progress of agriculture and commerce, particularly with regard to entails with absentee or negligent owners. We have subjects of his majesty here who possess hundreds of square leagues – enough to form a small kingdom – but who produce little of value.'

e. At the top of New Spain there was a privileged upper class, with a sumptuary lifestyle. Differences in status – a hereditary aristocracy, privileged groups of clergy and military with tax exemptions and legal immunities, an Indian population without rights or opportunity – meant that there was much less entrepreneurial vigour than in the British colonies. The elite in New Spain were rent-seekers with a low propensity to productive investment.

f. In the government of New Spain, power was highly concentrated on the centre, whereas in British North America there were 13 separate colonies, and political power was fragmented, so there was much greater freedom for individuals to pursue their own economic interests.

g. Another source of advantage for North America was the vigour of its population growth because of the rapid inflow of migrants. The population of the USA rose 38-fold from

1700 to 1820, while that of Mexico rose less than half. Economic enterprise was more likely to flourish in a society where the market was expanding so rapidly.

It is not possible to estimate the growth performance of the economy of New Spain in the colonial period as a whole, if only because of the uncertainty about population growth. If Rosenblat's estimate of 4.5 million is accepted for 1519, there was a net population increase of about half over three centuries or about 0.14 per cent a year. If the Berkeley estimate for 1519 is accepted, then there was a decline in population of about three-quarters. My own judgement is that the Rosenblat figure is probably closer to the truth.

Clearly the economic and class structure of New Spain was very different from that of the Aztecs, but given the superiority of Spanish technology in agriculture and mining, the reduction in internal warfare and abolition of human sacrifice, the capacity to sustain the *peninsulares* and *criollos* (about 18 per cent of the population) at a high standard of living, to maintain a big church establishment and to remit almost 3 per cent of GDP out of Mexico, I would judge that average productivity and real product per capita were significantly higher than under the Aztecs.

3)   The first phase of independence 1821–1877

The colonial grip on New Spain was weakened by the Napoleonic wars in which Spain was occupied by the French, and became subject to liberal influences. These metropolitan changes were unpopular with conservative Spaniards in the administration in Mexico, and their loyalty to the metropole waned rapidly. The *criollo* group saw independence as an opportunity to take over the top echelon from the *peninsulares*. At a lower level there was an awakening of Indian resentment against the exploitative social system, which led to the first overt acts of rebellion. Thus diverse forces contributed to the move towards independence which lasted from 1810 to 1821. It involved considerable bloodshed and economic costs, including the ruin of the mining industry through flooding.

The main consequences of independence were the disappearance of the Spanish crown as the fountainhead of authority and the rapid decline in economic and social power of the peninsular Spanish elite. A conservative *criollo* group took over political power, but they were opposed by *criollo* liberals who wanted bigger changes in the social order. The mestizo group also wanted a share of the spoils, power, and offices of state. The disappearance of the old bureaucracy and the weakening of church power removed the basis of the long-standing internal *pax hispanica*. The new Mexico was a federal state with little effective central power. There was a breakdown of law and order and tax yields fell. Though tribute was no longer remitted to Spain, resources were absorbed in internal rebellions and in combating external aggression. As the main export was silver coins used as currency elsewhere in the world (China, the Caribbean, Malaya and the Philippines) the new government was not in a position to issue paper currency or to debase the coinage, so it borrowed abroad and clawed property and income from the church. By 1852, the foreign debt was already $53 million. Financial weakness led to default which was a major factor in the foreign intervention which forced the Emperor Maximilian on Mexico. He paid the French war expenses with bonds, so by 1865 the foreign debt was $182 million. After the defeat of Maximilian and the restoration of Juarez, this debt was repudiated. In retaliation, the UK, the major creditor, broke off diplomatic relations for two decades.

Table 3   Comparative Growth Performance in Mexico, Brazil and USA

	Mexico	Brazil	USA
		Population (000s)	
1700	4,500	300[a]	250[a]
1820	6,590	4,507[a]	9,618[a]
1877	9,666	11,099	47,141
1910	15,160	22,216	92,407
1940	19,654	41,114	132,122
1992	89,520	156,012	255,482

Note: a)   excludes indigenous population

	Per Capita GDP (1990 'international' dollars)		
1820	760	670	1,290
1877	726	751	2,594
1910	1,435	796	4,971
1940	1,556	1,302	7,020
1992	5,112	4,637	21,608

Sources: Maddison and Associates (1992) and Maddison (1994).

As a result of the political chaos, Mexico had 71 rulers in the period 1821–76, including two emperors, many presidents (unelected and elected), a governing council, and a council of regency (see Banamex, 1986, pp. 353–4). These rulers had over 200 Ministers of Finance. The USA in the same period had 4 years of civil war but otherwise a regular succession of 14 elected presidents and 26 secretaries of the Treasury (Morison and Commager, 1942, Vol. 2, p. 736). The long period of instability had an adverse impact on per capita income which was lower in 1877 than it had been at the beginning of the century.

During this period, Mexico lost more than half of its territory to the United States. Although the areas ceded were very large and have since become some of the most prosperous parts of the USA, there were relatively few Mexicans living in them at the time of the cession, so the loss did not have much immediate economic impact. (For 1803, Humboldt gives a figure of 144,000 in those territories, i.e. about 2.5 per cent of the population at that time.)

At the time of independence the clergy, like the civil administration was dominated by peninsular Spaniards and part of this group joined the general Spanish exodus. The church, which had already been weakened in the last phase of the colonial epoch, had its legitimacy further reduced by the refusal of the Vatican and Spain to recognise Mexican independence until 1836. As a result important bishoprics remained vacant. The Inquisition was finally ended in 1820 and its assets sold by the state together with some other assets of missions in California, and the properties taken over by the 1804 legislation.

Nevertheless the church still held about a quarter of the national wealth in landed property and urban residences, as well as its income from tithes (see Bazant, 1971). This wealth was an attractive target for a government in need of revenue, particularly as the clergy had been declining in number since independence.

In 1856 the urban and rural real estate of the church was disentailed, but such was the government's need for cash that it sold off much of it at a substantial discount to the richer members of the local population and to some foreign interests (the French and British being the most prominent of these). This appropriation of church land sparked off a civil war in which the conservative and clerical group lost, but soon afterwards in 1863 the French invaded in support of the conservative interest and imposed Maximilian as emperor from 1864 to 1867. After the French withdrawal and the execution of Maximilian, the liberal regime of Benito Juarez consolidated the sales of church land, confiscated and sold the property of Mexicans who had supported the French invasion, and sold off large areas of vacant land. The Juarez brand of liberalism embodied in the 1857 constitution, was intended to modernise Mexico. It established procedures for civil marriage, separated church and State, and removed barriers to land alienation, including Indian land. However, given the existing distribution of wealth and power, the land sold went to the wealthiest groups in the population. With large amounts coming on the market at once, much of it went for a fraction of its long-term value.

The processes of independence, political upheaval and invasion had nevertheless shaken up the social structure of Mexico. The power and wealth of the church had been removed, the hierarchical barriers which had cut mestizos out of the bureaucratic political elite had faded – indeed Juarez himself was a full-blooded Indian (a Zapotec, from Oaxaca). However, the quiescence of the Indian population had not been greatly disturbed.

In the first period of independence the population rose by about half, but per capita income fell. The estimates for income in Table 3 are very rough, but Coatsworth (1978) and Reynolds (1970) both share the view that there was a fall.

4)   The Porfiriato 1877–1911

Porfirio Diaz, a general who had fought with distinction against the French, ended the turbulence and disorder by establishing himself as a dictator for over three decades. The *pax* of the Porfiriato was achieved by buying off the groups capable of armed opposition, by giving them most of the 27 state governorships, and by judicious rotation of generals. The army was reinforced by the creation of local forces of *rurales* to repress dissent. The central power and fiscal revenue were greatly strengthened, the mestizo group came to dominate the political scene, and the anti-clericalism of the previous liberal regime was toned down.

Diaz favoured foreign direct investment and local entrepreneurs in agriculture, mining and industry. The government improved ports, built railways, removed local tolls and barriers to trade, drained the valley of Mexico, changed the old Spanish law on subsoil rights so that petroleum and coal rights were vested in landowners, and established law and order. The tariff was liberalised and rationalised with explicit protection for textiles, and duty-free entry for capital goods. As a result this period was one of rapid economic growth and even greater inequality. The economy became much more closely oriented commercially and financially to the USA.

When Diaz came to power there were only 640 kilometres of railway: at the end there were over 19,000 (as compared with 25,000 today). These railways not only increased internal communication but linked with ports and with the US network of railways. The railways constructed by Diaz did a great deal to improve the operation of a market economy and stimulated economic growth in many ways. Before that internal freight transport was confined to mules or lumbering wooden *carros* and passenger transport was on foot, mules, horses or horsedrawn carriages. Coatsworth (1981) has argued, using the counterfactual technique of the new economic history, that the 'social saving', i.e. the relative contribution of railway freight transport to Mexican growth potential, was much greater than that of railways in the USA, UK or Russia. Private investors in the railways did relatively badly, because of frozen freight rates and other regulations (see Pletcher 1958).

Apart from railways, the Diaz administration improved ports and started a system of telegraphs and telephones. These, like the railways, helped promote economic activity but also were instruments of law and order, which helped the central administration to exercise effective power, transport troops, and monitor local developments with much greater accuracy.

The land policy of Diaz did not depend much on new legislation. He simply used the framework created by the liberals in the 1857 Constitution. The Diaz regime took over 85 per cent of the Indian communal lands, which were distributed to cronies, or to wealthy local and foreign investors. Under the laws of 1883 and 1894 land was given to survey companies, much of it land which Indians had held without a clear title. Survey companies got 24 million hectares in this way. 55 million hectares of communal land were sold at an average price of 32 cents a hectare. Most of the land went to very large holders, so that by 1910, 834 haciendas possessed 90 per cent of the land. W.R. Hearst alone owned 3 million hectares in Chihuahua and 10,000 Americans had ranches in Mexico. During the Diaz regime, there was a big increase in the output of raw materials for domestic industry and for export, and of livestock production. The hitherto underdeveloped areas in the North of the country and in Yucatan were opened to large-scale agriculture. Some observers have suggested that food production suffered from land reallocation, but Coatsworth (1976) argues that per capita food production rose during the Porfiriato.

Foreigners were allowed to exploit Mexican mineral resources without paying taxes except a stamp duty. As a result the oil industry was dominated by three foreign groups under Doheny, Rockefeller and Lord Cowdray. Duties on the export of minerals were abolished. Mineral and manufacturing output boomed during this period. Mineral exports were greatly diversified and the value of textile sales rose from 8 million pesos in 1876 to 30 million in 1892.

Silver output more than doubled in the last two decades of the regime, and other minerals rose much faster. Mineral output as a whole rose by 7 per cent a year in the Porfiriato. This is all the more striking as output in the 1880s had been no higher than in 1810. The Porfirian expansion of mineral output depended on the growth in railways and a switch from sixteenth- to nineteenth-century mining technology.

During the Porfiriato, exports rose in volume by 6.1 per cent a year – a great deal faster than GDP. Exports were greatly diversified from the 1890s onward. Non-precious metals rose from 21 per cent of exports in 1877 to 54 per cent in 1911.

By 1911 Mexico had attracted close to $2 billion of foreign investment, or about five times as much as in 1877. Vernon (1963) suggests that foreign investment provided two-thirds of the capital in the industrial and service sectors. Half of it came from the United States.

About half of the foreign investment was in railway or government bonds – a good many of these were defaulted and equivalent to grants. More profitable for foreigners were investments in mining – precious metals, copper, lead, zinc, graphite and antimony – or in cattle, hides, cotton, chickpeas, rubber, vanilla, sugar, guayule (a source of rubber), henequen (sisal), chicle and ixtle (a hard fibre), which became export products. Vernon reports on an enquiry in 1914 which shows some measure of foreign ownership in 25 of 27 large manufacturing concerns in Mexico.

Mexican exports and industry were stimulated during the Porfiriato by accidental external changes which were by no means the result of Mexican policy. The *de facto* devaluation of the peso greatly increased the profitability of mineral and agricultural exports. For more than two centuries the relationship of gold and silver prices had been stable. But in the 1870s, Germany and several other countries demonetised silver and put large amounts of it on the market, and US production of silver increased greatly so that the price fell by half. The ratio of silver to gold value by weight was 16:1 in 1870 and fell to 34:1 in 1905 (Ortiz Mena, 1942). This led to a corresponding fall in the value of the peso against the major world currencies. During this period, Mexican money wages remained fairly stable, partly because of the repression of the labour movement and the expulsion of Indians from the land.

There were, however, some adverse effects from the continuous devaluation of the currency and a Monetary Commission was set up which led to a change in policy. The Commission found against the existing system for the following reasons (Casasus, 1905). The continuous rise in import prices was beginning to have inflationary effects in Mexico and threatened to set off a spiral of wage and price increases such as had been induced by paper money and floating exchange rates in Argentina. Inflation would eventually damage the competitive position of Mexico. Devaluation raised the burden of foreign debt service. The fluctuations and uncertainty about exchange rates created difficulties for banks, foreign investors and for government revenues. Mexico introduced sliding-scale import duties in 1902 to compensate for this. The Commission suggested that if Mexico adopted the gold standard, it would help to stabilise the silver price.

Limantour, the Finance Minister from 1893 to 1911, dominated economic policy, and ran a series of budget surpluses from 1894 to 1910 with a cumulative total of about 150 million pesos. He greatly increased Mexico's credit rating, and was able to reduce the interest rate on foreign debt from 8 per cent in 1888 to 4.4 per cent in 1910. From the 1880s onwards banking was greatly expanded under the influence of the 1884 Code of Commerce and the 1897 Banking Law. In 1884 the Banco Nacional de Mexico, a Franco-Egyptian venture, was set up. This bank, and others, were empowered to issue banknotes. There was no central bank of issue.

In 1905, Mexico adopted the gold standard at a parity of 1:32, suspended free coinage of silver, prohibited import of coins, created paper money, and set up a currency stabilisation fund. In the next two years $60 million of silver was exported. By 1911, silver constituted only 10 per cent of the currency. This policy had a short-term deflationary impact on economic activity and its expected long-term impact was interrupted by the Mexican revolution.

During the 33 years of the Porfiriato, GDP grew at 3.5 per cent a year (Table 3) and per capita real income almost doubled. Inequality increased, land holding became even more concentrated in the hands of large proprietors, and about a seventh was in the hands of foreigners by 1910. Mining and manufacturing were substantially expanded, but ownership was largely foreign. The Indian population lost most of its communal land, and a bigger proportion had to enter the labour market as peons or labourers, thus putting a downward pressure on wages. The regime did little for popular education, reserving most of the opportunities there were for the elite. Three-quarters of the population were illiterate. The military became smaller in number, but the old generals who dominated politics shared the lavish spoils available, and operated a repressive political system. The new bureaucratic elite of *cientificos* nurtured by Limantour were influenced by contemporary ideas of Comte and Spencer about the survival of the fittest. Hence there was a more or less racist contempt for the Indian population and a willingness to put key sections of the economy in the hands of more 'civilized' foreigners.

5) The revolution, its aftermath and consolidation 1911–1940

By 1910, Diaz was 80 years old, and many of his cronies in the ruling political elite were also reaching geriatric status. There were therefore all the normal stirrings from (a) ambitious people who wanted to step in their shoes without necessarily wanting to change the system. There were also (b) liberals (like Madero, Diaz' successor) who aspired to a more democratic political system or a more integrated society than the *cientificos* wanted. There was (c) a nationalist element which felt that too many of the benefits of the Diaz regime went to foreigners, and finally (d) the confiscation of Indian lands and impoverishment of Indians made this underclass ready to revolt in some regions, particularly the South, when a charismatic leader like Zapata was there to lead them.

Thus it was a combination of interests which pushed Diaz into exile in 1911 and gave the Presidency to a succession of men who up to 1934 might be said to have represented mainly interests (a) and (b) above. However, the dynamics of revolution brought many parts of the country into armed revolt, with populist leaders like Villa taking effective power away from the centre, and US intervention complicating the situation further.

The power of the Presidency was weak. Between 1913 and 1931, two presidents (Madero and Carranza), and one president elect (Obregón) were assassinated, one was shot at and many leaders disappeared violently. Between 1911 and 1920 Mexico was in a state of civil war.

As a result, political compromises were made which obscured the nature of the polity. Thus President Carranza, a conservative landowner, accepted the 1917 constitution which prescribed land reform, national ownership of subsoil rights, free education, the rights of labour, popular welfare and democracy. These progressive provisions of the constitution were successfully advocated by the leading leftist and nationalist politicians of the day.

There was indeed some action towards land reform and popular education under the 'bourgeois' presidents, but, no effective element of socialism or even very strong action against foreign interests outside the agrarian sector, until the Presidency of Cárdenas in 1934–40. During the revolution there had been little ideology and no dominant party, but rather a diffused process of struggle for power by improvised political groups, regional and local bosses and self-appointed generals.

The revolution had very damaging effects on the economy. More than a million people were killed. Agricultural and manufacturing output fell. The traditional mining sector was so adversely affected that output in 1921 was only 60 per cent of that in 1910. However, there was an amazingly large growth of petroleum production from 0.5 million tons in 1910 to a peak of 26 million in 1921 when Mexico became the largest producer outside the United States.

During the revolution, the various governments took to issuing paper currency on a large scale. Most of the banking system was bankrupt. Public finance was in chaos and by 1916 the exchange rate had fallen to less than a tenth of its 1910 level. All foreign debt was in default.

The 1920s was a period of stabilisation and deflationary policy in which per capita output showed little progress at all. Mexican oil became less profitable in the 1920s after the new wells in Venezuela came on stream. Foreign investment in oil was adversely affected by Mexico's foreign debt record, by nationalist legislation, and the limitation of company rights in the subsoil. By 1929 oil output had fallen three-quarters from the 1921 peak.

During the presidency of Calles and of the two provisional and one elected presidents who succeeded him under his tutelage, the government managed to run a budget surplus in most years, not by increasing revenue but by reducing expenditure. The government was continuously urged to cut expenditure by the foreign creditors organised in the Committee of Foreign Bondholders in 1919, but in spite of much negotiation, foreign debt service was not resumed. The gold standard had been restored in 1918, and a good deal of paper money was replaced by gold and silver coins. In keeping with the general deflationary climate, the demands of labour unions were suppressed. Very little land was distributed to peasants.

The response to the 1929–33 crisis was a deflationary one. Monetary policy was tightened and government expenditure was cut further. However, the tariff was raised in 1930 and the gold standard was abandoned in mid-1931 when the exchange reserve had run out. The exchange rate fell from 2.15 pesos to the dollar to 3.6 by 1933. Total output fell by 20 per cent from 1929 to 1934. The purchasing power of exports, of which minerals were a major portion, declined by 50 per cent.

Under Calles, the nature of the Mexican political system began to change. It was he who effectively created the basis for a monolithic party as the institutional bedrock of political power, thus overcoming centrifugal local and regional political forces. Calles also ended the political power of the army and the church. In fact he persecuted the church to a degree which sparked off the Cristero wars in the central plateau in the late 1920s. A crude attempt to persecute religion and the church in the Southeast was the subject of Graham Greene's novel, *The Power and the Glory*.

Calles formalised the party structure by giving corporatist-type representation to peasant interests (with all *ejido* members being theoretical members), to labour (in the officially favoured trade unions) and to civil servant and professional interests. There was originally an army section in the party, but this was later merged with the third section. This third section of the PRI, today called CNOP (Confederacion Nacional de Organizaciones Populares) brings together the middle-class professional organizations and all sorts of associations for political purposes which do not fit into the labour or peasant sections.

It was in the 1920s that military expenditure was cut down to the low level it has since maintained, local armed unrest was ended, the power of the central government was consolidated, the financial mechanism was greatly strengthened, agricultural research was started, and there was some improvement in sanitation, irrigation and roads. In the 1920s, the first steps were taken to create a technocratic civil service which was politically committed to the existing government, capable of wielding significant power, and with career prospects which could lead to major public office and substantial financial rewards. The beginnings of a system of popular education were created by Vasconcelos.

In the 1920s and 1930s Mexico created many powerful financial institutions to foster development. The Bank of Mexico started operations in 1925 and came to have much wider functions than a normal central bank, with a very able and powerful staff of economists and engineers. In 1926 the Agricultural Credit Bank was set up, and in the 1930s the Cárdenas administration created the Nacional Financiera, the Banco de Credito Ejidal, Banco Nacional de Fomento Cooperativo and the Banco Nacional de Comercio Exterior. In many ways the control of these financial institutions over the economy resembled that of similar organisations in Mussolini's Italy. But in the developing world, Mexico was a pioneer. Turkey also developed a number of development banks at this period, but none of them was as powerful as the Nacional Financiera, and they were not as well staffed as in Mexico. From the first, Mexico paid great attention to training the higher personnel of these institutions and gave many scholarships for study abroad, particularly in the USA.

The Presidency of Cárdenas in 1934 represented a change in regime. He embarked on a policy of public works, moderate budget deficits and greatly eased monetary policy. The discount rate fell from 7 per cent in 1931 to 3 per cent in 1937, and there was massive creation of credit. The supply of paper money and bank deposits rose from 259 million pesos in 1929 to 864 million in 1940. In 1935–36 the limit on the issuing power of the Bank of Mexico was removed. There was a six-year plan for 1934–40. A great deal of land was distributed to the peasants and labour unions were encouraged to enrol as many urban workers as possible. The public works programme for 1935–40 involved expenditures of over a billion pesos through special public agencies – 165 million went on roads, 144 million on irrigation and 190 million on rural credit. This provided a good basis for later expansion of output, but the output growth in the Cárdenas period was not impressive by the standards of later years. Total output in 1940 was less than 20 per cent higher than in 1926.

Total land redistribution from 1915 to 1940 was 25.6 million hectares, which is a good deal less than the 79 million hectares in sales and gifts by Porfirio Diaz. The basic law on land distribution dates from 1915. It indicated that the allocation of landed property and natural resources was a matter for the nation to decide in the light of social justice and the public interest. It annulled the title to a good many of the lands acquired under the Diaz regime, it prohibited foreigners from holding land within 100 kilometres of frontiers and 50 kilometres of the coast, and reaffirmed the prohibition of church landholdings. Later, the Agrarian Code gave the right to expropriate private land within a seven kilometre radius of the beneficiary village. Within this area small private properties ('pequenas propiedades') were protected, but they were defined rather generously as units of 150 hectares of irrigated cotton land up to 5,000 hectares for the cultivation of guayule.

Private holdings for livestock pasture were permitted up to 50,000 hectares. The land which was redistributed was not handed over to individual peasants, but was destined to create collective 'ejidos'. Within these, land was allocated to individual peasants but it could not be sold, mortgaged or transferred. Pasture and forest land of ejidos remained collective property. In some ejidos, cultivation was done collectively. This was intended to be a return to the traditional patterns of Indian landholding. It was felt that distribution to individuals might lead to resale on a large scale and negate the distributive objectives. This pattern of landownership also gave the government political leverage. But it had clear disadvantages from the standpoint of agricultural credit and production incentives.

Table 4   Land Redistribution 1915–64 and Land Distribution Resolutions 1964 onwards

President	Term ended	Hectares Distributed (000s) By term	Cumulative Distribution	Percent of Mexican Surface area By term	Cumulative Percentage of Mexican Surface Area
Carranza	May 1920	168	168	0.1	0.1
De la Huerta	Sep. 1920	34	202	–	0.1
Obregón	Nov. 1924	1,100	1,302	0.6	0.7
Calles	Nov. 1928	2,973	4,275	1.5	2.2
Portes Gil	Feb. 1930	1,708	5,982	0.9	3.1
Ortiz Rubio	Sep. 1932	945	6,927	0.5	3.5
Rodríguez	Nov. 1934	791	7,718	0.4	3.9
Cárdenas	Nov. 1940	18,786	26,504	9.6	13.5
Avila Camacho	Nov. 1946	7,288	33,791	3.7	17.3
Alemán	Nov. 1952	4,633	38,425	2.4	19.6
Ruiz Cortines	Nov. 1958	6,057	44,482	3.1	22.7
López Mateos	Nov. 1964	8,870	53,352	4.5	27.2
Díaz Ordaz	Nov. 1970	24,738	78,090	12.6	39.9
Echeverría	Nov. 1976	12,774	90,864	6.5	46.4
López Portillo	Nov. 1982	6,398	97,262	3.3	49.7
De la Madrid[a]	Nov. 1988	1,558	98,819	0.8	50.5

Note: a)   Figures as of February 18, 1985.

Source: INEGI (1985), Vol. I, Table 7.4. Figures for 1964 onwards apparently refer to Presidential Resolutions; distributions since 1964 were probably a good deal smaller than the Resolutions, e.g. about 9 million hectares under Díaz Ordaz.

Cárdenas built on the political foundations which Calles had created and pushed the political system in a leftist nationalist direction from which it has since retreated *de facto* but still upholds rhetorically. He gave official sanction to the indigenous movement which stressed the value of the Indian element in Mexican culture. There were support programmes for Indian communities, dramatic murals on public buildings and a new emphasis on archaeological evidence of the Indian civilisations. This was designed to promote national integration and to mitigate the sense of anomie in the Indian population which had been considered an inferior race in the colonial period and in the Porfiriato.

Cárdenas reinforced the constitutional power and legitimacy of the presidency, by exiling Calles and ensuring that former presidents could not be reelected or continue to exercise power over their successors. He honoured this principle by handing over his own office constitutionally to a handpicked successor who was well to the right of himself in the political spectrum. Non-reelection had been a tenet of the Madero uprising in 1910, at the end of the long Diaz rule. It was broken only once, by Obregón, in 1928 but he was assassinated before reassuming office.

Cárdenas transferred nearly one-third of the haciendas' arable land to Indians and the poorer mestizos. Most of the land taken by the state for redistribution was seized without compensation. A very small amount was paid for in bonds which were worth a fraction of their nominal value. The *ejidos* received their land free. Much greater compensation was paid to foreign than to Mexican landlords after protracted negotiations which ended only in the 1950s. This land reform effort helped to legitimise the Mexican political system.

Cárdenas satisfied Mexican nationalist aspirations by taking over the foreign-owned oil companies in 1938. This led to a break in diplomatic relations with the UK in 1938, and severe strains on relations with the USA. However, the US government under Roosevelt was bent on a 'good neighbour' policy towards Latin America, and did not pursue the interventionist policy of its predecessors. After 1938, Mexico did not allow foreign investment in oil. This had substantial economic costs, but an element of nationalist pride was a major part of the new political system, and acted as a substitute for other types of socialist experiment. It did not prevent Mexico from subsequent borrowing abroad on a massive scale, and only partially cut off access to foreign technology, because there has been large foreign direct investment in Mexican industry, in spite of governmental restrictions.

Cárdenas endorsed the Calles policy of building up indigenous financial institutions and administrative capacity, and also stressed the role of the state in planning major investment decisions and in allocating capital.

Although the Cárdenas policies were not particularly favourable to domestic capitalist interests, and were distinctly pro-labour, there were no acts of nationalisation *vis-à-vis* the domestic industrial sector, and Cárdenas picked a successor, Avila Camacho, who was much more favourable to private sector interests in both industry and agriculture. The private sector was subsequently favoured by many types of government action and by the docility of government trade unions with regard to wage levels. Hence the Cárdenas moves to change the distribution of property and power were not socialist, but were minimal requirements for a new political system with greater legitimacy and staying power than anywhere else in Latin America, in an economy which still remained very unequal.

Between 1910 and 1940, GDP growth was much slower than in the Porfiriato, at 1.1 per cent a year. Population growth was slower because of deaths (and births foregone) in the revolution. Per capita growth was less than 0.3 per cent a year compared with 2.1 per cent during the Porfiriato.

The main institutional consequences of this period of revolution and political change were:

a. the creation of an effective one-party government encompassing most of the interest groups in the population, making policy through discreet processes of consultation, consensus and cooptation. Enormous power is concentrated in the President who, since 1934, has been elected for a single six-year term. The traditional colonial sources of power – the church and the army – no longer exercise political influence;

b. a substantial role for government in the production process and government dominance of the financial system. Administration of this direct state economic role and consultation with the private sector is exercised by a group of highly paid *tecnicos* who are often educated abroad at government expense;

c.   a private sector protected and favoured by government and cooperating quite amicably through discreet corporatist channels. Because of the open border, it is able to export substantial amounts of capital quickly when its fears are aroused;

d.   a chary attitude towards foreign direct investment, whose sphere of activity is carefully regulated with a pragmatic view of the national interest;

e.   the assertion of a national identity in which Indians are (at least in theory) fully integrated, a populist emphasis on the welfare of the masses via instruments controlled by government, particularly the communal *ejido*, education, health and other social welfare benefits.

Finally, in view of the reemergence of the debt problem since 1982, it is useful to recall Mexico's previous experience with this problem which had been a running sore in relations with foreign powers since the 1850s, and which was successfully cleared up in the 1940s.

Mexico had a long history of debt negotiation after the suspension of debt service in 1914. The International Committee of Bankers on Mexico was founded in 1919 to represent the collective interests of United States, French and United Kingdom bondholders and other creditors who respectively held 29, 28 and 21 per cent of Mexican debt. Their main negotiator was T.W. Lamont of the J.P. Morgan Bank. The bankers put strong pressure on Mexico to follow a deflationary policy and cut government expenditure. Lamont signed four agreements with successive Mexican Ministers of Finance (de la Huerta) in 1922, (Pani) in 1925, (Montes de Oca) in 1930, and (Suarez) in 1942. In the first of these Mexico agreed unrealistically to pay fully all capital and capitalized interest on government and railway debt (around $707 million), and in return was given five years' grace and 40 years (1928–68) to pay for amortization. In the 1925 agreement the railway assets and the corresponding debt were returned to private hands, so that the capital was scaled down. In the third agreement, interest arrears were written off, and debt service was geared to capacity to pay. In 1931 debt service was paid in blocked pesos and in 1932 it was suspended. In the final 1942 agreement, the foreign public debt claims were written down from $510 to $50 million. In 1943, in another agreement the $500 million foreign petroleum companies' claims for their nationalized assets were settled for $24 million (plus $13.5 million already paid to the Sinclair interests in 1940), and in 1946 the $558 million railway company claims were settled for $51 million (see Bazant, 1968).

References

O. Altimir, 'La medicion de la poblacion economicamente activa de Mexico, 1950–1970', *Demografia y Economica*, vol. VIII (i), 1974, pp. 50–83.

P.J. Bakewell, *Silver Mining and Society in Colonial Mexico, Zacatecas 1546–1700*, Cambridge University Press, 1971.

Banamex, *Mexico Social 1985–1986*, Mexico, 1986.

Bank of Mexico, *Indicadores Economicos*, May 1986.

A. Bauer, 'The Church and Spanish American Agrarian Structures, 1765–1865', *The Americas*, July 1971.

J. Bazant, *Historia de la Deuda Exterior de Mexico 1823–1946*, El Colegio de Mexico, 1968.

J. Bazant, *Alienation of Church Wealth in Mexico*, Cambridge University Press, 1971.

M.D. Bernstein, *The Mexican Mining Industry 1890–1950*, State University of New York, 1964.

L. Bethell, ed., *Cambridge History of Latin America*, Vols I, II, Cambridge University Press, 1984, Vol. III, 1985.

W. Borah, *New Spain's Century of Depression*, University of California Press, Berkeley, 1951.

W. Borah and S.F. Cook, *The Aboriginal Population of Central Mexico on the Eve of the Spanish Conquest*, University of California Press, Berkeley, 1963.

D.A. Brading, *Miners and Merchants in Bourbon Mexico 1763–1810*, Cambridge University Press,1971.

N. Butlin, *Our Original Aggression*, Allen & Unwin, Sydney, 1983.

J. Canga Argüelles, *Diccionario de Hacienda*, Calero y Portocarrero, Madrid, 1834.

J.D. Casasus, *Currency Reform in Mexico, Reports Presented to the Monetary Commission*, Mexico, 1905.

F. Chevalier, *Land and Society in Colonial Mexico: The Great Hacienda*, University of California Press, Berkeley, 1963.

J.H. Coatsworth, 'Anotaciones sobre la Producción de Alimentos Durante el Porfiriato', *Historia Mexicana*, vol. XXVI 1976.

J.H. Coatsworth, 'Obstacles to Economic Growth in Nineteenth Century Mexico', *American Historical Review* (83), 1978.

J.H. Coatsworth, *Growth Against Development: The Economic Impact of Railroads in Porfirian Mexico*, Northern Illinois University Press, Dekalb, Illinois, 1981.

J.D. Cockcroft, *Mexico: Class Formation, Capital Accumulation, and the State*, MRP, New York, 1983.

A. Collantes de Téran, *Sevilla en la Baja Edad Media: la ciudad y sus hombres*, Ayuntamiento de Sevilla, 1977.

N.D. Cook, *Demographic Collapse in Indian Peru, 1520-1620*, Cambridge University Press, 1981.

S.F. Cook and L.B. Simpson, *The Population of Central Mexico in the Sixteenth Century*, University of California Press, Berkeley, 1948.

H. Cortes, *La Conquête de Méxique*, Maspero, Paris, 1982.

D. Cosio Villegas, *Historia moderna de Mexico. El Porfiriato: vida economica*, Hermes, Mexico, 1965.

R.T. Davies, *The Golden Century of Spain*, Macmillan, London, 1964.

W.M. Denevan, ed., *The Native Population of the Americas in 1492*, Wisconsin, 1976.

E. Florescano, 'La politica mercantilista españolo y sus implicaciones economicas en la Nueva España', *Historia Mexicana*, January–March, 1968.

A.G. Frank, *Mexican Agriculture 1521–1630: Transformation of the Mode of Production*, Cambridge University Press, 1979.

C. Gibson, *The Aztecs Under Spanish Rule*, Stanford University Press, 1964.

P. Gregory, *The Myth of Market Failure*, Johns Hopkins, Baltimore, 1986.

E.J. Hamilton, *American Treasure and the Price Revolution in Spain 1501–1650*, Harvard University Press, 1934.

R.D. Hansen, *The Politics of Mexican Development*, Johns Hopkins, Baltimore, 1971.

I. Herrera Canales, *El Comercio Exterior de Mexico 1821–1875*, Colegio de Mexico, 1977.

A. de Humboldt, *Ensayo Politico sobre el Reino de la Nueva España*, Porrua, Mexico, 1978.

INEGI, *Anuario Estadistico de los Estados Unidos Mexicanos*, Mexico D.F., 1984.

INEGI, *Estadistícas Históricas de Mexico*, 2 vols, Mexico D.F., 1985.

J.I. Israel, *Race, Class and Politics in Colonial Mexico 1610–1670*, Oxford University Press, 1975.

A.V. Judges, 'Educational Ideas, Practice and Institutions', in A. Goodwin, ed., *The New Cambridge Modern History*, Vol. VIII, *The American and French Revolutions 1763–93*, Cambridge University Press, 1965.

D.B. Keesing, 'Employment and Lack of Employment in Mexico, 1900–70' in J.W. Wilkie and K. Ruddle, *Statistical Abstract of Latin America Supplement 6*, UCLA, Los Angeles, 1977.

T. King, *Mexico: Industrialization and Trade Policies Since 1940*, Oxford University Press, 1970.

D.M. Ladd, *The Mexican Nobility at Independence 1780–1826*, University of Texas, Austin, 1976.

A. Lavrin, 'The Execution of the Law of Consolidacion in New Spain: Economic Aims and Results', *Hispanic American Historical Review*, February, 1963.

F. Lopez Camara, *La estructura economica y social de Mexico en la epoca de la Reforma*, Siglo Veintiuno, Mexico, 1967.

A. Maddison, *Monitoring the World Economy 1820–1992*, OECD Development Centre, Paris, 1994.

A. Maddison and Associates, *The Political Economy of Poverty, Equity and Growth: Brazil and Mexico*, Oxford University Press, New York, 1992.

L.H. Morgan, *Ancient Society*, Holt, New York, 1877.

M. Morineau, *Incroyables Gazettes et Fabuleux Metaux*, Cambridge University Press, 1985.

S.E. Morison and H.S. Commager, *The Growth of the American Republic*, 2 vols, Oxford University Press, New York, 1942.

R. Ortiz Mena, *La Moneda Mexicana*, UNAM, Mexico, 1942.

D.M. Pletcher, 'The Fall of Silver in Mexico 1870–1910 and its Effect on American Investment', *Journal of Economic History*, Spring, 1958.

J.M. Quiros, *Memoria de estatuto. Idea de la riqueza que daban la masa circulante de Nueva España* (Vera Cruz 1817) reprinted in *Coleccion de documentos para la historia del comercio exterior de Mexico* (Mexico 1959), VI.

C.W. Reynolds, *The Mexican Economy: Twentieth Century Structure and Growth*, Yale, 1970.

A. Riding, *Distant Neighbours*, Knopf, New York, 1985.

W. Robertson, *The History of America*, T. White, Cork, 1778.

A. Rosenblat, *La Poblacion Indigena de America Desde 1492 Hasta la Actualidad,* ICE, Buenos Aires, 1945.

A. Rosenblat, *La Poblacion de America en 1492*, Colegio de Mexico, Mexico D.F., 1967.

F. Rosenzweig, ed., *Fuerzo de Trabajo y Actividad Economica Por Sectores, Estadistícas Economicas del Porfiriato*, El Colegio de Mexico, Mexico D.F., no date (1960?).

F. Rosenzweig, 'La economia Novo-Hispaña al comenzar el siglo XIX', *Revista de Ciencias Politicas y Sociales*, UNAM, July–September, 1963.

F. Rosenzweig, 'El desarrollo economico de Mexico de 1877 a 1911', *El Trimestre Economico*, July–September, 1965.

W.T. Sanders, 'Population, Agricultural History, and Societal Evolution in Mesoamerica', in B. Spooner, ed., *Population Growth: Anthropological Implications*, MIT, Cambridge, 1972.

W.T. Sanders, 'The Population of the Central Mexican Symbiotic Region, the Basin of Mexico, and the Teotihuacán Valley in the Sixteenth Century', in: Denevan (1976).

A. Smith, *The Wealth of Nations*, Cannan's ed., Chicago, 1976.

P.H. Smith, *The Labyrinths of Power*, Princeton University Press, 1979.

L. Solis, 'La influencia del mercantilismo español en la vida economica de America Latina: Un intento de interpretacion', *El Trimestre Economico*, April–June, 1969.

L. Solis, *La Realidad Mexicana: Retrovision y Perspectivas*, Siglo Veintiuno, Mexico, 1984.

J. Soustelle, *La Vida Cotidiana de los Aztecas*, Fondo de Cultura, Mexico D.F., 1977.

J.J. TePaske and H.S. Klein, 'The Seventeenth Century Crisis in New Spain: Myth or Reality?', *Past and Present*, February, 1981.

R.P. Thomas, 'A Quantitative Approach to the Study of the Effects of British Imperial Policy upon Colonial Welfare: Some Preliminary Findings', *Journal of Economic History*, March, 1965.

E. van Young, *Hacienda and Market in Eighteenth Century Mexico*, University Of California Press, Berkeley, 1981.

J. Vazquez Gomes, *Prontuario de Gobernantes de Mexico, 1325–1976*, Edicion del Autor, Mexico City, 1977.

R. Vernon, *The Dilemma of Mexico's Development*, Harvard University Press, 1963.

R. Vernon, ed., *Public Policy and Private Enterprise in Mexico*, Harvard University Press, 1964.

J.W. Wilkie, *The Mexican Revolution: Federal Expenditure and Social Change since 1910*, University of California Press Berkeley, 1970.

E. Wolf, *Sons of the Shaking Earth*, University of Chicago Press, 1959.

R.A. Zambardino, 'Mexico's Population in the Sixteenth Century: Demographic Anomaly or Mathematical Illusion?', *Journal of Interdisciplinary History*, Summer, 1980.

Modern Asian Studies **23**, 4 (1989), pp. 645–670. Printed in Great Britain.

Dutch Income in and from Indonesia 1700–1938

ANGUS MADDISON

University of Groningen

I. Introduction

This paper attempts to establish broad orders of magnitude for the colonial period as a whole, and the results are necessarily rough and tentative. Nevertheless, this kind of quantitative macroestimation is useful in illuminating the plausible size of the magnitudes which are usually implicit in qualitative assessment.

II. Summary

The principal findings are that Dutch income in and from Indonesia probably amounted to about 1.4 per cent of Indonesian domestic product in 1700 and rose to about 17 per cent in 1921–38 (see Table 1). Until 1870, about 90 per cent of this Dutch income in Indonesia was remitted out of the country. After that the economy was opened up to private enterprise, the non-governmental Dutch presence grew, and a higher proportion of Dutch income in Indonesia went to local con-

TABLE I

European Income in Indonesia

Percentages of Indonesian net domestic product					
	All 'European' income		All 'European' income	Income of 'European' residents	Other 'European' income
1700	1.4	1870	7.6		
1780	1.2	1913	14.2		
1820	2.4	1928	20.2		
1830	2.0	1938	15.5		
1840	7.1	Average 1921–38	16.9	12.2	4.7

Source: 1921–38 from Polak, other figures from Table B1 below; 1921–38 figures are at current prices other figures at constant 1928 prices.

0026–749X/89/ $5.00 + .00

TABLE 2
Indonesian Exports and Export Surplus per Head of Total Population of Indonesia

	Annual Averages				
	Commodity exports per capita in current guilders	Adjusted export surplus per capita in current guilders	Adjusted export surplus per capita in 1928 guilders	Adjusted export surplus as percent of NDP in 1928 prices	Commodity exports as percent of NDP in 1928 prices
1698–1700	0.47	0.18	0.33	0.7	1.8
1778–1780	0.54	0.30	0.45	0.9	1.7
1838–1842	2.73	1.46	3.32	6.3	17.9
1868–1872	3.80	2.14	3.90	7.4	18.4
1911–1915	13.34	4.64	4.81	7.6	21.9
1926–1930	25.19	8.55	8.55	10.3	29.4
1921–1938		6.67		10.6(a)	

(a) at current prices.

Source: 1838 onwards estimated from Appendices B and C, from Mitchell, and Elson; 1698–1780 derived from Glamann adjusted by Van Stuijvenberg and Vrijer wholesale price movement. For 1925–38 the export surplus (from Polak's balance of payments table) is already adjusted for movements of treasure (gold and silver). These averaged 5 per cent of the commodity trade surplus in 1925–29, so for earlier years, we reduced the trade surplus by 5 per cent to eliminate the possible effect of an inflow of treasure to Indonesia.

sumption and accumulation of asset claims. In 1921–38 about 62 per cent of it was remitted—about 10.6 per cent of Indonesian domestic product (see Table 2). In spite of the long and large net drain of income from Indonesia over more than three centuries, foreign claims on assets in Indonesia were about 150 per cent of Indonesian GDP in 1937 (Callis, p. 36).

Income remitted from Indonesia represented a 1 per cent addition to Dutch domestic product in 1700, about 5 per cent from 1840 to 1870 and rose to around 8 per cent in 1921–38 (see Table 3). From 1840 onwards this flow was the bulk of Dutch foreign income, whereas in the eighteenth century, when total income from abroad was proportionately just as high, the Indonesian contribution was much smaller.

In India, where the literature on the colonial 'drain' is much more voluminous, the flow to the colonial power was relatively much smaller and the economy much less involved in international trade. In the interwar period, 1921–38 (at its peak), British income in India was about 5 per cent of Indian domestic product, and the remitted part was about 1.7 per cent (see Table 4). In the same period this income represented an addition of about 0.8 per cent to U.K. domestic product

DUTCH INCOME IN AND FROM INDONESIA   647

TABLE 3
Dutch Income Derived from Indonesia 1700–1938

	Adjusted Indonesian export surplus at current prices annual averages million guilders	Dutch net domestic product at current prices million guilders	Indonesian surplus as ratio of Dutch NDP (per cent)	All income from abroad as per cent of Dutch NDP
1698–1700	(2.5)	237 (a)	1.1	n.a.
1778–1780	(5.0)	287 (b)	1.7	6.8
1868–1872	56.1	1,103 (c)	5.5	n.a.
1911–1915	222.9	2,566	8.7	8.8
1926–1930	494.8	5,574	8.9	10.9
1921–1938	403.3	5,054	8.0	8.6
1948–1950		15,117		1.0

(a) 1700; (b) 1780; (c) 1870.

Source: Export surpluses calculated as described in Table 2 for 1838 onwards. For 1698–1700 and 1778–80 derived from Glamann as described in text. Dutch NDP 1700–1870 from Table 8; 1911–38 from CBS 1970. Total income from abroad is available for 1900 onwards from CBS 1970. For 1780 I used Riley's p. 84 figure of 350 million guilders for Dutch holdings of foreign loans. This capital was assumed to yield 4 per cent, i.e., 5.5 per cent of NDP. In addition, there was East India Company income and some smaller income from the West India Company.

TABLE 4
Indian Exports and Export Surplus per Head of Total Indian Population

	Commodity exports per capita in current rupees	Balance on trade and treasure per capita in current rupees	Balance on trade and treasure per capita in current guilders	Balance on trade and treasure as per cent of NDP at current prices	Commodity exports as per cent of NDP in current prices
1838–1842	0.58	0.17	0.21	n.a.	n.a.
1868–1872	2.17	0.43	0.53	1.0	5.2
1911–1915	7.28	1.08	0.87	1.3	9.0
1926–1930	9.28	0.91	0.83	0.9	9.6
1921–1938	7.51	1.34		1.7	9.6

Source: Commodity Exports from Chaudhuri, 1983, pp. 833, 873, 837 and 839 for successive periods. Treasure from Dutt, vol, 2, p. 114. Chaudhuri, p. 873 and Statistical Abstracts for British India. The data refer to fiscal years.

(about one-tenth of the importance of the Indonesian flow to the Netherlands). The U.K. also had very substantial income from abroad from other sources in prewar years, of which the Indian contribution was only about one-sixth (see Table 5).

TABLE 5
British Income from India 1838–1938

	Indian surplus on trade and treasure at current prices £ million annual averages	UK net domestic product at current market prices £ million	Indian surplus as ratio of British NDP (per cent)	All property income from abroad as a ratio of British NDP
1838–1842	3.7			
1868–1872	10.9	976 (a)	1.1	3.6 (a)
1911–1915	21.9	2,339	0.9	8.0
1926–1930	22.4	4,273	0.5	5.5
1921–1938	33.9	4,317	0.8	4.5

(a) 1870

Source: Export surplus as in Table 4. Net domestic product and all property income from abroad calculated from Feinstein T12–13 (compromise estimate of GDP at factor cost), T8–9 (indirect taxes and subsidies) T4–7 (capital consumption), and T10–11 (property income from abroad).

III. The Merchant Capitalist Period (1602–1780)

The Dutch established themselves in Indonesia at the beginning of the seventeenth century by pushing out the Portuguese who had themselves displaced many of the indigenous and oriental traders whose Asia-wide trade had flourished before the arrival of the Europeans.

It is not clear whether Indonesian exports at the end of the merchant capitalist period were any more important proportionately than they were before the Europeans arrived, though the Dutch did introduce new export crops (sugar and coffee) in the eighteenth century.

The vehicle of Dutch expansion was a joint stock company of Dutch merchants (VOC founded in 1602). The East Indian Company operated on a monopolistic basis and did a more effective job than the Portuguese in destroying indigenous competitors.

Unlike the Portuguese, the Dutch never considered themselves to have a civilizing or evangelical role in Asia, but operated entirely on a commercial basis. This reduced the frictions with native rulers in Indonesia and also made inter-Asian trade easier. Thus they established a monopoly in trade with Japan via a trading post in Deshima after the Japanese had expelled the evangelical Portuguese. This privileged position in Japan lasted until 1853.

The VOC quickly established a territorial base in the Indies (Batavia 1619). This, together with trading posts in India, Formosa,

Japan, Ceylon and South Africa served as a centre for the so-called 'country' (inter-Asian) trade in which the Dutch played the biggest role in the seventeenth and most of the eighteenth century. The Batavian foothold also served as a base for territorial influence in most of Java. Control was first established in the coastal area (pasisir), in Bantam and the coffee growing area in the Preanger, and was gradually extended elsewhere in Java.

When the Dutch arrived in Java there were important sultanates in Bantam and Cheribon, and a central Javan kingdom of Mataram, but none of these had the extensive territorial range of the Moghul empire because their administrative and military organization was weaker, inland communications were poorer, and the institutional arrangements by which the ruling class squeezed a surplus from the population were also more feeble. The economy was much less monetized than that of India. Fiscal levies were in kind or in the form of labour services rather than land tax. The incidence of these was rather arbitrary and depended on local conditions. Within Indonesian villages, the control mechanisms for extracting tribute were weaker than in the caste-bound Indian villages with their clearer hierarchy and stronger religious sanctions. As a consequence of this, peasants probably worked less in Indonesia than in India, and also found it easier to migrate or overthrow rulers who imposed too great a squeeze.

It seems doubtful that in the merchant capitalist period the Dutch did much to increase the overall rate of fiscal squeeze. Their income was derived by capturing the income from trade previously enjoyed by Asian trading communities in coastal areas, and by appropriating to themselves part of the tribute previously levied by indigenous rulers in Java.

Glamann's figures on the value of trade, adjusted by the price indices of Posthumus and Van Stuijvenberg and Vrijer, suggest that the VOC's cargoes arriving in Amsterdam from the East as a whole rose in volume by 1.7 per cent a year in the 79 years from 1619–21 to 1698–1700. In the following 80 years to 1778–80, the expansion was much slower (0.1 per cent a year). Nevertheless the relative importance of the Eastern trade rose in the eighteenth century because non-colonial trade actually fell by 0.2 per cent a year (see Johan de Vries, p. 27).

By 1780, the Asian trade was about 12.5 per cent of total Dutch trade (Johan de Vries and Brugmans), and Brugmans suggests that the Indonesian component of this was about half. As the goods were collected from Indonesia with an increased degree of coercion, the profit margin was probably larger than in 1700. Imports from

Indonesia were probably about 3 per cent of Dutch domestic product and the favourable balance in 1780 represented about 1.7 per cent of Dutch GDP compared with about 1 per cent in 1700 (see Table 3).

The VOC went bankrupt at the end of the eighteenth century. This was partly because of bad trading results during wars with the U.K. but it was also induced by the fact that the servants of the company in the East were a thieving lot without adequate supervision in their work. They traded extensively on their own account and found various illicit channels to remit their profits unbeknown to the VOC.

Chaudhuri's (1978) figures suggest that the British East India Company's trading volume rose much faster (at about 1 per cent a year) than that of the Dutch Company from 1698–1700 to 1758–60 and by 1780 British EIC activity was bigger than that of the VOC.

There do not appear to be any estimates of the percentage of Indonesian trade and profits actually controlled by the VOC but it is significant that the British East India Co. controlled only a quarter of India's exports after the end of the eighteenth century (Chaudhuri 1983, p. 817).

Although the VOC monopoly was more strictly enforced in Indonesia than that of the EIC in India, Adam Smith (1776, Book IV, chapter 7) suggested that the role of private traders was significant:

Of all the expedients that can well be contrived to stunt the natural growth of a new colony, that of an exclusive company is undoubtedly the most effectual. This, however, has been the policy of Holland, though their company, in the course of the present century, has given up in many respects the exertion of their exclusive privilege.

IV. The Transition Period 1780–1830

The end of the eighteenth century was a bad period for the Dutch economy because the overall volume of trade was adversely affected by war, investment income from foreign bonds fell, the reopening of the port of Antwerp brought new competition, and the British eventually took control of all the major Dutch colonies whilst the Netherlands was under French hegemony. The U.K. took over a good deal of the previous Dutch role in inter-Asian trade.

The transition period 1780–1830 saw major changes in the Dutch territorial role in Indonesia particularly under Governor-General Daendels who centralized the administration in Batavia, ended the separate governorship in Semarang, abolished the sultancies of Bantam and Cheribon and strengthened the status of Dutch representatives at the successor states to Mataram (Jogjakarta and Soerakarta). When Raffles took over as Governor during the interlude of British power he continued these Westernizing principles in administration and law and introduced legislation for land taxation. This was the period when the British East India Company was also under the influence of philosophic Radicals determined to Westernize Asia. This attitude was changed in British India by the Mutiny of 1857. Thereafter the British gave up Westernization and temporized with Asian traditional law and custom.

In Indonesia the setback to Westernization occurred earlier. The Diponegoro revolt of 1825–30 was the Indonesian equivalent of the Indian Mutiny. Thereafter the Dutch stuck consistently to a policy of dual administration, using traditional rulers, law and custom as a major instrument of their rule.

It was also clear that Indonesia under a Westernized and liberal commercial system was unlikely to be profitable to the Netherlands. An open trading system would mean that most of the trading profits would be taken by more powerful British or American traders.

V. Fiscal Tribute, Bureaucratic Restrictions and Favouritism: 1830–1870

In response to these problems Governor Van den Bosch introduced the Cultivation System in the 1830s. In a non-monetized economy it was obviously difficult to raise the degree of exploitation quickly by raising land taxes, so the Netherlands exercised its claims on Indonesian income by mobilizing and increasing the traditional form of tribute of Indonesian rulers—forced deliveries of crops or labour services in lieu of land taxation. From 1816 to 1914 movement and residence of the indigenous and Chinese populations was controlled by a system of pass-laws designed to maintain labour discipline and enforce ethnic 'apartheid'.

The Cultivation System was remarkably successful in raising the income flow from Indonesia. In the 1830–70 period half of it went directly to the Dutch government as a fiscal tribute arising from production under the Cultivation System and from the profits of the Consignment System which gave a monopoly on transport of exported government crops to the NHM shipping company started by the Dutch king. In addition, the state derived substantial revenue by selling monopoly franchises ('farms') to dealers in opium and other products. The opium franchises were not ended until 1904.

Although private production was restricted and regulated, cultivation permits were granted to cronies and favourites of the authorities with a good many given by officials to themselves. Those with freest scope were the owners of the 'partikuliere landerijen', which were areas sold freehold either by the VOC or the Daendels and Raffles administrations to private individuals (European or Chinese) who thereafter were free of land tax and had all the labour service claims of native rulers. The native rulers in Jogjakarta and Soerakarta also granted leases to Europeans under government supervision, and government leases were given elsewhere for coffee cultivation on 'waste land' (an administratively elastic concept). Government dominated production in sugar and coffee, but most of the tobacco crop was in private European hands. The government was particularly generous in subsidizing the favoured individuals who constructed sugar factories (there were between 93 and 112 of these sugar contracts outstanding between 1840 and 1860). Not only did they enjoy high revenues because of guaranteed supplies of cane and sales outlets, but their enterprises were often started with interest-free government loans. Because of these loan expenditures, the government was actually making substantial losses on sugar until the mid 1840s. Finally the government made substantial incentive payments to its own officials (binnenlands bestuur) according to the yields of sugar, coffee, and indigo.

There were also substantial and bigger government incentive payments of this kind to officials of the parallel native administration (inlandsch bestuur), as well as less licit opportunities for squeeze all the way down fron the 76 Regents to the 34,000 village heads in Java. This last element of profit from the regime was not part of the drain from Indonesia, but probably strengthened class differentiation within the indigenous population. Traditional sanctions of authority in levying tribute on village society were reinforced by the more efficient Dutch bureaucratic techniques.

Fasseur has shown in detail how the system worked for the interests of the Dutch government and its favourites. By 1849, the non-crop income of the Dutch authorities in Indonesia (from opium, salt, tax farming and land rents) was more than adequate to cover local administrative expenses, so the whole proceeds of the crop levies were then available for the Netherlands. In 1844 Indonesia was allocated a fictitious debt of 236 million guilders to cover the costs of liquidating the VOC's debts (134 million guilders) and the costs of colonial wars. This fictitious debt was amortized by 1865 in yearly annuities, but the flow from Indonesia was much bigger than this and the residual 'Batig Slot' was cheerfully added to Dutch state revenue. In fact, after 1840 there was little increase in the volume of crops exported, but prices for export crops rose and the competitive strength of Indonesia was increased after the abolition of slavery in the Caribbean in the 1830s which ruined the sugar industry there. The abolition of the slave trade also raised the price of slaves in the coffee economy of Brazil. From 1831 to 1850 (Fasseur, p. 118), the Netherlands treasury proceeds from Indonesia amounted to 234 million guilders, and from 1851 to 1870, 491 million (19 per cent and 31.5 per cent respectively of Dutch state income for these periods). In these two periods, the total export surpluses were 483 and 977 million guilders, so the fiscal tribute was half of the total drain.

The proportionate burden of the Cultivation System varied from one part of Java to another. In some regions there were unsuccessful experiments with new crops which yielded little, so the peasantry's labour on them was not enough to fulfil their land tax obligations and they had to make cash payments in addition. In other areas, where the yield was better, there were actually net 'wage' payments to the peasantry because the yields were bigger than the land tax obligation. In this so-called system virtually all price and wage fixing was done arbitrarily by government, the administration had no cadastral guidelines to permit a fair distribution of the tax burden and in view of communication difficulties (until 1845 when a new postal service was available via Egypt, the minimum delay for a two-way communication with the Netherlands was 4 months) and the fact that the Ministers of Colonies were usually ex-officials or beneficiaries of bureaucratic cronyism, supervision from the Hague was poor.

When the Netherlands acquired a more democratic political system in 1848, criticism of this primitive tribute system and bureaucratic cronyism grew steadily. The government's coercive methods and the monopolistic practices of the private sector were not particularly conducive to productivity growth, and the increase in output from 1840 to 1870 was slow.

In 1870, when the opening of the Suez canal and the growing importance of steam shipping made it clear that Indonesian potential was not being fully used, the country was finally opened up to Dutch and foreign private enterprise and investment (although freehold purchase of land from natives was forbidden throughout Dutch rule).

Europeans were now allowed to acquire heritable leaseholds for plantations for a 75-year period, and the size of the Dutch community in Indonesia grew very fast. The government crop system was not immediately abolished, but its role declined rapidly. In 1870, the government had been responsible for 55 per cent of export crop production; by the early 1890s this dropped to zero. The drain from Indonesia became increasingly attributable to the private sector, though Dutch bureaucrats and military continued to draw income locally and to remit substantial sums for savings, pensions, etc.

The impact of the Cultivation System on Indonesians is a matter of considerable controversy which lies outside the scope of this paper, but as my estimates of the growth of Indonesian domestic product in appendix B imply a view on this issue, I would simply state my hypothesis that in Java as a whole the impact was not to reduce average Indonesian per capita food production, but rather to increase the labour input needed to maintain a given level of real income. I therefore assume provisionally that Indonesian per capita product was stable. Basically, this assumption is inspired by a Boserup–Myint type view of Indonesia's indigenous production potential rather than the Malthusian view underlying the work of Boeke and Geertz.

VI. Colonial Capitalism and the Liberal Order 1870–1928

From 1870, as private enterprise established itself in plantation agriculture on a commercial basis, costs and benefits were assessed more rationally and agronomic research helped to raise yields, particularly for sugar.

From the turn of the century, there was also a rapid development of petroleum, rubber and tin exports from Sumatra, which had by then been fully incorporated into the Dutch East Indies as a result of a tradeoff with the British (who ceded their claims in Sumatra against those of the Dutch in the Gold Coast) and a costly 30-year war between the Dutch and the Atjehnese.

The six decades of capitalist expansion in Indonesia were not interrupted by the First World War in which the Netherlands was a neutral, and in the postwar years the Dutch sensibly stayed out of restrictive schemes for rubber which the British imposed in Malaya. According to my rough estimates (see Table 6), Indonesian per capita domestic product rose by about 0.8 per cent a year in this period, a good deal better than performance in India. My estimation technique is

TABLE 6
Indonesian Population, GDP and GDP per Head

	Population 000s	GDP index	GDP level in 1970 $ million at US relative prices	Per capita GDP in 1970 $ at US relative prices	NDP level in 1928 guilders	NDP per capita in 1928 guilders
1700	13,103	20.73	2,263	173	636	48.5
1780	15,243	24.02	2,623	172	737	48.4
1820	16,443	26.34	2,875	175	808	49.1
1830	17,573	28.00	3,057	174	859	48.9
1840	18,785	32.14	3,509	187	986	52.5
1870	26,528	45.47	4,964	187	1,395	52.6
1913	48,150	100.00	10,918	227	3,068	63.7
1928	58,946	160.10	17,480	297	4,907	83.2
1929	59,830	155.11	16,935	283	4,754	79.5
1937	67,398	177.46	19,375	287	5,439	80.7
1938	68,409	177.16	19,342	283	5,430	79.4
1939	69,435	189.98	20,742	279	5,823	83.9
1950	76,746	138.20	15,088	197	4,236	55.2
1965	104,756	226.44	24,722	236	6,940	66.3
1973	124,242	417.39	45,570	367	12,793	103.0

Source: Appendices A and B for prewar, World Bank. 'World Tables', Washington DC, 1983 for 1950–73, and Muljatno (1960) for link 1938 to 1953 GDP. Indonesian per capita product in $ calculated in same way as described for other countries in Maddison (1970) Appendix A and revalued from 1965 to 1970 prices from Maddison (March 1983).

described in Appendix B. The results are consistent with Van Laanen's estimates (1984) which were derived by a different method. But both Van Laanen and I have a lower growth figure than Zimmerman (1962) hypothesized.

In the 1870–1928 period there seems to have been an increase in indigenous Indonesian income, judging from Polak's evidence, and the evidence of smallholder participation in exports which Anne Booth uses. It seems clear, however, that the growth in indigenous per capita income was more modest than that of Europeans which was largely geared to the export sector where trade volumes rose rapidly.

In the last decade or so of the nineteenth century there was extensive discussion of the likelihood that popular welfare had declined in Indonesia. The timing of the discussion coincided with a general concern in the developed world with the alleged Great Depression which was in fact largely a price phenomenon. The voluminous official studies on this question produced little evidence that there had been a decline in welfare. But the discussion helped to draw attention to the highly exploitative nature of the colonial regime, which was drawing criticism from journalists and politicians on the left of the political spectrum. To meet these new concerns, the government embarked upon the so-called Ethical Policy after 1900 which in theory was intended to raise native welfare. The authorities were all the more willing to increase their spending and to tighten surveillance of their allies in the native administration, as there had just been a major colonial war in Sumatra, and there was an increasing need to deal with nationalist political activity.

The main impact of the Welfare Policy was to increase the size and the pay scales of the existing bureaucracy, to add new corps of specialist technical services, and to raise government investment. A good deal of the extra investment went on irrigation works, and the benefits from these flowed mostly to Western sugar plantations. Unlike British practice in India, water was not sold, but supplied free. During the heyday of the 'welfare' period, the government maintained a coolie labour ordinance (1880–1932) which bolstered the supply of cheap labour for plantations (mainly in Sumatra) and enforced penal sanctions for runaway workers. Levels of spending on social services for the indigenous inhabitants, and particularly on education remained abysmally low. In 1930, according to the census, only 6.4 per cent of the indigenous population were literate, and only 0.32 per cent were literate in the Dutch language. This neglect of indigenous education was a major reason why Indonesians were in a weak position to get higher-paid jobs in the colonial economy. In fact, Indonesian literacy levels and life expectation were no better than in British India, which never claimed to be following a welfare policy.

At the end of the colonial period, the Dutch presence in Indonesia was much denser than the British presence in India (about 8 times as big relative to population). This can be seen clearly in Table 10. The number of European army personnel was about the same relative to total population in the two countries, but the number of Europeans in the Dutch civil administration was nearly 15 times the ratio in India. The Dutch presence in the private sector (particularly in mining and plantations) was much bigger than that of the British in India. They also had a higher tendency to be settled as families, with a higher proportion born in Indonesia. The higher dependency rate is one of the reasons the relative per capita income of the British was higher in India. They had 5 per cent of Indian NDP with 0.05 per cent of the population, or an average income 100 times the Indian average, whereas the Dutch had 16.9 per cent of Indonesian NDP, 0.4 per cent of

DUTCH INCOME IN AND FROM INDONESIA   657

TABLE 7
Indian Population, GDP and GDP per Head

	Population 000s	GDP index	GDP level in 1970 $ million at US relative prices	Per capita GDP in 1970 $ at US relative prices	NDP current rupees billion
1700	170,300	49.27	34,226	201	
1780	195,000	56.42	39,193	201	
1820	208,600	60.35	41,923	201	
1840	217,575	62.90	43,694	201	
1870	253,215	78.87	54,788	216	11.04
1913	303,700	100.00	69,466	229	24.47
1928	329,700	107.68	74,801	225	36.63
1938	376,100	114.87	79,796	212	25.22
1946	415,200	129.80	90,167	217	
1946*	341,868	129.80	74,242	217	
1950*	359,000	128.35	73,412	204	
1965*	485,000	212.42	121,493	251	
1973*	580,000	282.86	161,820	279	

Source: Population 1700–1820 Habib 1982, pp. 166–7, thereafter from Maddison 1971. GDP 1870–1900 from Heston 1983, 1900–38 from Maddison, 1985, 1700–1870 per capita income assumed stable. Estimates of NDP in 1900–38 current rupees from Maddison 1985 adjusted by Sivasubramonian implicit NDP deflator, for 1870 from Heston NDP and price index quoted by McAlpin. Estimates are for fiscal years for 1870 onwards (i.e. centred on October 1st). The figures for 1900–46 refer to the Indian subcontinent excluding Burma. Asterisked figures 1946–73 refer to post independence India. Figures of per capita GDP in 1970 dollars derived from Maddison (1970) Appendix A, revalued in 1970 prices (see Maddison March 1983).

the population, and their average income was 42 times the average Indonesian per capita income.

The Dutch managed to integrate the enfeebled remnant of the native ruling class into their bureaucratic system by running a dual administration with European officials in the 'binnenlands bestuur' and a parallel native administration with hereditary regents at the top and quasi-traditional methods of job allocation lower down the scale. Control was exercised by having a specially thick layer of European officials who spent a good deal of their time as watchdogs over the native administration whose ostensible dignity and regalia camouflaged their basic role as Dutch puppets. The European administration proclaimed explicitly its 'big-brother' role.

The native states in Indonesia (Vorstenlanden) had 20.6 per cent of the population in 1930 compared with 24.2 per cent of the Indian population in native states. Indian states had more autonomy than the 'Vorstenlanden', their rulers had bigger incomes and maintained separate armed forces.

TABLE 8

Netherlands Population, GDP and GDP per Head

	Population 000s	GDP index	GDP level in 1970 $ million at US relative prices	Per capita GDP in 1970 $ at US relative prices	NDP current million guilders	NDP constant 1928 million guilders
1600	1,500					
1700	1,900	13.79	1,083	570	237	495
1780	2,026	13.23	1,039	513	287	475
1820	2,344	15.31	1,202	513	453	550
1870	3,607	40.60	3,188	884	1,103	1,458
1913	6,164	100.00	7,851	1,274	2,535	3,591
1928	7,679	158.50	12,444	1,621	5,691	5,691
1938	8,685	171.60	13,472	1,551	4,993	6,161

Source: Maddison, 1982, with interpolations and revision; 1700–1820 levels of GDP and GDP per head have been revised upwards in the light of recent revisions of U.K. real product and occupational structure (Crafts 1983, Lindert and Williamson 1982). For details see Maddison (September 1985). Current price NDP 1900–38 from CBS, 1970, p. 119 linked to earlier years derived from my volume index and Van Stuijvenberg and Vrijer 1982 consumer price index to 1870, and their wholesale price index for earlier years.

TABLE 9

U.K. Population, GDP and GDP per Head

	Population 000s	GDP index	GDP level in 1970 $ million at US relative prices	Per capita GDP in 1970 $ at US relative prices
1700	8,400	4.71	3,196	380
1780	12,640	8.51	5,774	457
1820	21,240	16.24	11,015	519
1870	31,393	44.60	30,257	964
1913	45,649	100.00	67,841	1,486
1913 (a)	42,622	100.00	65,359	1,533
1928 (a)	45,578	108.70	71,045	1,559
1938 (a)	47,494	132.50	86,601	1,823

(a) The figures below the line exclude Southern Ireland.

Source: Maddison 1982, with interpolations and revision; 1700–40 population revised in line with Wrigley and Schofield 1981, Dickson, Ogràda, and Daultrey, Lee, and Flinn. GDP 1700–1831 revised in line with Crafts 1983.

In 1930, total government expenditure in Indonesia was 783 million guilders (Creutzberg, vol. 2, p. 67) or 17 per cent of NDP. In 1930–31 total public expenditure of British India was 2,086 million rupees (Kumar in Kumar and Desai 1983, p. 926) or 9.9 per cent of my

TABLE 10

Dutch Presence in Indonesia (1930) Compared with British Presence in India (1931)

	Indonesia (000s)	India (000s)
Europeans in employment	78.3	96.5
Europeans outside labour force	162.1	71.5
Resident Europeans	240.4	168.0
Europeans in civil administration	11.7	4.4
Europeans in armed forces	9.0	59.7 (a)
Non-governmental European employment	57.6	33.4
of which agriculture and mining	18.9	4.7
	(per cent)	(per cent)
Europeans as per cent of total population	0.4	0.05
Employed Europeans as per cent of European residents	32.6	57.4
Per cent of Europeans employed outside government	73.6	34.6
Europeans as per cent of civil administration	2.53	0.17
Total civil administration as per cent of population	0.76	0.76
Europeans as per cent of armed forces	16.6	30.0 (a)
Armed forces as per cent of population	0.09	0.06 (a)

(a) In India, the rulers of native states had armed forces of 140,000 compared with 200,000 in the Indian Army. The native state forces are not included in the above.

Source: Indonesia (1930) from Polak, pp. 96–7; India (1931) from Banerji, pp. 128–9. See also Hutton (1933) and Maddison (December 1983). In the above figures, the term 'Europeans' refers to whites and those of mixed blood with assimilated status by the standards of the census. There was more miscegenation in Indonesia than India; 134,000 of the 'Europeans' in Indonesia were Eurasians, compared with 30,000 'Anglo-Indians who are not handicapped by excessive pigmentation' in india. In addition there were 138,395 persons in India who returned themselves as Anglo-Indians but who were not treated as Europeans by the census, because in British practice, they did not have assimilated status.

estimate of British India's NDP in that year. This excludes government spending on railways, whereas the Indonesian figure includes this, but the Indonesian ratio would be even higher if we excluded the income of the population in the 'Vorstenlanden' from the denominator, to match the exclusion of income in native states in India.

The cost of government in Indonesia was therefore proportionately about twice as high as in India.

VII. The Depression Years 1929–38

This paper is not concerned with cyclical problems or fluctuations in prices and terms of trade, and these, of course, are what dominated this period. The Polak national income figures and deflators lead to an

ANGUS MADDISON

TABLE 11

The Dimensions of Foreign Presence in Asian Colonies in the 1930s

	'Europeans', metropolitan nationals, and those of assimilated status (a)	Percentage of total population
Dutch colony		
Indonesia (1930)	240,162	0.40
British colonies		
Burma (1931)	34,000	0.23
Ceylon (1929)	7,500	0.15
India (1931)	168,134	0.05
Malaya (1931) (incl. Singapore)	33,811	0.77
Everybody's colony		
China (1921)	267,000	0.06
French colony		
Indochina (1937)	42,345	0.18
Japanese colonies		
Korea (1930–35)	573,000	2.62
Taiwan (1930)	228,000	4.96
U.S. colony		
Philippines (1939)	36,000	0.15

(a) Includes Eurasians in Indonesia (134,000); in Malaya (16,043); and in Indochina (approx. 14,000). The Philippines figure includes 10,500 Japanese. but excludes U.S. military personnel and 200,000 Hispano-Philippino mestizos.

Source: Maddison (1983).

index of national income which incorporates the impact of the sharp decline and recovery in terms of trade, i.e. it exaggerates the cycle in output.

During the recession, the Netherlands, being part of the gold bloc, did not devalue the guilder until 1936, which led to a deterioration in the competitive position of exports after the British and Japanese devaluations in 1931, and the U.S. devaluation in 1933. Policy was highly deflationary, and the fall in the general price level in Indonesia was extreme even by the standards of the time. Taking 1929 as the base for the index, the NDP deflator fell to 44.4 per cent by 1936, compared with 78.6 in the Netherlands, 67.1 per cent in India, and 91.0 per cent in the U.K.

The depression saw a decline in the income of those Europeans and companies exporting primary products, and particularly sugar, which was the product worst affected. Profits of foreign enterprise fell drastically. People holding fixed interest debt of the Indonesian government did best out of the recession, because Indonesia as a colony was not able to default as Latin American countries and China did, and the real value of fixed debt rose in a time of general price decline.

Civil servants had their salaries cut 25 per cent, but this was much less than the fall in prices and represented a substantial rise in real terms. New recruitment was curtailed, and some personnel were cut.

The world conjuncture improved in the second half of the thirties onwards which led to a recovery of business profits. This was further enhanced by the change in economic policy after devaluation and after the imposition of quantitative controls discriminating against Japanese and in favour of Dutch products.

VIII. Some Problems of Macroquantification

The present essay in quantitative analysis has concentrated on macro aggregates, using secondary sources (with substantial adjustment) for the key benchmark years, which other, mostly qualitative, evidence suggested to be turning points. There are obvious weaknesses in such analysis but several of them can be remedied by further research. The problems are as follows:

(a) The estimates of NDP rely heavily on the validity of the population figures. For 1920 onwards the official estimates are reliable, but for earlier years it is generally agreed that they are too low, particularly the early nineteenth-century estimates of Raffles. For 1850–1920 I have used Boomgaard's estimates (see appendix A). These show a growth rate of 1.5 per cent for Java, and 1.3 per cent for Indonesia as a whole. For earlier years I relied on Peper and Reid who show much slower growth of indigenous population which seems more plausible to me. For 1780–1850, my figures, derived from these two authors, show a population growth rate of 0.4 per cent a year for Java compared with Boomgaard's 1.2 per cent.

This is a wide range of disagreement, and the scope for difference of opinion on the Outer Islands is even greater than for Java, given the weakness of the evidence. The demographic question has obviously been of fundamental importance in interpretations of Indonesian history, and is worth a good deal more research. The traditional view that Javanese growth was precociously fast bolstered the old colonial view of Dutch success in developing the Indies, and also influenced the Malthusian type pessimism inherent in Boeke and Geertz. In my picture, Java's early growth does not look so special in the Asian colonial context.

(b) My estimates of NDP are derived by backward extrapolation of assumed per capita income by three ethnic groups for the period prior to the Polak estimates, i.e. before 1921. For Dutch income I assume the trend to have been dominated by export volumes, and I am reasonably satisfied with this method, though the export volume index itself is capable of improvement. I am also reasonably happy with my assumption that Chinese per capita income moved on average at a rate between that of Indonesian and European. For Indonesian real income and real product the estimates are weakest. Although it is clear that over the long run the increase in Indonesian standards must have been very modest, my assumptions need to be checked against indices of total food supply which may be derivable from the studies of Scheltema (1936) and Boomgaard (1984). Relative income shares of ethnic groups and the movement of real income as opposed to real product for Indonesia as a whole can be better estimated when long-term price indices are available. Van Laanen has provided a very valuable alternative estimate of long-term growth in real product which is compatible with my findings, but long-term growth trends will be much clearer when the quantitative research programme of the Royal Tropical Institute is consummated, and GDP has been calculated from the production side.

(c) Pending estimates of long-term balance of payment trends, I have relied on estimates of the adjusted trade balance (exports f.o.b. minus imports c.i.f.) to represent the size of the net transfer from Indonesia. Although this is very crude, it has met a couple of crosschecks. The trade surplus for 1921–38 corresponds to the findings of Derksen and Tinbergen (1945) for Dutch income from Indonesia in 1925–34. In the case of India, the surplus on trade and treasure for 1921–38 is virtually identical with my earlier estimate of the 'drain' from India for the same period derived from Banerji's detailed payments estimates (see Maddison 1970). The assumption that virtually all of the Indonesian drain went to the Netherlands also needs to be tested. Remer's estimates of interwar Chinese transactions suggest that remittances to China were running at only 25 million guilders in 1930.

Remittances by non-Dutch 'Europeans' were much smaller than Dutch and were offset to a greater degree by investment in Indonesia, so I think my assumption may be reasonably valid.

Appendix A: Population

The estimates in Tables A-1 and B-1 were built up by backward extrapolation from the reliable 1920 figures in CBS (1941), which was the source for 1920 onwards.

a) Indigenous Population

For the nineteenth century, it now seems generally agreed that the official figures supplied by Raffles for 1815 understated population substantially and gave rise to the impression that Javanese population growth was extraordinarily high (see J. C. Breman 1963), B. Peper (1970) and Widjojo (1970).

For Java 1850–1920 I used figures supplied by Peter Boomgaard. For 1820–50 which was a period of war, disease, and increased exploitation, I used a slower rate of growth, i.e. the middle of Peper's (1970) range (0.75 per cent a year). For 1700–1820 I assumed that population rose by 0.19 per cent a year, in line with Reid's estimate (1983b) for 1600–1800.

For the Outer Islands, CBS (1941) was used for 1920 onwards, but for earlier years the picture is murky. The 1905 official estimate is too low and there were no official estimates before that. For 1850–1920, I used Boomgaard's estimates. For 1820–50 I assumed that population grew by 0.5 per cent a year (two thirds of the rate in Java) and from 1700–1820 I assumed that growth was 0.19 per cent a year in line with Reid.

TABLE A-1
Rough Estimate of Breakdown of the Indigenous Population 1700–1938 (000s)

	Java and Madura	Outer Islands	Total
1700	7,955	5,060	13,015
1780	9,260	5,890	15,150
1820	9,990	6,355	16,345
1830	10,765	6,680	17,445
1840	11,600	7,022	18,622
1870	16,730	9,470	26,200
1913	32,667	14,615	47,282
1929	40,287	17,977	58,264
1938	46,064	20,555	66,619

b) Non-Indigenous Population

For the European and 'Other Asiatic' (mainly Chinese) population, I relied on CBS (1941), p. 5 for 1860–1930. For 1820, Peter Boomgaard kindly supplied estimates of non-indigenous population. For 1780 Baudet and Fasseur, p. 313 suggest that the VOC had 15,000 land-based personnel in South Africa and Asia, Furber p. 300 suggests that about half of them were in Indonesia so this is what I assumed. I assume that their number (7,500) was the same in 1700 as in 1780.

Population figures by major ethnic group are shown in Table B-1 below. A rough breakdown of the indigenous population in Java and the Outer Islands is shown in Table A-1. Obviously the figures for Java are more reliable than for the Outer Islands.

Appendix B: Indonesian Real Product and Income, Total and per Capita by Ethnic Group

For 1921–39 I used the estimates of J. J. Polak (1943). Polak's constant price series (p. 81) for ethnic groups were augmented by government export income and remittances (p. 70) deflated by the European cost of living index (p. 80).

For earlier years, I made a crude backward extrapolation by ethnic group, using Polak's 1928 per capita levels as a benchmark. In the indigenous sector I assumed a small increase in real per capita income after 1870. From then onwards the country was opened up to foreign trade, and there was a good deal of foreign investment. Although the Dutch squeezed a bigger surplus from Indonesia than the British from India, per capita product in the subsistence sector is not likely to have fallen, as Boeke and Geertz once suggested, given the fact that peasants could move from swidden to sawah and then double crop. What probably did happen was that peasants had to work harder.

I grouped the income of Europeans in Indonesia together with government income and remittances, and assumed that in real terms this income moved parallel to volume of exports.

For Chinese and other Asiatics, I assumed that per capita real income rose at the average rate for Europeans and Indonesians in the years prior to Polak estimates.

I arrived at total income by summing my rough estimates for the three ethnic groups (as Polak did).

TABLE B-1
Growth of Population and Real Income by Ethnic Group

	Indonesians			Foreign Asiatics			'Europeans'		
	Population 000s	Total income million 1928 guilders	Per capita income 1928 guilders	Population 000s	Total income million 1928 guilders	Per capita income 1928 guilders	Resident population 000s	Total income of European residents or available for remittances abroad million 1928 guilders	Total 'European' income per resident European 1928 guilders
1700	13,015	614	47.2	80	12.5	156	7.5	9	1,245
1780	15,150	715	47.2	85	13.3	156	7.5	9	1,245
1820	16,345	771	47.2	90	17.4	193	8.25	19.3	2,339
1830	17,445	823	47.2	116	18.9	163	11.8	17.0	1,443
1840	18,622	879	47.2	146	37.2	255	16.8	70.1	4,173
1870	26,200	1,237	47.2	279	52.2	187	49.0	106	2,163
1913	47,282	2,454	51.9	739	177	240	129.0	437	3,389
1928	57,403	3,524	61.4	1,320	393	298	223.0	990	4,439
1929	58,264	3,421	58.7	1,334	401	301	232.0	932	4,017
1937	65,634	3,968	60.5	n.a.	505	n.a.	n.a.	966	n.a.
1938	66,619	4,037	60.6	n.a.	554	n.a.	n.a.	839	n.a.
1939	67,618	4,277	63.3	n.a.	537	n.a.	n.a.	1,009	n.a.

Appendix C: Indonesian Export Volume and Values, 1825–1950

We present a crude index of export volume for benchmark years from 1825 to 1950. The figures for individual products at 1928 prices are shown in Table C1. As the coverage of Table C1 was not the same over the whole period, I chained the indices for periods where the coverage was the same to get a volume index for the whole period (see Table C2).

TABLE C-1
Exports of Indonesia at Constant (1928) Prices (000s guilders)

	1825*	1830	1840
Sugar	308	995	9,156
Coffee	15,009	13,824	53,325
Tobacco	1,873	359	8
Total of above	17,190	15,178	62,489

	1870	1913	1928	1937	1939	1950
Sugar	21,747	217,848	375,796	167,372	201,301	4,315
Tea	3,140	37,430	98,210	94,062	103,685	43,848
Cinchona	2	5,561	4,866	128,235	100,805	1,543
Rubber (dry)	0	8,497	278,050	522,605	450,965	786,549
Palmoil	0	(15)	9,197	62,725	73,773	30,933
Coffee	61,121	20,450	80,935	69,862	46,550	9,540
Tobacco	11,930	119,383	95,823	66,689	48,168	16,854
Copra	n.a.	49,776	106,490	117,003	116,862	60,966
Pepper	n.a.	27,618	42,870	54,957	123,276	n.a.
Maize	n.a.	3,962	12,950	17,241	7,627	n.a.
Cassava	n.a.	3,563	33,775	85,670	42,501	n.a.
Petroleum	0	24,720	108,482	187,625	191,670	174,580
Tin	17,688	74,088	96,555	108,440	78,853	118,852
Total	115,628	592,911	1,343,999	1,682,486	1,586,036	1,229,852

*Annual average for 1823–27.

Source: This table was prepared by Fons Feekes from various colonial sources available at the Royal Tropical Institute in Amsterdam.

TABLE C-2
Indonesian Export Volume and Values (Selected Commodities, Total and per Capita)

	Export value at 1928 prices	Succes-sive period volume indices	Chained volume index	Value of total exports at current prices 000 guilders	Volume of total exports at 1928 prices[+] 000 guilders	Per capita exports current prices guilders	Per capita exports 1928 prices guilders
	Three Products			All Products			
1825*	17,190	100.0	100.0	14,055	30,725	0.83	1.81
1830	15,178	88.29	88.29	9,950	27,127	0.57	1.54
1840	62,489	363.52	363.52	49,162	111,692	2.62	5.95
1870	94,798	551.47	551.47	92,793	169,441	3.50	6.39
	Six Products						
1870	115,628	100.0	551.47	92,793	169,441	3.50	6.39
1913	474,760	410.49	2,264.28	671,433	695,706	13.94	14.45
	Thirteen Products						
1913	592,911	100.0	2,264.28	671,433	695,706	13.94	14.45
1928	1,343,999	226.68	5,132.67	1,577,926	1,577,026	26.77	26.77
1937	1,682,486	283.77	6,425.35	951,194	1,974,205	14.11	29.29
1939	1,586,036	267.50	6,056.95	746,327	1,861,014	10.75	26.80
	Ten Products						
1939	1,412,632	100.0	6,056.95	746,327	1,861,014	10.75	26.80
1950	1,229,852	87.06	5,273.25		1,620,220		21.11

* average for the years 1823–27.

(+) assumes the volume movement for uncovered items in each period was parallel to the movement for the items covered. It would probably be preferable to assume that the unit values for uncovered commodities moved parallel with the average for those included, but as values for individual covered items for each year are not available in Creutzberg, this was not possible here.

Literature

Books

Banerji, A. K. 1963. *India's Balance of Payments*, Bombay: Asia Publishing House.
Berkhuysen, A. P. H. 1948. *De Drainagetheorie voor Indonesië*, Leiden.
Boeke, J. H. 1947. *The Evolution of the Netherlands Indies Economy*, Haarlem: Willink.
Boserup, E. 1965. *The Conditions of Agricultural Growth*, London: Allen and Unwin.

Callis, H. G. 1976. *Foreign Capital in Southeast Asia*, reprint of 1942 edition, New York: Arno Press.

C.B.S. 1941. *Statistical Pocket Book of Indonesia*, Batavia.

1970. *Zeventig Jaren Statistiek in Tijdreeksen 1899–1969*, The Hague.

Chaudhuri, K. N. 1978. *The Trading World of Asia, and the English East India Company 1660–1760*, Cambridge.

Creutzberg, P. (ed.) 1975. *Indonesia's Export Crops 1816–1940*. The Hague: Nijhoff.

Dutt, R. 1963. *Economic History of India*, Delhi: Publications Division, Govt. of India.

Fasseur, C. 1978. *Kultuurstelsel en koloniale Baten*, Leiden.

Feinstein, C. H. 1972. *National Income, Expenditure and Output of the United Kingdom 1855–1965*, Cambridge.

Furber, H. 1976. *Rival Empires of Trade in the Orient, 1600–1800*, Oxford.

Furnivall, J. S. 1967. *Netherlands India*, Cambridge.

Glamann, K. 1981. *Dutch–Asiatic Trade 1620–1740*, The Hague: Nijhoff.

Geertz, C. 1963. *Agricultural Involution*, Berkeley.

Hutton, J. H. 1933. *Census of India 1931, Volume I, India, Part I, Report and Part II, Imperial Tables*, Delhi.

Maddison, A. 1970. *Economic Progress and Policy in Developing Countries*, London: Allen and Unwin, and New York: Norton.

1971. *Class Structure and Economic Growth: India and Pakistan since the Moghuls*, London: Allen and Unwin.

1982. *Phases of Capitalist Development*, Oxford.

Mitchell, B. R. 1982. *International Historical Statistics: Africa and Asia*, London: Macmillan.

Polak, J. J. 1943. *The National Income of the Netherlands Indies, 1921–1939*, New York: Institute of Pacific Relations. Reprinted in vol. 5 of Creutzberg, P. (ed.) (1979), *Changing Economy in Indonesia*, The Hague: Nijhoff.

Posthumus, N. W. 1943. *Nederlandsche Prijsgeschiedenis*.

Prange, A. J. A. 1935. *De Nederlandsch Indische Betalingsbalans*, Leiden.

Raffles, T. S. 1965. *The History of Java*, Oxford (reprint), Kuala Lumpur.

Remer, C. F. 1933. *Foreign Investments in China*, New York: Macmillan.

Riklefs, M. C. 1974. *Jogjakarta under Sultan Mangkubumi 1749–1792: A History of the Division of Java*, Oxford.

1981. *A History of Modern Indonesia*, London: Macmillan.

Riley, J. C. 1980. *International Government Finance and the Amsterdam Capital Market 1740–1815*, Cambridge.

Scheltema, A. M. P. A. 1936. *The Food Consumption of the Native Inhabitants of Java and Madura*, Batavia: Institute of Pacific Relations.

Sivasubramonian, S. 1965. *National Income of India 1900–01 to 1946–47*, mimeographed, Delhi: Delhi School of Economics.

Sutherland, H. 1979. *The Making of a Bureaucratic Elite: The Colonial Transformation of the Javanese Priyayi*, Singapore: Heinemann.

Vries, Johan de 1968. *De Economische Achteruitgang der Republiek in de Achttiende Eeuw*, Leiden: Stenfert Kroese.

Widjojo Nitisastro 1970. *Population Trends in Indonesia*, Ithaca: Cornell University Press.

Wrigley, E. A. and Schofield, R. S. 1981. *The Population History of England 1541–1871: A Reconstruction*, London: Arnold.

Articles or Contributions to Books

Baudet, H. and Fasseur, C. 1977. 'Koloniale bedrijvigheid' in: J. H. van Stuijvenberg (ed.), *De economische geschiedenis van Nederland*, Groningen: Wolters-Noordhoff.

Boomgaard, P. 1984. 'Java's Agricultural Production 1775–1875', mimeographed, Groningen.

Booth, A. 1984. 'Exports and Growth in the Colonial Economy: 1830–1940', mimeographed, Groningen.

Breman, J. C. 1963. 'Java, Bevolkingsgroei en Demografische Structuur', *Tijdschrift van het Koninklijk Nederlandsch Aardrijkskundig Genootschap*.

Brugmans, I. J. 1948. 'De Oost-Indische Compagnie en de Welvaart in de Republiek', *Tijdschrift voor Geschiedenis*, pp. 225–31.

Chaudhuri, K. N. 1983. 'Foreign Trade and Balance of Payments (1757–1947)' in: D. Kumar and M. Desai, *Cambridge Economic History of India*, vol. 2, Cambridge.

Crafts, N. F. R. 1983. 'British Economic Growth, 1700–1831: A Review of the Evidence', *Economic History Review* (May).

Derksen, J. B. D. and Tinbergen, J. 1945. 'Berekeningen over de economische betekenis van Nederlandsch Indië voor Nederland', *Maandschrift, C.B.S.* (Oct./Dec.).

Dickson, D., O'Grada, C. and Daultrey, S. 1982. 'Hearth Tax, Household Size and Irish Population Change 1672–1821', *Proceedings of the Royal Irish Academy*, vol. 82, C, No. 6, Dublin.

Elson, R. E. 1983. 'Peasant Poverty and Prosperity under the Cultivation System in Java', mimeographed, ANU Conference on Indonesian Economic History, Canberra (December).

Golay, F. H. 1976. 'Southeast Asia: The "Colonial Drain" Revisited' in C. D. Cowan and O. W. Wolters, *Southeast Asian History and Historiography*, Cornell.

Habib, I. 1982. 'Population' in: T. Raychaudhuri and I. Habib, *Cambridge Economic History of India*, vol. 1, Cambridge.

Heston, A. 1983. 'National Income' in: D. Kumar and M. Desai, *Cambridge Economic History of India*, vol. 2, Cambridge.

Kumar, D. 1983. 'The Fiscal System' in: D. Kumar and M. Desai, *Cambridge Economic History of India*, vol. 2, Cambridge.

Laanen, J. T. M. van 1984. 'Per Capita Income Growth in Indonesia, 1850–1940', mimeographed, Groningen.

Lee, J. 1981. 'On the Accuracy of the Pre-Famine Irish Censuses' in: J. M. Goldstrom and L. A. Clarkson (eds), *Irish Population, Economy and Society*, Oxford.

Lindert, P. H. 1982. 'Revisiting England's Social Tables 1688–1812', *Explorations in Economic History*, 19.

Maddison, A. 1983. 'A Comparison of Levels of GDP per Capita in Developed and Developing Countries 1700–1980', *Journal of Economic History* (March).

1983. 'Dutch Colonialism in Indonesia: A Comparative Perspective', mimeographed, ANU Conference on Indonesian Economic History, Canberra (December).

1985. 'Alternative Estimates of the Real Product of India, 1900–46', *Indian Economic and Social History Review*, 22, 2 (April–June).

1985. 'Recent Revisions to British and Dutch Growth', paper presented at the Groningen Workshop in Quantitative Economic History (September).

McAlpin, M. 1983. 'Price Movements and Fluctuations in Economic Activity (1860–1947)' in: D. Kumar and M. Desai, *Cambridge Economic History of India*, vol. 2, Cambridge.

Muljatno, 1960. 'Perhitungan Peadpatan Nasional Indonesia Untuk 1953 dan 1954', *Ekonomi dan Keuangan Indonesia* (March–April).

Niel, R. van 1964. 'The Function of Landrent under the Cultivation System in Java', *Journal of Asian Studies* (May).

1972. 'Measurement of Change under the Cultivation System in Java, 1837–1851', *Indonesia* (October).

Peper, B. 1970. 'Population Growth in Java in the Nineteenth Century', *Population Studies*.

Reid, A. J. 1983a. 'Low Population Growth and its Causes in Pre-Colonial South East Asia', mimeographed, ANU Population Workshop, Canberra (December).

1983b. 'The Pre-Colonial Economy of Indonesia', mimeographed, ANU Conference on Indonesian Economic History, Canberra (December).

Stuijvenberg, J. H. van and de Vrijer, J. E. J. 1982. 'Prices, Population and National Income in the Netherlands 1620–1978', *Journal of European Economic History*, vol. 11, no. 3 (Winter).

Vries, Jan de 1984. 'The Decline and Rise of the Dutch Economy, 1675–1900' in: G. Saxonhouse and G. Wright (eds), *Forms and Methods in Economic History: Essays in Honor of William N. Parker*, Greenwich, Conn.: Jai Press.

Zimmerman, L. J. 1962. 'The Distribution of World Income, 1860–1960' in: E. de Vries (ed.), *Essays on Unbalanced Growth*, The Hague: Mouton.

PART V

THE ROLE OF GOVERNMENT POLICY IN THE PERFORMANCE OF ADVANCED CAPITALIST COUNTRIES

Part V: The role of government policy in the performance of advanced capitalist countries

The three essays in this section deal with the role of economic and social policy in affecting the performance of advanced capitalist countries.

Essay 13 (Maddison, 1983) is concerned with the degree to which Western economies have realised their economic potential. In the postwar period, Western growth was so buoyant that many observers thought we had entered a new world where enlightened government macropolicy could secure sustained prosperity. Unemployment was minimal in Western Europe, growth rates surpassed all historical records, inflation was generally regarded as modest, and the business cycle seemed obsolete. Domestic macropolicy was given a large degree of credit for these outcomes and strengthened international cooperation was clearly an important buttress.

The policy aims of full employment and rapid growth were an innovation compared with those of prewar years but the role of enlightened policy should not be exaggerated. The payoff to higher levels of demand was greater than expected because of the effect of recovery and catch-up which speeded productivity growth, and induced an investment boom. This 'virtuous' circle was bolstered by circumstances which restrained inflation: the climate of wage bargaining was mild as real income was rising fast; expectations of inflation were temporarily dampened by money illusion, key commodity prices were stable, and labour supply was eased by migration.

The situation changed sharply in the early 1970s due to the collapse of the Bretton Woods fixed exchange rate system, the erosion of price constraints, the emergence of strong inflation expectations, the jump in oil prices, the much greater international volatility of capital movements, and the erosion of some of the special supply side factors.

Force of circumstance required a new emphasis in policy, but the change in the macropolicy consensus was itself an important ingredient of the new situation, with major priority being given to price stability, dampening inflationary expectations, curbing budget deficits, maintaining the exchange rate. The full employment objective disintegrated, and governments accepted very large rises in unemployment as a cost of fulfilling their new objectives. There was in fact a return, in important respects, to policy objectives of prewar years. The main exceptions were (a) the remarkable fidelity to neoliberal trade policies developed in the golden age and to the habit of international cooperation; and (b) the attempt to cushion the social impact of deflationary macropolicy by compensatory and often contradictory micropolicy which led to big increases in social transfer payments and subsidies to threatened industries.

Essay 13 analyses these issues. Although it was published in 1983 I think its conclusions on the changed nature of economic policy objectives and the role of the new 'establishment consensus' are still valid.

Essay 14 (Maddison, 1984) surveys the reasons for the huge growth in government expenditure on the welfare state since Bismarck inaugurated it more than a century ago. The welfare state played an important role in legitimising capitalism and making society fairer. It has made capitalist property relations and the operation of market forces more acceptable by mitigating inequality and removing most of the grievances which motivated proponents of a socialist alternative. It strengthened the forces making for economic growth and stability. But the mix of programmes grew in response to very mixed and sometimes muddled policy objectives – some of which were redistributive, some of an insurance character or simply a response to interested lobbies. To finance the programmes governments raised revenue mainly by a large increase in social security levies with a regressive incidence. There is a substantial 'churning' of income as governments collect taxes and pay out transfers to the same people. There are also serious moral hazards which induce people to change their patterns of behaviour in order to qualify for benefits.

Essay 15 (Maddison, 1974) deals with the role of educational policy. The notion of education as human capital which was put forward by Schultz in 1961 was of major theoretical interest to economists interpreting sources of economic growth, and it was also taken up enthusiastically by educationalists who found its central argument a useful support in bolstering educational budgets. In this complex field there is a paucity of sharp evidence, so that new policy initiatives may involve reckless experimentation. This article was an attempt to clear my own mind about the major social and economic policy issues in this field, and about the role of education in growth.

References

Maddison, A. (1974), 'What is Education For?', *Lloyds Bank Review*, April.
Maddison, A. (1983), 'Economic Stagnation since 1973, Its Nature and Causes: A Six Country Survey', *De Economist*, **131**, 4.
Maddison, A. (1984), 'Origins and Impact of the Welfare State, 1883–1983', *Banca Nazionale del Lavoro Quarterly Review*, March.
Schultz, T.W. (1961), 'Investment in Human Capital', *American Economic Review*, **51**, 1–17.

[13]

DE ECONOMIST 131, NR. 4, 1983

ECONOMIC STAGNATION SINCE 1973, ITS NATURE AND CAUSES: A SIX COUNTRY SURVEY

BY

ANGUS MADDISON*

1 THE STAGNATION EXPERIENCE AND ITS CAUSES

After 1973, the growth of our sample of six western economies slowed down sharply. The average rise of real product for 1973–1982 was 1.9% a year compared with 5.3% for 1950–1973 (see table 1). The check to real income growth was bigger, because of the substantial terms of trade loss. There were two clearly marked and widespread cycles of recession in 1974–1975 and

TABLE 1 – RATES OF GROWTH OF GDP IN CONSTANT PRICES

	annual average compound growth rates				
	1870–1950	1950–60	1960–73	1973–82	1929–38
France	1.4	4.6	5.6	2.4	−0.4
Germany	2.1	8.0	4.5	1.7	3.8
Japan	2.2	8.8	9.8	3.6	4.7
Netherlands	2.3	4.5	5.0	1.5	0.3
U.K.	1.6	2.8	3.1	0.6	1.9
U.S.A.	3.5	3.3	4.0	1.8	−0.7
Average	2.2	5.3	5.3	1.9	1.6

Source: A. Maddison, *Phases of Capitalist Development*, Oxford, 1982, Appendix A, *National Accounts 1951–1980*, OECD, Paris, 1982, *Quarterly National Accounts*, No.1, 1983, and for 1982 in Netherlands, *Economic Outlook*, July 1983. The estimates are adjusted to exclude the impact of frontier changes.

* Professor of Economics, University of Groningen, The Netherlands. I am grateful to Jan Kregel, Simon Kuipers and Jan Pen for comments on an earlier draft.

TABLE 2 – YEAR TO YEAR PERCENTAGE CHANGE IN REAL GDP

	1973	1974	1975	1976	1977	1978	1979	1980	1981	1982	1983ᵃ
France	5.4	3.2	0.2	5.2	3.1	3.8	3.3	1.1	0.2	1.7	-0.5
Germany	4.5	0.7	-1.6	5.4	3.1	3.1	4.1	1.9	0.2	-1.1	0.5
Japan	8.8	-1.0	2.3	5.3	5.3	5.0	5.1	4.9	4.0	3.0	3.3
Netherlands	5.7	3.5	-1.0	5.3	2.4	2.7	2.1	0.9	-1.2	-1.4	-0.3
U.K.	7.5	-1.0	-0.7	3.6	1.3	3.7	1.6	-2.0	-2.0	1.2	1.8
U.S.A.	5.5	-0.7	-0.7	4.9	5.2	4.7	2.4	-0.3	2.3	-1.7	3.0
Arithmetic Average	6.2	0.8	-0.3	5.0	3.4	3.8	3.1	1.1	0.6	0.3	1.3

Source: OECD, *Economic Outlook*, July 1983.
ᵃ Forecast.

1981–1982 with high unemployment and underutilised plant, and the second recession started from a level where output was demonstrably below capacity (see tables 2 and 3).

This deceleration had three main causes:

1. a longer-term decline in productivity growth potential as the follower countries (Europe and Japan) converged on the performance levels of the leader (the U.S.A.);
2. inevitable 'cyclical' losses in output and employment as countries adjusted to important 'system shocks';
3. losses due to a change in the 'establishment view' of macropolicy tasks and instruments.

1.1 *The Longer-Term Productivity Deceleration*

European countries and Japan enjoyed unusually high rates of growth in the 1950's and 1960's because they were able to exploit the 'opportunities of backwardness.' This is clear from the evidence of tables 4 and 5. It was inevitable that this abnormal productivity bonus would evaporate as they drew closer to U.S. productivity levels.

In 1973–1982, productivity growth in our six countries averaged only 2.7% a year compared with 5.3% in 1960–1973. This is still considerably

TABLE 3 – GROWTH OF THE NONRESIDENTIAL FIXED CAPITAL STOCK

	annual average compound growth rates			
	1913–50	1950–60	1960–73	1973–80
France (net)	1.0	2.9	5.9	4.5
Germany (net)	1.0	6.6	6.5	4.0
Japan (gross)	3.3	5.1	12.1	6.8
Netherlands (gross)	n.a.	6.5	6.9	4.3
U.K. (net)	0.5	2.5	4.8	2.9
U.S.A. (net)	1.9	3.4	4.3	2.9
Arithmetic Average	1.5	4.5	6.8	4.2

Source: Generally from official sources as described in A. Maddison, *Phases of Capitalist Development*, Oxford, 1982. For the Netherlands, the estimate was derived as described in A. Maddison and B.S. Wilpstra (eds.), *Unemployment: The European Perspective*, London, 1982. For the U.S.A., the figures for 1929 onwards are from *Fixed Reproducible Tangible Wealth in the United States 1925–79*, U.S. Dept of Commerce, Washington D.C., 1982 with revisions and updating kindly supplied by John C.Musgrave. Japan 1973–80 from *Flows and Stocks of Fixed Capital*, OECD, Paris, 1982.

TABLE 4 – GROWTH OF GDP PER MAN HOUR

	annual average compound growth rates			
	1870–1950	1950–60	1960–73	1973–82
France	1.9	4.4	5.5	3.6
Germany	1.5	6.9	5.3	3.2
Japan	1.6	5.7	9.3	3.2
Netherlands	1.4	3.4	5.4	2.6[a]
U.K.	1.4	2.2	3.9	2.6
U.S.A.	2.3	2.5	2.5	1.0
Average	1.7	4.2	5.3	2.7

Source: A. Maddison, *Phases of Capitalist Development*, Oxford, 1982, updated.
[a] 1973–81.

TABLE 5 – LEVEL OF GDP PER MAN HOUR

	1870	1950	1960	1973	U.S.A. = 100 1982
France	64	46	55	81	101
Germany	66	36	55	77	94
Japan	27	16	22	49	60
Netherlands	111	56	62	88	98[a]
U.K.	120	59	58	68	79
Average for 5 countries	78	43	50	73	86
U.S.A.	100	100	100	100	100

Source: As for table 4.
[a] 1981.

higher than the average attainment of 1.7% a year from 1870 to 1950, but earlier performance has been surpassed because the rate of growth of the capital stock, though reduced, remains high by historical standards, the growth in the stock of human capital is still rapid, a relatively greater proportion of collective resources in more countries is devoted to R and D, and these economies are more open than in 1870–1950 to transmission of pro-growth influences and ideas through trade and capital markets.

The productivity slowdown also has a cyclical component due to lower investment and less efficient resource allocation in stagnating economies, so that the longer-term component of growth deceleration since 1973 is less than the observed productivity slowdown. This is particularly true in Japan where the extremely sharp productivity slowdown since 1973 reflects some degree of labour hoarding. This is greater there than in the other countries because of greater flexibility in wage structures and a greater government policy effort to keep unemployment low.

The most intriguing aspect of the productivity slowdown is that which has occurred in the U.S.A. The deceleration there may be due entirely to cyclical or *ad hoc* causes, but it may also be due to longer-term forces as the structure of demand is increasingly concentrated on the service sector where productivity growth is slowest.[1]

1.2 *Inevitable Costs of System Shocks*
Economic performance since the early 1970's has been adversely affected by 'system' shocks. These were the collapse of the Bretton Woods fixed exchange system and the twelvefold increase in oil prices. They were big enough to require changes in the discretionary weapons of macroeconomic policy, and in the rules of the game by which central banks and finance ministries had operated. Big enough too to change expectations within the private sector.

On any reasonable accounting, the most sophisticated governments could be expected to lose output in dealing with these shocks, because they involved new risks for policy, and transition problems in devising and learning to use new policy weapons, such as floating exchange rates. This is equally true of entrepreneurial and trade union decison-makers whose reactions significantly affect macroeconomic outcomes.

1.3 *Changes in the 'Establishment View'*
To some degree, the slowdown in growth since 1973, and particularly since 1979, has been due to a deliberate cautiousness in policy. The policy consensus has changed from what it was in the Golden Age before 1973 as described in section 4 below.

---

1 For an analysis of the longer-term elements in the productivity slowdown, see A. Maddison, 'Comparative Analysis of the Productivity Situation in the Advanced Capitalist Countries,' in: J.W. Kendrick (ed.), *International Comparisons of Productivity and Causes of the Slowdown*, American Enterprise Institute, Washington D.C., 1983; E.F. Denison, *Accounting for Slower Economic Growth*, Brookings, Washington, 1979; the articles by Lindbeck, Giersch and Wolter, and Denison in *Economic Journal*, March 1983, and R.C.O. Matthews (ed.), *Slower Growth in the Western World*, London, 1982.

It is not possible to give any scientific measure of the impact of policy changes on the slowdown. Comparing 1973–1982 with 1960–1973 we know that GDP growth is down 3.4 points from 5.3 to 1.9, and we acknowledge that longer-term factors and inevitable disturbance from shocks were important, so the influence of cautious or, as I feel, overcautious, policy in slowing growth performance is probably less than 1 percentage point a year of average GDP growth. Before pursuing the discussion of the policy changes in section 4, we describe the nature of the 1973–1982 situation in more detail in section 2, and the new openness of these economies in section 3.

2   THE NATURE OF THE 1973–1982 EXPERIENCE

2.1 *Demand Components*
It is clear from table 6 that the weakest element in demand has been investment, which fell by almost 1% a year on average compared with a 6.7% a year growth in 1960–1973. Since 1973, the investment picture has been very similar in all western countries, whereas in 1929–1938 the divergence in national policies was much greater and so was the intercountry variation in investment experience.

The strongest element has been exports, which are down from the high growth rates of 1960–1973, but very much better sustained than in the 1930's, when intratrade of these countries was reduced by erection of trade barriers, and trade with the rest of the world was drastically reduced by the falling purchasing power of countries whose earnings were hit by the price collapse, and whose capacity to borrow had virtually vanished because of a collapse of the world capital market. In 1973–1982 exports were buoyed by high OPEC spending and by the huge borrowings of the third world and East European countries. In 1975 and 1982, there was, however, a decline in world trade (see table 12) which interrupted the exports of these countries.

Government consumption has been a modest sustaining force in all countries. But its role was much less dynamic than in the 1930's, and every country showed a slowdown from the momentum in 1960–1973.

Private consumption was down everywhere quite substantially on 1960–1973 growth, on average better than in 1929–1938, but not always so.

2.2 *Labour Markets*
There has been a big increase in unemployment since 1973, with a rise in the average level from 2.5% in 1973 to 9% in July, 1983. There were two major

STAGNATION SINCE 1973: A SIX COUNTRY SURVEY   591

TABLE 6 – MOVEMENTS IN THE VOLUME OF DEMAND 1929–38 AND 1960–82

annual average compound growth rates

	Gross investment			Private final consumption		
	1960–73	1973–82	1929–38	1960–73	1973–82	1929–38
France	7.4	0.4	−3.2[a]	5.6	3.4	0.5
Germany	3.9	−0.7	5.1	4.7	1.8	1.0
Japan	13.6	1.7	8.9[a]	9.2	3.0	2.0
Netherlands	5.6	−1.7	−3.2	5.6	2.1	2.0
U.K.	4.5	−2.7	3.6	2.8	1.0	1.7
U.S.A.	5.0	−1.1	−9.0	4.2	2.5	−0.3
Average	6.7	−0.7	0.4	5.4	2.3	1.2

	Exports of goods and services			Government consumption		
	1960–73	1973–82	1929–38	1960–73	1973–82	1929–38
France	9.4	5.0	−5.0	3.9	2.8	4.2
Germany	7.9	5.1	−7.9	4.7	2.5	12.6
Japan	14.0	10.8	8.2	6.1	4.3	7.9
Netherlands	9.1	2.2	−3.6	2.8	2.4	2.5
U.K.	5.1	2.5	−2.9	2.5	1.6	6.0
U.S.A.	6.7	4.8	−1.9	2.8	1.6	4.6
Average	8.9	5.1	−2.2	3.8	2.5	6.3

Sources: 1960–82, *National Accounts of OECD Countries*, OECD, Paris, various issues. France 1929–38, estimates for public expenditure, investment and exports from J-J. Carré, P. Dubois and E. Malinvaud, *La Croissance Française*, Seuil, Paris, 1972, p. 316; consumption derived as a residual using the GDP growth figure on p. 35 and the 1938 weights for GNP in OEEC, *Statistics of National Product and Expenditure 1938 and 1947 to 1955*, OEEC, Paris, 1957, p. 59. Germany 1929–36 from D. Keese, 'Die volks-wirtschaftlichen Gesamtgrössen für das Deutsche Reich in den Jahren 1925–1936' in W. Conze and H. Raupach, (eds.) *Die Staats und Wirtschaftskrise des deutschen Reiches*, Klett, Stuttgart, 1967, p. 43 linked for 1936–8 to R. Erbe, *Die nationalsozialistische Wirtschaftspolitik 1933–1939 im Lichte der modernen Theorie*, Polygraphischer Verlag, Zürich, 1958, p. 100, deflated by consumer price index. Japan 1929–38 from K. Ohkawa and M. Shinohara, *Patterns of Japanese Economic Development*, Yale, 1979, p. 258. Netherlands 1929–38 from *Tachtig Jaren Statistiek in Tijdreeksen*, CBS. The Hague, 1979, pp. 144–5, and G.J.T. Vorstman, 'Een econometrische analyse van de Nederlandse volkshuishouding', CPB, The Hague, mimeographed, 21/3/74. U.K. 1929–38 from C.H. Feinstein, *National Income, Expenditure and Output of the United Kingdom 1855–1965*, Cambridge, 1972, p. T16. U.S.A. 1929–38 from *The National Income and Product Accounts of the United States, 1929–74, Statistical Tables*, U.S. Dept. of Commerce, p. 324.
[a] Fixed investment only.

leaps in 1973–1976 and 1979–1983, with an interval in 1976–1979 when the situation was stabilised. The unemployment situation is most egregious in the Netherlands and U.K., the two countries with least excuse for deflationary policy, given their unusually favourable energy and payments position.

Unemployment is the most obvious form of labour slack, but the fall in use of labour capacity can also be seen in the movement of total labour input. In 1973–1982 this fell by nearly 0.7% a year compared with a rise of 0.15 in 1960–1973 even though labour supply grew at a similar (0.9% per annum) pace in 1973–1982 as in 1960–1973 (see table 9). Thus the unemployment figures somewhat understate the actual degree of labour slack.[2]

The biggest sectoral shift in labour use since 1973 has been the weakening demand for workers in industry. Before that, the U.K. was the only large country with a substantial fall in the absolute level of industrial employment. Now this phenomenon of deindustrialisation has also affected France, Germany and the Netherlands on a very significant scale, and even in Japan and the U.S.A., where industrial employment had previously been substantial, stagnation has set in (see table 7). Both long-term and conjunctural factors have been at work. The elasticity of demand for industrial products is weaker than in earlier postwar years, productivity growth is rapid in this sector and competition from newly industrialising countries in the third world has increased. On top of this there has been the conjunctural slack in demand for industrial products, particularly for investment goods.

2 Economic slack is in my view bigger than labour slack, because the deceleration in labour productivity includes an element of productivity slack. There is also unused capital capacity in the economy because the rate of growth of capital stock, though slower than in 1960–1973, has continued at rates well above the historical norm. Some downward adjustment to capital stock growth after 1973 (as conventionally measured) is necessary because the OPEC price shocks rendered some capital stock prematurely obsolete. In my view once-for-all 'structural' losses of this type probably reduced capital stock by something of the order of 5%. Others would put the loss higher, *e.g.* M.N. Baily, 'Productivity and the Services of Capital and Labor,' *Brookings Papers on Economic Activity*, I, 1981, relates real capacity to stock market valuation of assets, and in the Netherlands adherents of the Hartog-Tjan thesis argue that there have been very large losses from the capital stock because excessively high wages have induced scrapping. From this, some people draw the further conclusion that unemployment in contemporary Western countries is similar to that in India, *i.e.* it is due to capital shortage. This position is just as implausible as the notion in some quarters that the rise in unemployment reflects an increased preference for leisure. For a statement of my position on the probable structural loss to capital stock and a critique of Baily, see my contribution to J.W. Kendrick, *op.cit.* and my contribution to A. Maddison and B.S. Wilpstra, *op.cit.* for a critique fo the Hartog-Tjan assumptions.

STAGNATION SINCE 1973: A SIX COUNTRY SURVEY   593

TABLE 7 – MOVEMENTS IN EMPLOYMENT BY SECTOR

| | 1960–73 | | | 1973–82 | | |
	Agri-culture	Industry	Services	Agri-culture	Industry	Services
			annual average compound growth rates			
France	−4.3	1.2	2.0	−3.2	−1.5	1.7
Germany	−4.6	−0.1	1.6	−3.9	−1.7	1.0
Japan	−4.8	3.4	2.7	−2.8	0.0	2.1
Netherlands	−3.1	−0.3	2.4	−1.5[a]	−1.9[a]	1.4[a]
U.K.	−2.6	−0.9	1.1	−1.3	−2.9	0.9
U.S.A.	−3.2	1.9	2.4	0.0	0.0	2.6
Average	−3.8	0.9	2.0	−2.1	−1.3	1.6

Source: O.E.C.D. *Labour Force Statistics.* Netherlands 1973–81 from OECD, *Economic Survey, Netherlands*, January 1983.
[a] 1973–81.

In services, the demand for labour has been much better sustained with substantial growth in employment since 1973. This reflects the lower cyclical sensitivity of demand, the higher long-term elasticity of demand and the slower growth of productivity in this sector.

TABLE 8 – GROWTH OF LABOUR SUPPLY, EMPLOYMENT OPPORTUNITY, AND TOTAL HOURS WORKED

| | annual average compound growth rates | | | | | |
| | 1960–73 | | | 1973–82 | | |
	Labour force	Employ-ment	Total hours worked	Labour force	Employ-ment	Total hours worked
France	0.78	0.67	0.03	0.70	0.07	−1.13
Germany	0.22	0.22	−0.79	0.10	−0.56	−1.45
Japan	1.23	1.26	0.47	0.90	0.78	0.35
Netherlands	1.15	1.00	−0.36	1.38[a]	0.60[a]	−0.70[a]
U.K.	0.29	0.24	−0.72	0.26	−0.72	−1.90
U.S.A.	1.84	1.94	1.46	2.29	1.62	0.75
Arithmetic Average	0.92	0.89	0.15	0.94	0.30	−0.68

Source: As for table 7.
[a] 1973–81.

TABLE 9 – UNEMPLOYMENT AS A PERCENTAGE OF THE LABOUR FORCE (YEARLY AVERAGES)

	1973	1974	1975	1976	1977	1978	1979	1980	1981	1982	July 1983
France	2.6	2.8	4.1	4.4	4.7	5.2	5.9	6.3	7.3	8.0	8.1
Germany	0.8	1.6	3.6	3.7	3.6	3.5	3.2	3.0	4.4	6.1	7.7
Japan	1.3	1.4	1.9	2.0	2.0	2.2	2.1	2.0	2.2	2.4	2.6
Netherlands	2.3	2.7	5.2	5.5	5.3	5.3	5.4	6.0	8.6	11.4	13.7
U.K.	3.2	3.2	4.7	6.0	6.3	6.3	5.6	7.0	10.6	12.4	12.6
U.S.A.	4.8	5.5	8.3	7.6	6.9	6.0	5.8	7.0	7.5	9.5	9.3
Average	2.5	2.9	4.6	4.9	4.8	4.8	4.7	5.2	6.8	8.3	9.0

Source: OECD, *Quarterly Labour Force Statistics*, No. 3, Paris, 1983, p. 77. Figures are standardised to enhance international comparability. It should be remembered that the unemployment figures in table 9, though adjusted to augment international comparability, do not fully portray the degree of labour slack in different countries because of the possibility of mitigating unemployment by sending foreign workers home, by cutting working hours or by reducing labour force participation. See A. Maddison, 'Monitoring the Labour Market,' *Review of Income and Wealth*, June 1980 which presents a full set of labour market accounts for France, Germany and the U.K., and A. Maddison and B.S. Wilpstra (eds.), *Unemployment: The European Perspective*, London, 1982, which presents similar accounts for the Netherlands. However, as the recession deepened, the relative importance of the various expedients for mitigating unemployment diminished, except in Japan.

Agriculture is now much less important than industry and services, but in all countries the rate of decline in agricultural employment was checked after 1973. This suggests a certain degree of labour hoarding which traditionally takes place in this sector in periods of weak demand.

2.3 Energy

A major concern of policy since 1974 has been to reduce demand for energy and stimulate the search for substitutes for OPEC oil. The most powerful instrument favouring such an outcome was, of course, the huge increase in oil prices engendered by the OPEC cartel's deliberate action in 1973–1974 and as a consequence of political upheaval in Iran after 1979. Unfortunately the U.S.A. delayed for some years before abandoning its control policies which encouraged consumption and discouraged the search for oil, but by 1982 a sharp decrease in energy consumption per unit of GDP had been achieved in all Western economies, and by the end of 1982 OPEC output had fallen to 14 million barrels a day – less than half the 1973 level of 31 million barrels. To some extent the cyclical weakness in demand has caused this OPEC weakness, and led to the drop in price from 34 to 29 dollars a barrel. But even with economic recovery in the west it seems that this spectre has been broken.

TABLE 10 – ENERGY CONSUMPTION PER $1000 OF REAL GDP (GDP IN 1975 U.S. RELATIVE PRICES, ENERGY IN TONS OF OIL EQUIVALENT)

	1950	1960	1973	1982
France	0.62	0.57	0.56	0.46
Germany	0.90	0.65	0.69	0.56
Japan	0.60	0.53	0.57	0.43
Netherlands	0.54	0.54	0.80	0.65
U.K.	1.04	0.84	0.78	0.61
U.S.A.	1.27	1.09	1.10	0.93
Average	0.83	0.70	0.75	0.61

Source: 1950 from W.S. and E.S. Woytinsky, *World Population and Production,* Twentieth Century Fund, New York, 1953, p. 941. For 1960 and later years from *Energy Policies and Programmes of IEA Countries, 1978 Review,* and subsequent IEA publications. GDP from I.B. Kravis, A. Heston and R. Summers, *World Product and Income,* Johns Hopkins, Baltimore, 1982.

3   THE OPENNESS OF WESTERN ECONOMIES

In the post-war years, western economies became much more open (see table 11). Except for France and Japan, the ratio of trade to GDP in 1982 was a good deal higher than in 1929, and the capital markets of all the major countries except France and Japan are also very open. These countries are committed to the liberal international economic order through reciprocal obligations in the European Economic Community, GATT *etc.*, and in spite of some backsliding, none of them has reacted to stagnation by the violently protectionist measures which characterised the 1930's. This is a major reason why their experience and policies have been more similar than in the 1930's. Openness facilitated post-war growth in important respects, but it has imposed noticeable constraints on expansionary policy since 1973.[3]

TABLE 11 – RATIO OF MERCHANDISE EXPORTS TO GDP AT CURRENT PRICES

	1929	1938	1950	1960	1973	1982
France	14.0	6.9	10.6	11.2	14.3	17.0
Germany	15.3	5.6	8.5	15.7	19.4	26.7
Japan	16.0	14.9	7.8	9.4	9.0	13.0
Netherlands	29.4	18.4	28.6	36.1	39.8	48.3
U.K.	15.5	8.4	16.7	13.9	17.1	20.5
U.S.A.	5.0	3.6	3.6	4.0	5.3	6.9
Average	15.9	9.6	12.6	15.1	17.5	22.1

Source: Exports f.o.b. from A. Maddison, 'Growth and Fluctuation in the World Economy,' *Banca Nazionale del Lavoro Quarterly Review*, June 1962; *Historical Statistics of Japanese Economy*, Bank of Japan, 1962, pp. 89–90; UN, *Yearbooks of International Trade Statistics* and *Monthly Bulletin of Statistics*. GDP 1950–81 except as specified from OECD, *National Accounts*, various issues, and 1938 from OEEC, *Statistics of National Product and Expenditure*, No. 2, Paris, 1957. Otherwise, France 1929 estimated from L. Fontvieille, *Evolution et Croissance de l'État Française 1815–1969*, ISMEA, Paris, 1976, p. 1743. Germany, 1929–38 from Statistisches Bundesamt, *Bevölkerung und Wirtschaft 1872–1972*, Kohlhammer, Stuttgart, 1972, p. 260. Japan 1929–60 from K. Ohkawa and M. Shinohara, *Patterns of Japanese Development*, Yale, 1979, pp. 252–4. Netherlands 1929 estimated from *Tachtig jaren statistiek in tijdreeksen*, CBS, The Hague, 1979. U.K. 1929–60 from C.H. Feinstein, *National Income, Expenditure and Output of the United Kingdom 1855–1965*, Cambridge, 1972. U.S.A. 1929–60 from 'The National Income and Product Accounts of the United States: An Introduction to the Revised Estimates for 1929–80,' *Survey of Current Business*, December 1980.

3 For a succinct analysis of the constraints of openness for macropolicy, see A. Lindbeck, 'Stabilization Policy in Open Economies with Endogenous Politicians,' *American Economic Review*, May 1976.

A major intercountry difference in post-1973 policy approaches was in the degree of acceptance of floating exchange rates. The U.S.A. endorsed them wholeheartedly and accepted with indifference the two-way volatility of exchange rates which others have called under- and overshooting. U.K. policy was generally similar though the deflationary Healey-IMF episode in 1976 was triggered by exchange rate concerns. Japan geared exchange rate and monetary policy to domestic needs and lived without great concern for big two-way fluctuations in the yen-dollar rate. Continental EEC countries attached greater importance to exchange stability, created a fixed rate system within the EMS and were willing to follow a degree of deflation (*i.e.* higher interest rates than the domestic situation warranted) to protect their exchange rates from too great a depreciation against the dollar.

A striking feature of the post-1973 situation at least until 1982 was the very large flow of western capital and recycled OPEC funds to the third world and to the communist countries.[4] This contrasts with 1929–1938

TABLE 12 – WORLD EXPORTS 1929–38 AND 1973-82

	World export volume	World export prices		World export volume	World export prices
1929	100.0	100.0	1973	100	100.0
1930	93.3	85.7	1974	105	140.9
1931	85.9	65.9	1975	100	151.6
1932	73.2	52.4	1976	112	154.6
1933	75.2	59.5	1977	116	168.2
1934	78.0	73.0	1978	122	184.9
1935	82.3	71.4	1979	131	218.2
1936	85.9	73.0	1980	134	260.6
1937	96.9	80.2	1981	133	254.6
1938	90.6	75.4	1982	130	243.1

Source: 1929–38 from A. Maddison, 'Growth and Fluctuation in the World Economy, 1870–1960,' *Banca Nazionale del Lavoro Quarterly Review*, June 1962. 1973–81 UN *Monthly Bulletin of Statistics*, 1982 from Bank for International Settlements *Annual Report*, Basel, June 1983, p. 85. 1973–82 figures exclude centrally planned economies.

4 See A. Lamfalussy, 'Changing Attitudes Towards Capital Movements,' in: F. Cairncross (ed.), *Changing Perceptions of Economic Policy*, London and New York, 1981 for an illuminating survey of post-war policy on international capital movements and a pragmatic willingness to contemplate controls. In this field there is also scope for a review of the current fiscal-regulatory mix which often gives greater incentives for foreign than for domestic investment.

when the international capital market broke down at the beginning of the world crisis and there was widespread debt default. However, the *de facto* 1982 default of Mexico on public debt to private banks, and subsequent moratoria for Argentina, Brazil and Venezuela have emphasised the risks underlying the vast web of debt. There are now powerful international organisations, like the IMF, to mitigate these problems, a greater sense of mutual responsibility and more mutual consultation than there was in the 1930's. Nevertheless, the recent moratoria mean that the flow of capital to the third world and communist countries will decline, and this combined with reduced OPEC income means that export markets outside western countries will be less buoyant.

4   CHANGES IN THE 'ESTABLISHMENT VIEW' OF ECONOMIC POLICY

In the course of the past decade the 'establishment view' of macroeconomic tasks and instruments has changed considerably. This change was not simply a response to events, but also helped to mould them. Cautious policy has been a significant cause of slower growth.

Any 'view' attributed collectively to the 'establishment' (by which I mean the top officials in finance ministries and central banks, together with those politicians holding office in such fields, and those academic economists currently caught in the web of policy as advisors, consultants *etc.*) must necessarily be eclectic, particularly if the group is defined to encompass several countries. But in the Golden Age of the 1950's and 1960's, one might reasonably have spoken of an AROMatic consensus (activist real output management). This reflected the functional convergence of several different ideological approaches. U.K. policy was Keynesian in inspiration with strong emphasis on demand management through fiscal instruments, augmented from time to time by incomes policy. France and Japan were more ambitious: their interventionist activism involved both demand and supply management. In Germany, Erhard's social market approach distinguished less between micro and macro problems, and stressed the virtues of competition and work incentives. A large influx of eager workers from East Germany and Southern Europe added to labour market flexibility. A powerful Bundesbank gave high priority to price stability and German success in maintaining high levels of activity was bolstered by buoyant exports. Nevertheless, Erhard and his state secretary Müller-Armack were also well aware of the virtues of demand management; they enacted the Growth and Stability Law in 1963, with a commitment to high employment policy which was subsequently extended in 1967. The Dutch approach was in essence not dissimilar to the German. The United States started the post-war era with a domestic Keynesian commitment, and an international policy heavily oriented to support economic growth. During the Eisenhower presidency there was an eight-year reversion to old-fashioned fiscal rectitude, in which economic growth and full employment received low priority. American policy reverted to Keynesianism from 1961 to 1979.

The consensus embodied liberalism in international trade and payments policy, and commitment to an extensive and regular network of international consultation and cooperation. A central institution was the fixed exchange system of Bretton Woods. This institution, together with the concept of a fairly predictable and cosy Phillips-curve trade-off between inflation and un-employment, did much to determine the rules of thumb or knee-jerk reactions of policy.

The simultaneous disappearance of Bretton Woods and the Phillips-curve 'norms' shattered the consensus.

In an attempt to preserve it, the establishment Keynesians, who ack-nowledged that inflation involved substantial welfare losses, suggested a variety of mechanisms for influencing the wage-price negotiating process which they regarded as sociopolitical in character.

Arthur Okun was the prototype of this group. He thought the welfare losses from inflation were substantial,[5] and his 'discomfort' index equated them with those of unemployment. The Keynesian tradition had always regarded wages and prices as sticky and stressed the likelihood of high unem-ployment and output losses if governments attempted to curb inflationary expectations by depressing demand. Okun developed this analysis further with new explanations of why labour and product markets were not of a clearing variety. His preferred direct-action weapon for mitigating inflation was the T.I.P., *i.e.* a tax-based incomes policy to provide fiscal rewards for price-stabilising firms.[6] This idea was only one of the new alternatives to or variants on incomes policy which had been the main earlier Keynesian direct-action weapon against inflation, but which had lost face because of the failure of statutory incomes policies in the Nixon administration in the U.S.A., and the Heath government in the U.K.[7]

5 See A.M. Okun, 'Efficient Disinflationary Policies,' *American Economic Review*, May 1978.
6 See A.M. Okun, *Prices and Quantities*, Brookings, Washington D.C., 1981. A.M. Okun and G.L. Perry (eds.), *Curing Chronic Inflation*, Brookings, Washington D.C., 1978, dis-cusses different kinds of T.I.P. arrangements including both penalties and rewards.
7 Other direct action Keynesian weapons include suggestions for reform of collective

However, this line of defence did not prove convincing because few people in the establishment were convinced that these Keynesian direct-action weapons could be successful without a social consensus, or that the more ingenious technocratic variants were workable.

An alternative defence of the AROMatic approach involved advocacy of cohabitation with the natural rate of inflation. This nonestablishment view was advocated strongly by Tobin,[8] in the early 1970's. He rated the welfare losses from inflation a good deal less than Okun, and had only modest faith in T.I.P. and other direct-action tools. This policy position involved a fair degree of accomodation of inflation, particularly in a period when exogenous shocks played a significant role. Keynesians of this persuasion have also suggested augmenting Keynesian remedies by measures to promote greater supply-side flexibility.[9]

As inflation worsened in the 1970's, Tobin himself edged a little closer to the Okun position,[10] and in any case, the 'establishment view' never embraced the Tobin argument because it feared what lay beyond the hitherto cosy Phillips-curve trade-off. The establishment accepted the two propositions of the 'Razor's Edge' theorem: (a) that accomodation of inflation beyond a certain point would lead inexorably to hyperinflation, (b) that hyperinflation will bring civilised life to an end.[11]

bargaining (J.E. Meade, *Wage-Fixing*, London, 1982), direct controls on prices and wages (J.K. Galbraith, *Money*, Houghton Mifflin, New York, 1975), and the advocacy of import controls by the Cambridge Economic Policy Group, see F. Cripps, 'Britain's Economic Crisis and Possible Remedies,' *Economic Policy Review*, Cambridge, April 1980. In Sweden the Rehn-Meidner advocacy of labour market policy had a similar intent.

8 See J. Tobin, 'Inflation and Unemployment,' *American Economic Review*, March 1972.

9 See Deepak Lal, 'Do Keynesian Diagnoses Need Revision,' in: A. Maddison and B.S. Wilpstra (eds.), *op.cit.*

10 For his appreciation of the state of theoretical dispute on macropolicy, see J. Tobin, 'The Monetarist Counter-Revolution Today An Appraisal,' *Economic Journal*, March 1981, and J. Tobin, *Asset Accumulation and Economic Activity*, Chicago, 1980.

11 See F. Modigliani, 'The Monetarist Controversy or Should We Foresake Stabilization Policies?,' *American Economic Review*, March 1977 for a critique of the first proposition. Analysis of the relation between inflation and hyperinflation is a Latin American speciality, and is still underdeveloped in the countries under review. Interpretation of this borderline area has been very heavily influenced by C. Bresciani-Turroni, *The Economics of Inflation*, London, 1937, which treated the 1923 German inflation as an uncontrollable monetary phenomenon. This experience is also frequently cited by amateur historians and sociologists as the prime cause of the Nazi rise to power, particularly by those who wish to downplay the influence of deflationary policy and mass unemployment in Germany between 1929 and 1933. A much superior analysis of this leading

Another major reason for the collapse of the AROMatic consensus was the vigour and cogency with which an alternative monetarist view had been prepared and propounded in the academic world, particularly by Milton Friedman. He had never accepted the Phillips-curve trade-off as a lasting phenomenon and predicted bigger inflation. He had advocated floating rates and a new policy armoury which was easy to understand. It laid major emphasis on monetary policy and monetary targets, it rejected discretionary demand management as fine-tuning, and involved disregard of unemployment and output losses, which were held to be natural and inevitable consequences of the previous overheating. These were in any case likely to be temporary, because this policy approach would allow the self-adjusting potential of the economy to reassert itself. International consultation was hardly necessary if exchange rates were allowed to float freely. Keynesian direct-action instruments such as incomes policies or T.I.P. were regarded as useless placebos at best, and the Tobin position was rejected by the Razor's Edge theorem. The distinction between potential and actual output disappeared.

The switch in the 'establishment view' was most extreme and sudden in the U.K., which had been the Keynesian heartland, and made a complete *volte face*. The change begin with the Callaghan government and was greatly reinforced by the Thatcher government. In other countries, the change was slower and more blurred. There was an eclectic McCrackenite period generally in the mid-1970's which was an attempt to blend the old approach with monetarism.[12] This view now lingers only in France. There was a recrudescence of structuralism (particularly strong in the Netherlands) which accepts the macro-deflationary essentials of the monetarist diagnosis, but combines it with activist micro-manipulation (tax kickbacks, subsidies, regulation *etc.*).

The hard core of the new 'view' is the monetarist programme, but also includes a revival of old-fashioned fiscal conservatism which is alarmed by unbalanced budgets (particularly important in the Netherlands), the backlash

example of Western hyperinflation can be found in F.D. Graham, *Exchange, Prices and Production in Hyperinflation in Germany 1920–1923*, Princeton, 1930, and in C.L. Holtfrerich, *Die deutsche Inflation 1914–1923*, Berlin, 1980. For a useful comparative survey of hyperinflations, see P. Cagan's contribution to M. Friedman (ed.), *Studies in the Quantity Theory of Money*, Chicago, 1956. A.J. Brown, *The Great Inflation 1939–1951*, Oxford, 1955 is another illuminating study of this gray area. See O. Eckstein, *Core Inflation*, Prentice Hall, 1981 for a recent attempt to decompose and dedramatise the inflationary process.

12 See P. McCracken *et al.*, *Towards Full Employment and Price Stability*, OECD, June, 1977.

TABLE 13 – ANNUAL PERCENTAGE CHANGE IN THE CONSUMER PRICE INDEX 1972–1983

	1972	1973	1974	1975	1976	1977	1978	1979	1980	1981	1982	1983[a]
France	6.2	7.3	13.7	11.8	9.6	9.4	9.1	10.8	13.6	13.4	11.8	9.0
Germany	5.5	6.9	7.0	6.0	4.5	3.7	2.7	4.1	5.5	5.9	5.3	3.0
Japan	4.5	11.7	24.5	11.8	9.3	8.1	3.8	3.6	8.0	4.9	2.7	2.7
Netherlands	7.8	8.0	9.6	10.2	8.8	6.4	4.1	4.2	6.5	6.7	5.9	2.5
U.K.	7.1	9.2	16.0	24.2	16.5	15.8	8.3	13.4	18.0	11.9	8.6	3.7
U.S.A.	3.3	6.2	11.0	9.1	5.8	6.5	7.7	11.3	13.5	10.4	6.1	3.5
Average	5.7	8.2	13.6	12.2	9.1	8.3	6.0	7.9	10.9	8.9	6.7	4.1

Source: OECD, *Economic Outlook*, July 1982, and *Main Economic Indicators*.
[a] May 1982–May 1983.

TABLE 14 – CURRENT BALANCE OF PAYMENTS AS PERCENT OF GDP 1960–1982

	1960–73 annual average	1974–82 annual average	1974	1975	1976	1977	1978	1979	1980	1981	1982
France	0.3	-1.0	-2.3	-0.0	-1.5	-0.7	0.6	0.0	-1.4	-1.4	-2.2
Germany	0.7	0.4	2.7	1.0	0.9	0.8	1.4	-0.8	-1.9	-1.1	0.5
Japan	0.5	0.2	-1.0	-0.1	0.7	1.6	1.7	-0.9	-1.1	0.5	0.7
Netherlands	0.7	1.2	3.0	2.3	3.0	0.7	-0.8	-1.1	-1.5	2.4	2.4
U.K.	-0.2	-0.3	-4.6	-2.0	-1.7	-0.1	0.5	0.0	1.6	2.4	1.5
U.S.A.	0.1	0.0	0.3	1.2	0.3	-0.7	-0.7	-0.1	0.3	0.1	-0.3
Arithmetical Average	0.4	0.1	-0.3	0.4	0.3	0.3	0.5	-0.5	-0.7	0.5	0.4

Source: OECD, *Economic Outlook*, July 1982.

against the welfare state and big government (particularly important in the U.S.A.). It has been reinforced by the influence of the rational expectations/ new classical economics, which rejects discretionary policy as impotent (rather than ineffective as the monetarists suggested), and has greater faith than the monetarists in instantaneous market clearing, so it holds out hopes of a rapid reversal of inflationary expectations if governments adopt 'credible' *i.e.* obviously masochistic policies. The policy implications of this position are very close to those of the prewar 'Austrian' school, which has also enjoyed a revival. For this school, the preferred and most creative business cycle situation is the recession which should be allowed to do its job in reallocating productive factors unhindered by government and trade union interference.[13]

This analysis of the general ideological drift is a stylized representation of reality. The 'establishment view' is not identical in all countries, and it is changing over time. My point in stressing it is that there has been an ideological change and that the stagnation of output and the rise in unemployment were in an important degree an intended outcome of policy. To an important degree the 'establishment view' is that the new policy mix has been successful, and this new ideology is therefore likely to slow down future growth.

The overriding preoccupation of the new orthodoxy has been to reduce the rate of price inflation. This goal was pursued with gradualist rather than big-bang tactics, so that the deceleration has been a long, drawn-out affair. By mid-1983, however, it was clear that a very substantial deceleration of inflation had been attained, with rates of price increase which were back within the 1960's norms in five of the six countries. In the AROMatic era this would have been the signal for vigorous policies of expansion, but the U.S.A. is the only one of the countries to take significantly expansionary measures. It has done this with a policy-mix which inhibits expansionary policy elsewhere, but this is not the only reason for lack of stimulative action elsewhere. The new orthodoxy waits for a self-starting recovery rather than one stimulated by policy.

A second major consideration of policy in the 1974–1982 period was the balance of payments. There was an obvious need for adjustment to meet the new deficits with OPEC countries, initial worries about the possibilities for recycling OPEC reserve accumulations, and caution about operating in the

13 See F.A. Hayek, *Monetary Theory and the Trade Cycle*, 1933 reprinted by Kelley, New Jersey, 1975, L. Robbins, *The Great Depression*, London, 1935, L. von Mises, Theory of Money and Credit, Cape, London, 1934, and M.N. Rothbard, *America's Great Depression*, New York, 1963.

604   A. MADDISON

new world of floating exchange. But except in France, the swing was rather small over the whole period, and in the Netherlands the current surplus was actually bigger than in 1960–1973. In fact, the balance of payments stance was too cautious. As a result reserves grew and these countries were able to extend or intermediate credits to the third world which rose from $119 billion in 1973 to $626 billion in 1982. It would have been healthier for both world output and finance if the big western countries had run smaller surplusus or bigger deficits and lent less.

5   MEASUREMENT OF THE POLICY STANCE

When we turn from my rather freewheeling characterisation of the 'ideological' switch in policy and try to document it by actual measurement of policy action, the evidence is, on the surface, rather weak. The most conventional indicator of the governmental posture and the one which figures most in political discussions, is the degree to which the government budget is in balance. A refined version of this indicator is given in tables 15 and 16, which show the 'fiscal outcome,' *i.e.* the overall balance of government transactions in relation to the total economy. This involves some degree of international standardisation because the numerator is not the balance of expenditure and taxation as shown in the budget (whose scope varies from country to country for institutional reasons), but is adjusted to include all those items of ex-

TABLE 15 – SUMMARY INDICATORS OF FISCAL AND MONETARY POSTURE

	Average fiscal outcome as percent of GDP		Average (end-year) discount rate	
	1960–73	1974–82	1960–73	1974–82
France	0.5	−1.1	5.3	9.8
Germany	0.6	−3.3	4.2	5.0
Japan	1.0[a]	−3.6	6.2	6.0
Netherlands	−0.5	−3.1	4.8	6.7
U.K.	−0.8	−3.6	6.9	12.5
U.S.A.	−0.0	−1.2	4.5	8.9
Average	0.1	−2.7	5.3	8.2

Source: OECD, *National Accounts,* and *Economic Outlook,* I.M.F., *International Financial Statistics.*
[a] 1970–73.

penditure and revenue which are classified as 'general government' transactions in the national accounts. The denominator is also standardized to
refer to the UN/OECD measure of gross domestic product.

It can be seen from table 16 that in all six countries budget deficits were a
good deal higher than in the 1960–1973 period.

At first sight it might seem that such a general increase in deficits reflected
a policy of economic stimulus. In fact total government expenditures rose
faster in relation to GDP from 1973 to 1982 than they had in 1960–1973.
But the growth in expenditure shares and deficits did not reflect governmental volition. The rise in government current and capital expenditure on
goods and services was in all cases slower than from 1960 to 1973; it was
transfer expenditure which showed the big increase. A good deal of the expansion was due to the built-in stability characteristics of social transfers in
advanced welfare states, and quite a significant part of apparently 'discretionary' increases was the result of social momentum to extend the coverage and
generosity of benefits which had built up in earlier years. The shortfall in tax
and social security levies because of unemployment, and higher expenditures
on debt service were further 'built-in' factors contributing to the deficits.

The comparison of fiscal policy stances can only be very crude, because of
differences in national economic situations, quality of data, problems in
interpreting objectives, and much bigger theoretical divergencies about the
nature and role of fiscal leverage than was the case in the 1960's.[14] However,
a Keynesian view would have been more concerned with the full employment
deficit, and less obsessive about the actual deficit. It would also have given
more weight to the fact that the impact of inflation was reducing the real
burden of government debt.

It is even more difficult to characterise the monetary policy stance in a
comparative way than it is for fiscal policy. In the 1970's, monetary policy
has been expressed in terms of control of monetary aggregates,[15] but comparison of growth of these between periods reflects mainly the price changes
which they validated rather than variations in the stringency of policy. We
therefore rely on a rather old-fashioned comparison of changes in discount
rates (see table 15).

This indicator is very crude because of institutional differences between

14 See A.I. Peacock and G.K. Shaw, 'Is Fiscal Policy Dead?,' *Banca Nazionale del
Lavoro Quarterly Review*, June 1978 for a useful review of this controversy.
15 See OECD, *Monetary Targets and Inflation Control*, Paris 1979, and *Budgetary
Financing and Monetary Control*, Paris, 1982 for an analysis of the development of
monetary policy instruments.

TABLE 16 – FISCAL OUTCOME – GENERAL GOVERNMENT NET LENDING AS PROPORTION OF GDP AT CURRENT PRICES

	1974	1975	1976	1977	1978	1979	1980	1981	1982	1983[a]
France	0.6	-2.2	-0.5	-0.8	-1.9	-0.7	0.3	-1.9	-2.6	-3.4
Germany	-1.4	-5.8	-3.6	-2.4	-2.5	-2.7	-3.2	-4.0	-3.9	-3.7
Japan	0.4	-2.6	-3.8	-3.8	-5.5	-4.8	-4.5	-4.0	-4.1	-3.4
Netherlands	-0.1	-2.7	-2.4	-1.4	-2.6	-3.7	-3.9	-4.8	-6.4	-6.9
U.K.	-3.8	-4.9	-5.0	-3.4	-4.2	-3.2	-3.3	-2.5	-2.0	-2.5
U.S.A.	0.5	-3.5	-1.5	-1.0	0.0	0.6	-1.3	-1.0	-3.8	-4.4
Average	-0.6	-3.6	-2.8	-2.1	-2.8	-2.4	-2.7	-3.0	-3.8	-4.1

Source: OECD, *National Accounts*, and *Economic Outlook*, December 1982, and July 1983.
[a] The OECD forecast in *Economic Outlook*, July 1983.

countries, and because the stringency of interest rates depends to some extent on how fast prices are rising. Nevertheless, it seems preferable to use nominal rather than deflated interest rates as an indicator because a big increase in nominal rates can reduce asset values in unindexed capital markets even if the real rate of interest has not risen. Using nominal rates, it is clear from table 15 that monetary policy in 1974–1982 was more restrictive than in 1960–1973 in all the countries except Japan.

Real interest rates reached rather high levels in 1982, and monetary policy was kept very tight in both the U.K.[16] and U.S.A., with both countries experiencing exchange rate appreciations. These countries have a predominating role in international capital markets, and their policies had the effect of keeping up interest rates in the EMS countries which wanted to protect their exchange rates. Since the autumn of 1982, the U.S. Federal Reserve Bank has eased monetary policy and this led to a general easing of monetary stringency as other western countries were quick to follow. There has also been a substantial fall in longer-term rates which should help revive demand for housing, which was particularly depressed by high mortgage rates.

6 THE OUTLOOK

After nine years of growth below potential, the objectives of deflationary policy have been largely achieved. Price momentum is back to 1960's magnitudes and the power of OPEC to impose another significant increase in real energy prices is gone. There is also large slack capacity in all the western economies, both skilled labour and physical capital. The liberal trading order has been kept more or less intact, the international capital market is wounded but survives as a substantial net lender, most western countries have ample exchange reserves, and there are very adequate arrangements for articulate international consultation of a type which did not exist in the 1930's.

Nevertheless, economic policy in western countries is extremely cautious, and the few big countries which tried a lonesome path to expansion – Germany in 1979 and France in 1981 – found it necessary to retract (Germany had misfortune in timing expansion to coincide with the second oil shock,

16 For a monetarist critique of the overtightness of British monetary policy for mistargeting on M3, see the testimony of David Laidler in *Monetarism in the United States and the United Kingdom, Hearings,* Joint Economic Committee, U.S. Congress, October 6, 1981, 1982. For a highly sophisticated critique of British policy from another perspective, see W.H. Buiter and M. Miller, 'The Thatcher Experiment: The First, Two Years,' *Brookings Papers on Economic Activity,* 2, 1981.

and France made its Keynesian objectives more difficult by simultaneous nationalisations and by overdefending its exchange rate). The unprecedented openness of these economies is a major reason why individual countries are unwilling to take much action on their own.

Hence the outlook is for a very weak expansion, and for little reduction in unemployment. The dangers of understimulus are rather obvious. They include (a) frittering away production potential by lowering investment in R and D and physical capacity; (b) leaving the large fraction of unemployed youth without the job experience which builds skills; (c) risks of nationalist beggar-your-neighbour attacks on the liberal trade regime; (d) weakening of the export markets and payments position of developing countries, with further risks for defauls in the international capital market; (e) the risk that the next general recession will be bigger than 1974–1975 and 1981–1982 because it will start from a weaker base.

Summary

ECONOMIC STAGNATION SINCE 1973, ITS NATURE AND CAUSES: A SIX COUNTRY SURVEY

This paper analyses the stagnation experience of the five biggest Western economies and the Netherlands since 1973 in historical perspective. It finds that the slowdown is due to three causes: (1) longer term productivity deceleration; (2) inevitable production/employment disturbance caused in absorbing the two OPEC shocks and the collapse of the Bretton Woods payments arrangements; (3) the switch to overcautious macropolicy as embodied in a new 'establishment view,' which keeps growth below potential, as did the 'Treasury view' which Keynes attacked in pre-war years.

[14]

Origins and Impact of the Welfare State, 1883-1983 *

I. From Nightwatch State to Welfare State 1883-1983

The capitalist epoch began around the time of Marx's birth, and until the 1880s, when he died, the state's role was primarily passive and permissive. Classical political economy advocated policies of *laissez-faire*, and these were generally pursued in both the social and the economic field. It was an era when technology offered large prospects for profit, when international markets were much more open to competition than in the preceding merchant capitalist epoch, when profits were untaxed, and there was an unlimited supply of cheap labour at more or less subsistence wages.

The distribution of the gains from capitalist development was unequal. The bourgeoisie grew in size. They and older landowning and professional élites were enriched. In the working class, average subsistence needs increased as the urban-rural ratio rose, but illiteracy, population pressure, a repressive poor law, legal constraints on union activity and political disfranchisement kept them hungry, insanitary, ragged and exploited.[1]

The state was a nightwatchman whose expenditure was concentrated on soldiery and police protecting property and the national frontiers. It seemed inevitable that such a system should someday crack, as its ultimate legitimacy was so threadbare.

Since then capitalism has not collapsed and the state's role has grown significantly in four main dimensions:

---

* A shorter version of this paper was presented at the Marx-Keynes-Schumpeter Symposium at the University of Gröningen in September 1983 and I am grateful to the participants for comments on that draft. I am also grateful to Friedrich Klau and Riel Miller for extensive discussions on this topic.
    [1] I am here simply making the point which seems incontestable, that inequality increased. I am not suggesting that working class standards did not increase in absolute terms from 1820 to the 1880s.

a) "welfare state" expenditures (i.e. income transfers and provision of services like education and health) have grown enormously and more or less continuously upward. They now average nearly 30 per cent of GDP in advanced capitalist countries;

b) state involvement in steering the economy through activist macroeconomic management to promote full employment became very substantial from the 1930s to 1970s but is now receding;

c) the state's role as a producer and employer has grown significantly over the long haul. But the process has not been monotonically upward and it has been less important than European socialist parties originally hoped or liberal pessimists (like Hayek, von Mises and Schumpeter) feared;

d) microeconomic intervention in resource allocation through legal prescriptions, regulation, taxes, subsidies and tax expenditures (tax dispensations) is much bigger than it was a century ago, but to a degree which is difficult to measure. Here too the increase in the state role has fluctuated, and has not been inexorably upward.

This paper is concerned with the first of these phenomena where the growth of state responsibility has been the most spectacular. It analyses the reasons for the emergence of the welfare state, and its impact on economic growth.

The classical economists who wrote in the century preceding the 1880s (Smith, Ricardo, Malthus and J.S. Mill) had a good deal to say about state intervention in economic life and its likely repercussions. They were all strongly in favour of minimal state action because they thought that market forces would promote a natural harmony of interests. In particular any sizeable state interference to redistribute income was expected to reduce incentives to work and save. Malthusian population diagnosis predicted an inevitable return to mass poverty because of the stimulus that charity would give to fertility and population growth.

The incentive problem connected with public poverty relief had been extensively discussed in England in the sixteenth century when the Protestant takeover reduced the capacity of the church to provide charity. The classical economists were reiterating views already arti-

Origins and Impact of the Welfare State. 1883-1983   57

TABLE 1

TOTAL GOVERNMENT EXPENDITURE AS A PERCENT OF GDP AT CURRENT PRICES

	1880	1913	1929	1938	1950	1960	1973	1981
France	11.2	9.9 (a)	12.0	21.8	27.6	33.9	38.8	48.7
Germany	10.0 (b)	17.7	30.6	42.4	30.4	33.4	41.2	47.7
Japan	9.0 (c)	14.2	18.8	30.3	19.8	20.9	22.9	34.1
Netherlands	n.a.	8.2 (d)	11.2	21.7	26.8	36.1	49.1	59.0
U.K.	9.9	13.3	23.8	28.8	34.2	32.9	41.5	46.4
U.S.A.	n.a.	8.0	10.1	18.5 (e)	22.5	27.9	32.0	34.4
Average		11.9	17.8	27.3	26.9	30.9	37.6	45.1

a) 1910-13; b) 1881; c) 1885; d) 1910; e) 1939.

Sources: 1950-81 generally from *National Accounts of O.E.C.D Countries*, various issues.

Otherwise as follows:

France: 1880-1938, numerator from L. FONTVIEILLE, *Evolution et Croissance de L'Etat Française 1815-1969*, ISMEA, Paris, 1976, pp. 2118, and 2124-9. The current price physical product denominator (p. 1743 for 1880-1929) was increased by a coefficient of 1.43 to convert it to a GDP basis, and 5 year averages were unscrambled by interpolation. 1938 GDP from *Statistics of National Product and Expenditure No. 2*, O.E.E.C., Paris, 1957.

Germany: 1881 and 1913 from S. ANDIC and J. VEVERKA, "The Growth of Government Expenditure in Germany since Reunification", *Finanzarchiv*, January 1964, p. 241-3.

Japan: 1885-1960 from K. OHKAWA and M. SHINOHARA, *Patterns of Japanese Development*, Yale, 1979, pp. 251-4 and 370-2.

Netherlands: 1910-38 very rough estimate derived from *Tachtig Jaren Statistiek in Tijdreeksen*, CBS, The Hague, 1979, pp. 144 and 150. Trend movement derived from "rijksuitgaven" divided by net national product at market prices, adjusted by the 1950 coefficient of this ratio to government expenditure/GDP ratio derived from OECD National Accounts for 1950.

U.K.: 1880 government expenditure from J. VEVERKA, "The Growth of Government Expenditure in the United Kingdom since 1790", *Scottish Journal of Political Economy*, 1963; 1913 from A.T. PEACOCK and J. WISEMAN, *The Growth of Public Expenditure in the United Kingdom*, NBER, Princeton, 1961, p. 164. GDP at market prices from C.H. FEINSTEIN, *National Income, Expenditure and Output of the United Kingdom 1855-1965*, Cambridge, 1972, pp. T 14-8.

U.S.A.: 1913-39 government expenditure from S. FABRICANT, *The Trend in Government Activity in the United States Since 1900*, NBER, New York, 1952, p. 27. 1913 GNP from J.W. KENDRICK, *Productivity Trends in the United States*, NBER, Princeton, 1961, p. 297; 1929 and 1939 GDP from "The National Income and Product Accounts of the United States: An Introduction to the Revised Estimates for 1929-80", *Survey of Current Business*, December 1980.

culated in preparing Elizabethan legislation, or by Locke and Defoe in the seventeenth and eighteenth centuries.[2] The classical views were expressed most harshly by Malthus, and most generously by J.S. Mill.[3] But, by modern standards, the gap between Malthus and Mill was rather small. Both believed that unless poverty relief was kept to meagre levels (involving material privation and constraints on the liberty of paupers) the economic results would be disastrous.

In 1883, therefore, most observers expected the state's role in economic life to remain minimal. The dominant official view was the *laissez-faire* "liberalism" of classical political economy, which we have just described. Marx viewed the state as an apparatus to reinforce the exploitation of the masses by the ruling class. He never conceived of the capitalist state significantly promoting growth or alleviating social tension. When he did back political action within a capitalist framework it was not to urge the potential for welfare expenditure, but for regulatory intervention to shorten working hours to 10 per day. Most other socialists (e.g. Robert Owen) in the first half of the nineteenth century wanted to solve the social problem via self-starting utopian experiments that did not require state action.

One exception to the received opinion was Adolph Wagner, who in 1883 enunciated his "law" of a steadily rising proportion of public expenditure. Wagner was a *Kathedersozialist* who like many professors before and since, was distilling a tendency which he wanted to see rather than describing a phenomenon based on empirical observation.[4] But Wagner in fact adumbrated the characteristics of a welfare state. He favoured progressive taxation, public education, state control of railways etc. Between 1820 and 1880 there was no observable tendency for increased public expenditure in capitalist countries, but Wagner's prediction was better than his history. "Welfare state" expenditures have grown from below 2 per cent of GDP in 1883[5] to a typical figure of

---

[2] For the sixteenth century texts see A.E. BLAND, P.A. BROWN, and R.H. TAWNEY, *English Economic History: Select Documents*, Bell, London, 1914, and for eighteenth century views, see D. MARSHALL, *The English Poor in the Eighteenth Century*, Kelley, New York (reprint) 1969.

[3] Mill was more optimistic because he believed that birth control could check the Malthusian spectre. He also favoured freedom for trade unions, encouragement to cooperatives, peasant landownership, wealth equalization through death duties, some limited subsidization of elementary education and regulation of working hours. See J.S. MILL, *Principles of Political Economy*, Sixth (people's) edition, Longmans Green, London, 1880.

[4] See A. WAGNER, "Three Extracts on Public Finance", in R.A. Musgrave and A.T. Peacock, eds., *Classics in the Theory of Public Finance*, Macmillan, London, 1967.

[5] The U.K. figure for 1890 was 1.9 per cent of GDP, see A.T. PEACOCK and J. WISEMAN, *Op.cit.*, p. 184. For other countries, the figure is more difficult to establish, but the German ratio

nearly 30 per cent in 1983, and now dwarf public expenditure on the traditional domain.

One of the remarkable things about the growth of the welfare state is that there has been rather little analysis by economists of the dimensions of its growth, the causes of the growth and its economic impact. As the average per capita output of capitalist countries has increased more than sevenfold since 1883, it is quite clear that the classical economists were wrong about the disincentives to growth arising from state welfare. Their type of critique was also weakened by the discredit into which Malthusian population theory and classical wage theories had fallen by the 1880s when economists such as Marshall and Sidgwick began to take a brighter view of welfare possibilities. From time to time liberal economists have continued to allege the disincentive impact of transfers. Robbins and Rueff suggested that prewar unemployment was caused in large degree by overgenerous unemployment insurance, but until recently, this was regarded as wild exaggeration. The liberal critics therefore concentrated their attack on biases in voting procedure which prevent the electorate from getting what it really wants,[6] or on the "free lunch" illusion by which populist politicians delink social benefits from the taxation required to finance them, or on the bureaucratic dangers that loom when state programmes grow.[7]

There has of course been a very large literature on public choice which has explored the microeconomic efficiency of government expenditure and taxation and its welfare impact, but there is very little on the state in the growth accounting literature or in that on the longer run macroeconomics of capitalist performance. Simon Kuznets, J.W. Kendrick and Dale Jorgenson have more or less ingnored the question, and E.F. Denison gives it very little weight. Colin Clark is an exception in that he published an article in 1945 predicting that tax levies beyond a threshold of 25 per cent of GDP would end the capitalist accumulation process. But Clark was proved quite wrong by subsequent experience.

---

in the 1880s seems to have been well below 2 per cent from the evidence in ANDIC and VEVERKA, *Op. cit.* It is interesting to note that the proportion was similar in England in the seventeenth century. According to Gregory King's calculation for 1688 the poorer half of population (51.4 per cent) were estimated to spend more than they earned by an amount equivalent to 1.4 per cent of national income. This includes dissaving, but most of it was presumably transfers. See G.E. BARNETT, *Two Tracts by Gregory King*, Johns Hopkins, Baltimore, 1936, p. 31.

  [6] See J.M. BUCHANAN and G. TULLOCH, *The Calculus of Consent*, University of Michigan, Ann Arbor, 1962.

  [7] See W.A. NISKANEN, *Bureaucracy and Representative Government*, Aldine, Chicago, 1971.

In the past decade, however, liberal critics of the welfare state have advanced much stronger allegations about its dysfunctionality and they have also gained greatly in political power particularly in the U.K. and U.S.A. Former welfare state supporters have manifested various kinds of disillusion about its ability to resolve social conflict. In both camps, old fashioned fiscal conservatism has reemerged rather strongly as the momentum of welfare state expansion has been largely responsible for creating sizeable budget deficits in the period of slow economic growth since 1973. Governmental action to dismantle the welfare state has as yet been very limited, and does not begin to match the victories which the "liberal" school has had in moving macroeconomic policy away from what were predominantly Keynesian guidelines. Meanwhile, the evidence on the economic impact of the welfare state remains fuzzy.

This paper is intended as a diagnosis of the growth of the welfare state since 1883. It examines the causal forces behind its expansion, and its impact in mitigating the social conflicts which Marx detected in the first decades of modern capitalist development. It also considers whether the welfare state has reached dysfunctional limits which impede economic performance and which might provide a rationale for its dismantlement.

On such broad issues, it is difficult to assemble convincing evidence. I have therefore augmented the historical record with cross-country analysis of development in the five big capitalist economies plus the Netherlands.

II The Sociopolitical Forces which Produced the Welfare State

Bismarck was the politician who pushed capitalism in a new direction. Given the Prussian tradition of paternalism and *Staatsräson* he had no *laissez-faire* inhibitions limiting state action in social and economic affairs. As the architect of German unification he had a clearer view of the need to legitimate his new creation than politicians in older countries who took this for granted. Germany also had the best organised socialist movement, and many academics, like Wagner, who felt that the state needed to play a more active role in mitigating the social tensions of capitalism.

Since Bismarck's day, the welfare state has expanded enormously under a variety of political pressures. It has grown incrementally, and not as a grand design or a neatly structured edifice which serves clearly defined goals.

The growth impetus has come from several different sources. On the right side of the political spectrum, we have Bismarck who regarded state provision of welfare as "system-legitimation" — a positive counterpart to the Anti Socialist laws. Marxist critics of welfare capitalism have continued to interpret it in this Bismarckian light. But, on the left, the welfare state has been supported by reformist socialists who have seen its growth as fulfilment of their distributive aspirations, i.e. as "system-modification". This possibility was suggested in 1889 by the English Fabian socialists who saw the possibility of using the state for redistributive purposes because extensions of the franchise would provide opportunities for the labour movement to lobby and govern, and the advancing "material wealth" which was by then discernible made such redistribution possible without wrecking incentives.[8]

Between Bismarck and Bernard Shaw, we find other pundits of the welfare state who occupy a middle ground in the political spectrum. As the franchise was extended and real income rose, populist politicians used the state's taxing power to provide both services and transfer incomes on a huge scale, in a succession of *ad hoc* attempts to mitigate social tension and meet the claims of competing social groups.[9]

In the following discussion, I have defined the welfare state to include government expenditure in kind on services which meet "merit wants" (education, health services, housing etc.), and expenditures on cash transfers (pensions, unemployment compensation, family allowances, cash sickness benefits etc.). I have also assumed that the notion of welfare state requires some consideration of the size and progressivity of tax burdens.

Germany pioneered state insurance with three pieces of legislation. Sickness insurance was legislated in 1883 (extended in 1888) and

---

[8] See BERNARD SHAW, *et al.*, *Fabian Essays*, Allen and Unwin, London Jubilee edition, 1948. Shaw made these points very clearly on pp. 171-3. Sidney Webb argued with a characteristic piece of gradualist history that the concept of a social organism had been developing since 1848 under the influence of J.S. Mill, and cited regulatory and public health acts which had been passed earlier in the course of the nineteenth century, as evidence of the eclipse of *laissez-faire*.

[9] For a description of the process from one who, by European standards, occupies the populist middle ground, but who sometimes describes himself as a reformist socialist, see J.K. GALBRAITH, *American Capitalism: The Concept of Countervailing Power*, 1952.

provided income maintenance payments for workers during sickness absence who earned below a certain income threshold. In 1884 there was legislation providing compensation for industrial injury in occupations where there were substantial risks of this nature, and in 1889 a system of old age and sickness pensions was introduced. The first two schemes involved compulsory contributions by employers and workers and covered 12 million workers in 1890. The pension scheme was the only one which involved a government subsidy.

In the period from these reforms until the first world war, Western European countries generally moved in the German direction. The U.K. held on to the Malthus-Ricardo-Mill tradition until 1909 when the Welsh populist Lloyd George introduced state coverage for similar risks and also introduced unemployment insurance (which Germany did not have until 1927).

The pressure for such reforms in the U.K. came from the labour movement which grew strongly after the easing of restrictions on trade union activity and the gradual extension of the franchise. The evidence of poverty collected in the first social surveys (Mayhew, Booth and Rowntree) also helped, as did the activism of Fabian reformers like the Webbs who conducted inquiries into the Poor Laws. Beveridge's 1909 enquiry into unemployment had a significant impact and he was later a very influential advocate for a comprehensive welfare state and Keynesian policies to promote full employment. [10]

The last quarter of the nineteenth century saw increased public provision of compulsory primary education, and in the beginning of the twentieth century some secondary education. There was limited state action to improve sanitation and promote public health, but generally no public provision of health services. The motivation for state action in these fields was similar to that in social insurance. There was also some awareness of education's role in improving human capital which in Europe probably went furthest in Germany which promoted higher education and R and D earlier than other European countries.

State education was resisted in ecclesiastical circles and helped to provoke the *Kulturkampf* in Germany and the controversy surrounding the Jules Ferry laicisation reforms in France. In all Western European countries there was a degree of compromise, by which the state left

---

[10] See W.H. BEVERIDGE, *Unemployment: A Problem of Industry*, Longmans, London, 1909, *Full Employment in a Free Society*, Allen and Unwin, London, 1944, and *Social Insurance and Related Services: Report by Sir William Beveridge*, HMSO, London, 1942.

some role for church education and usually contributed substantially to finance it.

In the U.S.A., the tradition of rugged individualism held strong until 1935 when the social security system was introduced as part of Roosevelt's New Deal. Although the American provision of social insurance still lags well behind that of European countries, the U.S.A. went much further than Europe as an early provider of public education. This was in part because as an immigrant country, education was viewed as a powerful vehicle for national integration. U.S. tradition since Jefferson has always given strong emphasis to social mobility rather than social equality, and there was also a greater awareness than in Europe of the role of education in contributing to the supply potential of the economy.

In Japan, which in spite of location, can appropriately be treated as a major bastion of Western capitalism, the role of the state in social insurance has been a good deal smaller than in Europe, partly because other social arrangements covered some of the risks. But the state has always played a major role in bolstering the supply potential. Ever since the Meiji restoration in 1867, Japanese government has promoted technical progress, industrial investment and spent heavily on a public education system which provides an ample supply of skills and social discipline. Since 1960, Japanese welfare state expenditures have risen very rapidly.

During the first world war, the role of the state increased enormously in absorbing resources directly for military purposes, in raising taxes, and in regulating resource allocation. The degree of mobilization was probably higher than in the Napoleonic wars, and the potential regulatory scope for state action within a capitalist framework was amply demonstrated. The outcome of the war was a shakeup in the social hierarchy, particularly in defeated countries such as Germany and Austria, the emergence of a communist state on the doorstep of Western capitalism, and a strong feeling after such large scale and in retrospect such pointless sacrifices, that the political legitimacy of all Western countries needed to be consolidated by universal suffrage in countries which had been subjected to general mobilization.

Thus the forces that had fostered social insurance in prewar years were strengthened. The wartime growth of the government's role in production and resource allocation was largely reversed, but the coverage of social insurance and public education grew. Most countries developed some kind of unemployment insurance and widened the

TABLE 2

COVERAGE OF PUBLIC PENSION INSURANCE 1900-1970
(Percent of Labour Force)

	France	Germany	Netherlands	U.K.
1900	8	51	0	0
1915	9	58	50	55
1930	15	64	55	90
1945	52	65	66	109
1960	93	82	169	99
1970	100	81	170	98

Source: P. FLORA and A.J. HEIDENHEIMER, *The Development of Welfare States in Europe and America,* Transaction Books, New Brunswick, 1981, p. 76.

coverage of "public assistance", i.e. non-insured social risks began to be covered with less of the stigma of older attitudes towards the "undeserving poor". In every country included in our table 1, government expenditure increased as a share of GDP between 1913 and 1929. The war also brought a substantial regulatory role for government in housing markets, and in some countries important public housing construction and rental programmes. In almost all countries, the tax structure had been extended in wartime to include income tax, and this feature persisted. In this sense, the expansion of war finance had a certain ratchet effect as suggested by Peacock and Wiseman. [11]

However, this ratchet was only a very partial reason for government expansion as experience subsequent to the 1929 recession demonstrated that government's role could make a major leap forward in peacetime. Between 1929 and 1938 there was a massive increase in the relative importance of public expenditure in all the countries covered in table 1. Germany and Japan both tilted sharply towards totalitarianism with much increased military spending and widespread control of industry. But in France, the Netherlands, U.K. and U.S.A.,

---

[11] See A.T. PEACOCK and J. WISEMAN, *The Growth of Public Expenditure in the United Kingdom*, Princeton, 1961.

massive unemployment led to increased social spending, to "structural" support programmes for industry, farm relief programmes etc.

The second world war involved many Western governments in even bigger resource mobilization efforts than the first, to higher levels of taxation, and to patterns of taxation which would produce a strong "fiscal dividend" in the subsequent conditions of rapid economic growth and inflation. This was one factor facilitating finance of public spending in the postwar era. Nevertheless, the average proportion of GDP spent by Western governments was lower in 1950 than in 1938. This was due in substantial measure to the dismantlement of the totalitarian state in Japan and Germany and to their demilitarization. In other countries the government role had grown. In the U.K. there was a substantial increase in public spending due to the implementation of Beveridge's comprehensive social insurance proposals by the postwar Labour government, to the introduction of a national health service and education expansion. In France too there was a broadening of social insurance and health coverage, as well as a very generous pro-natal system of family allowances.

Progress in these directions also occurred in the Netherlands, but it was only later that it became the top government spender, when the natural gas bonanza put large extra resources (about 6 per cent of GDP) into the hands of government. In the U.S.A., the increased role of government by 1950 was due to high military spending and the cold war. Social expenditure had not increased.

In the golden years of fast economic growth to 1973, the growth of government expenditure was concentrated in health, education, housing, the new area of "environment", and on social transfers. Expenditure on traditional public goods such as defence actually declined as international tensions eased.

In providing merit goods and social transfers, there was a certain "bandwaggon effect". Once these programmes grew beyond a certain size and involved large tax levies, there was a tendency for their coverage to become universal rather than to remain restricted to beneficiaries who would otherwise be in hardship. Middle class voters could see that there were substantial benefits from participation in schemes which they had in any case to help finance, and the stigma of indigence which may have formerly been involved in participation in such schemes disappeared when their coverage was enlarged and benefits came as cheques in the mail rather than cash in the post office.

The growth of welfare expenditure was encouraged by changes in demographic structure. In the 1880s, people aged 65 and more were on average only 5 per cent of the population of our six countries. Now they are 13 per cent of the population and count rather heavily in voting for both pensions and health services from which they are the main beneficiaries.

The persistent incidence of inflation and general practice of rent control made it difficult to make private provision for retirement or risk contingencies via insurance or small investments. This produced a greater reliance on indexed inflation-proof public schemes.

Another significant influence in raising the welfare share of GDP was the fact that measured productivity in education and health services was declining. There was pressure from professional bodies to increase manning levels, e.g. the teachers' unions pressed for smaller classes, medical personnel in hospitals rose in numbers relative to the patients. In a period of rapid economic expansion, teachers and doctors were also able to preserve rather favourable salary scales.

Finally, an important reason for expansion in transfer payments in the 1960s was the widened concern with poverty whose nature was redefined. In the 1950s, the British tended to think that the postwar expansion of their welfare state had virtually abolished poverty and that progressive taxation had produced much greater equality. In 1951, Rowntree and Lavers found only 2 per cent of the population of York in poverty compared with nearly 18 per cent in 1936.[12] But in the 1960s British poverty was rediscovered and redefined. Titmuss[13] was the leader of the movement in the academic world but it had wide support amongst the growing number of sociologists and social workers who formed the major lobby for the expansion of social coverage on a non-insurance basis, e.g. supplementary benefits. In 1970 Atkinson, after a careful survey of the evidence concluded that 9 per cent of the British population were living in poverty.[14]

---

[12] See B.S. ROWNTREE and G.R. LAVERS, *Poverty and the Welfare State*, Longmans, London 1951 on poverty levels. DUDLEY SEERS had also argued that there had been a major shift in income distribution because of tax changes, *Bulletin of the Oxford Institute of Statistics*, Vol. 12, no. 10. This induced C.A.R. CROSLAND to downplay the importance of distributional issues in his influential, *The Future of Socialism*, Cape, London, 1956, pp. 42-53. At the same time and using the same evidence J. STRACHEY, *Contemporary Capitalism*, Gollancz, London, 1956 produced a Marxist revisionist analysis of the historical development of welfare states and progressive taxation as social progress obtained by pressure of the labour movement in parliamentary democracies.

[13] See R.H. TITMUSS, *Income Distribution and Social Change*, Allen & Unwin, London, 1962.

[14] See A.B. ATKINSON, *Poverty in Britain and the Reform of Social Security*, Cambridge, 1970. This new awareness of poverty was also present in other European countries, as reflected e.g. by the creation of the Swedish Low Income Commission or L. STOLERU's book, *Vaincre La Pauvreté Dans les Pays Riches*, Flammarion, Paris, 1977.

The rediscovery and redefinition of poverty also occurred in the U.S.A. In 1952 Galbraith wrote "in recent times, for most people the biological minimums of food, clothing and even shelter have been covered as a matter of course. By comparison the further wants are comparatively unimportant".[15] But in 1962 Harrington claimed that a majority of Americans was poor and later Jencks defined poverty as a relative not an absolute level of living.[16] The academic lobby played a smaller role in influencing the Lyndon Johnson welfare expansion (Food Stamps, Medicaid, Medicare and AFDC) than academics did in the U.K. The main reason was the widespread rioting by the black population in the cities, who wanted something more material to supplement civil rights legislation.

In the 1960s and 1970s there was a general move to universalize social benefits, so that the distinction between social insurance and social transfers has become rather blurred in Europe, and in the Netherlands has virtually disappeared. In the U.S.A. where social insurance programmes are run on a trust fund basis, there is still a sharp distinction between insurance and "welfare" payments, and the latter have less political legitimacy than in most of continental Europe. The U.K. is in a somewhat intermediate position with supplementary income payments and various *ad hoc* benefits playing a major role.

Since 1973, there has been another substantial leap forward in government expenditure. This has generally been smaller than in the 1930s, and has occurred because of the built-in stabilizer characteristics of advanced welfare states, even though the macropolicy stance of governments has generally been restrictive. Unemployment compensation has obviously risen, though by less than would seem warranted by the extent of the problem. Other social transfers have risen, to some extent to disguise unemployment. Hence Dutch payments for "handicapped" workers removed from the labour force rose from 2 to 4.3 per cent of GDP from 1973 to 1980. In other countries there have been substantial extra payments for "pensions" to workers persuaded to retire prematurely, and many supplementary (non insurance) programmes have grown to augment the income of the unemployed.

---

[15] See J.K. GALBRAITH, *American Capitalism*, Penguin, London, 1952, p. 116.
[16] See M. HARRINGTON, *The Other America*, Penguin, London, 1962, and C. JENCKS, *Inequality*, Harper, New York, 1972.

III. Government Spending Levels in the 1980s

Table 3a classifies the present structure of government expenditure. The traditional domain of "public" wants is not much larger now than it was in the 1880s. The big difference is in "merit" wants,[17] and income maintenance, which together absorb amounts varying from 20 per cent of GDP in Japan and the U.S.A. where the government commitment is weakest to nearly 40 per cent in the Netherlands where it is highest.

Table 3 defines government in a national accounting sense, and therefore excludes public enterprise activity. The importance of this varies between countries a good deal, being now biggest in France amongst the countries listed and smallest in the U.S.A.[18]

Another problem of inter-country comparability arises from "tax expenditures" i.e. derogations deliberately built into the normal system of tax liability as a form of subsidy for certain types of spending. Thus the U.S. gives tax derogations to people with children or for private pensions, health insurance and education spending. These are a substitute for some of the government expenditure on these items which occur in other countries. Table 3 may therefore somewhat understate the U.S. governmental role compared with that of Europe. In Germany tax expenditures amounted to 1.9 per cent of GDP in 1980 and in the U.S.A. federal "tax expenditures" alone were bigger at 5.7 per cent of GDP in 1979.[19] However, it is very difficult to compare "tax expenditures" (a) because they are a tax foregone rather than a tax collected: (b) they require definition of the "normal" tax structure from which a derogation is granted, and (c) a definition of "normal" income as distinct from expenses incurred in producing it.

---

[17] The terms "public" wants and "merit" wants are taken from R.A. MUSGRAVE, *The Theory of Public Finance*, McGraw Hill, New York, 1959. Public goods must be provided by the State because they benefit everyone, and it is not possible to restrict access to them. They could not be financed by voluntary contributions, because the great majority would choose to be "free riders". Unlike "public goods", "merit goods" flow in some degree to individuals who could be required to pay personally for the services received.

[18] In 1975-9, employment in public enterprise was estimated to be 4.4 per cent of total employment in France, 7.9 per cent in Germany, 8.2 per cent in the U.K. and 1.6 per cent in the U.S.A., see L. PATHIRANE and D.W. BLADES, "Defining and Measuring the Public Sector: Some International Comparisons", *Review of Income and Wealth*, September 1982, p. 273. Since the 1981 nationalizations, French public enterprise employment has risen to around 10 per cent of the labour force.

[19] See DEUTSCHER BUNDESTAG, *Achter Subventionsbericht*, Bonn, 1981 and the annual U.S. reports on this topic.

Origins and Impact of the Welfare State, 1883-1983   69

TABLE 3(a)

STRUCTURE OF GOVERNMENT EXPENDITURE AS PERCENT OF GDP AROUND 1980

	France 1980	Germany 1980	Japan 1981	Netherlands 1978	U.K. 1979	U.S.A. 1978	Average
Total	46.9	48.5	34.1	57.8	43.4	33.8	44.1
TRADITIONAL COMMITMENTS							
Debt Interest	1.7	1.9	3.6	4.0	4.6	2.7	3.1
"Public Wants" (Defence and General Government)	7.4	8.5	4.2	10.3	8.7	8.5	7.9
MODERN COMMITMENTS							
Economic Services	3.4	5.3	6.0	3.8	3.9	3.4	4.3
"Welfare State" (Merit Wants and Income Maintenance)	34.4	32.8	20.3	39.7	26.2	19.2	28.8

TABLE 3(b)

DETAIL OF WELFARE STATE EXPENDITURES AS PERCENT OF GDP AROUND 1980

	France 1980	Germany 1980	Japan 1981	Netherlands 1981	U.K. 1979	U.S.A. 1978	Average
"Merit Wants"	15.9	13.8	12.6	(18.7)	13.9	9.0	13.8
a) Education	5.7	5.1	5.0	7.1	5.4	5.7	5.7
b) Health	6.2	6.5	4.7	6.6	4.7	2.5	5.2
c) Housing	3.2	1.4	2.4	} (5.0)	3.3	0.4	} 2.9
d) Other	0.8	0.8	0.5		0.5	0.4	

	France 1981	Germany 1981	Japan 1981	Netherlands 1981	U.K. 1981	U.S.A. 1981	Average
Income Maintenance	18.4	16.8	7.7	19.3	10.5	9.0	13.6
a) Pensions	11.9	12.5	4.8	13.0	7.4	7.4	9.5
b) Sickness Cash Benefits	1.2	0.7	0.1	1.9	0.3	0.1	0.7
c) Family Allocations	2.2	1.2	1.6	2.0	1.4	0.5	1.5
d) Unemployment Compensation	1.9	1.4	0.4	1.0	1.4	0.5	1.1
e) Other	1.2	1.0	0.7	1.4	0.0	0.5	0.7

Source: OECD Statistics Division, OECD *National Accounts,* and Ducth national sources.

Other problems in defining the scope of government expenditure arise from government loan guarantees or other devices to disguise off-budget loan activity.[20] However, table 3 is based on national accounting conventions which are more comparable between countries than "budgets", and less likely to conceal governmental off-budget loan activity.

It should be noted that the state is not nearly so important proportionately as an employer or producer as it is in terms of expenditure. Public employment averages about a sixth of total employment in our six countries, and government carries out a somewhat bigger proportion of production.[21]

Table 4 shows the structure of government current revenue in 1950 and 1980 which provides a rough idea of how government finances its expenditure. In 1980 roughly equal amounts were raised from social security levies, direct and indirect taxation (another 4 per cent being raised from miscellaneous current revenue, and in that year all the countries ran a budget deficit). However the situation varies by country. Social security levies are three times as high in the Netherlands as in the U.K. The Netherlands is also in the lead for direct taxes, and "other" sources of revenue; the U.K. is the leader for indirect taxes, levying almost three times the proportion of Japan. Since 1950 all countries have raised the tax burden considerably with the biggest leap in the Netherlands.

IV. The Social Impact of Government Action

It is not easy to give an authoritative assessment of the role of government in social progress over the past century, because it is not possible to reconstruct a counterfactual framework, without this very pervasive influence. However, there can be little doubt that government has improved and equalized social welfare by mitigating the hardships associated with unemployment sickness and old age and by improving health and education.

---

[20] See *The Underground Federal Economy: Off-budget Activities of the Federal Government*, JOINT ECONOMIC COMMITTEE, U.S. CONGRESS, April 1982, which argues that more comprehensive measures of government produce a less alarmist view of budget deficits.

[21] See *Employment in the Public Sector*, OECD, Paris, 1982, p. 12.

TABLE 4

CATEGORIES OF GOVERNMENT CURRENT REVENUE AS A PROPORTION OF GDP

	Total Current Revenue	Social Security Levies	Direct Taxes	Indirect Taxes	Other
			1950		
France	32.9	9.3	5.6	15.3	2.7
Germany	31.6	7.7	9.0	13.4	1.5
Japan[a]	21.9	1.9	8.9	9.7	1.4
Netherlands	33.0	4.3	13.4	12.7	2.6
U.K.	33.5	3.4	13.8	16.0	0.3
U.S.A.	24.0	2.4	13.2	8.3	1.0
Average	29.5	4.8	10.7	12.6	1.6
			1980		
France	45.4	18.3	8.6	14.7	3.8
Germany	42.8	14.1	12.6	12.8	3.3
Japan	28.2	7.4	11.0	7.6	2.2
Netherlands	55.4	18.4	16.1	12.1	8.8
U.K.	40.6	6.2	14.4	16.2	3.8
U.S.A.	32.7	7.9	14.8	8.2	1.8
Average	40.9	12.1	12.9	11.9	4.0

(a) 1952.

Source: National Accounts of OECD Countries 1950-68 and 1963-1980 editions, OECD, Paris.

The average person in 1983 has a life expectation of around 73 years in the advanced capitalist countries as against 46 a century earlier. Most of this improvement would probably have occurred without much change in government's role, because of progress in medicine and pharmacology. But the rather sharp division of life into three stages of schooling, work and retirement would not have been as marked without the heavy government commitment to both compulsory and postcompulsory education, its provision of pensions and retirement rules. Now the average person gets 10 years of schooling and 8 years of retirement, and government has helped to institutionalize this.

Similarly the average person now works only 1700 hours a year, because of shorter hours, time off for paid vacations and paid sickness absenteeism. Collective bargaining helped to bring this about, but so did government action. The intercountry differences in this field — five week holidays in France and 1 week in Japan clearly reflect different government attitudes.

Kuznets has suggested that capitalist development at first involved increased inequality[22] and then took a U-turn towards increased equality. This conclusion is certainly correct for disposable income after taxes and transfers though it is less true for primary income.

Governments have helped equalize primary income over the past century by provision of more equal educational opportunity and permitting greater freedom for trade union bargaining. The bargaining power of workers was also strengthened by the termination of what Arthur Lewis called the phase of unlimited supply of labour (i.e. the wilting supply of labour from agriculture, and in the U.K. case, from Ireland).[23] This was not due to government action but is probably one of the main reasons why the bargaining power of workers is stronger in advanced capitalist countries than in the third world.

However, in the past two or three decades, the availability of social transfers has tended to increase inequality in primary income because it induces people to stop working and to set up separate household units which are only sustainable because of the existence of social transfers.

When post-tax, post-transfer incomes are considered, the most powerful equalizing instrument is cash transfers provided by social security and welfare schemes. The tax systems of Western countries do much less to promote equality than their apparently progressive structures would suggest, as the big expansion of social transfers since 1950 has been financed mainly by rather regressive social security levies (see table 4).

The relative role of the factors influencing income distribution is shown in table 5. It is clear that transfers reduce the inequality of original income most. The decile ratio for "original" income is 49:1 and

---

[22] See S. KUZNETS, "Economic Growth and Income Inequality", *American Economic Review*, March 1955. See F. KRAUS' contribution to FLORA and HEIDENHEIMER, *Op. cit.* for an extensive review of the literature on distribution and of causal influences.

[23] See W.A. LEWIS, "Economic Development with Unlimited Supplies of Labour", *Manchester School of Economic and Social Studies*, May 1954. For an interpretation of Japanese experience from this perspective, see R. MINAMI, *The Turning Point in Economic Development: Japan's Experience*, Kinkuniya, Tokyo, 1973. The abandonment of classical (subsistence) wage theory in favour of marginal productivity theory occurred at about the time of the Lewis transition in European countries.

Origins and Impact of the Welfare State, 1883-1983   73

TABLE 5

RATIO OF TOP TO BOTTOM INCOME DECILE

	Original Income	Pre-Tax Post-transfer Income	Post-Tax Income	Distributive Impact of Transfers	Distributive Impact of Direct Taxes
France	33.7	20.7	21.7	13.0	−1.0
Germany	34.1	12.4	10.8	21.7	1.6
Japan	n.a.	9.9	9.1	n.a.	0.8
Netherlands	n.a.	13.5	10.7	n.a.	2.8
U.K.	66.8	11.8	9.4	55.0	2.4
U.S.A.	61.8	23.7	17.7	38.1	6.0
Average	49.1	15.3	13.2	32.0	2.1

Source: M. SAWYER, "Income Distribution in OECD Countries", *Occasional Studies, Economic Outlook*, OECD, Paris, July 1976.

the post transfer ratio is 15:1. The tax system, by contrast only reduces the post-transfer range from 15:1 to 13:1.[24]

Over the past century, the distribution of wealth has also become more equal mainly because of the spread in house-ownership, but the inequality of wealth is very much greater than that for income. Wealth taxes are small, inheritance tax can often be bypassed, and there have been no revolutionary confiscations of wealth as in Eastern Europe. The U.K. Gini coefficient for wealth distribution in 1971 was .84 compared with .34 for pre-tax income. In the U.S.A. the comparable figure for wealth in 1962 was .76, and .41 for income (in the 1970s).[25] The wealth picture is more equal if future pension rights are considered as capital,

---

[24] The only country which produces a regular survey of the overall distributional impact of the welfare state including public services in kind such as health and education is the U.K. British education and health expenditures were found to be redistributive but to a milder degree than for transfers. See "The Effects of Taxes and Benefits on Household Income, 1981", *Economic Trends*, December 1982.

[25] See *Social Trends*, No. 4 for U.K. wealth distribution, and D.S. PROJECTOR and G.S. WEISS, *Survey of Financial Characteristics of Consumers*, 1966, p. 30 for U.S. wealth distribution. Income distribution is from M. SAWYER, *Op. cit.* The Gini coefficient ranges from zero (complete equality) to 1 (complete inequality where the top person has all wealth or income).

but few people would consider non-negotiable rights in state pensions (or other social benefits) as part of their wealth.[26]

One of the egalitarian arguments for increased educational expenditures has been the expectation that it would contribute to social mobility. This is an area where change is very difficult to measure, but the evidence suggests that the changes have been rather modest. Thus a major U.S. study concluded that social mobility did not change much in the first half of the twentieth century and sociologists in other countries have reached similar conclusions.[27]

V. Has the Welfare State Reached Dysfunctional Limits?

Around 1960, there was a spate of literature claiming that the welfare state had created social harmony within Western capitalism,[28] and that class conflict had disappeared because levelling processes had produced a middle class social continuum in which the ruling class had been dismantled and the working class had acquired bourgeois status and aspirations. There was a widespread tendency in such circles to reject the word "capitalist" as an appropriate epithet to describe Western society, and to come up with labels like "post-industrial", "post-capitalist", etc.

In retrospect these views of social harmony seem naïve, although Marx's prediction of continuous sharpening of class antagonism and material welfare between rich and poor has not proved correct.

In the 1960s and 1970s, conflicts within Western society became more obvious, though they were not of the type which Marx predicted. Major race riots in the United States were a reminder that the melting

[26] See ROYAL COMMISSION ON THE DISTRIBUTION OF INCOME AND WEALTH, Report No. 1, *Initial Report on Standing Reference*, HMSO, London, 1975, pp. 86-92 shows the bottom 80 per cent of the population owning 17.6 per cent of conventional wealth, but 40.7 per cent if the capitalized value of occupational and state pensions is included. This calculation does not deduct the capitalized value of future contributions.
[27] P.M. BLAU and O.D. DUNCAN, *The American Occupational Structure*, Wiley, New York, 1967, A. MADDISON, "Education, Inequality and Life Chances: The Major Policy Issues", in *Education Inequality and Life Chances*, OECD, Paris 1975, J.A. BRITTAIN, *The Inheritance of Economic Status*, Brookings, Washington D.C., 1977, and J.A. BRITTAIN, *Inheritance and the Inequality of Material Wealth*, Brookings, Washington D.C. 1978.
[28] See G. MYRDAL, *Beyond The Welfare State*, Duckworth, London, 1960, D. BELL, *The End of Ideology*, Free Press, New York, 1960.

pot theory was a myth[29] and that major U.S. cities were not harmonious communities but ethnic ghettoes, replete with crime. Student disturbances almost toppled the Gaullist regime in France in 1968, and New Left student radicalism shook universities to their foundations in many countries. Urban terrorism became an important menace in Germany and Italy. The Women's Liberation movement gained momentum. Union militancy became greater in many countries.[30]

In the 1970s, there was a sharp acceleration in the rate of inflation and a general failure of attempts to deal with this problem by techniques of social accommodation such as incomes policies and social contracts.

Thus the rosy 1960s views about the degree of social harmony achieved by the welfare state had begun to fade. The difficulty of abolishing poverty (when it is defined as relative deprivation) became clear and a series of studies showed that tax-transfer structures were full of inequities, notches and "poverty traps". In the early 1970s there was a growing realization that a tax-transfer system which had grown piecemeal and involved so many people, was very difficult to reform or rationalize. The Nixon Administration had a first try at simplifying the U.S. tax and social security system by introducing a kind of negative income tax, but failed in this objective, and similar intentions in the U.K. were abandoned at an earlier stage.[31]

These kinds of disillusion were reinforced after 1973 by the substantial budget deficits and growing public debt which were the consequence of slower economic growth in countries with a heavy commitment to income maintenance (see tables 6 and 7). In conditions of stagnating income, there has been greater electoral resistance to high taxation and greater hostility to programmes for the "undeserving poor" than in the earlier postwar decades of rapid growth. This has helped to bring radical conservative governments to power in the U.K. and U.S.A. which are committed to cutbacks in the welfare state. But they are not alone in this, because old-fashioned fiscal worries about budget deficits and increased government debt have induced many other Western countries to envisage similar moves.

---

[29] See N. GLAZER and D.P. MOYNIHAN, *Beyond the Melting Pot*, MIT Press, Cambridge, Mass., 1963 for a realistic survey of blacks,Puerto Ricans, jews, Italians and Irish in New York City.
[30] See C. CROUCH and A. PIZZORNO, *The Resurgence of Class Conflict in Western Europe Since 1968*, Macmillan, London, 1978.
[31] For U.S. experience, see D.P. MOYNIHAN, *The Politics of A Guaranteed Income*, Vintage Books, New York 1973, and H.J. AARON, *Politics and the Professors*, Brookings, 1978. For the U.K., see *Proposals for a Tax Credit System*, Cmnd. 5116, HMSO, 1972. For the aspirations of a Giscardist minister, see L. STOLERU, *Vaincre La Pauvreté*, Flammarion, Paris, 1977. The OECD also gave consideration to this kind of arrangement, see *Negative Income Tax*, OECD, Paris, 1974.

TABLE 6

FISCAL OUTCOME – GENERAL GOVERNMENT NET LENDING AS PROPORTION
OF GDP AT CURRENT PRICES

	Average 1960-73	Average 1974-82	1983
France	0.5	−1.1	−3.4
Germany	0.6	−3.3	−3.1
Japan	1.0(a)	−3.5	−3.4
Netherlands	−0.5	−3.1	−8.1
U.K.	−0.8	−3.5	−2.7
U.S.A.	−0.0	−1.2	−3.8
Average	0.1	−2.6	−4.1

(a) 1970-3

Source: 1960-77 derived from *National Accounts of OECD Countries,* 1960-71, 1961-78 and 1962-79 editions, and from OECD *Economic Outlook,* December 1983, p. 33.

TABLE 7

RATIO OF NATIONAL DEBT TO GDP
end year debt in nominal value divided by GDP for year stated

	1960	1973	1982
France	28.6	7.5	11.2 (a)
Germany	7.4	6.7	19.3
Japan	6.2	6.7	26.4 (b)
Netherlands	43.9	23.1	39.5
U.K.	110.3	52.6	52.7(c)
U.S.A.	46.7	25.9	32.6

(a) 1981; (b) 1979; (c) 1978.

Source: Debt from IMF, *International Financial Statistics,* except U.K. from *Annual Abstract of Statistics,* HMSO, London, adjusted to end-year basis. GDP from OECD National Accounts Statistics.

Within the academic world, economists of "liberal" persuasion
have grown hugely in number and have revived the long moribund
Ricardo-Malthus spirit in a frontal attack on the welfare state. One of

the most formidable of these is Martin Feldstein, who is Chairman of Mr. Reagan's Council of Economic Advisors. He has claimed that income-transfer programmes have "exacerbated the instability of family life", that social security has reduced U.S. personal saving by half, caused the capital stock to be two fifths smaller than it might otherwise have been, and that unemployment compensation has raised unemployment.[32]

On the macroeconomic level, there is no clear evidence that the growth of the welfare state has had adverse effects on economic performance. The welfare state absorbs the same proportion of resources in Japan and the United States but these two countries have had very different growth records and very different investment rates. The welfare state is bigger in all the European countries than in the U.S.A., and they have also had more rapid growth and much bigger investment rates. The vigour of postwar economic growth was not noticeably impeded up to 1973 by growth of the welfare state, and it would be hard to prove that the welfare state had a major role in the general growth slowdown since 1973.

Nevertheless it is clear that the expansion of the welfare state, which has strengthened the legitimacy of capitalism and modified its social content in the past century, has now produced characteristic problems which affect all six countries to some degree:

Merit Goods

(i) In health and education services, the "output" is largely provided by highly organised professional groups who are used to relatively high incomes and to finding employment for virtually all their members. As a result measured productivity in terms of pupil/teacher and patient/doctor ratios has fallen continuously. This has been a major reason for the increasing relative cost of public services (see table 8) and for accusations of overmanning,[33] though this relative price effect has been smaller since 1973;

---

[32] See M. FELDSTEIN, *The American Economy in Transition*, NBER, Chicago, 1980, p. 3; "Social Security, Induced Retirement, and Aggregate Capital Accumulation", *Journal of Political Economy*, September-October 1974; "The Economics of the New Unemployment", *Public Interest*, Fall 1973.

[33] See R. BACON and W. ELTIS, *Britain's Economic Problem: Too Few Producers*, Macmillan, London, 1978, who stress, wrongly in my view, that overmanning is a peculiarly British problem. In fact the U.K. health service has been able to check costs and ration demand more effectively than other countries have done with different arrangements.

TABLE 8

RATES OF PRICE INCREASE IN THE PUBLIC AND PRIVATE SECTOR
(per cent)

	Government Consumption		Private Consumption	
	1950-73	1973-80	1950-73	1973-80
France	7.5	12.7	5.3	10.7
Germany	5.6	5.7	2.8	4.7
Japan	9.0[a]	9.5	4.7[a]	9.1
Netherlands	8.2	8.6	4.2	7.3
United Kingdom	6.1	17.9	4.3	15.5
United States	4.5	8.1	2.7	7.9
Average	6.8	10.4	4.0	9.2

(a) 1952-73
Source: OECD, *National Accounts*, 1950-68 and 1963-80 editions.

TABLE 9

MANNING LEVELS IN HEALTH AND EDUCATION

	Population Per Physician		Pupil Teacher Ratios in Primary Education	
	1960	1980	1950	1979
France	1,024	463	28.4[b]	20.0
Germany	699	442	47.7	19.6
Japan	971	785	36.6	25.2
Netherlands	909	545	35.0	24.3
U.K.	1,130[a]	956	29.8	19.4[c]
U.S.A	718	498	31.0	19.3[d]
Average	909	615	34.8	21.3

(a) 1956; (b) 1955; (c) 1978; (d) 1977.
Source: UNESCO *Statistical Yearbooks*, WHO, *World Health Statistics*, and OECD Dept. of Social Affairs.

(ii) Public health and education services are generally provided free or with user charges very much below cost. This has inflated demand particularly for the most expensive kind of medical services which are both skill and capital intensive. The problem is much more acute in health than in education, because public health expenditure is concentrated on services where the demand is difficult to distinguish from private consumption, and where externalities are not present. In most countries supply is privately organized as well, and governments which finance the services cannot ration their availability. The managerial problems under (i) and (ii) are not confined to government services but have also been felt acutely in private insurance. In fact government is ultimately better placed to handle these problems than are private insurance schemes.

(iii) The third "merit" good provided by government is housing, and in this area there is very wide variation between countries. Dutch government housing expenditure is proportionately ten times as high as in the U.S.A. It is obviously a field where there are environmental externalities, but these can usually be achieved by regulatory intervention, and it is quite clear that the bulk of housing consists of private goods privately provided. Public policy in this area has hindered labour mobility, distorted capital markets, encouraged extravagantly high demand in some areas of accommodation and created scarcities in others. Apart from these efficiency losses, there is no evidence that the impact of public housing and public subsidies is equitable. Indeed the biggest one, which is tax relief on mortgage interest, is regressive in its impact.

Transfers and Work Incentives

(iv) It is alleged that social transfers have been pushed to the point of serious "moral hazard", where the levels of benefit are generous enough to induce the characteristics whose adverse effects they were intended to mitigate. As a result they have weakened the incentive to work. The classical argument here concerns unemployment insurance. Robbins and Rueff argued in the 1930s that U.K. unemployment was due in considerable degree to overgenerous unemployment compensation, and this argument has recently been disinterred by

Benjamin and Kochin.[34] It is true that U.K. unemployment benefits were better than in other countries at that period but this school exaggerates the value of benefits as can be seen by a simple comparison of total unemployment compensation payments and the size of unemployment. In fact U.K. unemployment benefits from 1920 to 1939 averaged 0.9 per cent of GDP and unemployment 9.4 per cent of the labour force which hardly suggests a generous enough average benefit situation to encourage much unemployment.[35]

At the beginning of the economic slowdown in 1974, when unemployment started its general rise, there were strong suggestions that a good deal of the extra unemployment was voluntary because the generosity of benefits had been increasing in the course of the 1960s. Analysis of this type did not suggest that increased benefits induced many people to become unemployed, but rather that it lengthened "spells" of unemployment by permitting people the luxury of more careful job search.[36] In spite of the problems inherent in this kind of analysis, particularly in getting an accurate average picture of the degree to which unemployment benefit replaces wages, it seems probable that there is some degree of voluntary unemployment. However, since 1974 unemployment has increased dramatically even though several countries have reduced benefits. It is clear that most of the increase is not voluntary.

Table 10 shows that the work disincentive impact of pensions is likely to be substantially higher than that for unemployment insurance because the income replacement ratios are higher. It is of course the intention of pension schemes to permit or even compel people to stop working, so one can hardly speak of moral hazard in this area. However, some countries now provide pensions to a growing number of people below age 65, and this is one of the reasons why the activity rate for males aged 55-64 has dropped. This problem is most

---

[34] See L. ROBBINS, *The Great Depression*, Macmillan, 1934, p. 93 refers to "colossal" expenditure as unemployment relief, but does not give this as much causal weight as J. RUEFF, "L'Assurance Chômage, cause du chômage permanent", *Revue d'économie politique*, March-April 1931, pp. 211-41. D.K. BENJAMIN and L.A. KOCHIN, "Searching for an Explanation of Unemployment in Interwar Britain", *Journal of Political Economy*, 1979, pp. 441-78 stick to Rueff's line.

[35] Figures on G.B. unemployment benefits are from *British Labour Statistics: Historical Abstract 1886-1968*, Dept. of Employment, London, 1971, p. 366. GDP (adjusted from U.K. to G.B. basis) from C.H. FEINSTEIN, *National Income, Expenditure and Output of the United Kingdom 1855-1965*, Cambridge, 1972, pp. T 11. Unemployment percentages from A. MADDISON, *Phases of Capitalist Development*, Oxford, 1982, p. 206 and are adjusted to show relation to labour force rather than to insured unemployed.

[36] See H.G. Grubel and M.A. Walker, eds., *Unemployment Insurance: Global Evidence of its Effects on Unemployment*, Fraser Institute, Vancouver, 1978 for a useful survey of the literature.

Origins and Impact of the Welfare State, 1883-1983   81

TABLE 10

RELATIVE SIZE OF PENSIONS AND THE "PENSIONABLE"POPULATION

	Government Financed Pensions as Percent of GDP 1981	Persons 65 and older as Percent of Population 1981	Income Compensation Ratio
France	11.9	13.7	86.9
Germany	12.5	15.3	81.7
Japan	4.8	9.2	52.2
Netherlands	13.0	11.6	112.1
U.K.	7.4	15.1	49.0
U.S.A.	7.4	11.4	64.9
Average	9.5	12.7	74.5

Source: OECD. Labour Force Statistics, and table 3b above.

TABLE 11

RELATIVE SIZE OF UNEMPLOYMENT COMPENSATION AND THE UNEMPLOYED POPULATION

	Unemployment Compensation as Percent of GDP 1981	Unemployed as Percent of Population 1981	Income Compensation Ratio
France	1.9	3.2	59.4
Germany	1.4	1.8	77.8
Japan	0.4	1.1	36.4
Netherlands	1.0	3.4	29.4
U.K.	1.4	4.9	28.6
U.S.A.	0.5	3.6	13.9
Average	1.1	3.0	40.9

Source: OECD Statistics Division for compensation and population; unemployment from U.S. Bureau of Labor Statistics. The income compensation ratio is column 1 divided by column 2. Averages are arithmetic averages of columns.

marked in the Netherlands where the number of people with permanent handicap pensions had reached 12 per cent of the labour force by 1980, and is perhaps the most outstanding case of moral hazard with regard to labour supply.

There are some other dimensions of labour supply where significant cases of moral hazard seem to be present, but which are difficult to compare between countries. However, there is some evidence that the Netherlands occupies an extreme position within our six countries, with 1.9 per cent of GDP going on sickness benefit, and a 10 per cent rate of sickness absence (roughly three times the U.S. rate of sickness absence).

The Tax Burden

(v) High taxes and social security levies and their unequal or arbitrary incidence are often cited as factors which weaken incentives to work, save or invest, and weaken tax morality, so that there are rapidly growing do-it-yourself, barter and underground economies which reduce overall efficiency and measured output.

It is difficult to accept these arguments in their most simple form because labour force activity rates are generally rising (with rising female participation big enough to offset falling male participation in most countries). The general fall in investment rates since 1973 is dominated by cyclical factors, and investment rates now in advanced welfare state conditions are still higher in most countries than they ever were in pre-war years. The theoretical basis for Feldstein's argument about U.S. savings is hotly disputed and his specific figures were invalidated by an important programming error.[37]

At first sight it is plausible that there is some point or range of taxation which would cause economic collapse because of incentive problems, but it is not clear where it lies. The view of "tolerable" burdens has increased with time as incomes have risen. In the nineteenth century, Giffen suggested 10 per cent of national income, in 1945 Colin Clark said that 25 per cent was the upper peacetime limit. Assar Lindbeck has recently advanced a new version of the argument and has suggested that advanced states like Sweden or the Netherlands, where the tax burden is around 60 per cent have reached a position of arterio-

---

[37] See H.J. AARON, *Economic Effects of Social Security*, Brookings, Washington, 1982 for a general review of this field.

sclerosis which acts as a major drag on productivity growth.[38] It is true that productivity growth has slowed down considerably since 1973 in all our countries, but difficult to prove that the welfare state has a major responsibility.[39]

The main weakness in the argument about ultimate taxable capacity is that it tends to view government as a black hole into which taxpayers' money disappears, whereas government does provide services and social transfer income in return. The tolerability of big government depends on whether its activity is publicly conceived to be efficient and equitable, rather than on its absolute size. There are clearly differences in tradition between countries which affect this public perception, because discontent with government is bigger in the U.S.A. than in the Netherlands, although the Dutch commitment to welfare is twice as big.

The growth of the underground economy is significant evidence of decline in tax morality, though its size is often exaggerated and its existence is a testimony to the vigour of the capitalist spirit rather than a herald of its collapse.

VI. Conclusions

It is difficult to reach strong conclusions on the influence of the welfare state on economic development because the evidence does not warrant them. Strong judgements on the question are influenced mainly by ideological positions, or predictions about what might happen in the future. The relative political strength of different ideological positions varies between countries, and is not related to the relative size of the welfare state. Five different ideological positions are currently distinguishable in most Western countries, and the following paragraphs attempt

---

[38] See PEACOCK and WISEMAN, *Op. cit.*, p. 66 for Sir Robert Giffen's view; C. CLARK, "Public Finance and Changes in the Value of Money", *Economic Journal*, December 1945; A. LINDBECK, "Work Disincentives in the Welfare State", Institute for International Economic Studies, Stockholm, Reprint 176 and A. LINDBECK, "The Recent Slowdown of Productivity Growth", *Economic Journal*, March 1983.

[39] For an alternative interpretation of the slowdown see A. MADDISON "Comparative Analysis of the Productivity Situation in the Advanced Capitalist Countries" in J.W. Kendrick, ed., *International Comparisons of Productivity and Causes of the Slowdown*, Ballinger, Boston. 1984

TABLE 12

LABOUR FORCE PARTICIPATION RATES
(per cent of age group in labour force)

	Males Aged 55-64		Males Aged 65 and over	
	1960	1982	1960	1982
France	75.0	59.9	30.5	5.9
Germany	82.0	68.1[a]	22.6	6.0[a]
Japan	86.1	84.9	56.0	38.8
Netherlands	87.7	60.5[a]	19.9	4.6[a]
U.K.	84.7	79.3	25.4	7.8[a]
U.S.A.	85.1	70.2	30.3	17.8
Average	83.4	70.5	30.8	13.5

(a) 1981.
Source: OECD, *Demographic Trends 1950-1990*, Paris, 1979 and OECD, *Labour Force Statistics 1970-1981*, Paris, 1983.

to characterize the current views of these groups — the liberals, the populist middle ground, the egalitarians, the neo-Marxists and the new left.

a) *The Liberals*

There is no evidence that high welfare state expenditure has been disastrous for economic incentives and economic growth as early nineteenth century *laissez-faire* liberals (relying heavily on Malthusian population assumptions) would have predicted. The recent emphasis of the liberal school on the dysfunctionality of the welfare state from the point of view of work incentives, savings and economic growth is a reassertion of the more fundamental type of critique which the *laissez-faire* school originally advanced. However, they have not produced acceptable evidence of very significant adverse impact on growth. Their persuasive power derives more from worries about fiscal deficits and current disillusion amongst former welfare supporters of other political persuasions than the power of their own argument. And the new radical governments in the U.K. and the U.S.A are as much concerned to increase inequality of rewards to property and work for their own sake as for their presumptive impact on economic performance.

b) *The Populist Middle Ground*

In the postwar period until the 1970s, support for the welfare state was general over a fairly wide spectrum of politicians and bureaucrats in Western countries for pragmatic reasons. Such measures added to the legitimacy of the state by providing programmes broadly in the public interest. Economic growth provided the finance for such schemes without much political effort. It was acknowledged that public transfers involved a fair degree of "churning", but bureaucratic dangers or incentive costs were not thought to be great. Within this group of political managers and administrators, attitudes have swung closer to the liberal school, because tax revenues are less buoyant now that stagnation has replaced growth, welfare state commitments are very large and have a momentum of their own which is difficult to control.

Members of this group are now apt to give more emphasis to the wastes involved in "churning",[40] but are very conscious of the practical difficulties of rationalizing transfers through negative income tax or social security reform and the problems of checking manpower growth in public services.

c) *The Egalitarians*

Amongst egalitarians, there has also been some disillusionment with the welfare state, though there can be little doubt that transfers (see table 5) have been highly equalizing.

As far as transfers are concerned, egalitarians complain that there is too much "churning", that the net distributive impact is small relative to the amount of gross tax and transfer activity.[41] Some of them would be content with smaller, more redistributive programmes.

---

[40] On "churning", see the remarks of H. HOUTHAKKER in *The Economics of Federal Subsidy Programs*, Joint Economic Committee, Part I, 1972 "we are gradually moving towards a situation where everybody is subsidizing everybody else. As we all know from birthdays and Christmas Eves, the exchange of gifts, even rather useless gifts, frequently helps stimulate good fellowship and a sense of community. One could be more sanguine about this trend, however if it did not contain an element of self-deception, in the sense that the beneficiaries of any particular program feel they are getting something for nothing".

[41] See W. BECKERMAN, *et al., Poverty and the Impact of Income Maintenance Programmes in Four Developed Countries*, ILO, Geneva, 1979.

In the merit goods field, there has also been a realization that there are inherent limitations on the degree to which delivery of education and health services can be manipulated to serve egalitarian goals.[42]

d) *The Neo-Marxists*

The neo-Marxists who have written about the welfare state have generally treated it as more than Bismarckian. They suggest that it has been necessary not only to make a capitalist economy legitimate or acceptable, but also that it was functionally necessary, e.g. public education and health services are required to provide the skills and strength needed in productive workers. But they hold that the welfare state now has strong elements of dysfunctionality because its growth has strengthened workers' bargaining power, and higher taxes have squeezed profits. Attempts to remedy these problems by cutting back on welfare will reduce capitalist legitimacy and ultimately lower the quality of the labour force. The argument seems to be that the welfare state has prolonged the duration of the capitalist epoch but that now is a time of crisis and that its heyday is over.[43]

e) *The New Left*

The various New Left views are to large degree a revival of the viewpoint of the utopian socialists with an equally diverse range of interests. They have in common a heavy stress on self-starting schemes involving local initiative, and an attack on government provision as bureaucratic in form and psychologically repressive. Their discontent is concentrated more on public services than on transfers. Ivan Illich is perhaps the most vociferous of this group and has attacked public education because it produces alienation, and public health services because they have created a significant degree of iatrogenic (doctor-made) illness.[44] It is difficult to characterize the policy implications of

---

[42] See C. JENCKS, *Inequality*, Basic Books, New York, 1972, on education, and J. LE GRAND, *The Strategy of Equality*, Allen and Unwin, London, 1982 on health.

[43] See I. GOUGH, *The Political Economy of the Welfare State*, Macmillan, London 1979, and J. O' CONNOR, *The Fiscal Crisis of the State*, St. Martin's Press, New York, 1973.

[44] See I. ILLICH, *Deschooling Society*, Harper and Row, New York, 1971, and *Medical Nemesis*, Calder and Boyars, London, 1975.

the New Left. Those derivable from Illich do not differ much from liberal programmes for privatization and vouchers such as Milton Friedman has advocated. In several countries, elements of the New Left have been incorporated into welfare state programmes in various ways. These range from leafraking measures to mitigate unemployment in the U.K. or U.S.A. to much wider participation in the Netherlands.

* * *

Although it is clear that the welfare state is no longer regarded as the triumph of social engineering it was widely thought to be in the 1960s, the combination of disillusion and hostility which has developed in the 1980s has thus far been too vaguely focussed to check its growth.

University of Groningen

ANGUS MADDISON

[15]

What Is Education For?

by Angus Maddison

In the past two decades, educational enrolment in Western countries has grown three times faster than population, teaching staffs have risen even more and education budgets have doubled their claim on national income. Until recently, it was generally felt that this expansion sustained economic growth, improved the quality of life and contributed to social mobility. But the climate has changed since the student revolts of 1968, and scepticism about the value of further expanding formal education is widespread. It is argued that education produces alienation rather than self-fulfilment, that home environment has a bigger impact on learning than schools, that education is not useful as an investment, and that it does not help social mobility. The new agnosticism is most prevalent in the USA, most muted in Britain, but has affected all countries in some degree. This article reviews the recent literature and the issues raised for public policy. The main conclusions are that the area of ignorance is surprisingly big, that until a great deal more research is done educational policies are, to a large extent, acts of faith and that many of the goals which education is supposed to achieve can be attained only by a much wider range of measures and a more sophisticated analysis of the interaction of the various instruments of social policy.

In the following review I cover the role of education in respect of five major goals, as: a means of personal fulfilment; an instrument for social continuity and cohesion; a mechanism for social mobility; a means to promote social equality; and as an 'economic investment' for individuals and society.

Education as a Means of Personal Fulfilment

The major purpose of education is to provide opportunities for self-fulfilment and personal development–a more complex process with humans than with

The author is a member of the Secretariat of the Organisation for Economic Co-operation and Development, but the views expressed here are purely personal. He is grateful to K Gannicott, N Postlethwaite and R Shannon for comments on an earlier draft.

19

animals because of the vast stock of knowledge we have accumulated. Access to this heritage is a basic human right which should yield satisfaction throughout life.

However, formal education is, in large measure, obligatory, a good many pupils get little current satisfaction from it, and the lifetime benefits from extending it beyond a certain point are doubtful for many people. Other possibilities for learning outside formal education have been considerably widened by the spread of television, radio, tape recorders, records, paperback books, foreign travel and better-educated parents. The schoolmen no longer monopolize access to knowledge.

Self-fulfilment often seems a less important aim of public education policy than other goals, such as examination success. Students complain about the stereotyped content of education, that they have little say in determining curricula and that their learning is channelled into acquiring paper certificates. These protests have occurred in secondary schools as well as in universities, though the stridency of protest varies from country to country. With the slackening in the labour market for graduates, entry into higher education has levelled out sharply in the UK, USA, Canada, Sweden and Japan, which suggests that the psychic attractions of formal education are not too powerful once the economic incentive weakens.

Attacks on the shortcomings of present public education systems in providing personal satisfaction have come from the New Left and from ultra-liberals like Milton Friedman. Marcuse and Reich criticize schools and universities because they produce 'alienation' by inculcating orthodox ideas and suppressing individuality. Illich[1] has gone further than them in suggesting alternative educational arrangements, though his ideological position as a frockless priest is more eclectic than that of the neo-Marxists. He quotes Friedman's advocacy of educational vouchers with approval. For Illich, schools are psychological prisons with a hidden curriculum inculcating conformity. The influence of schools is reinforced by their power to award certificates, which is used to provide labour market rewards for conformists. Therefore, 'inquiries into man's learning history must be made taboo', and he would abolish compulsory education. Instead, people would get a lifetime credit card to finance their own informal learning. One might well feel that children would not know how to use such freedom, but Illich argues that children have as much (or as little) capacity for rational choice as adults. The role of government is to provide facilities for the 'autonomous assembly of resources under the personal control

---

[1]See H Marcuse, *One Dimensional Man*, Sphere Books, London, 1968; C A Reich, *The Greening of America*, Penguin, London, 1972; I D Illich, *Deschooling Society*, Calder and Boyars, London, 1972.

of each learner', but the details and feasibility of this are not stated very rigorously. He suggests that computer dating can be used to match learners and teachers who want to discuss problems of mutual interest. The computers would be supplemented by bulletin boards and classified ads (though he does not explain how people would learn to read these in the first place).

Illich's criticism of school alienation is undoubtedly valid for the adolescent slum-dwellers with whom he has worked. The widespread problem of drop-out and drug addiction in the United States indicates that there is great disillusion with the school environment. It is useful to be reminded that education is a means to satisfy personal needs, that decisions are usually taken on a paternalistic basis by parents, teachers and the state, and that the product is often regarded with distaste by many of the supposed beneficiaries. There is an obvious need to provide more flexible options in education and to give more heed to individual wishes. The further compulsory education is pushed into the adolescent years the stronger the reaction of unwilling learners. However, one could hardly expect any society to leave as many of the decisions to young children as Illich suggests and the vehemence of his argument would seem very out of place if applied, for example, to British primary education, which gives considerable emphasis to child-centred learning. Illich exaggerates the extent to which learning can be autonomous. It is, after all, a process of social adaptation and acquisition of a cognitive heritage which systematic instruction can greatly facilitate. It is also a fallacy to suppose that education can be a panacea for the problems of alienation Illich describes. Under his system, slum-dwellers would probably end up without any education at all, whereas the rest of the community would probably persuade their children to undergo more formal instruction.

The interesting thing about this recent discussion is that the old idea that continuous extension of compulsory formal schooling is a means to personal fulfilment has now been abandoned in many places on the political spectrum. There is a feeling in many countries that people will gain more satisfaction from a wider range of facilities for post-formal education than from an extension of compulsory education. Hence the growing support for educational voucher schemes which would give everyone the possibility of taking time off during working life for sabbatical study. In France, for instance, the right to educational leave has been given to workers and the compulsory school age has been reduced. However, there is not enough experience to know how well these new ideas will work, and there may well be a return to the notion of longer compulsory education but with greater flexibility of choice for adolescent pupils.

21

Lloyds Bank Review

Education as an Instrument for Social Continuity and Cohesion

Education is usually financed and provided by governments because they consider it important in promoting or establishing social continuity and cohesion, a role more explicit in new countries or in those with new ideologies than it is in Western Europe. In the USA, education has been traditionally regarded as a powerful instrument for forging a strong and homogeneous society from an immigrant population. This aim is also important in African countries, which are usually split by ethnic and linguistic diversity. In all societies, education is the major instrument for transmitting the cultural and social heritage between generations. Durkheim was thinking of these goals when he said:

> Society can survive only if there exists among its members a sufficient degree of homogeneity; education perpetuates and reinforces this homogeneity by fixing in the child from the beginning the essential similarities which collective life demands. . . . Society finds itself with each new generation faced with a *tabula rasa*, very nearly, on which it must build anew.

The problem about this is that, once universal literacy is attained and enough scholars are available to preserve past accumulations of knowledge, it is not possible in Western societies to get agreement on the 'essential similarities of collective life'. There is an openmindedness about ethical standards and accepted truths which did not exist in previous generations; and there is now great doubt about the efficacy of education as a social melting pot. Once the education system has reached a certain stage of development, its social role merges rather closely with the humanistic goal of personal fulfilment. Education is no longer a force for social cohesion, a bulwark of church and state, but rather a source of dynamic and unpredictable social change.

Education as an Instrument for Social Mobility

Since the French revolution, liberals everywhere have supported educational expansion on meritocratic grounds. It was generally felt that free access to education was a powerful instrument of social mobility. For this reason, governments have provided free public education and tried to ensure that facilities at a given level of education are equal for all pupils. In most Western countries, the whole population gets compulsory education to age 15 or 16; while in Western Europe about a quarter of the younger generation, and in the USA about half the population, now have access to some form of higher education.

22

What Is Education For?

However, the limited evidence which sociologists have mustered suggests that the large-scale provision of post-compulsory educational facilities has been very unevenly used by children from different social classes,[1] even though it may have been very helpful to a small *élite* of gifted children from poorer families. Well over half of public education spending in Western countries now goes on post-compulsory education and the benefits of these expensive forms of education are disproportionately concentrated on children from the upper and middle classes. This is true even in California, where attendance rates in publicly-financed higher education are higher than anywhere else in the world. There are two main reasons why 'free' schooling does not provide equality of opportunity.

First, open access and no fees do not mean that education is really free. Poorer families are unable to use these opportunities fully because they can often not afford to sacrifice the wages which their children can earn. Higher education can usually be financed by those with low-income parents because there are grants or loans, but for the 16–19 age-group maintenance facilities are much less generous and this is the age at which the drop-out rate for children of poor families is most serious. If equal educational opportunity is to be real rather than rhetorical, it is necessary either to extend compulsory education or to broaden the range of maintenance support at secondary level. Most governments provide family allowances and tax privileges which encourage voluntary attendance at school and some countries give substantial grants or loans for secondary school attendance. However, these are not big enough to offset the earnings which can be gained from work, so that economic constraints on access to education are still operative, even when education is nominally free.

The other problem for children from poorer families is that they do not seem to do as well in school on average as those from middle- and upper-class homes. There is no unanimous view as to why this happens; nor is its importance fully documented.

Recent evidence from the Coleman Report in the USA, the Plowden Report in the UK and the massive international studies carried out by the IEA (International Association for the Evaluation of Educational Achievement)[2]

---

[1]See *Group Disparities in Educational Participation and Achievement*, OECD, Paris, 1971 which reviews the parental background of students in most Western countries, and T Husen, *Social Background and Educational Career*, OECD, Paris, 1972.
[2]J Coleman and Associates, *Equality of Educational Opportunity*, US Dept of Health, Education and Welfare, Office of Education, Washington DC, 1966; *Children and Their Primary Schools*, 2 vols, Central Advisory Council for Education (England), HMSO, London, 1967; T Husen, ed *International Study of Achievement in Mathematics*, Wiley, New York, 1967 and *International Studies in Evaluation*, vols I-IX (six subject study), J Wiley, New York, 1973–4.

suggests that in several countries schools are not nearly so effective as had been imagined in eliminating learning handicaps that derive from unequal home backgrounds. The Coleman report was a big survey sponsored by the US Office of Economic Opportunity, designed mainly to see what difference there was in school facilities for black and white students, and whether any such difference affected ability to learn. The report showed, rather unexpectedly, that educational facilities per pupil did not vary much between black and white pupils within particular regions (though they were worse in the South, where black pupils are most heavily concentrated), and that the lower performance of black pupils was due largely to inferior home background. The evidence in the Plowden report also indicated that schools do not offset the learning disadvantages of those with deprived home backgrounds, and Douglas' studies came to the same conclusion for the UK[1]. All of these reports have tended to weaken the hopes that access to equal facilities can create equality of opportunity. Their impact has probably been most depressing in the USA.

However, there are several reasons for thinking that the Coleman report's pessimism about the equalizing possibilities of schooling is exaggerated. In the first place, it based its conclusions on tests of verbal ability, where home background is more influential than it is in other subjects. This has been shown in the IEA studies of proficiency in foreign languages and science, where the school influence is much more important. Secondly, the technical methods used in the Coleman and IEA reports to distinguish the influence of home from that of school exaggerate the former because most of the interaction between home and school is attributed to the home. Thirdly, and most important, all of the data used in the Coleman, Plowden and IEA reports refer to students whose experience of school has been much more homogeneous than their home background. If one could get samples of children with wider ranges of educational experience, including those with no education at all, one might reach quite different conclusions about the relative impact of home and school. In most Western countries, such samples are not and will not be available, because no one is likely to permit children to be deprived of all schooling for experimental purposes. However, the range of testing could be extended to cover some of those who have dropped out of school, as well as those in school, and such tests might produce very different results.

It is rather paradoxical that, in a period when the role of school in learning has been under challenge, educational radicals have broadened the egalitarian goal: they argue not simply for equality of access and treatment, but for positive

---

[1] J W B Douglas, *The Home and the School*, MacGibbon & Kee, London, 1964; J W B Douglas, J M Ross and H R Simpson, *All Our Future*, P Davies, London, 1968.

discrimination in favour of those with the greatest learning difficulties[1]. The extent of such discrimination which is advocated varies according to the degree of radicalism, but all the radicals want to achieve at least a substantial reduction in the present differences in average learning performance of students from different social groups.

At the moment, educational resources tend to be most lavish for the brightest pupils and our experience of the effectiveness of compensatory policies is rather limited. There is considerable uncertainty about the impact of factors which affect learning, such as size of class or length of study. Critics, such as the authors of the British 'Black Papers', who are more interested in raising the level than in reducing the differences in performance, have argued that there are likely to be substantial losses of efficiency (worse performance of bright pupils) as a result of comprehensive education schemes, and they would presumably object even more to stronger programmes of positive discrimination in favour of those with learning difficulties. However, Torsten Husen, perhaps the leading member of the radical school, has produced a good deal of international evidence to show that the brightest pupils perform in the same way in almost any kind of school system.

The argument for levelling-up was in the past concentrated on the need for positive discrimination in facilities within formal education, but more recently emphasis has been given to the development of pre-primary education and to 'second chance' opportunities for people who have left school. Hence, the rapid growth of pre-primary facilities in many countries, the creation of the Open University in the UK, the law giving workers the right to educational leave in France, the new emphasis on work experience as a qualification for university entrance in Sweden, or the US Carnegie Commission's endorsement of the right to two years' education 'in the bank'.

In spite of the Coleman, Plowden and IEA reports mentioned above, there is still a case for believing that extra resources spent on schooling and on the development of pre- and post-formal education can contribute to greater equality of learning achievement, though direct measures to improve the home background, such as income supplements and housing subsidies, may sometimes be more effective. However, a good deal of the concern with inequality in learning skills arises from the assumption, not always explicit, that educational attainment is a major factor in economic success, and this assumption has been seriously challenged by Jencks and his colleagues at Harvard, (see page 29).

---

[1]See T Husen, *Social Background and Educational Career*, OECD, Paris, 1972.

Lloyds Bank Review

Education as an Instrument for Social Equality

An important element in the support for education has been the belief that its expansion would produce greater equality of earnings, by increasing the supply of educated and reducing the supply of less-educated people. This would decrease the relative wages of the former and raise those of the latter. This is a rather simplified theory, because earnings by level of education will be affected by the rate of capital formation, changes in technology, trade union pressure, migration and other factors. Furthermore, the empirical evidence is poor; in most countries historical series on earnings by level of education are not available. In the USA, however, where there are figures for four decades, the relative earnings of graduates did not weaken, in spite of the large growth in their numbers.

The basic weakness in the 'more education means more equality' argument is the mistaken assumption that growth in the stock of education necessarily leads to greater equality in its distribution between persons. Existing inequalities in the distribution of the 'stock' of education between persons are large, and educational expansion does not necessarily reduce them. The younger generation have more education than their predecessors thirty years ago but the spread between the best- and the least-educated has not decreased even in an egalitarian country like Sweden. For the UK, if one takes simply the cumulative *number of years* of formal education of the population, then inequalities between the best- and least-educated are not too great. But, if allowance is made for differences in the *cost* of providing instruction at different levels, inequality in the distribution of educational capital is very striking. A year of primary education cost the government £125 in 1971–72, but a year of university education cost £1 250. Public education therefore endows people with very unequal amounts of educational 'capital'. Although educational inequality is so large—and the fact deserves more recognition—it would not be a rational policy to try to eliminate it by topping up everyone's education to graduate or PhD level. This would be extremely costly and produce a lot of discontent when people found the effort of study had no economic pay-off. It would be more reasonable to levy some sort of wealth tax on those with the most educational capital.

Education as an Economic 'Investment'

That education adds to the productivity and earning power of the individual and can raise a nation's output has long been recognized. However, the full implications of treating education as an investment in human capital, analogous

26

to that in physical capital, have been spelled out only in the past fifteen years. The basis of the argument is the empirical evidence from many countries that there are systematic differences in lifetime earnings of people with different levels of education.

The 'Chicago school' of economists has been the most active in developing a theory of human capital. On the assumption of competition in labour markets, they have taken variations in earnings by level of education as a measure of its economic benefit and they have used information on earnings and costs of education (including earnings lost through not being at work) to calculate private and 'social' rates of return on educational investment. Governments were thus provided with guidelines as to whether expenditure on education, or certain types of education, should be contracted or expanded. The calculus of cost and benefit has been carried out in more than thirty countries, including the UK.[1] Generally speaking, these studies have shown education to have been a worth-while investment (compared with alternative investment in physical capital) and they have shown that further expansion of educational facilities is warranted in most countries, except at postgraduate level.

Other economists, the 'manpower planners', have also stressed the role of education as an investment, and have offered rather more detailed policy advice to governments. Instead of showing rates of return, they have provided coefficients linking manpower requirements more directly to certain levels of output or rates of economic growth. This approach has been used in Soviet planning since the 1920s, by Indian and Swedish planners, and also in Britain, to forecast demand for scientific and medical manpower and for schoolteachers. In its crudest form, the manpower approach is rather mechanistic and can go seriously wrong because of the ease with which one type of educated labour can be substituted for another. In circumstances where earnings data are not available and governments make the decisions on allocation of educated labour, there is no real alternative to the manpower approach, but if data are available on earnings by level of education and if market forces are important in allocating human resources, the human capital approach may be a better guide to policy.

The most important practical problem for those who take the human capital approach seriously is the poor quality of information on training beyond formal education. The little evidence at present available would suggest that such training may cost half as much again as formal education, so the scope for

---

[1]See G Psacharopoulos, *Returns of Education*, Elsevier, Amsterdam, 1973, and *Economic Trends*, May 1971.

exaggerating the returns on formal education is large. Better information on post-formal education (a good deal of which is not carried out by ministries of education), would make it possible to make more rational decisions about where education should be expanded. More information is also needed on fringe benefits and conditions of employment by level of education. These are usually more significant the higher the level of education, and any calculation of the economic benefits of education which ignores them can be misleading. More frequent information is also needed on earnings by level of education. Changes in earnings differentials by level of education mean that predictions of the outcome of educational investment based on historical data may not be very reliable.

Some critics who accept the idea that education is a useful economic investment would argue that its importance cannot be measured in practice, because they deny that earnings reflect productivity. This judgement can be advanced on several levels. Labour markets are imperfect because some groups of people get monopoly income by restricting entry to their profession; adjustments of supply and demand are 'sticky', so that lags and imperfections will always prevent actual wages from reaching their true equilibrium rate; a large part of employment (particularly of the higher-educated) is in the government sector, which is not trying to maximize profits. It is true that the government's wage structure is strongly influenced by market decisions in the private sector, but many of the best-educated people in the private sector work for large corporations which remunerate on quasi-bureaucratic principles. Critics can point also to the acknowledged facts of sex and race discrimination and old-boy networks as evidence that earnings do not reflect productivity.

A newer line of criticism comes from those who argue that there is no very close connection between the content of most people's education and the jobs they do. Their economically useful skills are nearly all learned on the job. The only or main economic significance of education, so it is argued, is to provide a screening device for employers to identify people who have a capacity to learn or to work efficiently. Viewed in this way, education is an expensive device which could be replaced by cheaper aptitude tests, but these are not adopted because the private costs of education are heavily subsidized by the state and because education costs employers nothing. A good deal of education is, therefore, a waste of time and money to provide credentials which are not socially useful.

However, the human capital theorists, unlike the manpower planners, have never claimed that education necessarily has a direct relation to the jobs people do. To some degree, the link is direct; doctors and lawyers study topics that have a direct bearing on their work. In other cases, the relevant thing is not the specific content of education but the exercise and discipline in learning processes which education provides. Education also induces habits of perseverance and order which are necessary in work. These views of education are compatible with the human capital approach because the three functions—relevant knowledge, general learning skills and work discipline—all affect productivity.

Ivar Berg, the American sociologist, is probably the most extreme critic of credentials. His book, *The Great Training Robbery,* argues that the existing supply of education is excessive and that employers react by upgrading paper qualifications demanded for lower level jobs. Although these qualifications are not really needed, people are forced to acquire them in order to get the jobs. Thus, there is a snowball effect, in which excess education steadily gets more excessive.

As evidence for his thesis, Berg compares skill and paper requirements for particular jobs, basing himself on US Department of Labor estimates, but it is difficult to prove clearly from this material whether there has been a significant amount of upgrading. Even if we accept Berg's hypothesis that there is a tendency to upgrade paper qualifications demanded for particular jobs in conditions of excess supply, this does not mean that the process of educational expansion will snowball indefinitely. If this did occur on a large scale, relative earnings of the more highly-educated would decline, for Berg does not suggest that employers upgrade pay to match increased paper qualifications. The fall in earnings would presumably act as a signal and deter some entrants to the higher levels of education. The recent falling-off in the growth rate for new entrants to universities shows that there are some self-adjusting mechanisms which make the snowball view unrealistic in its extreme form. But it is, of course, true that the signalling mechanisms could be substantially improved, and that the likelihood of wasteful over-expansion would be reduced if the cost of higher education were more obvious, eg financed by loans rather than grants. It is desirable to establish a more rational pattern of subsidies for post-compulsory education and training. At the moment, the most prestigious credentials are sometimes the cheapest to acquire: university students are more favoured, for example, than students in secretarial or hairdressing schools, who have to finance more of their education themselves.

The most extreme attack on the idea of education as an investment has come from CR Jencks and his associates in Harvard in *Inequality: A Measurement of the Effect of Family and Schooling in America.* Jencks believes that schools are not the main influence on learning and that educational attainment has little

29

Lloyds Bank Review

impact on economic success. He argues that education is important only as a source of personal satisfaction and that other social goals which educationists thought they could aim at are best approached more directly by other policy instruments, such as the redistribution of income and wealth, family planning, housing subsidies and so on. He argues, quite seriously, that social success (as measured by earnings) is largely a matter of luck and depends very little on education, family background or IQ, putting forward evidence that the variations in the earnings of men who are identical in all these respects are only 12 to 15 per cent less than those of the population in general.

Jencks's evidence is presented in a very devious way and has failed to convince most of the people who reviewed the book in a special issue of the *Harvard Educational Review*. The important and legitimate point he makes is that education is a risky investment for any particular individual. The differences in average earnings between people with different levels of education are subject to very wide dispersion for particular individuals. For example, in the USA in 1971, nearly 12 per cent of high-school graduates had incomes greater than the mean income of those with four or more years of college, and 30 per cent of the latter had incomes less than the mean for high-school graduates.

Jencks's book has attracted wide attention in the USA and has naturally annoyed those who look to education as a panacea for most social problems. Although he greatly exaggerates the economic unimportance of education and underrates the importance of schools in learning, his book rightly points to the need for more direct methods to tackle some of the problems education has been expected to solve.

It is clear that the goals of education are multiple, hard to measure and sometimes conflicting. This makes it difficult to find rational criteria for policy-making, because there are no universally-agreed concepts of efficiency or equity. The problem is further complicated by the high degree of ignorance about the learning process. The research of the past decade, though it has led to few clear conclusions, has at least deflated some of the mythology and introduced a greater degree of professionalism into analysis of educational policy. Perhaps the most important conclusion one can derive is the need for intensified research on the pedagogic, economic and social role of education, and for more explicit consideration of the relationship between education policy and other measures.

30

PART VI

[16]

Confessions of a Chiffrephile *

ANGUS MADDISON

Family influences

My interest in economics started early. Until I was six, I lived in Newcastle-on-Tyne, where the main industries were shipbuilding and coal-mining. A large proportion of the work force were unemployed throughout the 1920s, and unemployment was massive in 1929-33. My father had a steady job as a railway fitter but I had two unemployed uncles, and there were many unemployed neighbours. The unemployed were not only poor but depressed. Many loitered aimlessly at streetcorners, looked haggard, wore mufflers and cloth caps and smoked fag-ends. Their children were often sickly or tubercular.

My father took me to Gateshead every Sunday to see my grandmother. The double-decker bridge across the Tyne had open-work iron girders with a long drop to a dirty river that flowed between laid-up ships and a long line of derelict factories. The bleak image of the dead economy was sharpened by the noise and vibration above. Trams rattled down the middle of the roadway, and trains rumbled ominously overhead. At the Gateshead end, the buildings were blacker, and the clusters of unemployed thicker than in Newcastle. I saw nowhere so depressing until visiting Calcutta thirty years later.

□ University of Groningen, Groningen (The Netherlands).

* Contribution to a series of recollections on professional experiences of distinguished economists. This series opened with the September 1979 issue of this *Review*.

BNL Quarterly Review, no. 189, June 1994.

In 1933, the railway workshops were relocated in Darlington. We only moved 30 miles but it was a different world with much less unemployment. I was also aware of other improvements, as I knew that food prices had fallen and that mortgages were affordable.

My parents both left school when they were 12 and were interested in improving their education and mine. My mother used to read to me at an early age, she taught me to play golf, we had competitions in spelling or guessing the title of operatic music we heard on the radio. She took me to movies with dancing or singing (Shirley Temple, Fred Astaire, Nelson Eddy and Jeannette Mc-Donald) and later we graduated to the Sadlers Wells ballet and opera when they appeared locally. My father had been in France from 1914 to 1918 as a paramedic, giving first aid and comfort to the wounded and dying. He continued this interest as a first aid instructor in evening classes for railwaymen. When I was young I often went along as the accident "victim" and was bandaged and splinted by the class. At the time I was an adolescent both my parents were active in the education activities of the Cooperative Movement which ran "week-end schools" once a month where my father was often the chairman. When I was about 12, I started to go with them to these sessions. The speakers gave lectures on British political or economic issues or on international affairs. Those I remember best were Hamilton Fyfe, Principal of Aberdeen University, J.M. (later Lord) Peddie, a Coop economist, Sir Walter Citrine, the trade union leader, and Bruno Halpern, an Austrian economist. About 30 regulars attended these sessions, and the discussions were usually animated. The people who came were nearly all industrial workers or their wives, who were active in trade unions or local labour politics.

One of these meetings, in 1940, was concerned with the political and economic consequences of the war. There were a couple of speakers, Cyril Joad, a philosopher, who dealt with the political issues, and Jack Hemingway, my history teacher, who explained how the war could be financed, basing himself on Keynes' new book, *How to Pay for the War*, which my father bought. This was the first book I read on economics and was more or less intelligible to a 14 year old. It advocated a compulsory levy to prevent inflation, and rationing to provide fair shares. The appendix on national income put the macroeconomic options in a simple quantitative framework. It was then that I began to realise that economics was a useful discipline for solving serious problems and wondered why peactime economic problems could not have been solved by the same approach Keynes applied to those of wartime. I followed up Keynes' reference to Colin Clark. I read his *Conditions of Economic Progress* in the public library and was fascinated at the way it quantified what was going on in so many countries. This first exposure to economics had a lasting effect on my subsequent research agenda and the contact with adult education gave me the idea that you get educated by forming your own networks and setting your own programme. I was never subsequently very respectful of formal curricula.

My mother was one of 10 children, a boisterous Scottish family, who bubbled with self-confidence. My most colourful relative was my uncle David who had some kind of chest trouble he had developed in the army. He had a small military pension and could not work at his trade as a french-polisher. He became a street corner politician, giving occasional talks on Fabian socialism on a soapbox on the Newcastle town moor. He always welcomed an audience and was quite willing to use a small boy as a foil for his skeptical ideas on politics and religion. My mother regarded him as a sage, so he became my guru. I imbibed a good deal of what he said without fully understanding it, and he got me to read Shaw and Voltaire.

School

When I was 11, I passed the examination to go to the grammar school. At that time, it was not free. The fees were equivalent to about 6 weeks of my father's take home pay, so it involved significant parental sacrifice. If I had not been the only child, they probably would not have been able to afford it.

At the grammar school, I was a successful pupil, and specialised in history, English and foreign languages when I entered the sixth form. I was also the editor of the school magazine and secretary of the debating society. There was no economics teaching, but a significant amount of economic history. During the war we had many women teachers, only a few years older than their pupils. My history teacher was Jack Hemingway. He was a friend of my father and took me under his wing. He had been a liberal parliamentary candidate and was active in adult education. He stressed that history was not a

set of facts about kings and queens, but that there were different
schools of historians, and different layers of past experience which
could be examined. He got me to read Adam Smith, Tawney, Cole,
Postgate, the Hammonds and the Webbs. Joan Clapton was also a
strong influence. She taught English literature and special history
subjects to sixth formers. She was a radical intellectual of 1930s
vintage, who roused my interest in Marxist literature, not so much the
economics, but the materialist interpretation of history, the notion of
exploitation and of class conflict.

My German teacher, Stephanie Hawthorn, fresh from Oxford,
helped turn us into Europeans. The sixth form classes were small –
for German there were usually three of us. My two classmates were
dedicated entirely to language studies and were deep into comparative linguistics. With the four languages we had studied, English,
French, German and Latin, we found we had a quick key to learning
related European languages. They dabbled in more exotic tongues
and I took an evening class in Russian. I improved my speaking
knowledge of German by listening to the BBC German service and to
the German radio. I also frequented a German-speaking Club for
Austrian, German, and Czech refugees who were released from
internment to join the Pioneer Corps of the British army.

One of the learning problems in a provincial town is access to
books, but I did not do too badly. There were the school and public
libraries, and I had a friend, Scottie (R.J. Scott) with a second hand
book business. He had a very large stock of books on history and
economics, and he let me borrow books, or gave me big discounts
when I could afford to buy them.

University studies

At the end of 1944, I won a scholarship in history to go to
Cambridge University (Selwyn College). I went in January 1945,
rather than wait for the next academic year, by which time I expected
to be in the army.

Student numbers were greatly reduced because the war was
still on, but the London School of Economics was evacuated to
Cambridge and added a large mix of female and foreign students. The

array of scholars offering lectures was impressive, and one was free to go or stay away from all of them. The University Library was near my college and there was open access to millions of books.

The most exciting of the economic history lectures were those of Michael Postan. He covered British history from medieval times to the nineteenth century. He used the same analytical tools for the whole period – a framework in which the size of the capital stock, changes in technology and demography figured large. He presented empirical evidence of a quantitative kind, made bold hypotheses where information was lacking, and managed to convey the impression that these were contentious topics of major interest. All this delivered with exotic Bessarabian showmanship.

I also attended R.H. Tawney's lectures on economic history at LSE. These were delivered without panache but their analytic content was as sharp as Postan's. Tawney covered very broad themes – how the institutions of the American and Russian economies differed from those of the UK, why peasants had not disappeared from European agriculture as Marx had predicted.

The most crowded lectures were those of Harold Laski, who was Professor of Political Science at LSE, and chairman of the Labour Party. Laski was a great raconteur, with a droll humour. He dealt with the evolution of British political institutions like parliament, the crown, local government etc. stressing that the way they worked depended on the locus of political and economic power.

At the beginning of June 1945 I went home and worked actively in the General Election of 5th July for the Darlington Labour candidate who won with a majority of more than 8000. In the neighbouring constituency of Stockton, my friend George Chetwynd (the husband of one of my schoolteachers), defeated Harold Macmillan by nearly 9000. The sweeping victory of the Labour party, the successful outcome of the war and the creation of the UN gave me a strong sense that the big issues that had preoccupied my parents were on their way to solution.

When I went back to Cambridge in 1945 the atmosphere was very different. The LSE had gone back to London, but the university was much more crowded. It was full of people demobilised from the armed forces, and generally speaking those with the highest academic merit had been released first. It was a stimulating peer group. To add to the variety, there were about 150 American and a few Canadian soldiers including Harry Johnson.[1] There was a reflux of dons from the war. Bertrand Russell came back from America, and replaced Laski as the star lecture room attraction.

I was more prosperous, as my grant had risen and I had two part-time jobs – teaching an evening class in one of the Cambridge village institutes and lecturing to German prisoners of war for the Foreign Office. In the summer I had passed the American examination for translation work at the War Crimes Tribunal at Nuremberg, but the British Foreign Office persuaded the Americans not to recruit British nationals. As compensation they gave me a job lecturing in PoW camps. Both of these lecture series were on problems of reconstruction in European countries.

I spent most of the summer of 1946 on European political issues. The Cambridge Labour Club held a conference for about 30 European social democrats organised by Robin Marris, Wat Tyler and myself in conjunction with Denis Healey, who was then international secretary of the Labour Party. At that time there was still a social democratic movement in East Europe, so the geographic scope was very wide. Then I went abroad for the first time, for six weeks. First to Tirol, where the Austrian students and the four occupying powers organised a two week seminar, then to Prague, Switzerland and Italy. In Paris I attended a meeting of the International Union of Socialist Youth, organised by Healey and Per Haekerrup, who was later Danish foreign minister. We stayed in the Ecole des Arts et Métiers in Montrouge, and were roused by a militant French activist in a blue shirt who shouted "c'est l'heure" so dramatically that we thought there was at least a fire if not a revolution.

In 1946, I switched from history to economics. This was a much tougher discipline than history and was made more challenging by the competition between different schools of thought. Dennis Robertson, the professor, gave an elegant and whimsical introductory course on pre-Keynesian lines, and Joan Robinson made most of the running for the Keynesians. She also ran a huge discussion group, which was a bit intimidating as she loved a fight and tended to demolish opponents. The hottest topics were theoretical, and almost entirely concentrated on what Cambridge economists had said. As Dharma Kumar paraphrased Joan Robinson, "time is a device to prevent everything

---

[1] H.G. Johnson, "Cambridge in the 1950s, memoirs of an economist", *Encounter*, January 1974, pp. 28-39.

happening at once, space is a device to prevent it all happening in Cambridge". There was not much attention to what people thought in Oxford, or LSE, in Scandinavia or the USA, and almost nothing on problems of economic growth, business cycles, the European economy, or economic development which later became my major interests.

Austin Robinson was an honourable exception to the neglect of the real world and gave a highly quantitative course on current problems of planning and resource allocation. He was one of the few lecturers who permitted the audience to ask questions.

My supervisor was Maurice Dobb, a scholarly Marxist who was the only prominent Cambridge economist interested in long run capitalist development. I used to read my weekly essays to him, and I often took the initiative in suggesting topics. He had the demeanour of a discreetly agnostic bishop who certainly did not push his own views. He was not very interested in the mainstream Cambridge controversies, but had a very wide range of interests in history and economics and a broad international perspective. He was a close friend of Piero Sraffa. They had been to Russia together, and at that time were editing Ricardo's correspondence. Sraffa would occasionally enliven the supervision by bursting in with a dazzling smile and a new discovery.

Economics students were generally much more dedicated to their subject than historians. Interaction with this peer group was as important in the learning process as the lectures and supervision. The two people who contributed most to my education in this respect were Wilfred Beckerman and Robin Marris.

There was some scope for discussion of non-Cambridge type topics in the Marshall Society, where I remember impressive presentations by Arthur Lewis on the nature of the innovative process and by Nicky Kaldor on how he had revamped Hungarian economic policy. I was also impressed by the style and content of Lionel Robbins' Marshall Lectures in 1947 which were about policy problems of war economics, postwar planning and the transition to market economies.

I was a member of the Political Economy Club set up by Keynes, and continued by Robertson, who selected the membership of about 20. It was the only seminar where students gave papers which were subject to discussion. I gave a paper on Anglo-American differences in industrial productivity, basing myself largely on Laszlo Rostas' new

book which came out in 1948.[2] This was the topic on which I wanted
to do my graduate work, so I was grateful for Robertson's hospitality.

In July 1948 I went into the Royal Air Force to do my military
service. This was more interesting than I had expected. I became an
education officer at a Group headquarters in York, giving talks on
current affairs to airmen, and lecturing on strategy to officers taking
promotion examinations. I made them read Julius Caesar, von
Clausewitz, Eisenhower, and the strategic bombing survey where a
bunch of economists[3] identified mistakes in British wartime strategy
which my pupils found hard to swallow.

In October 1949 I sailed to Montreal in a crowded Cunarder, and
started graduate study at McGill University. The graduate school had
useful courses on new topics like game theory and linear programming,
but students got little guidance or supervision. However there was
expertise on output and productivity measurement at the Dominion
Bureau of Statistics in Ottawa where official statisticians were both
accessible and helpful, so I managed to do the basic statistical part of
my research which was intended to enlarge the Rostas comparison of
UK and US industrial performance to include Canada. It was
fashionable to attribute a good deal of the large US productivity
advantage over the UK to economies of scale, and I hoped to test this
by looking at Canada, where productivity was higher than in the UK,
but where the scale of production was smaller.

In December 1949 I went to the meetings of the American
Economic Association in New York, which was a huge affair, with
many simultaneous sessions, about 1000 economists, and the great
stars of the time including Schumpeter who was the chairman. I had
bought his *Capitalism Socialism and Democracy* in 1945, and was
fascinated by its breadth of vision and originality. It was interesting to
experience his wit and sparkle. He introduced Seymour Harris, the
great anthologist of the epoch, by saying to the audience "many of
you have read his works, most of you have written them".

In 1950 I moved to Johns Hopkins University in Baltimore.
There were about 20 graduate students in economics, with close
supervision of research and compulsory graduate courses. The faculty

---

[2] L. Rostas, *Comparative Productivity in British and American Industry*, Cambridge
University Press, Cambridge, 1948.

[3] U.S. Strategic Bombing Survey, *The Effects of Strategic Bombing on the German War
Economy*, October 1945 (the authors included Kenneth Galbraith, Paul Baran, Edward
Denison, Tibor Scitovsky, and Nicholas Kaldor).

included Fritz Machlup, Evsey Domar, Clarence Long and Al Harberger, and there was a steady stream of visitors including Bergson, Kuznets and Viner. There was also a large US government research programme on Soviet economic performance.

My research supervisor was Clarence Long, who had lengthy experience with the National Bureau of Economic Research, and followed their policy of intensive manuscript criticism. I wrote a 20 page paper on Canadian industrial productivity and a few days later, to my astonishment, he gave me 15 typewritten pages of commentary, with fully documented criticism of my sloppy reasoning, weak evidence, poor table layout, vague headings, inadequate sources and woolly conclusions. I had never previously been subjected to such close scrutiny, but it was, of course, exactly what graduate students need and usually do not get. Another person who was extremely helpful was Irving Siegel, who worked on the Russian project and had done a good deal of work on productivity in government agencies before the war.

Machlup gave the compulsory graduate course twice a week. He not only lectured but crossexamined his class, and gave us written tests to find out if we had absorbed his message. He was an eclectic and original economist with enormous charm and dedication. His main concern was to inculcate the virtues of clarity and precision.

Although I found the discipline at Hopkins very useful, I did not think I would profit much from another year of it, nor did I want to settle in the USA, so I got an academic job in the UK, at the University of St. Andrews in Scotland, where I had very light duties teaching a course in American economic history. I was able to write up the research I had done as a graduate student and published three articles.

In September 1952, I got a temporary three month assignment with the Food and Agriculture Organisation of the United Nations in Rome. I worked for Gerda Blau in the economics department on problems of the world wheat market, and she also sent me to GATT for three weeks to analyse non tariff barriers to agricultural trade. I could probably have stayed in FAO where I earned more than five times what I was paid as a lecturer in Scotland, but as the horizons were limited to agricultural problems I moved to Paris in January 1953, where the salary was lower, but the work promised to have wider scope.

OEEC: work on advanced capitalist countries

OEEC was created in 1948 to foster economic recovery in Western Europe. It was a major instrument in assessing requirements for American aid under the Marshall Plan and coordinating its distribution. When I came, the character of the Organisation had changed. There was clearly scope for further activity in liberalising trade and in provision of liquidity through the European Payments Union, but part of the original *raison d'être* had disappeared with the termination of Marshall Aid.

Up to 1952, the emphasis had been on the establishment and monitoring of detailed quantitative goals – rebuilding iron and steel capacity, creating transport networks, improving energy supplies etc. The OEEC had a large network of "vertical" committees with a sizeable secretariat for consideration of these problems in individual industrial sectors, in energy and agriculture. This was the area where the loss of momentum was most perceptible, but this was also true to some extent of the Economic Committee[4] serviced by the Economic and Statistics Directorate which I had joined.

In 1953 the Economic Committee had three regular jobs: *a)* annual reviews of economic policy in individual Member countries, *b)* an annual report on the European economy, and *c)* vetting the annual reports of the committees covering industrial, agricultural and energy problems. The country reviews involved experts from capitals on lines which are still followed. This was not true of the two areas where my own work was concentrated.

My boss was François Walter, the Director of Economics. He was a French civil servant on secondment (from the Cours des Comptes), without formal training in economics. He had spent the war in England and his anglophilia extended to writing in English. He had feverish energy and needed a factotum with the stamina to check his economic arguments and polish his English. Wilfred Beckerman had done this before I came, and was glad to move on to the National Accounts Division. In theory we worked five and a half days a week, but Walter did not believe in squandering Saturday afternoons on leisure pursuits. In these conditions I learned to work

---

[4] See Eric Roll, *Crowded Hours*, Faber and Faber, London, 1985, chapter 6 on the work of the Programmes Committee of which he was chairman. The Programmes Committee was the predecessor of the Economic Committee.

hard and draft quickly, and constant contact with Walter improved my French a good deal.

The worst chore was the annual report where every paragraph was subject to detailed scrutiny and approval by the Economic Committee. Walter did not draft the whole report before presenting it, but gave the committee a chapter at a time. The result was a great deal of rewriting and a patchy structure. However, it was a good training exercise for me, because one had to try to capture the essence of what was happening in the European economy as a whole and at the same time accommodate the often discordant points made by members of the national delegations.

My second task was as secretary of the subcommittee which vetted the annual reports of the industry committees. We had to eliminate the expression of protectionist views, try to inculcate some of the virtues of liberalism into the chairmen of the committees and the respective parts of the secretariat and check the validity of their economic reasoning.

Although this was a laborious and sometimes painful process, it was reasonably effective. The chairman, Dr. Horst Robert, read all the reports carefully, and was meticulously briefed. There were occasional crises, *e.g.* when the textiles committee wanted to publish a strongly protectionist report, but we won these battles, as we had strong support from Robert Marjolin, the Secretary General.

There was clearly a need for a more sophisticated forum than the Economic Committee to monitor the macro-economic conjuncture, to assess growth performance, to exchange ideas on policy options and to improve the diagnostic quality of our statistics. All of these tasks were undertaken successfully in the course of the next few years, but there was no grand design – the improvement happened gradually. It is clear from Marjolin's memoirs,[5] that he did not see progress in this direction as a priority. His mind was concentrated on progress towards a European customs union.

An opportunity for improving our policy analysis occurred when the Group of Economic Experts was created. The first meeting was intended mainly as an encounter between the economic side of the new US administration and the Europeans. The first session was not enlightening from an analytical point of view, but it was clear that the Eisenhower team was interested in regular exchange of views on

---

[5] Robert Marjolin, *Architect of European Unity, Memoirs 1911-1986*, Weidenfeld and Nicolson, London, 1989.

economic policy options and the interaction of the American and European economies at a reasonably high level. The US delegate was Gabriel Hauge, who had been on Eisenhower's political campaign staff and was his personal economic assistant. The French delegate was Paul Delouvrier, then the chief French official for economic cooperation and later Governor General of Algeria. The other members were high level economic professionals, notably Robert Hall from the UK and Otmar Emminger from the Bundesbank (or Bank deutscher Länder as it then was). It was agreed to follow up on a regular basis, under Hall's Chairmanship. He was economic advisor to the UK government, a slow speaking Australian of great wisdom and professional competence. He was a master of the meaningful grunt and an excellent chairman of the Group until 1961.

The core of the group was Robert Hall, Otmar Emminger, Etienne Hirsch, head of the French Plan from 1952 to 1959 (later Pierre Uri or Jacques Donnedieu de Vabres), Jan Tinbergen (later Jan Pen and/or Pieter de Wolff) from the Netherlands, Arthur Burns (later Raymond Saulnier) from the US Council of Economic Advisors, and varying representation from the Bank of Italy. In the long run the type of dialogue they developed revolutionised the character of our work and strengthened the Organisation substantially.

There was a very wide range of views in the Group. Tinbergen was a social engineer and model builder. Hirsch was a planner but a very flexible one. Hall was a pragmatic Keynesian. Emminger was the most articulate. He was primarily concerned with financial stability and payments equilibrium. He was not interested in microeconomic questions which were to be solved by market mechanisms set in train by macro-policy. The German position was not one of *laisser faire* and was concerned with employment as well as price stability. This was certainly the case for Alfred Mueller-Armack, Erhard's state secretary in the Ministry of Economics. The Germans were usually very well briefed on business conditions as they had five conjuncture institutes. Burns was least concerned with employment and growth. He pushed the US government away from Keynesian activism in favour of price stability and budget balance. Nevertheless, Burns with his NBER background was interested in close monitoring of performance of the leading economies and their mutual interaction. Hall avoided methodological confrontations. It was agreed that the best way to develop the dialogue was to set up future sessions with an analytical paper from the Secretariat on the nature of current conjunctural problems, to analyse the policy options for stability and growth, and discuss issues where the interaction of the economies was likely to cause problems. The emphasis was almost entirely macroeconomic. It marked a complete change from the detailed allocation problems which had preoccupied OEEC in earlier years.[6]

In 1955 there was a major change at the top of the Organisation when Marjolin and his two deputies resigned. Marjolin was a man of luminous intelligence. He believed in using the force of ideas to change the world by pragmatic action. Starting from very humble origins, leaving school at fourteen, he restarted his formal education when he was 20 and attained high academic honours. He was a successful economic journalist in prewar France, had an important wartime role as Jean Monnet's Deputy in Washington, was a major actor in implementing the Marshall Plan and later in creating the European Community. His successor René Sergent (an Inspecteur de Finance, and previously Deputy Secretary General of NATO) did not have Marjolin's intellectual power, vision and drive. However, Sergent was an agreeable and intelligent man with a disarming humility and willingness to take advice. He responded very positively to our initiatives to strengthen the analytic work of the Organisation, particularly as his period of office was wracked by unsuccessful attempts to use the OEEC as a vehicle for a Europe-wide free trade area.

François Walter left at the same time as Marjolin. He was replaced by Eivind Erichsen, a Keynesian economist with wide experience in the Norwegian Ministry of Finance. Milton Gilbert, the director of Statistics and National Accounts, became the overlord of Economics as well as Statistics.

The change brought a big improvement in the quality of our work and the efficiency of our Directorate. Milton was an economist and statistician of the highest calibre. He had played a major part from 1940 in organising and defining the scope of the official US

---

[6] See the (May 5th 1955) comment of Hall in A. Cairncross, ed., *The Robert Hall Diaries 1954-61*, Unwin Hyman, London, 1991, p. 35 on the significance of the expert group: "These meetings are really something quite exceptional for economists and I should think are quite new in the history of the world, in the sense that economic experts, if they existed at all as Government advisers, were not generally very important people until Keynes's ideas had been commonly accepted in the West. So that there were not the people to meet as we do: now we have 7 or 8 or 9 people who are by and large the chief professional advisers of the main Western Governments except Canada – all have more or less the same professional training in that they understand how to maintain the level of activity and what forces operate on it".

national accounts.[7] Marjolin took him on around 1950 to introduce national accounting techniques to OEEC countries and he was the only American in the OEEC Secretariat. He worked closely with Richard Stone in Cambridge in training a new breed of official statistician and establishing a standardised system of accounts. He had built up a highly competent National Accounts division under Geer Stuvel to check the procedures followed in the different countries in implementing the new system and to produce standardised accounts for all Member countries. He had also inaugurated a series of path-breaking comparisons of purchasing power of currencies and comparability of real product levels.[8] This national accounts work was the bedrock on which our future analysis of comparative growth performance was based. It provided a yardstick for assessing the success of policy which had never existed before. Gilbert was also active in the creation of the International Association for Research in Income and Wealth, where Simon Kuznets stimulated academic researchers in many countries to create a historical counterpart to the postwar national accounts. Apart from his work on national accounts, Milton had once been editor of the *Survey of Current Business* in the US Department of Commerce, so he was well qualified for the work on policy issues and the monitoring of the short term economic situation in the OEEC area, to which he now switched his attention.

Gilbert had a relaxed easy-going manner and did not write much himself; but when we had to prepare discussion papers for the experts, we would spend hours trying to clarify the major issues. I gave him a draft on the lines we had agreed, he went over it slowly, carefully and orally, making the text as succinct as possible, trying to find words with the exact nuance of meaning in order to get a document that was lucid and creatively pungent with regard to policy options. He had an eagle eye for tables, making sure that they were

---

[7] See S. Kuznets, "Discussion of the new department of commerce income series. National income: a new version", and "Objectives of national income measurement. A reply to professor Kuznets", by M. Gilbert, G. Jaszi, E.F. Denison and C.F. Schwartz in *Review of Economics and Statistics*, August 1948. For Gilbert's role in developing the accounts, see C.S. Carson, "The history of the United States national income and product accounts", *Review of Income and Wealth*, June 1975.

[8] M. Gilbert and I.B. Kravis, *An International Comparison of National Products and the Purchasing Power of Currencies*, OEEC, Paris, 1954; M. Gilbert and Associates, *Comparative National Products and Price Levels*, OEEC, Paris, 1958; D. Paige and G. Bombach, *A Comparison of National Output and Productivity*, OEEC, Paris, 1959.

the most appropriate we could produce, and elegantly presented.[9] Over the next five years I learned a good deal from these long sessions. Under the new dispensation we could also prepare much better annual reports, with some thematic unity,[10] and we got a better chairman, Roger Ockrent, for the Economic Committee.

In the summer of 1958 I spent a month on leave of absence (as a NATO Fellow) in Washington and New York, where I was able to brief myself rather fully on US techniques of policy analysis and pick up ideas for improving our analytical work. I had long talks with Paul McCracken and David Lusher in the Council of Economic Advisors, with Julie Shiskin who prepared their business indicators, with George Terborgh and Raymond Goldsmith on measurement of capital stock, with Ed Denison on techniques of analysing economic performance and Senator Paul Douglas on the work of the Joint Economic Committee of Congress of which he was then the chairman. In New York I saw Sol Fabricant and Geoffrey Moore in the NBER, Sanford Parker of *Fortune* magazine and Bill Butler of the Chase Manhattan Bank on techniques of monitoring US economic performance. I also started a fruitful relationship with the team of economists at United Nations headquarters who wrote the part of the UN's *World Economic Report* on advanced capitalist countries.

We sharpened our analysis of long term growth potential and productivity performance by using the national income statistics and our new publication on manpower statistics to create a more systematic framework of growth accounts. We first made use of these macro accounting techniques in a major study on growth problems and prospects which was published in the 8th annual report. The quality of our business cycle analysis was substantially upgraded. Our current economic indicators were improved through introduction of US seasonal adjustment techniques. In 1960 the Department started a new publication, *Main Economic Indicators*, incorporating about 100 seasonally adjusted series, which was a much more sophisticated vehicle for short term conjunctural analysis than we had previously had.

These analytic improvements were fed into our work for the Economic Experts which was gradually transformed into the Econ-

---

[9] See comments on Gilbert's style in Murray Rossant's foreword to M. Gilbert, *Quest for World Monetary Order*, J. Wiley and Sons, New York, 1980, p. VIII.

[10] *Europe Today and in 1960*, OEEC, Paris, 1957; *A Decade of Cooperation: Achievements and Perspectives*, OEEC, Paris, 1958; *Policies for Sound Economic Growth*, OEEC, Paris, 1959; *Europe and the World Economy*, OEEC, Paris, 1960.

omic Policy Committee in 1959. This had a higher status than the Economic Committee, it met every 4 months and consisted of fiscal and monetary policy officials from all Member countries. In April 1961 it was further augmented by the creation of a working party on policies to stimulate economic growth, and another one (more influential but with a restricted membership) on payments issues and the fiscal monetary mix (with Emile van Lennep[11] as chairman). A little later another working party was created to deal with problems of inflation and production costs. The impetus for the new working parties came from the new Kennedy administration. Walter Heller and Jim Tobin from the Council of Economic Advisors created a new atmosphere of intellectual cooperation, Bob Solow was a very effective contributor to the new work on growth, and Bob Roosa to the discussions on payments issues.

This committee structure is still the hard core of OECD's economic policy work. The analyis was strengthened later when the Economic Department developed forecasting models, quarterly national accounts, and created the twice yearly *Economic Outlook*, but the work we did in 1955-60 was of fundamental importance in strengthening cooperation between the advanced capitalist economies, and in creating an articulate dialogue which helped them avoid the mistakes of diagnosis and policy they made in the interwar years of conflict and beggar your neighbour policy. It was important that the USA was fully involved in this process. It strengthened OEEC in a period when it was under great strain on the trade front.

In the course of 1960-61 there were major changes in preparation for the creation of a new organisation. The US and Canada were to join as full members, and procedures for Japanese entry were begun. There was pressure from the USA to instigate work on development, with a view to persuading European countries to increase or initiate aid to developing countries. The time was propitious as the process of decolonisation was reaching completion and there was increasing competition from the USSR to win the allegiance of the third world, with notable success in the case of Egypt and Cuba.

I became the secretary of the Development Assistance Group which was a forerunner of the development aid activities to be carried out by the new organisation. The first task was to set up a comprehensive statistical monitoring system to measure the flow of different

---

[11] See E. van Lennep, *Herinneringen van een internationale Nederlander*, Stenfert Kroese, Leiden, 1991.

categories of financial resources to developing countries (official loans and grants, private credits and direct lending, export credit guarantees, etc.) from each of the 14 countries which were deemed to be developed. Most of the countries had no comprehensive view of such flows. We could get a rough aggregate cross-check from balance of payments statistics but we had to go to central banks, finance ministries, export credit agencies, the World Bank and IMF to break down the different categories. The results were sometimes unexpected, *e.g.* the flow from France was very much bigger proportionately than in the USA, but as expected the flows were small from Germany, Japan and Scandinavia. This first report (*The Flow of Financial Resources to Countries in Course of Economic Development*) was carried out at breakneck speed and published in April 1961. It set the main guidelines which the Development Assistance Committee still uses for collecting data from its Member countries.

At that time it seemed to me that the basis for analysing growth and stability in advanced capitalist countries had been reasonably firmly established, and that the problem of development was an exciting new field. I therefore decided to switch jobs, but I first took six months leave of absence in the second half of 1962 to write my first book, *Economic Growth in the West*,[12] where I tried to explain the postwar acceleration of growth in Western Europe, and the greater stability of the growth path. I pushed the historical perspective back to 1870, using the same type of quantitative national accounting evidence we had been using in OEEC for the postwar period. When I was writing it, I realised how far my horizons had widened over the research agenda I had as a graduate student. I was still trying to explain why some countries achieved faster growth or higher income levels than others, but I had a broader view of causality (particularly the role of domestic and international policy), a firmer and bigger array of macroeconomic evidence for a wider group of countries, and a longer time horizon. I also had a strong belief in the usefulness of the international cooperation in which I had been engaged, and in the efficacy of postwar macroeconomic policy in improving capitalist economic performance.

---

[12] A. Maddison, *Economic Growth in the West*, Allen and Unwin, London, 1964.

Work on economic development

I worked almost exclusively on development problems from the early 1960s to 1971. In 1963 I was director of the OECD's technical assistance programme which mainly involved economic advisory assistance to Greece, Portugal, Spain, Turkey and Yugoslavia. In 1964-66 I was a Fellow of OECD's new Development Centre. In 1967, I left OECD for 5 years, first on a research project for the Twentieth Century Fund, and then in 1969-71 to work for Harvard University's Development Advisory Service in Pakistan and Ghana.

The Development Centre was created to involve OECD more directly with developing countries in order to understand their policies better and to operate as some sort of intellectual intermediary between them and the OECD.

The first President was Robert Buron, a French politician with wide connections in the third world, who regarded politics as "le plus beau des métiers". After a prewar career in the Chamber of Commerce for chocolate makers and wartime public relations for the French movie industry, he became an MRP politician and held a number of ministerial posts in the Fourth and Fifth Republic – notably Minister of Colonies (d'Outre Mer) for Mendès France and Minister of Transport for de Gaulle. Buron was not interested in research but in seminars for ministers and senior officials in countries where there was scope for a dialogue on development problems and policies. Raymond Goldsmith was made Vice-President to oversee research. He had made pioneering theoretical contributions to the study of capital, wealth, savings and financial flows and had produced massive comparative empirical studies in these fields. He picked a very good librarian for the Centre and helped start work on national accounts for developing countries in order to monitor their economic growth,[13] but in most respects he was a loner. He did not create a research team but got on with his own work. He let the Fellows choose their own topics, insisting only that they be related in some way to foreign aid.

My first instinct was to attempt a general survey explaining comparative development experience in quantitative and historical

---

[13] The Development Centre started to collect national accounts information from developing countries in 1964, held a few seminars on their comparability, and produced its first regular estimates in 1968, *National Accounts of Less Developed Countries 1950-1966*.

perspective in the way I had done for the OEEC countries. I decided to postpone this for several reasons. In the first place, the statistical basis for such a venture did not then exist. A second reason was that the developing world was much more heterogeneous in institutions, ideologies, policy objectives and weaponry, cultural and political heritage, social structure and level of real income. Given the huge range of these countries and my relative ignorance of them, it seemed sensible to familiarise myself with problems of countries where I had sufficient *entrée* to get a feel for the policy making process and which would represent different types of political-institutional heritage. The Centre offered plenty of scope for this and it was quite compatible with my official commitment to research on foreign aid.[14]

Brazil

Brazil was the country where I developed the widest range of contacts and saw most of the policy-making process. I went to Rio in October 1964 at the invitation of Roberto Campos, Minister of Planning in the military regime which had just overthrown the populist government of Goulart. Campos was an economist-diplomat with very wide experience. He was born in a monastery in the backwoods of Mato Grosso and was a seminarist before he joined the foreign ministry in 1939 as a junior consul. On his way up, he got a Ph.D. in economics from Columbia University, was one of the Brazilian delegates to Bretton Woods, helped make the development plan of President Kubitschek, was head of the Brazilian Development Bank and Ambassador to the United States. Campos was by far the most powerful minister, strongly supported by Octavio Bulhoes as Minister of Finance. Campos had a team of outstanding young economists in his ministry, including Mario Simenson and João Paulo dos Reis Velloso who later became ministers. The mentor of both Campos and Bulhoes was Eugenio Gudin (1886-1986), a *laisser faire* liberal of penetrating intellect and irreverent humour, who had founded the academic study of economics in Brazil after a career as an engineer.

---

[14] My contribution to the Centre's work on aid consisted of two books: A. Maddison, *Foreign Skills and Technical Assistance in Economic Development*, OECD Development Centre, Paris, 1965, and A. Maddison, A. Stavrianopoulos and B. Higgins, *Foreign Skills and Technical Assistance in Greek Development*, OECD Development Centre, Paris, 1966.

The main preoccupation of the economic team was a stabilisation exercise to put a halt to hyperinflation, reduce the budget
deficit, reform the tax system, get rid of a distorted set of price
controls and subsidies, liberalise foreign trade, create a new exchange
rate mechanism and reform financial institutions. The stabilisation
exercise was an outstanding success in laying the foundations for a
subsequent decade of very fast economic growth and it was carried
out in gradualist fashion in 1964-67, without pushing Brazil into
recession. I was able to observe this operation at close quarters in the
research department of the Planning Ministry where I was a con-
sultant. I also had contact with the research group in the Vargas
Foundation, which performed some of the functions of a statistical
office, producing both the national accounts and the price indices as
well as providing short term business cycle analysis in its journal
Conjuntura. I went to Brazil six times in 1964-67, visited a good many
parts of the country, acquired some modest competence in Portuguese, as well as learning the samba and bossa nova.

I was very impressed by the vigour and originality of Brazil. The
population has cosmopolitan roots, with significant immigration of
Italians, Germans, Japanese, Lebanese as well as the original mix of
Portuguese settlers and African slaves. As there are several very large
cities, its intellectual life is multipolar. It has been blessed with much
gentler political transitions than most of Latin America, so the tone of
discussion on economic policy issues was less bitter than in some
other places. It is a frontier country with a high degree of self
confidence without a chip-on-the-shoulder feeling of exploitation by
powerful neighbours. Added to this was the fascination of the
economic problems they were tackling. I had had no previous experience of such an inflationary economy, such boldness in institutional innovation, or such an elaborate set of institutions for co-
existence with inflation. The Campos approach to these problems was
basically liberal and (except for his gradualism) not too different from
that of the World Bank and IMF in the 1980s, but at that time it
went counter to the prevailing policy views in other Latin American
countries.

The most disconcerting thing about Brazil was the very high
degree of inequality. Regional variance in per capita income in the
twenty states ranged from nine to one, and the horizontal variation of
income was also very sharp and noticeable, particularly in Rio with its

impoverished ramshackle *favelas* poised on slippery hillsides behind luxurious beachfront apartments. It was also very noticeable that the black population was completely absent from the seats of power or any well paid activity except sport and entertainment.[15]

Guinea

In January 1965, four of the Development Centre fellows, Edmond Janssens, Nino Novacco, Göran Ohlin and I, went to Conakry for a month with Buron and Goldsmith. In the first week, we talked to Sékou Touré, the President, Ismael Touré his brother, who was Economic Development Minister, Siafoulaye Diallo, the Minister of Finance and Planning, who appeared to be second man in the regime, and Keita Fodeba, a professional dancer and founder of the national ballet, who had become a highly original Minister of Defence. Buron made a speech to the national assembly and then we had all the senior economic officials in a seminar for three weeks.

In the colonial period, Sékou Touré, who started life as a postal worker, had been a Communist (CGT) trade union leader and a member of the French parliament. He was the great grandson of a warrior chief, Samory, who fought the French between 1879 and 1898. In the 1950s, he went to Czechoslovakia to a school for party *cadres*. In Guinea he had organised political life on a single party basis. Virtually all adults were expected to join. The party had nearly 8000 committees and when we visited outlying regions we found roomfuls of villagers who had come to palaver – often with very searching questions such as why a colonial power like Portugal was in OECD. One of the functions of the party was to reduce the significance of ethnic divisions which were physically very marked. Sékou was a very dark skinned stocky Malinke, whereas Saifoulaye was a tall lanky Peul with light brown skin and semitic features.

The Guinean situation was unique in Africa as the French had abandoned the country when it opted for independence in 1958.[16] There was no neocolonial apprenticeship as there was elsewhere in

---

[15] See A. Maddison and Associates, *The Political Economy of Poverty, Equity and Growth: Brazil and Mexico*, Oxford University Press, New York, 1992.

[16] See Elliott J. Berg, "Socialism and economic development in Tropical Africa", *Quarterly Journal of Economics*, 1964, for an excellent analysis of the roots of African socialism.

French Africa which became independent in 1960. In a population of
3 million, there were less than 50 Guineans with higher education.
There had been 600 Frenchmen in government service, several
thousand French soldiers, and about 2500 expatriates in productive
and service enterprises who all left abruptly. As a result, the administration, health services and modern economy had collapsed. The
country was excluded from the franc area to which its neighbours
belonged. Ministers (virtually all without higher education) had had
to improvise an administration from scratch, getting technical assistance from wherever they could. The radio (*La Voix de la Révolution*) was run by a beautiful Hungarian lady. The only newspaper,
Horoya, had a circulation of 8000 every 2 or 3 days but the East
Germans had built the Patrice Lumumba printing plant with a
capacity of several hundred thousand newspapers a day. Military
advice and incompatible equipment came from China, Czechoslovakia, and the German Federal Republic. The military effectiveness of
the army seemed doubtful, but they did useful work on development
projects. They made shoes, clothing and suitcases, mended roads and
trained rural animateurs. The Defence Minister was also responsible
for security and police. It had a crack unit of glamorous women who
served as traffic police in Conakry and doubled as a night club
orchestra. Before we came, the army had had a visit from Franz
Joseph Strauss, the German Defence Minister, and when we were
there they had another from Che Guevara, the Cuban specialist on
guerilla warfare.

The Guinean ministers and civil servants were friendly, without
guile, ready to answer all questions, and several of them dressed in
traditional Muslim robes. We visited the big bauxite and aluminium
operation in Fria, a banana and pineapple plantation, a match factory
and a model state farm run by a group of ministers. The farm was
littered with Soviet tractors and other machinery, but had no visible
output. When I asked the Minister of Planning about this, he replied
"Tu sais, j'ai pas la tête pour les chiffres" (I have no head for figures).
The state trading organisation had taken over French shops, which
were almost completely empty, and plantation agriculture was
faltering. In spite of the chaos, it was a lively and interesting place. It
survived by virtue of a robust subsistence economy, widespread
smuggling by ethnic groups with relatives in neighbouring countries,
and rich deposits of bauxite and iron ore which attracted foreign

investment. The mixed bag of foreign aid was quite sizeable, and, on balance, was probably helpful but some of the projects seemed very dubious, *e.g.* the Chinese match factory imported huge Chinese trees to provide its raw material.

In July 1965 there was a seminar on supposedly similar lines in Teheran, but it was totally different from Guinea. We met elegant officials and junior ministers with sleeked hair and expensive suits, who listened politely and said little. Hoveida (later executed by Khomeini) was the only interesting one, but we did not learn much about the country. When I tried to discuss the oppressive atmosphere of the place with Buron, he shut me up, as he suspected that his chauffeur might be listening and reporting on us.

Mongolia

In January and early February 1967 I undertook a bizarre and picaresque mission for my friend Herbert Philips of UNESCO. I visited Outer Mongolia and Cambodia to investigate the role of science in economic development. I was mainly interested in the Mongol part of the trip, as I had taken a course on Mongol history at Johns Hopkins, where Owen Lattimore had a project including the exiled head of the Mongolian buddhists, the Gegen Dilowa Hutuktu, and two Mongol princes. My companion on the trip was Ratchik Avakov, a Soviet Armenian who had worked in IMEMO in Moscow and who was then working in UNESCO. At first he was a bit suspicious of me but after a month together and 25000 miles of travel in climates ranging from 30 degrees below zero to about 80 above, we ended up like brothers.

I began to realise Ratchik's value in Moscow when he got the Mongol ambassador out of bed early in the morning and demanded that he give me a visa. That way we got an Aeroflot plane the same day that landed at Omsk and Tomsk and finally deposited us in Irkutsk, where we waited a long time for the two engined Antonov of Mongol Air. By mistake I picked up what I thought was the only British passport in Irkutsk and met its owner, the wife of the British ambassador to Mongolia, who was on the same plane.

There was only one hotel in Ulan Bator, a city where a large proportion of the population still lived in yurts (felt tents). The adult inhabitants had deeply lined faces from constant exposure to the extreme climate. A large proportion were bow-legged – having spent a good deal of their lives in the saddle in a country with two and a half million horses and only one million people. They drank fermented mare's milk (kumiss) which they boiled with tea, and they ate a good deal of horsemeat, often steaks sliced off the haunch of a living animal. The food in the hotel was abysmal. The Yugoslav cook had gone insane trying to improve the local diet. There had been a big expansion in cereal output, so he had put bread on the menu, but it came in damp, heavy, unsliceable chunks. Fortunately, Heath Mason, the British Ambassador, invited me to dinner a couple of times. The Embassy was in the hotel, and he got a regular monthly supply of Yorkshire steak and kidney puddings, delivered in the diplomatic pouch by two Queen's messengers who helped eat them.

The country had broken away from Chinese rule in the early 20th century and had been in the Soviet sphere of influence since the 1920s as a buffer state. The princely class, and the large population of Lamaistic Buddhist monks had been obliterated. The old cursive script, written in vertical columns was replaced by cyrillic, written horizontally. The political system was organised on the Soviet model, with large amounts of Soviet aid and technical assistance, and there was a large Soviet military presence. In the Summer of 1939, these Soviet forces had repulsed a Japanese invasion in the battle of Khalkhin-Gol.

Chirendev, the head of the Academy of Sciences, was an atomic physicist and told us about its major research projects. The biggest was on agriculture, a second on mathematical and natural sciences, with a much smaller commitment to social sciences. There was also research activity in the University of Ulan Bator and in the geological institute. In all, there were 9000 people with higher education and a thousand of these were in research institutes. We also talked to the ministers of labour and education, the rector of the university, the planning ministry and the statistical office. It was difficult to assess the impact of science and technical change on growth, but there had clearly been large changes over the previous forty years. Communication was sometimes a bit difficult. I asked Mrs. Lchamsoryn, the president of the State Commission on Labour and Wages, how many people were unemployed. The interpreter told me it was a silly question. I persisted, and was told that "under socialism there can be no unemployment".

We made a field trip about 30 kilometres out of Ulan Bator to a collective farm where there were a lot of yurts huddled together surrounded by wooden fences to mitigate the cold wind. Here as elsewhere, there were hundreds of horses. We went to an outlying brigade, a kilometre or so from the farm headquarters, to have some boiled tea and interview an old peasant. I asked him what difference socialism had brought, and he said, echoing Lenin, that socialism meant electricity. It was only then that I noticed an electric wire from the main camp to his yurt. As Mongols move their herds and yurts around to different pasture in the course of the year, I wondered if the electricity moved with them.

We managed to get enough statistical material for our report and left after a week. Getting out was difficult as the electrical system in the aircraft failed just after take off. We managed to glide back and the elderly pilot spent several hours unsuccessfully working on it with a spanner. Eventually he borrowed the presidential plane, which looked the same outside, but inside had a salon and a bedroom configuration rather than serried rows of seats. We got to Irkutsk about 10 hours late. After the usual halts in Omsk and Tomsk, we spent a freezing day in Moscow visiting IMEMO, then flew to Delhi and Bangkok for stop-offs before going on to Phnom Penh for our next mission, where we swapped our fur covering for straw coolie hats.

USSR and Japan

In mid-1965 Goldsmith was replaced as Vice President of the Centre by Ian Little. Ian brought in a new team of Fellows (Tibor Scitovsky and Maurice Scott) to work together on a common project on industrialisation and trade. As I was not part of this project, I was able to spend a good deal of time on a study of Japanese and Soviet growth. Both of these countries had attempted to accelerate their growth performance and catch up with the advanced countries, so it seemed useful to assess what they had achieved and how they did it.

In 1964 I had visited Moscow and Leningrad to collect material for work on Soviet growth. I contacted IMEMO (the Institute for World Politics and Economics) in Moscow (which was the main institute of the Academy of Sciences for studying western economies), and found myself unexpectedly welcome as their Deputy Director,

Manoukian, had just translated my book, *Economic Growth in the West*. The most outspoken and interesting of their economists was Stanislav Menshikov, who became a good friend.

It was more difficult to meet economists working on the Soviet economy, but with some difficulty I got the telephone number of Gosplan and contacted Valentin Kudrov who had translated the OEEC real income studies into Russian. Kudrov came, with a minder, to meet me at the Metropole Hotel. In his halting English and my very limited Russian, we managed to have a dialogue in which I sounded his opinion of several US Kremlinologists whose work was my main quantitative source, and we had an exchange of views on problems of measuring real product and growth which we still continue.

Apart from this I managed to take in something of the flavour of Soviet society, being accosted by people wanting Beatles records, looking at museums, watching the May Day parade in Red Square, with Kruschev, Ben Bella and Oginga Odinga on Lenin's tomb.

In 1965, I visited Japan for a few weeks to collect material on Japanese growth. Here it was possible to have a much deeper dialogue than in Moscow, and statistical information was readily available. I already had friends in Hitotsubashi University, particularly Kazushi Ohkawa, who was starting to publish 13 volumes on Japanese quantitative economic history. Saburo Okita opened the doors of government agencies such as the Bank of Japan, the Economic Planning Agency, the Ministry of Agriculture, and the Ministry of Education where one could often find ten economists in a room all fresh and eager to talk after their morning callisthenics. Apart from the sophistication of these people I was struck by the strong discipline and an organisation that operated like clockwork. I had had the same impression about Japanese industry on my first trip in 1961 when I had visited the Sony radio factory, and found the foremen had Ph.D's and all the operatives had high school education.

During 1966, when I was writing up the Japan-Russia study, I was fortunate in having fairly frequent contact with Arthur Lewis. I visited him a couple of times in Princeton, he spent 6 weeks in the Centre in the Summer of 1966 and we met from time to time afterwards as members of an OECD expert group on technical assistance. Arthur was probably the brightest economist to work on development and as a West Indian, had a lifetime familiarity with the problems. I profited greatly from contact with him, both in our daily luncheon sessions in Paris, and from his written comments on my drafts which were always forthright, penetrating and enlightening.

Economic progress and policy in developing countries

At the beginning of 1967 I left OECD, and wrote the general survey of postwar development experience I had considered doing three years earlier. This was financed by the Twentieth Century Fund of New York. For the next two and a half years I worked at home in Paris, with a couple of brief spells as a visiting academic, in Berkeley in 1968, and in Montreal in 1969.

At that time, I became strongly influenced by Edward Denison's comparative growth accounting approach which incorporated the theoretical insights of Bob Solow and Ted Schultz. I made some departures from Denison in giving a bigger weight to capital and introducing domestic policy and foreign aid as part of the explanatory framework. The book covered 29 countries and involved a great deal of statistical groundwork, to estimate comparative levels of real GDP, stocks of physical and human capital as well as comparable estimates of growth of GDP and for major sectors.

The rest of the book dealt largely with policy issues concerning reasons for instability of the growth path, problems in agricultural, industrial and trade policy and attitudes to population growth. Although country performance varied widely, the tone of the book was optimistic about the significant acceleration in postwar growth. A major shortcoming was that it neglected the social impact of growth, something I felt should be next on my research agenda.

Social policy in Pakistan and Ghana

Pakistan

I went to Pakistan for the Harvard Advisory Group[17] at the end of June 1969, to work on social problems in the Planning Commission in Islamabad.

---

[17] See George Rosen, *Western Economists and Eastern Societies: Agents of Change in South Asia 1950-1970*, Johns Hopkins, Baltimore, 1985 for a description of the Harvard Group's experience in Pakistan.

I already had some knowledge of the country. I had met the Chief Economist, Mahbub ul Haq, in Bangkok in 1962 when we were members of a UN expert group which produced a report on *Methods of Long Term Projections*.

He arranged a visit I made to Pakistan in May 1965 when I met several other very bright and well trained Pakistani economists, notably Nurul Islam, Sartaj Aziz and Khalid Ikram. I attended a conference in Harvard in 1965 on Pakistani economic development where I met American economists who had worked on Pakistan including Edward Mason, Hollis Chenery, Gus Papanek and Kenneth Galbraith.

As Pakistan got a good deal of foreign aid, its administration was more open to foreign advisors than most. Indeed part of the advisory work was to brief the continuous stream of World Bank missions. There was a political change shortly before I went which seemed to promise some scope for advance in social policy. From 1958 the military government of Ayub Khan had had a doctrine of functional inequality: "The underdeveloped countries must consciously accept a philosophy of growth and shelve for the distant future all ideas of equitable distribution and welfare state. It should be recognised that these are luxuries which only developed countries can afford".[18]

Ayub was toppled in March 1969 by workers and students in a climate of social unrest. Political opposition was gathering strength in East Pakistan because of the uneven allocation of foreign aid and the fruits of development. The new military dictator, Yahya Khan, took a number of measures to appease discontent, suspending 15 per cent of high level civil servants for corruption, raising the minimum wage, chastising business tax evaders, promising more resources to education and to East Pakistan.

The Planning Commission was the central agency coordinating economic policy and foreign aid in the new capital, Islamabad (designed by Doxiadis). It was part of the Presidential Secretariat, the President being the Minister to whom we reported, with M.M. Ahmad as Deputy Chairman. Ahmad was a moderate, doleful, and reserved chap who was hereditary leader of a small religious sect, the Ahmadiyas. I had the impression that he carried less weight than his

---

[18] Mahbub ul Haq, *The Strategy of Economic Planning: A Case Study of Pakistan*, Oxford University Press, Karachi, 1966, p. 30.

predecessor Said Hasan who had worked for Ayub. Mahbub had a very powerful role with direct access to the President when necessary. The defender of the corporate interests of the old bureaucracy was Qamar-ul-Islam, a top member of the Civil Service of Pakistan (CSP), an *élite* group descended directly from the Indian Civil Service (ICS) of colonial days.

In the Commission my main job was to scrutinise policy proposals for education, health, housing, urban water supply, and family planning that came from the relevant ministries and the regional planning agencies in Dacca and Karachi. I had to get a perspective of what was feasible from whatever documentary evidence I could collect, cross-examining my colleagues, and occasional visits to hospitals or public works projects. Apart from Nafees Sadek, who produced a brilliant report on family planning, the Commission was not rich in expertise on these matters, but Charles Benson of the Ford Foundation was a knowledgeable colleague on education.

My work did not involve particularly sophisticated comparisons of costs and benefits but it provided fascinating insight into the social situation and the systematic biases in resource allocation which derived from the character of the power *élite*. I never had any problem with Mahbub in being forthright on such issues, and parts of my drafts emerged in several chapters of the plan. Whether I had much impact on what happened is another issue, but I may have contributed something to checking programmes I thought were misguided.

Pakistan's social structure was still strongly influenced by the heritage of the British raj. The nationalist forces which had created Pakistan had no element of socialism or social reform as in India, nor were they particularly religious. Their religious content was primarily anti-Hindu and certainly not Islamic in any fundamentalist sense. The Pakistan Jinnah created was Viceregal and the primary locus of power was the bureaucratic-military *élite*. The organisational framework of this group was still the one created by the British and their working language was English. Their houses, clubs, cantonments, life style and idioms were British colonial. The group was much bigger than in colonial days. The armed forces numbered 300000 with 7000 officers compared with 100 Muslim officers in the smaller Indian army of the British period. There were 500 members in the *élite* CSP and about 1150 Class I officers under them. This was more than ten times the number of top Muslim officials under the British. These people got the major benefits of government housing expenditure. Urban improvements were concentrated in their cantonment areas. They benefitted substantially from expenditure on secondary and higher education. The benefits also went to the new class of businessmen who also got subsidised loans, licenses to import scarce goods and other perquisites. The traditional landlord *élite* was virtually untouched by land reform except in East Pakistan where most landlords had been Hindus. Landlords in West Pakistan were major beneficiaries of government expenditure on irrigation, particularly the new waters that became available after the construction of the Tarbela dam on the Indus river – a World Bank project intended to replace potential water losses to the Indian Punjab.

The bulk of the population were extremely poor. The average weight of an adult Pakistani was 120 lbs., *i.e.* about 30 lbs. less than the average European. Their average haemoglobin count was two thirds of that in Europe, and in this anaemic state they were readily prone to tuberculosis, pneumonia and influenza. At any one time, a third of the population suffered from intestinal disorders, the rural population was infected by hookworm, and prone to typhoid. Eighty-five per cent of the population were illiterate and most women had a very low status, hidden behind veils with very few opportunities to get a job.

Many of the proposals we got would have bypassed these people, *i.e.* major expansions in secondary and higher education, medical training for doctors who emigrated on graduation, housing and urban facilities for the bureaucracy and military. There had been some progress in areas where welfare gains were cheap. Malaria, dysentery, and smallpox eradication programmes, together with access to simple drugs had prolonged average life expectation from 30 to 50 years in the two decades since independence, and there was plenty of scope for further cheap gains by expanding and improving primary education, better water and sewerage, birth control programmes, better trained teachers and nurses, better rural health centres.

At the beginning of 1970, political criticism of the government increased, particularly in East Pakistan. The Jama'at-i-Islami party (a fundamentalist group advocating violent forms of action) alleged that the Harvard Advisory Group were foreign spies. After this we adopted a lower profile, our workload dropped considerably, and in mid 1970 the Group's work in Pakistan was discontinued.

In this period of increased leisure, I started a history of India and Pakistan, *Class Structure and Economic Growth.*[19] This explained the emergence of the postcolonial *élite* from the heritage of Hindu, Moghul and British rule, and showed how the new distribution of power had affected the character of postwar policy and the nature of economic growth. I visited East Pakistan and India for a few weeks to gather more material. Then I went to Harvard for six months, to write up the book and collect further material in the Widener Library. There I attended Alexander Gerschenkron's economic history seminar regularly and went occasionally to lectures by John Fairbank on Chinese history, and by Simon Kuznets on economic growth.

I was more satisfied with the book on India and Pakistan than with most of the other things I had written on development because I had worked for much longer in the country, had had the daily experience of running a household (Harvard gave me a large house and 5 servants) and had close access to the policy making process. Even the workaday environment of the Commission was enlightening with its 4 segregated lifts for different categories of civil servant, stairs which only the sweepers used, the bearers who lost documents because they could not read the names of the addressees, and the all-male group of one-finger typists.

Most members of the Harvard Group were congenial colleagues. There were very interesting places to visit, Lahore (a Moghul capital), Harappa (the seat of the Mohenjo Daro civilisation), Taxila (a town built by Alexander the Great), old British hill stations like Murree and Abbottabad, and the road up the Khyber to Kabul, with stop-offs in Peshawar, Landi Kotal, and Jallalabad.

Ghana

At the end of 1970 I went to Ghana to work in the Ministry of Finance and Planning on social policy. I had been interested in broadening my knowledge of Africa, which, apart from a brief visit to Nigeria, was confined largely to ex-French colonies.

Ghana was the first British African colony to become independent, in 1957, about a year before Guinea broke away from

---

[19] A. Maddison, *Class Structure and Economic Growth*, Allen and Unwin, London, 1971.

France. Ghana had the same aspirations to break with colonial tradition and create a variety of African socialism. The transition to independence was much easier in Ghana, which inherited large sterling balances from the colonial administration, had a very much larger stock of educated people, and some political experience before independence (with Kwame Nkrumah as prime minister). It was not cut off from the rest of the Commonwealth or aid from the metropole as Guinea had been. The Gold Coast had been run as a coherent entity, whereas Guinea was carved out of a much larger French administrative area on the eve of independence.

Ghana was unusual in Africa in having built up a very large export sector of relatively prosperous peasant cocoa farmers. White settler agriculture was virtually non-existent, because the climate is extremely unattractive. It was a rather egalitarian country as access to land was easy, and there were no barriers of religion or caste to impede social mobility. Women were much freer in Ghana than was the case in Pakistan or in Islamic Guinea. Conjugal ties are informal, and it was quite common to find successful businesswomen with several children who had never had a husband. Because of the relative abundance of land and the steady nature of the climate, hunger was not a significant problem.

Nkrumah had expanded the government sector of the economy considerably. There had been a big push for industrialisation. In agriculture he created state farms, there was large investment in infrastructure projects, *e.g.* the large new port in Tema, the highway between Accra and Tema, and lavish facilities for Pan African conferences. He provided aid to some other African countries, Guinea in particular. He greatly extended the education network and the size of the administration. He spent the sterling balances, accumulated foreign debt, and squeezed the income of cocoa farmers. Many of the investment projects were ill conceived, and some were disastrously wasteful. The result was economic stagnation, substantial inflation, balance of payments crisis, and allocation of resources by licensing which led to inefficiency and corruption.

In 1966, Nkrumah was overthrown by the armed forces and went into exile in Guinea. The military have ruled the country off and on ever since, but I went there during a brief interval when Kofi Busia was prime minister, after elections in August 1969.

The objectives of economic policy were not very clear when I was there. It was felt that Nkrumah had made major errors and that his thrust in policy should be stopped. However, there was no policy to remedy the balance of payments problems, there had been little reduction in the state's economic commitments, and there was still a large network of administrative controls. Official interest in the social sectors was desultory and the Finance Minister, Mensah, took decisions without much reference to his staff. Busia, the Prime Minister exercised little control over his ministers. He was a mild mannered ex-professor, in rather poor health. He was keen on European advisors, particularly if they came from Oxford, and he did not trust his own people much.

I found the government's housing policy had the same bias as in Pakistan. The top civil servants and army officers aspired to colonial style bungalows on quarter acre plots with two car garages. Most of governmental expenditure on housing went into buildings which approached these standards. There were about 60000 government houses. They represented only about 6 per cent of the total housing stock but 60 per cent of the houses which did not have mud walls. They were allocated by the state housing corporation, the armed forces and police, the Tema Development Corporation, Ministries of Education, Health, etc. All these authorities were making big losses because they charged only 7 per cent of the occupants' salaries in rent. Gross rents from these houses were about 5 million cedis whereas I estimated a private developer would need 40 million cedis to make a reasonable return.

I recommended a large cutback in building of such houses, an increase in rents and diversion of the money to better provision of water and sewerage, and research on improved ways of building and roofing the mudwalled tin-roofed housing in which 90 per cent of the population lived.

As I could find no way to get the Minister of Finance to read my report, I gave it to the Prime Minister, who, to the consternation of the civil service and army, decided to implement my recommendation to double the rents of government owned housing. I had suggested that the increase be phased in gradually, but he did it at one swoop. This was probably the greatest influence I ever had as an advisor, but its implementation helped to topple Busia.

At about the same time my Harvard colleagues persuaded the Prime Minister not to implement the 30 per cent increase in government salaries which he was well known to be contemplating, on the grounds that such a policy would raise prices rather than real incomes.

The juxtaposition of two unpopular decisions in one prime ministerial speech sparked off riots and Busia's fall seemed increasingly probable. On the 10th July, he gave a banquet for top level officials of the central and provincial government, the police and the military. He told them they should work harder, be less corrupt, and pointed with pride to a tiny enclave of foreign advisors who were serving him so well. At this time, I resigned, partly for health reasons, and partly because of the obvious dangers of foreign advisors giving advice which was subject to virtually no filtering processes before being implemented. The organisational and policy basis for putting the country back on its feet seemed extremely feeble. Busia was deposed by the military about six months later, the economy went downhill over the next decade, and in spite of some recent gains, per capita income is still below the 1950 level.

Social policy in OECD countries: education

In August 1971 I returned to OECD and to the end of 1978 worked on social policy issues, mainly education, income distribution and employment problems.

The notion of education as human capital analogous to physical capital had been put forward by Schultz in 1961 and received a warm welcome from economists. The idea was also taken up enthusiastically by educationists who found its central argument a useful support in bolstering educational budgets. However by the 1970s, serious doubts had started to arise about the private and the social returns obtained from the very rapid expansion of education in the 1960s.

The sceptics included those who argued that education was to an important degree a screening device, that there was overemphasis on formal credentials, that it was difficult to distinguish the role of intelligence, family background and education in determining earnings, and there were people with new and radical policy messages (such as Jencks and Illich) who cast strong doubts on the contribution of formal education.

In this complex field there is a paucity of sharp evidence, and unlike the OECD economic committees where there is some degree of professional discourse, meetings on education involved civil servants and policy makers with very diverse background and training. As a result, it seemed to me that new policy initiatives sometimes involved reckless experimentation.

I felt my most useful contribution to rational policy making would be to improve the quality and comparability of the quantitative evidence on earnings and education, on educational costs and benefits, on levels of formal educational achievement and enrolment. In pursuit of this aim we created a committee on educational statistics which produced the first OECD *Yearbook of Education Statistics* in 1974. This was designed to show the flow of pupils through different levels of formal education in the framework of demographic accounts, so that one could easily compare the enrolment situation in the different countries by sex and age. It also showed stocks of educated people in the population broken down by age, and public expenditure on education. The analysis was backed by a standardised classification of education in OECD countries which appeared in 10 volumes from 1972 to 1975 and provided a detailed basis for comparing equivalent levels of educational provision. We made pilot studies of total public and private expenditure by level of education (including earnings foregone of students in postcompulsory education) and made a beginning in assessing participation in and expenditure on training and adult education.[20]

The major gap in the indicators was a measure of the cognitive performance of pupils over time and at different levels. The IEA (Institute of Educational Achievement) had gathered a great deal of useful comparative evidence by organising a massive series of tests in 22 countries for secondary education, but was reluctant to consolidate its findings to provide an aggregate picture of educational performance. There was in fact a good deal of resistance in educational circles to studies which might make it possible to judge the quality of teachers and curricula.[21]

---

[20] L. Lévy Garboua, S. Newman, T. Noda, A. Peacock, T. Watanabe and M. Woodhall, *Educational Expenditure in France, Japan, and the United Kingdom*, OECD, Paris, 1977. The work on educational statistics has now been institutionalised in the publication *Education at a Glance*, OECD, Paris, 1993. However, the work on statistics of the stock of educated persons, which is particularly useful for growth accounts, has been dropped.

[21] The situation now seems to have changed, as OECD has recently begun to publish comparative statistics on the cognitive achievement of students.

At that time, governments were concerned with the distributional impact of education, but it was clear that people had very different conceptions of its equalising potential. Some had meritocratic goals in mind and wanted to achieve a gradual downward expansion of opportunity, giving bright children from poorer families a chance to rise in the social hierarchy. Others saw expansion of education as a process for changing the social structure, and reducing income dispersion by a massive increase in the proportion of people with higher education. Some were primarily interested in changing attitudes. They wanted to use the education system as a vehicle of fraternity – reducing status differentials and other kinds of social distance. I tried to assemble evidence on these issues and organised a major conference which involved a confrontation between eminent economists, sociologists and educationalists.[22] On the whole I found education a disappointing field for effective international cooperation because of the difficulties of measuring performance and the power of interest groups to resist the production of relevant evidence.[23]

The welfare state

In 1974-75, there was a sharp recession which affected the USA and Japan as well as virtually all the European countries. This was accompanied by a burst of inflation whose intensity was unparalleled in peacetime. In the event, it turned out that the Western economies had entered a new phase of development, where growth was much slower and less stable than in the postwar golden age.

These unprecedented developments led to a disturbing reorientation in the macroeconomic policy objectives and armoury of OECD countries, but they also led to a reexamination of the size and structure of government social spending and social transfers.

By the early 1970s, government spending in European countries had risen to an average of about 40 per cent of GDP. The bulk of this

---

[22] See OECD, *Education, Inequality and Life Chances*, Paris, 1977.
[23] See A. Maddison, "What is education for?", *Lloyds Bank Review*, April 1974, for a general survey of educational objectives.

went on social programmes. Further expansion in these was triggered automatically in recession as payments for income support rose and indexed benefits kept pace with inflation. There were also large expenditures on industrial subsidies.

These programmes had expanded in the earlier period of rapid economic growth in response to mixed policy objectives, some of which were redistributive, some of an insurance character, some simply a response to the pressure of interested lobbies. In order to finance these programmes, governments had increased their revenue mainly by a large increase in social security levies with a regressive incidence. There was a substantial degree of income churning in which governments collected taxes and paid out transfers to the same people without much net effect on income distribution.

Nevertheless, the welfare state had strengthened the forces making for economic growth and stability. It had also made capitalist property relations and the operation of market forces more legitimate by removing most of the grievances which motivated proponents of a socialist alternative. As a result the "socialist" parties in these countries had generally abandoned the aim of nationalising industry or significantly interfering with the operation of market forces.

Between 1974 and 1978 I spent a good deal of time on problems of the equity and efficiency of tax-transfer systems. We created a committee on social aspects of income transfer policy with Ian Byatt, of the UK Treasury, as chairman. The committee explored a wide range of distributive issues: incomes policies, poverty traps, incentives, unemployment compensation, minimum wages, distribution of income and wealth, tax and social security reform. We also did a pilot survey of the tax transfer systems of France, Italy, the Netherlands and the UK.

The time was propitious for such research. The OECD fiscal committee put out a number of very useful comparative studies on the structure of taxation, tax incidence by income level and its effect on incentives. The economics directorate published a series of studies on various kinds of public expenditure, and income distribution.[24] In the UK, the Royal Commission on the Distribution of Income and Wealth issued 8 major reports from 1976 to 1979, and the Swedish Low

---

[24] M. Sawyer, "Income distribution in OECD countries", *OECD Economic Outlook, Occasional Studies*, July 1976.

Incomes Commission had put out a 12 volume report in the early 1970s. In the USA, the Brookings Institution (animated by Joe Pechman and Henry Aaron) carried out a vast array of studies on tax incidence and social security. Together with Alice Rivlin as Director of the new Congressional Budget Office they worked as an effective pressure group for reform in these areas. In France, the Giscard government gave prominence to distributive issues in its early stages, particularly in the preparations for the seventh plan.

In the 1980s, political attitudes on these issues changed a good deal. The Thatcher governments in the UK and the Reagan-Bush administrations in the USA rejected the egalitarian bias in the distributive policy of earlier governments, made big reductions in the incidence of direct taxes and succeeded in bringing substantial increases in inequality. The policy switch in other countries was less extreme, but the political interest in monitoring these problems was sharply diminished, and the results of several of our studies were not published.[25] In fact the size of the welfare state has risen since the 1970s. Popular support for it is very firmly embedded in European countries, so there were "automatic" increases in benefits when unemployment rose and there was an influx of poor immigrants from outside the area. Furthermore governments tended to cushion the social impact of anti-inflationary macro-policy by expanding programmes to disguise unemployment (such as the large expenditure on early retirement in France or the huge expansion in the number of people drawing "handicapped" benefits in the Netherlands). Hence the problems of balancing equity and efficiency in social spending are just as sharp as they were in the 1970s, and the usefulness of internationally comparable monitoring exercises are rather clear.

Unemployment and labour market analysis

The recession and slowdown in economic growth in the OECD economies in the 1970s had major implications for the labour market.

---

[25] I set out my own views in "Origins and impact of the welfare state", in this *Review*, March 1984.

Unemployment had been at frictional and seasonal minima in the 1960s, and cyclical unemployment had virtually disappeared. But by 1978, European unemployment was two and a half times as large as in 1973 and would have been significantly higher if governments had not taken measures to check immigration, to entice people to leave the labour force or to work part-time. The OECD Committee on Manpower and Social Affairs therefore found its agenda full of new and pressing problems and the importance of the issues caused it to be raised to ministerial level in 1976.

There was clearly a need to improve comparative monitoring of the situation in the labour market. OECD already had a regular publication (*Labour Force Statistics*) which I had always used for analysing labour input in comparative macroeconomic accounts, but the definitions of unemployment differed considerably from one country to another. They were derived from different sources (mostly administrative as labour force sample surveys were then far from general) and governments sometimes changed the definitions for political purposes.

As a first step in improving the situation, I asked the US Bureau of Labor Statistics (BLS) in 1975 to lend us one of their experts (Connie Sorrentino) to examine the intercountry variance in definitions of unemployment and make recommendations for standardisation. We then set up a committee of labour statisticians to consider more closely the possibilities for improved labour market monitoring. BLS provided the chairmanship of the committee. We followed up the Sorrentino report by a more detailed study, *Measuring Employment and Unemployment* (1979) which analysed in full detail the scope of the different national unemployment and employment statistics. This provided a basis for improved monitoring for the ministerial committee, but there was a need to push the analysis further by looking at dimensions of labour "slack" other than unemployment, *e.g.* measures to encourage a reverse flow of immigrant workers, reductions in activity rates through increased provisions for early retirement, classification of less efficient workers as handicapped, incentives to promote short time working and cut working hours, or incentives to firms to hoard workers. Germany was a rather extreme case where unemployment in 1978 was 3.8 per cent of the labour force, but "labour slack" was 8.6 per cent. I therefore proposed the adoption of a systematic set of labour market accounts which would put labour market participation into a demographic framework,[26] and measure labour input in terms of total hours worked. The advantage of this for labour market analysis was obvious, and the measure also had more general application for growth and productivity accounts. Such accounts necessarily involve merger of data from different sources, and in their full version also involve assessment of deviations of actual labour input from "normal" (for migration, activity rates, working hours, and unemployment). Labour statisticians are much less used to data merger and imputations of this kind than are national accountants, so progress in this area has been slow. Nevertheless, several countries now have accounts of this kind, *e.g.* Finland, France, Germany and Sweden.

My basic feeling about the social policy issues on which I worked in OECD was that the analytical basis for policy decisions was rather poor. Consequently decision-making relied too much on hunches or reactions to interested pressure groups. There was a need for monitoring frameworks analogous to the growth accounts and cyclical indicators available for macroeconomic policy, and I tried to develop something appropriate in each of the three fields. What I did was slow to make an impact, but not without long term influence. There were frustrations when one was rowing against the stream, but there were also opportunities for doing something new if one took the right initiatives, used the appropriate networks and picked the right chairperson for intergovernmental committees. The possibilities for freewheeling initiatives and conjuring up research funds were in fact greater than in OECD macropolicy work where governmental interests and perceptions were more clearly focussed.

---

[26] See "Monitoring the labour market: a proposal for a comprehensive approach in official statistics (illustrated by recent developments in France, Germany and the UK)", *Review of Income and Wealth*, June 1980. My proposals for a functional classification of manpower and employment budgets can be found in my Shell Lecture "Why Do Unemployment Rates Differ?", University of Buckingham Employment Research Centre, October 1983. In 1988, the OECD in *Employment Outlook* (pp. 84-114) for the first time published comparative labour market budgets for 22 OECD Member countries, with a functional breakdown not unlike that which I had suggested.

Academic life in Groningen

My main reason for leaving the OECD and entering academic life was to have more freedom to pursue my own research agenda. The University of Groningen was the ideal spot for me. It was founded in 1614, and has over 20000 students in a picturesque old town of 150000, with canals, a 16th century cathedral and a night life which can compete with the boulevard St. Michel and the rue St. Denis in Paris. There are about 200 economists teaching in the faculties of economics, econometrics and business science. Most of the teaching I did has been at graduate level on economic growth and development in different parts of the world economy. There is plenty of scope for interdisciplinary cooperation with economic historians and sociologists who are also part of the economics faculty. The graduate students are exceptionally well qualified for comparative quantitative work, as they are computer literate, fluent in two or three languages and willing to learn more. There is a research school for Ph.D. students. I have supervised 12 of them, and most of their theses have been published.[27]

Since I went there in 1978, I have written 2 books which covered the development of 16 advanced capitalist countries in a comparative framework of historical growth accounts. I tried to analyse both the supply side possibilities and to see the influence of policy and the international economic order in determining economic performance. The analytical framework of these books and associated articles[28] was strongly influenced on the supply side by John Kendrick, Edward Denison, and Moses Abramovitz with whom I have had frequent contact in various ways.

---

[27] The most recent are C. de Neubourg, *Unemployment, Labour Slack and Labour Market Accounting*, 1987; T. Elfring, *Service Employment in Advanced Economies*, 1988; E. Bax, *Modernisation and Cleavage in Dutch Society*, 1988; J. Reijnders, *The Enigma of Long Waves*, 1988; S. Manarungsan, *The Economic Development of Thailand 1850-1950*, 1989; B. van Ark, *International Comparisons of Output and Productivity*, 1993; D. Pilat, *The Economics of Catch-Up. The Experience of Japan and Korea*, 1993; and P. van der Eng, *Agricultural Growth in Indonesia since 1880*, 1993.

[28] See *Phases of Capitalist Development*, Oxford University Press, 1982, *Dynamic Forces in Capitalist Development*, Oxford University Press, 1991, "Growth and slowdown in advanced capitalist economies: techniques of quantitative assessment", *Journal of Economic Literature*, June 1987, "Ultimate and proximate growth causality: a critique of Mancur Olson on the rise and decline of nations", *Scandinavian Economic History Review*, No. 2, 1988.

I continued to work on lower income countries in a comparative economic context, both to quantify their economic performance and to assess the influence of indigenous institutions and colonialism in explaining their relative economic backwardness. I extended my analysis to cover world economic performance in two books published by the OECD Development Centre.[29]

In the past 10 years or so, the Groningen research programme in my field has had two main branches: growth analysis and level analysis.

In the first field I created a network of researchers on historical growth accounts in the Club des Chiffrephiles.[30] We organised four international workshops on quantitative economic history in Groningen in 1984, 1985, 1989 and 1994 and I also persuaded the International Association for Research in Income and Wealth to renew its interest in historical national accounts in seminars in 1987 and 1992. More recently we started to reexamine the long-run estimates of growth performance of the East European economies and China. In this way it has been possible to widen the scope of historical national accounts to cover the bulk of the world economy well back into the nineteenth century, and some of our associates have pushed back the quantification much earlier.

In comparative economic history, it is necessary to measure levels of performance as well as growth. The second major focus of our Groningen research effort has therefore been on international comparisons of real product by industry of origin. This is a complement to the expenditure side estimates initiated by Kravis, Heston and Summers, and it is more useful for growth and productivity analysis. The analytical statistics we get from such work help to sharpen analysis of the causes of economic growth, catch-up and convergence, lead-country/follower-country phenomena, and the locus of technical progress. Since 1983, this ICOP (International Comparisons of Output and Productivity) programme has produced

---

[29] See A. Maddison, *The World Economy in the Twentieth Century*, OECD Development Centre, Paris, 1989; A. Maddison and G. Prince, *Economic Growth in Indonesia 1820-1940*, Foris, Dordrecht and New York, 1989, A. Maddison and Associates, *The Political Economy of Poverty, Equity and Growth: Brazil and Mexico*, Oxford University Press, New York, 1992; A. Maddison, *Monitoring the World Economy 1820-1992*, OECD Development Centre, Paris, 1994.

[30] "Chiffrephile" is a word I invented to characterise economists and economic historians, who, like myself, have a strong predilection for quantification.

more than 60 publications. The history and methodology of the approach are set out in Maddison and van Ark 1988 and 1994.[31] The basic data on value added, productivity and purchasing power are derived from censuses of production. Our interests have been worldwide, but we did not aspire to comprehensive coverage. We were satisfied to concentrate our efforts on relatively large countries which provide a representative picture of world population and output covering a very wide range of income levels. The estimates have so far covered 13 countries for agriculture and mining and 21 countries for manufacturing. For the core countries Argentina, Brazil, China, France, Germany, Indonesia, Japan, Korea, Mexico, the Netherlands, the UK and USA we have developed a network of associated researchers, and more recently have extended the work to East European countries. As the methodology has been clearly articulated and our worksheets are as transparent as possible, the basic approach is now rather easy to replicate and such comparisons have attracted visiting researchers from Australia, Bulgaria, China, Finland, Portugal and Russia.

---

[31] My interest in this kind of comparative work goes back a long way, see "Productivity in Canada, the United Kingdom and the United States", *Oxford Economic Papers*, October 1952, *Economic Progress and Policy in Developing Countries*, Norton, New York, 1970. The ICOP work began with "A comparison of levels of GDP per capita in developed and developing countries 1700-1980", *Journal of Economic History*, March 1983. The ICOP methodology is set out in A. Maddison and B. van Ark, *Comparisons of Real Output in Manufacturing*, World Bank, Washington, D.C., 1988, and A. Maddison and B. van Ark, "The international comparison of real product and productivity", Research Memorandum, Groningen Growth and Development Centre, Groningen, 1994. See also A. Szirmai, B. van Ark, and D. Pilat, eds., *Explaining Economic Growth: Essays in Honour of Angus Maddison*, Elsevier, North Holland, 1993 for the nature of Groningen research activity.

Name index

Aaron, Henry 470
Abramovitz, Moses 36, 127–30, 473
Abul Fazl 262
Adams, Brooks 257
Agherli, B.B. 167
Ahmad, M.M. 460
Ahmad, Sultan 227
Akbar 258, 260, 262, 267–8, 275, 287
Alemán, Miguel 326
Alexander the Great 463
Andic, S. 387, 389
Anstey, Vera 257, 286
Ark, Bart van 120, 125, 128, 137, 140, 204, 228–30, 243, 247, 475
Ashbrook, A.G. 195
Astaire, Fred 434
Atkinson, A.B. 396
Aubrey, Henry 196, 317
Auerhan, Jan 19
Aurangzeb 258, 267, 307
Avakov, Ratchik 455
Avila Camacho, Manuel 326–7
Ayub Khan 460–61
Aziz, Sartaj 460

Babur 258
Backhouse, E. 261
Bacon, R. 191, 407
Baily, M.N. 368
Bairoch, Paul 76, 189–92, 194, 200
Bakewell, P.J. 314
Ballance, Robert 204, 227
Banerji, A.K. 278, 345, 348
Baneth, Jean 227
Baran, P.A. 269
Barnett, G.E. 389
Barro, R.J. 129–30
Baudet, H. 349
Bauer, A. 315
Bauer, P.T. 199
Baumol, William 39, 128
Bazant, J. 319, 328
Beckerman, Wilfred 191, 439, 442
Ben Bella, Ahmed 458
Benjamin, D.K. 410
Bennett, M.K. 191, 286, 288
Benson, Charles 461
Berg, Ivar 428

Bergson, A. 130, 441
Beveridge, W.H. 273, 392
Bhatia, B.M. 288
Bismarck, Otto von 390–91
Blades, Derek 36, 137–8, 204, 227, 398
Bland, J.O.P. 261
Blau, Gerda 441
Block, H. 228
Blomme, J. 129
Boeke, J.H. 340, 347, 350
Bolona Behr, C.A. 196
Bombach, G. 194, 202, 205, 207, 229–30, 235–7, 241, 244–5, 248
Boomgaard, Peter 347–9
Booth, Anne 341
Booth, Charles 392
Borah, W. 310–11, 314–15
Boserup, E. 266, 340
Bowles, Samuel 68
Bowring, Sir John 197
Brading, D.A. 314
Braithwaite, S. 191
Breman, J.C. 349
Bresciani-Turroni, C. 376
Brinkman, Henk-Jan 78
Broadberry, S.N. 145
Brugmans, I.J. 335
Buchanan, D.H. 294
Buchholz, E.W. 197
Bulhoes, Octavio 451
Burns, A.F. 231, 444
Buron, Robert 450, 453, 455
Bush, George 470
Busia, Kofi 464–6
Butler, Bill 447
Butlin, Noel 308, 311
Byatt, Ian 469

Cairncross, A. 445
Callaghan, James 377
Calles P.E. 324, 326–7
Callis, H.G. 332
Campos, Roberto 451–2
Canga Argüelles, J. 315
Cárdenas, Lazaro 323, 325–7
Carranza, V. 323, 326
Carré, Jean-Jacques 37, 40, 43, 48–51, 54, 62, 75–6, 78–9, 146, 367

476

Casasus, J.D. 322
Caves, R.E. 124, 229
Chacko, K.C. 280
Chandler, Alfred 123–4
Chaudhuri, K.N. 333, 336
Chenery, H. 129, 460
Chetwynd, George 437
Chevalier, F. 314
Chirendev 456
Choi, Kwang 90
Christensen, Laurits 37–8, 41–2, 44, 47, 49–50
Chung, William 37, 40, 47, 54
Cipolla, C.M. 129
Citrine, Sir Walter 434
Clapton, Joan 436
Clark, Colin 40, 191, 389, 412, 435
Clive of India (Robert Clive) 262, 268–9, 304
Coatsworth, John 308, 316, 320–21
Cole, G.D.H. 436
Collantes de Téran, A. 311
Commager, H.S. 319
Commons, John R. 86–7
Comte, Auguste 323
Contador, C.R. 195
Conze, W. 367
Cook, N.D. 311
Cook, S.F. 310–11
Cornwallis, Lord 269
Cortés, Hernan 309, 311
Cowdray, Lord 321
Crafts, N.F.R. 129, 344
Creutzberg, P. 344, 353
Crosland, C.A.R. 396
Cummings, Dianne 37–8, 41–2, 44, 47, 49–50
Curzon, Lord 297

Daendels, H.W. 336, 338
Dalhousie, Lord 271
Darby, Michael R. 69, 72
Darling, M.L. 283
Daultrey, S. 344
Davies, S. 208, 229–30, 236, 241, 244, 248
Davies, Stephen 227
Davis, K. 264, 287
De la Huerta, Adolfo 326, 328
De la Madrid, Miguel 326
De Long, J. Bradford 128
Dean, A. 167
Dean, G. 137
Deane, Phyllis 189–90
Defoe, Daniel 388
Delahaut 191
Delouvrier, Paul 444

Denevan, W.M. 310–11
Denison, Edward F. 7, 12, 22, 24, 36, 37, 39–40, 42–4, 47–52, 54, 57–62, 64, 66, 92, 129, 389, 447, 459, 473
Derksen, J.B.D. 348
Desai, R.C. 282, 344
Dewhurst, J. Frederick 80
Dholakia, Bakul 38
Diallo, Siafoulaye 453
Diaz Alejandro, Carlos 189, 195, 197
Díaz Ordaz, Gustavo 326
Diaz, Porfirio 308, 320–21, 323, 325, 327
Dickson, D. 344
Digby, W. 257, 269, 288
Dobb, Maurice 439
Doheny 321
Domar, Evsey 441
Donnedieu de Vabres, Jacques 444
Douglas, Paul 45, 447
Doxiadis, Constantine 460
Drechsler, Laszlo 227
Dubois, Paul 37, 40, 43, 48–51, 54, 62, 75–6, 78–9, 146, 367
Duesenberry, J.S. 29
Durkheim, Emile 421
Dutt, Romesh 257, 261, 269, 275, 288, 333

Easterlin, R. 130
Echeverría, Luis 326
Eddy, Nelson 434
Edwardes, M. 273, 302
Edwards, I. 228
Ehrlich, E. 124
Eisenhower, Dwight D. 375, 440, 443–4
Elfring, Tom 204
Elson, R.E. 332
Eltis, W. 407
Emminger, Otmar 444
Engerman, S.L. 145
Erbe, R. 367
Erhard, Ludwig 374, 444
Erichsen, Eivind 445

Fabricant, S. 231, 387, 447
Fairbank, John 463
Fasseur, C. 338–9, 349
Feekes, Fons 352
Feinstein, Charles 37, 40, 43, 48–9, 51, 54, 75–6, 78, 137, 139–40, 147, 334, 367, 372, 387
Feldstein, Martin 407, 412
Ferry, Jules 392
Field, A.J. 142, 145
Flinn, M.W. 344

Flora, P. 394
Fodeba, Keita 453
Fogel, Robert 50
Fontvieille, L. 372, 387
Frank, J.G. 229
Frankel, M. 229–30, 235
Franklin, Benjamin 317
Friedman, Milton 170, 377, 417, 419
Fukami, Hiroaki 80
Furber, H. 277, 349
Fyfe, Hamilton 434

Gaathon, A.L. 11
Gadgil, D.R. 262
Galbraith, J.K. 87, 397, 460
Galenson, W. 229–30, 235
Gallmann, R.E. 143, 145, 147
Ganguli, B.N. 267
Gannicott, K. 418
Gaulle, Charles de 450
Geertz, C. 340, 347, 350
George III 261
Gerschenkron, A. 129, 463
Ghengis Khan 258
Ghosh, Arun 227
Gibbon, Edward 103
Giffen, Sir Robert 412
Gilbert, Milton 40, 194, 203, 445–6
Giscard d'Estaing, V. 470
Glamann, K. 332–3, 335
Goldsmith, Raymond 42–3, 51, 137, 189, 447, 450, 453, 457
Gollop, Frank 38, 44, 56
Gordon, David 68
Goulart, J.B.M. 451
Gowing, M.M. 147
Graham, D.H. 197
Granier, Roland 36, 74
Grant 277
Greene, Graham 324
Griffiths, R.T. 147
Griliches, Zvi 58
Groote, Peter 137
Gudin, Eugenio 451
Guevara, Che 454
Guinchard, P. 229
Gusmao Veloso, Maria Alice de 204, 223, 227

Habib, Irfan 343
Haddad, C.L. 195
Haekerrup, Per 438
Hall, Robert 444–5
Halpern, Bruno 434

Hamilton, C.J. 289
Hamilton, E.J. 313, 315
Hancock, W.K. 147
Hansen, B. 195, 197
Harary, Micheline 36
Harberger, Al 441
Harbison, F. 19
Harrington, M. 397
Harris, Seymour 440
Hartog, H. den 146, 368
Hassan, Said 461
Hastings, Warren 268–9, 302
Hauge, Gabriel 444
Hawthorn, Stephanie 436
Hayami, Y. 126, 205–7
Hayek, Friedrich 90, 386
Healey, Denis 373, 438
Hearst, W.R. 321
Heath, Edward 375
Heath, J.B. 229
Heaton, H. 290
Hedges, Janice 73–4
Heidenheimer, A.J. 394
Heller, Walter 448
Helliwell, John 37, 42, 47, 49, 57, 62
Hemingway, Jack 434–5
Heston, Alan 92, 94, 129, 140, 191–6, 198–200, 202, 227–9, 242–3, 247, 343, 371, 474
Hirsch, Etienne 444
Hitchens, D.M.W.N. 208, 229–30, 236, 241, 244, 248
Hoffman, Walter 54
Hofman, André 128, 137, 140, 308
Hooley, R.W. 196
Horioka, C.Y. 170
Hou, Chi-Ming 281, 295
Houben, Aerdt 36, 227–8
Houthakker, H. 415
Hoveida 455
Humayun 258
Humboldt, A. de 196, 315–17, 319
Husen, Torsten 424
Hutton, J.H. 345

Ikram, Khalid 460
Illich, Ivan 416–17, 419–20, 466
Ingram, J.C. 197
Islam, Nurul 204, 460
Islam Shah 258
Israel, J.I. 314

James, J.A. 145
Janssens, Edmond 453

Jefferson, Thomas 393
Jehangir 258
Jencks, C. 397, 424, 428–9, 466
Jinnah, M.A. 461
Joad, Cyril 434
Johnson, Harry 438
Johnson, Lyndon B. 397
Jones, D.T. 228–9
Jones, Sir William 302
Jong, Gjalt de 128, 137
Jorgenson, Dale 37–8, 41–2, 44, 47, 49–50, 52, 56, 58, 64, 129, 228–9, 389
Juarez, Benito 318, 320
Judges, A.V. 317
Julius Caesar 440

Kaldor, N. 29, 122, 142, 439
Keese, D. 367
Kendrick, John W. 36–7, 39–40, 42–5, 47–52, 54, 56, 58, 62, 76, 78, 82, 137–8, 387, 389, 473
Kenessey, Z. 228–9
Kennedy, John 448
Keynes, John Maynard 29, 170, 296, 384–5, 434–5, 439, 445
Khambata, K.J. 278
Khanin, G. 130
Khomeini 455
Kim, Kwang-Suk 38, 196–7
Kindleberger, Charles P. 130
King, Gregory 389
Kirner, Wolfgang 51, 137, 146–7
Kirschen, E. 191
Kirsten, E. 197
Klau, Friedrich 385
Klein, H.S. 315
Klodt, Henning 39, 228–9
Kochin, L.A. 410
Köllmann, W. 197
Kondratieff, N.D. 126
Krause, L.B. 124
Kravis, Irving 40, 189, 191–4, 196, 198–200, 202–3, 227–9, 242–3, 247, 371, 474
Kregel, Jan 361
Krijnse-Locker, Hugo 137, 227
Kruschev, Nikita 458
Kubitschek, Juscelino 451
Kudrov, Valentin 227, 229–30, 244, 458
Kuipers, Simon 361
Kumar, Dharma 344, 438
Kumar, Jagdish 204, 227
Kundu, Arabinda 227
Kunze, Kent 73–4
Kuroda, M. 229

Kux, Jaroslav 227
Kuznets, Simon 40, 51, 91–2, 129, 137, 167, 170, 189–91, 194, 200, 202–3, 228–9, 389, 402, 441, 446, 463

Laanen J.T.M. van 341, 348
Ladd, D.M. 317
Lal, Deepak 105
Lamartine Yates, Paul 308
Lamont, T.W. 328
Landes, David 104, 189–92, 194, 200
Langoni, Carlos 38
Laski, Harold 437–8
Lattimore, Owen 455
Lavers, G.R. 396
Lavrin, A. 315
Lchamsoryn 456
Lebergott, Stanley 72, 76
Lee, J. 344
Leff, N.H. 195
Lenin 457–8
Lennep, Emile van 448
Lewis, Arthur 9, 108, 402, 439, 458
Lewis, C. 277, 280–81
Limantour, J.Y. 322–3
Lindbeck, Assar 39, 412
Lindert, P.H. 344
Little, Ian 457
Liu, T.–C. 195
Lloyd George, David 392
Locke, John 388
Long, Clarence 441
López Mateos, Adolfo 326
López Portillo, José 326
Lucas, R.E. 129
Lundberg, E. 129
Lusher, David 447
Lützel, H. 137, 140

Macaulay, T.B. 301–2
Machlup, Fritz 441
Macmillan, Harold 437
Maddison, Angus 10, 17, 19, 38, 40, 42, 45, 48–9, 51, 53, 60, 62, 69–70, 72–4, 77–8, 81–2, 94, 100, 103, 105, 109, 115–20, 123, 126, 128–30, 138, 140–41, 143, 146, 167, 179, 181–2, 190–91, 193, 195–8, 200, 202, 205, 207–8, 210, 212, 228–30, 235, 247–8, 308, 319, 341, 343–6, 348, 361, 363–4, 370, 372–3, 451, 475
Madero, Francisco 323, 327
Maital, Shlomo 39
Maizels, A. 229

Malinvaud, Edmond 37, 40, 43, 48–51, 54, 62, 75–6, 78–9, 146, 367
Malthus, Thomas 111, 386, 388, 392, 406
Mann, H.H. 283
Manoukian, A.A. 458
Marcuse, H. 419
Marczewski, Jean 189–90
Marjolin, Robert 443, 445–6
Mark, Jerome 227
Marris, Robin 438–9
Marshall, Alfred 389
Martin, John 36
Marx, Karl 385, 388, 390, 404, 437
Marzouk, G.A. 195, 197
Mason, Edward 460
Mason, Heath 456
Matthews, Robin 36–7, 40, 43, 48–9, 75
Maximilian, Emperor 318, 320
Mayhew, Henry 392
Mayo, Lord 286
McAlpin, M. 343
McCracken, Paul 447
McDonald, Jeannette 434
McGreevey, W.P. 197
McLennan, Kenneth 39
Meer, Cees van der 204–6, 208, 215, 220–22, 227
Meidner, Rudolf 376
Meltz, Noah 39
Mendès-France, P. 450
Mensah 465
Menshikov, Stanislav 458
Mensink, G.J.A. 205, 207, 230, 235
Merrick, T.W. 197
Mill, J.S. 386, 388, 391–2
Mill, James 271
Miller, Riel 385
Mills, F.C. 231
Mitchell, Brian R. 80, 181, 332
Modigliani, F. 170
Monnet, Jean 445
Montes de Oca 328
Moore, Geoffrey 447
Moreland, W.H. 266, 275, 287
Morgan, L.H. 311
Morineau, M. 315
Morison, S.E. 319
Morley, Lord 297
Morris, M.D. 285
Mowery, D.C. 122, 130
Mueller, B. 181
Mukherjee, M. 304
Mulder, Nanno 137, 167, 308
Mulhall, M.G. 197

Muljatno 341
Müller-Armack, Alfred 374, 444
Murshid Quli 265
Musgrave, John 78, 137, 363
Musgrave, R.A. 398
Mussolini, Benito 325
Myers, C.A. 19
Myint, Hla 340

Nadir Shah 268–9
Naik, J.P. 264
Naraoji, D. 275, 277
Neale, W.C. 285
Needham, J. 105
Neef, Arthur 227
Nehru, J. 262
Nelson, R. 128
Niewaroski, D.H. 191
Nishimizu, M. 229
Nixon, Richard 375, 405
Nkrumah, Kwame 464
Novacco, Nino 453
Nurullah, S. 264

Obregón, Alvaro 323, 326–7
O'Brien, Patrick 64
Ockrent, Roger 447
Odling-Smee, John 37, 40, 43, 48–9, 75
Ó Gráda, C. 344
Ohkawa, Kazushi 37, 40, 43, 48–51, 54, 58, 69, 75–6, 78, 81, 146, 151, 367, 372, 387, 458
Ohlin, Göran 453
Okita, Saburo 458
Okun, Arthur 62, 375–6
Olson, Mancur 86–90
O'Mahony, Mary 138, 140
Ooststroom, Harry van 208, 210, 212, 227–8, 248
Ortiz Mena, A. 322
Ortiz Rubio, Pascual 326
Owen, Robert, 388

Paige, D. 194, 202, 205, 207, 229–30, 235–7, 241, 244–5, 248
Pani, A.J. 328
Papanek, Gus 460
Park, Joon-Kyung 38
Parker, Robert 227
Parker, Sanford 447
Parniczky, G. 204
Pathirane, L. 398
Peacock, A.T. 387–8, 394
Pechman, Joe 470

Peddie, J.M. (Lord Peddie) 434
Pen, Jan 36, 227, 361, 444
Pencavel, John 36
Peper, B. 347, 349
Perkins, D.H. 197
Perkins, D.W. 195
Philips. C.H. 276
Philips, Herbert 455
Pilat, Dirk 125, 137, 227, 229
Pletcher, D.M. 321
Polak, J.J. 331–2, 341, 345, 348, 350
Portes Gil, Emilio 326
Postan, Michael 437
Postgate, Raymond 436
Posthumus, N.W. 335
Postlethwaite, T. Neville 418
Prais, S.J. 124, 227–9
Prasada Rao, D.S. 204–5, 208–9, 215, 217–21
Psacharopoulos, George 48

Quiros, J.M. 317
Qureshi, I.H. 261, 267

Raffles, Sir Thomas Stamford 337–8, 347, 349
Raupach, H. 367
Raychaudhuri, T 267
Reagan, Ronald 407, 470
Rehn, Gösta 376
Reich, C.A. 419
Reid, A.J. 347, 349
Remer, C.F. 348
Reynolds, C.W. 196–7, 317, 320
Ricardo, David 386, 392, 406, 439
Riley, J.C. 333
Ringstad, V. 58
Rivlin, Alice 470
Robbins, L. 389, 409, 439
Robert, Horst 443
Robertson, Dennis 438–40
Robertson, W. 311
Robinson, Austin 439
Robinson, Joan 64, 438
Rockefeller, John D. 321
Rodríguez, Abelardo 326
Roemer, M. 196–7
Romer, Paul 92, 129
Roosa, Bob 448
Roosevelt, Franklin D. 327, 393
Rosenberg, N. 122, 126, 130
Rosenblat, Angel 310–11, 315, 318
Rosenstein-Rodan, Paul 108, 189
Rosenzweig, F. 316–17

Rosovsky, Henry 37, 40, 43, 48–51, 58, 69, 75, 81, 146
Rostas, Laszlo 229–30, 235, 439–40
Rostow, Walt W. 9, 108, 129, 190
Rowntree, B.S. 392, 396
Roy, A.D. 228–9
Roy, D.J. 229, 241
Rueff, J. 389, 409
Ruiz Cortines, Adolfo 326
Russell, Bertrand 438
Ruttan, V.W. 126, 204
Ruttan, Y. 205–7

Sadek, Nafees 461
Salou, Gérard 37, 42, 47, 49, 57, 62
Salter, Billie 189
Salter, W.E.G. 130
Samory 453
Sanders, W.T. 310–11
Saulnier, Raymond 444
Sawyer, M. 403
Scheltema, A.M.P.A. 348
Schiphorst, José 78
Schmidt, L. 138
Schmookler, Jacob 50, 126
Schofield, R.S. 344
Schroeder, G.E. 228
Schultz, Theodore W. 22, 48, 108, 459, 466
Schumpeter, Joseph A. 126, 385–6, 440
Scitovsky, Tibor 457
Scott, Maurice 457
Scott, R.J. 436
Seers, Dudley 396
Sergent, René 445
Shah Jehan 258, 260, 268
Shah, K.T. 278
Shannon, R. 418
Shaw, Bernard, 391, 435
Sher Shah 258
Shinohara, Miyohei 51, 54, 69, 76, 78, 146, 151, 229, 367, 372, 387
Shiskin, Julie 447
Shoemaker, Robbin 204
Sidgwick, Henry 389
Siegel, Irving 441
Simantov, Albert 204
Simenson, Mario 451
Simpson, L.B. 310, 314
Sinclair 328
Sinha, N.K. 265, 277
Sivasubramonian, S. 278
Skinner, J.S. 145
Slicher van Bath, B.H. 262

Smith, A.D. 208, 229–30, 236, 241, 244, 248
Smith, Adam 129, 311, 317, 336, 386, 436
Smith, Anthony 227
Snodgrass, D.R. 16
Solow, Robert M. 8, 49, 448, 459
Sorrentino, Connie 471
Soustelle, J. 311
Souza, Angelo de 227
Spencer, Herbert 323
Sraffa, Piero 64, 439
Stuijvenberg, J.H. van 332, 335, 344
Stone, R. 40, 231, 446
Strachey, J. 396
Strauss, Franz Joseph 454
Strumilin, S.G. 22
Sturm, Peter 36–7, 42, 47, 49, 57, 62
Stuvel, Geer 446
Suarez, Eduardo 328
Suh, Sang-Chul 196–7
Summers, Robert 92, 94, 129, 140, 191–4, 196, 198–200, 202, 227–9, 242–3, 247, 371, 474
Szereszewski, R. 195
Szirmai, Eddy 137, 227, 229

Tatom, John 59
Tawney, R.H. 436–7
Temple, Shirley 434
TePaske, J.J. 315
Terborgh, George 447
Turluin, I.J. 205–6, 209, 222
Thatcher, Margaret 377, 470
Thomas, R.P. 316
Tibbetts, Thomas 227
Timur 258, 268
Tinbergen, Jan 45, 137, 348, 444
Titmuss, R.H. 396
Tjan, T.S. 146, 368
Tobin, J. 376–7, 448
Touré, Ismael 453
Touré, Sékou 453
Tyler, Wat 438

Ul Haq, Mahbub 460–61
Uri, Pierre 444
Urquidi, Victor 227, 308

Van den Bosch, J. 337
Vasconcelos, J. 325
Velloso, João Paulo dos Reis 451

Vernon, R. 321–2
Veverka, J. 387, 389
Villa, F. 323
Viner, J. 441
Voltaire, François 435
Von Clausewitz, Karl 440
Von Mises, Ludwig 386
Vorstman, G.J.T. 367
Vries, Johan de 335
Vrijer, J.E.J. de 332, 335, 344

Wagner, Adolph 388, 390
Wallis, J.J. 145
Walter, François 442–3, 445
Ward, Michael 43, 55, 137, 227–8
Warriner, Doreen 14
Webb, Sidney 391
Weber, Adolf 204
Weber, Max 86, 103
Wee, Herman van der 129
Weisskopf, Thomas 68
West, E.C. 229–30, 235–6, 244–5
Wickizer, V.D. 286, 288
Widjojo, Nitisastro 349
Wieringa, Paul 204, 227
Williamson, J.G. 344
Wilpstra, Bote 51, 78, 363, 370
Wiseman, J. 387–8, 394
Wolff, E.N. 128
Wolff, Pieter de 444
Worden, Gaylord 227
Woytinsky, E.S. 80, 371
Woytinsky, W.S. 80, 371
Wrigley, E.A. 344

Yahya Khan 460
Yamada, Saburo 204–6, 208, 215, 220–22
Yamey, B.S. 199
Yeh, K.–C. 195
Young, E. van 314
Yukizawa, K. 229–30, 235, 244
Yun, Bartolomé 308

Zambardino, R.A. 310–11
Zanden, J.L. van 147
Zapata, Emiliano 323
Zerkowsky, Ralph 227
Zimmerman, L.J. 195, 341

Economists of the Twentieth Century

Monetarism and Macroeconomic Policy
Thomas Mayer

Studies in Fiscal Federalism
Wallace E. Oates

The World Economy in Perspective
Essays in International Trade and European Integration
Herbert Giersch

Towards a New Economics
Critical Essays on Ecology, Distribution and Other Themes
Kenneth E. Boulding

Studies in Positive and Normative Economics
Martin J. Bailey

The Collected Essays of Richard E. Quandt (2 volumes)
Richard E. Quandt

International Trade Theory and Policy
Selected Essays of W. Max Corden
W. Max Corden

Organization and Technology in Capitalist Development
William Lazonick

Studies in Human Capital
Collected Essays of Jacob Mincer, Volume 1
Jacob Mincer

Studies in Labor Supply
Collected Essays of Jacob Mincer, Volume 2
Jacob Mincer

Macroeconomics and Economic Policy
The Selected Essays of Assar Lindbeck, Volume I
Assar Lindbeck

The Welfare State
The Selected Essays of Assar Lindbeck, Volume II
Assar Lindbeck

Classical Economics, Public Expenditure and Growth
Walter Eltis

Money, Interest Rates and Inflation
Frederic S. Mishkin

The Public Choice Approach to Politics
Dennis C. Mueller

The Liberal Economic Order
Volume I Essays on International Economics
Volume II Money, Cycles and Related Themes
Gottfried Haberler
Edited by Anthony Y.C. Koo

Economic Growth and Business Cycles
Prices and the Process of Cyclical Development
Paolo Sylos Labini

International Adjustment, Money and Trade
Theory and Measurement for Economic Policy, Volume I
Herbert G. Grubel

International Capital and Service Flows
Theory and Measurement for Economic Policy, Volume II
Herbert G. Grubel

Unintended Effects of Government Policies
Theory and Measurement for Economic Policy, Volume III
Herbert G. Grubel

The Economics of Competitive Enterprise
Selected Essays of P.W.S. Andrews
Edited by Frederic S. Lee and Peter E. Earl

The Repressed Economy
Causes, Consequences, Reform
Deepak Lal

Economic Theory and Market Socialism
Selected Essays of Oskar Lange
Edited by Tadeusz Kowalik

Trade, Development and Political Economy
Selected Essays of Ronald Findlay
Ronald Findlay

General Equilibrium Theory
The Collected Essays of Takashi Negishi, Volume I
Takashi Negishi

The History of Economics
The Collected Essays of Takashi Negishi, Volume II
Takashi Negishi

Studies in Econometric Theory
The Collected Essays of Takeshi Amemiya
Takeshi Amemiya

Exchange Rates and the Monetary System
Selected Essays of Peter B. Kenen
Peter B. Kenen

Econometric Methods and Applications (2 volumes)
G.S. Maddala

National Accounting and Economic Theory
The Collected Papers of Dan Usher, Volume I
Dan Usher

Welfare Economics and Public Finance
The Collected Papers of Dan Usher, Volume II
Dan Usher

Economic Theory and Capitalist Society
The Selected Essays of Shigeto Tsuru, Volume I
Shigeto Tsuru

Methodology, Money and the Firm
The Collected Essays of D.P. O'Brien (2 volumes)
D.P. O'Brien

Economic Theory and Financial Policy
The Selected Essays of Jacques J. Polak (2 volumes)
Jacques J. Polak

Sturdy Econometrics
Edward E. Leamer

The Emergence of Economic Ideas
Essays in the History of Economics
Nathan Rosenberg

Productivity Change, Public Goods and Transaction Costs
Essays at the Boundaries of Microeconomics
Yoram Barzel

Reflections on Economic Development
The Selected Essays of Michael P. Todaro
Michael P. Todaro

The Economic Development of Modern Japan
The Selected Essays of Shigeto Tsuru, Volume II
Shigeto Tsuru

Money, Credit and Policy
Allan H. Meltzer

Macroeconomics and Monetary Theory
The Selected Essays of Meghnad Desai, Volume I
Meghnad Desai

Poverty, Famine and Economic Development
The Selected Essays of Meghnad Desai, Volume II
Meghnad Desai

Explaining the Economic Performance of Nations
Essays in Time and Space
Angus Maddison

Economic Doctrine and Method
Selected Papers of R.W. Clower
Robert W. Clower

Economic Theory and Reality
Selected Essays on their Disparity and Reconciliation
Tibor Scitovsky

Doing Economic Research
Essays on the Applied Methodology of Economics
Thomas Mayer

Institutions and Development Strategies
The Selected Essays of Irma Adelman, Volume I
Irma Adelman

Dynamics and Income Distribution
The Selected Essays of Irma Adelman, Volume II
Irma Adelman

The Economics of Growth and Development
The Selected Essays of A.P. Thirlwall
A.P. Thirlwall

Theoretical and Applied Econometrics
The Selected Papers of Phoebus J. Dhrymes
Phoebus J. Dhrymes

Innovation, Technology and the Economy
The Selected Essays of Edwin Mansfield (2 volumes)
Edwin Mansfield

Capitalism, Socialism and Post-Keynesianism
Selected Essays of G.C. Harcourt
G.C. Harcourt